THE AUTONOMY OF LABOUR LAW

To what extent is labour law an autonomous field of study? This book is based upon the papers written by a group of leading international scholars on this theme, delivered at a conference to mark Professor Mark Freedland's retirement from his teaching fellowship in Oxford. The chapters explore the boundaries and connections between labour law and other legal disciplines such as company law, competition law, contract law and public law; labour law and legal methodologies such as reflexive governance and comparative law; and labour law and other disciplines such as ethics, economics and political philosophy. In so doing, it represents a cross-section of the most sophisticated current work at the cutting edge of labour law theory.

The Autonomy of Labour Law

Edited by
Alan Bogg
Cathryn Costello
ACL Davies
and
Jeremias Prassl

HART PUBLISHING

OXFORD AND PORTLAND, OREGON
2017

Hart Publishing
An imprint of Bloomsbury Publishing Plc

Hart Publishing Ltd
Kemp House
Chawley Park
Cumnor Hill
Oxford OX2 9PH
UK

Bloomsbury Publishing Plc
50 Bedford Square
London
WC1B 3DP
UK

www.hartpub.co.uk
www.bloomsbury.com

Published in North America (US and Canada) by
Hart Publishing
c/o International Specialized Book Services
920 NE 58th Avenue, Suite 300
Portland, OR 97213-3786
USA

www.isbs.com

First published in hardback, 2015
Paperback edition, 2017

British Library Cataloguing-in-Publication Data
A catalogue record for this book is available from the British Library.

ISBN: PB: 978-1-50991-414-2
HB: 978-1-84946-621-9

Typeset by Compuscript Ltd, Shannon
Printed and bound in Great Britain by
Lightning Source UK Ltd

EDITORS' PREFACE

The chapters in this volume were first presented at a conference entitled *Oxford Labour Law: Past, Present, Future* held at St John's College, Oxford, in July 2012. The conference was held to mark the retirement from formal teaching duties of Professor Mark Freedland, and the contributors to this volume are his former colleagues or students (or both). In the course of the conference, we also had occasion to acknowledge the remarkable partnership of Paul Davies and Mark Freedland over four decades, and its enduring imprint both on Oxford labour law and the discipline itself. We are grateful to the many other friends and colleagues who attended the conference and contributed to two days of lively and good-humoured discussion, and particularly to those who chaired sessions (Catherine Barnard, John Bowers QC, Simon Deakin, Sir Patrick Elias and Sir John Mummery). We acknowledge the generous financial support of Oxford University's John Fell Fund, the Oxford Law Faculty and St John's College for the conference, the encouragement of the Dean of the Oxford Law Faculty, Professor Timothy Endicott, and the practical help of Marianne Bièse and the staff at St John's. In preparing the volume for publication we have benefited from research assistance from Joelle Grogan, Ioannis Katsaroumpas and Paolo Ronchi, and we would like to thank Richard Hart, Rachel Turner and colleagues at Hart Publishing for their enthusiastic support for this project from the outset.

Although this project began as an examination of the contribution of Oxford colleagues to the academic study of labour law, we hope it has a much broader story to tell about the normative, institutional and substantive autonomy of labour law as a discipline, a story we develop in the Introduction. At the same time, we hope that the volume is a fitting tribute to the inspiration the contributors have derived from their connection, at different times and in different ways, with labour law at Oxford. In this vein, we would like to record our particular gratitude to Paul and Mark.

Alan Bogg
Cathryn Costello
Anne Davies
Jeremias Prassl

14 July 2014

CONTENTS

LIST OF CONTRIBUTORS

Diamond Ashiagbor is Professor of Law at the School of Oriental and African Studies, University of London.

Lizzie Barmes is Professor of Law at Queen Mary, University of London.

Alan Bogg is Professor of Labour Law at the University of Oxford and Fellow and Tutor in Law at Hertford College, Oxford.

Alice Carse is a barrister specializing in employment law at Devereux Chambers.

Hugh Collins is Vinerian Professor of English Law at the University of Oxford and a Fellow of All Souls College, Oxford.

Cathryn Costello is Andrew W Mellon University Lecturer in International Human Rights and Refugee Law in the Refugee Studies Centre at the Oxford Department of International Development. She is also a Fellow of St Anthony's College, Oxford.

Nicola Countouris is a Reader in Law at University College London and co-ordinator of the UCL Labour Rights Institute.

Anne CL Davies is Professor of Law and Public Policy at the University of Oxford and Fellow and Tutor in Law at Brasenose College, Oxford.

Paul L Davies is the Allen and Overy Professor of Corporate Law at the University of Oxford and a Fellow of Jesus College, Oxford.

Sandra Fredman is the Rhodes Professor of the Laws of the British Commonwealth and the USA at the University of Oxford, and a Fellow of Pembroke College, Oxford.

Mark Freedland is Professor Emeritus of Employment Law at the University of Oxford and a Senior Research Fellow of St John's College, Oxford.

Deirdre McCann is Reader in Law at the University of Durham.

Christopher McCrudden is Professor of Law at Queen's University, Belfast.

Jill Murray is Associate Professor of Law at LaTrobe University, Melbourne.

Wanjiru Njoya is Assistant Professor of Law at Queen's University, Canada.

Tonia Novitz is Professor of Labour Law at the University of Bristol.

Jeremias Prassl is a Fellow and Tutor in Law at Magdalen College, Oxford.

Phil Syrpis is Reader in Law at the University of Bristol.

INTRODUCTION: EXPLORING AUTONOMY

ALAN BOGG, CATHRYN COSTELLO,
ACL DAVIES and JEREMIAS PRASSL

The contributions in this volume are the result of a conference held in July 2013 to celebrate the *Past, Present and Future of Labour Law in Oxford*. Over the course of two days, it quickly became apparent that the idea of the autonomy of labour law was a unifying theme of many contributions. This autonomy theme served not only as a lens or prism through which to view a trajectory which had begun nearly fifty years ago, but also helped to tie our discussions into broader current debates within labour law, far beyond the parochial limits of Oxford labour law.

In this introduction, we therefore take up the autonomy of labour law as a key topic, different facets of which recur throughout subsequent chapters.[1] Whilst individual contributions range widely in methodology and perspective, there are also striking continuities and resonances. Part I briefly surveys each contribution in turn, setting the backdrop for an exploration of three levels of autonomy in Part II. At the meta-level, first, the normative dimension reflects an opening up of discourse on a plurality of values. At the mid-level, the range of institutions considered comprises not only the familiar contract of employment, collective labour law and personal work relations, but also the new governance mechanisms of the European employment strategy, positive equality duties and a range of aspects of corporate governance. On substantive autonomy, finally, the theme of 'common law' scepticism recurs in particular. Yet here too there is increasing differentiation in relation to 'negative autonomy'. In so doing, all contributions look to a wide range of aspects, including the common law of obligations, company law, human rights law and many other domains to reach progressive outcomes in labour law. A third part returns to the past, present and future of labour law in Oxford, by exploring the history of the subject since its inception in the teaching of Otto Kahn-Freund.

[1] Countouris (Ch 7, this volume), drawing on N Countouris, 'European Social Law as an Autonomous Legal Discipline' [2009] *Yearbook of European Law* 95.

I. The Autonomy of Labour Law

The 'autonomy of labour law' may seem like an odd rallying cry to those unfamiliar with the trajectory of labour law scholarship in the last century. In what sense is any field of law autonomous, if law as a whole is to be regarded as forming a system? The autonomy claim has several elements, but is at the outset perhaps best understood within a particular intellectual tradition. Professor Lord Wedderburn is usually credited, in his article 'From Here to Autonomy' in 1987,[2] with drawing the notion into Anglophone labour law scholarship. He drew in particular on the account of French jurist Paul Durand, who described the evolution from distinctiveness (*particularisme*) to autonomy of labour law in France.[3] Wedderburn's approach sought to separate labour law in particular from the ordinary common law, and from the influence of ordinary judges imbued with a common law mindset through training, experience and tradition. However, as Mark Freedland puts it in the opening chapter to this collection, entitled 'Otto Kahn-Freund, the Contract of Employment and the Autonomy of Labour Law', although he did not use the term 'autonomy of labour law', Kahn-Freund was a 'supreme exponent of the autonomy of labour law *avant la lettre*'. This looked less at the notion of juridical autonomy of labour law as a regulatory system, and more to the autonomy of the social forces in collective bargaining. Autonomy in this sense denoted the freedom of social groups to determine their own norms, facilitated by a freedom *from* state interference and control in the processes and outcomes of collective negotiation.

As even the historical emergence of 'autonomy' as a concept suggests, the 'autonomy of labour law' has various aspects. First of all, at the meta-level, there is the issue of whether labour law rests on or embodies a specific or distinctive set of normative precepts or ideals. Secondly, at the mid-level, there are two quite distinct strands. As exemplified in Kahn-Freund's concerns for the autonomy of social actors from the state, there are concerns to ensure 'political autonomy'. In particular, he asserted the idea of the 'autonomy' of social forces from state control.[4] Ensuring the autonomy of social actors from the potentially overweening or even authoritarian state was a central theme, understandable given Kahn-Freund's arrival in Britain as a German Jewish scholar seeking refuge from a fascist regime. As Kahn-Freund was acutely aware, the dependence of the German trade union movement on the German state had weakened the resistance of civil society to the tragic eclipse of liberal-democratic norms. The other mid-level strand concerns 'institutional autonomy' *stricto sensu*, in particular ensuing that the institutions charged with elaborating, enforcing and, in particular, adjudicating labour law were suitable to realize its particular aims

[2] Lord Wedderburn, 'Labour Law: From Here to Autonomy?' (1987) 16 *Industrial Law Journal* 1.
[3] ibid fn 2, citing P Durand, 'Le Particularisme du Droit du Travail' [1944] *Droit Social* 276.
[4] On this political sense of autonomy, see A Bogg *The Democratic Aspects of Trade Union Recognition* (Oxford, Hart Publishing, 2009) ch 1.

or normative commitments. Thirdly, there is a substantive dimension, referring to a distinctive set of legal rules and principles regulating an identifiable social phenomenon. Here, we find a commitment to examining the micro-level, working from empirical realities and phenomena, and so a commitment to socio-legal and empirical methods.

Different scholars emphasize different interrelationships between the different levels. To illustrate a classic starting point, a strong theme is what Freedland terms the 'negative dimension' of autonomy. This was a major theme in Kahn-Freund's theory of political autonomy as freedom from state interference in the social forces. It is also exemplified in Wedderburn's take, where autonomy means freedom from outside influence, ie substantive autonomy of labour law, in particular from the common law and its judges. Wedderburn's prescriptions lead him directly to questions of institutional autonomy of labour law. He refers to this as the 'agony at the point of a new departure', the recognition that even a new labour code 'would not, experience suggests, be administered according to its purposes by the existing common law courts'.[5] Accordingly, new (autonomous) law would need new procedures and new labour tribunals. In contrast, other approaches emphasize a positive approach to autonomy. Often the starting point of these other approaches is a commitment to the particular aims and normative commitments of labour law, whilst showing greater openness to the capacity of outside rules, principles and institutions to help realize these aims.

A. Labour Law's Autonomy: Theory and Methodology

Mark Freedland's contribution focuses on two distinct phases in the work of Kahn-Freund. The evolution in Kahn-Freund's thinking is revealing, as it reflects important realizations about the importance and significance of labour law's autonomy. At the outset, while Kahn-Freund acknowledged the potential problems with rooting labour law in the contract of employment, he saw it as holding much promise in the defence of 'collective *laissez-faire*'—not least as a way of making the terms of collective agreements enforceable through their incorporation into individual contracts. Disillusionment only followed at a later stage, when the common law had clearly failed to develop as originally envisaged, notably by continuing to ignore inequality of bargaining power. It had therefore become a threat to labour law's autonomy, because of its 'paradoxically antithetical' insistence on a notion of formal equality between the parties, whilst at the same time requiring the employee's subordination as a defining characteristic. He later railed against common law conservatism, in particular the dead weight of the master and servant construct, which prevented the contract of employment from fully integrating worker-protective legislation as part of its mandatory, non-derogable content.

As regards the autonomy claim, Freedland notes that while asserting the

[5] Wedderburn (n 2) 28.

autonomy of labour law can helpfully dislodge common law assumptions of equality of bargaining power, the master–servant institution is immanent in labour law. This point is also made by Hugh Collins, who evocatively characterizes as bitter 'vinegar' the residue of master–servant thinking which precludes a progressive development of the common law on the contract of employment.[6] Collins' chapter on 'Contractual Autonomy' thus tackles the autonomy claim head-on, albeit at 'mid-level'. In order to delineate the discipline of labour law, a task distinct from identifying overarching purposes of labour law, he seeks to develop a 'mid-level theory regarding the core ingredients of the legal subject'. This task goes to the substantive content of labour law, which is identified by distinguishing its core and peripheral elements.

In tracing the transition of English labour law from 'collective autonomy' to 'contractual autonomy', Collins draws heavily on the work of Davies and Freedland on the decline of collective *laissez-faire*.[7] With that decline came the centrality of the contract of employment as the legal institution around which the subject is built. In contrast to his earlier work on the structure of labour law,[8] Collins' account thus focuses on the distinctive legal institutions of labour law, rather than being driven by a particular normative vision. The contract has a decisive role throughout the employment relationship, and meets the requirement of internal conceptual coherence. However, this raises the evident 'dilemma of contractual autonomy', namely that the common law of contract is not particular to labour law at all. On this point, Collins again turns to Freedland's lead in *The Personal Employment Contract*.[9] The route therein identified is towards a restatement of the common law on the contract of employment.

However, as Collins notes, that route seems to have been abandoned in Freedland and Kountouris' *The Legal Construction of Personal Work Relations*. In embracing personal work relations not founded on a contract of employment, they simply assert the employment contract's lack of centrality. As the 'personal work relation' is not a legal concept, Collins contends that it fails to provide the legal basis for an autonomous legal subject. So there are two routes—either expand the contract (ie the contractual autonomy route) or work towards the creation of the personal work relation as a legal institution. Collins treats autonomy as established when a legal subject has three characteristics: it must be distinctive, independent and self-regulating. The third requirement means that the subject must have its own special internal logic and so function as 'an autopoetic subsystem of law'.[10] Whether these characteristics are present requires examination of both the external views of the practice of labour law,

[6] Collins (Ch 2, this volume).

[7] P Davies and M Freedland, *Labour Legislation and Public Policy: A Contemporary History* (Oxford, Clarendon Press, 1993), drawing on the phrase first used in O Kahn-Freund, 'Labour Law' in M Ginsberg (ed), *Law and Opinion in England in the 20th Century* (London, Stevens, 1959) 224.

[8] H Collins, 'Labour Law as a Vocation' (1989) 105 *Law Quarterly Review* 468.

[9] M Freedland The Personal Employment Contract (Oxford, Oxford University Press, 2003).

[10] G Teubner, *Law as an Autopoietic System* (Oxford, Blackwell, 1993).

and its internal logic. While the normative perspective is important, the focus is principally on legal reasoning, institutions and doctrinal concepts.

In this respect, his approach differs sharply from that of Alan Bogg, who explicitly uses normative ideals to identify the central case. In contrast to Freedland and Collins, his starting point is a rights-based theory of labour law, which in turn dictates the appropriate internal structure. Bogg's chapter 'Labour Law and the Trade Unions: Autonomy and Betrayal' asks why in an era when union membership, collective bargaining coverage and collective action are all in sharp decline, should labour lawyers continue to concern themselves with collective labour law? Like Collins, Bogg seeks to identify labour law's central elements. However, unlike Collins, Bogg contends that purportedly value-free approaches cannot truly determine which practices are central. Accordingly, Bogg contends that a normative approach is required. The question 'what is labour law?' must be reformulated as 'why labour law?',[11] with descriptive reflection on the structure of labour law continuous with, rather than autonomous from, an account of ethics and the human good. To this end, Bogg surveys various recent rights-based accounts, contrasting the 'capability approach' with Freedland and Kountouris' recent theorization of 'personality in work'.[12] He identifies two distinctive capability theories in labour law, the modest version of Deakin, Browne and Wilkinson,[13] and Langille's over-reaching account.[14] In part due to the under-specified nature of capability theory, he finds both accounts lacking. Like Collins, he turns to Freedland and Kountouris' theorization of 'personality in work', in it finding a compelling normative base for a rights-based approach to labour law. Bogg offers an important addition to their account, clarifying the connection between personality in work and collective rights. He suggests that the concept of 'subsidiarity' be used to support such a connection. The 'central case' analysis places collective rights as human rights at the structural core of labour law.

In her chapter 'Common Law Confusion and Empirical Research in Labour Law' Lizzie Barmes urges sustained empirical research into the common law of employment. Such work could build on existing traditions of openness in labour law research—both as regards methodological questions, and the understanding that labour law does not exist in the abstract—in order to stimulate political interest in relevant legislative projects and to shed light on existing incoherence and confusion. The latter in particular is driven by a significant chasm between common law adjudication of employment disputes and the increasingly

[11] Employing the 'central case' methodology of John Finnis: J Finnis, *Natural Law and Natural Rights*, 2nd edn (Oxford, Oxford University Press, 2011) ch 1.

[12] MR Freedland and N Kountouris, The Legal Construction of Personal Work Relations (Oxford, Oxford University Press, 2011).

[13] S Deakin and F Wilkinson, *The Law of the Labour Market* (Oxford, Oxford University Press, 2005); S Deakin and J Browne, 'Social Rights and Market Order', in T Hervey and J Kenner (eds), *Economic and Social Rights under the EU Charter of Fundamental Rights: A Legal Perspective* (Oxford, Hart Publishing, 2003).

[14] B Langille, 'Labour Law's Theory of Justice' in G Davidov and B Langille (eds), *The Idea of Labour Law* (Oxford, Oxford University Press, 2011) 104.

complex realities of working life, as seen, for example, in the ongoing controversy surrounding the relationship between the regimes of (common law) wrongful and (statutory) unfair dismissal, or the determination of workers' status.

Against this backdrop, a broader methodological approach is needed to develop a fuller understanding of how employment adjudication works, and how the resulting norms interact with broader social and economic institutions. Such work at the micro-level, she contends, would furthermore have significant instrumental benefits—not least for doctrinal scholarship, the focus of which would shift from individual, potentially anomalous, cases to larger sets of decisions. An empirical analysis of common law adjudication would furthermore stimulate public dialogue as to political responsibility to intervene in problems the judiciary cannot resolve. It would, finally, provide the necessary background for a critical understanding of the legal process, in particular the influence of the judiciary's demographic homogeneity on employment-related decision-making—for example in areas such as behavioural conflicts at work, the comparative adjudication of (interim) injunction applications, and even more heavily statute-based areas such as judicial review of public sector equality considerations. The empirical work she undertakes and advocates has the capacity to reveal whether traditional labour law scepticism about judicial attitudes and institutional propensities is well-founded. In this sense, she urges that this facet of autonomy discourse be subject to empirical investigation and refinement, rather than treated as dogma.

In her chapter 'Evaluating the Reflexive Turn in Labour Law' Diamond Ashiagbor examines what, if anything, is gained by reformulating labour law as a field of reflexive law and governance. As both collective *laissez-faire* and statutory intervention have had their heyday, she asks whether 'reflexive law' is an appropriate frame to understand new forms of labour market governance, particularly those rooted in the social and employment policy of the EU. The hallmarks of a reflexive law include indirect steering and a focus on second-order effects, based on an assumption that law and the economy are discrete systems, and an attendant focus on proceduralization. Reflexive law marks a decisive shift away from top-down, rule-based, centralized, 'command-and-control' approaches, with the state becoming decentred as other actors take on a greater regulatory or self-regulatory role. She notes that in reflexive law scholarship, there is sometimes a tendency to conflate the descriptive and normative usages of the term.

She concludes that reflexive law approaches do have some explanatory power, and capture some, but not all, features of both the European Employment Strategy and UK positive equality duties. Examining these positive equality duties through a reflexive lens[15] reveals that they are a hybrid, entailing both traditional individual rights enforcement, and broader institutional responsibility to mainstream equality. She argues that absent clearly delineated duties, there is a difficulty of translating public goals into managerial norms, with equality

[15] C McCrudden, 'Equality Legislation and Reflexive Regulation: A Response to the Discrimination Law Review's Consultative Paper' (2007) 36 *Industrial Law Journal* 255.

morphing into a business-friendly version of diversity. Ultimately, she contends that there is an imperfect 'fit' between theories of reflexive law and the new forms of labour law and governance she examines. Furthermore, these new forms often seem to lack normative underpinnings, raising the concern that reflexive regulation may not differ significantly from de-regulation or non-regulation.

Ashiagbor considers two different senses of the autonomy claim. First, in systems theory, on which reflexive law approaches draw, it is assumed that law and the economy are self-referential and self-reproducing systems. While some scholars have suggested that labour law is a discrete subsystem, she rejects this notion in favour of an understanding of labour law as an inextricable part of the legal system.[16] Notably, while she draws on Collins in this context, the latter's chapter identifies the criteria for labour law to be an autonomous sub-system, drawing on Teubner's notion of autopoiesis.[17] Ashiagbor's second sense of the autonomy claim relates to institutional autonomy. Reflexive law aims to trigger the self-regulatory process within the economy, providing only a framework, a set of background rules, leaving actors to operate, deliberate or bargain in the shadow of the law. Law thus becomes 'a system for the coordination of action within and between semi-autonomous social subsystems'.[18] On this account, the autonomy of the social partners is a modest claim, admitting the distinctive structuring and steering role of law. In this sense, she contends that reflexive labour law is 'autonomous' in the same way and to the same degree that collective *laissez faire* could be understood to have been autonomous. 'Pure' autonomy is a fiction. It can only be understood as a relative concept.

B. Labour Law's Autonomy: Core Organizing Concepts

The next part examines controversies concerning core organizing concepts in labour law through the lens of autonomy.

Jeremias Prassl's chapter 'Autonomous Concepts in Labour Law? The Complexities of the Employing Enterprise Revisited' returns to the suggestion, first made in the joint work of Mark Freedland and Paul Davies,[19] that some of the most pressing challenges to the scope of employment protective legislation could best be understood as driven by a unitary notion of the employer. He explores the extent to which employment law's rigid attachment to this notion is the result of the discipline's attachment to concepts which have become autonomous from the broader common law. The key factors that shaped the unitary notion of the employer are identified, including received language and fact patterns, the

[16] H Collins, 'Book Review of Rogowski and Wilthagen (eds) Reflexive Labour Law: Studies in Industrial Relations and Employment Regulation' (1998) 61 *Modern Law Review* 916, 919.

[17] G Teubner, 'Substantive and Reflexive Elements in Modern Law' (1983) 17 *Law and Society Review* 239, 242.

[18] ibid 242.

[19] P Davies and M Freedland, 'The Complexities of the Employing Enterprise' in G Davidov and B Langille (eds), *Boundaries and Frontiers of Labour Law* (Oxford, Hart Publishing, 2006) 273.

common law's bilateral conception of the contract of employment, and company law's understanding of the corporate veil of limited liability companies. This received understanding causes deep problems for the scope of employment law. To resolve them, he looks outside labour law, to developments in the general law of obligations and company law. As the law has advanced considerably in each of these areas, he finds flexible solutions in response to complex modern-day fact patterns. The privity doctrine, for example, is no longer seen as the end point into the enquiry of two parties' relationships, with tort law increasingly stepping into the breach (even in the complete absence of contractual relationships). The corporate veil has similarly become qualified by a long list of context-specific exceptions. On the basis of these examples, it is suggested that employment law's unitary notion of the employer is a problematic case of conceptual autonomy, which only an openly functional notion of the employer could overcome.

Nicola Countouris' chapter on the 'Uses and Misuses of "Mutuality of Obligations" and the Autonomy of Labour Law' returns to 'one of [Mark Freedland's] most important contributions to the modern understanding of the contract of employment', the notion of mutuality of obligation, as a key locus in which to explore whether, and if so, in what sense, labour law can be understood to constitute an autonomous discipline. Labour law, Countouris suggests, never sought to conflate autonomy with isolation; which may explain the extent to which its core notions, such as mutuality and the contract of employment, have been subject to the gravitational force of the English law of obligations. Mutuality of obligation first emerged in Mark Freedland's work as a technical device to conceptualize the operation of the contract of employment, in particular as regards the rules surrounding breach and termination. In the hands of the senior judiciary and through the influence of contractual principles (such as consideration) and contract law reasoning, however, this analytical-descriptive device soon morphed into a *requirement* for the existence of a contract of service—thus leaving increasing numbers of workers in fragmented or short-term work arrangements outside the scope of employment protective norms. By embarking on a comparative analysis of mutuality of obligation, Countouris demonstrates that there is no inherent link between the legal construction of employment relationships as contracts of employment and English law's notion of mutuality of obligation. He critiques the English approach as 'hardly reconcilable with the autonomous function and rationale that was originally attached to the concept'. He urges that the courts should abandon it, and the notion should be restored to its original, purely analytical, purpose.

Cathryn Costello's chapter 'Migrants and Forced Labour: A Labour Law Response' looks at migrant workers and the contemporary empirical evidence concerning forced labour amongst migrant workers in the UK. Looking at forced labour brings many other branches of law crowding in—immigration law, criminal law and human rights law in particular. Her central contention is that forced labour should be regarded as a labour law problem, with a labour law solution. She identifies three elements to a labour law approach to migrant workers' vulnerability to labour exploitation and forced labour. The first move would be to insulate labour law from matters of migration status. The second would be to regulate labour intermediaries, taking into account the particular vulnerabilities to migrant workers in the labour supply chain. Thirdly, she advocates developing greater institutional protections for labour rights, given the significant enforcement deficit for migrant workers' rights. Her desiderata have a strong autonomous ring to them, urging greater normative and institutional autonomy for labour law, to protect both migrant and local workers.

These three contributions share a focus on key constructs in labour law. Prassl argues that conceptual autonomy has thwarted progressive development of labour law, at least in assuming a unitary notion of the employer. Instead of representing a 'Faustian pact with the English Common Law Devil',[20] common law developments might thus be seen as offering the conceptual building blocks for a progressive move towards a functional notion of the employer. Costello's chapter also looks outside labour law. Drawing on her collection co-edited with Freedland,[21] to which many Oxford colleagues contributed, she examines the impact of immigration law and the migration process on work relations. Yet, her prescriptions seek to reassert the substantive and institutional autonomy of labour law, in particular aiming to ensure that labour rights are insulated from immigration law. In contrast, Countouris critiques the judicial development of the notion of 'mutuality of obligation'. The trajectory he identifies, judicial distortion of a distinctive labour law concept, has a Wedderburnian ring to it. That judicial distortion came as the notion was transfigured into an employment-law-specific apparatus, loaded with value judgements and potentially duty-laden.

C. Labour Law's Autonomy: Labour Law, Public Law and Human Rights

The third part looks at the significant bearing of public, human rights and equality law on labour law.

Anne Davies in her chapter 'Labour Law as Public Law' revisits Paul Davies' and Mark Freedland's 1997 article,[22] in which they identified the 'modes' of UK public law with a clear influence on labour law, namely the individualist and constitutional-rights-based modes. Davies applies their framework to recent developments, refining and developing it as she goes. The 'individualist' mode refers to the protection of the individual from encroachment by powerful actors, normally the state. In labour law, this mode is evident in courts' assessment of employers' decisions on both procedural fairness and reasonableness grounds.

[20] Freedland on Otto Kahn-Freund, ch 1 below.

[21] C Costello and M Freedland, *Migrants at Work: Immigration & Vulnerability in Labour Law* (Oxford, Oxford University Press, 2014) (forthcoming).

[22] P Davies and M Freedland, 'The Impact of Public Law on Labour Law, 1972–1997' (1997) 26 *Industrial Law Journal* 311.

Across various contexts, she finds that courts are much more rigorous in their application of procedural fairness duties in public law than in labour law, a finding she shares with Davies and Freedland. The 'constitutional rights-based' frame has become more important with the incorporation of the European Convention on Human Rights (ECHR) into UK law with the Human Rights Act 1998. She traces its impact by focusing on domestic UK case law on Article 11 ECHR on freedom of association. She concludes that while the HRA has contributed to robust judicial review in the public law context, the labour law approach is more cautious. Her additional novel and important contribution concerns the contracting out of public services to the private sector. Although this was not part of Davies and Freedland's 1997 analysis, it has been a central theme of Freedland's public law scholarship.[23] Labour law, via the Acquired Rights Directive (ARD), has by 'happy accident' been interpreted so as to ensure its continuity in various outsourcing situations.[24] In contrast, in public law, the courts have been reluctant to treat private entities as undertaking public functions.

Overall, the three scenarios support her general thesis that there is judicial reluctance to extend public law scrutiny beyond purely public situations. Labour law case law generally embodies greater deference to employer prerogatives than public law does to the state. She suggests two main explanations. In public law, the courts aim to keep the government in check, a task that increasingly eludes Parliament. In contrast, in labour law, the courts still regard Parliament as having the primary responsibility for striking a balance between the interests of employers and workers, and are more reluctant to interfere. Relatedly, courts defer to employers' assessment of their economic interests. Her conclusion advocates the institutional autonomy of labour law, invoking Wedderburn.[25] She suggests that the courts tend to defer to employers' economic freedom in a way that sits uneasily with labour law's traditional concern for *limiting* the employer's economic freedom, though it is a disposition that sits rather more easily with the common law's concern to protect property rights.

In her chapter 'Equality Law: Labour Law or an Autonomous Field?' Sandra Fredman notes that absent a written constitution and bill of rights in the UK, anti-discrimination law developed as an integral part of labour law in the UK. Although UK statutes prohibited discrimination in other contexts from the outset, the employment context dominated. However, with incorporation of Article 14 ECHR into domestic law, a human right to equality, albeit limited in scope to the ambit of other ECHR protections, is now part of UK law. EU

[23] MR Freedland, 'Government by Contract and Public Law' [1994] *Public Law* 86; 'Privatising *Carltona*: Part II of the Deregulation and Contracting Out Act 1994' [1995] *Public Law* 21; 'The Rule Against Delegation and the *Carltona* Doctrine in an Agency Context' [1996] *Public Law* 19, 'Public Law and Private Finance—Placing the Private Finance Initiative in a Public Frame' [1998] *Public Law* 288.

[24] Council Directive 2001/23/EC of 12 March 2001 on the approximation of the laws of the Member States relating to the safeguarding of employees' rights in the event of transfers of undertakings, businesses or parts of undertakings or businesses [2001] OJ L82/62.

[25] Wedderburn (n 2).

discrimination law too has matured and been extended beyond the work context. She argues that the right to equality unsettles the assumptions in both labour law, where the focus is on an employer–worker relationship, and human rights law, which emphasizes the relationship between the state and individual. But whereas human rights law has gradually been overcoming these limitations, labour law in the UK has been moving in the opposite direction. Hers is ultimately a plea for the specificity of equality law. She argues that an appropriate understanding of the nature of non-discrimination duties justifies their application beyond the employment realm.

Fredman notes that in the two recent leading cases on the scope of UK anti-discrimination rules, *Jivraj*[26] and *X v Mid Sussex CAB*,[27] the courts took a traditional employment law approach to the question of the scope of non-discrimination. She shares Freedland and Kountouris's critique of *Jivraj*[28] for unduly restricting the scope of non-discrimination duties. She argues that the focus on the employment relationship, traditionally understood, is particularly discordant in equality law. In her view, all those who are capable of discrimination should be subject to equality law duties, with modulated justifications to accommodate competing rights and interests at stake. In particular, limits on the duty not to discriminate should not be based on an employer's economic interests. Appropriate limits to the right not to be discriminated against should derive from human rights considerations, particularly the need to protect the rights and interests of others.

Chris McCrudden in his chapter 'Labour Law as Human Rights Law: A Critique of the Use of "Dignity" in Freedland and Kountouris' engages deeply with the foundational concepts of the *The Legal Construction of Personal Work Relations*.[29] In Freedland and Kountouris's view, the functions of labour law are to maximize workers' dignity, optimize their capabilities, while ensuring the importance of stability in the work relations.[30] Although their account is based on this triumvirate of values, McCrudden focuses on dignity alone, noting the recent surge in dignitarian theorizing in labour law, often drawing on human rights theory. He notes that although 'dignity' features in international human rights and labour rights instruments, Freedland and Kountouris do not draw on any particular legal conception, but rather a general philosophical account. McCrudden contends that their vision of dignity, a composite or amalgam of autonomy and equality, is perilously under-theorized. For instance, he points out that they cite James Griffin, whose individualist account of dignity as a foundation for human rights denies the label 'human rights' to some well-established labour rights along with collective rights.[31] While McCrudden acknowledges that

[26] *Jivraj v Hashwani* [2011] UKSC 40, [2011] 1 WLR 1872.

[27] *X v Mid Sussex Citizens Advice Bureau* [2012] UKSC 59, [2013] 1 All ER 1038.

[28] M Freedland and N Kountouris, 'Employment Equality and Personal Work Relations—A Critique of *Jivraj v Hashwani*' (2012) 41 *Industrial Law Journal* 56.

[29] Freedland and Kountouris (n 12).

[30] ibid 49.

[31] J Griffin, *On Human Rights* (Oxford, Oxford University Press, 2008).

under-specification may leave room for appropriation, contestation and dialogue, his concern is that tacitly their account may be 'personalist'. Although personalism is itself a set of highly differentiated accounts of the value of the human person, McCrudden notes that it tends to be duty-laden. Indeed, some personalist accounts lead to highly authoritarian conceptions of the role of the state.

Finally, McCrudden expresses concern that by grounding labour law in dignity, the authors will contribute to labour law being treated as human rights law. However, he notes that the European Court of Human Rights tends to treat as a violation of human dignity only extreme human rights violations, such as torture and inhuman and degrading treatment, or slavery, servitude, and forced labour. In this context, in his view, they may unintentionally be 'risking the crown jewels' of labour law, that is

> sacrificing labour law's collectivist and solidarity based roots for a much thinner set of individualist foundations, and at the same time risking a significant loss of labour law's autonomy by encouraging the importation of human rights principles into areas of labour law that seem unsuited to human rights as they are currently understood.

The future challenge McCrudden sets is to provide that richer conception of dignity, one that sets it apart from the more attenuated understanding of dignity that human rights are sometimes seen as based on. This challenge is, at least in part, met by Bogg's chapter, which aims to establish a clear basis for collective rights by fleshing out the relationship between dignity and capabilities. It may also be the case that the composite interaction between a plurality of values, dignity amongst others, is capable of securing an appropriate sense of labour law's autonomy. After all, Freedland and Kountouris are concerned to articulate a base for labour law of 'personality *in work*' rather than personality as such.

Turning to EU law, in their chapter 'The EU Internal Market and Domestic Labour Law—Looking Beyond Autonomy' Phil Syrpis and Tonia Novitz focus in particular on the profound effects of the Court of Justice's development of internal market law. Their analysis begins by sketching out the developing objectives of the Union's internal market law: following a long period where the Court avoided direct collisions between domestic labour laws and EU norms (notably by insulating collective bargaining against the provisions of competition law), the much-discussed decisions in *Viking* and *Laval* brought the two systems into head-on conflict.[32] These rulings subordinate workers' right to take industrial action to the internal market freedoms. A second section explores the increasingly complex relationship between Treaty provisions and secondary legislation seeking to balance the European Union's social and economic goals, and suggests that the disappointing trend continues in this sphere, with the latter continuously ending up subordinated to the former. In rejecting the resulting claims for an autonomous insulation of employment put forward by many labour lawyers, Novitz and Syrpis suggest that the discipline should instead engage much more

[32] M Freedland and J Prassl (eds), *EU Law in the Member States:* Viking, Laval *and Beyond* (Oxford, Hart Publishing, 2014) (forthcoming).

directly with EU internal market law, which has come to permeate large parts of domestic legal systems. They suggest a number of ways in which this could be achieved; from critiquing the case law of the Court within the existing Treaty framework (particularly following the Lisbon Treaty's amendments in favour of the 'social' within the Treaties) to addressing the legislative and political institutions beyond the Court of Justice.

Like the preceding discussions of European human rights norms, Syrpis and Novitz assume that EU norms and institutions are open to being infused with labour law values. But like Ashiagbor, they identify the risk that in the particular institutional context of the EU internal market, the economic tends to be privileged over the social.

D. Labour Law's Autonomy: Labour Law, Commercial Law and Economic Theory

The fourth and final part looks to commercial law and economic theory.

In questioning the normative implications of understanding labour law as the law of the business enterprise, Alice Carse and Wanjiru Njoya, in their chapter 'Labour Law as the Law of the Business Enterprise', turn to the role of workers as corporate stakeholders in modern enterprise, against a backdrop of recent scholarship which sees the corporation as a resource contributing to overall societal welfare. With particular reference to the contexts of job security in economic dismissals and the extent to which directors' fiduciary duties include the taking into account of employees' interests in conflict with other stakeholders' claims, they suggest that the law of the business enterprise might be seen as a valuable repository for the doctrinal development of labour law. At the outset, they admit that this approach may lead to excessive judicial deference to managerial power. However, in the longer term, they suggest that a bringing together of the two domains of business enterprise and labour law may lead to an evolution in favour of workers' interests, offsetting any short-term drawbacks resulting from a loss of the special treatment workers' interests enjoy in labour law. In particular, by reconceptualizing the firm as operating in the broader societal interest, and ensuring that directors' duties are understood not merely through their role as shareholders' agents, but rather as trustees of or mediators over claims to the corporation's assets, workers' legitimate expectations may increasingly come to be protected through their status as corporate constituents.

Jill Murray's chapter 'Conceptualizing the Employer as Fiduciary: Mission Impossible?' examines the interface between the common law of employment and the equitable concept of fiduciary obligation, conceptualizing the employer as owing a fiduciary obligation to the employee. Her central contention is that the engagement of labour, whether through a contract of employment or otherwise, necessarily involves a relationship of trust and confidence requiring the employing entity to place the interests of the worker above their own within a particular, narrow sphere. She admits her approach is 'heretical' in that usually the fiduciary aspect of employment law, if any, is conceived as the duty of employee to employer. Fiduciary obligations are rooted in trust, where the trustee undertakes to act in the interest of another. The rationales for the employee's fiduciary obligations vary, with the implied contractual duty of fidelity nowadays providing 'a kind of scaffolding' for the fiduciary duty, allowing the fiduciary duty to be grounded in contractual agreement.

Treating the *employer* as fiduciary, in contrast, is more conceptually challenging. In particular, there is no expectation that the employer act in the interests of employees, nor is there a contractual basis for fiduciary obligations towards employees. However, she argues that a case can be made for the employer as fiduciary, based on the ways in which the employment relationship is treated within orthodox equitable principles. As equity imposes fiduciary obligations to protect the employer's business from illegitimate competition, an argument for the employer's fiduciary obligation to the employee may be grounded on a similar acknowledgement of the need to protect the 'integrity' of the employee as an 'economic being'. With this insight in mind, Murray examines four core aspects of labour law: the employer's power over the content of the contract and mode of contracting; the employer's power during the performance of the contract; the employer's power to manipulate corporate form; and the exercise of workplace power in the absence of contract. Under the first category, she considers sham self-employment, triangular labour relations and intermittent contracts. In all these instances, she suggests a possible corrective role for equitable approaches to thwart abuse of employer power. Concerning employer power during the performance of the contract, she suggests a role for equity where employers permit the exercise of actual power for their own benefit, and then rely on the contract to avoid legal responsibility. Here she suggests that the actions should be viewed as unconscionable. Thirdly, concerning the employer's power to manipulate corporate form, she identifies some egregious evasive manipulations of the corporate form. Finally, she identifies work scenarios where there may be no contract (or no valid contract, as in *Hounga v Allen*[33]), where the equitable 'clean hands' doctrine can play a role. While some of these applications would be highly unorthodox, she argues that this equitable approach could apply easily to the protection of accrued employee entitlements and possibly even to the manipulation of corporate form to avoid common law liabilities.

Paul Davies' chapter 'Efficiency Arguments for the Collective Representation of Workers: A Sketch' understands efficiency as 'arranging governance rights in the company so as to minimise its cost of production', thus maximizing the enterprise's overall contribution to society at any given level of production. His argument begins by questioning the assumption in traditional accounts found in law and economics scholarship that it is usually efficient to withhold control rights from employees, as shareholders collectively are the group with the

[33] *Hounga v Allen* [2014] UKSC 47, [2014] ICR 847.

strongest incentive to reduce a company's production costs. Given the open-ended contractual nature of the employment relationship, however, these claims deserve to be scrutinized closely: if employees' interests can be said to include the long-term competitive efficiency of their employing enterprise, the allocation of certain governance rights to workers may well create value for both employees and employers. This is especially so if those rights operate both at board and sub-board levels, institutionalizing effective co-operation. He then turns to a comparative analysis of the German system of employee involvement in corporate governance, which involves a complex set of interrelationships between employee representatives in a variety of arrangements, from board-level representation and works councils to collective bargaining. A survey of recent empirical evidence on the efficiency of that approach suggests the emergence of long-term implicit contracts between management and labour, with an impact on production costs which is 'not negative and may well be positive'. In concluding, Davies explores the extent to which Germany's multi-level codetermination approach may be generalized.

Deirdre McCann's closing chapter concerns the evolution of normative orders at the international level, where the increasingly sophisticated literature on regulatory theory has precipitated an important shift in the World Bank's conceptualization of labour regulation. In this respect, she traces a trajectory whereby the World Bank has created theoretical space—a plateau—for legitimate labour market regulation. While the simplistic antinomy between market efficiency and labour regulation now seems to have been discarded by the World Bank—indeed, it was scarcely coherent given the necessary market-constituting function of legal norms—the normative consequences of this reconceptualization are still unclear. Indeed, and paradoxically perhaps, McCann speculates that one effect of this shift in the World Bank's approach might be the destabilization and degradation of the institutional role of the International Labour Organization (ILO) in the sphere of international labour standards. The effect of this may radiate far beyond the boundaries of the ILO itself, calling into question the persuasive authority of ILO norms in other fora such as the European Court of Human Rights.

The contributions by Carse and Njoya, and by Murray, seem, at least implicitly, to assume the worker-protective aim of labour law, yet look to other fields to vindicate that aim. Carse and Njoya look to the law of the business enterprise as a source of greater worker protection. However, their account also demands an important reconceptualization of the corporation qua resource contributing to overall societal welfare. Murray similarly looks to equity, but acknowledges that institutionalizing the employer's fiduciary duties to the employee is quite a leap from current practice. Davies' approach, in contrast, assumes the value of efficiency. While this value is often assumed in public discourse to be in tension with worker-protective aims, he examines the evidence that efficiency aims may support the institution of collective representation of workers. Similarly, McCann invokes the economic benefits of labour law, but notes the challenge for traditional institutions of labour law, such as the ILO, when international economic institutions such as the World Bank encroach on its territory.

II. Three Levels of Autonomy

The contributions reflect highly diverse takes on the normative dimension of autonomy. At the meta-level we find, unsurprisingly perhaps, a proliferation of values: efficiency, dignity, freedom, equality, capabilities, basic goods. We find such value pluralism in Freedland and Kountouris' distinctive notion of personality in work, which rests on a plurality of three core values: dignity, capability and stability. We might say that these values are of such ubiquity that their invocation in the labour law context is unsurprising. Nonetheless, this normative territory is relatively uncharted because of the historical dominance of focusing on social and institutional autonomy (the mid-level in our framework), namely a paradigm focused upon the institutions of labour law, typically collective bargaining, the contract of employment and the personal employment relation. However, there are older constitutional currents in labour law that also align with universal values, such as industrial democracy or the dignity of labour. It is perhaps fair to say that these older currents were eclipsed in British labour law in the middle decades of the twentieth century as scholars marvelled at the virtue of an organic system of voluntary collective bargaining that owed more to the practical activities of working people than the ethical reflections of philosophers. After 1979, of course, there was no question that those normative debates now needed to be joined in public and scholarly discourse.

As Bogg's contribution makes explicit, these values are not unique to labour law. They represent rather the extension into the world of work of ideas of general social value. So too, Paul Davies claims, with the value of efficiency. Opening up this normative contestation is to raise many questions with which the contributors grapple, although by no means resolve. We could ask whether efficiency is a value like the others, or if it is, is it of merely instrumental rather than intrinsic value, or a mere subordinate side-constraint? The disintegration of labour law's autonomy in this sense, and the proliferation of values, certainly makes the theoretical task a challenging one. As McCrudden's intervention shows, committing to a dignitarian basis for labour law raises deep concerns about the substantive implications of this move.

Once labour law admits of this plurality of values, an idea virtually all of the contributors endorse or assume, the focus on the institutional and substantive autonomy comes to the fore. What of the autonomy of social actors, such a strong theme in Kahn-Freund's work? The roots of his variant of autonomy were, it will be recalled, strongly anti-statist, reflecting pluralist political thought. In some of the contributions, there is a distinct shift to assuming that equality and human rights duties, in particular, should be extended to all powerful private actors. This leads to a reconfiguration of the state's role, and the technique of state coercion, which prompts difficult normative questions about the appropriate reach of state compulsion. Fredman, for instance, explicitly defends the view that equality duties cut across the public–private divide. The question of who is the duty-bearer prompts different responses throughout the volume, not only depending on whether the state, corporation or individual is at issue, but also as different accounts of the basis of obligation are identified. It also depends on regulatory technique, for it is perhaps the case that justifications for imposing reflexive duties, which create spaces for autonomous action, might be different to non-reflexive techniques, with implications in turn for broader normative questions of the appropriate limits of state intervention.

On the institutional front, Barmes' contribution is a powerful plea for greater empirical work to understand the actual practices of the legal institutions, a reminder that these are often under-investigated. With the proliferation of institutions with a role in labour law comes concerns about fragmentation and dilution of the normative focus on worker protection. Ashiagbor's assessment of two forms of new governance in labour law, the European Employment Strategy and positive equality duties, echoes a concern that these institutional mechanisms may all too easily lack normative rigour. Costello reminds us that the institutional disarray concerning enforcement of labour rights in the UK leaves many workers vulnerable to extreme exploitation and abuse, but in advocating greater institutional protections, notes that the insulation of labour from immigration law therefore becomes even more important.

Concerning substantive autonomy, the Wedderburnian current of scepticism about the common law, and common law judges in particular, recurs throughout the collection, notably in Anne Davies' contribution which illustrates the courts' reluctance to constrain employer prerogatives in key fields. This negative take on autonomy also appears in Costello's argument that migration status, ie status derived from immigration law, should have no bearing on the enjoyment of labour rights. In particular, the application of the common law doctrine of contractual illegality to deny vulnerable migrant workers the protections of equality, human rights and labour rights would seem to embody all the worst elements of the common law 'vinegar'.[34]

Yet, for other contributors, porosity with the wider common law is productive rather than pernicious. Barmes cites the example of the public sector equality duties as an example of a field requiring empirical elucidation, a technique also discussed by Ashiagbor. Prassl looks to other features of the common law in order to develop a functional concept of the employer. Murray looks to equity to identify areas where the law ought to constrain employer prerogatives. Murray's chapter is a further illustration that the 'negative' concept of autonomy is too hasty if it treats private law as a unified category. Nor should we imagine that the common law is impervious to progressive development driven by labour law,

[34] Collins (n 6).

as the leading Supreme Court ruling on sham transactions illustrates.[35] Carse and Njoya, and Paul Davies look to the institutional form of the legal institution that is the corporation in order to identify and rationalize important duties to workers. Engagement with disciplines other than labour law is par for the course in labour law scholarship, yet the autonomy claim persists. This is not a paradox, but rather a reflection of the importance of having a filtering mechanism to ensure that borrowings are normatively and institutionally fitting.

Throughout the collection, then, we find concern that labour law should engage with other domains, albeit cautiously. This holds in particular for human rights law. McCrudden, for instance, warns that human rights law may bring a heavily individualist focus within the judicial protection of human rights (in particular at the ECtHR), thereby undermining the collectivist values of labour law. The perils in subsuming labour law into human rights law are also present in the contributions of Anne Davies and Costello. For Davies, the human rights case law may be too deferential to employer prerogatives. For Costello, the current approaches to the states' positive duties to combat forced labour are thus far excessively focused on criminalization. The inclusion of the prohibition of human trafficking into Article 4 ECHR is also problematized in her chapter, and she suggests a labour law reading of Article 4 ECHR.

The key issue then becomes to develop filtering criteria to assess whether a particular borrowing or even influx from another legal domain is apt to fulfil or undermine labour law's aims and functions. To illustrate that filtering process, consider the immunity of collective agreements from competition law, a prime example where labour law is insulated from another field.[36] In this context, given that the values and institutions of competition law are antithetical to the workings of collective agreements altogether, nothing but full insulation is appropriate. In contrast, Novitz and Syrpis argue in their contribution that the full insulation of labour law from EU internal market norms is not required, reassuring as that might appear post *Viking* and *Laval*. Rather they advocate various strategies to ensure that the social and labour dimensions of the internal market are properly developed. It is tempting to reflect upon how Wedderburn might have responded to this analytical move. Is 'internal market law' not simply Europe's common law? If it is, then labour law's traditional concern with substantive autonomy might yet have some vitality in this context, though the debates remain keenly contested.[37]

The scholarly protégées of the 'radical and refugee'[38] Kahn-Freund of various generations thus continue to reap the rewards of his rich thinking. The present volume ranges across all facets of the autonomy claim, from the normative to the

[35] *Autoclenz Ltd v Belcher* [2011] UKSC 41, [2011] ICR 1157. See further A Bogg, 'Sham Self-Employment in the Supreme Court' (2012) 41 *Industrial Law Journal* 328; ACL Davies, 'Sensible Thinking About Sham Transactions' (2009) 38 *Industrial Law Journal* 318.

[36] Collins (Ch 2, this volume).

[37] A Bogg, '*Viking* and *Laval*: The International Labour Law Perspective' in Freedland and Prassl (eds) (n 32).

[38] C Glasser 'Radicals and Refugees: The Foundation of the Modern Law Review and English Legal Scholarship' (1987) 50 *Modern Law Review* 688.

institutional and substantive elements. The autonomy of labour law is a rallying cry not for insulation, but engagement—with other legal fields, scholarly disciplines, practical politics and lived realities.

III. Autonomy and the Past, Present and Future of Labour Law Teaching in Oxford

There is, in conclusion, one further factor that unites all contributors to this volume: their early study and research work under Paul Davies and Mark Freedland. The latter's retirement from (formal) teaching duties thus provides an opportune moment briefly to explore the history of labour law teaching and research in the University of Oxford, in the development of which Mark and Paul were involved from the very beginning. In explaining their motivation in writing *Labour Legislation and Public Policy* they noted that

> the subject lacked all coherence unless one had obtained a good grasp of the tumultuous history of the recent legislation in this area. Those who have lived through the evolution of the subject over the past thirty years have acquired this useful knowledge by accretion, but for students who were born only well after the development of modern labour law was under way, there seemed to us to exist no full-scale treatment of these matters.[39]

The same point is perhaps true for the history of the teaching of the subject, each student taking the status quo at the moment when she first began to study labour law as a point of departure, with little knowledge by accretion from earlier periods. The concluding paragraphs of this introduction hope to remedy this with a brief overview to sketch out some of the highlights of the past 45 years, without however purporting to provide a full-scale treatment of these matters, or even a comprehensive list of all the practitioners and academics across the disciplines who fondly recall being taught, or teaching with and for Mark and Paul—whether as students, doctoral researchers, early career fellows or long-term colleagues.[40] Against certain constants (notably as regards the shape of the introductory labour law course, taught today to final-year undergraduates), three broad phases emerge: the establishment of labour law in Oxford under Otto Kahn-Freund, a move from collective *laissez-faire* to the legal regulation of collective bargaining, and most recently the opening up into international and European law, as well as many other disciplines.

[39] P Davies and M Freedland, *Labour Legislation and Public Policy: A Contemporary History* (Clarendon Press, Oxford 1993) i.

[40] We are deeply grateful to all those who have spoken to us in the preparation of this account; in particular Hugh Collins, Nicola Countouris, Paul Craig, Judy Fudge, John Gardner, and of course Paul Davies and Mark Freedland themselves. All historical errors are, of course, entirely ours.

A. The Early Years: Otto Kahn-Freund and Labour Law in Oxford

The history of Oxford labour law begins in 1964, with Otto Kahn-Freund's move to Oxford to take up the Chair of Comparative Law.[41] His interests in labour law were, at first, confined to his London origins, where he had already taught labour law at the LSE,[42] and where he continued to be based part-time through his work as a member of the Royal Commission on Trade Unions and Employers' Associations from 1965 to 1968 (the Donovan Commission).[43] Otto's first course in Oxford explored comparative family law, before moving on to comparative tort law, with an increasing focus on workers' compensation claims in subsequent years.

Labour law teaching itself began through an informal seminar series at Brasenose, and it was not until 1968 that Kahn-Freund 'breached a certain last bastion by introducing the teaching of labour law in the University of Oxford',[44] when a labour law course appeared on the books as a BCL (taught masters course) subject. In what Mark Freedland has termed 'a less than totally welcoming environment',[45] the course was designed to offer students a general introduction to the subject, with a particular focus on the following four areas:

> (a) The mutual contractual and statutory rights and obligations of employers and employees …;
> (b) Collective bargaining and the law …;
> (c) Trade disputes and the law …;
> (d) Trade unions and the law … .[46]

Mark Freedland arrived in Oxford in 1966. Having been introduced to labour law at University College London by Roger Rideout, he spent a year as a graduate student at Brasenose College, before being elected to a Junior Research Fellowship (JRF) at St John's College in 1967. The topic of his doctoral research,[47] as Hugh Collins suggests in this volume, was significantly ahead of its time,[48] and

[41] We take the account of Otto Kahn-Freund's life in the following primarily from M Freedland, 'Otto Kahn-Freund (1900–1979)' in J Beatson and R Zimmermann (eds), *Jurists Uprooted: German-Speaking Emigré Lawyers in Twentieth Century Britain* (Oxford, Oxford University Press, 2004), as well as a special edition 'Sir Otto Kahn-Freund, QC, FBA 1900–1979' (1979) 4 *Industrial Law Journal*.

[42] Following in the footsteps of Sir William Robson who had begun to teach the topic at LSE in the 1920s and 1930s. 'As a subject of academic study, [however, labour law] had grown from most modest beginnings in the preceding thirty years almost entirely as the result of Kahn-Freund's inspiration and enthusiasm': Freedland (n 41) 300, 307.

[43] See H Clegg, 'Otto Kahn-Freund and British Industrial Relations' in W Wedderburn of Charlton, R Lewis and J Clark (eds) *Labour Law and Industrial Relations: Building on Kahn-Freund* (Clarendon Press, Oxford 1983).

[44] Freedland (n 41) 317.

[45] Freedland (Ch 1, this volume).

[46] University of Oxford, *Examination Regulations* (Oxford, Oxford University Press, 1968).

[47] M Freedland, 'The Application of the General Principles of the Law of Contract to the Termination of the Employment Relationship' (Doctoral Thesis, University of Oxford, 1970). Published, with significant additions, as M Freedland, *The Contract of Employment* (Clarendon Press, Oxford 1976).

[48] Collins (Ch 2, this volume).

would turn out to become the cornerstone of a lifelong interest in the contract of employment. [49] The teaching of labour law in those early years took place as much at the Oxford Branch of the Workers' Educational Association at Rewley House (today part of the University's Continuing Education Department) as it did at the faculty itself.

Otto retired from the Comparative Law Chair in 1970, the year of Mark's election to a Tutorial Fellowship at St John's.[50] This retirement, much like those marked by the publication of this collection, was however entirely nominal, as he remained fully and intensely active in academic teaching or research until his death in 1979, as evidenced, for example, by the 1972 Hamlyn Lectures on *Labour and the Law*, and a significantly reworked edition in 1976.[51]

Paul Davies came to the Oxford law faculty as a Tutorial Fellow at Balliol College in 1974, soon joining Mark in teaching the BCL labour law course. Whilst their interests may at times have had slightly different focal points (individual labour law for Mark, collective matters for Paul; perhaps reflected to a certain extent in a focus on micro- and macroeconomic interests), there was never any division of labour. The course soon drew an enthusiastic crowd of students, many of whom fondly remember the young academics' contrasting and complementary teaching styles. The early BCL labour law course also led to the first major co-writing project, the publication in 1979 of the first edition of *Labour Law: Text and Materials*.[52]

The Examination Regulations of 1980 marked an important change, as labour law was for the first time listed as a subject for *both* the undergraduate exam (Final Honour School, FHS) and the BCL. This change was the result of two years' careful lobbying effort to allow the introduction of labour law as an undergraduate option. An initial proposal the year before had been voted down by the faculty—though whether this was due to ideological and methodological opposition to a subject perceived as politically charged and straying beyond black-letter analysis of the common law, or a fear of what was then perceived to be an unnecessary proliferation of option courses—remains unclear. Once a subsequent survey indicated that at least 60 undergraduates would be interested in taking up the new option subject, that opposition could be overcome, and course numbers would routinely exceed 60 students at undergraduate level and 20–30 BCL students, enough to fill the law faculty's board room during seminars.

It is perhaps a testament to Otto's prescience, as well as Mark and Paul's careful development of the subject, that in basic outline many aspects of the undergraduate course have been evolving organically ever since. The second

[49] M Freedland, *The Personal Employment Contract* (Oxford, Oxford University Press, 2003); M Freedland and N Kountouris, *The Legal Construction of Personal Work Relations* (Oxford, Oxford University Press, 2011); M Freedland, A Bogg, H Collins, N Countouris, A Davies, S Deakin and J Prassl (eds), *The Contract of Employment at Work* (Oxford, Oxford University Press, forthcoming).

[50] Becoming the University Lecturer in Labour Law the following year.

[51] O Kahn-Freund, *Labour and the Law* (London, Stevens for the Hamlyn Trust, 1972).

[52] P Davies and M Freedland, *Labour Law: Text and Materials* (London, Weidenfeld & Nicolson, 1979).

edition of their textbook in 1984, for example, shows significant revisions in terms of structure as well as content in order to keep pace with developments in the law.[53] This continued with a major reform of the way the course was organized and examined in the mid-1990s, making it one of the first option subjects in Oxford where lectures, seminars and tutorials ran in a co-ordinated fashion.

B. From Collective Bargaining and the Law to Legal Regulation and Collective Bargaining

With the introduction of labour law as an undergraduate course, the core module could thus move to the FHS, leaving space for the creation of a specialized option at BCL level. In 1981 (for first examination in 1982), precisely such a course was introduced under the title of Collective Bargaining and the Law.[54] This title was astutely in line with legislative and political developments from the 1970s onwards, reflecting the increasing importance of seeing even collective bargaining through the lens of its legal regulation. In terms of content, the nature of the graduate course allowed more time and space to focus on theoretical aspects of the subject as well as its interaction with other disciplines; legal knowledge was mostly assumed. The broad outline of the course was set down as follows:

> Collective Bargaining and the Law: The impact of collective bargaining and legislation upon the formation, content and termination of the employment relationship, and in particular:
> (a) the growth of collective bargaining in Great Britain from 1850 to 1960
> (b) the development of governmental regulation of the employment relationship in Great Britain from 1960 onwards;
> (c) the interaction of collective bargaining and labour legislation in Great Britain from 1960 onwards.

In its teaching methodology, the course was very much focused on understanding labour law in its wider political, sociological and economic context. In that sense it stood firmly in the Kahn-Freund school of an institutional, rather than doctrinal, understanding of our subject—an understanding that continues to inform our work to date, for example in a pronounced focus on labour law's regulatory techniques.[55] More than one student vividly recalls hours spent puzzling over latest government pronouncements, trade union strategies, and technical questions of macroeconomics such as the Phillips curve of unemployment.[56]

[53] P Davies and M Freedland, *Labour Law: Text and Materials*, 2nd edn (London, Weidenfeld & Nicolson, 1979).

[54] University of Oxford, *Examination Regulations* (Oxford, Oxford University Press, 1981).

[55] Ashiagbor (Ch 5, this volume).

[56] A Phillips, 'The Relationship between Unemployment and the Rate of Change of Money Wages in the United Kingdom 1861–1957' (1958) 25 *Economica* 283.

This interdisciplinary focus was furthermore not just limited to course design, but also indicative of Oxford labour law's broader relationship with the so-called 'Oxford school of industrial relations', key members of which included Alan Fox (a fellow of Nuffield College from 1958), Allan Flanders (Nuffield 1964–69) and Hugh Clegg (Nuffield 1949–67). Otto Kahn-Freund's background at the LSE meant that he was deeply familiar with interdisciplinary work, as opposed to Oxford's traditional emphasis on the common law alone—it is no surprise, perhaps, that the very term 'collective *laissez-faire*' had been coined in a broader industrial relations book.[57] In Oxford, he soon found a good friend and ally for this line of research in Hugh Clegg, an association continued by Mark and Paul.

The focal point for these collaborative discussions was a weekly series of industrial relations seminars organized from 1971 onwards by Bill (Lord) McCarthy, fellow of Nuffield College from 1959, and Mark and Paul, each Hilary (spring) term at Nuffield College.[58] Many students during those years remember their seminars on Fridays at 5 pm, which under the title of 'Labour Law and Labour Relations: Recent Trends and Future Possibilities' brought together law, PPE (politics, philosophy and economics) and industrial relations students and academics to hear from and discuss with a wide range of practitioners.

The first significant research output from this period is the preface to the third edition of *Labour and the Law*.[59] Written at a point in time where the industrial relations system had changed beyond what Otto had described, it nonetheless carefully preserves key elements of his legacy and thinking, in particular his 'conviction … that the social and economic function of a given body of law could be entirely transformed behind a curtain of ostensible legal continuity'.[60]

At around the time of the miners' strike of 1984–85, the BCL course was renamed The Legal Regulation of Collective Bargaining to reflect the changing legal and political landscape; with the publication of Mark and Paul's *magnum opus*, *Labour Legislation and Public Policy*,[61] in the Clarendon Series in 1993 marking the end of the work on this course as well as the Nuffield College seminars, which came to an end soon thereafter.

C. European and International Employment Law and Beyond

Whilst undergraduate teaching continued to develop with continuity, the BCL course was to change significantly. In 1991, Legal Regulation of Collective Bargaining morphed into International and European Employment Law, where

[57] O Kahn-Freund, 'Legal Framework' in A Flanders and H Clegg (eds), *The System of Industrial Relations in Great Britain—Its History, Law and Institutions* (Basil Blackwell, Oxford 1954).

[58] See W McCarthy, 'Introduction: The Changing Limits of Legal Intervention' in W McCarthy (ed), *Legal Intervention in Industrial Relations: Gains and Losses* (Oxford, Basil Blackwell, 1992) xv.

[59] P Davies and M Freedland (eds), *Kahn-Freund's Labour and the Law*, 3rd edn (London, Stevens & Sons, 1983).

[60] Freedland (n 41) 305.

[61] Davies and Freedland (n 39).

> Candidates [were] expected to show knowledge of the procedures and functions of the International Labour Organization and (in so far as they relate to the regulation of employment) of the Council of Europe and the European Communities, and of the scope, interpretation, and application of the regulatory instruments pertaining to employment which have been adopted by these bodies.

This new tack reflected a growing interest in future avenues for the development of labour law in European Union law, in the standards set by the International Labour Organization (ILO), and the Council of Europe's European Convention of Human Rights and European Social Charter. Mark and Paul's research during this period could also draw on their wide network of international contacts, especially in France, Germany and the European University Institute (EUI) in Florence.[62]

With Paul Davies' move to London take up a chair at the LSE in 1998, his work started increasingly to focus on company law;[63] without however abandoning a strong interest in labour law, as evidence by the publication in 2006 of the successor volume to *Labour Legislation and Public Policy*, *Towards a Flexible Labour Market*.[64]

In Oxford, labour law teaching continued to evolve. The BCL and undergraduate courses developed and taught by Mark and Paul had always been supplemented by a range of related options, notably a Comparative Human Rights paper, as well as less formal courses. Hugh Collins, for example, offered a course on Marxism and Law,[65] and, together with Mary Stokes, a course on Power in the Corporation, attended on occasion by both Mark and Paul. Over time, new research areas became increasingly prominent, as seen in an increased focus on feminist, human rights and globalization perspectives of labour law in the teaching of Sandra Fredman[66] and Christopher McCrudden.[67]

This diversification of interests led to significant growth in the BCL course materials, with different groups of students attracted to each part. As a result, two BCL courses were on offer from 1999: European Employment Law (later also known as European Employment and Equality Law), modelled on the International and European Law syllabus already set out, and International Economic

[62] Culminating in the publication of S Sciarra, P Davies and M Freedland (eds), *Employment Policy and the Regulation of Part-Time Work in the European Union* (Cambridge, Cambridge University Press, 2003).

[63] Most notably as editor of *Gower & Davies' Principles of Modern Company Law*, 9th edn with S Worthington (London, Sweet & Maxwell, 2012); *The Anatomy of Corporate Law: A Comparative and Functional Approach*, 2nd edn with R Kraakman et al (Oxford, Oxford University Press, 2009); and *An Introduction to Company Law*, 2nd edn (Oxford, Clarendon Press, 2010).

[64] P Davies and M Freedland, *Towards a Flexible Labour Market: Labour Legislation and Regulation since the 1990s* (Oxford, Oxford University Press, 2006).

[65] H Collins, *Marxism and Law* (Oxford, Oxford University Press, 1982).

[66] eg S Fredman, *Women and the Law*, Oxford Monographs in Labour Law (Oxford, Oxford University Press, 1997).

[67] eg C McCrudden, *Buying Social Justice: Equality, Government Procurement, and Legal Change* (Oxford, Oxford University Press, 2007).

Law and Labour Rights (subsequently Globalisation and Labour Rights). In the latter,

> Candidates [were] expected to show knowledge of the procedures and functions of the International Labour Organization and more generally of the role of labour standards in the normative structures of world trade.

There was therefore little overlap between the options, which allowed interested students to study both courses; those on the MJur course with first degrees from civil law jurisdictions could furthermore offer the undergraduate labour law paper as a third subject. In 2011, the courses were fused back together, eventually reverting to the 1991 title; with the present authors (as well as many others) once again teaching international and European labour law.

In conclusion, it is important to note how throughout the past forty-five years, there has never been one sense of autonomy of Oxford labour law. It had, of course, been a significant achievement early on to establish labour law as an autonomous subject within the Oxford law curriculum, free from and independent of the teaching of the classic common law subjects, and marked by a dedication to and development of Kahn-Freund's interest in understanding the 'practices and functions, rather than doctrines or structures'[68] of labour law. At the same time, however, Oxford labour law has always found itself intensely tied up in interdisciplinary work, whether in economics, sociology and politics, or even—as the manifold contributions in this volume show—as a discipline within law.

[68] Freedland (n 41) 311.

Part I

Labour Law's Autonomy: Theory and Methodology

1

Otto Kahn-Freund, the Contract of Employment and the Autonomy of Labour Law

MARK FREEDLAND

I. Introduction

This chapter, in parallel with others in this volume, has its origins in a paper delivered at the conference held in July 2013 on the topic of the Past, Present and Future of Labour Law in Oxford.[1] In that paper, my choice was to focus my attention upon the Oxford legacy of Professor Sir Otto Kahn-Freund, that is to say his influence upon labour law studies in Oxford and the significance of the work of his Oxford years within the totality of his contribution to labour law scholarship; and I further chose to concentrate upon his thinking, especially during those years, about the treatment of the contract of employment in English law. In this chapter, in accordance with the declared aims of this symposium volume, I seek to recast that earlier paper around the idea of the autonomy of labour law. I have found that the necessity to make that transformation has been a productive one; the English law of the contract of employment has for me turned out to be a quite unexpectedly fruitful field in which to reflect upon the autonomy of labour law, and the autonomy theme has seemed to provide quite a powerful optic through which to view Kahn-Freund's work in that field. Accordingly, after a brief recapitulation of my original tribute to his Oxford legacy, I turn to an evaluation of his engagement with the English law of the contract of employment from the perspective of the idea of the autonomy of labour law.

For a project of charting the past, present and future of labour law studies in Oxford, there could be no more appropriate starting point than to consider the transcendent role of Otto Kahn-Freund. He was beyond doubt the founding

[1] In writing this chapter, I have benefited greatly from discussion at and since the conference of the paper on which it has been based, and, in particular, from comments by Prof Alan Bogg and Prof Anne Davies on the draft of the chapter.

father of those studies, both in the intellectual and the practical sense. In the practical or operational sense, it was he who introduced the subject to the Oxford law curriculum in the shape of an option in the BCL graduate taught course, which was offered from the end of the 1960s onwards. He accomplished that feat in a less than totally welcoming environment, so that we can feel sure that his colossal standing was instrumental in securing agreement to this dangerous innovation. His successors had to wait and campaign for a good many years after that for the subject to be admitted to the syllabus of the undergraduate law course, the Final Honours School of Jurisprudence.

That also makes the point about the magnitude and significance of Kahn-Freund's intellectual role in providing an analytical and ideological or narrative framework for labour law studies in Oxford. He of course played that role more widely, indeed both on a national and an international stage; the purpose of the paper from which this chapter derives was to consider the direction and the distinctiveness which he imparted to the subsequent development of labour law by those of us who first sat at his feet and then continued to labour in the vineyard which he had laid out and planted in Oxford. An obvious path to take in pursuit of the Kahn Freund's legacy to Oxford labour law would have been to look again at his articulation and development of the notion of 'collective *laissez-faire*'. That doctrine will certainly be hovering in the ether throughout this exposition; but I have, perhaps counter-intuitively but I hope not perversely, chosen to concentrate on another aspect of Kahn-Freund's thinking in the labour law field, namely his perspective upon the contract of employment and in particular upon the English law of the contract of employment.

If I say that this choice to focus on Kahn-Freund's treatment of the contract of employment might seem counter-intuitive or perverse, that is because Kahn-Freund's fame as the doyen of British labour lawyers is especially based upon his preoccupation with collective industrial relations and their embodiment in labour law. In that domain, his voluntarist stance was a determined and consistent one. In real contrast, Kahn-Freund's approach to the contract of employment is much less clear, positive or declamatory—it was, on the contrary, ambivalent, often rather negative and prone to twists and turns which could sometimes seem slightly mysterious. In the original paper, I suggested that it is those very qualities which render Kahn-Freund's engagement with the contract of employment especially fascinating and particularly creative of his legacy to Oxford labour law studies. In this chapter, I now argue that these creative complexities can be best understood if seen through the lens of the idea of the autonomy of labour law. The next section of this chapter advances a suggested way of understanding the idea of the autonomy of labour law, arguing that the law of the contract of employment is central to that understanding; in subsequent sections, that understanding is taken as the basis of an evaluation of Kahn-Freund's approach to the contract of employment as it evolved through the course of his career as the pre-eminent labour law scholar of his time and probably the greatest formative influence upon labour law scholarship of all time.

II. The 'Autonomy of Labour Law' and the Role of the Contract of Employment

In order to use the idea of the 'autonomy of labour law' as a critical tool in the development of labour law theory, we need a working definition or working understanding of it. Views will differ as to how this is best to be provided, and various possibilities are on display in this volume; I set out my own suggestion here, with its bearing on the English law of the contract of employment specially in mind. It was Professor Lord Wedderburn who famously, in the 'From Here to Autonomy' article published in 1987,[2] inserted the idea into the common parlance of labour law scholarship in the English-speaking world, drawing upon the work of the French jurist and doyen of French labour law Paul Durand, who had written about an evolution from *le particularisme du droit du travail* to *l'autonomie du droit du travail*—from distinctiveness to autonomy.[3] Bill Wedderburn there articulated the idea in terms of the separation and separateness of labour law, and it is that upon that notion of separateness that I base my own understanding of the autonomy of labour law.

My own understanding of autonomy as a desired ideal for labour law consists of the assertion that labour law, if it is to attain a satisfactory level of functional coherence, needs to evolve and operate as an independent subsystem of the general legal system within which it is located, be that a national or supranational or subnational one. There are of course difficulties and dangers with the acceptance of this as a desideratum for labour law—difficulties in deciding what independence means and how it is to be achieved, and dangers that complete independence might bring with it intellectual enclosure, autopoiesis[4] or self-referentiality; but it nevertheless seems to me to be useful to accept the systemic independence of labour law as a good and positive value, in the context at least of certain legal systems, and to search one's mind as to how best to realize that ideal. In that pursuit, I find it useful firstly to identify two dimensions of the autonomy of labour law, a normative one and a procedural or methodological one, and secondly to identify two aspects of the development of the autonomy of labour law, a negative one and a positive one. I proceed to enlarge upon that set of suggestions.

Firstly, then, I suggest that the ideal of autonomy of labour law has two dimensions or aspects, a normative one and a procedural or methodological one, in the sense that in order to realize that ideal it is necessary both to recognize a distinctive set of normative goals for labour law and to ensure that the institutional structuring, administration and adjudication of labour law are specially

[2] Lord Wedderburn, 'Labour Law: From Here to Autonomy?' (1987) 16 *Industrial Law Journal* 1.
[3] See ibid, fn 2 citing P Durand, 'Le Particularisme du Droit du Travail' [1944] *Droit Social* 276.
[4] See generally, G Teubner, *Law as an Autopoietic System* (Florence, The European University Institute Press, 1992).

adapted and suited to achieving those goals.[5] It is in that dual sense that the autonomy of labour law consists in constituting it as a distinct subsystem of the legal system or systems within which it exists and functions. Secondly, I suggest that the development of an 'autonomous' system of labour law in that dual sense needs to have two aspects, a negative and a positive one. In its negative aspect, the autonomy of a labour law system is developed by separation and differentiation from the larger legal system in which it exists, either generally or from some element or elements in that larger legal system which are inimical to the coherent development of labour law—this is, as it were, the aspect of 'autonomy from' or 'autonomy of'. In its positive aspect, the autonomy of a labour law system is developed by the articulation and execution of its own proper tasks and its own proper mission—this, by the same token, is the aspect of 'autonomy in' or 'autonomy for'.

Within that framework, individual theorists articulate the idea of the autonomy of labour law in widely varying and context-specific ways, both as to the elements upon which emphasis is placed, as to the formulation of each element, and as to the strictness with which autonomy is asserted. Thus while Bill Wedderburn found his starting points for expounding the notion of the autonomy of labour law in the writings about French labour law of Paul Durand and Gerard Lyon-Caen, he was very conscious that the idea played out differently in the context of English law.[6] Indeed, the very point of his argument was to assert that the vindication of the autonomy of labour law would be even more of an uphill struggle in the English legal environment than in the French one. So Wedderburn noted the way in which French labour law had achieved a fair degree of *particularisme*, both in the separation of the *Code du Travail* from the *Code Civil* and in the relative independence of the labour law judiciary from the general civil and commercial law judiciary; and he implicitly contrasted with that state of affairs in France the situation in the United Kingdom in which, in his very convincingly argued view, labour law had continued to be infused with the spirit of the common law and dominated by the common law judiciary. So for him, the Herculean task of realizing the autonomy of labour law in the context of English law would require a root-and-branch expulsion of 'the common lawyers' from a domain in which their influence had gone almost unchallenged; his focus was upon the negative aspect of the autonomy of labour

[5] It might be wondered whether I am entitled to advance this claim to the normative autonomy of labour law, given the way that I have, with Nicola Kountouris in our work on *The Legal Construction of Personal Work Relations* (Oxford, Oxford University Press, 2012) proposed the normative notion of 'personality in work', which seems to be regarded by some, eg Professor McCrudden (cf his critique in the present volume), as too strongly rooted in universal human-rights-based values such as dignity, autonomy and equality to qualify as an authentic rationale for autonomous labour law. I would counter-claim that I am not arguing inconsistently, since our notion of 'personality *in work*' (emphasis added, but strongly implicit) is as I see it, in its intention at least, essentially anchored within and specific to labour law itself.

[6] See Wedderburn (n 2) 1–2.

law, that is to say the intellectual and practical ground-clearing which would be necessary in order to achieve it.[7]

In Bill Wedderburn's account of what would be involved in that exercise in liberation, which he saw as essential to the realization of the autonomy of labour law in the context of English law, he gave a striking prominence to the law of the contract of employment. Rightly enough in my own view, he identified that body of law as one of the principal seats and locations of the 'common law control' of English labour law. He could see all the signs and indications that the common law judiciary, so long as they remained the primary exponents of the law of the contract of employment, would continue to regard and fashion and deploy the contract of employment according to an implicit paradigm of the 'master–servant' relation which their predecessors had evolved over a very long period of time but especially during the nineteenth century.[8] In his rather absolutist way, building upon but somewhat going beyond recent work, particularly by Roger Rideout[9] and Bob Hepple,[10] he issued what amounted to a clarion call for the extrusion of the common law of the contract of employment from the core of English labour law in the name of realizing the latter's autonomy from control by common law.

By that slightly circuitous route, I arrive at the central question which this chapter seeks to answer. It is the question of how Otto Kahn-Freund's thinking and writing about the contract of employment might be regarded as contributing to the debate about the autonomy of labour law. The answer is, of course, an essentially complex one. On the one hand, Kahn-Freund did not particularly, to the best of my recollection, invoke the language of 'the autonomy of labour law' as such. On the other hand, we might regard him as the supreme exponent of the autonomy of labour law *avant la lettre*, that is to say before that terminology became common currency. Was it not he who promulgated to English lawyers the distinctive rationale of redressing the inequality of bargaining power inherent in the making and administration of the individual contract of employment, and the equally distinctive institutional methodology of 'collective *laissez-faire*'? But even if we do regard him as an exponent of 'the autonomy of labour law' in all but name, that does not tell us how he would have located the English law of the contract of employment within a coherently 'autonomous' framework of labour law.

My suggested answer to that question—of necessity a somewhat speculative one—is that Kahn-Freund was somewhat internally conflicted (as I must say I have always found myself) about the rightful place of the law of the contract of employment within the kind of normatively adequate and coherent framework

[7] Compare, for example, his ringing statement that '[I]t is no good asking the common law how to render void the unjust dismissals of ordinary workers. The answer to that problem must be the one given to the man who asked the way to York: "you do not start from here"' (ibid 7).

[8] This is a point made especially powerfully by Alan Fox in his seminal work *Beyond Contract: Work, Power and Trust Relations* (London, Faber & Faber, 1974) 186–90.

[9] R Rideout, 'The Contract of Employment' [1966] *Current Legal Problems* 111.

[10] B Hepple, 'Restructuring Employment Rights' (1986) 15 *Industrial Law Journal* 69.

for English labour law which he constantly sought to devise and promote. His view on this was I think always less absolutist than the approach which I have attributed to Bill Wedderburn.[11] He was as keenly aware as Wedderburn that the English law of the contract of employment was in need of *reform* if it was satisfactorily to serve the proper aims of labour law as he viewed them; but I think that, in early days at least, Kahn-Freund was more open than Wedderburn to the feasibility of a gradualist and consensual approach to such reform. However, I believe that his assessment in this respect did change over time, becoming a somewhat more pessimistic one; but I think that this evolution in his thinking brought him to a profoundly interesting set of conclusions which are very instructive and full of meaning for those of us who find ourselves thinking about the role of the contract of employment in the 'autonomy of labour law' more than thirty years later. The next sections of this chapter are devoted to depicting that evolution.

III. Kahn-Freund and the Contract of Employment (1)

Pursuing the line of argument upon which I embarked in the previous section, in this and the next section of the chapter I survey the main points in his writing at which Kahn-Freund took up a position with regard to the contract of employment, and in particular English law's treatment of it. I think that we can depict this as an evolution through two contrasting phases. There was a first phase during which Kahn-Freund theorized the contract of employment as a difficult notion but one that could be put to good service in the maintenance of collective *laissez-faire*. This was succeeded, however, by a second phase during which Kahn-Freund experienced serious disillusionment at the unwillingness of English common lawyers to approach the contract of employment in the way that he regarded as functionally appropriate.

These evolutions had their precursors in Kahn-Freund's earlier career in the Weimar Republic in Germany, in many ways the cradle of twentieth-century labour law. At that time, it seems to me that he was not himself primarily interested in the legal theory of the contract of employment, being, as always, much more concerned with the social phenomena of collective bargaining and collective labour relations. I think he was content at that stage to leave the theorizing and development of the law of the contract of employment to his mentor Hugo Sinzheimer. His memorial essay on Sinzheimer indicates that he regarded him as having arrived at a theory of the contract of employment which elegantly reconciled the competing views of individual employment relations as relations

[11] David Howarth offered an eloquent critique of the absolutism of Wedderburn's approach in 'The Autonomy of Labour Law: A Response to Professor Wedderburn' (1988) 17 *Industrial Law Journal* 11.

of exchange on the one hand and personal subordination on the other,[12] and I think this was not high on the list of his problems or preoccupations in the labour law field during his Weimar period. This is in my view in and of itself informative with regard to Kahn-Freund's thinking about the role of the law of the contract of employment; it signifies to me that, in the German labour law of that period, the contract of employment simply did not have a pivotal role in giving, or for that matter denying, effect to the basic infrastructure of worker-protective norms which were in his view essentially and necessarily derived from collective bargaining even if they had been to an important extent embedded into the legal constitution of the Weimar Republic.[13]

It was a very different story when Kahn-Freund came to England in the 1930s and gradually set about constructing a theory and practice of labour law as, in the language of the present work, a distinctive or autonomous discipline, in this extremely different legal, social and normative environment. His thinking about and handling of the law of the contract of employment in this new national context provides for me quite a tense piece of intellectual theatre, in which competing approaches become the subject of truly dramatic conflict. There is a particular reason for this dramatic tension; in the new legal and industrial relations environment in which Kahn-Freund found himself, for which he would by 1959 have coined the new currency of 'collective *laissez-faire*',[14] the contract of employment would move right to centre stage as the key legal institution to sustain the whole voluntarist structure. That is to say, if the fabric of labour law was to be woven primarily from collective agreements which were not themselves to constitute legally enforceable contracts, and if that fabric were to be framed by deliberately minimalist employment legislation playing a secondary or auxiliary role, the contract of employment would have to provide the mechanism by which a set of primarily extra-legal norms could be transposed into existing legal forms and structures both in a theoretical as well as in a practical sense. The dramatic choice for Kahn-Freund was whether he could trust English common lawyers, and most especially the English common law judges, to approach the contract of employment on that set of understandings—he faced a kind of prisoner's dilemma in having to base his own strategy for labour law upon a set of predictions as to how they would behave.

In what I like to think of as his first Oxford moment, Kahn-Freund decided to take the risk. This was in 1953/54 in the 'Legal Framework' chapter which he contributed to the symposium work edited by Allan Flanders and Hugh

[12] O Kahn-Freund, 'Hugo Sinzheimer 1875–1945' translated by J Clark as ch 2 of R Lewis and J Clark (eds), *Labour Law and Politics in the Weimar Republic* (Oxford, Basil Blackwell, 1981), see 91–93 'The Analysis of the Contract of Employment'.

[13] As to which see generally the invaluable article by Ruth Dukes, 'Constitutionalizing Employment Relations: Sinzheimer, Kahn-Freund, and the Role of Labour Law' (2008) 35 *Journal of Law & Society* 341.

[14] O Kahn-Freund 'Labour Law' in M Ginsberg (ed), *Law and Opinion in England in the 20th Century* (London, Stevens and Sons, 1959) 224.

Clegg on *The System of Industrial Relations in Great Britain*.[15] It was his first Oxford moment in the sense that this was his first significant collaboration with colleagues in Oxford, in this case with the leading members of the emerging 'Oxford School of Industrial Relations'. In that context, and at what in retrospect appears to have been almost the high noon of undisputed collective *laissez-faire*, Kahn-Freund was willing to identify the individual employment relationship taking the legal form of the contract of employment or contract of service as 'for the lawyer … the cornerstone of the edifice [and upon which] everything hinges' and moreover, I think he was willing even to regard it as a benign rather than a malign legal institution.

Even as he made it, I am sure that Kahn-Freund found this a difficult concession. He was acutely aware of the paradoxes which he had to swallow, the Faustian pact with the English common law Devil which he had to make, in order to assume this posture. For him it meant then and would always mean accepting an essentially individualistic analysis of employment relations in order to provide a legal framework for a social system of which for him the significant dynamics were always the collective ones. It meant subscribing to the lawyers' insistence upon the formal equality between contracting parties, as a condition of access to a contractual discourse which might admit the possibility of correcting an imbalance of bargaining power which was special to the individual employment relationship.

There were, I think, several factors which explained why he was thus willing in that particular intellectual and historical context. First and probably foremost, he was addressing an audience not of lawyers but of students of industrial relations, who would understand that he was on their side in regarding the social phenomena of collective action as the primary and real and virtuous ones, and the lawyers' individualized constructs as the secondary and artificial and suspect ones; he was not in danger of being misunderstood in this respect. Secondly, despite all those misgivings, he did genuinely regard the approach of English common lawyers to the contract of employment as creating a legal bastion against involuntary servitude. His soul had stirred to the beat of Lord Atkin's ringing declaration in *Nokes v Doncaster Amalgamated Collieries Ltd* that:

> I had fancied that ingrained in the personal status of a citizen under our laws was the right to choose for himself whom he would serve, and this right of choice constituted the main difference between a servant and a serf.[16]

Kahn-Freund accepted that the contractual analysis of the employment relationship embodied that commitment, and Lord Atkin's implicit contrast, drawn in the dark hours of August 1940, with Nazi oppression in full swing across the

[15] O Kahn-Freund, 'Legal Framework' in A Flanders and H Clegg (eds), *The System of Industrial Relations in Great Britain* (Oxford, Basil Blackwell, 1954).

[16] *Nokes v Doncaster Amalgamated Collieries Ltd* [1940] AC 1014 [HL] 1026.

Channel, had justly found its mark in Kahn-Freund's considerable capacity for empathy with British libertarianism.[17]

There were yet two further factors which I think inclined Kahn-Freund towards a positive development of the law of the contract of employment at that time. The first consisted in the fact that he saw and took up the opportunity for some 'legal engineering' in furtherance of his grand project of securing an appropriate place for collective bargaining within the framework of British labour law. Having apparently resolved that the way forward did not consist in asserting the direct legal enforceability of collective agreements, he was in search of a doctrinal basis for the automatic incorporation of the terms and conditions of employment established by them into individual contracts of employment. In 'Legal Framework' he identified an ingenious solution which would draw upon the notion, long-established in the general law of contract, of incorporation into contracts of 'customary' terms based upon applicable customs which were 'certain, notorious and reasonable'; he advanced the argument that collective agreements could be regarded as 'crystallizing' the customary terms and conditions for a particular trade or occupation in a particular locality in such a way as to satisfy the requirements for their incorporation into individual contracts.[18] This analysis has since been superseded by the requirement of provision of statutory particulars of terms to be incorporated from collective agreements, but nevertheless remains as a monument to Kahn-Freund's creative engagement at that time with the English law of the contract of employment.

The final factor that reconciled Kahn-Freund to a positive approach to the English law of the contract of employment was his conscious decision that the juridification or embodiment in legislation of the institutions of collective representation in enterprise management would actually work to undermine them rather than to protect them. Running with the grain of contractual analysis of individual employment relations therefore made good sense, even if that involved overlooking the artificiality of that analysis. As he himself put it: 'The voluntary principle is sufficiently valuable to be purchased at the price of lack of realism in the law.'[19] The next section of this paper will try to chart in detail how Kahn-Freund gradually came to feel that this had been a bad bargain, indeed in a sense no longer a bargain at all once the 'voluntary principle' itself was discarded by governments from 1970 onwards, and how he came to think that the English law of the contract of employment had negative rather than positive value in the development of worker-protective labour law.

[17] It is well worth bearing in mind, in this connection, that when Kahn-Freund first adumbrated his famous characterization of British industrial relations and labour law as imbued with the spirit of 'collective *laissez-faire*', he was at pains to locate the labour and trade union movement's participation in that ethos as being at least as much derived from a nineteenth-century liberal, and libertarian, tradition as from a socialist one: cf his chapter on 'Labour Law' in Ginsberg (ed) (n 14) 224.

[18] See O Kahn-Freund (n 15) 48–49 and 58–59.

[19] ibid 51.

IV. Kahn-Freund and the Contract of Employment (2)

With the long hindsight which is afforded from the vantage point of 2013, we can see that the significant changes in Kahn-Freund's attitude to the English law of the contract of employment which occurred in the 1970s were in truth a reaction to the long decline in the power and coherence of the system of collective bargaining which was starting to manifest itself from the later 1960s onwards. In this section, I argue that, during that final decade of his life, Kahn-Freund's perception of the mounting juridification both of collective labour relations and individual employment relations caused him to have growing misgivings about the role and impact of the common law of the contract of employment. I go on to argue that these misgivings were prescient ones, and that they were highly pertinent to our reflections upon the 'autonomy of labour law' in today's yet further transformed legal, social and economic environment.

In this evolution of Kahn-Freund's views about the role and normativity of English law concerning the contract of employment, there is an interesting mid-point, or staging-post along the way, in a set of lectures which he gave in Canada in 1967 and which were published in 1968 under the title of *Labour Law: Old Traditions and New Developments.*[20] This was, therefore, at the very time at which Kahn-Freund was engaged in the deliberations of the Royal Commission on Trade Unions and Employers Associations (the 'Donovan Commission')[21] which reported in May 1968, in which Kahn-Freund's essential mission was to sustain the collective bargaining system in the face of the mounting political and economic pressures under which it was placed at that time. It was by this stage evident to him that legislation was beginning to take over from collective bargaining as the principal source of regulation of terms and conditions of employment for most workers, a development which he attributed to the growth of the 'white collar' employment sector in which levels of trade union membership and organization were much lower than in the 'blue collar' sector.

At this juncture, he was prepared to be cautiously optimistic about the effect which the new wave of labour legislation—which he could see as having to be regarded as directly 'regulatory', rather than as merely 'auxiliary' to collective bargaining—would have upon the contract of employment. He regarded the Contracts of Employment Act 1963 and the Redundancy Payments Act 1965 as having on the whole effected an ameliorative 'reshaping' of the contract of employment itself. He was especially approving of the way in which the 1963 Act, in imposing upon employers the requirement to provide employees with written particulars of the main terms and conditions of their employment within

[20] O Kahn-Freund, *Labour Law: Old Traditions and New Developments* (Toronto and Vancouver, Clarke, Irwin and Company Ltd, 1968).

[21] *Report of the Royal Commission on Trade Unions and Employers' Associations* (1968) Cmnd 3623.

thirteen weeks of the start of their employment, had managed to formalize the process of recruiting for employment without going to the lengths of requiring the contracts themselves to be in writing. He also liked the way in which the redundancy payments provisions of the 1965 Act were susceptible to variation by ministerial order where a different but no less worker-favourable redundancy payments scheme had been embodied in a suitable collective agreement; he thought this was a good way of creating regulation which was *jus cogens*, mandatory law, in relation to the contract of employment, but *jus dispositivum*, optional law, in relation to the collective agreement. At this stage, one feels that he could envisage the contract of employment, remoulded by such regulatory legislation, as becoming a benign institution in the new world of labour law and industrial relations.

There was I think a perceptible shift towards a more negative view of the role of the law of the contract of employment on Kahn-Freund's part in *Labour and the Law*,[22] the first edition of which was published in 1972.[23] On this occasion, regarding it as too soon to gauge the future effect of the Industrial Relations Act 1971, Kahn-Freund chose instead to focus upon the shortcomings of the common law's regulation of employment relations in general, and the limits of the law of the contract of employment in particular. He was especially concerned to emphasize the *marginal* nature of common law's regulation of the contract of employment, which he ascribed to its *ex ante* functioning, and its failure to take control of the normal operation of employment relations, dealing only with 'pathological situations', and leaving it to collective bargaining and regulatory legislation to fill the vacuum. At first it therefore appears that Kahn-Freund's misgivings about the common law of the contract of employment are primarily methodological ones; but then it emerges that he has a deeper normative concern, namely that 'the common law … ignores any disequilibrium of power which results from normal social relations, as distinct from abnormal personal conditions'.[24] He remarks that the law of restraint of trade represented the only aspect of the employment relationship 'which did induce the courts to lift the veil of equality and to allow the fact of subordination to impinge upon the validity of contractual promises'.[25]

However, I find it notable that Kahn-Freund's concluding reflections on the role and character of the common law of the contract of employment were even more bleak. These were embodied in his Blackstone Lecture for 1977, published

[22] O Kahn-Freund, *Labour and the Law* (London, Stevens for the Hamlyn Trust, 1972).

[23] We can see that Kahn-Freund was already firmly inclining in this direction by 1969 in his Sidney Ball lecture of that year, published as 'Industrial Relations and the Law—Retrospect and Prospect' (1969) 7 *British Journal of Industrial Relations* 301–16; he there takes the view that 'the law and the lawyers have simply fallen down on their jobs in the area with which I am concerned' (311), by which it becomes apparent that he meant that that the common law of the contract of employment was incapable of remedying the increasingly visible deficiencies of the system of collective bargaining, and that statutory reform was not progressing quickly enough to bridge the gap.

[24] Kahn-Freund (n 22) 26.

[25] ibid 27.

in the *Law Quarterly Review* at the end of that year as 'Blackstone's Neglected Child: The Contract of Employment'.[26] I have for a very long time found this lecture rather mysterious, but I think that I have at last understood exactly where he was tending. The invitation to give that lecture provoked a long historical reflection on his part on the role and orientation of the common law in regulating the employment relation, with Blackstone himself squarely the object of his severe historical critique. The argument of that lecture is, as the title implies, that Blackstone's account of employment relations was fundamentally flawed by his failure or refusal to envisage them as archetypally taking the legal form of the contract of employment—he having chosen to present them as relations between master and servant which for him formed part of the law of persons, thereby in Kahn-Freund's view indelibly stamping them with the character of a status of servitude.

This might on the face of it suggest that Kahn-Freund had remained in the same posture vis-à-vis the contract of employment as in 1954, still convinced that its inherent vindication of freedom of entry into and exit from the employment relation was, although more than somewhat artificial in its detailed implications, nevertheless of supreme totemic value. I am now convinced, however, that by 1977 his main sentiment was one of disillusionment with what English common lawyers had eventually made of the contract of employment; and on this occasion his contrivance was to blame much of this on Blackstone, reproaching him for having failed to tend and nurture the slender roots of *contractual* thinking about 'master and servant relations' in the mid-eighteenth century. Nevertheless, I equally believe that Kahn-Freund's real concern was not so much that English common lawyers had never accepted the contract of employment, but that, somewhat to the contrary, once they had accepted it, they had nevertheless shown themselves unable or unwilling to implement a vision of the contract of employment into which worker-protective legislation was fully integrated as part of its mandatory and non-derogable content.

This becomes manifest, as the real point of the whole argument, almost at the end of the piece, where he says:

> I cannot even begin here to go into the complexities, both substantive and procedural, which arise from the co-existence of statutory and contractual claims. Are we not entitled to say that such difficulties would have been avoided if English labour law had not, as it were, *ab initio* been paralysed by the inability to see employment and employment legislation in a contractual frame, and especially to see oppressive as well as protective statutes as mandatory norms operating on the contract?[27]

He becomes really fierce with Blackstone about this, declaring that:

> 'To ascribe this fundamental defect of legislative method to the influence of Blackstone would be ludicrous. But what can be said is that the same defect was inherent in his

[26] O Kahn-Freund, 'Blackstone's Neglected Child: The Contract of Employment' (1977) 93 *Law Quarterly Review* 508.

[27] ibid 527. I respectfully suggest that Kahn-Freund meant to say 'especially to see protective as well as oppressive statutes as mandatory norms …'.

> failure to treat the contract of employment as the general foundation of the service relation. Like other expounders of the common law, he was intellectually helpless in the face of legislation, unable to see statute law and common law as a whole. … To use EM Forster's word, he suffered from a congenital inability to 'connect' so common among lawyers.[28]

I truly think this was an expression of a deep disenchantment with the English common law approach to the contract of employment upon which he had earlier pinned a great deal of hope. With habitual gallantry, Kahn-Freund concluded about Blackstone in the following conciliatory terms:

> I cannot think that, by seeing his shortcomings, we are doing a disservice to the memory of a distinguished commentator on the common law. They cannot detract from the great and imperishable services he did to legal education in this University and in this country in general.[29]

Nevertheless, the critique which Kahn-Freund developed in that lecture was a deeply felt one; and it has important implications for our reflections upon the 'Autonomy of Labour Law' in general and the role of the law of the contract of employment in particular—implications which I seek to tease out in the concluding section of this chapter.

V. Conclusion

This chapter, as I indicated at the outset, has developed out of a paper cast in terms of assessing 'the Oxford legacy' of Otto Kahn-Freund. I briefly return to that theme, because it is relevant to my conclusions about Kahn-Freund's contribution to the idea of the autonomy of labour law, and about the role of the law of the contract of employment in that whole discussion. Having begun by asserting his foundational significance to labour law studies in Oxford, I conclude by acknowledging that we have to be careful not to over-claim him for Oxford. He came to Oxford late in his life and late in his career, consciously an intellectual torchbearer from the schools of social science of Weimar Germany and the London School of Economics. He was and remained at heart a rebel against the Oxford Law School, the home of stalwarts of the common law such as Dicey or Anson or Pollock. He was from and for the *Modern Law Review*, not the *Law Quarterly Review*.

However, perhaps by making that acknowledgement we get to the very point of his legacy to labour law in Oxford, and indeed in the United Kingdom at large. For Kahn-Freund, labour law was one area in which he could import (could one say 'transplant'?) into Oxford his own brand of critical and realist jurisprudence,

[28] ibid 528.
[29] ibid.

and his own normative view of legal studies as primarily comparative and above all sociolegal ones. This was a project of ensuring that the social and economic realities of collective industrial relations, coupled with the worker-protective impulses which when it was necessary expressed themselves in parliamentary legislation, constantly shaped and informed a body of law which, he could increasingly clearly see, would otherwise default towards what were for him the individualist and ultimately reactionary attitudes of the common lawyers.

This was for Kahn-Freund a continuing struggle, eventually probably in his eyes a losing battle, and in 'Blackstone's Neglected Child' he was in my view expressing the effort and frustration which that caused and cost him. But although those reflections were for him genuinely difficult and painful ones, I think that they have much to offer to our present debate about the autonomy of labour law. In the language of that debate, he had understood all too clearly by 1977 that the law of the contract of employment was a location in which that autonomy was crucially undermined by the infusion of not just one but two common law approaches or attitudes. The first of those two, the importance of which he had identified, as we have seen, in *Labour and the Law*, consisted of the common law's insistence upon respect for the formal equality which was dogmatically asserted to exist between the contracting parties. The second of those two, which is emphasized in 'Blackstone's Neglected Child', consists in the imposition of an equally firm insistence upon the subordination of the employee to the employer as a defining characteristic of the contract of employment—an insistence that might be relatively innocuous if it amounted to no more than a formal way of identifying the contract of employment, but has actually been of far greater consequence because it imports a set of hierarchical norms, about discipline and obedience and loyalty, redolent of the master–servant relations which had formed Blackstone's archetype for this body of law.[30]

It was I think Kahn-Freund's realization of the propensity of the common law judiciary to combine those two almost paradoxically antithetical approaches in their handling of the law of the contract of employment which made him sound so pessimistic in a set of notes in 1977. In particular I think he could both observe and foresee that it was proving and would continue to prove to be difficult to harness the common law of the contract of employment, informed

[30] It is, of course, quite appropriate to ask whether this is a distinctively English development; it might be thought comparative analysis would show that norms of obedience and fidelity are at the historical core of the idea of the contract for subordinate or dependent employment in most if not all European legal systems, indeed that such norms might be even more strongly maintained in those legal systems which import the obligation of 'good faith' into such contracts in the way that English contract law has as a matter of general principle refrained from doing. I think that Kahn-Freund would have been quite prepared to agree to that generalization; his point, however, was that when this rigorously hierarchical 'master and servant' approach was eventually moderated by legislative reform in each of those legal systems, most such systems were willing to modify their vision of the law of the contract of employment by integrating the newer legislative norms into it, whereas English lawyers insisted on adhering to an older notion of the 'common law contract of employment' which in their view survived intact beneath a statutory superstructure. The subsequent evolution of the English law of the contract of employment only serves, in my view, to demonstrate how right he was.

by that combination of attitudes, to the service of the newly created apparatus of worker-protective employment legislation in the way that the legislators had assumed and intended. I think he was quite right in that view and that prediction, especially but by no means solely with regard to the new body of statute law of unfair dismissal; and I also think that he was thereby leaving us with very important messages about how best to understand and pursue the idea of the autonomy of labour law.

The first message of that kind which I derive from these particular writings is that the 'autonomy of labour law' is a very difficult ideal to pursue in the context of English law, at least according to the established way of understanding that ideal. Secondly, on the other hand, those same writings also suggest to me a different possible way in which to understand and pursue that ideal in that same context. The first of those two messages, about the sheer difficulty of pursuing the 'autonomy of labour law' in English Law, communicates itself to me from Kahn-Freund's observation of the way in which those *two* common law approaches, the 'formal equality approach' and the 'master and servant approach', both infused the law of the contract of employment. He had come to think that both those two approaches were locked into the core of our system of labour law, almost beyond the reach of his normative concern with the sustaining and nurturing of the system of collective bargaining and worker-protective labour legislation.

In particular, that observation of the concatenation of those two common law approaches to the contract of employment serves to convince me that the autonomy of labour law cannot be realized by what I take to be the normally imagined method, namely an assertion of independence from the general civil or private law system in question. That might suffice to liberate the law of the contract of employment from the 'formal equality approach', which is indeed a feature of the common law of contracts in general; but it would not serve to displace the 'master and servant approach' because that is *already* a distinctive feature of the law of the contract of employment, and therefore lodged *within* the stockade of labour law rather than safely outside it.

However, even if Kahn-Freund was by the end of his academic and actual life feeling rather discouraged by these phenomena, his writings about the English law of the contract of employment, taken in their entirety, also convey to me a more positive message about the possibility of a different approach to the realization of the autonomy of labour law. Taken as a whole, those writings suggest to me that he would have regarded 'the autonomy of labour law', had he chosen to deploy that particular rhetoric, as being most effectively pursued from *within* the general legal system in question, rather than by sharp contradistinction from that system. He certainly believed that labour law needed its autonomous ideal of redressing the inequality of power between employees and employers, and that the realization of that ideal generally required a distinctive administration of justice for employment issues; but I think that he always preferred to suggest positive paths for the doctrinal development of labour law from within the general law than to demand a declaration of independence from it.

If we accept that these are the messages which Kahn-Freund left for us with regard to the autonomy of labour law and the role of the law of the contract of employment, how might those messages sound in our ears rather more than thirty years later? The constitution of the labour market, and indeed the whole social and economic landscape, have been greatly transformed in the intervening years, and the labour law system itself has undergone equally momentous transformations, most of which would have worried him considerably. It is very debatable as to how much and in what directions the law of the contract of employment has altered during that time. One might argue that there has been just the kind of departure from the 'formal equality approach' which Kahn-Freund would have hoped for, especially manifested in the *Autoclenz* decision of the Supreme Court;[31] and one might also take the view that the 'master and servant approach' has been more fully consigned to the repository of discredited history.

On the other hand, one might in 2014 feel many of the concerns that Kahn-Freund felt in 1977 about the state of English law concerning the contract of employment, and feel them no less sharply than he did then. My own feeling is that it is a body of law which continues to support and facilitate the infliction of many forms of precarity, exploitation and legal exclusion upon large and growing sectors of the labour force. I would see the task of socializing and balancing the law of the contract of employment, therefore, as a struggle that continues to confront us no less urgently than in the late 1970s. Many of us in the community of labour law scholarship have tended in recent years to see the struggle as taking us *beyond* the contract of employment in various senses; Kahn-Freund's writings leave us with a set of reasons for returning to the study and refinement of the law of the contract of employment itself. I hope to have shown that such a study would both follow from and pursue a concern with the autonomy of labour law.

[31] *Autoclenz Ltd v Belcher* [2011] UKSC 41. See especially A Bogg, 'Sham Self-Employment in the Court of Appeal' (2010) 126 *Law Quarterly Review* 166 and by the same author 'Sham Self-Employment in the Supreme Court' (2012) 41 *Industrial Law Journal* 328.

2

Contractual Autonomy

HUGH COLLINS

One concern about 'the autonomy of labour law' focuses on the question of what are, or ought to be, the essential ingredients of the subject of labour law that is taught in most British law schools. What holds it together as a legal subject and explains its focus? The question differs from the issue of the ultimate aim or principal purpose of labour law. Reflection about a general aim, such as combating the inequality of bargaining power in the employment relation, will illuminate the subject of labour law in general, but it will not prove an adequate guide to a more detailed middle-level theory regarding the core ingredients of the legal subject. The present examination of the autonomy of labour law is at once more mundane and more complex. Although it is influenced by normative perceptions of the legitimate purposes of labour laws, the key task in formulating a conception of the autonomy of labour law is to explicate how labour law reasons about the social practices involved in work relations, and to use that understanding of legal reasoning to ascertain what should lie at the core of the subject, what legal concepts and institutions hold it together, and what should be regarded as peripheral matters. This approach assumes that legal subjects such as labour law cannot be reduced to detailed expressions of aims or goals for the subject, because the demands of consistency and coherence in legal reasoning inevitably separate legal analysis from the underlying and motivating moral and political aspirations of advocates of the subject.

Having considered in more detail the methodology required to develop a conception of the autonomy of labour law for this purpose of defining the legal subject, the enquiry proceeds to investigate how conceptions of the autonomy of labour law have radically changed during the past half century in Britain. In charting that historical change, we can draw heavily on the influential historical account advanced by Paul Davies and Mark Freedland of the decline of 'collective *laissez-faire*',[1] but the central question addressed here is what can be regarded today, in the twenty-first century, as providing the essential ingredients of the

[1] P Davies and M Freedland, *Labour Legislation and Public Policy: A Contemporary History* (Oxford, Clarendon Press, 1993), drawing on the phrase first used in O Kahn-Freund, 'Labour Law' in M Ginsberg (ed), *Law and Opinion in England in the 20th Century* (London, Stevens, 1959) 224.

autonomy of labour law. The claim put forward is that the contract of employment, as a legal concept or legal institution, may now provide the essential conceptual underpinning for the autonomy of labour law. This historical change in the conception of the autonomy of labour law may be described as a transition from 'collective autonomy' to 'contractual autonomy'.

Having advanced that claim by means of drawing heavily on the scholarship of Mark Freedland, the concluding part of the chapter acknowledges and explores some of the difficulties in elaborating such a conception of labour law. For a start, it should be admitted that the paradigm of contractual autonomy remains very much a work in progress. The rules and principles of the law of the contract of employment developed in the nineteenth century are at best rudimentary tools for constructing a modern version of the autonomy of labour law. During recent decades, labour lawyers and judges have to some extent been refashioning those archaic tools for the purpose of developing a modern law of the contract of employment, which in turn may provide the conceptual foundation for the autonomy of labour law. A central dilemma in constructing this modern restatement of the law of the contract of employment is the extent to which this law should, on the one hand, borrow from the general law of contract applicable to commercial and consumer contracts, and on the other, differentiate itself from those general rules in order to tailor a special law for the contract for employment. This chapter argues for a mixture of these approaches to help to articulate the idea of 'contractual autonomy' for labour law. In the conclusion, however, I examine the extent to which Mark Freedland has himself abandoned the project of constructing a paradigm of contractual autonomy by replacing it with the idea of a personal work relation, and assess the prospects for success of this alternative.

I. Constructing a Paradigm

A. External and Internal Perspectives

To speak of 'the autonomy of labour law' implies a claim that the subject is distinctive, independent and self-regulating. Like a person's face, labour law as a legal subject is distinctive in so far as it possesses certain characteristics that, in their unique combination, mark out that subject as different from others. The independence of the subject requires it to be self-standing and separate from the other branches of the legal system, not simply comprising a part of a broader whole in the way that liability for negligent breach of a duty of care is part of the law of torts. For a legal subject to be self-regulating, it must possess to a significant degree its own system of legal reasoning and its own concepts or legal institutions, or at least use legal rules and concepts in idiosyncratic ways.

In other words, to be autonomous, labour law must think about issues within its own special logic, it must have its own sphere of meaning, or function as an autopoietic subsystem of law.[2]

Assertions regarding the autonomy of labour law are not usually made in the context of attempts to provide an accurate description and taxonomy of the legal system and the place of labour law within it. On the contrary, an assertion of the autonomy of labour law has been commonly advanced as part of a normative argument that labour law ought to be more independent from other branches of law. Lord Wedderburn, for instance, drawing on French debates on a similar issue concerning the relation between labour law and the Code civil, identifies the essential problem as the continuing dominance of the common law over labour law, especially the general law of contract and how it is applied to the contract of employment: '[I]t is the very function of the common law to preserve subordination inherently within employment, and if necessary to do it creatively.'[3] Independence for labour law is demanded owing to a concern that the insertion of the rules from other branches of law, such as tort, property and contract, will subvert or undermine the integrity and successful functioning of labour law as a specialized subsystem of the law. For instance, the full application of competition law to the field of collective labour relations would probably lead to the prohibition of collective agreements as cartels, as happened under the Combination Acts,[4] even though effective collective agreements are normally regarded by labour lawyers as an integral element of any functioning labour law system. The idea of the autonomy of labour law therefore typically presents both a descriptive claim—that there is a distinctive, independent and self-regulating subject—and a normative claim that the independence of this subsystem of the law should be respected and enhanced. These two aspects of this idea of the autonomy of labour law will, however, be connected in most analyses: views about what constitutes the autonomous subject of labour law will be influenced by views about its proper or ideal functions and purposes.

Nevertheless, labour law will inevitably be like other things. After all, in its very name it reveals that it must resemble other branches of the law. It has evolved as a subsystem of the legal system. Furthermore, labour law inevitably includes rules and principles borrowed or transplanted from other branches of the law, such as company law, human rights law, property law, contract law and the remainder of the law of obligations. At the same time, however, labour law may differ from other branches of the law by, for instance, deploying certain unique concepts or legal institutions, or by using particular legal techniques of regulation and adjudication. A list of similarities and differences between labour law and other branches of the law could never persuasively establish its autonomy; it would just be a list. It would tell us that labour law contains

[2] G Teubner, *Law as an Autopoietic System* (Oxford, Blackwell, 1993).

[3] Lord Wedderburn, 'Labour Law: From Here to Autonomy' (1987) 16 *Industrial Law Journal* 1, 9.

[4] Combination Acts 1799 (39 Geo III, c 81), 1800 (39 & 40 Geo III c 106), 1825 (6 Geo 4 c 129); cf in France, *Loi Le Chapellier*, 14 June 1791.

rules and principles that find their parallels or origins in other branches of the law such as contract and tort, but also some doctrines and concepts that seem unique to labour law. Those unique elements will prove especially interesting to the task of identifying the distinctiveness of labour law, but they are likely to appear too scattered to help us understand labour law as an integrated and autonomous subject.

Instead, following a standard sociological method[5] that is frequently adopted implicitly in theories of law and legal doctrines,[6] a better approach is to identify a central case or paradigm of labour law, which describes the constitutive elements of the subject. Through the selection of legal materials, claims for the autonomy of labour involve the construction of a paradigm or central case,[7] which corresponds to the practices of labour lawyers and their internal viewpoint about the identity of the subject,[8] and a normative perspective of the theorist regarding the proper aims and justifications for labour law. The construction of such a paradigm or central case of labour law is a delicate enterprise. To be successful it must merge both external and internal points of view.

The external point of view looks from a sociological perspective at the subject. It gathers information about its features from the practices of lawyers who consider themselves to be practising labour law or employment law or writing about the subject.[9] This external viewpoint can observe what areas of social life are characteristically subject to those practices, such as employment relations and collective relations between trade unions and employers. The external viewpoint also observes the forms of regulation that are used in labour law, the composition of the significant regulators and adjudicators, and the values expressed by proponents of the subject. The external viewpoint can take us a long way towards discovering the features of labour law that make it appear distinctive and independent. However, these external features that serve to identify labour law in practice are not sufficient to help to construct a theory of the autonomy of labour law.

For a paradigm of labour law to meet the third requirement of autonomy, ie the self-regulating or autopoietic character of the subject, it has to identify the distinctive legal concepts and methods of legal reasoning that are used within labour law. The law of trusts, for instance, establishes its autonomy in

[5] M Weber, *Economy and Society*, ed Guenther Roth and Claus Wittich (Berkeley, University of California Press, 1978).

[6] R Cotterrell, 'Why Must Legal Ideas Be Interpreted Sociologically?' (1998) 25 *Journal of Law & Society* 171; Nicola Lacey, 'Philosophical Foundations of the Common Law: Social not Metaphysical' in J Horder (ed), *Oxford Essays in Jurisprudence*, 4th series (Oxford, Oxford University Press, 2000) 17.

[7] J Finnis, *Natural Law and Natural Rights*, 2nd edn (Oxford, Oxford University Press 2011) ch 1, provides a rigorous analysis of the methodology in theories of law. (This methodology is explored more thoroughly in Alan Bogg, in this volume).

[8] H Collins, 'Legal Classifications as the Production of Knowledge Systems' in P Birks (ed), *The Classification of Obligations* (Oxford, Clarendon Press, 1997) 57.

[9] To that extent the 'external viewpoint' is partly 'internal' in that it uses evidence from practising lawyers about what they subjectively regard as labour law.

this sense through the distinctive pattern of rights and obligations that arise in the special legal institution of a trust. No doubt there will be troublesome borderline instances such as constructive trusts, but the fiduciary duties of the trust provide a core concept that maintains the integrity and autonomy of the subject. The construction of a useful paradigm for the autonomy of labour law requires the combination of the external viewpoint—essentially an examination of the practices of a group who regards themselves as working in the field of labour law to see what is distinctive and independent about those practices—and the internal view, which examines the special characteristics of how labour law thinks about issues and disputes.

Finally, one should acknowledge the importance of the normative perspective of the theorist who constructs a conception of the central case or paradigm. Even where there is broad agreement about the relevant legal practices and concepts that constitute labour law, the final decisions regarding the salience of some particular features, or what lies at the core of the subject and what lies at the penumbra, and the outer limits of its scope, depend ultimately on (often unexpressed) normative judgements regarding the essential features of the subject, its virtues, or its vocation. Choices about salience and inclusion are influenced by the normative perspective of the theorist and consequent views about the constitutive significance of different parts of labour law and the proper scope of the subject. These normative perspectives on labour law are likely to focus on considerations of justice, so that the chosen paradigm will emphasize the role of the law in securing and policing what is regarded by the theorist as a fair distribution of power and wealth in connection with personal work relations.

It should be stressed, however, that in this investigation of the autonomy of labour law as a subsystem of law, the focus is not on normative perspectives, but rather on legal reasoning itself and how labour law displays some unique institutions and concepts through which it seeks to resolve disputes or social and economic problems. By way of analogy, consider the law of contract. A popular view about the aims of the law of contract holds that its main aim is to uphold the morality of keeping one's promises,[10] or at least to protect this convention from being undermined.[11] Even assuming that these analyses of the aims are correct, it must be acknowledged that the common law of contract goes about its task by employing a distinctive set of legal doctrines, such as the requirements of agreement composed of offer and acceptance and of consideration to support that agreement. By applying those doctrines, the courts will inevitably decline to enforce some promises such as donative promises that lack consideration,[12] and may end up enforcing implied agreements where there is no evidence of any explicit promise at all.[13] This possible mismatch between general aim and

[10] Charles Fried, *Contract as Promise* (Cambridge, MA, Harvard University Press, 1981).

[11] J Raz, 'Promises in Morality and Law' (1982) 95 *Harvard Law Review* 916; D Kimel, *From Promise to Contract* (Oxford, Oxford University Press, 2003).

[12] M Eisenberg, 'Donative Promises' (1979) 47 *Uunversity of Chicago Law Review* 1.

[13] *Paal Wilson & Co A/S v partenreederei Hannah Blumental (The Hannah Blumenthal)* [1983] 1 AC 854 (HL).

legal reasoning arises because legal reasoning is relatively autonomous from moral and political reasoning. Though always influenced by moral and political considerations, the law has its own logic or integrity. This chapter investigates the question of what legal concepts or institutions form the core or paradigm for labour law such that it possesses autonomy in the sense of being a distinct branch of legal studies.

B. Contextualism

One immediate challenge to any theory of the autonomy of labour law of this kind comes from the contextual approach to the delineation of legal subjects. From a contextual perspective, it may be said that, unlike other mainstream legal subjects such as contract law or the law of torts that are conventionally considered to comprise doctrinal categories, labour law is inherently a contextual subject, which considers a diverse collection of legal matters that are more or less closely related to employment relations. On this view, a contextual subject such as labour law is said to have no need of a distinctive conceptual framework, because it is a rag-tag collection of bits of other subjects—tort, contract, public law, human rights law—which can be sewn together to make a patchwork quilt.[14] From this contextualist viewpoint, the subject derives its coherence, if it possesses any at all, from its exclusive focus on a particular context: employment or personal work relations. On that view, labour law cannot be autonomous in the sense being investigated here, because it lacks a unique system of what has been called here self-regulation or autopoiesis. Instead of evolving its own system of legal concepts and developing them through legal reasoning, labour law is presented by the contextualist as a bundle of legal rules and principles that are stitched together by little more than the social field of employment relations to which they are applied.[15] The contextualist proposes a purely external point of view, which makes no attempt to understand or construct an internal view of the logic of labour law, and which implicitly denies the autonomy of labour law.

The sole effective response to a contextualist is to present a convincing account of the autonomy of labour law from the internal point of view as possessing its own legal concepts and system of legal reasoning. But it is possible, as a prelimi-

[14] It is important to distinguish the enterprise of the study of the law in context, which has always been a feature of labour law studies, from a definition of the subject of labour law by reference exclusively to context. The choice of context itself presents its own difficulties: H Collins, 'The Productive Disintegration of Labour Law' (1997) 26 *Industrial Law Journal* 296. I should acknowledge, however, that a definition of the subject by reference to context forms a starting-point of my discussion of the scope of labour law in H Collins, 'Labour Law as a Vocation' (1989) 105 *Law Quarterly Review* 468, 473, though the point of that essay is devoted to a consideration of normative aims for the subject.

[15] An important extra element is likely to comprise membership of different types of clubs: people who self-identify themselves as labour lawyers are likely to attend particular conferences, join particular societies, publish in particular journals, etc, all of which serves to create a profession that helps to bind the subject together as well as the contextual focus: Collins (n 8) 58–60 'The Imperialism of Professional Cohorts'.

nary matter, to chip away at some of the assumptions behind the contextualist challenge to the project of establishing the autonomy of labour law as a legal subject. The first assumption lies in the division between contextual subjects and the more traditional doctrinal subjects that, in possession of an internal legal logic, can claim autonomy. This assumption may be challenged by questioning whether the legal subjects described as doctrinal are not also determined by their context. Contract law, for instance, is usually held up as an autonomous doctrinal subject, but it can be argued that the selection of the rules and principles of what are regarded as the essential components of the subject is influenced to a considerable extent by what is regarded as its appropriate context, which is discrete market transactions such as sales of goods. As it is generally defined, in the books and in teaching, contract law excludes contracts that create associations (including trade unions and companies), contracts within the family, and contracts involving interests in real property. There is nothing wrong in excluding such topics, for they clearly raise all kinds of distinctive issues, but the point is rather that they will not be excluded for doctrinal reasons—there will be an offer, acceptance and consideration in those situations as well—but for contextual reasons. If contract law in general can present itself as an autonomous and coherent body of legal doctrine whilst being ultimately contextual, why not labour law? Whilst the contextual framing of a legal subject may be a matter of degree, all legal subjects share this dimension of determining their scope by reference to context, which makes labour law only different in its degree of contextualization, but not different in kind.

Moreover, the idea that labour law simply borrows its ideas from other parts of the law and sews them together into a patchwork surely undervalues the conceptual contribution of labour law itself to the remainder of the law. Legal examination of the employment relation has generated its own concepts, such as the notion of constructive dismissal[16] and its handmaiden, the implied term of mutual trust and confidence.[17] Similarly, the notion of prohibitions on indirect discrimination was first conceived in the context of the workplace and applicants for jobs,[18] though it has since been exported to many other fields of social life such as sales to the public and landlord and tenant.[19] To assume that labour law is merely a contextual subject without its own legal concepts and institutions does not fit the evidence very well. Furthermore, the contextualist viewpoint effectively denies that labour lawyers have anything distinctive to contribute to legal analysis and therefore, implicitly, that labour law is not a subject worth studying in itself as part of an education in legal reasoning. Before we endorse the contextualist explanation of labour law in its entirety, therefore, it is worth considering more deeply whether any claim can be made for labour law to be

[16] *Marriott v Oxford Co-operative Society Ltd (No 2)* [1970] 1 QB 186 (CA).
[17] *Mahmoud and Malik v Bank of Credit and Commerce International SA* [1997] ICR 606 (HL).
[18] *Griggs v Duke Power Co* 401 US 424, 91 S Ct 849 (1971); Sex Discrimination Act 1975 s 1.
[19] Equality Act 2010, pts 3 and 4.

a doctrinal subject, at least to no lesser extent than most other subjects taught in universities.

This is the question to be considered here: can labour law be presented as a system of law, bound together not merely by a context such as its focus on the employment relation but also by a distinctive conceptual framework of law? In other words, does labour law reason in a particular way about its field of interest by analysing problems within its own terms and concepts and by producing solutions that fit consistently and coherently within that framework of law? Is labour law a system or was it never more than patchwork?

C. Dynamic Subject

There is no reason to suppose, however, that the most useful and plausible paradigm for the purposes of understanding the autonomy of labour law has remained static. On the contrary, the paradigm has arguably shifted considerably during the past half century. The next section of this paper seeks to reconstruct the paradigm of fifty years ago, and having done so, charts its fall. While labour lawyers may regret and resist the demise of that paradigm, described by some as the death of labour law,[20] the task in recent years has been to construct a new one. Without a new paradigm that both corresponds to the practice of labour lawyers and grasps the internal logic of the reasoning of labour law, claims for the autonomy of labour law will prove unconvincing.

II. The Original Paradigm: Collective *Laissez-faire*

Although it may be hard to secure agreement on the current characteristics of labour law, thanks to the work of Kahn-Freund, the picture of the subject in the 1960s in the United Kingdom was sharply focused and broadly accepted. For the vast majority of employment relationships, the institution of collective bargaining provided the key method of regulation and a central concept in the paradigm of labour law. Leaving aside senior managers, professionals and some marginal groups of workers, collective agreements provided essential terms of employment and rules and procedures to govern management's power to direct labour. As Kahn-Freund said: 'The principal purpose of labour law, then, is to regulate, to support, and to restrain the power of management and the power of organised labour.'[21] But he added that the role of the law was essentially auxiliary: to protect the existence of independent trade unions, to promote collective

[20] K Ewing, 'The Death of Labour Law' (1988) 8 *Oxford Journal of Legal Studies* 293.
[21] O Kahn-Freund, *Labour and the Law* (London, Stevens, 1972) 5.

bargaining, to protect effective bargaining on the part of the workforce by means of industrial action, and by various mechanisms to extend the outcomes of collective agreements to the bulk of the nation's workforce.[22] This auxiliary framework was provided by statute, not the common law. Judge-made law played a marginal role in the enforcement of contracts of employment, which in practice was largely confined to the award of damages in cases of the unjustified summary dismissal of well-remunerated employees, and in the judicial development of those economic torts that were inevitably committed by union leaders in calling for industrial action. This statutory framework established voluntary collective bargaining as the core method for the regulation of employment relations. It permitted workers to form trade unions, to organize, to bargain collectively, and to back up claims with industrial action within the framework of the statutory immunities against claims in tort and against criminal offences. With only a few exceptions, the detailed regulation of employment relations and the terms and conditions of employment was not supplied directly by the law, but by collective self-regulation established by collective agreements between employers and trade unions. Labour law established procedures and constraints on action by capital and labour, but the detailed rules governing employment relations were largely determined by non-legal processes such as collective bargaining and its shadowing institutions such as Wages Councils. In Kahn-Freund's influential view, 'This attitude of abstentionism was the outstanding virtue of British law.'[23]

This image of labour law advanced by Kahn-Freund matched the insights of the sociology of industrial relations, in which the British system was regarded as mature and functional, permitting both sides of industry to strike a fair balance of interests that achieved a measure of social justice whilst ensuring that workers had a democratic voice at work. The law was perceived as serving the function of constructing and stabilizing this industrial relations system at a structural level without interfering in its day-to-day autonomous operations. The test advanced for good labour law was whether it supported the role of autonomous collective bargaining in the settlement of the terms of employment relations.

Labour lawyers could therefore claim that their subject was not merely a contextual subject connected to the employment relation. Labour law concerned some unique social institutions and legal concepts such as trade unions, collective bargaining and industrial action, and labour law offered a distinctive 'voluntaristic' approach towards the regulation of these social institutions. At the same time as labour law secured the foundations of the system, it refrained from determining the substantive outcomes of the collective bargaining. In other words, the legal framework provided institutional support for a unique system of self-regulation that governed a major part of the nation's economic activity. At its core, labour law avoided general contract law, distrusted tort law, largely ignored public law[24] and abstained from detailed substantive regulation of the labour

[22] ibid ch 3.
[23] ibid 270.
[24] The influence of public law, though rare before 1970, became more significant for a time in

market. Unlike the emerging laws of landlord and tenant, consumer law, and other branches of the law aimed at protecting weaker parties to contracts, labour law eschewed mandatory legal rules to govern employment relations. Labour law carved out its own idiosyncratic and reflexive route to legal regulation,[25] using concepts and institutional mechanisms unknown elsewhere in the law. Labour law could claim that it taught an innovative and unique doctrinal system that governed a field of great public importance. Its claim to be an autonomous subject in its own right was surely unchallengeable. In this context, claims for the autonomy of labour law, such as those voiced by Lord Wedderburn, were essentially arguments against the introduction by judges into the autonomous field of labour law the legal doctrines that were familiar to them from other areas of private law, such as contract and tort.

In the half century of labour law teaching at Oxford (and the full century at the London School of Economics), the subject has been transformed almost beyond recognition. Continuities in the contextual subject matter of labour law and perennial concerns about the tasks for legal regulation have maintained a recognizable identity for labour law, but the changes in the direction and techniques of labour law, wrought mostly by prolific legislation, amount to more than wrinkles on an old familiar face. Of course, the subject remains concerned broadly speaking with the same context: legal relations formed in the context of employment. Within employment relations, such as other contracts involving weaker parties such as consumers, the attention of labour lawyers continues to be focused on problems arising from the power relation between the employer and employee, though labour lawyers still maintain that the degree of subordination of the typical worker to the employing organization raises distinctive issues concerning respect for human dignity and personal autonomy ('labour is not a commodity'). It is probably also true that most teachers and students who are drawn to the subject of labour law share the vocation of its original proponents, which was to combat the outcomes of the economic and personal domination that is structurally present in contracts of employment.[26] But that shared vocation has certainly had its grip on the subject shaken over the past half century. Its predominance has been challenged by other powerful claims such as those regarding equity as between different groups of workers that were manifested in part as anti-discrimination laws. The aim of combating inequality of bargaining power was also rivalled by a divergent political agenda that viewed improvements to business competitiveness and labour market efficiency as a

the 1980s and 1990s, partly as a result of membership of the European Economic Community. See P Davies and M Freedland, 'The Impact of Public law on Labour Law 1972–1997' (1997) 26 *Industrial Law Journal* 311; S Sedley, 'Public Law and Contractual Employment' (1994) 23 *Industrial Law Journal* 201.

[25] G Teubner, 'Substantive and Reflexive Elements in Modern Law' (1983) 17 *Law and Society Review* 239; G Teubner (ed), *Dilemmas of Law in the Welfare State* (New York, Walter de Gruyter, 1988).

[26] Collins, 'Labour Law as a Vocation' (n 14).

preferable touchstone for labour law.[27] Labour law could also be viewed as part of a broader welfare and security strategy to promote work opportunities and to protect the economic security of workers throughout their lives.[28] Nevertheless, most conceptions of labour law, as evidenced in textbooks and teaching programmes, still seem to taking their bearings from the gravitational pull of the need to redress the economic and social domination present in employment relations. Despite this continuity in views about the normative aims of the subject of labour law, it is nevertheless evident that the legal framework has changed substantially since Otto Kahn-Freund arrived in Oxford in 1964.

The character of the social institutions that surround the employment relationship has undergone a seismic shift during those fifty years. The most obvious change in the social institutions has occurred as a consequence of the decline of collective bargaining as the principal mechanism for combating the inequality of bargaining power between employer and employee and for regulating the terms of jobs. That gradual deterioration in the role of collective regulation of employment itself appears to be in part associated with the structural transformation of the UK economy from industrial production towards a much greater reliance on the service sector. That structural transformation in the economy has created an increased demand for jobs that were initially described as 'non-standard', because they did not fit the predominant pattern established under industrial production in the twentieth century of full-time indefinite employment; these 'non-standard' forms of employment relation, such as part-time, fixed-term or freelancers, are frequently preferred by service sector employers as they offer flexibility in terms of hours and size of workforce. So not only was collective bargaining a declining force in establishing terms and conditions of employment, but the other social institution of the standard employment relation was also declining in its prevalence and being replaced by more precarious kinds of contractual relations for work.

Even though Parliament started experimenting with radically different legal frameworks for labour law from 1971 onwards, the prevailing wisdom among labour lawyers, including Kahn-Freund, for at least another decade was that most of these initiatives were ultimately misguided, counterproductive, damaging to the law or marginal to the central concerns of the subject.[29] At the time of writing a paper on the 'Productive Disintegration of Labour Law'[30] in 1997, it was plain to me that the game was up. The centre of gravity of labour was no longer

[27] H Collins, 'Regulating the Employment Relation for Competitiveness' (2001) 30 *Industrial Law Journal* 17.

[28] Alan Supiot et al, *Beyond Employment—Changes in Work and the Future of Labour Law in Europe* (Oxford, Oxford University Press, 2001).

[29] Kahn-Freund (n 21) 270: '[W]e shall see whether legal compulsion or its threat is capable of remoulding industrial relations. I have not tried to conceal my own skepticism—nor my fear that this experiment may do harm to industrial relations and to the law itself.'

[30] Collins, 'Productive Disintegration' (n 14). Others had been raising similar questions: R Mitchell (ed), *Redefining Labour Law: New Perspectives on the Future of Teaching and Research* (Melbourne, Centre for Employment and Labour Relations Law, University of Melbourne, 1995).

what Kahn-Freund had called 'collective *laissez-faire*' supported by auxiliary legal structures. Nor were the changes that were occurring simply a restructuring of the legal framework for collective bargaining achieved through a revision of the rights of ownership of the means of production and the bargaining rights of the participants. Although that revision of the legal framework for bargaining had certainly happened under Prime Minister Thatcher, what was becoming clear by 1997 was that more radical changes were afoot. Legal abstentionism in the field of labour relations was dead, though labour lawyers, still in a state of shock at their bereavement, were uncertain about how to start afresh or indeed whether they wished to do so.

From 1971 onwards, with the advent of the law of unfair dismissal, legislation was subtly changing its focus from the bargaining process to the setting of the substantive terms and rules of the employment relationship. By the 1980s, legal rights conferred on individual employees, such as rights to claim unfair dismissal and redundancy payments, to claim protection from direct and indirect discrimination on an expanding list of protected characteristics, and to claim for deductions from wages, now comprised the bulk of litigation related to the employment relation and dominated the practice of labour lawyers. In a sense, the decline of collective bargaining as an effective system of regulation can be measured by the rise of individual claims before tribunals. Legal abstention was replaced by detailed regulation. Statute law had moved from process to outcome, from the auxiliary periphery to the detailed regulation to terms of employment, and judge-made law became increasingly important as the vehicle for the authoritative interpretation of complex statutes and elaborate written contracts of employment in order to determine the legal claims of workers.

These developments could not be ignored by labour law teachers and nor, ideally, could they be sidelined into a different subject called employment law. Instead of a prolonged focus on the law of collective bargaining as the principal and most effective tool for combating the inequality of bargaining power in the employment relation, by the close of the twentieth century a labour law course had to stretch over many legal rights of individual employees governing wages, hours, dismissal and discrimination, and, at the same time to include a multi-level system of law that encompasses European Union law and transnational human rights law. What formerly lay at the core of the subject of labour law—the auxiliary law of collective bargaining—is now at best a declining fraction of the subject. Labour law had evidently lost its paradigm in collective *laissez-faire*, but could an autonomous labour law be revived in a new form? What would be the key organizing topics in this post-abstentionist world? The entity of labour law seemed to have lost its identity. Or had there been a transfer of the undertaking of autonomous labour law to a new paradigm?

III. A Contribution from Oxford

Near the beginning of the teaching of labour law at Oxford, in August 1970, a young scholar, MR Freedland, presented his doctoral thesis in Oxford with the title: 'The Application of General Contract Principles to the Termination of the Employment Relationship'. At a historical moment when collective bargaining had become not only the dominant regulatory mechanism for work relations, but also ideas of social compacts in tripartite mechanisms between the elected government, employers and trade unions suggested that this voluntary regulatory mechanism might be used for the entire governance of the country, it might be thought that this topic for a labour law thesis was splendidly irrelevant and arcane. The common law of the termination of employment, the law of wrongful dismissal, was irrelevant for the vast majority of workers, because at that time the normal course for challenging dismissals was negotiation between employer and trade union representatives in the shadow of the threat of industrial action. The topic was arcane because it required an investigation of the precedents of the common law, many of which were drawn from a pre-industrial age and articulated in the language of master and servant. Understandably, it may have seemed to bemused onlookers at places such as the London School of Economics that, during the transfer of the subject of labour law from the University of London, Oxford had imposed its traditional stamp on the subject by confining its enquiries to judge-made common law and the search for systematic doctrine in those precedents. Perhaps intoxicated by the sight of the dreaming spires or perhaps submerged under the Blackstonian doctrinal tradition, had Kahn-Freund and his protégé gone native on moving to Oxford?[31]

In the subsequent book of the thesis, entitled *The Contract of Employment*,[32] now expanded to include the formation of contracts of employment, the young scholar acknowledges some discomfort with its focus. By 1976, the year of publication of the book, the Conservative government had collapsed under pressure from the trade unions opposed to the Industrial Relations Act 1971, and the new Labour government had largely restored the regime of collective *laissez-faire* but had gone further than ever before (or since) to promote collective bargaining through the Employment Protection Act 1975. Although some of these momentous events for labour law are mentioned, mostly in an appendix, the book resolutely keeps its focus on the common law of the contract of employment. In the introduction, it is admitted by the young scholar that, although there was a flow of small claims for wages and damages for wrongful dismissal in the inferior courts, these were scarcely of any importance or relevance to the system of industrial relations. Insofar as the law of the contract of employment

[31] The story of the ambiguous attitude of Kahn-Freund towards the contract of employment is brilliantly explored in M Freedland, 'Otto-Kahn-Freund, the Contract of Employment and the Autonomy of Labour Law', in this volume.

[32] M Freedland, *The Contract of Employment* (Oxford, Oxford University Press, 1976).

regulated the individual employment relationship, the young scholar confessed that it was an apparatus that was somewhat 'rudimentary and obsolescent'.[33] Why, then, was it worth the time and energy of writing a book on this irrelevant and apparently archaic topic?

The answer proffered by the young scholar to this conundrum lay in Kahn-Freund's insight that the contract of employment provided the legal framework on which everything else in labour law was built.[34] With its assumption of the formal equality of the parties, this legal framework may have been deeply unsatisfactory in many respects, but the legal analysis has to start somewhere, and the contract of employment provides in English law what we might call the initial juridical act, the elementary legal bond on which the legal material of labour law is built. This foundational quality of the contract of employment for labour law was evident even in the new statutory rights enacted during those years, such as the rights to claim a minimum period of notice, a redundancy payment, equal pay and unfair dismissal. Although those statutes conferred legal rights on employees that increasingly supplanted the common law in practice, nevertheless those legal rights were always premised on the existence of the contract of employment at common law. This foundational quality of the contract of employment could also be identified, though with more difficulty, in the operation of the system of collective bargaining, for to the extent that collective agreements had legal effects, it was through the vehicle of incorporation into the contract of employment. Without that vehicle of the contract of employment, the legally unenforceable collective agreement would be no more than a legal black hole.

Even so, though one must concede that the contract of employment could be described as a foundation stone for the whole of labour law and therefore deserving some attention, it was also true that this foundation stone was deeply buried underground, seldom disinterred, and when it was examined by the judges and the textbooks, it provided limited information about the issues presented, little more indeed than the words inscribed on the foundation stone laid by the Victorian judges: freedom of contract. Compared to the high-profile litigation wars being conducted in the courts in the 1960s over the scope of the economic torts and the immunities for industrial action, the legal measures designed to support and extend the reach of collective bargaining, and the emerging crisis of governance linked to wage-linked hyperinflation, the neglected topic of the contract of employment seemed to deserve its oblivion. With his unwavering eye on the ball, when Otto-Kahn Freund delivered his Hamlyn lectures in 1971 on the subject of 'Labour and the Law', a series of lectures that provided at that time a definitive restatement of the subject, he dismissed the contract of employment early on as a necessary fiction for distinguishing the subordination of employment from compulsory labour,[35] a fiction scarcely to be mentioned again. Viewed

[33] ibid 4.

[34] O Kahn-Freund, 'Labour Law' in A Flanders and H Clegg (eds), *The System of Industrial Relations in Great Britain* (Oxford, Blackwell, 1954) 45.

[35] Kahn-Freund (n 21) 15.

in this historical light of the 1970s, whatever one's views about the subject of labour law, a doctoral thesis on the topic of the contract of employment in 1970 seemed unlikely to promise a valuable contribution to the subject.

And yet, things have not turned out that way. In contemporary labour law in Britain, the contract of employment and the law governing it has assumed a pivotal position. It occupies a leading position in the textbooks.[36] These days, issues connected to the law of the contract of employment are at the heart of most of the labour law cases that reach the Supreme Court and the Court of Appeal. It is no longer just an indispensable figment of the legal imagination. The law of the contract of employment has been exposed above the surface and now provides a substantive and procedural framework for employment relations. It is no longer just a foundation stone, a juridical presupposition with no concrete effects, but the scaffolding for the whole legal edifice.

IV. The Centrality of the Contract of Employment

To appreciate just how pivotal the common law of the contract of employment has become in contemporary labour law, it is worth recalling briefly some of its crucial roles in the contemporary regulation of employment relations. The common law supplies vital ingredients in the determination of rights and obligations from the inception to the conclusion of employment relations.

A. Existence, Enforceability and Scope

An initial question that arises is whether a worker has a contract of employment or any kind of contract at all with the supposed employer. That issue arises mainly with respect to the application of statutory rights that depend upon the existence of a contract of employment or an employment-like arrangement. For instance, casual workers and interns may lack any kind of binding contractual agreement at all, which will defeat all potential claims brought under statute, from the right to a minimum wage to protection from unfair dismissal.[37] If the contract is unenforceable for illegality, the employee is unlikely to be able to claim any statutory rights at all unless those rights can be established completely independently of the existence of a contract.[38] Statutory employment rights only

[36] eg S Deakin and GS Morris, *Labour Law*, 6th edn (Oxford, Hart Publishing, 2012), ch 3; H Collins, KD Ewing and A McColgan, *Labour Law* (Cambridge, Cambridge University Press, 2012) ch 3.

[37] *O'Kelly v Trusthouse Forte* [1984] QB 90 (CA); *Carmichael v National Power* [1999] ICR 1226 (HL).

[38] *Hall v Woolston Hall Leisure Ltd* [2001] ICR 99 (CA); *Hounga v Allen* [2012] EWCA Civ 609.

apply to particular kinds of contractual arrangements, such as the contract of employment, and the courts decide the scope of those categories by reference to the traditional distinctions of the common law, such as the contrast between contracts for services (independent contractors) and contracts of service.[39] In all these legal issues, the common law plays a vital role, because it determines the existence of the contract, its legal enforceability, and its classification. Statutory employment rights are therefore parasitic on the common law of contract.

B. Interpretation

The common law of contracts determines the interpretation placed upon employment relations, so that it shapes the respective obligations of the parties through the general categories of express and implied terms. The ordinary principles for the interpretation of standard form contracts are applied to the proliferation of standard form contracts of employment, with only an occasional concession to the point that these are adhesion contracts, drafted and offered on a take-it-or-leave-it basis by the employer, which typically construct a one-sided description of the obligations arising under the contract.[40] Whilst demanding absolute obedience from the employee to a complex set of detailed rules and duties, these standard form contracts grant employers broad discretion through flexibility clauses and unilateral variation clauses, so much so that the employer can lawfully alter its own obligations virtually at will.[41] In fidelity to the principle of freedom of contract, the common law permits the employer to dictate the terms and to create a relation of subordination, whilst reserving the right to engage in opportunism.

The express terms can be supplemented by default rules, which have been devised by common law judges over the centuries. By creating the implied terms that impose upon employees duties of obedience, loyalty, good faith in performance, and carefulness, the courts provided default rules that back up or even constitute a relation of subordination.[42] True, the courts also developed implied terms that imposed duties upon employers, in particular the duty to take reasonable care of the health and safety of employees,[43] and not to, without good reason, act in a way calculated to destroy mutual trust and confidence.[44] But the courts were not tempted to create default rules that required the employer to act reasonably, fairly or with respect for employees, for that would suggest a general power of the courts to supervise managerial decisions with respect to

[39] *Lane v Shire Roofing Company (Oxford) Ltd* [1995] IRLR 493 (CA).

[40] *Autoclenz Ltd v Belcher* [2011] UKSC 41.

[41] *Bateman v ASDA Stores Ltd* [2010] IRLR 370 (EAT).

[42] *Lister v Romford Ice and Cold Storage Co Ltd* [1956] AC 583 (HL) (carefulness); *British Telecommunications plc v Ticehurst* [1992] ICR 383 (CA) (good faith); *Nottingham University v Fishel* [2000] IRLR 471 (QB) (loyalty).

[43] *Candler v Crane, Christmas & Co* [1951] 1 All ER 426 (CA).

[44] *Mahmoud and Malik v Bank of Credit and Commerce International SA* [1998] AC 20 (HL).

their staff. Hence, the limits of managerial power are only determined by the complex and to some extent unpredictable idea of mutual trust and confidence.

The express and implied terms shape the entire contractual relation. Parliament has occasionally intervened by granting mandatory rights in a form that either explicitly (in the case of equal pay)[45] or implicitly (in the case of working time)[46] amounts to the insertion of a mandatory term in the contract of employment, which overrides any contrary provision. However, normally statutory employment rights are independent from the terms of the contract, parasitic on the existence of that contract, but providing separate entitlements that in general should prove superior to those afforded by the terms of the contract. That leaves largely undisturbed the contract of employment as the central legal institution governing employment relations.

C. Termination

The common law continues to determine many legal questions arising with respect to the termination of the contract of employment. Under the common law, the contract could normally be terminated unilaterally by either party giving notice and that rule persists today except that by statute certain minimum periods of notice apply to termination by employers.[47] Alternatively, under the common law, a contract of employment could be terminated bilaterally by one party accepting a repudiatory breach or fundamental breach of contract committed by the other party.[48] Those common law rules have been used to interpret the statutory concept of dismissal, which was created to govern the law of unfair dismissal and redundancy payments. For instance, the interpretation of the idea of constructive dismissal has been founded on the common law. Constructive dismissal is described in the statute as a situation where 'the employee terminates the contract under which he is employed (with or without notice) in circumstances in which he is entitled to terminate it without notice by reason of the employer's conduct'.[49] This statutory notion was interpreted to require the employer to commit a repudiatory or fundamental breach of contract, as had been required by the common law of wrongful dismissal. To prevent employees from resigning and claiming unfair dismissal in circumstances where the employer was merely behaving unreasonably, harshly, capriciously or unfairly, the courts insisted that constructive dismissal only arose when the employer committed a fundamental breach of contract, in effect washing his hands of the employment relation.[50] Many other examples of how the common

[45] Equality Act 2010, s 66.
[46] *Barber v RJB Mining Ltd* [1999] ICR 679 (QB).
[47] Employment Rights Act 1996 s 86.
[48] *Société Général, London Branch v Geys* [2012] UKSC 63.
[49] Employment Rights Act 1996 s 95(1)(c).
[50] *Western Excavating v Sharp* [1978] ICR 221 (CA).

law concepts arising in the contract of employment have been employed to curtail the potential protective effect of legislation might be given.[51]

D. Remedies for Dismissal

Under the common law of wrongful dismissal, an employee who had been unjustifiably dismissed without notice could claim damages for the loss of wages during the notice period. For professional or managerial employees with a contractual term of lengthy notice, the sum might be substantial, but for most workers on weekly or daily contracts, this compensation would be minimal. Nor could an employee obtain specific performance of the contract or an injunction against dismissal. Although the precise rationale of *Addis v Gramophone Co Ltd*[52] remains ambiguous even after a century has passed, there was no doubt in the minds of the judges that it ruled out any compensation for the unpleasant or harsh manner of dismissal. In effect, under the common law, an employer could dismiss at any time, for any reason, in any manner, with the minimal requirement to pay wages until the expiration of the payment period of a day or a week.

During the twentieth century, this legal framework increasingly failed to match the expectations of continuity of employment shared by both employers and employees. Most jobs were regarded as permanent, with the expectation that in the absence of serious misconduct an employee would keep the job. The statutory law of unfair dismissal responded to this situation by protecting job security through a requirement that an employer should not dismiss an employee unless it was reasonable to do so.[53] Breach of that requirement would result in a 'just and equitable' award of compensation, which unlike the common law, was expressly stated to include the losses caused by the dismissal, and those losses could include not only the wages during the period of notice but also loss of income during a period of unemployment consequent upon dismissal.[54] Although the statute apparently created a clean break with the common law of wrongful dismissal, the gravitational force of the common law is still evident. For instance, when interpreting the requirement that the compensation for the statutory claim for unfair dismissal should be an amount that was 'just and equitable', the courts resurrected the common law rule against compensation for distress caused by the manner of dismissal.[55]

[51] SD Anderman, 'The Interpretation of Protective Statutes and the Contract of Employment' (2000) 29 *Industrial Law Journal* 223.

[52] *Addis v Gramophone Co Ltd* [1909] AC 488 (HL).

[53] Employment Rights Act 1996 pt X, originally created in the Industrial Relations Act 1971.

[54] Employment Rights Act 1996 s 123.

[55] *Dunnachie v Kingston upon Hull City Council* [2004] UKHL 36, [2004] ICR 1052.

E. The Ascription of Responsibility to the Employer

The idea of the contract of employment also determines who is regarded as the person or legal entity that is responsible for breaches of employment rights.[56] The common law assumes that at one end of the contract of employment there must be a single entity that is responsible for paying wages and for compliance with labour rights. In practice, however, that simple bilateral relation will often not correspond to the organizational framework around the performance of work.[57] In the case of two companies, a parent and a wholly owned subsidiary, an employee may be directly employed by the subsidiary, but the management of both companies, at least in the relevant respects, may be located in the parent company. The parent company may set wages, determine levels of manpower, and control health and safety practices. Unless the employee can succeed in some kind of claim in tort,[58] the contractual framework of responsibility restricts liabilities under contract or statute to the immediate employer, in this instance the subsidiary company. A similar problem arises in the frequent use of subcontracting of the peripheral activities of a business. Although the subcontractor enters the contract of employment with the worker, the principal business is likely to control many aspects of the business of the subcontractor, including for instance whether the employee will be made redundant. In an analogous triangular situation, a business may recruit its staff from an agency, under which arrangement the agency selects staff, pays them and dismisses them. It is unlikely that a court will find any direct contractual link between the business client of the agency and the worker,[59] any more than it will pierce the corporate veil and discover a contract between the parent company and the employee of the subsidiary. This common law framework, based on a model of a bilateral contract between two parties, determines the allocation of responsibility within these more complex economic arrangements or networks, even though the formal legal framework hardly matches the real allocation of power and decision-making. The general principle of the common law is simple: no direct contractual link between the employing entity and the worker, no responsibility.

F. Autonomy through the Contract of Employment

The above list of situations where the common law of the contract of employment exercises a decisive influence on the shape and content of labour law could be multiplied with more examples extending over a broader range of issues. Yet it still would remain a list, albeit a long one. The question posed at the outset

[56] See Jeremias Prassl in this volume.

[57] H Collins, 'Ascription of Legal Responsibility to Group in Complex Patterns of Economic Integration' (1990) 53 *Modern Law Review* 731.

[58] eg *Chandler v Cape Plc* [2012] EWCA Civ 525.

[59] *James v Greenwich London Borough Council* [2008] EWCA Civ 35.

was whether the contract of employment should be regarded as the key legal institution, or at least one of the key institutions, that enables us to comprehend the autonomy of labour law. To answer that question, more than a list is required. In particular, what is needed is an account of distinctive concepts and institutions of legal reasoning, viewed from an internal point of view, that constitute the paradigm of the subject of labour law. Can the law of the contract of employment meet that requirement?

The way in which the legal principles and concepts derived from the common law of the contract of employment seem to permeate every aspect of the regulation of the employment relation in the above list begins to make the case for regarding the contract of employment as providing the distinctive legal concept that shapes the whole subject. If we ask the question how does labour law think about a particular dispute between an employer and employee, the starting-point of the legal enquiry is frequently one that directs attention to the rights and obligations of the parties under the common law of the contract of employment. Less obviously, but more crucially, the common law's perception of what the employment relation is like is vital in structuring the law's understanding of the dispute. The common law insists that the dispute lies between the employer as a single legal entity and an individual employee. Collective dimensions of the dispute, such as the fact that the dispute arose in the context of collective industrial action or of collective claims for equal pay, rarely form part of the legal analysis. Moreover, the dispute is characterized as one that arises in the context of a contractual relation, so that the legal analysis immediately focuses on the explicit and implicit undertakings in that contractual relation. The contractual framework also determines the limits of responsibility for breaches of obligations by confining the legal enquiry to the parties to the contract and excluding third parties. Even when statutory rules appear to regulate a dispute, those rules depend for their application and are frequently interpreted through the prism of the background rules of the common law of contract. Indeed, throughout the subject of labour law it is frequently the concepts drawn from the legal analysis of the contract of employment that orient legal reasoning and provide the concrete framework for the construction of legal argument. This is the nub of the case for the 'contractual autonomy' of labour law. But there is a powerful objection to this conception of the autonomy of labour law as a legal subject.

V. The Dilemma of Contractual Autonomy

The principal objection to the notion of contractual autonomy is that it may provide no autonomy at all. The problem is that, in the development of the common law of the contract of employment, the judges have indubitably drawn extensively upon the rules and principles of the general law of contract. If the content of the law of the contract of employment differs hardly at all from the general law of contract, it cannot be convincingly maintained that labour law is autonomous from the internal perspective, namely that it thinks about legal issues in a distinctive way. On the contrary, the dominance of the general law of contract in legal reasoning would lead ineluctably to the conclusion that labour law lacks autonomy as a legal subject, because the subject is merely the application of the general law of contract to a particular type of contract. But is that description of the law of the contract of employment correct?

Again we need to turn to the work of that young scholar in Oxford, Mark Freedland, for instruction, though by 2003, when he answers this very question in *The Personal Employment Contract*,[60] he merits the title Professor of Employment Law in the University of Oxford. It is an oversimplification, but not, I suggest, a seriously misleading one, to describe the agenda of that later book as one to establish the contractual autonomy of labour law in the sense described here. His central argument is, I believe, that, first, he recognizes the validity of the characterization made above that the law of the contract of employment now provides the legal institution at the heart of almost every aspect of labour law and determines to a considerable extent how the law reasons about issues arising in employment relations. Second, however, he seeks to distance the paradigm of the law of the contract of employment both from the general law of contract and from the ancient laws of master and servant. He appreciates that, if the law of contract of employment merely applies the general law of contract, the problem arises, as I have argued, that the contractual autonomy of labour law is destroyed. On the other hand, he does not seek to align the modern law of the contract of employment too closely with the traditional law of master and servant, for the values or 'ideology' of that legal framework were hardly emancipatory or protective of the downtrodden servants, no matter how appropriate those rules might have seemed to judges seeking to buttress managerial disciplinary powers during the industrial revolution.[61]

The route beckoning us out of that dilemma is clear. The third step in the argument must be the creation of a third conception of the legal institution of the contract of employment, one that is neither the simple application of the general law of contract to the employment relation nor the resuscitation of the eighteenth-century structures of domination and subordination of the law of master and servant. This third step in the argument draws Professor Freedland outside the normal comfort zone of legal scholarship, for, as he acknowledges in the Introduction to *The Personal Employment Contract*, the creation of a new conception of the legal institution of the contract of employment must involve not only interpretation of the law but a normative orientation in which some aspects of the law must be rejected and replaced. He offers what he terms a 'restatement' of the law of the contract of employment, in which 'important prescriptive or policy choices' are made in the development of the legal concepts

[60] M Freedland, *The Personal Employment Contract* (Oxford, Oxford University Press, 2003).
[61] A Fox, *Beyond Contract: Work, Power, and Trust Relations* (London, Faber & Faber, 1974).

in order to achieve 'clarity, coherence, and functionality', the latter term being interpreted broadly to require the law to extend and adapt itself so that it is 'in harmony with the realities of the contemporary world of work, and can command respect as a coherent basis for the regulation of that world of work'.[62]

Although the explicit normative orientation of this project may to some eyes make it a questionable exercise in legal scholarship (though as I made clear earlier I do not share that concern), the deeper, structural reason why this position is so exposed lies in the need to wage war on two fronts. The second stage of the argument outlined above requires the proposed restatement of the law of the contract of employment to distance itself both from the general law of contract and the old law of master of servant. The risk here is that the arguments will cancel each other out and the position will collapse.

The problem is that to distance the law of the contract of employment effectively from the general law of contract, it will be necessary to highlight certain features of employment that appear to make it distinctive or autonomous. For instance, with respect to termination of the contract of employment, it is evident that the language of employment law often differs substantially from that used in the general law of contract. Instead of talking about repudiation, fundamental breach and acceptance of repudiation, as happens in connection with commercial contracts, the judges speak of lawful and wrongful dismissal, giving notice and constructive dismissal. Professor Freedland seizes upon this contrast to justify the separation of the law of the contract of employment from the general law of contract.

> In particular, we suggest that the whole vocabulary of 'dismissal', with its variants of 'summary dismissal', 'lawful dismissal', and 'wrongful dismissal' evolved, in the context of the action or claim for wrongful dismissal, quite autonomously from that of the general law of contract, so that, for example, an equation of the notion of 'wrongful dismissal' with that of 'repudiation by the employer' is a palpably false one.[63]

If that claim is correct, however, the danger is that what makes the law of the contract of employment autonomous is that it is still embedded in the old law of master and servant from whence the law of wrongful dismissal originates. In order to counter that unattractive conclusion, it might be argued that those ancient legal concepts such as summary dismissal have been modified in order to align them with the general law of contract. But that escape route risks putting an end to the venture of establishing contractual autonomy for labour law. Professor Freedland candidly recognizes the dilemma and points to the only way out that is left.

> When writing the original version of this work [ie the book published in 1976], the present author was of the view that a convergence of these two discourses [ie the general law of contract and the law of master and servant] was taking place, and

[62] Freedland (n 60) 11–12.

[63] ibid 402. I acknowledge that I have already in this chapter made that 'palpably false' equation on several occasions.

> that its theoretical completion should be attempted or encouraged. That enterprise seemed to be both feasible and useful as a modernization of the law of the contract of employment, a distancing of it from the archaic trappings of the law of master and servant. Now the present author takes a different view. In the intervening years, there has been extensive development of the law of personal employment contracts as a specialized discourse in which the two vocabularies interact with each other, and produce something which is different from each of its constituent parts. It would be artificial to present this body of law entirely or even predominantly according to the terms and concepts of the general law of contract, although those terms and concepts remain very influential in its formulation.[64]

The proposed route out of the dilemma is a blending of the general law of contract and the law of master and servant, which, unlike oil and vinegar, it is asserted will combine to form a new molecule, a legal entity, the contract of employment (or more precisely the 'personal employment contract' or 'personal work contract') that will provide the legal foundation for the autonomy of labour law. To this mixture are added references to employment legislation, such as the law of unfair dismissal, which, it is suggested, can serve to orient the restatement of the common law of the contract of employment in line with modern values and understandings of work relationships.[65]

Ultimately, however, I do not think that Professor Freedland pursues exactly this proposed route out of the dilemma in that book. There is good reason to reject it. The vinegar of the old law of master and servant seems far too bitter to be permitted to contaminate the mix. In many instances, the application of ordinary principles of contract law serves to exclude that contamination completely with beneficial effects for clarity, consistency and functionality. For instance, the application of the general law of contract requiring the employee to accept a repudiatory breach of an employer before the contract of employment is terminated serves many interests of the employee in terms of job security, fair treatment, and full compensation for termination of the contract.[66] This effect should not surprise us: commercial law in general prides itself on the equal treatment of the parties, hates being used as an instrument to escape contractual undertakings, and is alert to the misuse of contractual powers for opportunistic purposes. In all these respects, general contract law or commercial law is likely to be superior to the old law of master and servant, so the predominance of the general law of contract to the exclusion of the old law of master and servant is likely in most instances to bring the law governing the contract of employment

[64] ibid 402–03.

[65] An important issue, outside the scope of the present essay, is the extent to which the common law can be regarded as having been influenced by modern statutes. One of the central themes of another book by Professor Freedland (along with Nicola Kountouris) observes how the common law, unlike continental civil law systems, has resisted modification in the light of statutes and has instead maintained a 'disaggregated' approach, under which at the least the starting-point of legal reasoning is that the content of statutes has in principle no bearing on the content of the common law: see M Freedland and N Kountouris, *The Legal Construction of Personal Work Relations* (Oxford, Oxford University Press, 2011).

[66] eg *Geys* (n 48).

closer into alignment with modern views about the standards applicable to the employment relationship.

Moreover, general contract law is no longer an undifferentiated body of legal doctrine focused predominantly on the discrete sale of goods. It is frequently recognized, for instance, that long-term contracts present special problems that may require tailored solutions involving such standards as disclosure of information, performance in good faith, and special rules governing termination such as a requirement of reasonable notice and a fair distribution of assets from a failed joint venture.[67] Many of those contracts also create power or authority relations under which one party exercises control over the other, which, it is sometime recognized, may necessitate interventions to prevent misuse of discretion and opportunism. Those aspects of the general law of contract may well have particular application to the law of contracts of employment, which are often long-term, co-operative ventures, requiring investments by both parties.[68] In his references to relational contracts and elsewhere, Professor Freedland often draws on these aspects of general contract law for inspiration in constructing a modern law of the contract of employment.[69] He also highlights how general contract law increasingly has to negotiate with statutory rules emanating from both the UK and the EU, so that a central problem in employment law of integrating contractual terms and statutory norms is replicated in many business sectors.[70]

Whilst the old law of master and servant may be best cast firmly aside, and whilst modern contract law may be a much more fertile and sensitive source of legal doctrine for the contract of employment than is commonly supposed, it has to be acknowledged that general contract law remains firmly attached to other principles that will surely remain an anathema to a functional modern law of the contract of employment. General contract law has a strict set of criteria for the formation of binding contracts, such as agreement and consideration, but many instances of work relations, particularly those that are informal and precarious, will struggle to fit their facts into the marked slots of offer, acceptance and consideration. General contract law also tends to be reluctant to insert implied terms or additional duties into commercial contracts, for such practices are hard to square with claims to be enforcing the intentions or agreement of the parties, and may be criticized for creating uncertainty, encouraging litigation and inappropriately inserting a covert fairness standard for transactions when efficiency generally favours freedom of contract. For employment relations,

[67] D Campbell and D Harris, 'Flexibility in Long-term Contractual Relationships: The Role of Cooperation' (1993) 20 *Journal of Law & Society* 166; IR Macneil, 'Contracts: Adjustment of Long-Term Economic Relations Under Classical, Neoclassical and Relational Contract Law' (1978) 72 *Northwestern University Law Review* 854.

[68] Hugh Collins, 'The Contract of Employment in 3D' in D Campbell, L Mulcahy and S Wheeler (eds), *Changing Concepts of Contract* (Basingstoke, Palgrave Macmillan, 2013) 65; RC Bird, 'Employment as a Relational Contract' (2005) 8 *University of Pennsylvania Journal of Labor and Employment Law* 148; D Brodie, 'How Relational is the Employment Contract?' (2011) 40 *Industrial Law Journal* 232.

[69] Freedland (n 60) 92.

[70] ibid 522.

however, it may be much more appropriate to insert implied terms, in part to flesh out what may be a relative informal contract in comparison to commercial contracts, but more especially to try to express the diffuse expectations of the parties regarding commitment, loyalty and performance in good faith. Moreover, ordinary commercial law seems to embrace the use of standard form contracts without compunction, recognizing that these non-negotiated terms are highly efficient in business transactions. Legislation tightly controls the misuse of one-sided standard terms in the context of consumer transactions and provides looser controls for commercial transactions, but there are hardly any statutory controls over unfair terms in the context of employment.[71] To some extent the courts may be able to combat harsh terms through careful interpretation of contract terms to align their meaning with the reasonable expectations of the parties, but the fundamental problem in this context is that the freedom for employers to use standard form contracts to shape the employment relation in accordance with the general law of contract is simply too one-sided and easy to manipulate. It produces express terms of the contract of employment that ensure domination, exploitation, and opens the door far too wide to opportunism. In these examples, which could be multiplied, it seems clear that a modern restatement of the law of the contract of employment would be best advised to cast a great amount of general contract law aside as well.

VI. Conclusion

The preceding discussion of the project of developing a paradigm for labour law in the idea of contractual autonomy reveals its dilemmas and complexities. Such a paradigm needs to draw on the general law of contract, including those aspects that make special provision for long-term and relational contracts, yet at the same time it needs to distance itself from the sharper rules of commercial law that link it tightly to free markets and freedom of contract, without taking into account the unique or typical features of the employment relation. While the project of developing a paradigm of contractual autonomy along those lines does not seem impossible, it is certainly complex and contestable at every point. The characteristic resistance of the common law to being persuaded to adopt statutory employment laws as a source of norms or principles creates a major obstacle to the development of such a restatement of the law of the contract of employment.

Grappling with that difficulty and many other puzzles for an adequate model of contractual autonomy, our Oxford labour law scholar, together now with his own protégé, seem almost to have abandoned the project in the latest work,

[71] H Collins, 'Legal Responses to the Standard Form Contract of Employment' (2007) 36 *Industrial Law Journal* 2.

The Legal Construction of Personal Work Relations.[72] Notice how the vital word 'contract' has been dropped from the title and replaced with the category, 'personal work relations'. This novel concept includes contracts of employment, but adds to them relations of personal work that may be regarded as entirely non-contractual in character or which may be regarded as partly contractual and partly non-contractual.[73] One potential advantage of this new 'framing concept' of personal work relations for the discussion about the autonomy of labour law lies in the way that it is no longer confined by the legal categories of contract or contract of employment, so that many kinds of work relations such as casual workers, dependent entrepreneurs like freelancers, and undocumented migrant workers can be included within the paradigm of the subject. Their inclusion reflects admirably the point that similar concerns about safety, fair treatment and the prohibition of discrimination apply to those arrangements as to standard contracts of employment. But there are other motivations in play behind the construction of this new paradigm for labour law. The authors boldly argue, with regard to the principal aim of labour law, that:

> the original notion, of the redressing of the inequality of bargaining power inherent in the individual contract for subordinate employment, has receded to being a largely symbolical or totemic ideal rather than a comprehensive statement of the practical purpose of labour law.[74]

In support of this claim, the authors observe correctly that the purposes of labour law have been increasingly described and conceptually organized around the protection of fundamental human rights and also by reference to a perspective on the regulation of the labour market that emphasizes what they describe as 'mutualisation of risks',[75] but which current governments tend to label a policy of 'flexicurity' that is supposed to support labour market participation and social protection during the lifetime of the worker in return for the acceptance by the worker of economic risks such as periodic unemployment or underemployment. These reorientations of the aims of labour law certainly may lend normative support to a fresh paradigm that focuses on the personal relations of work.

But where does that argument leave the project of 'contractual autonomy'? As the authors ask: '[D]o we risk shaking in a dangerous way the conceptual foundations of labour or employment law itself?' Their robust answer is to deny any serious risk, 'if only because the contract of employment has quite long since ceased to be the foundation or cornerstone of labour or employment law in the sense in which it once could be so regarded'.[76] This response seems to me to be inadequate to meet our concern.

At the commencement of this chapter, I sought to prise apart the question of the aims of labour law from the question about the conceptual autonomy of

[72] Freedland and Kountouris (n 65).
[73] ibid 434.
[74] ibid 438.
[75] ibid 439.
[76] ibid 436.

labour law within the legal system. It was argued that labour law, as a subsystem of the legal system, obtains its autonomy by constructing its own self-regulating or autopoietic concepts, institutions and modes of reasoning. What provided autonomy for labour law in the mid-twentieth century was the unique regulatory system described as 'collective *laissez-faire*'. That conceptual basis for the autonomy of labour law could in theory be true regardless of the aims of labour law, though the match between the aim of providing a 'countervailing force' against the inequality and subordination of the contract of employment certainly afforced the claim for autonomy and helped to establish this dominant paradigm for the subject. The crucial problem presented by the notion of the 'personal work relation' for the conceptual autonomy of labour law is not that it may or may not match contemporary revised aims for labour law, but rather that a 'personal work relation' is not a legal concept. And it is not possible to organize a legal subject around a legal institution or legal concept that does not exist.[77]

That conclusion does not put an end to the proposed venture of reorganizing labour law around the paradigm of a personal work relation. It is true that we might conclude that we should stick to the legal concepts that we have already and that, despite its manifest problems as the conceptual anchor for labour law, we continue to recognize the contract of employment as the foundation stone for the subject. That is the project of contractual autonomy. The alternative is to declare that, if the concept of a personal work relation does not yet exist in the law, we should make it happen. That task should be performed by discovering the necessary elements of the concept of a personal work relation in the existing fabric of the law and then proposing a reconfiguration of those elements into a modern legal institution. That process of discovery and reconstruction is a perennial dimension of the evolution of legal systems, which enables them to adjust to new social conditions. It is not merely a legal enquiry, but rather an exercise in 'sociological jurisprudence',[78] through which new legal concepts and institutions are developed and shaped to address new social and economic problems. Whilst not ruling out that innovative agenda as a theoretical possibility, we need to recognize that the invention of new legal concepts requires formidable legal skills, persuasive and cogent arguments, and, above all, patience while the new concept takes root in the legal system. The book *The Legal Construction of Personal Work Relations* embarks on that heroic journey, but it has only just commenced.

[77] The same problem arises in the context of networks, see RM Buxbaum, 'Is "Network" a Legal Concept?' (1993) 149 *Journal of Institutional and Theoretical Economics* 698; G Teubner, *Networks as Connected Contracts*, edited by H Collins with an introduction, trans M Everson (Oxford, Hart Publishing, 2011) 73, and in the same book Collins, 'Introduction to Networks as Connected Contracts', 18.

[78] Collins, ibid 18–21; G Teubner, '*Coincidentia Oppositorum*: Hybrid Networks Beyond Contract and Organisation' in M Amstutz and G Teubner (eds), *Networks: Legal Issues of Multilateral Co-operation* (Oxford, Hart Publishing, 2009) 3.

3

Labour Law and the Trade Unions: Autonomy and Betrayal

ALAN BOGG*

Yet there is good reason for trade unionists in every continent to hold their heads high. There is even greater need for their message to reach the honest, inquiring eyes of our daughters and sons who are not yet warped by an increasingly competitive society. In that tradition, the authors of a labour law reform pledged to expand freedom for working people, touched by new frontiers of human rights, will pass to their heirs a finer testament in action, endorsed with Winstanley's preface to the Diggers: 'When these clay bodies are in grave, and children stand in place, / This shows we stood for truth and peace and freedom in our days.' Lord Wedderburn[1]

I. Introduction

In an era of dwindling union membership, collective bargaining coverage in precipitous decline and plummeting levels of strike action, why should labour lawyers continue to concern themselves with the legal framework of collective labour relations?[2] The fundamental right to freedom of association might be regarded as something of an irrelevance to the day-to-day working lives of most workers, quite unlike the contract of employment, unfair dismissal protection or the right to a minimum wage. In this vein, Cynthia Estlund has observed in the US context that 'the health and vitality of labor law, both as a body of law and as a field of scholarly enquiry, hinges on the vitality of the institutions that define

* I owe an embarrassingly large range of debts to friends and colleagues who have very kindly discussed the ideas in this chapter or commented on drafts. Many thanks to my co-editor Anne Davies, and to Nick Barber, Hug Collins, Guy Davidov, Ruth Dukes, Mark Freedland, Judy Fudge, Tarunabh Khaitan, Brian Langille and Virginia Mantouvalou. The usual disclaimers definitely apply in this case.

[1] Lord Wedderburn, 'Freedom and Frontiers of Labour Law', in *Labour Law and Freedom* (London, Lawrence & Wishart, 1995) 410.

[2] For a recent summary of trade union density levels in a range of countries, see the OECD figures at www.stats.oecd.org/Index.aspx?QueryId=20167.

labor law: labor unions and collective bargaining. Therein lies the problem.'[3] Perhaps motivated by similar concerns, Richard Mitchell concludes his thoughts on future directions for the field of labour law scholarship with the following question: 'Does one continue to focus on the details of collective bargaining, trade unions, strike law and so on when these do not reflect the reality of how labour markets are operating?'[4] Some labour law scholars would now answer in the negative. Such an answer need not involve any normative hostility towards trade unions and collective bargaining. Indeed, one might consistently reject a collective orientation in relation to the boundaries and priorities of the discipline of labour law, while at the same time endorsing the normative value of collective action.

How should we decide which elements are central (and hence which elements are peripheral) to the canon of a legal discipline? Labour lawyers have generally approached this structural enquiry in one of two ways. The first approach insulates the descriptive enterprise from the theorist's own ethical commitments. The identification of labour law's structure as a legal discipline should proceed in a spirit of neutrality rather than political judgement. In some respects, Kahn-Freund's sociological theorization of 'collective *laissez-faire*' was imbued with this spirit. The discipline of labour law was structured around the collective institutions of work regulation in recognition of the empirical fact that collective bargaining, with its autonomous creation of social rather than legal norms, was the predominant method of job regulation for most British workers. The joint work of Paul Davies and Mark Freedland, especially as represented in *Labour Legislation and Public Policy*, was imbued with this same methodological spirit.[5] As legislative priorities shifted in the post-war period, and the autonomy of collective bargaining ceased to be the leitmotif of governmental strategies for labour market regulation, the disciplinary structure of labour law required modification in order to keep pace with these important changes.

The second approach fuses the descriptive enterprise with ethical commitment. The identification of labour law's internal structure cannot proceed without understanding labour law as a regulatory activity that is continuous with a theory of fundamental rights, distributive justice, and basic human goods in the sphere of work. Note that this approach is not especially concerned with what legislators (or judges or trade union leaders) happen to *think* labour law is for, or with what legislators (or judges or trade union leaders) happen to *think* really matters. Instead, the theorist is concerned with an account of what is truly just,

[3] CL Estlund, 'The Death of Labor Law?' (2006) 2 *Annual Review of Social Science* 105. It should be noted that there are important terminological differences between English and US labour law. In the US, 'labor law' is used to describe the body of doctrine that applies specifically to the collective institutions. By contrast, usage in the UK uses 'labour law' to describe the entire set of norms, individual and collective, that regulate employment.

[4] R Mitchell, 'Where Are We Going in Labour Law? Some Thoughts on a Field of Scholarship and policy in process of change' (2011) 24 *Australian Journal of Labour Law* 45, 59.

[5] P Davies and MR Freedland, *Labour Legislation and Public Policy* (Oxford, Clarendon Press, 1993).

what labour law is *really* for, and what *really* matters. This is to treat the articulation of labour law's theory of justice as an objective enquiry into reason and value.[6] Hugh Collins' work on 'Labour Law as a Vocation' is an exemplar of this tradition,[7] as is Keith Ewing's 'Democratic Socialism and Labour Law',[8] and Lord Wedderburn's particular rendering of 'collective *laissez-faire*'.[9] It is also possible to detect this moral orientation in Freedland and Kountouris' *Legal Construction of Personal Work Relations*.[10] Such approaches tend to locate collective rights as structurally central, regardless of whether legislators happen to view trade unions as peripheral, irrelevant or even deviant.

These debates are fiercely contested. Understandably so, for as the quotation of Lord Wedderburn that opened this chapter suggests, much is at stake. To assert labour law's autonomy from ethical and political theory might be regarded as a betrayal of values, the betrayal of a vocation no less, and collective rights are often the first casualties in this act of betrayal. This chapter offers an exploratory engagement with these methodological debates, with a particular focus on how best to execute the structural task of identifying labour law's central elements. Section II sets out two methodologies—naturalism and descriptivism—that are faithful to this insulation of the descriptive enterprise from moral commitment. It questions whether the specific task of identifying labour law's central structural features is amenable to these non-normative approaches. The causal empiricism of naturalism is simply ill-suited to providing any kind of answer to this sort of question. The descriptivist approach runs the risk of arbitrariness in choosing which perspective to adopt in formulating criteria of significance and importance. These doubts lead me to support a more normative approach, based on the 'central case' methodology developed in John Finnis' work on natural law theory.[11]

In Section III, I distinguish between three different ways of elucidating a legal subject's internal structure: institutional, instrumental and rights-based theories of legal structure. Given the recent interest in 'rights-based' theories in labour law, and private law theory more generally, Section III evaluates some recent attempts to deploy the 'capability approach' as the basis for a 'rights-based' theory. So far, these attempts have not been successful, though much of this is attributable to features of the 'capability approach' as a full-blown normative theory, rather than its specific execution by labour lawyers. As an alternative, Freedland and Countouris' recent theorization of 'personality in work' as a normative base for a rights-based approach to labour law is considered.

[6] For a recent engagement with this view, see B Langille, 'Labour Law's Theory of Justice' in G Davidov and B Langille (eds), *The Idea of Labour Law* (Oxford, Oxford University Press, 2011) 104.

[7] H Collins, 'Labour Law as a Vocation' (1989) 105 *Law Quarterly Review* 463.

[8] K Ewing, 'Democratic Socialism and Labour Law' (1995) 24 *Industrial Law Journal* 103.

[9] Lord Wedderburn (n 1) ch 1.

[10] MR Freedland and N Kountouris, *The Legal Construction of Personal Work Relations* (Oxford, Oxford University Press, 2011).

[11] See particularly J Finnis, *Natural Law and Natural Rights*, 2nd edn (Oxford, Oxford University Press, 2011) ch 1.

This has distinct advantages over the 'capability approach', though 'personality in work' requires further developmental work to articulate a clearer connection with collective rights. To this end, the chapter suggests that the concept of 'subsidiarity' might be used to support such a connection. In Section IV, I suggest that any normative theory of rights should be able to accommodate the fact of deep normative disagreement about labour rights in pluralistic societies, and that the normative theory of 'personality in work' is capable of accommodating such disagreement.

II. Two Methodologies of Labour Law: Naturalism and Descriptivism

The task of identifying labour law's central structural elements is certainly evaluative. At the very least, this task depends upon an evaluative judgement of which elements are important and significant.[12] It has already been suggested that there are two kinds of approach in the labour law literature, distinguished by their attitude towards moral values in the descriptive enterprise. These methodological debates are in fact well developed in the jurisprudential literature.[13] For this reason, it may be helpful to draw upon those debates in general jurisprudence in order to better clarify what is at stake in the more localized concerns of labour lawyers. Some caution is needed, of course. Legal theorists are often concerned with identifying the central case of particular concepts, an explanatory task that may be similar to but not identical with the labour lawyer's structural concern to identify which features should be regarded as central to the discipline. Yet it is nevertheless striking how the methodological distinctions in labour law mirror similar fault lines in legal theory.

For example, Brian Leiter distinguishes between 'epistemic' and 'moral' values in jurisprudence, corresponding to two styles of legal theory. The first set of approaches would be committed to the view that only 'epistemic' values, such as 'evidentiary adequacy … simplicity, … explanatory consilience',[14] are needed to perform this task of demarcating the central case. This might involve the application of scientific methods in the philosophical study of social phenomena, as in the philosophical approach that has been described as 'naturalism'. Alternatively, it might involve applying the techniques of conceptual or linguistic analysis. Yet each of these approaches is aligned with the view that the descriptive task is morally neutral towards its object. The second set of approaches would be committed to the view that epistemic values alone do not suffice. Instead, it is

[12] For an excellent overview of the debates in legal theory concerning the role of evaluation in descriptive theories, see J Dickson, *Evaluation and Legal Theory* (Oxford, Hart Publishing, 2001).

[13] B Leiter, *Naturalizing Jurisprudence: Essays on American Legal Realism and Naturalism in Legal Philosophy* (Oxford, Oxford University Press, 2007) esp chs 1, 6.

[14] ibid 168.

necessary for the theorist to bring moral values and commitments to bear on the making of judgements of importance and significance. We cannot know what is truly important and significant without knowing what is truly good for persons, hence moral evaluation is necessary for describing social phenomena in a way that is descriptively illuminating.[15]

This section will evaluate epistemic methodologies as they have been developed in recent work in labour law theory. There are many excellent examples of epistemic approaches doing important work in the field of labour law. When epistemic enquiries are directed at appropriate questions, they can offer analytically powerful insights. However, the section will conclude by suggesting that the structural enquiry into labour law's central elements is unlikely to be advanced where the enquiry is guided only by epistemic values.

A. The 'Naturalistic' Approach

'Naturalism' in philosophy encompasses a variety of positions.[16] Most relevant to understanding naturalism in legal philosophy is 'methodological naturalism' which stands for the view that philosophical theories should be 'continuous with the sciences either in virtue of their dependence upon the actual results of scientific method in different domains or in virtue of their employment and emulation of distinctively scientific ways of looking at and explaining things'.[17] This countenances a rigorous empiricism in legal theory, one that would draw upon the scientific methods of disciplines such as sociology, anthropology, political science or psychology. The theoretical aim is to identify causal propositions about the world, with explanatory and predictive power, that may be verified through empirical enquiry. This has obvious relevance to 'legal realist' attempts to formulate scientific causal laws that explain and predict the patterns of 'outputs' in judicial decision-making by reference to the sociological or psychological characteristics of judges.[18] The naturalist approach would not, however, be confined to a theory of adjudication. For example, theoretical accounts that identify causal patterns explaining and predicting the development of labour laws by reference to factors such as economic development, constitutional structure or 'legal family' would also be examples of the scientific approach defended by natu-

[15] Moral values can figure in different ways. For an exploration of these distinctions, particularly the distinction between what she terms 'moral justification' and 'moral evaluation' approaches, see Dickson (n 11) esp chs 2 and 4. This chapter will focus on the 'moral evaluation' thesis that is associated with the natural law work of John Finnis. For a labour law application of the 'moral justification' thesis associated with the work of Ronald Dworkin, see H Collins, *Justice in Dismissal* (Oxford, Oxford University Press, 1992).

[16] See B Leiter, 'Naturalism in Legal Philosophy' *The Stanford Encyclopaedia of Philosophy* (July 2012) plato.stanford.edu/entries/lawphil-naturalism/. See also B Leiter, 'Naturalism and Naturalized Jurisprudence' in B Bix (ed), *Analyzing Law: New Essays in Legal Theory* (Oxford, Oxford University Press, 1998).

[17] ibid 'Naturalism in Legal Philosophy'.

[18] Leiter (n 13) ch 1.

ralists.[19] Conversely, measuring the causal effects of labour laws on economic efficiency would likewise fit the naturalist research agenda.[20] The 'naturalistic' approach has perhaps had its greatest direct influence in the field of comparative labour law. The most influential statement of this naturalistic approach can be found in the comparative theory developed by Hepple:

> The temptation for labour law scholars is to focus their energies on developing an ideal theory of labour rights or social justice. But any theory is sterile unless we first try to understand why real employers, workers, politicians, and judges act as they do in practice. Labour Law is not an exercise in applied ethics. It is the outcome of struggles between different social actors and ideologies, of power relationships.[21]

This is a strong claim, and one that seems on the face of it to be internally inconsistent. For if labour law is the outcome of struggles between competing political ideologies, there is already quite a bit of 'applied ethics' happening without which competing visions of the just society—ideologies—could not even get off the ground. Nevertheless, there is little doubt that this form of theorization has been extremely fruitful. As Brian Langille has observed, such causal accounts illuminate 'how labour law turns out at the level of legal and institutional detail in various places at various times' in a way that other theoretical approaches do not.[22] And in some contexts, *more* naturalism in labour law theorizing would certainly be a good thing too. For example, a 'legal realist' research agenda in the analysis of common law adjudication in employment is urgently needed.[23] While it is true that 'the doctrines and concepts of the common law are surely evolving' in some worker protective ways, there are also examples of highly regressive common law developments; it also seems true that 'the demographic and professional background of common law judges in appellate courts probably differs little from a generation ago'.[24] The halting progress of the common law of employment is unlikely to be explicable in purely doctrinal terms. Naturalism therefore has an important role in advancing knowledge in respect of labour law adjudication and the causes of judicial decisions.

Despite this, the naturalistic approach is sometimes dependent upon other forms of enquiry in order for naturalistic methods to be deployed. Even in respect of very basic boundary questions, such as whether a particular regulation is properly regarded as a labour law norm, we will need something other than

[19] See S Deakin, P Lele and M Siems, 'The Evolution of Labour Law: Calibrating and Comparing Regulatory Regimes' (2007) 146 *International Labour Review* 133. For an excellent discussion of the methodological implications of naturalism in constitutional theory, see NW Barber, *The Constitutional State* (Oxford, Oxford University Press, 2010) ch 1.

[20] See eg R La Porta, F Lopez-de-Silanes and A Shleifer, 'The Economic Consequences of Legal Origins' (2008) 46 *Journal of Economic Literature* 285.

[21] B Hepple, 'Factors Influencing the Making and Transformation of Labour Law in Europe' in G Davidov and B Langille (eds), *The Idea of Labour Law* (Oxford, Oxford University Press, 2011) 30.

[22] Langille (n 6) 104.

[23] See the chapter by L Barmes in this volume.

[24] A Bogg and T Novitz, 'The Techniques of Voice: Prospects for Continuity and Change' in A Bogg and T Novitz (eds), *Voices at Work: Continuity and Change in the Common Law World* (Oxford, Oxford University Press, 2014).

naturalism to enable the causal enquiry to proceed. Thus, Hepple and Veneziani observe that 'a comparative historical study of this kind rests on the assumption that a common definition of "labour law" can be found'.[25] Causal empiricism cannot assist in this task, and this suggests that (*pace* Hepple) there is something else first needed before the causal enquiry can proceed. In his study of methodology in constitutional theory, Nick Barber makes a similar point in relation to causal theories about the origin of the state: without 'sufficient agreement about the nature of the phenomena being investigated', the causal debates might be at cross-purposes where different theorists are working with different accounts of the state.[26] We need some concepts in place before causal enquiries can even get off the ground, and naturalism is unable to do that preliminary theoretical work but is itself dependent upon other methods and approaches.[27]

In this way, naturalism should be regarded as having an important role to play in illuminating important problems in labour law, such as the causes of judicial decision-making or the causal determinants of labour law change over time. But in no sense can naturalism be regarded as having some kind of methodological priority, as is implied in Hepple's statement. While its methods are extremely fruitful in answering *some* important questions in labour law, there is absolutely no reason to think that it can answer *all* of the important questions that we might think of asking. In particular, it is difficult to see how naturalism would have anything to say one way or another about the centrality and significance of collective labour rights in labour law's internal structure. Even if epistemic criteria such as 'statistically normal usage', 'evidentiary adequacy' and 'explanatory consilience' might enable us to explicate the central case of certain kinds of concept,[28] they shed no light on the delicate normative judgements that seem necessary to elevate or demote particular norms within the internal structure of a legal discipline. This is not so much a criticism of naturalism as a criticism of over-extending its reach beyond the questions it is well suited to addressing.

B. The Descriptivist Approach

Other epistemic approaches seek an explanation of social phenomena through the techniques of 'ordinary language' philosophy or conceptual analysis. As an

[25] B Hepple and B Veneziani, 'Introduction' in B Hepple and B Veneziani (eds), *The Transformation of Labour Law in Europe* (Oxford, Hart Publishing, 2009) 12.

[26] Barber (n 19) 5.

[27] A point made well by J Coleman, *The Practice of Principle* (Oxford, Oxford University Press, 2001) 211. Langille (n 6) offers an interesting critique of B Hepple's defence of a causal approach in labour law theory, suggesting that the causal approach is *necessarily* parasitic on an ethical theory of justice. According to Langille, without such a theory of justice, the phenomena to be studied cannot be demarcated. This seems mistaken, however, in not allowing for the possibility of ethically neutral conceptual or linguistic analysis to demarcate those phenomena. Yet I would agree with Langille that ultimately a normative approach is likely to be more fruitful, even if it is not the only approach in town.

[28] See Leiter's dialogue between a descriptivist and a natural lawyer on the concept of 'city' (n 13, 168–70).

example of this descriptivist approach, in a recent and important contribution to the philosophy of discrimination law Khaitan has deployed the conceptual method to postulate the identity conditions of individual norms of discrimination law. This uses a method of reflective equilibrium, moving to and fro between considered intuitions and particular cases, to identify necessary and sufficient conditions that must be satisfied in order for a norm to be characterized as a component of the domain of discrimination law.[29]

Might Khaitan's theoretical project be adopted by labour lawyers so that we use this reflective method to identify the identity conditions of 'norms of labour law'? Having identified the set of norms that are within the domain of labour law, this might be an important prelude to the task of organizing those norms into an ordering of structural priority. The first observation that one might make is that the task of isolating the identity conditions of norms of labour law seems less pressing in labour law when compared with discrimination law. Whatever else might be contested or controversial about labour law, we *do* know that labour law is concerned with the legal regulation of a distinctive kind of human activity, of *work*. So if a norm is concerned with the regulation of work, then it seems uncontroversial to characterize it as a norm of labour law. By contrast, discrimination law lacks that particular focus in that it is not centred on regulating one particular kind of activity. For example, it is unclear whether discrimination law should extend beyond the regulation of state action. To the extent that it should, which other spheres of activity should it encompass? Work? Provision of goods and services? Intimate relationships? Religious communities? Since the boundaries of discrimination law are so controversial, elucidating the identity conditions of individual discrimination law norms is an important philosophical task, and a prelude to other forms of philosophical reflection on the domain of discrimination law.

There are of course difficult questions about the meaning of 'work' too: does it include unpaid caring activities within its scope? Are we concerned with work that is undertaken within particular categories or types of personal work relation? Perhaps Khaitan's sophisticated conceptual methodology might have real value here in helping us to determine whether legal norms governing unpaid care work or the dependent self-employed should be treated as norms of labour law or allocated instead to a different regulatory domain. It seems unlikely, however, that a conceptual analysis of 'work' is likely to help very much in resolving these very difficult questions. Often labour lawyers are not especially interested in developing a conceptually rich account of 'work' in isolation from a wider set of questions about whether and if so how to regulate it, and to what ends. For this reason, labour lawyers who engage with the issue of caring activity as

[29] T Khaitan, 'Prelude to a Theory of Discrimination Law' in D Hellman and S Moreau (eds), *Philosophical Foundations of Discrimination Law* (Oxford, Oxford University Press, 2014).

a concern of labour law,[30] or of the relational scope of labour law protections,[31] do so from a strongly normative perspective. This is because the underlying regulatory questions are themselves strongly normative. When we move to the question of how to rank norms in terms of their relative importance or significance within a regulatory domain, which is also strongly normative, it is difficult to see how a conceptual method can really advance this particular kind of enquiry. We probably do not need the assistance of a conceptual method to agree that norms relating to collective labour relations are norms of labour law. When we disagree about the structural priority to accord to those norms within labour law's domain, this seems to invite a normative dialogue rather than a dialogue about the meaning of concepts.

Perhaps the most influential example of the descriptivist approach in mainstream labour law is the joint work of Paul Davies and Mark Freedland. Although they do not rely upon abstract philosophical methods, nevertheless they emphasize the distinction between epistemic and moral values, and their affirmation of the primacy of epistemic values is characteristic of the descriptivist approach. What is especially important about the Davies and Freedland approach is its attempt to formulate criteria of centrality in a 'detached' way. The first clear statement of this perspective was set out in the editors' introduction to the third edition of Kahn-Freund's *Labour and the Law*, where they challenge 'the definitive description of a framework of labour law organized around the concept of collective bargaining'.[32] The authors argued for a distinction between normative commitment and descriptive adequacy. Even if the priority of voluntary collective bargaining could be defended 'as a statement of values', it was no longer reliable 'as a guide to the proper confines of the subject of labour law'.[33] This was because it failed to acknowledge the macroeconomic agendas of successive governments in the post-war period, which led to an undermining of labour law's descriptive adequacy in making sense of the rapidly changing world of work. It was a methodological theme that was deepened some years later in their introduction to *Labour Legislation and Public Policy*.[34] The authors argued that 'the enterprise of writing about labour law and politics is made feasible if one realizes that political scientists can write in an *acceptably detached way* about politics, as their works (or, rather, the best of them) demonstrate'.[35] They also accorded explanatory significance to the method of legislation as a way of understanding the development of labour law in the post-war period. This was

[30] See eg the rich normative account in N Busby, *A Right to Care? Unpaid Care Work in European Employment Law* (Oxford, Oxford University Press, 2011) chs 1 and 2.

[31] Freedland and Kountouris, exploring the role of dignity in respect of the relational scope of fundamental employment rights.

[32] PL Davies and MR Freedland (eds), *Kahn-Freund's Labour and the Law*, 3rd edn (London, Stevens & Sons, 1983) 2.

[33] ibid.

[34] Davies and Freedland (n 5).

[35] ibid 3 (emphasis added).

because 'legislation has been overwhelmingly the major source of new principles in labour law' so that labour law was now 'predominantly a statutory subject'.[36]

This moral neutrality of Davies and Freedland's descriptive approach is evident in two ways. First, the political basis of labour law is acknowledged, but the descriptive theorist must engage with this political dimension in a 'detached' rather than a committed way. The dependence of labour law upon politics is a feature to be described and explained by the theorist. Political detachment enables the theory to be sensitive to different political programmes and their regulatory manifestations, whereas political commitment might impede the analysis especially where the theorist's political values are at variance with governmental values. In this situation, bias and hostility might distort the analysis of legal norms in their political context. It might also lead the theory to be insensitive to the significance of legislative events judged by the ethical standards of the architects of legal change. This might entail a loss of explanatory power of the theory. Secondly, the choice of which perspective to adopt for the purposes of theory construction is also based upon a neutral criterion. As Hugh Collins has noted, a fundamental theoretical question for labour lawyers is

> determining which theory and whose understanding of practice would influence the legal analysis. Would the theory be that espoused by the revolutionary worker on the shop floor, or that held by the bosses from their perspective of the grouse moor, or perhaps even the vision of the hippies who regarded all work as a degradation of the human spirit?[37]

For Davies and Freedland, it is the legislator's understanding of practice which is accorded descriptive priority. This preference is defended on the neutral basis that legislation has been the dominant form of legal intervention in labour law in the post-war period.

This method can certainly provide an account of labour law's central features, with centrality determined by the political agenda set by the government. This has attracted the important objection that it permits 'the Government to set the agenda for scholarship and to define the terms of debate', a form of political interference in the scholarly vocation,[38] though similar objections might be levelled if we were to choose the perspective of the revolutionary shop steward or the boss on the grouse moor as the basis for our judgements of what is important and interesting in the regulation of work. So which perspective should we adopt, and how should we choose in a way that avoids the charge of arbitrariness? There seems no particularly compelling reason to elevate the governmental view of labour law and its priorities. According to John Finnis, the theorist should adopt the viewpoint of the person who is

> consistent; attentive to all aspects of human opportunity and flourishing, and aware of their limited commensurability; concerned to remedy deficiencies and break-downs,

[36] ibid 4.
[37] H Collins, 'The Productive Disintegration of Labour Law' (1997) 26 *Industrial Law Journal* 295, 296.
[38] Collins (n 7) 482.

> and aware of their roots in the various aspects of human personality and in the economic and other material conditions of social interaction.[39]

This is a perspective that seeks a descriptive-explanatory account of social phenomena based upon a *sound* understanding of human values and *true* norms of justice and rights. It would lead us to ask 'whether, and if so why, and when, we—or more precisely each one of us—should favour introducing, having, endorsing, maintaining, complying with, and enforcing' laws such as labour laws.[40] This may be reformulated as 'why labour law?' as a basis for understanding 'what is labour law?' It rejects the moral neutrality of descriptivism, but in so doing it is elevated above the fray of politicization that comes from adopting the worker's or the employer's or the judge's or the legislator's perspective as the uniquely privileged vantage point for structuring labour law.

It is important to be careful in not over-extending our criticisms of Davies and Freedland, and it would be mistaken and inappropriate to suggest that this methodological approach leads them into being apologists for unjust governmental activity. Davies and Freedland might argue that an uncluttered understanding of legislative activity, informed by a detailed and sensitive understanding of governmental objectives, is the demystifying prelude to clear-headed moral critique of legislation. There is no reason at all, therefore, why the descriptive theorist cannot also be a trenchant moral critic: it is simply that one ought not to do those two things simultaneously. The descriptivist is not bound to be an apologist for unconscionable legislative acts, even if the governmental perspective is central to theory-construction.

This is an important point. There is nevertheless an important loss in maintaining this separation between epistemic and moral values. Consider the appropriate scholarly response to the legislative attack on freedom of association under the Conservative government between 1979 and 1997. We might first wonder whether some normative commitment is needed in order to determine which aspects of the legislative agenda should be regarded as particularly significant for descriptive purposes. Those aspects which go against the common good, as intentional attacks on freedom of association, would seem to stand out as being of particular significance and importance for descriptive purposes. Otherwise, how else should we choose? Even so, the descriptivist might deplore its justifications and social effects on working people, and may be candid in saying such. Yet it would not be open to the descriptivist to characterize this legislation as defective *as labour law*. We see a similar distinction in legal theory between legal positivism and natural law, and the theoretical treatment of evil law. For the legal positivist, an evil legal system can be criticized as evil, but it is no less an instance of law as a good legal system. For the natural lawyer, committed to a central case of law as directed at justice and the common good, an evil legal

[39] Finnis (n 11) 15.

[40] J Finnis, 'Describing Law Normatively', in J Finnis, *Collected Essays*, vol IV: *Philosophy of Law* (Oxford, Oxford University Press, 2011) 23.

system would be defective *as law*, a corrupted version of the central case. For a labour lawyer to criticize legislative attacks on freedom of association as a defective instance of labour law, such a claim presupposes a central case of regulatory activity, of flourishing labour law in its focal sense which is concerned to uphold fundamental rights, of which the government's activity is a corrupted instance.[41] This way is blocked to the descriptivist, however, for there are no criteria of centrality for descriptive purposes that are external to the government's own priorities. And the claim that a piece of legislation is defective *as labour law*, it seems to me, captures a rather different quality of normative criticism than is open to the descriptivist constrained by the hermetic separation of description and moral evaluation.

To recap, we have evaluated two descriptivist strategies that might be used to identify labour law's central structural features. First we explored Khaitan's sophisticated analysis of the identity conditions of norms of discrimination law and assessed whether that kind of approach might enable us to advance the enquiry into labour law's central case. We identified important differences between, on the one hand, the task of determining the identity conditions of individual norms of labour law and, on the other hand, determining the structural priority of those norms. The latter enquiry seemed intractable to Khaitan's conceptual methodology. We then explored Davies and Freedland's elevation of the governmental perspective in making judgements of centrality. This approach was rejected in favour of a normative approach, given the arbitrariness in elevating the governmental perspective on labour law for the purposes of descriptive-explanatory theory. Difficult questions remain, of course. Which normative theory should we adopt? And would such a theory lose its power as a descriptive-explanatory theory, especially where legal developments involve injustice and the violation of fundamental rights? We shall address those questions in the next section.

III. In Defence of Normative Theory

The theoretical task of constructing labour law's central case is best viewed as a normative one. The distinction between epistemic and moral values is not the only dimension that needs be addressed, however. It is also possible to distinguish between three approaches to identifying labour law's internal structure: institutional theories; instrumentalist theories; and rights-based theories.[42] Institutional

[41] For an example of this kind of approach, see Lord Wedderburn, 'Freedom of Association and Philosophies of Labour Law' (1989) 18 *Industrial Law Journal* 1.

[42] The concepts of 'instrumentalist' and 'rights-based' theories is taken from D Nolan and A Robertson, 'Rights and Private Law' in D Nolan and A Robertson (eds), *Rights and Private Law* (Oxford, Hart Publishing, 2012), which offers a sophisticated analysis of these distinctions within the context of private law theory.

theories orientate their enquiries around the rule-making and dispute-resolving institutions in the sphere of work regulation, and the structure of the discipline reflects judgements about which of those institutions are identified as particularly central and significant. Collective *laissez-faire* in the 1950s represented the heyday of the institutional approach, with the institutions of collective bargaining located at the centre of the discipline.[43] Later institutional theories came to regard the individual contract of employment as the institutional centrepiece of labour law, reflecting the rise of statutory employment rights, and individual litigation as a mode of dispute resolution, operating from the platform of the contract of employment.[44] Instrumentalist theories, by contrast, configure the structure of labour law around its instrumental role in promoting particular goals.[45] Sometimes these goals are welfarist, such as the amelioration of subordination or unequal bargaining power.[46] Sometimes these goals are economic, such as the promotion of efficiency, productivity or competitiveness.[47] Finally, 'rights-based' theories are non-instrumentalist in characterizing the structure of labour law as based upon a coherent set of fundamental rights.[48] Rights-based theories have become more prominent in recent years in labour law, reflecting the dominance of rights-based theories in private law theory more generally.[49] There has been an explosion of interest in exploring the connections between labour rights and human rights,[50] developing normative criteria for identifying a coherent group of fundamental rights for labour law,[51] and elucidating the analytical aspects of rights-claims and their interrelationship with other concepts such as duties and powers. These rights-based theories also force us to rethink certain assumptions about the differences between 'contextual' subjects such as labour law as compared with 'pure' private law subjects such as contract or tort law. For if labour law's internal structure is based predominantly around a spine of fundamental rights and norms of corrective justice, there may be more structural similarities between labour law and other legal disciplines than we have been accustomed to acknowledging.[52]

[43] The classic text is AD Flanders and HA Clegg (eds), *The System of Industrial Relations in Great Britain* (Oxford, Blackwell, 1954).

[44] As early as 1979, P Davies and MR Freedland described the contract of employment as 'the central legal institution of our labour laws', a claim supported by the increasing significance of individual employment rights as a mode for channeling dispute resolution: see P Davies and M Freedland, *Labour Law: Text and Materials* (London, Weidenfeld and Nicolson, 1979) 2; see also the chapter by H Collins this volume.

[45] For a general overview, see G Davidov, 'The Goals of Regulating Work: Between Universalism and Selectivity' (2014) 64 *University of Toronto Law Journal* 1.

[46] H Collins, in 'Labour Law as a Vocation' (n 7), seems to advance this as a normative claim.

[47] H Collins, 'Regulating the Employment Relation for Competitiveness' (2001) 30 *Industrial Law Journal* 17, which seems based significantly on the non-normative consideration that competitiveness had been elevated as a particular policy concern in recent governmental activity in work regulation.

[48] For discussion, see Nolan and Robertson (n 42).

[49] See eg R Stevens, *Torts and Rights* (Oxford, Oxford University Press, 2007).

[50] V Mantouvalou, 'Are Labour Rights Human Rights?' 3 *European Labour Law Journal* 151.

[51] H Collins, 'Theories of Rights as Justifications for Labour Law' in G Davidov and B Langille (eds), *The Idea of Labour Law* (Oxford, Oxford University Press, 2011) 137.

[52] For an approach that seems to assume a distinction between contextual and non-contextual

It is of course possible to engage in each of these structural enquiries from a normative or a non-normative perspective. Nor should we regard the boundaries as fixed or rigid. At different points, Hugh Collins has experimented with all three conceptions of structure, and from both normative and non-normative perspectives. Mark Freedland's early collaborative work with Paul Davies might be characterized as institutionalist and non-normative; his more recent work with Nicola Countouris in *Legal Construction of Personal Work Relations* is strongly normative and rights-based. It is impossible to assess each of these structural enquiries comprehensively within the constraints of a single chapter, so my aims here are more modest. I propose to assess the 'capability approach' which has emerged in recent years as a dominant paradigm in labour law. Its dominance reflects the rising prestige of normative rights-based theories of labour, and the capability approach is best understood as a framework for developing a coherent set of fundamental labour rights that provide a structure for labour law's central case. In my view, there are reasons to be very cautious before labour lawyers adopt the 'capability approach' as a framework for rights-based theories of labour law. The section will conclude by suggesting that Mark Freedland and Nicola Countouris' sophisticated articulation of a theory based upon the concept of 'personality at work' provides a more satisfactory normative base for a rights-based structure for labour law.[53] In so doing, I suggest some additions to their argument in order to make the linkages with fundamental collective rights clearer and more compelling than it is in the original argument.

A. The Capability Approach Assessed

The last decade has been marked by the striking influence of Sen's capability approach in theorizing the normative basis of labour law. According to Robeyns, the capabilities approach is

> a theoretical framework that entails two core normative claims: first, the claim that the freedom to achieve well-being is of primary moral importance, and second, that freedom to achieve well-being is to be understood in terms of people's capabilities, that is, their real opportunities to do and be what they have reason to value.[54]

Before evaluating the application of Sen's theory to the labour law context, there are four points that should be noted which give us reason to be cautious in placing significant weight on Sen's work as a *normative* theory. First, Sen's work is primarily directed at the elaboration of a metric for measuring comparative human development within and across countries, and as an alternative to human development measures based either on GDP or the allocation of 'primary goods'

disciplines in this respect, see S Deakin and F Wilkinson, *The Law of the Labour Market* (Oxford, Oxford University Press, 2005) 298–302.

[53] Freedland and Kountouris (n 10) 369–82.

[54] I Robeyns, 'The Capability Approach', in *The Stanford Encyclopedia of Philosophy* (April 2011) available at http://plato.stanford.edu/entries/capability-approach/.

such as income.[55] Secondly, it follows from this that Sen's work is *not* concerned with elaborating a full theory of justice in normative political philosophy.[56] Judy Fudge has rightly drawn attention to these limitations in Sen's theory.[57] Sen himself concedes that the capabilities approach tells us little 'about the fairness or equity of the processes involved, or about the freedom of citizens to invoke and utilize procedures that are equitable', which would be an important element in a theory of justice.[58] Furthermore, as Brighouse observes, the capabilities approach is fundamentally an argument about what it is that we should be concerned to distribute, and it falls short of elaborating a comprehensive set of rules beyond the notion of a basic threshold of minimum capabilities to guide distributive policies.[59] Nussbaum has done significant work in elaborating Sen's work as a basis for normative theory, and she acknowledges that her own much thicker version of the capabilities approach is itself a theory of 'minimal social justice'.[60]

Thirdly, Sen avoids engaging in a normative elaboration of which capabilities should be demarcated as 'fundamental' and hence warranting heightened political support and protection. For Sen, this elaboration should occur in particular contexts democratically through deliberative social choice procedures. This avoidance of prescriptive stipulation preserves the liberal orientation of the theory; and it ensures that the capabilities approach can speak to a broad range of cultural, social and geographical contexts. It also hinders the ability of the theory to provide any normative content to the capabilities.[61] Fourthly, it follows from this that Sen's account of capabilities is unable to provide a full account of fundamental human rights. While Sen argues that human rights can usefully be viewed as entitlements to capabilities, he also acknowledges that capabilities are unable to provide a complete account of the rights that we have.[62] Indeed, without an account of which capabilities are fundamental, it is impossible to determine which human rights (as entitlements to capabilities) should be regarded as fundamental.

All of which should sound a clanging alarm bell in respect of inflationary

[55] I Robeyns, 'The Capability Approach in Practice' (2006) 14 *Journal of Political Philosophy* 351.

[56] For a critical view of Sen's engagement with the question of justice, see J Gardner, 'Amartya Sen's *The Idea of Justice*' (2011) 6 *Journal of Law, Philosophy and Culture* 241.

[57] A Sen, *The Idea of Justice* (London, Penguin, 2009) 296, discussed in J Fudge, 'Labour as a "Fictive Commodity": Radically Reconceptualizing Labour Law' in G Davidov and B Langille (eds), *The Idea of Labour Law* (Oxford, Oxford University Press, 2011) 128, fn 48.

[58] As Sen himself concedes: see A Sen, 'Elements of a Theory of Human Rights' (2004) 32 *Philosophy and Public Affairs* 315, 336.

[59] H Brighouse, *Justice* (Cambridge, Polity, 2005) 68.

[60] M Nussbaum, *Creating Capabilities: The Human Development Approach* (Cambridge, MA, Belknap Press, 2011) 71.

[61] It is worthwhile to compare Nussbaum's approach, which uses the notion of dignity to articulate a much richer and more prescriptive set of capabilities based upon the notion of a threshold for a human life worthy of human dignity. See M Nussbaum, *Women and Human Development: The Human Capabilities Approach* (Cambridge, Cambridge University Press, 2001) ch 1. The list is life; bodily health; bodily integrity; senses, imagination, and thought; emotions; practical reason; affiliation; connection with other species; play; and political and material control over one's environment.

[62] A Sen, 'Human Rights and Capabilities' (2005) 6 *Journal of Human Development* 151.

claims for Sen's capability approach as a basis for a 'new normativity' for labour law; for even in its thickest forms it claims to do no more than provide an account of 'minimal social justice'; Sen's account declines to specify a list of core capabilities that political communities have particular reason to value; and hence is unable to elaborate an account of our fundamental social rights. It is, in Robeyns' terms, 'radically *underspecified*' as a normative theory.[63] We can distinguish between two kinds of usage of capabilities in general labour law theory: the 'immodest' version of Langille; and the 'modest' version in the collaborative work of Deakin, Browne and Wilkinson. While each approach displays great sophistication, both attempts are likewise 'radically underspecified' as theories of labour law's normative basis.

B. Langille's Immodest Capabilities Approach

Brian Langille is much taken with Sen's work on capabilities.[64] According to Langille, the virtue of Sen's work is that it engages in a uniquely deep way with the question of our 'true ends'. When we ask what are our 'true ends', we discover 'that the point of all our striving is human freedom'.[65] Langille's recent work promises no less than a full theory of justice and a complete account of labour law's normative foundations. According to Langille, this also explains why freedom of association and collective bargaining are regarded as fundamental rights in labour law, given their role in harnessing the self-governing capacities of workers to take charge of their own fates in the labour market. In this way, the substantive matters such as wages, working time, and health and safety are more likely to be respected and even ratcheted up through workers exercising their associational freedoms, in a kind of virtuous circle effect.[66] Since the capabilities approach, even by the admission of its leading proponents Sen and Nussbaum, offers at most only a 'minimal' theory of justice, Langille's extravagant project seems odd. But let us leave that reservation to one side for a moment and examine Langille's main arguments.

There are two core claims in Langille's 'new normativity' argument. First, there is a reiteration of his earlier argument that 'real human freedom' is 'an end in itself'.[67] But not merely *an* end. It is then variously described as 'our true end';[68]

[63] Robeyns (n 55) 353.

[64] Langille's first serious engagement with the capability approach of Sen was his use of it to rationalize the core labour rights in the ILO Declaration of Fundamental Rights and Principles 1998, and as a basis for international labour law's functions more generally. See particularly the very engaging paper: B Langille, 'Core Labour Rights—The True Story (Reply to Alston)' (2005) 16 *European Journal of International Law* 409. This is broadened out into a normative base for labour law more generally in Langille (n 6).

[65] Langille, 'Core Labour Rights' (n 64) 432.

[66] ibid 434–35.

[67] Langille (n 6) 118.

[68] ibid.

'our real goal';[69] and the 'intrinsic and ultimate end' of political action.[70] Secondly, not only must political action promote the goal of substantive human freedom as an 'intrinsic and ultimate end': it must also be directed at 'the maximizing of human freedom'.[71] Now there is little doubt that Sen's work is susceptible to this interpretation. As Nussbaum acknowledges, 'Sen sometimes speaks as if all capabilities were valuable zones of freedom and as if the overall social task might be to maximize freedom.'[72] Each of these claims should, however, be resisted.

Let us start with the idea that our 'true' and 'intrinsic' and 'ultimate' end is substantive human freedom as such.[73] When we engage in valuable activities and practices, do we do so for the sake of freedom? That seems untenable. I spend time with friends for the sheer fulfilment that arises out of the intrinsic good of friendship; I visit the art gallery for the sake of aesthetic and spiritual contemplation. Substantive freedom is very important, of course, in enabling citizens to make their own judgements about what is valuable; furthermore, it is very often the case that the value to be realized in an activity can only be realized through autonomous participation.[74] According to Kymlicka,

> [L]iberals do not say that we should have the freedom to select our projects for its own sake, because freedom is the most valuable thing in the world. Rather, our projects and tasks are the most important things in our lives, and it is because they are so important that we should be free to revise them, should we come to believe that they are not worthwhile.[75]

It might be added to this that most liberals rarely care about 'liberty' or even 'substantive human freedom' in an undifferentiated way. As Nussbaum observes, the promotion of human freedom (with or without the 'substantive' qualification) cannot itself be a sensible political goal: some freedoms are noxious (such as the freedom of employers to sexually harass workers); some freedoms are of little consequence (the freedom of workers to eat pistachio ice-cream during their rest periods); and some freedoms matter a great deal (the freedom from forced servitude or slavery).[76] What is missing from Sen's (and therefore Langille's) account is an account of specific human capabilities that are especially important and demarcate fundamental aspects of human flourishing, such as Nussbaum's elaboration of central capabilities as marking the minimum threshold for leading a life worthy of human dignity.[77] Without this specificity, it is impossible to begin the

[69] ibid 112.
[70] ibid 114.
[71] ibid.
[72] See Nussbaum (n 60) 70. Nussbaum rejects this maximizing approach as flawed.
[73] For a pertinent philosophical discussion of the general issues raised by this claim, see J Finnis, 'Action's Most Ultimate End', in J Finnis, *Reason in Action: Collected Essays*, vol I (Oxford, Oxford University Press, 2011) ch 10.
[74] W Kymlicka, *Liberalism, Community and Culture* (Oxford, Oxford University Press, 1989) 11–13.
[75] W Kymlicka, *Contemporary Political Philosophy*, 2nd edn (Oxford, Oxford University Press, 2001) 222.
[76] Nussbaum (n 60) 72–74.
[77] Nussbaum (n 61) 78–80.

task of enumerating fundamental social rights as a basis for protecting the really important human capabilities. Without an account of fundamental social rights, we cannot even begin to offer an account of justice, not even a minimal one.

The idea of 'maximizing' human freedom is also flawed. If we evaluate this claim from the perspective of a single agent it certainly makes no sense. It is obviously not true that a human life lived with maximal freedom is a better or more fulfilled life. On the contrary, such a view

> is false, and indeed perverse. It quickly leads to the existential view that we should wake up each morning and decide anew what sort of person we should be. This is perverse because a valuable life is a life filled with commitments and relationships. These give our lives depth and character.[78]

A life of maximal freedom would be as exhausting as it was unfulfilling. The goal of freedom maximization fares little better as a political rather than a personal ideal. In his famous critical engagement with John Rawls' *A Theory of Justice*, HLA Hart demolished Rawls' early commitment to liberty maximization. Such an approach would seem to lead even to 'forbidding the institution of private property, since to own anything privately is to have liberty to use it in ways denied to others'.[79] These criticisms led Rawls to reformulate his liberty principle as an equal right 'to a fully adequate scheme' of liberties rather than any commitment to a maximal scheme of liberties.[80] Furthermore, Nussbaum's development of the capabilities approach is concerned to identify the basic threshold conditions for a life worthy of human dignity rather than any attempt at maximization. Indeed, once we begin the necessary task of specifying fundamental capabilities such as 'bodily integrity' or 'play' or 'affiliation',[81] the fact that these different forms of human flourishing appear to be incommensurable renders the very idea of maximization incoherent.[82]

C. Deakin, Browne and Wilkinson's Modest Capabilities Approach

In essence, these authors present an argument that 'social rights can be understood as mechanisms for enhancing the substantive economic freedoms of individuals to achieve a wide range of functionings. … Social rights are the foundation of a market order'.[83] Thus, Deakin and Wilson argue that social

[78] Kymlicka (n 75) 222–23.

[79] HLA Hart, 'Rawls on Liberty and its Priority', in HLA Hart, *Essays in Jurisprudence and Philosophy* (Oxford, Oxford University Press, 1983) 227.

[80] J Rawls, *Political Liberalism* (New York, Columbia University Press, 1993) 291.

[81] Nussbaum (n 61) 78–79.

[82] For further discussion of incommensurability and its rendering of goods maximization 'senseless', see Finnis (n 11) 115.

[83] S Deakin and J Browne, 'Social Rights and Market Order', in T Hervey and J Kenner (eds), *Economic and Social Rights under the EU Charter of Fundamental Rights: A Legal Perspective* (Oxford, Hart Publishing, 2003) 27, 42.

rights perform a critical 'market-creating' function in ensuring that citizens are provided with the social, economic and institutional means to participate effectively in labour markets and achieve higher levels of economic functioning.[84] As such, this is a version of the capabilities approach that is being developed very specifically within the domain of labour market regulation discourse.[85] It is not an exercise in reasoning *from* general political values *to* particular normative conclusions about the regulation of work as a human activity of profound moral significance. This starting point for theorization of social rights, from within labour market discourse rather than from general politics or ethics, might be thought to skew the conception of social rights at the outset by coupling *social* rights to the realization of *economic* freedoms. The authors are likewise scrupulous in observing Sen's own observations about the limits of his capabilities approach. Thus, they observe that Sen's approach does not 'prescribe any particular set of outcomes for a given society or group of societies';[86] it is not a 'full theory of justice';[87] nor does it provide a list of privileged capabilities properly regarded as fundamental.[88] Consequently, and following Sen, it is suggested that 'attention is focused instead on social choice procedures by which the content of capability sets can be collectively determined in particular contexts'.[89] This creates a wide democratic space for the specification of which social rights should be adopted. Indeed, the theory is not even 'prescriptive about the mechanisms that should be employed' to implement social rights.[90] All of this enables a 'reflexive' approach to the specification of social rights and even their modes of regulatory implementation: everything, it seems, is up for grabs in a deliberative process of 'social learning' that eschews dogmatism.[91] In this respect, there is a modesty of aspiration that does not constrain Langille's use of capabilities.

Judy Fudge, while expressing a healthy degree of scepticism about the capability approach in general, is certainly more welcoming of Deakin, Browne and Wilkinson's version of it. She suggests that it 'provides for a much more robust set of social rights' than Langille's thin account of capabilities, which potentially include substantive rights such as maternity pay and minimum wage as well as procedural rights such as collective bargaining.[92] It also provided an account that appears to bridge the chasm between market-proponents and social-rights-proponents, by identifying a common normative base.

Nevertheless, there are reasons to be very cautious before endorsing this alternative account of capabilities. First, economic freedom even in its substantive

[84] Deakin and Wilkinson (n 52) 347–48.
[85] ibid 345.
[86] ibid 347.
[87] Deakin and Browne (n 83) 37.
[88] ibid.
[89] ibid 38.
[90] Deakin and Wilkinson (n 52) 352.
[91] ibid.
[92] J Fudge, 'The New Discourse of Labor Rights: From Social to Fundamental Rights?' (2007) 29 *Comparative Labor Law and Policy Journal* 29.

formulation is remarkably thin as a normative basis for social rights. Compare Nussbaum's much richer account of human capabilities rooted in an account of the diverse forms of human flourishing, which provide the basis to a dignified life: life; bodily integrity; senses, imagination and thought; emotions; practical reason; affiliation; relations with other species; play; control over one's political and material environment.[93] Should we configure the social right to collective bargaining as merely a procedural mechanism for translating human capital into higher levels of economic functioning? Or should we configure it in dignitarian terms as a space where citizens can participate in the goods of affiliation, practical reason and the exercise of shared political control over one's working environment?[94] The latter seems to be a richer and more appealing basis for the relevant social right. The choice has a vital practical significance because the dignitarian approach also justifies the view that some social rights should properly be regarded as inderogable, in a way that the economic freedom approach cannot. It might be that some central capabilities are so basic and fundamental that waiver of them would lead to a life not worthy of human dignity.[95] This circumvents an enquiry into whether scope for derogation augments or negates substantive economic freedom, though clearly the matter of respect for the human agent's practical reasoning will be relevant on the dignitarian approach in delimiting the zone of inderogability.[96]

The second point against the Deakin, Browne and Wilkinson approach is its collapse into proceduralism as regards the specification of social rights. It seems part of a broader trend in labour law theory to conceptualize the discipline more as a structured dialogue rather than a set of concrete and highly specified rights or values.[97] The truth is that (and *pace* Fudge) we simply do not know whether the social rights generated by this approach will be thin, thick or something in between. While this might suffice for Sen's theoretical purposes, engaged as he is in the comparative measurement of human wellbeing in the sphere of development studies, it will not suffice for a normative agenda in labour law. There are three reasons to think that the proceduralism in this theorization of capabilities is excessive, undermining its appeal as a normative theory for labour law.

First, the formal idea of 'capabilities' deployed in the modest conception is too empty to provide a structure for any democratic processes that might be used to specify and develop social rights. Without a connection to a value such as dignity, such as might be used to provide some normative direction to demo-

[93] Nussbaum (n 61) 78–80.

[94] For a thoughtful exploration of Nussbaum's thought in respect of collective labour rights, see T Novitz, 'Information and Communication Technology and Voice: Constraint or Capability?' in A Bogg and T Novitz (eds), *Voices at Work: Continuity and Change in the Common Law World* (Oxford, Oxford University Press, 2014).

[95] Nussbaum (n 61) 90–96.

[96] ibid.

[97] This view may be detected in B Langille, 'Imagining Post "Geneva Consensus" Labor Law for Post "Washington" Consensus Development' (2010) 31 *Comparative Labor Law and Policy Journal* 523.

cratic deliberation about social rights, there is a risk that the deliberative process will be ethically unstructured. There is then a danger that the vacuum will be filled up with arguments based upon narrow economic imperatives driven by powerful corporate actors. Given the abstractness of a value such as dignity, the normative tethering that it would provide to the deliberative process would still leave significant discursive space for participants to engage in a genuine dialogue about the specific content of social rights. But its presence would give some normative direction and context to deliberation, hence generating some (modest) constraints on the deliberative agendas, process and outcomes. Secondly, if so much is being entrusted to the democratic process, it is imperative that a theoretical account is also provided of the constitutional context of labour law-making. This touches upon another dimension of labour law's autonomy: its interface with constitutional law.[98] One of the most striking developments in the aftermath of the global financial crisis has been the assault on the political voice of workers, especially in the UK and the US, through the medium of campaign finance reform.[99] Yet without political voice based upon democratic equality, workers and their organizations are unable to exercise credible democratic control over the regulatory structure of work. Given that the democratic process in this account of social rights is carrying so much argumentative weight, it is not sufficient to configure labour law as 'the law of the labour market'. The locus of the discipline must be wider still to encompass 'the law of labour market governance', taking in the full range of constitutional doctrines as they regulate the exercise of workers' (and capital's) political voice.

Thirdly, in view of the central role for a democratic process in the specification of social rights, there is also insufficient engagement with democratic theory in the modest conception of capabilities. It would seem that the Deakin, Browne and Wilkinson approach is committed to a deliberative model of democracy, with the specification and implementation of social rights entrusted to a process of 'mutual learning' through discursive engagement. There is now a significant literature on the deliberative conception of politics, and the institutional supports that are necessary to support its practical realization. The starting point for analysis is often Habermas' positing of an 'ideal speech situation' which would require a framework of basic rights upon which citizens can rely.[100] These rights would certainly include the core civil liberties such as freedom of association, freedom of assembly and freedom of speech. However, they may also extend to a richer range of social rights and a programme of wealth redistribution in order to ensure the substantive democratic equality of citizens in the deliberative

[98] An interface explored brilliantly in K Ewing, 'The Importance of Trade Union Political Voice: Labour Law meets Constitutional Law' in A Bogg and T Novitz (eds), *Voices at Work: Continuity and Change in the Common Law World* (Oxford, Oxford University Press, 2014).

[99] Ewing ibid. See also J Logan, 'The Movement to Eliminate Labor's Political Voice: Proposition 32 and "Paycheck Protection" in the United States' in A Bogg and T Novitz (eds), *Voices at Work*, ibid.

[100] J Habermas, *Between Facts and Norms: Contributions to a Discourse Theory of Law and Democracy*, trans W Rehg (Cambridge, MA, MIT Press, 1997) 104. See also J Cohen, 'Reflections on Habermas on Democracy' (1999) 12 *Ratio Juris* 385, 391.

process.[101] It is therefore difficult to funnel *all* of our determinations regarding rights into a deliberative process, for deliberation itself is dependent upon a guarantee of social rights. Once again, a 'law of the labour market' is not sufficient to support the proceduralism on offer in the modest conception of capabilities. Enquiry into the complex interrelationship between deliberation and social rights will only be facilitated by a 'law of labour market governance', which is a much more ambitious project than the one offered by Deakin and Wilkinson.

As Nussbaum's work on capabilities demonstrates, proceduralism is not an inevitable consequence of adopting the capabilities approach. Deliberative processes themselves depend upon a structure of social rights to ensure that the preconditions of a fair deliberative process are guaranteed. It is therefore difficult to entrust the formation of social rights to 'mutual learning' through deliberation without a precise account of how deliberative processes are to be constructed and supported, and whether there might be social rights that provide a framework for the deliberative stage of resolution (and hence not a subject of deliberation in the way that other social rights might be). And there might be some social rights, such as freedom from forced labour, that are so incontrovertibly fundamental, with a settled protective core, that it would be inappropriate to subject them to a deliberative process with unknown outcomes.

At points Deakin and Browne seem to imply that Sen's prioritization of a deliberative social choice procedure to specify the capabilities provides an analogy with or connection to 'constitutional guarantees of freedom of association and collective representation'.[102] Yet the intersection between collective bargaining and deliberative theory remains highly contested, with some scholars sceptical of the deliberative model in the sphere of collective bargaining.[103] The capabilities approach offered by Deakin, Browne and Wilkinson is certainly modest when compared with Langille's. Yet for all its modesty, and perhaps even because of its modesty, it is also dangerous in what it leaves unresolved. We are effectively being asked to write a blank cheque and hand it over to a democratic process. As such, it is no less faulty as a basis for a 'new normativity' for labour law than Langille's immodest approach.

To summarize the argument thus far, both versions of the capability approach argued that freedom of association should be regarded as a fundamental labour right at the structural core of labour law. However, the capability approach is problematic for three reasons. First, both versions fail to provide a coherent account of our fundamental rights, either because the theory does not specify which exercises of freedom we have particular reason to value (Langille) or because the theory allocates the particular resolution of fundamental rights to a

[101] J Cohen, 'Procedure and Substance in Deliberative Democracy' in J Bohman and W Rehg (eds), *Deliberative Democracy* (Cambridge, MA, MIT Press, 1997) 407, 422.

[102] Deakin and Browne (n 83) 38–39.

[103] See eg S McCrystal and T Novitz, 'Democratic' Preconditions for Strike Action—A Comparative Study of Australian and UK Labour Legislation' (2012) 28 *International Journal of Comparative Labour Law and Industrial Relations* 115; and cf A Bogg, *The Democratic Aspects of Trade Union Recognition* (Oxford, Hart Publishing, 2009) ch 6.

democratic procedure (Deakin et al). Secondly, both versions fail to provide an account of justice in the sphere of employment. This is unsurprising, for even on Nussbaum's rich account of human capabilities (which is far richer than anything on offer in Langille's or Deakin, Browne and Wilkinson's work) she concedes that her theory of justice is nothing more than 'minimal'. Finally, as Judy Fudge has argued powerfully, the capabilities approach articulated by Sen is inattentive to relations of power and domination in spheres of activity such as employment. As Sen himself has observed, the capabilities approach tells us little 'about the fairness or equity of the processes involved, or about the freedom of citizens to invoke and utilize procedures that are equitable'.[104] Cumulatively, these considerations should give labour lawyers considerable pause for thought before endorsing the recent turn towards capabilities as a new normative basis for labour law.

D. 'Personality at Work' as a Basis for a 'New Normativity'

In a recent work on the legal construction of personal work relations, Freedland and Countouris propose a new understanding of labour law's normativity, one that is based in the notion of 'personality in work'.[105] This notion of personality in work is composed of three core values: dignity, capability and stability. According to Freedland and Countouris, this provides the following set of justifications for protective labour laws:

> (1) *dignity* and decent conditions for workers; (2) maximizing workers' access to the labour market and opportunities for skills development and *capability* building; and (3) controlling the costs and risks for employing entities and workers alike of entering into such arrangements by introducing and promoting elements of *stability*.[106]

These notions, dignity in particular, are formulated at a very high degree of abstraction.[107] According to them, dignity is itself an amalgam of notions of autonomy and equality without too much specificity being accorded to each of these separate values.[108] The framework envisages a dynamic interaction between these normative elements. For example, they offer an account of the capability approach 'from a predominantly *normative* perspective', which envisages the specification of capabilities 'for the purposes of fostering human autonomy and equality at work, and a rewarding existence'.[109] It may perhaps be added that the normative ideal of stability, one suffused with notions connected to the rule of law, would also provide shape and content to the capabilities. The authors envisage that this account will create a 'springboard' for social rights protections, which will extend to 'respect of the fundamental rights of freedom of associa-

[104] Sen (n 58).
[105] Freedland and Countouris (n 10) 369–82.
[106] ibid 372.
[107] For a critique on this basis, see the chapter by McCrudden in this volume.
[108] Freedland and Countouris (n 10) 374–75.
[109] ibid 378.

tion, collective bargaining, and strike action, as well as for the societal support for forms of collective organization across the various layers of the increasingly segmented modern workforce'.[110]

In many ways, this provides a much more fruitful basis for reconceiving labour law's normativity than either the immodest or the modest conception of capabilities. Against the immodest conception offered by Langille, the notions of dignity and stability in Freedland and Countouris' argument can provide some normative guidance to the task of determining which forms of life we have reason to value. This can then assist us in identifying which rights we should properly regard as fundamental. Against the modest conception offered by Deakin, Browne and Wilkinson, there is no doubt that Freedland and Countouris' notion of 'personality' leaves significant space for democratic procedures to specify the content and shape of social rights, given their desire not to be 'overly prescriptive' in respect of normative values such as equality.[111] Yet the values of dignity and stability provide a basis for steering and structuring democratic procedures. The democratic discourse revolves around the enquiry into the normative consequences of dignity and stability for determining the capabilities of workers; it is not a democratic discourse untethered to any set of structuring values.

Nevertheless, it is a fair criticism that Freedland and Countouris are not especially clear in specifying how they derive freedom of association as a fundamental labour right from their composite notion of 'personality in work'. Of course, there is an ambiguity in the extent to which 'personality in work' is offered as a unifying value for labour law as a whole, as distinct from a more particular role in the narrower domain of personal work relations. In my view, there are distinct advantages in treating it as a unifying value, not least that this operates as a much-needed solvent for the overly rigid separation of the 'individual' from the 'collective' in labour law. In this spirit, I want to suggest the following as a supplement to their theory, and one that is based on McCrudden's 'personalist' reading of Freedland and Countouris.[112] It is a reading that I find plausible and appealing in its own right. It is based in a notion of the human person as an individual with unique value and dignity, who finds her fulfilment in self-constituting action guided by reason in community with others. Once we see this notion of 'personalism' at work in 'personality in work', this points to the related idea of subsidiarity.[113] Subsidiarity may be regarded as 'a fundamental aspect of general justice that common enterprises should be regarded, and practically conducted, not as ends in themselves but as a means of assistance, as ways of helping individuals to "help themselves" or, more precisely,

[110] ibid 379.

[111] ibid 374.

[112] See the chapter by McCrudden in this volume.

[113] On the connections between personalism and subsidiarity, see A Follesdal, 'Subsidiarity' (1998) 6 *Journal of Political Philosophy* 190, 207–10. See generally NW Barber, 'The Limited Modesty of Subsidiarity' (2005) 11 *European Law Journal* 308.

to constitute themselves.'[114] Understood in this way, freedom of association is a vital fundamental right that supports the associational spaces where individuals engage in forms of mutual 'self-help' and a life of self-constituting action.

E. Freedom of Association and the Argument from Subsidiarity

Integral human fulfilment is mostly realized through participation in the communal life of associations, such as families, political groups, artistic or scientific associations, churches, or trade unions. The principle of subsidiarity

> affirms that the proper function of association is to help the participants in the association to help themselves or, more precisely, to constitute themselves through the individual initiatives of choosing commitments (including commitments to friendship and other forms of association) and of realizing these commitments through personal inventiveness and effort in projects.[115]

This envisages that tasks and functions should be allocated to the lowest level of association possible, with centralization of tasks and functions only warranted where these tasks could not be performed efficiently at the lower level.[116] It also envisages that the point of all associational activity is to enable individuals to lead a life of dignity and self-respect, realized through autonomous commitment and action. This is something more than a principle of efficient governance or administration, however. Properly understood, it is only where the lower level of association is unable to reach a threshold of efficiency that reallocation of tasks and functions should be contemplated. It need not be the most efficient form of governance.

Thus stated, subsidiarity sheds fresh light on some old and familiar themes, especially as represented in Kahn-Freund's seminal work. Historically, labour lawyers were intensely preoccupied with the question of *how* substantive labour standards were formulated and implemented. Under the old dispensation, this was a matter of *moral* significance rather than a matter of mere technical interest. Theoretical reflection on the political norm of subsidiarity provides a way of making sense of this preference for collective bargaining over legislation as a source of protective norms, of workers forging their own norms rather than being passive recipients of statutory rights. It marked the difference between, on the one hand, a fully authentic and dignified human life of self-constituting action and, on the other hand, a life blighted by the corrosive effects of passive dependence on benign governments or benign employers. Furthermore, subsidiarity's occupation of a political space between statist socialism and *laissez-faire* individualism, and its commitment to a norm of group liberty as a bulwark

[114] Finnis (n 11) 169. It should be noted that this notion of subsidiarity is distinct from the structural principle deployed in the context of European law and governance: on the differences between the personalist and the European conception of subsidiarity, see Barber (n 113).
[115] Finnis (n 11) 146.
[116] ibid 147.

against totalitarianism, provides an elegant political rationalization of 'collective *laissez-faire*'.[117] Carozza has emphasized the structural connections between the principle of subsidiarity and the theory and practice of fundamental human rights.[118] As he observes, international human rights instruments

> stress that human society amounts to more than simply the individual and her unmediated relationship to a single whole, the state. The communal aspects of human rights are directed toward the protection of a wide variety of intermediate bodies and associations, from the family to labor organizations to religious communities and political associations.[119]

Freedom of association is thus critical as an underpinning to the principle of subsidiarity, and it should be regarded as a human right of fundamental importance. It is likewise understandable that the insights of subsidiarity have been deployed as a critical tool in charting the human consequences of the erosion of collective bargaining as a way of doing labour law.[120]

The erosion of collective bargaining in no way implies the erosion of freedom of association's normative importance in the scheme of labour law. On the contrary, if we care about the things that really matter, namely the dignity of workers as human beings, a concern that lies at the base of personalism and subsidiarity, the erosion of collective bargaining positions freedom of association as a focal point of scholarly enquiry with renewed urgency. Furthermore, once refracted through the lens of subsidiarity, freedom of association begins to take a particular shape against the backdrop of recent debates. It helps us to understand how freedom of association is about much more than *being* in association. Legal protections must also extend to *doing* in association with others, whether that means acting as a trade union representative on behalf of others, or taking strike action in solidarity with co-workers. This reflects subsidiarity's basis in the significance of self-constituting action to the dignified life. It also helps us to understand how collective bargaining should be protected as an integral element of freedom of association, for it is only through this special form of concerted activity that workers 'can help themselves by their own private efforts and initiatives'.[121] This encompasses more than a negative duty on the state to refrain from impeding collective action, requiring the state to positively support the self-governing activities of associations such as trade unions.[122] Finally, the norm of subsidiarity would support a norm of presumptive respect for the internal organizational autonomy of associations, though such a norm does not preclude

[117] For discussion, see PG Carozza, 'Subsidiarity as a Structural Principle of International Human Rights Law' (2003) 97 *American Journal of International Law* 38, 41.

[118] Carozza, ibid 56.

[119] ibid 47.

[120] TC Kohler, 'Individualism and Communitarianism at Work' (1993) *Brigham Young University Law Review* 727.

[121] Finnis (n 11) 169.

[122] Carozzo (n 117) 43–44.

regulation of an association's internal affairs in appropriate cases (eg harming the common good through a violation of a member's fundamental rights).[123]

On this approach, freedom of association takes its place as a fundamental labour right of special importance. Perhaps many of those who would argue for the relegation of 'collective' matters in the structuring of the discipline might agree with that as a normative proposition. But one can imagine the following line of argument. What is normatively appealing might not be descriptively perspicuous, particularly when successive governments (and most of the English judiciary) do not share those normative commitments. By structuring the discipline around fundamental rights, there is a danger of 'deafness' to legislative and judicial activity. We might fail to grasp the nature and importance of the new labour law by failing to understand it in its own terms. Worst of all, we might be led to denounce legislation or judgments as 'irrational or wicked'.[124]

There is a delicate line here. We should not discount the opposite worry of the legislator setting the scholarly agenda,[125] which might lead us to be critical of recent work that has marginalized collective labour rights in the discipline of labour law simply because collective labour rights were marginalized in the particular legislative agenda of 'New Labour'.[126] But in any event, the 'deafness' critique would miscarry here because it fails to appreciate the suppleness of a 'central case' methodology, articulated with great power by John Finnis.[127] This enables normative theories to perform descriptive-explanatory tasks in legal and social theory. According to Finnis, we can only understand concepts through understanding flourishing instances of those concepts: we understand 'father' by understanding what a good father looks like; we understand 'tutor' by understanding what a good tutor looks like; and so forth. But we also understand that bad or deficient fathers and tutors are still instances of the concept being studied, even if corrupted and so peripheral instances. And so it is with law. To identify legislation that violates basic elements of the fundamental human right to freedom of association, to critique it in those terms, perhaps even to characterize it as 'irrational or wicked' precisely because it is an intentional attack on a basic human right, might lead us to regard the legislator's activity as a peripheral or corrupted instance of proper legislative responsibility in the sphere of work and its regulation. But this is not the same thing at all as 'deafness', for the study of peripheral cases 'is illuminated by thinking of them as watered-down versions of the central cases'.[128] These borderline instances are interesting in their

[123] J Finnis, 'Reflections and Responses' in J Keown and RP George (eds), *Reason, Morality and Law: The Philosophy of John Finnis* (Oxford, Oxford University Press, 2013) 515.

[124] The 'deafness' and 'wickedness' objections may be distilled from Collins (n 37) 297.

[125] A worry articulated in Collins' earlier methodological reflections in 'Labour Law as a Vocation' (n 7).

[126] See eg H Collins, 'Is There a Third Way in Labour Law?' in J Conaghan, RM Fischl and K Klare (eds), *Labour Law in an Era of Globalisation: Transformative Practices and Possibilities* (Oxford, Oxford University Press, 2004) ch 23.

[127] Finnis (n 11) ch 1.

[128] ibid 11.

own right, though reflection upon them may also enable us to see elements of the central case in a new and interesting light. So a 'detached' descriptive-explanatory account of the statutory recognition procedure that prioritized the perspective of competitiveness-based social partnership as an analytical tool[129] might make contact with some of the explicit policy concerns motivating legislators and judges from time to time. Yet it is in the corresponding loss of moral indignation that we might lose a vivid sense of what is *really* at stake here, what *really* matters, namely the just treatment of workers and consideration for their ability to lead a dignified life of self-constituting action.

The 'central case' analysis would point to the fact that there has been a flagrant and intentional attack on workers' human rights, particularly in the collective sphere, by legislators and judges motivated by merely instrumental considerations such as 'competitiveness'. It would identify the ways in which legal norms impede or damage the realization of human rights. It would engage critically with the elevation of 'competitiveness' as an overarching concern of legislators, highlighting its purely instrumental character and its tenuous relationship to forms of human flourishing that are intrinsic. It might even explore how 'partnership' itself, regarded as an instance of the good of friendship, can be understood as a concept with its own focal and peripheral meanings.[130] The form of 'social partnership' that fixates on competitiveness seems like an attenuated version when compared with a version that emphasizes reciprocity and a fair distribution of the benefits and burdens of productive activity, just treatment of workers for its own sake, and respect for fundamental rights. Thus conceived, natural law theory is not blind to the fact that often 'legislative debate … turns on matters only mediately related to the criteria of justice, for example on the efficiency with which alternative schemes or perspectives can be implemented and their expense'.[131] Realistic appraisal of legislators and courts is entirely possible within a 'central case' framework structured by moral commitment.

IV. Labour Law and Disagreement

One final matter must be addressed. There is a danger that any normative theory of labour law, especially where that theory is rights-based, might be incapable of responding to the fact of reasonable normative disagreement in liberal and pluralistic societies. Like any other kind of right, labour rights are not immune to the fact of reasonable disagreement. Kahn-Freund once said of the 'balance of collective forces' in collective bargaining that 'to maintain it has on the whole been the policy of the legislature during the last hundred years or so. … This

[129] See H Collins, *Employment Law*, 2nd edn (Oxford, Oxford University Press, 2010) ch 6.
[130] Finnis (n 11) 11.
[131] ibid 182.

is a sentiment shared, it is to be hoped, by all political parties represented in Parliament.'[132] This indicated the profound importance of *consensus* to Kahn-Freund's theory of collective *laissez-faire*. Even in 1983, when these words were printed in the final edition of *Labour and the Law*, this assumption of a normative consensus on the value and parameters of collective labour rights was already untenable.

The terrain of collective labour relations was characterized, if anything, by deep normative *disagreement*. Much of this normative disagreement revolved around the nature of freedom of association: did it rest upon freedom or some other value such as solidarity or equality? If freedom, was it aligned with negative or positive liberty? Did it protect trade union membership? If so, was this protection merely from state interference or from acts of employer interference as well? Did its protection extend to trade union activities such as collective bargaining? Did it encompass only individual rights or did it extend to collective rights for trade unions as independent right-holders? The spectrum of possible answers to these difficult questions was as richly varied as the underlying political orientations of the protagonists. Labour law needed to take this normative disagreement seriously, and collective laissez-faire in the hands of its leading protagonists was not especially geared up to this theoretical task. We need to ascertain whether the adoption of a normative theory, such as 'personality in work', is able to respond in a more satisfactory way to the existence of reasonable disagreement about rights. If it cannot, then its credentials as an appealing theory of labour law may be questioned.

It is possible to identify two strategies to deal with normative disagreement in labour law. The first strategy might be described as democratic proceduralism. It acknowledges that we disagree, and often disagree *reasonably*, about matters of justice and rights. We disagree about the content of rights; we disagree about the specific practical implications of various rights; we disagree about the normative foundations of rights; and we even disagree about which rights there are. In Waldron's terms, everything seems to be 'up for grabs' in discourse about rights.[133] For theorists such as Waldron, this has profound implications for our democratic institutions. In a subtle and wide-ranging set of arguments, Waldron builds a positive case for entrusting the articulation and protection of our fundamental rights to well-functioning democratic legislatures rather than to constitutional courts with powers to strike down 'unconstitutional' legislation.

The spirit of Waldron's work is well represented in labour law theory. Its instincts seem to chime with the procedural approach of Deakin et al to capabilities as a basis for labour law. It also perhaps underlies Brian Langille's subtle account of international labour law as creating a deliberative space for civic dialogue about rights rather than as generating a prescriptive set of enforceable labour rights.[134] Whatever the merits of this approach as a principled position, it

[132] Davies and Freedland (n 32) 12.
[133] J Waldron, *Law and Disagreement* (Oxford, Oxford University Press, 1999) 302.
[134] Langille (n 97).

should be resisted as an approach to real politics in the world in which we live. As Waldron himself acknowledges, his principled argument is dependent upon a range of assumptions about democratic institutions. One of those assumptions is that democratic institutions are structured in a way that respects democratic equality.[135] Under current political conditions in many countries there are serious distortions of political equality, especially in the field of 'labour law'-making. There have been systematic attempts to silence workers' political voices through campaign finance reform in many countries,[136] and clear evidence of the 'capture' of governmental processes by powerful corporate actors using the leverage of threatened capital flight.[137] Under these conditions, constitutional courts have often been the only forums in which workers' voices have been heard so as to impede the legislative curtailment of freedom of association rights.[138] As Waldron himself acknowledges, political philosophers must attend to the reality of politics as it is, rather than some idealized or sanitized conception of it.[139] For this reason, the strategy of democratic proceduralism as a response to normative disagreement under current democratic conditions would be utter folly.

The second strategy might be described as a strategy of denial or minimization. On this approach, the scope for *reasonable* disagreement about collective labour rights is curtailed in various ways. Those who argue against, say, collective bargaining as a fundamental labour right are regarded as engaging in unreasonable disagreement, like climate change deniers or flat earth believers. We might simply dismiss such a position as one involving a disguised attempt to promote economic self-interest, perhaps in thrall to some agent or other of capital.[140] We might question the good faith of the protagonist, and the extent to which she is applying her reason with appropriate attitudes, such as openness to truth and the persuasive force of good arguments, to a genuine problem of justice.[141] We might simply give up on dialogue with particular interlocutors, such as 'neo-liberals', on the basis that it is an alien ideology that is beyond the reach of progressive discourse.[142] Or we might allow only for 'borderline' disa-

[135] J Waldron, 'The Core of the Case against Judicial Review' (2006) 115 *Yale Law Journal* 1346, 1361–62.

[136] For discussion, see Ewing (n 98).

[137] B Walker and R Tipples, 'The Hobbit Affair: A New Frontier for Unions?' (2013) 34 *Adelaide Law Review* 65.

[138] See eg constitutional litigation in the Canadian context on freedom of association and collective bargaining, discussed in A Bogg and K Ewing, 'A (Muted) Voice at Work? Collective Bargaining in the Supreme Court of Canada' (2012) 33 *Comparative Labor Law and Policy Journal* 379.

[139] Waldron (n 133) 158.

[140] See S Besson, *The Morality of Conflict: Reasonable Disagreement and the Law* (Oxford, Hart Publishing, 2005), for a rich analysis of disagreement and its many forms. On the distinction between disagreements about justice and mere conflicts of interest, see Besson, 20–21.

[141] ibid 97–98.

[142] Lord Wedderburn, while emphasizing the importance of engaging in democratic debate about freedom of association (and not 'taking to the hills'), also points to the fact that 'assumptions are no longer freely shared' with neoliberal interlocutors such as Hayek: Lord Wedderburn, *Employment Rights in Britain and Europe: Selected Papers in Labour Law* (London, Lawrence & Wishart, 1991) 228.

greements about freedom of association and its outer limits, but hold that there is no scope for 'pivotal disagreement' that goes 'deep into the *core of a concept*'.[143]

None of these moves seem satisfactory, however. Disagreements about freedom of association, for example, are usually 'pivotal'; interlocutors approaching the issue do so in good faith on the basis of reasoned opinions about value rather than self-interest; and it is simply false to imply that the underlying concepts deployed by 'neo-liberals' are somehow alien or unrecognizable to a progressive audience. For example, freedom might be described as an 'essentially contestable' concept.[144] We might disagree with 'neo-liberal' understandings of it; we will likely offer our own understanding in response; but there will be sufficient agreement and understanding for the conversation to get off the ground, even where the disagreement is 'pivotal'. At its worst and its most extreme forms, the strategy of denial or minimization is incompatible with basic principles of academic freedom. It is certainly not a tenable response to the fact of disagreement in labour law, much of which is properly characterized as reasonable normative disagreement.

Where does the normative theory of Freedland and Countouris fit between these two approaches to disagreement? Superficially, at least, it might seem more naturally aligned with the strategy of denial or minimization. If there are fundamental rights, based in forms of human flourishing that are objectively good, this evinces a commitment to moral truth. If there can be moral truth about our rights, then there can be moral error. The trick is to pick the side of moral truth. This would be too simplistic a presentation, however. There is another possibility that avoids the excesses of both democratic proceduralism and denial/minimization. It is therefore an appealing theoretical basis for labour law in circumstances of reasonable disagreement about rights.

Following Aquinas, Robert George sets out two ways in which the conscientious legislator translates the requirements of natural law into positive law.[145] First, there is a direct process of deduction from the moral principle to the legal norm, as might occur in the legal prohibition of a grave moral wrong such as rape or murder. Secondly, there is a process of *determinatio* whereby the legislator enjoys a creative freedom in specifying the requirements of positive law in order to further human wellbeing. This creative choice is not entirely free. Sometimes legislative schemes are unjust and so should not be chosen at all. Often, though, there will be many reasonable (but incompatible) schemes that may be implemented. In other words, in respect of *determinatio* there will be scope for *reasonable* disagreement about what ought to be done. Nor should we assume that the scope for *determinatio* is severely limited in respect of fundamental rights. As Finnis observes,

[143] Besson (n 140) 51.

[144] For a full discussion of this as it relates to disagreement, see Besson (n 140) ch 3.

[145] R George, 'Natural Law and Positive Law', in R George, *In Defense of Natural Law* (Oxford, Oxford University Press, 1999) 102.

> [L]aws and decisions declaring and giving effect to human rights have the complexity characteristic of positive law. Some of them stand to the right in question as a simple application or deductive conclusion. More commonly they stand to the right in question as determinations, that is, specifications and delimitations which when reasonable could nonetheless reasonably have been different.[146]

This kind of distinction is certainly compatible with the theory of 'personality in work'.

In relation to freedom of association, then, there is a plateau of agreement that is needed in order for the conversation to begin. The interlocutors must agree that there is such a thing as 'freedom of association' and that it is a fundamental right. There will also be a core of fundamental elements within freedom of association that are direct deductions from the natural law. Beyond this, however, there will be fertile scope for reasonable disagreement about how to further specify the elements of the fundamental right in positive law. So the 'fundamentality' of freedom of association is not 'up for grabs'. Nor are its core features, those matters derived by way of deduction from natural law. Beyond this, however, there is significant scope for a dialogue about freedom of association, and it is a dialogue that labour law must make space for. The following matters would, in my view, be located within the scope of such a dialogue:

(i) What is the normative basis of freedom of association? Freedom or some other value such as solidarity, equality or civic participation? If freedom, should we understand freedom in terms of negative liberty, positive liberty, non-domination or 'capabilities'?
(ii) Does freedom of association encompass a negative freedom to disassociate? If it does, what is its extent? Does negative freedom to disassociate relate only to membership as such, or can it be asserted as a freedom not to bargain collectively or a freedom not to strike?
(iii) What degree of 'thickness' does freedom of association display?[147] Does it extend to certain 'activity-rights' such as the right to collective bargaining or the right to strike? What package of freedoms, claim-rights, powers and immunities does freedom of association encompass? To the extent that it grounds certain claim-rights, which duties are correlative to those claim-rights?
(iv) Who are right-holders under freedom of association? Individuals? If individuals, may those rights be confined to those working under particular kinds of personal employment contract or should it extend to persons as such? Are there collective rights for groups such as trade unions? If so, do corporations also enjoy collective rights under freedom of association?
(v) Under what circumstances can freedom of association be limited?
(vi) Should freedom of association be constitutionalized? Should we envisage

[146] J Finnis, 'Introduction' in J Finnis, *Human Rights and Common Good, Collected Essays*, vol III (Oxford, Oxford University Press, 2011) 3.

[147] Bogg and Ewing (n 138).

constitutionalizing only its 'core' elements? If it is constitutionalized, should its interpretation be entrusted to constitutional courts? Or should it be safeguarded in the ordinary legislative process and be subject to popular democratic control?

(vii) Given the contraction of traditional forms of association such as trade unions, how can freedom of association be developed to sustain new forms of association and collective action? Should freedom of association protect 'basic' forms of concerted action (X *and* Y present a grievance to their employer) regardless of a connection to trade union activity?[148] Should the study and teaching of strike law extend to other forms of popular protest and mobilization that occur outside 'official' trade union channels, such as new anti-capitalist movements and 'days of action'?

V. Conclusion

To what or to whom do labour lawyers owe loyalty? To a scholarly discipline? To particular dogmas treasured by the high priests of the discipline? To the trade union movement? To employers? To the state? To 'labour as a class'?[149] We prize any one of these particular attachments at our peril. Our loyalty should be to a compelling account of human flourishing, fundamental rights and the requirements of justice in a political community based on the common good. This is what it means to reclaim 'labour law as a vocation'. This repudiates a particular understanding of 'autonomy' in the sphere of labour law, one that asserts that labour law should be autonomous of controversial theories of justice, rights and human goods. Instead, labour law should be fully connected to normative theory.

This normative perspective provides the underpinning to a rights-based theory of labour law's structure, where freedom of association takes its legitimate place as a fundamental labour right in a coherent set. This is certainly not to say that freedom of association is the *only* fundamental right that matters. Nor is it necessarily to say that freedom of association matters *more* than other fundamental rights (though strong trade unions are usually instrumentally significant in the formulation and enforcement of other fundamental labour rights). It is to say that freedom of association matters a great deal, and that it may without any embarrassment at all take its place alongside more individual rights such as the right not to be unjustifiably dismissed, the right not to be discriminated against for illegitimate reasons, or the right to fair and just working conditions. Freedland and Countouris' joint work has provided a bold engagement with

[148] A Bogg and C Estlund, 'Freedom of Association and the Right to Contest: Getting Back to Basics' in A Bogg and T Novitz (eds), *Voices at Work: Continuity and Change in the Common Law World* (Oxford, Oxford University Press, 2014).

[149] Mitchell (n 4) 59.

that vital task of theorizing labour law's rights-based internal structure from a normative perspective.

There is a tendency for many labour lawyers to emphasise labour law's *normative* autonomy as a basis for its *doctrinal* autonomy, particularly from the general common law of contract.[150] This chapter has offered a set of arguments that would counsel some caution in this regard. Even normative justifications that are ostensibly 'internal' to labour law, such as 'inequality of bargaining power', depend upon a wider set of normative ideas in general political theory. 'Inequality of bargaining power' is, in itself, normatively inert without understanding what kind of equality we are interested in, and equality of what, and equality for whom, and why subordination might itself be an objectionable relational state of affairs, and so forth. This requires labour lawyers to reach beyond their discipline to the realm of value and reasons, though these values and reasons must of course be sensitive to contextual features of work as a distinctive kind of human activity.

True reasons based upon a sound understanding of fundamental rights and justice, are good reasons for everyone, employers, workers and governments alike. Mark Freedland's contribution to scholarship is an exemplar of this approach, with a scholarly legacy that is both anti-dogmatic and unremittingly humane in its concern for justice, dignity and fundamental rights. It is in the betrayal of *those* epistemic and moral values that we see the betrayal of a discipline.

[150] See the chapter by Freedland this volume.

4

Common Law Confusion and Empirical Research in Labour Law

LIZZIE BARMES

I. Introduction

The question I address in this chapter is whether there should be more empirical enquiry to illuminate the twin current phenomena in the UK of, on the one hand, confusion and incoherence in common law doctrine affecting employment, and, on the other, political indifference to this amidst otherwise frenetic legislative activity related to working life. I argue that more research by labour law scholars could usefully be directed to systematic examination of the functioning in practice of the common law system. My contention is that this has an unusual capacity to deliver a range of instrumental benefits, including of a doctrinal nature. Development in this direction would also build on labour law research traditions that have emphasized the interconnectedness of law with other phenomena, in particular through methodological openness and by conceiving of law as best understood in interaction with its social, economic, political and institutional environments.

II. Conceptual Problems in Common Law Doctrine in the UK

Conceptual problems in the UK with common law doctrine affecting working life seem to be getting worse. This is no doubt to some extent a reflection of the growing complexity and variety of both law and working practices and of the interactions between these variables nationally, regionally and globally. In these circumstances it is inevitable that courts are increasingly required to engage with novel and challenging factual and doctrinal dilemmas. This makes it yet more important that the institutional settings in which judges operate are such that they do not reliably have good information on which to base their decisions, whether regarding the 'fit' of different potential outcomes with surrounding law or about broader empirical learning on the issue before them. Instead a huge amount is left to the intellectual style of individual judges and to what they either happen to know or that advocates chose to inform them about. These are decision-makers, moreover, whose knowledge and ideas about the world, and indeed about thinking itself, have largely been formed by the very particular experiences, practices and cultures of the legal world in which they trained and had their professional careers. They are also drawn, especially at the upper echelons, from an extraordinarily narrow demographic group and their composition very poorly reflects British society as a whole, for example in the number of female judges and of those from minority ethnic and cultural groups.

It is unsurprising in these conditions that examples are accumulating of common law decision-making about work that breaches basic coherence norms and makes no sense to non-lawyers. The most striking example is the curious distinctions that successive House of Lords and Supreme Court judgments have made, on the one hand, between common law and statutory rules about termination of employment, and, on the other, between events in the lead up to this.[1] First, if contractually wrongful or tortious conduct by an employer, including seemingly in breach of express contractual terms, occurs very close to termination of the contract, it will give rise to potential liability only for the statutory wrong of unfair dismissal and not at common law. While there is some doubt as to how the rules work regarding express terms, it seems generally to remain possible, however, for claimants to apply for common law injunctive relief from even a termination-related breach and also that contractual damages will exceptionally be recoverable where a contract specifies that they will be.[2]

Secondly, in situations where even identical wrongful conduct occurs sufficiently far away from termination, there will potentially be liability both for unfair dismissal and at common law. Yet the basis on which this vital temporal distinction should be made has been left unclear by the case law. Moreover, there is the further complication that losses and expenses flowing from pre-dismissal breaches will not be recoverable in any unfair dismissal action[3] and those resulting from termination will be disallowed at common law.[4]

[1] *Johnson v Unisys* [2001] UKHL 13, [2003] 1 AC 518; *Eastwood v Magnox Electric plc, McCabe v Cornwall CC* [2004] UKHL 35, [2005] 1 AC 503; *Edwards v Chesterfield Royal Hospital NHS Foundation Trust* & *Botham v Ministry of Defence* [2011] UKSC 58, [2012] 2 AC 22.

[2] The doubt arises from the failure in *Edwards v Chesterfield* (n 1) of an overall majority to agree on the basis for the exclusion of common law liability for breach of express terms in a contract of employment in the context of a termination. See further L Barmes, 'Judicial Influence and *Edwards v Chesterfield Royal Hospital NHS Foundation Trust* and *Botham v Ministry of Defence*' (2013) 42 *Industrial Law Journal* 192.

[3] See *GMB Trade Union v Brown* [2007] UKEAT 0621_06_1610 and *GAB Robins (UK) Ltd v Triggs* [2008] EWCA Civ 17, [2008] ICR 529.

[4] This was the position reached in *Eastwood v Magnox* (n 1) when it was made clear that some common law actions escaped the 'Johnson exclusion zone' even if contractual termination later

The peculiar practical consequences are legion.[5] They include that the law sometimes requires ex-employees to bring separate claims in different court systems to recover all their compensatable losses and expenses consequent on the same wrongful conduct. Carefully negotiated contracts of employment will also apparently sometimes be ignored, even if they were agreed before *Edwards* broached the exclusion of compensation claims for termination-related breach of express terms. At the same time, there are instances of common law claims for personal injury damages in which, without explanation, no one seems to have paid any attention to these complexities,[6] and of others in which arguably obvious doctrinal errors were made by the courts hearing them.[7]

It may be that the existence of compulsory employers' liability insurance has had some influence regarding personal injury cases, although in theory that should have made no difference. Equally the complexity and counter-intuitiveness of the rules seem a likely spur to doctrinal mistakes by litigants, their lawyers and even judges. Perhaps most importantly, putting legal norms and decisions governing analogous fact situations side by side, it has become very hard to fathom the point or purpose of the relevant complex of statutory and common law rules. This is not to say that the stages by which we arrived at this point cannot be explained. Each step in the legislative and case law evolution can be accounted for as an isolated event, perhaps even justified. My point is that common law adjudication, interacting with legislative interventions, has made the overall legal position confusing, arbitrary and inaccessible to employers, employees and anyone else whose behaviour the rules are seeking to influence. After all, those regulated by employment law are not free to choose which categories of legal norms and court decisions to be bound by. The current state of affairs, however, makes it challenging to find a logically coherent internal structure to this area of law, let alone to extract clear and constructive general messages about how workplace relations ought to be conducted.

Another prominent example of common law confusion consists in the rules

ensued. After the decisions in *Edwards* and *Botham*, however, it is yet harder to know how the courts will determine which common law claims are still possible.

[5] See further L Barmes, *Bullying, Harassment and Other Behavioural Conflict at Work: Individual Rights and the Missing Collective Dimension* (forthcoming).

[6] A prominent example is *Horkulak v Cantor FitzGerald International* [2003] EWHC 1918 (QB), [2004] ICR 697, from which there was a partially successful appeal on quantum, [2004] EWCA Civ 1287, [2004] ICR 402.

[7] *Monk v Cann Hall Primary School* [2013] EWCA Civ 826, [2013] IRLR 732 recently illustrated multiple doctrinal mistakes by litigants and the High Court (HC) that were only picked up on appeal to the Court of Appeal (CA). The respondent school and Council first admitted liability in tort for personal injury caused to Mrs Monk by the way she was excluded from school premises. They subsequently withdrew that admission and persuaded the HC that the common law personal injury claim was within the 'Johnson exclusion zone'. Mrs Monk then won her appeal to the CA (and was permitted to re-plead her claim) because the events complained of in fact appeared very likely not to have constituted a dismissal, rendering *Johnson* etc irrelevant. See also *Smith v Housing Trafford Trust* [2012] EWHC 3221 (Ch), (2013) IRLR 86 in which the potential implications of *Edwards* were ignored by the HC despite their apparent relevance to the (admittedly unusual) factual and litigation history.

about categorizing work contracts. A difference here is that Parliament, through statute, has positively accorded judges a prominent role in determining whether or not the myriad working arrangements thrown up by the modern economy attract or avoid statutory legal protections for those subject to them. A further difference from my first example is that the case law is not characterized by internal incoherence to the same degree. The problems rather lie in the unpredictability of decision-making and the difficulty of relating the law and its underlying premises to working life.[8] The decision in *Autoclenz v Belcher*[9] is interesting in this regard. In a case in point, the Supreme Court was faced with inconsistent lines of authority about sham employment transactions as high up as the Court of Appeal.[10] It boldly cut through the unreality of some of that decision-making to decide that what mattered was the 'true agreement'.[11] This welcome acknowledgement of the meaninglessness of some written work contracts was, however, neither connected to clear guidance about when courts should look behind the paperwork nor to any indication of whether aspects of the contract other than its categorization were potentially affected. In particular, could *Autoclenz* allow courts sometimes to determine what was truly agreed in order to decide whether a contract had been breached? There seems no logical reason why not, at least where the written documentation is found to constitute a sham. Yet this would add a further layer of difficulty in reconciling decision-making in this area.[12]

There are also many further illustrations of adjudication on employment status being unstable on basic issues and of the frequent incapacity of the legal rules meaningfully to interpret modern arrangements by which people sell their labour. These include varied attempts in the last decade to rationalize the legal position of long-term agency workers,[13] ongoing oscillations about when someone is only a 'worker'[14] and the recent disagreements of fundamental principle between Employment Tribunals (ETs), the Employment Appeal Tribunal (EAT) and the Court of Appeal about how the employment status of a lap dancer ought to be analysed.[15]

It is easy to think of other illustrations of common law confusion about working life. One is decision-making about whether to incorporate contrac-

[8] See L Dickens, 'Fairer Workplaces: Making Employment Rights Effective' in L Dickens (ed), *Making Employment Rights Effective, Issues of Enforcement and Compliance* (Oxford and Portland, Oregon, Hart Publishing, 2012) 211 on the difficulties arising from the complexity of modern employment legislation, citing as one cause: '[U]ncertainties for employers which arise through the legislature choosing to leave key aspects of the coverage of rights to judicial interpretation', which is 'characterized currently by lack of a coherent approach.'

[9] *Autoclenz Ltd v Belcher & Ors* [2011] UKSC 41, [2011] 4 All ER 745.

[10] ibid [28].

[11] ibid [30].

[12] See *Qantas Cabin Crew (UK) Ltd v Lopez & Hooper* [2013] IRLR 4 for circumstances in which the EAT refused to take this step having found the paperwork to be, in effect, genuine.

[13] These arguably culminated in the decision in *James v London Borough of Greenwich* [2008] EWCA Civ 35, [2008] ICR 545.

[14] *Hospital Medical Group v Westwood* [2012] EWCA Civ 1005, [2012] IRLR 834 usefully summarized these, while illustrating the complexities of the issues in the modern labour market.

[15] *Quashie v Stringfellows Restaurants Ltd* [2012] EWCA Civ 1735, [2013] IRLR 99.

tual terms from external sources, especially collective agreements, works handbooks and now staff intranets, including as influenced by the widespread use of standard-form contracts and the practical effects of legislation about the statutory statement of terms and conditions.[16] Judicial pronouncements that were at least in part empirical assertions about contracting practice were in fact significant to the majority analyses in both *Johnson* and *Edwards*, albeit with no consideration of the evidence or lack of it to support these.[17] Another is the vexed question of the relationship between express and implied terms in ongoing contracts of employment, in which there are varied lines of authority to choose between.[18] I could go on, but I hope this brief sketch is enough to make good the claims that the common law as it affects employment is increasingly beset with conceptual uncertainty, if not outright inconsistency and illogicality, and that this is often allied to the difficulty of fitting the law to the reality of working lives.

An important corollary to these observations concerns the role of UK governments and Parliament. It is not that conceptual problems with common law rules about work have multiplied in a period in which the legislature has been inactive. Rather, as has been commonplace since at least the 1980s, there has been a kind of legislative hyperactivity over the last 15 or so years. Some of this originated in the EU, but a great deal was 'homegrown'. It has spanned an extraordinary range of subject-matters, from the enactment by Labour governments from 1997 to 2010 of many new individual rights, culminating in the Equality Act 2010, to the creation in the same period of a statutory recognition procedure, significant recalibration of the rules about transfers of undertakings, implementation of major EU Directives about information and consultation, enactment of the cross-cutting Human Rights Act 1998 and successive attempts to reform the ET system. Since the coalition government came to power in 2010 there has been yet more change, with various alterations to existing legislation, the Equality Act 2010 especially, and a thorough-going further attempt to alter

[16] See the recent twists in this judicial tale in *Malone v British Airways plc* [2010] EWCA Civ 1225 [2011] IRLR 32 on collective agreements and *Bateman v Asda Stores Ltd* [2010] UKEAT 0221_09_1102 on works handbooks, each criticized for inconsistency with prior authority in, respectively, R Russell, '*Malone and others v British Airways plc*: Protection of Managerial Prerogative?' (2011) 40 *Industrial Law Journal* 207 and F Reynolds QC and J Hendy QC, 'Reserving the Right to Change Terms and Conditions: How Far Can the Employer Go?' (2012) 41 *Industrial Law Journal* 79.

[17] *Johnson v Unisys* (n 1) [63]–[66] (Lord Hoffmann) and *Edwards v Chesterfield* (n 1) [37]–[39] (Lord Dyson), [94] (Lord Mance). Consider the following comment by Lord Phillips at [79] about that reasoning, explaining his concurrence with Lords Dyson, Mance and Walker on the outcome only: 'The courts ascribe to Parliament an intention that the relevant legislation will bear a meaning that is rational and coherent. The "intention" is thus somewhat artificial. It is even more artificial in the present context to impute to every party to a contract of employment the same intention that Lord Hoffmann and Lord Dyson JSC have ascribed to Parliament in relation to the effect of disciplinary codes.'

[18] Contrast, for example, the approaches to the relationship between express and implied terms in *Gogay v Hertfordshire County Council* [2000] IRLR 703, [2001] 1 FLR 280 (CA); *Reda v Flag Ltd* [2002] UKPC 38, [2002] IRLR 747; and *Rutherford v Seymour Pierce Ltd* [2010] EWHC 375 (QB), [2010] IRLR 606.

the ET system focused, as the Labour changes were before, on reducing the number of ET claims.

In none of this has anything been done about the problems with the common law, either those outlined above or any others. This may signal that successive governments and legislatures are content with the current position. Yet this would be easier to infer if the issues were at least acknowledged. Much as judges have commented on the urgent need for reform,[19] however, difficulties in this area of employment law appear not even to register outside legal circles. Indeed it would not be that surprising if ministers, other politicians and their advisers were a further group which is confused by how the various categories of rule fit together and interact.

III. Research Traditions, Empiricism and Common Law Adjudication about Labour Law

It seems to me that established research traditions in labour law can point the way to a better understanding of this state of affairs and to solving doctrinal muddle. I have in mind two broad features of scholarly endeavour in the field, both strongly present in the UK and elsewhere. The first is methodological variety, with a powerful emphasis on research experimentation and disciplinary openness. This has famously and substantially encompassed historical enquiry, comparative and international law, political and moral philosophy, legal, social and economic theory, as well as internal legal doctrinal analysis. The second feature of labour law scholarship, no doubt linked, is the depiction of law in its relationships to a wide range of other phenomena. This conveys that labour law is best understood not just by decoding legal texts, but by uncovering its role in a legal system's historical evolution, perceiving interactions with changing social and economic practices and finding the influence of philosophy, ideology and politics, all illuminated by comparison between nations and situated in a regional or global context.

Drawing inspiration from this, my contention is that contemporary labour law scholars, faced with the dichotomy I have outlined, could usefully strike out in new ways to make sense of what is happening. It seems to me that the situation I have identified is crying out for a further period of methodological innovation directed at building a fuller empirical picture, first, of how adjudication is working on its own terms and, secondly, of how it, and law more generally, are interacting with society, politics and the labour market. It may well be that in earlier times functionally equivalent data about the operation of labour law came from routinely gathered evidence about workplace practices and industrial relations. Yet as individual legal rights have grown in number and collective work-

[19] See eg *Eastwood v Magnox* (n 1).

place power has reduced, a need has emerged for new kinds of evidence about the relationships between, on the one hand, law and adjudication and, on the other, working lives and society more generally.

There are important examples of empirical research into law's impact by labour law scholars[20] and a growing sociological literature,[21] all of which is significant, not least in the opportunities it creates for interdisciplinary collaboration. There remain, however, major knowledge gaps, in the UK and beyond, which certainly encompass the substance and effects of adjudicative practice and endure despite recent developments in the empirical literature.[22] It is additionally striking that individual common law rights are largely ignored by UK policy-makers and non-lawyer researchers working on employment law, with the unspoken premise seeming to be that the ET system covers the range of relevant entitlements. This arguably supports the possibility adverted to above that our politicians and policy-makers lack understanding of the common law courts, their epistemic approach and the interactions between common law and statutory rules. Equally, it may reflect a curious separation of policy-making and law about, on the one hand, health and safety and, on the other, personal injury. Whatever the reasons for the sidelining in the UK of empirical investigation into common law adjudication and its effects, however, it is clear that labour law scholars are well placed to supply the lacunae in the evidence. In fact I would contend that thoroughgoing understanding and familiarity with the convoluted law in this field is necessary to the design and conduct of the kind of research I am advocating.

As such, my suggestion is that the common law problems identified above call for methodologically sound empirical work[23] by lawyers, first, more completely to document the conceptual crises within the common law, including any patterns in substantive decision-making, and, secondly, to use social scientific tools to investigate the causes and consequences of this, including in the attitudes of judges, the impact on workplaces and the responses of policy-makers. I give

[20] See eg C McCrudden, D Smith and C Brown, *Racial Justice at Work: the Enforcement of the 1976 Race Relations Act in Employment* (London, Policy Studies Institute, 1991); C McCrudden, R Ford and A Heath, 'Legal Regulation of Affirmative Action in Northern Ireland: An Empirical Assessment' (2004) 24 *Oxford Journal of Legal Studies* 363.

[21] See for helpful recent reviews of relevant evidence and analysis, W Brown, A Bryson, J Forth and K Whitfield, *The Evolution of the Modern Workplace* (Cambridge, Cambridge University Press, 2009); L Dickens (ed), *Making Employment Rights Effective, Issues of Enforcement and Compliance* (Oxford and Portland, Oregon, Hart Publishing, 2012). See also the outcomes of the ESRC Seminar Series in 2012–13, 'Reframing Resolution—Managing Individual Workplace Conflict', www.uclan.ac.uk/workplaceconflictseminars (accessed 17 March 2014).

[22] See S Deakin, 'Labor and Employment Laws' in P Cane and H Kritzer (eds), *Oxford Handbook of Empirical Legal Research* (Oxford, Oxford University Press, 2010) 326, commenting that: 'There is a small but growing literature looking at the judicial resolution of labour law disputes from a behavioural perspective.'

[23] See for a very rare example of research of this kind, A Brown, A Erskine and D Littlejohn, *Review of Judgments in Race Discrimination Employment Tribunal Cases* (London, DTI, 2006) the main aim of which was 'to identify any persistent patterns in the written judgments of Race Relations Act … cases that might explain why these claim are relatively unlikely to succeed at tribunal'.

some concrete examples below, but I would contend the major concerns to be, first, that we have so very few systematic quantitative and qualitative investigations into common law adjudication in the labour law field, or, secondly, data on how this and ET enforcement activity feed back into attitudes and interact with other legal and quasi-legal influences on workplaces and elsewhere. This is despite both having a wealth of rich data, going back years, about ET litigation and that public and political debate and action is so often rooted in (dubious) hypotheses about the effects of labour law enactments and enforcement.[24]

What I am advocating undoubtedly harks back to American legal realist ideas.[25] It is important to be clear, however, about the respects in which this is and is not the case. The central influence is in methodological terms, from the prominence in that tradition of social scientific investigation of adjudication and the impact of law more generally. The idea of examining case law to extract the recurrent features of decision-making in a particular field certainly owes much to mid-twentieth-century research experimentation by scholars such as Llewellyn.[26] Equally, my argument evokes the central theoretical concern of the realists with documenting and explaining the distance between law 'on the books' and in practice.

I explicitly would not, however, hypothesize that the empirical findings of any one or more American legal realist obtain in respect either of modern UK adjudication in common law cases or of understanding more generally of how labour law is currently functioning here. This is the case moreover in respect of earlier realist scholarship, such work that is associated with the critical legal studies movement[27] and the outcomes of the ongoing resurgence in the US of related lines of enquiry.[28] In fact I regard not presuming the truth of any substantive position deriving from this scholarship as flowing from the insight that law can only be fully understood if viewed as it operates in a particular field. In my view it follows that experimental assumptions ought not to be made about the impact of context and local variation. By the same token, if there are resonances between different times and places in what is found, this would all the more powerfully suggest something transcendent had been captured about the nature of law and legal process.

[24] For a detailed review see Barmes (n 5) ch 2.

[25] See generally W Twining, *Karl Llewellyn and the Realist Movement*, 2nd edn (Cambridge, Cambridge University Press, 2012).

[26] See especially K Llewellyn, *The Common Law Tradition—Deciding Appeals* (Boston and Toronto, Little, Brown and Company, 1960).

[27] In any event there was less emphasis on empirical work in this movement, on which see C. McCrudden, 'Legal Research and the Social Sciences' (2006) 122 *Law Quarterly Review* 632, 638 commenting that: '*Methodologically*, although not politically, CLS tended to be relatively conservative, usually resorting to doctrinal analysis in practice, though one leavened with social theory, an external perspective and a radical political agenda.'

[28] See, first, B Leiter, *Naturalizing Jurisprudence, Essays on American Legal Realism and Naturalism in Legal Philosophy* (Oxford, New York, Oxford University Press, 2007) for an overarching interpretation of American legal realism and a 'reconstruction' of its philosophical components and, secondly, so-called new legal realist empirical studies over the last decade or so, in the employment and equality field by, for example, L Edelman, S Sturm and their collaborators.

For present purposes, however, my focus is not only the antecedents of what I advocate nor its implications more widely. It is also the instrumental reasons for more research in the UK in this tradition and particularly about the common law. I explore several below, all of which would be augmented by studies being conducted on a comparative basis.

A. Enhancing Doctrinal Understanding

The first tangible benefit of work on this model relates to the content of law. It is arguable that traditional internal legal scholarship does what is needed in terms of discovering incoherence in common law doctrine, with no need to worry about the social scientific validity of findings or of fitting them into an overall account of adjudication, legal process and law.[29] The premise to this view is that the common law operates as a presumptively complete system of rules, such that there is no need to identify patterns of logical error to make the case for correction. What matters is simply that errors of coherence and consistency are discovered and ranked according to which of them does the most mischief to the reasoning structure as a whole. One issue I have with this approach on its own terms is that it invites endless dispute that is essentially unsolvable because of the 'thickness' and variability of judgments as data.[30] There is so much choice as to which strains of case law, and which strands of reasoning within them, to emphasize that the same sources can produce apparently valid ideas of legal rightness and wrongness while contradicting one another in fundamental ways.[31]

But that is not the only reason I think a more systematic approach to at least some case law analysis would be an appropriate supplement to traditional doctrinal scholarship.[32] There is a positive case for researchers to use social scientific tools qualitatively to analyse either whole 'populations' of cases, in the

[29] For a helpful account of this approach to scholarship see McCrudden (n 27) 633–35.

[30] See C O'Cinneide, 'Democracy, Rights and the Constitution—New Directions in the Human Rights Era' (2004) 57 *Current Legal Problems* 177, 180–81 about the impoverishing effect on debate about judicial review of the selective use of case law to support competing viewpoints.

[31] Aside from this observation being another way in which my perspective is reminiscent of American legal realism, given its explorations of indeterminacy in legal reasoning, it is worth pointing out that this phenomenon is a feature of all the labour law controversies mentioned above. An especially stark recent example was moreover provided by the divergent case law analyses in *Société Générale v Geys* [2012] UKSC 63, [2013] 1 AC 523 by the four Justices in the majority and Lord Sumption in dissent. See further A Burrows, 'What Is the Effect of a Repudiatory Breach of Contract' (2013) 42 *Industrial Law Journal* 281.

[32] I am not arguing that all doctrinal scholarship ought to adopt a more sociologically grounded approach to methodology, just that more of it should. The restatement approach is an interesting example of doctrinal work that arguably has a valuable role to play, with its intriguing way of claiming both to state the law and to enable it to develop, all from an internal point of view (albeit with participation, frequently, by varied legal actors). Indeed the role of this kind of work in legal development calls for empirical investigation in its own right, including for the indirect influence it gives to the wider group sometimes asked to participate. See in relation to the common law of the contract of employment, M Freedland, *The Personal Employment Contract* (Oxford, Oxford University Press, 2003) and in relation to restitution, A Burrows, *A Restatement of the English Law of Unjust Enrichment* (Oxford, Oxford University Press, 2012).

sense of the entire subset of decisions on a particular subject-matter, or at least a defensibly representative sample of those decisions. It is that case law analysis on this design is revelatory of much more about errors of coherence than the anatomy of the particular mistake and its place in the internal framework of law. It shows, for example, where categories of error recur and equally where courts are more reliable in their decision-making. Not only does this make it possible to diagnose elements of adjudication that are working better or worse, but it becomes possible to see more clearly how this is related to wider phenomena, such as substantive and procedural legal complexity and the characteristics of individuals, organizations and fact situations that get to courts. A more nuanced, multi-layered case can thereby be made for change, with more contextualized, tailored prescriptions for solving doctrinal puzzles.

To take the boundary disputes as between the ET system and the ordinary courts mentioned above, this kind of analysis would reveal if the problem implicates boundaries between others causes of action and also document the practical outcomes for different kinds of litigants, perhaps reinforced by qualitative research with claimants and respondents. This would broaden the basis on which the case for change could be assessed, moving beyond arguments from internal coherence and constitutional principle, to ones also based on a fuller knowledge of the scale of the problem and a more finely grained sense of what would work to solve it.

B. Uncovering State Responsibility

The second reason for such work concerns authorship and responsibility for errors in legal reasoning. So long as judge-made law about work continues to be ignored by governments and Parliament, the impression is reinforced that common law rules are merely technical 'law stuff' and the sole responsibility of judges. The implication if that area of law gets into a mess is that this is an unfortunate risk inherent in our constitution and nothing to do with the legislature. My argument is that the more the functioning in practice of the system of common law rules is uncovered, the more the ultimate responsibility of politicians is highlighted. If there are recurrent problems of a particular type with adjudication, this gives a strong indication that only the legislature can step in and engineer a solution. If a problem is endemic to the common law system, which repetition would tend to indicate, leaving it to judges to solve is like asking them to haul themselves up by their own bootstraps. Individual cases provide no perspective from which they can fully perceive the difficulty, nor do they have either the capacity, let alone the legitimacy, to come up with a systematic solution even if they could see the problem.

The various examples mentioned above illustrate this phenomenon. For example, having made individual decisions about the boundaries between contract and statute claims that look arbitrary from a broader perspective, and that create strange practical effects, the judges have no mechanism through which to reconsider the whole area, to unravel what was done in earlier cases and to find a better outcome. In any event, and paradoxically so far as it is accepted that the boundary problems have been judicially created, the constitutional concerns that started judges on this path suggest they ought not even to try. Equally, it is inevitable that case-by-case application by different courts of somewhat archaic language to determine who is and is not an employee will give rise to inconsistent, unsettled decision-making, as well as some quite surreal characterizations of working life. Again, however, there is nothing overarching that courts are in a position to do to retrieve this.

By the same token, research designed as I have suggested uncovers the functionality that law and legal process can have for the agendas of politicians. This kind of analysis points in a different direction to more traditional doctrinal work, presenting legal conundrums not only as technical difficulties but as the means by which legal discourse, intentionally or accidentally, is sometimes a means to an end of politicians ducking, deflecting or indirectly steering difficult public policy decisions. I have argued elsewhere that leaving the scope of statutory protections for working people to judge-made law is functional to governments and politicians avoiding urgent economic, political and social dilemmas.[33] A similar argument can be made that problems with effective adjudication of the very broad range of individual rights now on the UK statute book enable governments to create such rights and to reap the attendant political benefits while anticipating they will not make much difference to the functioning of the labour market. Indeed, another way that somewhat empty enactments of this kind may operate to maintain the status quo, or indeed to reinforce managerial freedom, is by giving employer lobbies additional bases on which to resist change which might have more impact. Yet only methodical documentation of how the system of individual employments rights actually works would enable the interactions of law and politics in this field really to be unravelled.

C. Probing Judicial Influence

The third worthwhile possible outcome of more research on this model concerns understanding the culture of legal process and especially the influences on judges in making and developing the common law. Thinking about research traditions in labour law highlights the variety of ways in which law is shaped, communicated and deployed. Formal legal process is only one means amongst many through which this takes place. There is teaching, supervising, mentoring, writing for different audiences, campaigning and the myriad interstitial exchanges amongst lawyers, academics, politicians, policy-makers, trade unionists, activists, human

[33] L Barmes, 'Learning from Case Law Accounts of Marginalized Working' in J Fudge, S McCrystal and K Sankaran (eds), *Regulating Legal Work: Challenging Legal Boundaries* (Oxford, Hart Publishing, 2012).

rights practitioners, working people and society at large. The question this gives rise to in this context is whether empirical research could illuminate what drives judges when they determine cases and how far such factors in turn translate to other spheres, such as the workplace, the classroom or political debate.

An urgent specific question in democratic terms is the effect on decision-making of the demographic homogeneity of many judges, especially at the higher levels. It seems almost inevitable that this must result in certain points of view being privileged and other, less elite, perspectives being crowded out.[34] If so, the challenge is for the system to become more inclusive, not only in the people appointed to the judiciary but in the openness of judicial discourse. We can only begin to work out how legitimately to achieve this, however, if we have a better sense of the extent to which current adjudicative processes marginalize certain voices and prioritize others.

I should say that the need for imaginative research design in paramount here and the difficulties cannot be overestimated.[35] There are already indications that investigating the impact of a single dimension of group identity, such as being a woman, will not show very much.[36] This is hardly surprising given the homogenizing effects of education and socialization as a lawyer, as well as the subsequent experience of a successful legal career. Indeed Griffith's work used case law analysis to develop a theory along these lines.[37] In any event, we are all bearers of a complex amalgam of influences related to class, politics, gender and sexual identity, ethnic, cultural or religious background, and indeed the infinite dimensions of human experience and propensity.

Nevertheless, there should be scope for devising effective research techniques,[38] for example combining ethnography and sociological analysis of case law,[39] first, to trace how judicial discourse and substantive decision-making are structured by dominant practices, preconceptions and beliefs; and, secondly, for excavating

[34] Consider the comment by Baroness Hale at the start of her dissent in *Edwards v Chesterfield* (n 1) [110] that: 'I should perhaps declare an interest, as the only member of this court to have spent a substantial proportion of her working life as an employee rather than as a self-employed barrister or tenured office holder.'

[35] See generally S Roach Anleu and K Mack, 'Trial Courts and Adjudication' in Cane and Kritzer (eds), *Oxford Handbook* (n 22) 545 and esp 564–65 about the difficulties of demonstrating links between judicial attitudes etc and particular outcomes, and also D Robertson, 'Appellate Courts' in Cane and Kritzer (eds), *Oxford Handbook* (n 22) 572 about the conceptual and methodological problems with the considerable US literature about the impact of attitude on, in particular, the constitutional decision-making of the Supreme Court.

[36] See on the findings about gender, K Malleson, 'Justifying Gender Equality on the Bench: Why Difference Won't Do' (2003) 11 *Feminist Legal Studies* 1 and more generally S Roach Anleu and K Mack (n 35) 553.

[37] JAG Griffith, *The Politics of the Judiciary*, 4th edn (London, Fontana Press, 1991).

[38] C Hunter, J Nixon and S Blandy, 'Researching the Judiciary: The Invisible in Judicial Decision-Making' (2008) 35 *Journal of Law & Society* 76 is a very helpful meditation on an innovative study of adjudication in possession cases, the design of which was notably challenging because decisions are taken extraordinarily quickly and with, at most, very quick oral reasons given.

[39] For an interesting recent example from the UK see, T Poole and S Shah, 'The Law Lords and Human Rights' (2011) 74 *Modern Law Review* 79, in which patterns of agreement and dissent, as well as voting records, were charted in a database of judgements from 1994 to 2007.

whether and how these intersect with membership of particular social and identity groups. Not least, this may be an area in which the growing literature on judicial biography can enhance the validity of empirical enquiry.

IV. Examples of Empirical Research into the Courts and the Common Law

In the space remaining I will illustrate how I think this kind of approach might work in relation to particular common law topics, adverting to an ongoing project of mine and sketching two other potential areas for enquiry.

A. Adjudication in the UK of Behavioural Conflicts at Work

I am coming towards the end of a study[40] an element of which has investigated adjudication in the UK from 1995 to 2010 about 'behavioural conflicts at work'. By this I mean disputes about how colleagues have behaved towards one another, whether or not there was also an issue about a particular workplace practice or decision. This categorization enabled me to isolate a significant proportion of the authoritative judgments (therefore excluding ET decisions) about this type of dispute in the period. These formed a worthwhile case study of adjudication of a broad range of individual employment rights, including ones deriving from contract and tort law. In classic US legal realist style, therefore, the research design tracked the application of law to a particular type of dispute, not how events are chopped up by different legal categories.

Detailed qualitative analysis of my final sample of about 150 cases disclosed several recurrent features of decision-making in this kind of conflict, irrespective of either the court in which the claim was made or the legal basis on which it was put. As suggested above regarding boundary disputes in labour law, the doctrinal analysis revealed the need for rationalization of the relevant legal rules to be more systemic and urgent than comes across from considering problems merely as missteps in the internal logic of the law. In so doing, the responsibility of politicians for taking an overarching view, and that they are best placed to put right deep flaws, emerged strongly. At the same time, my method demonstrated some positive features of the detailed factual analysis of complex work situations undertaken by courts. This made a case for imaginative thinking about how judicial endeavour might be put to more optimal use, including through distilling and disseminating the often highly accessible, consistent messages that were immanent in the judgments and which another aspect of my project indicated do not get through to workplaces.

[40] See further Barmes (n 5).

B. Comparative Adjudication of Injunction Applications

Another illustration is in the form of an idea for a comparative research project. This came to me from discussion with Judy Fudge about her and Eric Tucker's recent study of the last hundred years of adjudication in British Columbia of applications for injunctions to restrain picketing.[41] There is an opportunity in the fact that the grant of labour injunctions in a wide range of jurisdictions depends on common law principles, even if the underlying claims derive from statute. This decision-making famously involves judges using open-textured, highly discretionary common law rules and procedures to intervene in charged, often politically contentious matters of widespread concern. Adjudication of these actions therefore provides fertile territory in which to uncover repeat tendencies in how labour law issues are framed and in the influences operating on judges.

There is an important tradition of scholarship of this kind within nations[42] that it seems to me is ripe for updating in the modern era and to which a comparative element would especially add a worthwhile dimension. In particular, differences and similarities between jurisdictions would enable more to be understood about how the law works, including specifically about whether the common law itself or more local phenomena have greater explanatory power. There would also be scope to extend comparison to civil law jurisdictions, thereby testing current theorizing that attributes significance to legal origins.[43]

C. Judicial Review of Public Sector Consideration of Equality

The last example arguably implicates the common law only to a limited extent, given the greater significance of recent statutory measures to analysis in the UK of public-sector decision-making about equality. These include, first, public-sector equality duties enacted over the years, and especially since creation of the 2000 race equality duty;[44] and, secondly, the provisions of the Human Rights Act 1998 that implicate equality rights.[45] The growth since the 1970s of the judicial

[41] J Fudge and E Tucker, '"Everybody Knows What a Picket Line Means" Picketing Before the British Columbia Court of Appeal' (2009) 162 *BC Studies* 53.

[42] See H Arthurs, 'Woe Unto You Judges: Or How Reading Frankfurter and Greene, *The Labour Injunction*, Ruined me as a Labour Lawyer and Made Me as an Academic' (2002) 29 *Journal of Law & Society* 657 for a lively autobiographical account of that tradition in North America and how it fits into American legal realism.

[43] See Deakin (n 22) 311–12.

[44] See Race Relations (Amendment) Act 2000, which inserted s 76 into the Race Relations Act 1976. The Disability Discrimination Act 2005 inserted s 49A into the Disability Discrimination Act 1995 to create a public sector disability equality duty, while the Equality Act 2006 inserted s 76A into the Sex Discrimination Act 1975 to do the same regarding gender equality. All of these were replaced and extended by the single public sector equality duty contained in s 149 of the Equality Act 2010.

[45] See in particular Arts 8, 9 and 14 of the European Convention of Human Rights 1950, setting out, respectively, the right to respect for privacy and family life, the right to freedom of thought, conscience and religion, and the provision for rights and freedoms under the Convention to be secured without discrimination.

review jurisdiction has nonetheless meant there is an easily identifiable set of judicial analyses of the place, if any, for equality considerations when public authorities exert power. This provides a valuable source of data through which to investigate how judges over time have required (or not) public bodies to take account of claims to equal treatment, and more generally to pursue equality. Indeed, comparison between purely common law judicial review reasoning and that under the various relevant statutory provisions might be revelatory in itself about how adjudication works. Imaginative research design may also permit learning about the influence of identity and experience on judicial decision-making.

There is, of course, existing work on which to build.[46] The developments I advocate are to ensure, first, that the entire dataset of judicial decisions is analysed, and, secondly, to undertake systematic qualitative analysis that codes from a fully external point of view. As noted above, this should still uncover doctrinal insight. Technical points would, however, be perceived in a different light, in that the recurrence of analogous issues and analytical tropes would reliably be revealed. At the same time, the confines of purely internal legal analysis would be avoided by drawing on, and indeed contributing to, methodological developments in the rest of the social sciences.

As with the other examples, there are also important possibilities for widening out the enquiry. First, there is scope for comparison with judicial decision-making about public-sector equality analyses in other countries, perhaps particularly where there has been experience both of common law and either statutory or constitutional intervention.[47] Secondly, collaborating with industrial relations specialists and political scientists would be a natural way to enhance what could be discovered. On the one hand, the variable developments regarding public sector equality duties over the last 15 years are promising in terms of finding out more about the impact of what judges decide on what actually happens at work.[48] On the other hand, dramatic changes in the same period to the global economic climate, and consequently to governmental approaches to public finance and spending, provide an ideal environment for testing hypotheses about whether judicial deference to governments, especially on money matters, alters according to background economic conditions.[49]

[46] See eg S Fredman, 'The Public Sector Equality Duty' (2011) 40 *Industrial Law Journal* 405; M Bell, 'Judicial Enforcement of the duties on public authorities to promote equality' [2010] *Public Law* 672.

[47] This would be able again to build on existing work and in particular on S Fredman, *Human Rights Transformed: Positive Rights and Positive Duties* (Oxford, Oxford University Press, 2008).

[48] See further about the case specifically for such enquiry in Barmes (n 5).

[49] In this regard see H Conley, 'Using Equality to Challenge Austerity: New Actors, Old Problems' (2012) 26 *Work, Employment and Society* 349.

V. Conclusion

A lurking question for me is whether the features I have drawn from traditions of labour law scholarship, of methodological innovation and disciplinary openness, are somehow related to the lived experience of studying and practising law as it relates to day-to-day working lives. Does this kind of encounter somehow make it harder to keep 'law stuff' sealed in its own epistemic box? Be that as it may, labour law scholarship is surely richer for that collision, including in being able more accurately to capture the nature of adjudication, legal process and law than any enquiry that emphasizes divides between legal and non-legal worlds.

There is a curiosity, however, in the relatively minor role accorded to primary empirical work by labour lawyers, in that documenting law's actual and potential impact on working life in a sense merely returns to the empiricist, sociological strand in Kahn-Freund's foundational work about collective *laissez faire*. As I have indicated, the explanation may lie in the easy availability in earlier times of data from other disciplines on which to base empirically grounded analyses of legal phenomena. In other words, law's role then could productively be examined and theorized without research of the kinds I have outlined above, with enquiry into common law adjudication appearing perhaps especially marginal. My argument may be seen therefore as tracing the implications in the modern era of preoccupations that animated earlier generations of labour law scholars. In present conditions in the UK, my contention is that the proliferation of law 'in the books', the extensive enactment of individual rights, and the resilience and increasing confusion of common law adjudication call for more lawyers to participate in the production and analysis of basic knowledge about how all this is functioning.

It is from this perspective that that I greatly welcome the increasing turn I perceive amongst labour law scholars to empirical work on a wide range of topics.[50] Most of all, empirical methodological innovation can break open debate about legal technicalities and, in so doing, illuminate general understanding of law and its processes, at the same time discovering effective means for getting out of seemingly intractable impasses. For the theme of this work, my analysis suggests that labour law calls in distinctive ways for openness and pluralism in how research is undertaken, while at the same time leaving open that what is discovered will be revelatory about other legal topics and, indeed, about law more generally.

[50] A good indicator is the April 2014 workshop organized by A Ludlow and A Blackham on 'New Frontiers in Empirical Labour Law Research'.

5

Evaluating the Reflexive Turn in Labour Law

DIAMOND ASHIAGBOR*

I. Introduction

The aim of this chapter is to interrogate what, if anything, is gained by reformulating labour law as a field of reflexive law and governance. The tradition of Oxford labour law scholarship stretching back to Kahn-Freund has not of course typically deployed the terminology of 'reflexive law', though it has been preoccupied—as reflexive law scholarship is—with the regulatory techniques of labour law. At its simplest, the reflexive turn in labour law is an attempt to speak to concerns about the effectiveness of the traditional regulatory techniques of labour legislation and administrative regulation in the context of changes in the institutional landscape, and changes to regulatory objectives in the areas of industrial relations and social policy.

What has changed since the heyday of, respectively, collective *laissez-faire* and statutory intervention, as the dominant techniques of labour market regulation, and how convincing is 'reflexive law' in its attempt to explain or rationalize the new forms of governance or law-making within the UK labour market, and more generally with reference to the social and employment policy of the European Union (EU)? This requires a threefold investigation: first, is reflexive law *descriptively* an appropriate means by which to understand the range of regulatory techniques being adopted across the field of employment and industrial relations? How accurate a description of regulatory change are theories of reflexive law, or related discourses of 'responsive', 'new' or 'experimentalist' governance? Second, is it right, *normatively*, to adopt or advocate a reflexive approach to regulation, to the extent that such an approach may well eschew a substantive content for labour law? Can a reflexive approach be inherently 'neutral' as to

* I am grateful to Alan Bogg and Anne Davies for their helpful comments, and to participants in the Oxford conference (July 2013) who discussed an earlier version of this chapter. The usual disclaimer applies.

(regulatory or labour market) outcomes? What of those criticisms of reflexive regulation which contend that the rise of reflexive (labour) law runs in parallel to and indeed reinforces the neoliberal turn in economic policy-making? Third, is there *empirical* evidence to show that a reflexive approach to regulation works in practice? Is it true to claim—as theorists of reflexive law, responsive regulation or new governance do—that regulatory interventions in the labour market are more likely to be successful in achieving their objectives if they avoid direct prescription of substantive social or distributive outcomes, and instead engage in what one might call 'second-order' regulation by creating frameworks within which social actors such as employers can negotiate?

As we shall see, there is, with some reflexive law scholars, a (deliberate) conflation of the use of reflexive law (and systems theory) as a descriptive and as a normative term. Where I consider it useful to think in terms of reflexive law and new governance is that such approaches can help to address the problem which Judy Fudge identifies with debates about the role of labour law, wherein a specific form of regulation at a particular moment in time has come to be seen as *the* form, rather than *a* form, of labour law.[1] What strikes me about this current form of labour law, if it is right to call it 'reflexive', is that the turn away from substantive norms and towards proceduralization coincides with a weakening in the institutions of social citizenship which had enabled a certain interventionist, regulatory model from the late 1960s onwards:[2] the erosion in support for industrial pluralism from its post-war heyday, the demise in the social power of trade unions and the decline of the welfare state.[3] It will be useful to explore the relationship, if any, between the procedural turn and the weakening of labour market institutions in answering the normative question above: are we seeing a hollowing out of the substantive content of labour law from the baseline of the 'social contract' period of the late 1970s, in part in response to or as a result of the fact that traditional actors, trade unions, are sliding out of the picture?[4] Finally, the paper will examine reflexive regulation as a response to employment discrimination, focusing on the empirical question of the conditions under which reflexive law might provide a more effective means to realize the substantive goals of anti-discrimination law.

[1] J Fudge, 'Labour as a "Fictive Commodity": Radically Reconceptualizing Labour Law' in G Davidov and B Langille (eds), *The Idea of Labour Law* (Oxford, Oxford University Press, 2011) 121.

[2] Davies and Freedland date the period of regulatory intervention from the late 1960s, when governments in the UK sought to introduce a 'floor of rights' by means of statutory intervention: P Davies and M Freedland, *Labour Legislation and Public Policy* (Oxford, Oxford University Press, 1993).

[3] ibid; see also S Fredman 'The New Rights: Labour Law and Ideology in the Thatcher Years' (1992) 12 *Oxford Journal of Legal Studies* 24.

[4] It is worth noting that a key part of the evolution of this substantive content of labour law was through its *individualization*, in the enactment of individual rights in particular equality rights (in part in response to the requirements of EU membership). That such expansion in the substantive content could so happily coincide with a period of deregulation makes sense if one understands that the overriding commitment was to decollectivization: to a reduction in the power of trade unions in the workplace and within industrial relations in general during the 1980s and 1990s.

What will become apparent throughout this paper is that there are a number of ways in which labour law might be understood to be 'autonomous' when seen through the lens of reflexive theory. First, by understanding *law* as a social subsystem with its own internal values (as distinct from, say, the economy or culture) reflexive approaches draw on systems theory to argue that subsystems such as the law and the economy are self-referential and self-reproducing. Accordingly, attempts to use law to 'steer' the economy or labour market are fated to be ineffective since the law exists autonomously of the groups it seeks to regulate. Can *labour law*, in keeping with this logic, be understood as autonomous, in the sense of comprising its own subsystem? Second, in addition to the 'systemic autonomy' of systems theory, (labour) law may be understood to be autonomous in the sense that the move away from dictating substantive outcomes and towards the proceduralization which is such a central feature of reflexive law means this form of governance is empty of normative content: reflexive (labour) law is thus untethered from the sort of distributive or redistributive goals that characterize state regulation of employment relations. A question here is whether this indirect steering, wherein parties may be said to 'bargain in the shadow of the law' may be seen as merely laying down a procedural framework within which substantive outcomes are determined, autonomously, by deliberative processes; or whether there do in fact remain some substantive minima within the scheme of reflexive regulation.

II. The Reflexive Turn: From Formal, to Substantive, to Procedural Law

The reflexive turn traces a trajectory within modern economies from formal, through substantive, to procedural law. The chief effort, with reflexive law theories and related approaches, is to capture what is seen as a gradual and general shift from the top-down, rule-based, centralized, 'command and control' approaches which have traditionally characterized regulation, including regulation of the workplace. In particular, that the state is seen to have become decentred, moving away from directly determining behavioural norms in the workplace; what Julia Black refers to as the more general phenomenon of the decoupling of *regulation* from *government*, and the 'post-regulatory' regulation of self-regulation.[5]

I shall be focusing on how the reflexive turn might cast light on how one conceptualizes domestic, as well as regional (EU), labour law. But a similar story could be told, using slightly different terminology, about the international context. If one understands, as Brian Langille posits, the true nature of inter-

[5] J Black, 'Decentring Regulation: Understanding the Role of Regulation and Self Regulation in a "Post-Regulatory" World' (2001) 54 *Current Legal Problems* 103.

national labour law not as an exogenous 'tax', constraining nations from acting in their self-interest, but rather as showing them where that self-interest lies in the first place, and assisting them in achieving it, then this rethinking of purposes has profound consequences for the content and processes of international labour law. In particular, it obviates the need for a regulatory model premised on the imposition of duty, external enforcement mechanisms and sanctions. It also suggests that the role of an international standard setter, namely the International Labour Organization (ILO), is instead to focus on technical assistance, the provision of expertise and incentives, 'promotion', benchmarking, learning, and the co-ordination of best practices—in other words, the deployment of techniques of soft law.[6] Indeed, it could be argued that the 1998 ILO Declaration on Fundamental Principles and Rights at Work has ushered in precisely such a form of governance, wherein the ILO retains its role in laying down universally applicable norms, albeit norms that are limited to the four 'core' fundamental principles.[7] Langille contrasts the 'ethic of substantive labour law', premised on a social agenda wedded to the achievement of distributive outcomes, with a vision of international labour law in which a more nuanced appreciation of the regulatory objectives of the ILO constitution leads to regulatory techniques underpinned by an 'ethic of procedural labour law', and to better, but self-determined, outcomes.[8] The crucial observation here is that there is a (welcome) trajectory, away from the 'standard and entrenched' view which sees 'labor standards as detailed, universal, comprehensive, top-down, one size fits all, all at once, a-contextual, imposed, centrally enforced, and backed up with clout'.[9]

This development can be seen as part of a broader trajectory. Following Weber's distinction between formal legal rationality and material legal rationality,[10] reflexive law theories contend that 'formal rationality' or legal formalism (the exclusion of non-legal considerations from law-making and adjudication) has given way to 'substantive rationality' in which law is used as an instrument for purposive, goal-oriented intervention.[11] This is an observation with which labour lawyers are familiar: formal legal rationality or legal formalism can be criticized

[6] B Langille, 'What is International Labour Law For?' (2009) 3 *Law & Ethics of Human Rights* 47.

[7] The ILO Declaration on Fundamental Principles and Rights at Work 1998 covers four fundamental principles and rights at work: freedom of association and the effective recognition of the right to collective bargaining; the elimination of forced or compulsory labour; the abolition of child labour; and the elimination of discrimination in respect of employment and occupation. Alston's, critical, view is that the emphasis on soft promotional techniques ushered in by the 1998 Declaration is likely over time to lead to a gradual downgrading of the ILO's traditional 'enforcement' mechanisms; further, that the ILO remains only nominally in charge, given that the system of oversight or monitoring of these four 'standards' has become decentralized: P Alston, '"Core Labour Standards" and the Transformation of the International Labour Rights Regime' (2004) 15 *European Journal of International Law* 457, 458.

[8] B Langille, 'Core Labour Rights—The True Story (Reply to Alston)' (2005) 16 *European Journal of International Law* 409, 429.

[9] B Langille, 'Imagining Post "Geneva Consensus" Labor Law for Post "Washington Consensus" Development' (2010) 31 *Comparative Labor Law & Policy Journal* 523, 533.

[10] M Weber, *Economy and Society* (Berkeley, University of California Press, 1978).

[11] G Teubner, 'Substantive and Reflexive Elements in Modern Law' (1983) 17 *Law and Society Review* 239.

for its assumption that the freedoms guaranteed by private law (in particular, property rights and contractual freedom) and the 'spontaneous' workings of the market are sufficient to ensure social justice. What we witness, in labour and other social spheres, is a transition from the 'rule orientation' of formal law, to the 'result orientation' of substantive law, as the legislature 'increasingly believes it is both necessary and legitimate to intervene [eg in markets], with the aim of steering economic and social developments in a direction which conforms with its own broad political and social objectives'.[12] Instead of being subject solely to the individual agreement of the contracting parties, labour ceases to be a commodity like any other and becomes subject to specific and binding legal regulations that limit the freedom of the contracting parties and 'steer' them in certain directions laid down by the state. Hence we see limits on child labour, or the imposition of maximum working hours or minimum wages. Labour law is perhaps the classic paradigm of this process of 'juridification', an arguably inevitable consequence of industrialization and of the welfare state.[13] Juridification is, however, a loaded term, not least because the (common) law is already involved in the structuring of markets ab initio; the individual agreement of contracting parties similarly depends upon law.[14] However, what may be helpful is to understand the term juridification in a narrower sense, to refer to the specific phenomenon of state intervention. For example, Hugh Collins uses the term to describe legislative intervention in a field

> hitherto unregulated by law to any significant extent. ... Juridification therefore denotes the advent of legal regulation in an area of social life previously left to private power, which, though indirectly constituted by laws ... was not itself directly colonized and moulded by law.[15]

However, according to theorists of reflexive law, there is also a crisis with substantive legal rationality at the heart of the process of juridification. The problem with this purposive orientation is that such state regulatory intervention can rigidify the social sphere—including labour law and industrial relations—in ways which limit the autonomy of individuals or groups to determine their own affairs. The juridification of law and state which has occurred as the welfare state has matured and law is used in an attempt to 'tame' markets leads to a crisis of regulation; the direct regulation of the behaviour of social actors simply reaches the limits of its effectiveness.

These limits to law arise, so a systems theory-inflected reflexive law contends, from the functional differentiation of modern society into separate systems (law,

[12] J Clark, 'The Juridification of Industrial Relations: A Review Article' (1985) 14 *Industrial Law Journal* 69, 70.

[13] S Simitis, 'Juridification of Industrial Relations' in G Teubner (ed), *Juridification of Social Spheres: A Comparative Analysis in the Areas of Labor, Corporate, Antitrust and Social Welfare Law* (Berlin/New York, Walter de Gruyter, 1987) 114–15.

[14] As Sunstein puts it, '[T]he rise of the modern administrative state was based largely on a rejection of common law ordering. For the proponents of the administrative agency, the common law system was hardly unchosen or neutral, but was instead highly partisan': C Sunstein, 'Status Quo Neutrality in Contemporary Law', in *The Partial Constitution* (Cambridge, MA, Harvard, 1993) 88.

[15] H Collins, *Justice in Dismissal* (Oxford, Oxford University Press, 1992) 36.

economy, culture), albeit systems that are cognitively open, and can learn from and respond to each other. Social theorists, such as Talcott Parsons and Niklas Luhmann,[16] have argued that early or pre-modern societies are characterized by a low degree of differentiation into social subsystems, whereas modern societies are characterized by structural differentiation into functional subsystems—such as the economic system, the political system, the legal system and the cultural system—each of which has its own specialized 'communications medium' or 'system reference' that determines the way it interacts with its environment. What Gunther Teubner refers to as the problem of 'mutual indifference'[17] is that these social systems become so complex internally that they seek their validity only by reference to their internal rules and values; economics, for example, does not seek its legitimacy by reference to legal rules. So as these systems become more autonomous of each other in modern society, it becomes harder for the state to use law to intervene to regulate areas of social life. This, in part, leads to a 'crisis of the regulatory state', since law can no longer be used to 'control' markets.

One way out of this crisis[18] is the possibility of a transition towards more indirect means of regulatory intervention, once the direct regulation of human behaviour reaches its limits. This sort of indirect legal regulation, Teubner considers, is more likely to lead to flexible solutions, given that there is a continued need for regulation. Thus, one has to abandon the idea of effective external control by law, and move towards more indirect means of regulatory intervention. The role of regulatory law must be seen instead as merely triggering the self-regulatory process within the economy—the regulation of schemes of self-regulation and the structuring of negotiating systems (here, one can see a link with collective bargaining). In this theory of 'reflexive law', Teubner tries to find a middle way between formalism and substantive law. Thus, reflexive or regulatory law operates to provide a framework, a set of background rules, leaving actors to operate, deliberate or bargain in the shadow of the law.[19] Law thus becomes 'a system for the coordination of action within and between semi-autonomous social subsystems'.[20]

This insight, that the legal order has moved from formal to substantive (or

[16] T Parsons, *The Social System* (Glencoe, IL, Free Press, 1951); N Luhmann, *Social System*, trans J Bednarz (Stanford, Stanford University Press, 1995).

[17] G Teubner, 'Juridification: Concepts, Aspects, Limits, Solutions' in Teubner (ed) (n 13).

[18] Teubner identifies a third facet to the crisis of law as an effective regulatory mechanism, what he refers to as a 'regulatory trilemma', namely the danger of 'legal disintegration through society'. What this means is that increased regulation of social spheres is problematic because the forced inclusion of political criteria within legal rules endangers the integrity of the law; law loses its autonomy from politics if its only role is to pursue social objectives. See Teubner (n 17) 25–26. Of course, legal realists (and, to some extent, critical legal scholars) would argue for an open articulation of the political values inherent in law: see FS Cohen 'Transcendental Nonsense and the Functional Approach' (1935) 35 *Columbia Law Review* 809. However, see D Kennedy 'Legal Formality' (1973) 2 *Journal of Legal Studies* 351, especially 377 et seq, where he argues, in the context of adjudication, that there is a 'third way', a judicial method distinct from both formal rule application and substantive rationality, namely reasoned elaboration.

[19] See below for further elaboration of the 'shadow of the law' metaphor.

[20] Teubner (n 11) 242.

purposive) rationality—exemplified by a shift towards post-regulatory law—is one which is shared by those, such as Nonet and Selznick, who characterize this transition from one type of law to another in terms of 'responsive' law, or responsive modes of regulation.[21] As with reflexive law, responsive law is another elusive concept,[22] which does not seek to offer operational precision.[23] But it can be understood, evolving from a legal order which Nonet and Selznick label as containing elements of repressive and autonomous law, as an account of a legal order which focuses on substantive outcomes and aspires to be facilitative, flexible and adaptive to social needs.[24] Despite being based on conflicting theoretical models, one can identify strong parallels between the intellectual approaches on either side of the Atlantic, from which can be derived common features of a postmodern legal rationality.[25] Whether described in terms of a post-bureaucratic society,[26] or a functionally differentiated society,[27] responsive and reflexive law theories share a common starting point and a similar observation about the move away from the interventionist state, a shift (to use the language of 'new' or 'experimentalist' governance) from government to governance or new governance.[28]

III. Reflexive Law and the Autonomy of Labour Law

Reflexive theory positions law as one of several 'self-contained epistemic subsystems' into which modern society has fragmented.[29] Thus, reflexive law speaks to the autonomy of *the legal system*; but what of the autonomy of *labour law*?

[21] P Nonet and P Selznick, *Law and Society in Transition: Toward Responsive Law* (New York, Harper, 1978).

[22] RA Kagan, 'Introduction to the Transaction Edition' in Philippe Nonet and Philip Selznick (eds), *Law and Society in Transition: Toward Responsive Law* (New Brunswick, Transaction Publishers, 2001) xii.

[23] ibid xiii.

[24] Nonet and Selznick (n 21) 77: 'We call it responsive, rather than open or adaptive, to suggest a capacity for responsible, and hence discriminate and selective, adaptation. A responsive institution retains a grasp on what is essential to its integrity while taking account of new forces in its environment. To do so, it builds upon the ways integrity and openness sustain each other even as they conflict. It perceives social pressures as sources of knowledge and opportunities for self-correction.'

[25] Teubner (n 11) 244. See also P Zumbansen, 'Law after the Welfare State: Formalism, Functionalism, and the Ironic Turn of Reflexive Law' (2008) 56 *American Journal of Comparative Law* 769, 787 et seq; C Joerges and D Trubek (eds), *Critical Legal Thought: An American-German Debate* (Baden-Baden, Nomos Verlagsgesellschafter, 1989).

[26] Nonet and Selznick (n 21).

[27] Luhmann (n 16).

[28] See below for a discussion of collective bargaining as a form of new governance. See also K Armstrong and C Kilpatrick, 'Law and New Approaches to Governance in the European Union: Law, Governance, or New Governance? The Changing Open Method of Coordination' (2007) 13 *Columbia Journal of European Law* 649.

[29] C Tomlins, 'How Autonomous Is Law?' (2007) 3 *Annual Review of Law and Social Science* 45, 55.

In Luhmann's sociological approach, it is law and politics that are seen as the two main societal 'function systems'.[30] Ralf Rogowski considers the possibility of classifying the industrial relations system as a functionally differentiated societal system on the same plane as the legal, the economic or the political;[31] and from there, he proceeds to conceive of labour law as a sub-field of the legal system—a separate field of regulation and discipline—which has co-evolved with the economic, political and industrial relations systems.[32] This approach, conferring an autonomy on labour law as a field or system, chimes with some of the ways in which labour law scholars have (perhaps over-optimistically) talked of the autonomy of labour law: that labour law might be able to develop autonomy from common law or civil law principles. However, as Lord Wedderburn cautions, no branch of law can be 'completely autonomous within the body of the juridical order as a whole'.[33] This claim to autonomy on behalf of labour law is revealed to be partial at best: not only must labour law break free from the underlying logic and procedures of the common law,[34] it would also need to assert independence from common law institutions, the courts and tribunals.[35]

A more modest claim to the autonomy of labour law lies in the recognition of the industrial autonomy of the social partners; that the responsibility for standard-setting and determination of terms and conditions of employment has lain with the collective parties—although the specialized concepts, rules and institutions of (collective) labour law must sit within the general legal system. As Alan Bogg explains, qualifying the common impression that collective *laissez faire* amounted to state neutrality or the abstention of law from industrial relations, the British experience of 'voluntarism' in fact amounted to 'a very distinctive legal structure that supported autonomous collective bargaining as its central regulatory method'.[36] In similar vein, Keith Ewing shows how '[w]hat is significant about labour relations in Britain … is not the absence of state intervention in industrial relations, but the nature and form of that intervention' which historically took the form of 'administrative regulation' which lent support to and promoted collective bargaining, rather than statutory intervention.[37]

I would contend that reflexive labour law is 'autonomous' in the same way and to the same degree that collective *laissez faire* can be understood to be autono-

[30] R Rogowski, *Reflexive Labour Law in the World Society* (Cheltenham, Edward Elgar, 2013) 3.

[31] R Rogowski, 'Industrial Relations as a Social System' (2000) 7 *Industrielle Beziehungen* 97.

[32] Rogowski (n 30) 23.

[33] P Durand, 'Le Particularisme du Droit du Travail' [1945] *Droit Social* 298, quoted in Lord Wedderburn, 'Labour Law: From Here to Autonomy?' (1987) 16 *Industrial Law Journal* 1.

[34] 'Within the stockade of employment protection in Britain, the erosion of workers' rights by common law orientations in meaning and interpretation (sometimes by the very adoption in the statute itself of common law terms) is now notorious': Wedderburn (n 33) 7.

[35] '[A]longside a new substantive code, a new framework for British labour law may need institutions not merely administrative like ACAS but judicial, too, which take their stand initially on some ground other than the common law': Wedderburn (n 33) 22.

[36] A Bogg, 'Worker Representation in Collective Bargaining: Voluntarism in the UK' (2006) 10 *Electronic Journal of Comparative Law* 1.

[37] K Ewing, 'The State and Industrial Relations: "Collective Laissez-Faire" Revisited' (1998) 5 *Historical Studies in Industrial Relations* 1, 11, 16 et seq.

mous. In my reading of systems theory, it is the legal system—not a subfield within it—which can make a meaningful, Luhmman-esque, claim to being a self-contained societal subsystem. The assertion by Rogowski that labour law can be understood as an independent subsystem is difficult to accept.[38] He concedes that the extent to which labour law can be said to have systemic autonomy varies between countries, in large part due to the extent to which labour courts are autonomous from the wider judicial order. But this concession seems to me to lend support to the reservations which Wedderburn forcefully highlighted, about the restricted space which an autonomous labour law could occupy.[39] Hugh Collins goes further:

> With respect to treating labour law as a system in the intended sense, the forces operating against this seem immense. The social importance of work renders it too vital a subject for the political system to refrain from constant intervention designed to recapture control from the legal system, and the legal system itself, for the same reason, resists the evolution of a sub-system. Thus the ordinary courts constantly block the operations of labour courts.[40]

At most, it seems to me, reflexive labour law can assert autonomy on a par with the operation of industrial autonomy. Indeed, several commentators have observed that collective bargaining can be understood as a form of new governance or reflexive regulation, not least because some forms of 'old' governance do indeed contain within them 'new' governance elements, such as decentred regulation and participatory decision-making. A case in point is the governance of EU social and employment policy, discussed in more detail below. To the extent that reflexive theories are descriptively correct, rather than a sharp shift from one method of governance to the other, we can instead discern an evolving process in which different forms of governance are used contemporaneously, and even the most innovative regulatory tools (such as the 'open method of coordination' in the case of the EU) are revealed to have long-standing antecedents. Referring to collective bargaining but also making a broader point about evolving modes of governance, Visser notes how 'innovations in governance are rarely path breaking, but nearly always a blending of "old" and "new"; that it is not always clear what is "old" or "new"; and that the most fascinating puzzles usually lie at the boundaries'.[41] Further, as Estlund explains, collective bargaining in the workplace within a publicly administered legal framework (old governance) has many features associated with new governance.[42]

[38] R Rogowski, 'Industrial Relations, Labour Conflict Resolution and Reflexive Labour Law' in R Rogowski and T Wilthagen (eds), *Reflexive Labour Law: Studies in Industrial Relations and Employment Regulation* (Deventer/Boston, Kluwer, 1994). For a sceptical discussion of the case for labour law as subsystem, see H Collins's review of Rogowski and Wilthagen (eds), ibid (1998) 61 *Modern Law Review* 916.

[39] Wedderburn (n 33).

[40] Collins (n 38) 919.

[41] J Visser, 'Beneath the Surface of Stability: New and Old Modes of Governance in European Industrial Relations' (2005) 11 *European Journal of Industrial Relations*, 287, 287–88.

[42] C Estlund, 'A Return to Governance in the Law of the Workplace (and the Question of Worker

IV. Is There a Normative Content to Reflexive or Responsive Regulation?

The strength of reflexive law is that rather than attempting to control markets or impose certain distributive outcomes, law is essentially procedural. According to systems theory, the real purpose of regulatory intervention is (and should be) to induce 'second-order effects' on the part of social actors, as a more effective route to achieving stated objectives than direct prescription. Law will instead be focused on the regulation of schemes of self-regulation and the structuring of negotiating systems so as to create a framework within which individuals or organizations interact, with the state indirectly 'steering' social actors to a desired goal.[43] With regard to labour law, the aim is to facilitate self-regulation in industrial relations and at company level.[44] Given the focus on self-regulation, and what this implies for the interventionist state, does reflexive law have a normative content? As De Schutter and Deakin ask, referring to fundamental rights, what is the relationship of reflexive governance to certain constitutive values?[45] More broadly, does reflexive law have an ideology? This question is seen as particularly pertinent by labour lawyers, following from a concern that 'scholars who draw on systems theory do not necessarily take strong normative or critical stands on the implications of the diminution of state regulatory power that they describe'.[46]

This could go one of two ways. It may be that there is nothing in systems theory, on which the reflexive approach draws, which inherently 'lend[s] itself to straightforward ideological appropriation'.[47] On the one hand, the view of the market and the state as separate worlds does resonate strongly with the rejection of state 'intervention', in the name of the efficient operation of the 'self-regulating' market economy. This would seem to suggest an alliance between the deregulatory agenda of neoliberalism and reflexive law's decentring of the state, a particular concern in relation to labour law. A decentred state alters power relations,[48] with the state no longer able or willing to provide a countervailing

Participation)' (2010) New York University Public Law and Legal Theory Research Paper Series, Working Paper No 10-39, http://papers.ssrn.com/sol3/papers.cfm?abstract_id=1640566 (accessed 12 March 2014); republished in D Levi-Faur (ed), *The Oxford Handbook of Governance* (Oxford, Oxford University Press, 2012).

[43] See S Deakin 'Two Types of Regulatory Competition: Competitive Federalism versus Reflexive Harmonisation. A Law and Economics Perspective on Centros' (1999) 2 *Cambridge Yearbook of European Legal Studies* 231, 245.

[44] R Rogowski and T Wilthagen 'Reflexive Labour Law: An Introduction' in Rogowski and Wilthagen (eds) (n 38).

[45] O De Schutter and S Deakin, 'Reflexive Governance and the Dilemmas of Social Regulation' in O De Schutter and S Deakin (eds), *Social Rights and Market Forces: Is the Open Coordination of Employment and Social Policies the Future of Social Europe?* (Brussels, Bruylant, 2005).

[46] K Kolben, 'Transnational Labor Regulation and the Limits of Governance' (2011) 12 *Theoretical Inquiries in Law* 402, 416.

[47] P Zumbansen, 'Post-Regulatory Law: Chronicle of a Career Foretold' (Faculty Seminar, McGill University Faculty of Law, 19 February 2009). See also Zumbansen (n 25).

[48] H Arthurs, 'Corporate Self-Regulation: Political Economy, State Regulation and Reflexive

force to the inequality of bargaining power within the employment relationship and wider labour market.[49] On the other hand, as Deakin and Rogowski note:

> Critiques of the means used to implement the egalitarian and solidaristic aims of post-1945 welfare states were undoubtedly combined, in some cases, with critiques of those aims. However, the link is not inevitable. The concept of reflexive law has been used, in numerous contexts, as a way into a debate about improving the effectiveness of labour law interventions, and thereby of responding to the neoliberal critique of labour law.[50]

My interest lies in how values may be institutionalized in the course of regulating self-regulation. The reflexive law approach, by placing such faith in self-regulation within subsystems, raises the question of whether safeguards need to be imposed, whether it might be necessary to institute substantive standards from above to limit the risk of abuse in power relationships.[51] Without returning to the sort of result orientation of substantive rationality which was rejected in favour of reflexive law, this form of regulation nevertheless still bears some of the hallmarks of juridification, since the state is indirectly 'steering' social actors to a desired goal; it would seem essential for the regulatory framework to have such normative underpinnings if it is not merely to replicate formal law. A helpful comparison with Teubner's threefold distinction between formal, substantive and reflexive law is Habermas' categorization of the paradigms of law. Habermas finds a solution to the 'hopeless competition' between the liberal paradigm and the welfare-state paradigm in the 'proceduralist' paradigm of law, and answers the question of how the proceduralist paradigm (or reflexive law) can revitalize the liberal democratic project, and provide scope for solidarity, without succumbing to the two extremes of 'market' or 'state':

> The proceduralist paradigm is not distinguished from the two earlier paradigms by its being 'formal' in the sense of 'empty' or 'poor in content'. In pointing to civil society and the political public sphere, it forcefully singles out points of reference from which the democratic process acquires a different weight and a role previously neglected in the realization of the system of rights. In complex societies, the scarcest resources are neither the productivity of a market economy nor the regulatory capacity of the public administration. It is above all the resources of an exhausted economy of nature and of a disintegrating social solidarity that require a nurturing approach. The forces of social solidarity can be regenerated in complex societies only in the forms of communicative practices of self-determination.[52]

Labour Law' in B Bercusson and C Estlund (eds), *Regulating Labour in the Wake of Globalisation: New Challenges, New Institutions* (Oxford, Hart Publishing, 2008) 29.

[49] P Davies and M Freedland (eds), *Kahn-Freund's Labour and the Law* (London, Stevens & Sons, 1983) 18.

[50] S Deakin and R Rogowski, 'Reflexive Labour Law, Capabilities and the Future of Social Europe' (2011) University of Warwick School of Law Legal Studies Research Paper No 2011/04, 7, http://papers.ssrn.com/sol3/papers.cfm?abstract_id=1780922 (accessed 11 March 2014).

[51] Schutter and Deakin (n 45).

[52] J Habermas, *Between Facts and Norms: Contribution to a Discourse Theory of Law and Democracy* (Cambridge, MA, MIT Press, 1996) 445.

Whilst the Habermasian perspective on the three paradigms of law does go some way towards answering the question as to the normative content of 'reflexive' or 'procedural' law, nevertheless, it is difficult to see in Teubner's reflexive theories a means by which values can be embedded. Teubner does, however, point out that:

> The term 'proceduralization' is easily misunderstood from a technical-legal point of view. To interpret it as a recommendation to a 'post-interventionist' legislator to do without substantive legal norms and rely exclusively on procedural law instead would be to miss the point. … It is obvious that every act of procedural regulation has substantive premisses and consequences.[53]

Relevant here is the metaphor of 'bargaining within the shadow of the law' which is deployed by both reflexive theorists and new governance theorists. Coined by Mnookin and Kornhauser to describe the law's influence on private ordering,[54] this term provides a way to think about the interaction between law and other norms. Thus, law 'casts a shadow' on negotiations and decision-making outside of the formal legal process, establishing the range within which informal settlements operate.[55] The crucial claim here is that law does more than merely dictate procedures, but does also have some sort of substantive content. Note Teubner's assertion that '[t]he mere existence of substantive law with its threat of sanctions creates negotiation positions for the parties … which ultimately affect the result of negotiation'.[56]

Nevertheless, in common with legal formalism, systems theory continues to assert the autonomy of law from other (value) systems, whereas Habermas argues that the responsibility for the failure of democracy in modern Western societies lies in part with the ethic of liberal legalism which has hidden behind a methodology that law is somehow a discipline distinct from politics and power.

V. New Governance in European Union Social and Employment Policy

Reflexive law remains, however, an ambiguous concept; there continues to be an unresolved tension in reflexive law theory between an equation of the normative with the factual on the one hand, and inclinations towards Habermasian regulative ideals on the other. This same tension is exhibited in many of the favourable

[53] G Teubner, *Law as an Autopoietic System* (Oxford, Blackwell, 1993) 66.

[54] RH Mnookin and L Kornhauser, 'Bargaining in the Shadow of the Law: The Case of Divorce' (1979) 88 *Yale Law Journal* 950.

[55] S Sturm, 'Law's Role in Addressing Complex Discrimination' in LB Nielsen and RL Nelson (eds), *Handbook of Employment Discrimination Research: Rights and Realities* (Berlin, London, Springer, 2005). Note, however, that Sturm critiques the 'shadow of the law' image as an adequate guide for shaping the relationship between law and norms, in particular, that Mnookin and Kornhauser's analysis focuses on law's formalistic aspects.

[56] Teubner (n 17) 34.

characterizations of recent experimentation within EU social and employment policy as examples of reflexive harmonization. In particular, in descriptions of the EU's regulatory experiment with the 'open method of coordination' or OMC—an experiment that is often characterized as an attempt to overcome the structural obstacles to pro-active EU policymaking, by resort to proceduralization.

Policymaking within the EU (in particular in the realm of labour law, social policy and employment policy) has long been constrained by conflicts between, on the one hand, state action (intergovernmentalism) and EU competence (supranationalism); and on the other, that between regulation and deregulation. Battles over the *existence* or *content* of regulation (rather than over the site or level of regulation) can be traced to the conceptions of the economy that have informed European integration. A particularly significant conception of the 'economic constitution' views the market economy as an essentially self-organizing system,[57] albeit one that requires a coherent legal framework to guarantee individual freedoms and the economic process. The ordoliberal conception of the competitive market order argues that the economy functions best when self-coordination of economic actors through market transactions or competition is left unimpeded by law. Although ordoliberal theory is by no means the only view of the economy underpinning European integration, it has shaped legal discourse, in particular in its view that the original treaties entrenched a particular version of the free market economic constitution.[58]

The dominant idea in ordoliberal and neoliberal thought, of the self-regulating market economy in which markets are natural or autonomous phenomena, finds an echo in systems theory, which also sees the law and the economy as separate though cognitively open systems. It is doubtless arguable that the adoption of a systems theory approach does not preclude an acceptance that law and social norms are constitutive of the economy. But alternative visions of the economy within legal discourse, which do allow for the possibility of market-correcting intervention, are essential if one is to construct a European polity able to move from economic rationality to social justice.

Given the difficulties of imposing regulatory solutions from the centre, the procedural turn has some appeal within an institutional context such as the EU. Several commentators have observed that the emergence of the open method as a technique of regulation in economic and social policy might best be understood in terms of reflexive theory,[59] whilst also at times acknowledging that

[57] ME Streit and W Mussler, 'The Economic Constitution of the European Community: From "Rome" to "Maastricht"' (1995) 1 *European Law Journal* 5, 8.

[58] See W Sauter, 'The Economic Constitution of the European Union' (1998) 4 *Columbia Journal of European Law* 27, 28.

[59] See D Ashiagbor, *The European Employment Strategy: Labour Market Regulation and New Governance* (Oxford, Oxford University Press, 2005) in particular ch 5; G de Búrca and J Scott (eds) *Law and New Governance in the EU and US* (Oxford, Hart Publishing, 2006); R Rogowski, 'Flexicurity and Reflexive Coordination of European Social and Employment Policies' in H Jørgensen and PK Madsen (eds), *Flexicurity and Beyond: Finding a New Agenda for the European Social Model* (Copenhagen, DJØF Publishing, 2007); M Dawson, 'The Ambiguity of Social Europe in the Open Method of Coordination' (2009) 34 *European Law Review* 55.

this reflexive approach might be a 'red herring'.[60] Put simply, the open method can be seen an example of the EU forsaking direct regulatory intervention in Member States, and instead seeking to achieve common goals not by imposing them, but through establishing a framework within which Member States are free to be 'self-regulating'. The open method is thus a form of regulation which aims to 'preserve spaces for experimentation in rule-making, and … promote regulatory learning through the exchange of information between different jurisdictional levels'.[61]

It is certainly true that the open method allows for regulation at one step removed. In one of the areas where the open method was first applied, the coordination of employment policies, the overall objectives are set by the European Council, but it is left to the Member States to set national and regional level targets to reach these objectives.[62] And where benchmarks or targets *are* set at European level, Member States are responsible for 'translating' these guidelines into national and regional policies, 'taking into account national and regional differences'.[63] Indeed, OMC is applied precisely in those areas where there is little or no Community/Union competence and where the main field of action is national, since it nevertheless enables Member States and the Union to co-ordinate their policies. OMC thus eases the tension between intergovernmentalism and supranationalism since it aims to achieve common goals without threatening jealously guarded national sovereignty. In sensitive political areas, the use of the classic 'Community method', with its centralization of policy formation is a problematic way of achieving policy convergence, whereas the open method would seem to be an ideal means of facilitating further Europeanization 'outside existing institutional forms'.[64] Employment policy co-ordination has forgone the traditional Community method of hierarchical lawmaking, in favour of the centralized setting of guidelines, benchmarks and indicators; their translation into national policies; and the periodic monitoring of such implementation by means, mostly, of peer review.

Further, as Claire Kilpatrick reminds us, traditionally within the EU, worker protection was associated primarily with hard law, whilst objectives such as job creation were to be achieved by means of soft law (for instance, through employ-

[60] 'The OMC should be rescued from its supporters as well as from its enemies. The literature is polarized between those who argue that the OMC is an architecture for reflexive learning in the EU … and those who think it is just another red herring': S Borrás and CM Radaelli, 'Recalibrating the Open Method of Coordination: Towards Diverse and More Effective Usages' (2010) Swedish Institute for European Policy Studies (SIEPS) Report No 7.

[61] C Barnard and S Deakin, 'Market Access and Regulatory Competition' in C Barnard and J Scott (eds), *The Law of the Single European Market: Unpacking the Premises* (Oxford, Hart Publishing, 2002) 218–19.

[62] Arts 145–50 Treaty on the Functioning of the European Union (formerly Arts 125–30 EC Treaty). See C de la Porte, 'Is the Open Method of Co-ordination Appropriate for Organising Activities at European Level in Sensitive Policy Areas?' (2002) 8 *European Law Journal* 38.

[63] Presidency Conclusions, Lisbon European Council, 23 and 24 March 2000, Bull EU-3/2000, 7–1, para 37, www.europarl.europa.eu/summits/lis1_en.htm (accessed 12 March 2014).

[64] D Hodson and I Maher, 'The Open Method as a New Mode of Governance: The Case of Soft Economic Policy Co-ordination' (2001) 39 *Journal of Common Market Studies* 719, 721–22.

ment policy, such as active labour market policies).[65] Since the worker protection and job creation goals were henceforth to be combined within the European Employment Strategy, there was a need for new regulatory tools—perhaps a hybrid between hard and soft law. It is difficult, for example, to envisage legislation on its own being a satisfactory mechanism by which to achieve job creation objectives such as 'full employment', 'employability' or improving investment in human capital. Thus, in the context of the Employment Strategy, an 'open' method of co-ordination arose which, in theory, allowed for flexible, decentralized, experimental management by objectives; this runs alongside the existing body of hard law measures aimed at worker protection—although in the years surrounding the launch of the Employment Strategy, few new legislative proposals were forthcoming from the European Commission.[66]

These new forms of governance can indeed be understood in part as a response to regulatory failure, in circumstances where Member States have been reluctant to cede control to the centre over social and employment policy. The difficult task of bargaining over divergent national interests in types and levels of regulation has been converted into a deliberative process, leading to 'non-hierarchical governance structures', and mutually acceptable standards.[67] Descriptively, the concept of reflexive law thus offers a valuable and promising analytical framework with which to understand the open method. But there remain several caveats. First, reflexive theories do not capture the entire reality of this co-ordination process. European policy-making is, after all, not concerned with self-regulation within subsystems, but rather, with the co-ordination of multilevel governance. OMC only partially fits into the paradigm model of governance envisaged by reflexive harmonization: it is arguable that the open method has not been fully internalized by key policy-makers;[68] there is a lack of 'ownership' of the open method, and of the (several times relaunched) Lisbon Strategy within which it sits.[69] The model of regulation favoured by theories of reflexive harmonization does not fully account for this reluctance on the part of the relevant actors to engage with the process in its entirety, or for the insufficient

[65] C Kilpatrick, 'New EU Employment Governance and Constitutionalism' in de Búrca and Scott (n 59) 127.

[66] For instance, the Commission envisaged the need to move 'from rigid and compulsory systems of statutory regulations to more open and flexible legal frameworks': European Commission 'Green Paper: Partnership for a New Organisation of Work' COM(97) 128 final.

[67] C Joerges and JNeyer, 'From Intergovernmental Bargaining to Deliberative Political Processes: The Constitutionalisation of Comitology' (1997) 3 *European Law Journal* 273.

[68] 'The governance of the Lisbon Strategy needs radical improvement to make it more effective and more easily understood. Responsibilities have been muddled between the Union and its Member States. There are too many overlapping and bureaucratic reporting procedures and not enough political ownership': European Commission 'Communication to the Spring European Council. 'Working together for growth and jobs: A new start for the Lisbon Strategy' COM(2005) 24, 10.

[69] For the most recent iterations of the European employment strategy, and OMC, see: Council Decision 2010/707/EU of 21 October 2010 on guidelines for the employment policies of the Member States [2010] OJ L308/46; European Commission 'EUROPE 2020: A strategy for smart, sustainable and inclusive growth' COM(2010) 2020; European Commission, 'Towards a job-rich recovery' COM(2012) 173 final.

involvement of stakeholders other than national governments. Further, account needs to be taken of the political reality of the operation of OMC, wherein Member States seek to conceal the European origins of certain policy initiatives. In the course of 'translating' European guidelines into national and regional policies, Member States appear reluctant to acknowledge the external sources influencing the domestic policy agenda, or seek to recycle existing domestic policies by adopting the rhetoric of the open method and the Lisbon Strategy to describe pre-existing policies. Such developments are inadequately accounted for in notions of 'mutual learning'.

Whilst the evolution of the open method of co-ordination and other 'new' forms of governance within the EU may provide a fit with certain aspects of reflexive or responsive theory, in that they prioritize experimentation in rule-making and the promotion of regulatory learning through exchange between different jurisdictional levels, 'self-regulation' is, I would contend, not an appropriate way to describe the relationship between the EU Member States and the supranational institutions. A better 'fit' can be discerned with those potential sites of reflexive labour law, such as voluntary corporate codes of conduct or the management of diversity within organizations, where the state is unable or unwilling to command changes in the behaviour of (private, economic) actors.

For these reasons, the normative question that arises from reflexive regulation's decentring of the state is less relevant in the EU context. There is a slightly different normative question; given the priority accorded to economic rationality within the European integration process, there is a risk that the outcomes of 'self-regulation' by Member States mirror the pre-existing priority accorded to the free market economic constitution. The open method of coordination of employment policy is modelled on—and, indeed subject to—coordination of economic and monetary policy for the Union as a whole, and particularly for Member States participating in the euro.[70] The version of OMC in operation for economic policy involves some rather 'hard' monetary policy co-ordination, especially in the context of the Stability and Growth Pact, enforced through multilateral surveillance and the excessive deficit procedure.[71]

What indirect steering does not appear to do in this instance is to provide a sufficiently robust normative framework to balance the economic policy discourse which continues to dominate EU employment policy. This has become even more apparent in light of the reforms to EU economic governance and

[70] See the 'Integrated Guidelines' for employment and economic policy: Council Recommendation 2010/410/EU of 13 July 2010 on broad guidelines for the economic policies of the Member States and of the Union [2010] OJ L191/28; Council Decision 2010/707/EU (n 69).

[71] At the heart of the EU's economic policy is the Stability and Growth Pact, a central part which is the Excessive Deficit Procedure, which seeks to enforce the requirement that Member States must not hold a budget deficit of more than 3% of GDP, or hold total government debt exceeding 60% of GDP. These limits are enshrined in Art 126 TFEU, and in Protocol 12 annexed to the Treaty. See J-VLouis, 'The Unexpected Revision of the Lisbon Treaty and the Establishment of a European Stability Mechanism' in D Ashiagbor, N Countouris and I Lianos (eds), *The European Union after the Treaty of Lisbon* (Cambridge, Cambridge University Press, 2012).

tightening of macroeconomic surveillance adopted since 2011—in particular in respect of those states which have received 'bail outs'.[72] The policy experimentation which is the hallmark of the open method in fact permits diversity only within a framework firmly wedded to sound public finances, comprehensive economic reform and restructuring of labour markets, thus limiting the extent to which Member States can depart from EU employment policy without also breaching economic policy guidelines and the Stability and Growth Pact. The European Employment Strategy, the Lisbon Strategy and the instruments of economic governance (the Broad Economic Policy Guidelines and the Stability and Growth Pact) establish the parameters within which Member States are free to be 'self-regulating'. In the absence of what might be labelled 'social benchmarking' or a strengthened framework of social rights, there is a danger that the open method will coalesce around the dominant criterion by which progress in employment policy has been evaluated, namely, an economic criterion.

VI. Reflexive Regulation of the Labour Market: The Case of Employment Discrimination

It is clear, not least from the high incidence of employer non-compliance with worker protective measures, that the traditional command and control approach to labour market governance, which has the state at its centre, has severe limitations. The numerous failings of such regulation are

> that the instruments used (laws backed by sanctions) are inappropriate and unsophisticated … that government has insufficient knowledge to be able to identify the causes of problems, to design solutions that are appropriate, and to identify non-compliance … that implementation of the regulation is inadequate … and/or that those being regulated are insufficiently inclined to comply.[73]

Reflexive law offers a solution based on decentring regulation. But it may be that earlier accounts of labour market regulation are of assistance here. Indeed, theories of collective *laissez-faire* sought to highlight, at a descriptive level, how the law played a comparatively minor role in British industrial relations, in particular in the 1950s and 1960, with the majority of the rules governing workplace relations emerging from collective bargaining between trade unions and employers rather than from statute. A crucial element of this story, though, to which the concern over the (absent) normative dimension of reflexive theory relates, is that even in this 'abstentionist' narrative, the state was far from *wholly*

[72] Presidency Conclusions, European Council, 24–25 March 2011, the 'Euro-Plus Pact', http://europa.eu/rapid/press-release_DOC-11-3_en.htm?locale=en (accessed 11 March 2014); C Barnard, 'The Financial Crisis and the Euro Plus Pact: A Labour Lawyer's Perspective' (2012) 41 *Industrial Law Journal* 98.

[73] Black (n 5) 106.

absent. Indeed, the state deployed law, and 'administrative regulation', as well documented by Keith Ewing,[74] to structure negotiating systems and to create a framework within which employers and trade unions could interact, and perhaps also facilitated solutions being reached through negotiation under the pressure of legal sanctions or in the shadow of the law.[75] The crucial point here is the state's role in structuring negotiating systems, even during the 'abstentionist' era, for example in its auxiliary support for union recognition; the question of how truly 'neutral and indifferent' the state was as to the *outcomes* of negotiations remains a pertinent one.[76]

One of the chief values in examining workplace law and regulation through the lens of reflexive law or 'new governance' is that it nudges legal scholars away from the over-preoccupation with 'old governance' measures, such as statutes, directives and the rule enforcement of 'hard law', as a means of achieving social policy goals.[77] At the level of the firm, the focus on litigation and ex-post rule enforcement has been inadequate to alter the behaviour of social actors or to restructure internal labour markets; it may be that such objectives will be better achieved through retaining legal remedies in the background, whilst 'mainstreaming' values such as equality. This seems to be particularly pertinent in the combating of discrimination, and for what Susan Sturm labels 'second-generation' employment discrimination, namely that which is less overt, deliberate or direct than first-generation discrimination, but rather involves manifestations of bias which are 'structural, relational, and situational'.[78] A plausible response to the failings of traditional command and control regulation is to focus on self-regulation, participatory decision-making and local problem solving, as regulatory solutions which are more likely than the external imposition of universal rules to lead to regulatory goals being internalized by the subjects of regulation.

Without returning to the sort of result orientation of substantive rationality which was rejected in favour of reflexive law, it would seem essential for the regulatory framework to have some normative underpinnings, such as respect for human rights or equality, if it is not merely to replicate formal law. Teubner describes reflexive law as structuring bargaining relations so as to equalize

[74] Ewing (n 37).

[75] Teubner (n 17) 34.

[76] A Bogg, *The Democratic Aspects of Trade Union Recognition* (Oxford, Hart Publishing, 2009).

[77] Although it is worth noting that some 'old' governance or hard law measures of EU social policy contain distinctly new governance elements, as with the case of 'social dialogue'. The social dialogue provisions (now contained in Arts 154–55 TFEU) not only oblige the Commission to consult with management and labour prior to the submission of legislative proposals; they also empower the social partners, if they so wish, to negotiate 'collective agreements' which can be implemented by Union instruments (Directives) or national practice. And not only does the process by which these Directives are drafted differ from the 'classic' method in which the Commission initiates legislative proposals, the actual content of the framework Directives so far produced under the social dialogue procedure has eschewed the prescriptive approach traditionally favoured in Directives. Such framework Directives do not aim at harmonization, but set out certain of the goals of European social policy, and leave a space for diversity and for self-regulation—either by management and labour, or at the national level.

[78] S Sturm, 'Second Generation Employment Discrimination: A Structural Approach' (2001) 101 *Columbia Law Review* 458, 460, 468–74. See also Sturm (n 55).

bargaining power, arguing that reflexive law in the context of the contract relation, for instance, seeks to 'subject contracting parties to mechanisms of "public responsibility" that are designed to ensure that bargaining processes will take account of various externalities'.[79] As Streeck warns, even in an entirely decentralized system, there exists an

> obligation of the 'higher level' of governance under the classical concept of subsidiarity to ensure the outcomes of self-regulation are compatible with general political objectives and norms of social justice, instead of being merely market outcomes or results of a contingent distribution of power.[80]

The anti-discrimination law regime provides a useful case study to illustrate this conundrum. The origins of the employment discrimination regime in the UK were very much marked by indirect regulation. Christopher McCrudden, examining the regulatory design of the Race Relations Act 1968, describes the model as one of 'enforced collective regulation … reinforced with a somewhat rudimentary command and control approach', only later on supplemented by statutory agencies and the individual rights/litigation model.[81] And more recently, the employment discrimination regime has witnessed a potentially game-changing shift to regulation which emphasizes the promotion of equality as opposed to mere 'legal compliance', the sharing of best practice between organizations, and the adoption of diversity management.

Through the introduction of what are known as 'equality duties' one can observe an attempt by legislators to deploy hybrid regulatory tools, entailing both the enforcement of individual rights, and the broader responsibility on institutions to 'mainstream' equality. These equality duties shift the onus from individuals to organizations, placing an obligation on public bodies to 'have due regard' to the need positively to promote equality, not merely to avoid discrimination. Prior to the introduction of equality duties, the emphasis of equality legislation had been on ex post rectification of cases of discrimination and harassment after they occurred, rather preventing such wrongs occurring in the first place. Existing legislation was geared towards responding to individual cases, rather than to addressing institutional-wide problems or organizational culture.

The public sector equality duties originate in the narrower race equality duty,[82] a response to the Macpherson Report into the murder of the black teenager, Stephen Lawrence.[83] Following failures in the investigation of Lawrence's murder, the report revealed institutional racism in the Metropolitan Police and highlighted the need for radical rethinking in the approach public sector organizations took towards addressing discrimination and racism in particular. According

[79] Teubner (n 11) 256.

[80] W Streeck, 'European Social Policy after Maastricht: The "Social Dialogue" and "Subsidiarity"' (1994) 15 *Economic and Industrial Democracy* 151, 171.

[81] C McCrudden, 'Equality Legislation and Reflexive Regulation: A Response to the Discrimination Law Review's Consultative Paper' (2007) 36 *Industrial Law Journal* 255, 257–58.

[82] Race Relations Act 1976, s 71 (inserted by the Race Relations (Amendment) Act 2000).

[83] Home Office, *The Stephen Lawrence Inquiry: Report of an Inquiry by Sir William Macpherson of Cluny* (Cm 4262-I, 1999).

to Macpherson: 'It is incumbent upon every institution to examine their policies and the outcome of their policies and practices to guard against disadvantaging sections of our communities.'[84]

For the short period between the implementation of the Macpherson recommendations and the coming into force of the Equality Act 2010, there were three separate public sector equality duties (PSEDs) covering race, disability and gender. The Equality Act 2010 replaced these with a new single equality duty covering race, sex, disability, sexual orientation, religion and belief, age, gender reassignment and pregnancy and maternity. The new PSED requires public bodies to 'have due regard' to the need to eliminate unlawful discrimination and harassment; to advance equality of opportunity between people who share a protected characteristic and those who do not; and to foster good relations between people who share a protected characteristic and those who do not.

Anticipating the introduction of the new equality duty in the government's 2007 proposal for a Single Equality Bill,[85] Christopher McCrudden interprets this development as part of an identifiable (if not necessarily intended) experiment with reflexive regulation.[86] The subsequent Equality Act 2010 not only imposed the single equality duty on specified public authorities (in their role as employers as well as in their performance of public functions) it also expanded the legal scope for all employers to engage in positive action.[87] There are hallmarks of reflexive regulation, at least in the 2007 Consultation Document, if not always in the 2010 Equality Act and subsequent regulations. For instance, rather than having a particular substantive goal imposed on them, second-order effects are to be induced by requiring public authorities—in the course of having 'due regard' to the need to promote equality—to undertake internal equality impact assessments, to consult and engage with stakeholders, and to construct their own solutions to inequality.[88] The focus is on consensus, partnership and mutual learning between organizations.[89]

[84] ibid para 46.27.

[85] Department for Communities and Local Government, *Discrimination Law Review: A Framework for Fairness: Proposals for a Single Equality Bill for Great Britain. A Consultation Pape*r (2007).

[86] McCrudden (n 81).

[87] '[P]ositive action is taken to be activity designed to improve the position, in terms of the distribution of benefits or dis-benefits, of a given social group or sub-group (or of several such groups), on the basis that its members suffer systematic disadvantage in that regard': L Barmes, 'Equality Law and Experimentation: The Positive Action Challenge' (2009) 68 *Cambridge Law Journal* 623, 623. Ss 158 and 159 Equality Act 2010 broaden the range of permissible positive action, allowing employers to 'enable or encourage' persons who share a particular protected characteristic (eg race, gender) to overcome or minimize identified disadvantage, or to permit more favourable treatment in recruitment and promotion of those with a particular protected characteristic if their participation is disproportionately low. The new public sector duties are set out in Equality Act 2010 ss 149–57.

[88] Department for Communities and Local Government, para 5.44. However, as Hepple notes, whilst draft regulations published in January 2011 required public authorities to publish details of the engagement they had undertaken when determining their equality policies, this requirement was abandoned in the final draft of the regulations in March 2011: B Hepple, 'Enforcing Equality Law: Two Steps Forward and Two Steps Backwards for Reflexive Regulation' (2011) 40 *Industrial Law Journal* 315, 326.

[89] Department for Communities and Local Government (n 85) para 5.100: '[F]urther action is

The question, however, is whether the preconditions for effective reflexive regulation are in place. First, whilst a hybrid model of regulation may be attractive to regulators as a means to overcome some of the limitations of the traditional command-and-control approach and its over-reliance on the individual complaints-based model, the current regulatory framework in the UK seems an ill-designed amalgam of old and new governance. As with the case of the EU Race Directive, the UK anti-discrimination law regime offers an intriguing prospect of hybrid regulation: a traditional old governance mechanism (such as a binding EU legislative act) which nevertheless contains within it the seeds for the development of new governance mechanisms (such as the scope envisaged by the EU directive for national equality agencies, ethnic monitoring and positive action).[90] However, in the context of the UK framework, as Lizzie Barmes cautions, regulatory innovation has been superimposed onto existing legal rules, resulting in measures that are 'poorly articulated with what is already there and in further inconsistent messages being given to the subjects of the various legal regimes'.[91] A particular example is the interaction between the gender and race duties which preceded the general PSED and the pre-Equality Act positive action provisions.[92] On the one hand, public authorities are required to be proactive in the pursuit of equality; on the other, in so doing, they risk contravening existing equality laws which are premised on a symmetrical model of equality and thus typically prohibit unfavourable treatment on grounds of an identity characteristic. It is not clear, however, that the extension of permissible positive action by the Equality Act 2010 has been sufficient to eliminate this potential incoherence between the public sector duty to promote and the symmetrical model of discrimination underpinning the prohibition of direct discrimination.

Second, the more reflexive elements of this regime, or rather the framework for providing a normative input, are arguably too weak or non-prescriptive to provide a sufficiently robust cue to steer organizations towards the attainment of substantive equality.[93] The new general PSED, with its requirement for relevant authorities to 'have due regard' to promote equality and eliminate unlawful discrimination does not prescribe a particular outcome, but defers to the exper-

needed to encourage good practice, simplify processes and explore the scope to develop streamlined approaches and minimise burdens on the private sector and public authorities alike. These might include encouraging good practice networks and considering the development of standard equality conditions for use in public sector contracts.'

[90] Directive 2000/43/EC of 29 June 2000 implementing the principle of equal treatment between persons irrespective of racial or ethnic origin [2000] OJ L180/22.

[91] Barmes (n 87) 635.

[92] Race Relations Act 1976, s 71 (inserted by the Race Relations (Amendment) Act 2000), and Sex Discrimination Act 1975, s 76A (inserted by s 84 of the Equality Act 2006). Section 49A of the Disability Discrimination 1995 (inserted by the DDA 2005) did not give rise to the same problems of 'fit' between public sector duties and positive action, as UK law on disability discrimination was never premised on a 'symmetrical' model of discrimination: thus, if the positive duty led a public authority to treat disabled persons more favourably than others, this would not amount to direct discrimination. See Barmes (n 87) 636–37.

[93] S Fredman, 'Breaking the Mold: Equality as a Proactive Duty' (2012) 60 *American Journal of Comparative Law* 265.

tise of local decision-makers. To do this, the given public body will need to understand the potential effects of its activities on different 'protected characteristics', which may necessitate some form of assessment or analysis, including the collection of equality data, for instance on the nature of its workforce or service users in order to understand them and better target policies or services.[94] However, as the Fawcett Society observes:

> [I]n the absence of clear statutory guidance and robust specific duties, there have … been mixed messages from government around the value and utility of equality impact assessments which has led to avoidable confusion amongst public bodies about what approach they should take in implementing the Equality Duty.[95]

In addition, government rhetoric has led to some uncertainty about what the 'due regard' standard means,[96] suggesting that public authorities can meet the equality duty without undertaking assessments, which are portrayed as 'onerous tick boxing exercises'[97] rather than meaningful consideration of equality impact. Indeed, the government-commissioned inquiry into the first two years of the operation of the PSED concluded that, whilst it was too early to make a final judgment about the impact of the equality duty, it was not achieving its aims in part because lack of certainty about what 'due regard' required was leading to public bodies being overly risk adverse and adopting unnecessarily onerous practices.[98] As Sandra Fredman's analysis of the case law on the PSED and on the earlier single equality duties has shown, judicial review of the 'due regard' standard reveals the courts' difficulty in reaching an appropriate balance between intervention on the one hand, and on the other, deference to decision-makers' conception of what equality requires.[99] The shadow of the law (the 'due regard' standard) has not been sufficiently robust to lead to the desired substantive consequences, wherein public bodies institutionalize equality norms. Nevertheless, the government review into the PSED declined to recommend the introduction of a statutory code of practice, despite the strong advice that such a code, in giving authoritative concise guidance on what the duty requires, would be the best way to reduce bureaucracy and over-engineering of compliance with the equality duty.[100]

[94] See Fawcett Society, *Policy Submission to the Review of the Public Sector Equality Duty* (2013) 16, www.fawcettsociety.org.uk/?attachment_id=2605 (accessed 12 March 2014).

[95] ibid 34.

[96] Prime Minister David Cameron's speech to the CBI, 19 November 2012, www.telegraph.co.uk/finance/economics/9687688/David-Cameron-CBI-speech-in-full.html (accessed 12 March 2014).

[97] Fawcett Society (n 94). See also Equality and Diversity Forum, *Submission to the Government's Equality Duty Review* (2013) para 22, www.edf.org.uk/blog/?p=22172 (accessed 12 March 2014).

[98] Government Equalities Office, *Review of the Public Sector Equality Duty: Report of the Independent Steering Group*, 6 September 2013, 11, 24; available at www.gov.uk/government/uploads/system/uploads/attachment_data/file/237194/Review_of_the_Public_Sector_Equality_Duty_by_the_Independent_Steering_Group.pdf.

[99] Fredman (n 93) 266: 'In attempting to prevent bodies from simply going through the motions of paying due regard to equality objectives, courts have intervened in specific decisions in ways which are unpredictable and inconsistent.'

[100] Equality and Human Rights Commission, *Response of the Equality and Human Rights Commis-*

Finally, if this experiment in reflexive regulation is to be effective, one would expect to see a mechanism by which the process of self-regulation is itself regulated. For Hepple, responsive or reflexive regulation in this context necessitates internal scrutiny by the organization, involvement of interest groups, and also crucially external monitoring or policing by an enforcement agency—in this case, the Equality and Human Rights Commission (EHRC)—the ultimate bearer of sanctions should voluntary methods fail.[101] This 'regulatory pyramid' is undermined where, as in the case of the government's proposed amendments to post-Equality Act 2010 regime, the powers, independence and budget of the EHRC are to be severely restricted.[102] The role and powers of the EHRC at present include the provision of information and advice; support for individuals and voluntary (advice) organizations; powers to conduct inquiries and investigations, for example, into discrimination in specific sectors of the labour market; assessment of compliance with the PSED; the issue of 'unlawful act notices' and 'compliance notices'; and the bringing of judicial review and other legal proceedings.[103] The EHRC's budget is to be reduced from a high of £70 million in 2007, to £26 million by 2015. In response to some of the changes mooted in the government's consultation process, the EHRC has countered that the proposed removal of the Commission's existing mediation and conciliation powers and aspects of its 'good relations mandate' could lead to an increase in 'lengthy and expensive' litigation by forcing private and public sector organizations down the more costly compliance rather than conciliation route.[104]

The Equality Act, at least as initially enacted, represents an attempt to move away from the prescriptive, rule enforcement approach of an individual rights strategy. This focus, on inserting equality considerations into organizational policymaking, is also manifest in the official encouragement given to organizations to adopt a 'diversity management' approach, not unlike the voluntary adoption of corporate codes of conduct.[105] As with these initiatives whereby private actors

sion to the Consultation. Equality Act 2010: The Public Sector Equality Duty: Reducing Bureaucracy (2011) www.equalityhumanrights.com/legal-and-policy/consultation-responses/response-to-public-sector-equality-duty-reducing-bureaucracy (accessed 12 March 2014).

[101] Hepple (n 88) 321.

[102] The future of the Equality and Human Rights Commission (EHRC) was considered as part of the Government's Review of Public Bodies in 2010. That review concluded that the EHRC should be retained but substantially reformed 'to focus it on the areas where it can add value'. See Government Equalities Office, *Response to the Consultation—Building a Fairer Britain: Reform of the Equality and Human Rights Commission Organisation* (2012) www.gov.uk/government/publications/response-to-the-consultation-building-a-fairer-britain-reform-of-the-equality-and-human-rights-commission (accessed 12 March 2014).

[103] Equality Act 2006, pt 1 'The Commission for Equality and Human Rights'.

[104] Equality and Human Rights Commission, *Commission's Response to the Government Consultation Paper: Building a Fairer Britain: Reform of the Equality and Human Rights Commission* (2011) para 27, www.equalityhumanrights.com/about-us/vision-and-mission/government-consultation-on-our-future (accessed 12 March 2014).

[105] Department of Business Innovation and Skills, *The Business Case for Equality and Diversity: A Survey of the Academic literature* (2013) www.gov.uk/government/publications/the-business-case-for-equality-and-diversity-a-survey-of-the-academic-literature (accessed 12 March 2014); European Commission, Directorate-General for Employment, Social Affairs and Equal Opportunities, *The*

take over responsibility from public regulatory agencies for setting and enforcing labour rights—through codes of conduct, labelling and investors' initiatives—the question arises as to legitimacy and effectiveness.[106] More specifically, in the case of employment discrimination, there is the concern that the business case for diversity typically contains ambiguity about the true role of anti-discrimination law.[107]

In recent years, and in particular since the Macpherson Report gave official recognition to institutional racism, diversity management programmes have been introduced into a range of public and private sector organizations in the UK, ostensibly to improve the participation and employment prospects of disadvantaged and/or underrepresented identity groups.[108] Seen through the lens of reflexive theory, one can characterize diversity management as the manifestation of a positive and voluntary effort on the part of organizations,[109] providing a framework for internalizing equality values.

However, the 'business case' for diversity is a common feature of both EU and UK equality discourse: we see this much in the UK government's consultation document which preceded the Equality Act 2010, as well as in the language of employer organizations, recognizing 'the benefits of effective diversity and inclusion policies' as providing 'sustainable competitive advantage'.[110] Not surprisingly, organizations seem to see the diversity rationale as being *primarily* about improving organizational competitiveness and efficiency.[111] In part as a result of this instrumental approach, there is a certain amount of 'conceptual slackness'[112] and confusion in the way the word 'diversity' is used in practice. A problem with the organizational management of diversity, as Lizzie Barmes and Sue Ashtiany note, is that the dominance of the business case occludes the origins of the equality guarantee in legal prescription. In their empirical study of diversity management in investment banks in the UK, Barmes and Ashtiany identify pitfalls, which would seem to undermine the aspiration of reflexive law theories to 'steer' social actors towards desired social goals by altering their mind-set. In particular, the very language of 'diversity' in contrast to 'equality' or 'anti-discrimination' can be understood as an a effort to distance organizational initiatives at creating a more diverse or inclusive workplace, from talk

Business Case for Diversity: Good Practices in the Workplace (2005) http://ec.europa.eu/justice/discrimination/document/index_en.htm#h2-4 (accessed 12 March 2014).

[106] See A Blackett, 'Global Governance, Legal Pluralism and the Decentred State: A Labor Law Critique of Codes of Corporate Conduct' (2001) 8 *Indiana Journal of Global Legal Studies* 401.

[107] L Barmes with S Ashtiany, 'The Diversity Approach to Achieving Equality: Potential and Pitfalls' (2003) 32 *Industrial Law Journal* 274, 278.

[108] A Lorbiecki and G Jack, 'Critical Turns in the Evolution of Diversity Management' (2000) 11 *British Journal of Management*, Issue Supplement s 1, S17.

[109] J Wrench, *Diversity Management and Discrimination: Immigrants and Ethnic Minorities in the EU* (Aldershot, Ashgate, 2007) 9.

[110] Confederation of British Industry, Preliminary submission to Discrimination Law Review (2006) in Department for Communities and Local Government (n 85) 8.

[111] Wrench (n 109) 3.

[112] ibid 4.

of equality or equal opportunities, 'given that those expressions are commonly associated with regulatory interventions'.[113]

Similarly, writing on the US experience, Lauren Edelman and her co-authors observe that broader management interests tend to dampen any commitment to workplace equality goals, with diversity management being used as means of achieving pre-existing employer goals, recasting grievances in ways that downplay legal issues, and avoiding some elements of the equality agenda. Ultimately, Edelman et al see employers as domesticating legal norms to serve their own managerial ends.[114] The problem of non-compliance, in particular with worker protective standards, motivates the appeal to reflexive theory to assist with rethinking regulatory design. And homing in on internal management systems as a target for regulation is a means to circumvent the inadequacies of command-and-control regulation.[115] But what the difficulty of integrating the legal and organizational perspectives in the example of diversity management illustrates is the problem of translating state goals (equality) into managerial norms (business-friendly diversity).

VII. Conclusion

There is, with some reflexive law scholars, a conflation of the use of reflexive law (and systems theory) as a descriptive and as a normative term. Teubner, on the one hand, offers a descriptive account of the crisis of regulatory/substantive law and the evolution of reflexive law; but on the other hand, argues that reflexive law should be seen as an answer to the crisis.[116] However, it is difficult to see in reflexive theories a means by which societies can institutionalize or embed values given that, in common with legal formalism, reflexive theories assert the independence of law from other (value) systems. My argument is that reflexive law approaches do have some explanatory power, and can help shed light, in particular on the genesis and ongoing evolution of hybrid or structural approaches to workplace governance, especially with regard to employment discrimination. Ultimately, though, I would contend that there is an imperfect 'fit' between theories of reflexive law and the development of new forms of labour law and governance within the UK and the EU. Further, the problem of lack of normative vision, for many, presents an objection to democratic experimentalist proposals in general, and in the employment discrimination context

[113] ibid 278.

[114] LB Edelman, S Riggs Fuller and I Mara-Drita, 'Diversity Rhetoric and the Managerialization of Law (2001) 106 *American Journal of Sociology* 1589.

[115] D Doorey, 'A Model of Responsive Workplace Law' (2012) 50 *Osgoode Hall Law Journal*, 47.

[116] 'Here my aim is to defend the dual character of the idea of reflexive law as both normative and analytic. Reflexion in law means both empirical analysis and normative evaluation': Teubner (n 53) 69.

in particular. What needs to be more convincingly articulated is the difference between reflexive regulation and deregulation or non-regulation.[117]

As in the case of corporate codes of conduct and other instances of private lawmaking, in what ways can we distinguish reflexive regulation from the mere exercise of corporate or institutional power, unless there is countervailing power granted to the other party in the bargaining arrangement, to ensure outcomes of deliberation are not merely market outcomes but reflect general political objectives and norms of social justice?

[117] See McCrudden (n 81) 258, arguing that the proposals for reform of the UK anti-discrimination law regime in the 2007 Consultation Document could equally be seen as an instance of neoliberal deregulation or non-regulation; see also Black (n 5).

Part II

Labour Law's Autonomy: Core Organizing Concepts

6

Autonomous Concepts in Labour Law? The Complexities of the Employing Enterprise Revisited

JEREMIAS PRASSL*

Writing in 2006 in a chapter entitled 'The Complexities of the Employing Enterprise', Paul Davies and Mark Freedland noted the importance of different perspectives in labour law, suggesting that the debate as to the appropriate scope of employment law coverage might

> best be understood from an unfamiliar perspective, indeed initially a counterintuitive one, [where the] problem lies not in the binary analysis of the worker, but in the unitary analysis of the employer.[1]

The present chapter hopes to return to this challenge. Its structure builds on previous work which has identified a range of factors that have come to shape a unitary notion of the employer, constituted as a single counterparty to the contract of employment in all circumstances:[2] from the original language and

* Parts of this contribution draw on my doctoral research, funded by the AHRC (AH/I012826/1). I am deeply grateful to my supervisor, Professor Mark Freedland, my examiners, Professors Paul Davies and Simon Deakin, and my fellow editors for comments and discussion. The usual disclaimers apply. For a fuller account of the notions developed, see J Prassl, *The Concept of the Employer* (Oxford, Oxford University Press, 2015) chs 5 and 6.

[1] P Davies and M Freedland, 'The Complexities of the Employing Enterprise' in G Davidov and B Langile (eds), *Boundaries and Frontiers of Labour Law* (Oxford, Hart Publishing, 2006) 273.

[2] J Prassl, 'The Notion of the Employer' (2013) 129 *Law Quarterly Review* 380. The present use of the word 'unitary' is not the only one seen in the literature. In Deakin's work on the evolution of the contract of employment, for example, 'unitary' denotes the single status that has emerged for all employees, distinct from that of independent contractors: S Deakin, 'The Evolution of the Contract of Employment, 1900 to 1950—The Influence of the Welfare State' in N Whiteside and R Salais (eds), *Governance, Industry and Labour Markets in Britain and France—The Modernising State in the Mid-Twentieth Century* (Routledge, 1998) 225.

fact patterns of early master and servant cases[3] to the role of the contract of employment[4] and limited liability companies.[5]

Following a brief exposition of these factors and the problems they cause for the scope of employment law, discussion will turn to scrutinizing each category in the light of recent developments in disciplines closely related to, but traditionally seen as autonomous from, labour law—in particular, the general law of obligations and company law. It will be suggested that the law has developed considerably in each of these areas, developing flexible solutions in response to complex modern-day fact patterns. Employment law's unitary notion of the employer is thus characterized as a problematic case of *conceptual* autonomy, resulting in 'constant and increasing counter-factuality'.[6] A concluding section briefly explores whether this development might be driven by the discipline's strong sense of *normative* autonomy,[7] and whether that link is an inherently necessary one.

I. The Unitary Notion of the Employer

Employment law's near-exclusive focus on the notion of the employee has played a significant role in shaping the unitary notion of the employer. This is not necessarily surprising, given the discipline's traditional focus on analysing and regulating the labour market from the position of the worker—in spite, perhaps, of Lord Wedderburn's famous remark that '[m]ost workers want nothing more of the law than that it should leave them alone'.[8] What started out as the purpose of employment law, in the sense of rebalancing the employee's inequality of bargaining power inherent in the employment relationship,[9] however, soon began to impact on the conceptual question as to which apparatus could best achieve that aim: a conceptual vacuum developed on the non-worker side of the employment relationship, filled by a vague notion reminiscent of old concepts such as the servant's master, and implemented through a conceptual apparatus befitting that period. Three factors in particular can be identified as having filled the conceptual void.

The unitary notion of the employer, first, maps closely onto the language and concepts surrounding *the master*, to be found in the common law long before a contract of service evolved.[10] That understanding was then carried over until

[3] S Deakin and F Wilkinson, *The Law of the Labour Market* (Oxford, Oxford University Press, 2005) 43.

[4] M Freedland, *The Personal Employment Contract* (Oxford, Oxford University Press, 2003) 40.

[5] R Coase, 'The Nature of the Firm' (1937) 4 *Economica* 386.

[6] Davies and Freedland (n 1) 274.

[7] H Collins, 'Labour Law as a Vocation' (1989) 105 *Law Quarterly Review* 463

[8] K Wedderburn, *The Worker and the Law*, 2nd edn (Harmondsworth, Penguin, 1971) 1.

[9] M Freedland and P Davies, *Kahn-Freund's Labour and the Law* (Stevens, 1983) 14, 69.

[10] A Merritt, 'Control v Economic Reality: Defining the Contract of Employment' [1982] *Australian Business Law Review* 105.

today by the role of contract as the key organizing device of the employment relationship, and the limited liability company as the predominant legal form of the employer.

In 1967, Lord Wedderburn famously referred to contract as the 'fundamental legal institution' of labour law.[11] Whilst Simon Deakin has convincingly challenged the traditional assumption that a common law system of employment law, based on freedom of contract, pre-dated the welfare state,[12] the institution of the contract and its connected doctrines have nonetheless had a fundamental effect on the perception of the employment relationship in general, and the employer as work-taking counterparty to a contract of service in particular. By looking at the vast majority of personal work relationships through the contractual prism, a unitary view of the employing entity is likely to emerge: if the exchange of wage and work is characterized as a bilateral contractual relationship, emphasis shifts to a single work-taking counterparty at the non-employee end. When used as the central category of personal work relationships, the contract of employment has a strong normative function. In substantive terms, the most significant influence of a contractual analysis in the employment context is its inherent emphasis on *bilateral* relationships between two individual parties. The nature of the implied contract under consideration in temporary agency work cases such as *James* illustrates this fundamental attachment to the notion of unilateral relationships: even clearly multilateral scenarios are tackled through several bilateral contracts.[13]

The perception of companies as anthropomorphic individual units as a result of separate legal personality is the third factor contributing to the historical assumption that the employer must be a singular entity, substantively identical across all different domains of employment law. Despite a multitude of actors, from employees and management to a board of directors and shareholders,[14] it has become a singular focal point for a unitary conception of the corporate entity, with powers and responsibilities perceived in anthropomorphic terms—a notion to which employment relationships then fasten. The legal boundaries of the company are thus set not at the economic remit of all those involved, but on a far narrower basis, shaped by two closely related doctrines: separate legal personality and limited liability.[15] The potential for abuse of this limited

[11] K Wedderburn, Cases and Materials on Labour Law (Cambridge, Cambridge University Press, 1967) 1.

[12] Deakin and Wilkinson (n 3).

[13] *James v London Borough of Greenwich* [2008] EWCA Civ 34, [2008] ICR 577 [5] (Mummery LJ). Despite dicta to the contrary in *Stephenson v Delphi Diesel Systems Ltd* [2003] ICR 471 (EAT) [53], the potential of multiparty contracts is not entirely barred: *Dacas v Brook Street Bureau (UK) Ltd* [2004] EWCA Civ 217, [2004] ICR 1437 [20], [78]; *Cable & Wireless Plc v Muscat* [2006] EWCA Civ 220, [2006] ICR 975 [41].

[14] A Berle and G Means, *The Modern Corporation and Private Property* (London, Macmillan, 1939) 119.

[15] *Salomon v Salomon & Co Ltd* [1897] AC 22 (HL). Though the rules for incorporation are found in statute. The Companies Act 2006, s 3(1)–(3) defines limited liability companies, and Part II of the Act sets out the incorporation process.

liability arrangement is rarely doubted; the courts have nonetheless provided clear affirmation of the 'right … inherent in our corporate law'[16] to rely on the principles expounded in *Salomon* in deliberately structuring corporate groups to parcel out liability.[17]

Given recent economic and social developments, the unitary notion of the employer as shaped by these historic factors increasingly poses significant regulatory problems, challenging the scope and application of employment law norms in complex multilateral scenarios—from the development of 'atypical' forms of work[18] to new economic models resulting from the vertical disintegration of enterprise.[19] The long-diagnosed crisis in the fundamental concepts of labour law[20] has therefore become 'if anything more serious, so far as employment contracts are concerned'.[21]

Whilst detailed conceptual work is beyond the scope of the present chapter, the need for more flexible solutions is clear—both as regards a broader understanding of the employment relationship in general,[22] and a more flexible, *functional* notion of the employer in particular.[23] One of the main difficulties with any such model, however, is its perceived incompatibility with the factors just identified. As the following section hopes to show, however, the unitary view is in fact very difficult to sustain once the employer is no longer seen as an autonomous concept in employment law: recent developments in all areas surveyed suggest that a far more flexible notion than has hitherto been assumed is possible, even necessary.

II. Revisiting the Unitary Notion

Within the narrow confines of employment law, the 'traditional focus on regulation within the confines of a single organization remains largely untouched'.[24] Any more flexible approach, identifying for example more than one entity as

[16] *Adams v Cape Industries Plc* [1990] Ch 433 (CA) 544D–E.

[17] P Davies and M Freedland, 'The Employment Relationship in British Labour Law' in C Barnard, S Deakin and G Morris (eds), *The Future of Labour Law: Liber Amicorum for Sir Bob Hepple QC* (Oxford, Hart Publishing, 2004) 137.

[18] S Fredman, 'Labour Law in Flux: The Changing Composition of the Workforce' (1997) 26 *Industrial Law Journal* 337.

[19] H Collins, 'Independent Contractors and the Challenge of Vertical Disintegration to Employment Protection Laws' (1990) 10 *Oxford Journal of Legal Studies* 353.

[20] K Wedderburn, R Lewis and J Clark (eds), *Labour Law and Industrial Relations: Building on Kahn-Freund* (Oxford, Clarendon Press, 1983) vi.

[21] Freedland (n 4) 26.

[22] ibid; M Freedland and N Kountouris, *The Legal Construction of Personal Work Relations* (Oxford, Oxford University Press, 2011).

[23] See J Prassl, *The Notion of the Employer in Complex Organisational Settings* (DPhil thesis, unpublished, Faculty of Law, Oxford 2012); J Prassl, *The Concept of the Employer* (Oxford, Oxford University Press, 2015).

[24] J Rubery, J Earnshaw and M Marchington, 'Blurring the Boundaries to the Employment Relationship: From Single to Multi-employer Relationships' in M Marchington et al (eds) *Fragmenting*

the employer, or even just an entity other than the immediate contractual counterparty, will at first glance appear to go against the three factors identified as crucial in shaping the received unitary notion of the employer.

First, there might be situations with more than one employer, or even different employers, depending on the specific regulatory domain in question: how does this sit with the meaning of 'the employer' in ordinary language and the historic evolution of fact patterns? A second implication of a more openly functional notion is that a search for a contractual link will no longer be the sole method of selecting the responsible party from an array of potential employers, which seems to go against the idea of privity, a crucial doctrine in the analysis of bilateral contracts. Third, in the context of complex corporate group 'employers', the idea of holding an entity that is not an immediate contractual counterparty liable could also be seen as a violation of each company's distinct legal personality. The following subsections turn to each of these three factors in order to demonstrate the absence of these perceived conflicts. Indeed, the opposite will emerge: in many respects, employment law's unitary notion of the employer is drawn much more strictly than general legal doctrine requires.

A. Language and Fact Patterns

Two factors have laid the foundations for a unitary notion: the singular, traditionally male, language used to describe '*the* employer', and the unitary fact patterns of early cases on the existence of a contract of service, which were soon applied as a fixed scheme to analyse more complex scenarios, even where that lead to highly artificial outcomes. Neither of these aspects, however, is conceptually as narrow as traditionally assumed.

The historic starting point from which the notion of the employer developed is the notion of the master, a single male individual in exclusive exercise of the control right over the servant: 'No man can serve two masters.'[25] Indeed, under the Master and Servant Acts the test of 'exclusive service' firmly entrenched that approach.[26] Even linguistically, the notion of the employer has, however, moved on, and can no longer be seen as admitting only of the current unitary interpretation of 'the *one* employer in all circumstances'.

Whilst it is not suggested that all departures from the unitary notion will map neatly onto everyday usage, there are two reasons why the gap between the legal concept and the general understanding will not be particularly large. Despite long-established assumptions,[27] there is no clear-cut law rule at common law

Work: Blurring Organizational Boundaries and Disordering Hierarchies (Oxford, Oxford University Press, 2005).

[25] *Yewens v Noakes* (1880–81) LR 6 QBD 530 (CA); *Sadler v Henlock* 119 ER 209, (1855) 4 El&Bl 570.

[26] Deakin and Wilkinson (n 3) 90.

[27] *Viasystems Ltd v Thermal Transfer Ltd* [2005] EWCA Civ 1151, [2006] QB 510 [76].

today 'that an employee cannot be the servant of two masters'.[28] As the discussion in the vicarious liability context of *Viasystems* showed, duality of employers is legally possible without creating much linguistic difficulty. Rix LJ, for example, embraced this 'possibility of dual responsibility' where '*[b]oth employers* are using the employee for the purposes of their business'.[29]

A second potential objection to address is the contention that the leading statutory definition of the employer in section 230 of the Employment Rights Act 1996 is firmly limited to single entities. The relevant subsections stipulate that:

> (4) In this Act 'employer', in relation to an employee or a worker, means the person by whom the employee or worker is (or, where the employment has ceased, was) employed.
> (5) In this Act 'employment'—
> (a) in relation to an employee, means (except for the purposes of section 171) employment under a contract of employment, and
> (b) in relation to a worker, means employment under his contract;
> and 'employed' shall be construed accordingly.

Upon closer inspection, this is not a direct, but an indirect definition of the notion, via the contract of employment. That model is more flexible than traditional analyses might suggest: there is nothing in principle to suggest that a contract of employment could not be a multilateral arrangement, therefore involving more than one party on the employer side.[30] The variety of different definitions offered in specific regulatory contexts, such as the extension in various discrimination statutes, is further evidence that even in its statutory definition, the notion is a flexible and context-sensitive one.

Seen from the perspective of the rules of statutory interpretation, 'the employer' is of course a technical term, as it is defined in various Acts of Parliament. A lack of congruence between a term's technical and ordinary meanings is not uncommon. Blackstone noted that whilst lawyers normally ought to see words in their 'usual and most known signification', technical terms should be 'taken according to the acceptation of the learned in each art, trade and science'.[31] In discussing this choice between ordinary and technical meaning, Lord Esher suggested that:

> If the Act is one passed with reference to a particular trade, business, or transaction, and words are used which everybody conversant with that trade, business or transaction knows and understands to have a particular meaning in it then the words are to be construed as having that particular meaning, though it may differ from the common or ordinary meaning of the words.[32]

[28] ibid [40], citing *Oceanic Crest Shipping Co v Pilbara Harbour Services Pty Ltd* (1986) 160 CLR 626 (HCA) [32].

[29] *Viasystems* (n 27) [77] (emphasis supplied).

[30] *James v Greenwich LBC* [2008] EWCA Civ 35, [2008] ICR 545 [20]; note also s 6(s) of the Interpretation Act 1978, which stipulates that in 'any Act, unless the contrary indication appears … words in the singular include the plural and words in the plural include the singular'.

[31] J Bell and G Engle, *Cross on Statutory Interpretation*, 3rd edn (London, Butterworths, 1995) 72, citing *Blackstone's Commentaries*, vol 1, 59.

[32] *Unwin v Hanson* [1891] 2 QB 115 (CA) 119.

Even if one were to disagree with what the words 'the employer' are capable of expressing in ordinary language, the focus for present purposes is on their specific meaning in employment law. Indeed, there is a clear presumption in favour of the technical meaning as long as the notion is deployed within the intended context.[33] The mere fact that a term has been defined in statute for some time, finally, does not suggest that its meaning cannot evolve:[34] 'There is … no inconsistency between the rule that statutory language retains the meaning it had when Parliament used it and the rule that a statute is always speaking.'[35]

The importance of fact patterns in shaping a unitary notion has similarly declined. Even if master and servant were historically an appropriate paradigm employment situation,[36] not all cases before the courts dealt with simple bilateral scenarios. As a result of the increasing vertical disintegration of enterprise[37] even the notion of a single company employer is no longer entirely accurate. The complexity of labour markets today has evolved drastically, to the extent that even relatively new models such as agency work can no longer be considered as atypical. As judiciary and academia take cognisance of these developments,[38] there is an increasing expression of unease as regards the 'morally … unattractive proposition[s]'[39] that may result from a strict unitary analysis of the facts.

The practical impact of these changes can be illustrated by reference to *Vamplew v Parkgate*.[40] The court there held that a worker killed at work had been an independent contractor, rather than a servant, emphasizing in particular that he had functioned as an employer vis-à-vis a group of men and boys engaged to work below him. The unitary conception as shaped by master–servant work patterns meant that by acting, in part, as an employer, Mr Vamplew could not at the same time also be an employee. Today, a similar analysis would not be followed, for example in the context of managerial employees. Whilst it is conceptually difficult to analyse the scenario with satisfactory analytical clarity,[41] there is no suggestion that a departmental manager in a large corporation, with the right to exercise a range of employer functions over his subordinates, would not *as a result thereof* be unable to qualify as an employee.

In summary, therefore, even though language and fact patterns were earlier noted as important historical drivers of a unitary notion of the employer, these

[33] F Bennion, *Bennion on Statutory Interpretation: A Code*, 5th edn (London, Lexis Nexis, 2008) 1206.

[34] D Greenberg, *Craies on Legislation*, 9th edn (London, Sweet & Maxwell, 2008) 702 et seq is the source of most of the following examples.

[35] *R (Quintavalle) v Secretary of State for Health* [2003] 2 WLR 692 (HL) [9].

[36] Deakin and Wilkison (n 3).

[37] Collins (n 19).

[38] *JGE v Portsmouth Roman Catholic Diocesan Trust* [2012] EWCA Civ 938, [2012] IRLR 846 [58]; E McKendrick, 'Vicarious Liability and Independent Contractors: A Re-examination' (1990) 53 *Modern Law Review* 770.

[39] *McDermid v Nash Dredging & Reclamation Co Ltd* [1987] AC 906 (HL) 912A.

[40] *Vamplew v Parkgate Iron & Steel Co Ltd* [1903] 1 KB 851 (CA).

[41] See Davies and Freedland (n 1) for a challenging further discussion of this point, which lies beyond the scope of the present chapter.

factors could today be seen as arguments in the opposite direction: employment law's concept is too narrow to capture the full spectrum of its economic and social significance.

B. Privity of Contract

The second factor identified as driving the unitary notion of the employer was the casting of employment relationships in contractual terms. The unitary view emerges as the result of analysing the employment relationship as a bilateral contractual exchange of wages and work, with a single party at either end. This is supported by the strict assumption that a bilateral contractual arrangement may have no impact on other parties: as a result of the strict rules of privity, the idea(l) of freedom of contract in this context is equated to freedom from contract.

In returning to an analysis of the role of contract law doctrine in shaping the notion of the employer, it should be kept in mind that the accuracy of Lord Wedderburn's characterization[42] of contract as the discipline's 'fundamental legal institution' is more limited than may at first be thought, both in its historical and potentially future significance.[43] That said, it is nonetheless important to engage with the underlying doctrine directly in order to show how it does not necessarily condition the current singular notion of the employer. Put at its most concise, the doctrine of privity in English law confines the effect of a bilateral contractual relationship to its two parties, who cannot impose a benefit or a burden on a third party.[44] As the following discussion shows, however, an exclusive emphasis on privity in contract law may frequently obscure the importance of other sources of multilateral obligations.

Whereas several continental jurisdictions have flirted with multilateral ideas such as network contracts to regulate the economic reality of multi-entity interdependency,[45] English law has eschewed these models for two reasons: privity, as just outlined, and a seemingly strong commitment to the principle of freedom of contract, in the sense of respecting the choice of group entities not to contract with employees or each other. Other ways of dealing with the issues raised by 'complex commercial and economic relations' can nonetheless be found.[46] Even before the introduction of a statutory avenue for the creation of

[42] K Wedderburn, *Cases and Materials on Labour Law* (Cambridge, Cambridge University Press, 1967) 1.

[43] L Barmes, H Collins and C Kilpatrick, 'Reconstructing Employment Contracts' (2007) 36 *Industrial Law Journal* 1 and subsequent articles in that special issue.

[44] But cf today the Contracts (Rights of Third Parties) Act 1999.

[45] G Teubner and H Collins, *Networks as Connected Contracts* (Oxford, Hart Publishing, 2011); J Morgan, 'Publication Review: Networks as Connected Contracts' (2012) 128 *Law Quarterly Review* 472.

[46] S Whittaker, 'Reciprocity Beyond Privity' in P Kincaid (ed), *Privity: Private Justice or Public Regulation* (Farnham, Ashgate, 2001) 180.

third party rights in 1999,[47] the courts had started to develop a series of 'juristic subterfuges'[48] in order to achieve the recognized need for flexibility. A notable example of this can be seen in the law of tort, and the tort of negligence in particular, allowing recovery for loss caused as the result of a contract, but not under the contract itself. Whilst a detailed discussion of the tort law exceptions and their particular problems (such as regards the recovery of pure economic loss, for example) is beyond the scope of the present discussion, several crucial lessons can nonetheless be learnt from the fact that even a contractual framing of a set of facts does not limit their legal analysis to a bilateral and unitary view.

Simon Whittaker has convincingly argued that 'true exceptions' to privity can, and already have been, developed by the courts. Whilst

> parties are free in principle to agree what contracts they wish, in most situations the law's response to this agreement is to classify it and regulate its consequences. … [W]here the consequences of a (voluntary) creation of a particular relationship fall to be determined by the law, there is no logical or conceptual reason why the law should not draw consequences for third parties from its creation not merely where this can be justified by the existence of an intention in the parties to do so, but also from the nature of the contract which the parties have entered.[49]

As a broader analysis of situations is thus both within the abilities and proper constitutional role of the courts, the question arises as to how and where such policy-driven exceptions should arise. There are two crucial limitations: context-specificity, and the need for clear-cut additional criteria. As regards the former, exceptions cannot become freely available, lest they subvert the doctrine of privity completely:[50] they can only be found in limited areas (such as employment law) in line with the demands of specific policy objectives.

The need for clear-cut criteria is expressed in the idea of *reciprocity*: 'qui sentit commodum sentire debet et onus; a person who enjoys the benefit must also bear the burden.'[51] Whittaker relies on the provisions of the Acquired Rights Directive (ARD), as implemented domestically by the Transfer of Undertakings (Protection of Employment) Regulations (TUPE Regulations),[52] as an illustration of this principle: with the acquisition of a business comes the acquisition of employment law obligations. Despite some controversy in contract law doctrine as to its precise terminology or mechanism, the principle underpinning the ARD

[47] Contracts (Rights of Third Parties) Act 1999.

[48] *Swan v Law Society* [1983] 1 AC 598 (HL), 611 (L Diplock); as quoted by Whittaker (n 46) 190.

[49] S Whittaker, 'Privity of Contract and the Tort of Negligence: Future Directions' (1996) 16 *Oxford Journal of Legal Studies* 191, 193.

[50] S Whittaker, 'Contract Networks, Freedom of Contract and the Restructuring of Privity of Contract' in F Cafaggi (ed), *Contractual Networks, Inter-Firm Cooperation and Economic Growth* (Cheltenham, Edward Elgar, 2011) 278, citing *Law Debenture Trust Corp v Ural Caspian Oil Corp Ltd* [1995] 1 All ER 157 (CA) 364 (Hoffman J).

[51] Whittaker (n 50) 261, quoting Coke, 1 Inst 230b.

[52] Council Directive (EC) 23/2001 on the approximation of the laws of the Member States relating to the safeguarding of employees' rights in the event of transfers of undertakings, businesses or parts of undertakings or businesses [2001] OJ L082/16; implemented in the United Kingdom today through the Transfer of Undertaking (Protection of Employment) Regulations 2006 (SI 2006/246).

and TUPE Regulations is a simultaneous transfer of benefit *and* burden. This is significant in two ways: the new employer, first, cannot take the benefit of an existing business without being subjected to the relevant 'burden', or employment law obligations. Second, 'it makes clear that for the future the employees' work for the new employer must be reciprocated by performance of an employer's obligations'.[53]

A strict unitary conception of the employer as an immutable entity is therefore not necessarily inherent in a contractual analysis of employment relationships. It should be noted that neither a particular context nor reciprocity between parties are in and of themselves enough to construe relationships beyond the contractual scope: reciprocity, for example, is *not* the justification for extending the relationship's scope; that element is primarily policy-driven. Taken together, on the other hand, these factors become very potent.[54] Their effect includes the imposition of clear outer limits in putting into effect these purposes: the reciprocity of rights and duties was at the core of the original relationship, so it should also form part of the additional benefits and obligations recognized by law as existing between contractual non-parties.[55]

Even if contract continues to play a central role in shaping the employment relationship, therefore, it does not have to play the limiting unitary effect traditionally ascribed to it within employment law: indeed, the courts are happy to move beyond it in a wide range of contexts, not least by relying on (and extending) tortious principles in the absence of contractual relationships and specific statutory regulation.

In *JGE*,[56] a victim who had been sexually abused by a priest whilst in a religious care home brought an action for tortious compensation. As the alleged abuser was no longer alive, a preliminary question arose as to whether the Diocese of Portsmouth (the trustees of the Diocesan Trust being sued for that purpose)[57] could be held liable vicariously. After an extensive review of the authorities,[58] Ward LJ unambiguously found that there was no contract of service between the bishop and the priest. His Lordship thus noted that '[b]ecause there [was] no relationship of employer/employee between them, then, if one [were] judging the question on conventional lines, the bishop is not vicariously liable for the tortious acts of the priest'. He nonetheless went on to enquire whether the bishop could 'be vicariously liable if the *relationship* [*was*] *akin to employment*? [Could] the law be extended that far?'[59]

In answering this question considerable reliance was placed on the decision

[53] Whittaker (n 50) 268.

[54] ibid 283.

[55] ibid 270.

[56] *JGE* (n 38).

[57] As the Roman Catholic Church in England has no legal personality as such, the judgment was framed in terms of the relationship between the clergyman and his bishop: ibid [18].

[58] Including *President of the Methodist Conference v Parfitt* [1984] QB 368 (CA); *Percy v Church of Scotland Board of National Mission* [2005] UKHL 73, [2006] AC 28.

[59] *JGE* (n 38) [31] (emphasis supplied).

in *Viasystems*, as clear evidence of the significance of the *role*, or function, of the employer in any particular area.[60] Indeed, '[t]he actual contract of employment [there] was treated as no more than an irrelevant distraction. Function triumphed over form.'[61] Ward LJ next recalled recent extensions of the second crucial ingredient in vicarious liability, actions within the 'scope of employment',[62] before turning to the policy considerations underpinning vicarious liability to emphasize the context-specificity of the notion of the employer: '[T]he time has come to recognise that the context in which the question arises cannot be ignored.'[63]

In order to determine whether the facts constituted a 'relationship akin to employment' for the purposes of vicarious liability, His Lordship extensively analysed how close the tortfeasor's relationship with the bishop was to one of contractual employment. Sufficient proximity was found, as the church could be equated to a multinational organization,

> with the Pope in the head office, with its 'regional offices' with their appointed bishops and with 'local branches', the parishes with their appointed priests. This looks like a business and operates like a business. Its objective is to spread the word of God. The priest has a central role in meeting that target.[64]

The 'relationship with his bishop [was therefore] close enough and so akin to employer/employee as to make it just and fair to impose vicarious liability.'[65]

It is interesting to note that whilst technically this decision was of course not a situation where an exception to privity had to be applied, it was nonetheless equally driven by the factors underpinning the proposed functional approach: context specificity, and a focus on the nature of a relationship rather than its form. Indeed, in that sense Whittaker's conclusion rings true in both scenarios: '[C]oncentration on one contract as the basis of liability in multi-contractual situations obscures the possibility of the creation of a bilateral entitlement between the parties beyond privity.'[66] Whereas earlier paragraphs showed how the *presence* of contract is not an obstacle to multilateral imposition of liability, the decision in *JGE* demonstrates how the courts have come to view that its *absence* is not necessarily a problem either.

C. Company Law

The third factor traditionally assumed to shape the received notion of the employer is the development a unitary conception of the corporate entity, with powers and responsibilities perceived in anthropomorphic terms—a notion

[60] eg ibid [39], quoting *Viasystems* (n 27) [55] (Rix LJ).
[61] *JGE* (n 38) [60].
[62] *Lister v Hesley Hall Ltd* [2001] UKHL 22, [2002] 1 AC 215.
[63] *JGE* (n 38) [59].
[64] ibid [77].
[65] ibid [81].
[66] Whittaker (n 49) 198.

to which employment relationships then fasten. From a legal perspective, the key driver here is the doctrine of separate legal personality and, as one of the consequences flowing from it, the idea of limited liability; that is to say, that shareholders can limit their economic and legal risk exposure to the value of their shares, and that claims can only be brought directly against the company itself.[67]

Exceptions to this rule have traditionally been characterized as the piercing or lifting of the corporate veil,[68] with labour law drawing on the traditional assumption that the common law is extremely hostile to the imposition of liability for a distinct legal entity's acts on the shareholders standing behind it: the veil may only be lifted (in the sense just outlined) in cases of fraud[69] or certain statutory provisions.[70] Whilst critics have noted the potential for abuse and artificial technicalities resulting from this approach,[71] a range of policy explanations have been adopted to support the strict line—most notably the idea that limited liability is necessary for the efficient functioning of public securities markets,[72] and the assignment of creditors to relevant economic units.[73]

The context changes significantly, on the other hand, where the shareholder is itself a legal person, ie a different company.[74] Such arrangements were not the paradigm situation at the origins of company law, with its emphasis on arm's-length dealing.[75] As Strasser notes, 'parent companies in fact present different policy issues and their limited liability should be determined by a different analysis.'[76] 'Changes to the profile of shareholders through the emergence of corporate groups and increased participation of institutional investors

[67] P Davies and S Worthington, *Gower and Davies' Principles of Modern Company Law*, 9th edn (London, Sweet & Maxwell, 2012) 207.

[68] S Ottolenghi, 'From Peeping Behind the Corporate Veil, to Ignoring it Completely' (1990) 53 *Modern Law Review* 338.

[69] The bar for which is set high: *Adams v Cape Industries Plc* [1990] Ch 433 (CA).

[70] For example in the Insolvency Act 1986, ss 213 and 214 (fraudulent and wrongful trading).

[71] O Kahn-Freund, 'Some Reflections on Company Law Reform' (1944) 7 *Modern Law Review* 54, 56; K Wedderburn, 'Multinationals and the Antiquities of Company Law' (1984) 47 *Modern Law Review* 87, 90.

[72] P Halpern, M Trebilcock and S Turnbull, 'An Economic Analysis of Limited Liability' (1980) 30 *University of Toronto Law Journal* 117 (as cited in Davies and Worthington (n 67)).

[73] The 'asset partitioning rationale' set out in H Hansmann and R Kraakman, 'The Essential Role of Organizational Law' (2000) 110 *Yale Law Journal* 387 (as cited ibid).

[74] P Blumberg, 'The Corporate Entity in an Era of Multinational Corporations' (1990) 15 *Delaware Journal of Corporate Law* 283, 285.

[75] K Hofstetter, 'Parent Responsibility for Subsidiary Corporations: Evaluating European Trends' (1990) 39 *International and Comparative Law Quarterly* 675, 576; J Borg-Barthet, *The Governing Law of Companies in EU Law* (Oxford, Hart Publishing, 2012) 58 on which the citations and structure of this passage build.

[76] K Strasser, 'Piercing the Veil in Corporate Groups' (2005) 37 *Connecticut Law Review* 637, 638; citing P Blumberg, 'Limited Liability and Corporate Groups' (1986) 11 *Delaware Journal of Corporate Law* 573, 575. I am grateful to Professor Jane Stapleton for drawing these articles, as well as further cases and materials on 'veil piercing' in the US context, to my attention: T Heiden, 'The New Limits of Limited Liability: Differing Standards and Theories for Measuring a Parent/Shareholder's Responsibility for the Operations of its Subsidiaries' in Practising Law Institute (eds), *Protecting the Corporate Parent: Avoiding Liability for Acts of the Subsidiary* (New York, PLI, 1993).

in the market for shares[77] provide a principled case for corporate shareholders to be treated differently from individual shareholders.'[78] This is compounded by the fact that employees (other than as wage creditors in insolvency) are a very specific group of claimants, who may appear to be voluntary creditors of the company, but who do not in reality enjoy the freedom to bargain for their protection as perceived in most economics literature.[79] The standard rationales become difficult to defend in situations where there is a clear economic unit across legally distinct entities, and the claimants in question cannot contractually adjust to this risk distribution. After some initial equivocation, the English courts, however, saw no reason to hesitate in extending the orthodox position to corporate groups.[80] It is therefore perhaps unsurprising that Davies and Freedland have concluded that 'ignoring the group structure will rarely be a policy available to the courts'.[81]

Upon closer investigation in line with the purpose of the earlier two subsections, however, the line may not be as clear-cut as it initially appears. In discussing exceptions to the doctrine of separate legal personality, Davies notes that there is only a narrow set of situations where such piercing may take place, in the sense of holding shareholders responsible for the debts or other liabilities of the company. While the rule in *Salomon v Salomon*[82] was intended to apply across the board, however, an 'impressively long' list of situations where the court have felt able to ignore separate legal personality has developed.[83] It is not surprising, then, that Easterbrook and Fischel find that '"Piercing" seems to happen freakishly. Like lightning it is rare, severe, and unprincipled.'[84] The problem is particularly acute in groups of companies. Writing in the US context, Cardozo J noted that '[t]he whole problem of the relation between parent and subsidiary corporations is one that is still enveloped in the mists of metaphor [which] starting as devices to liberate thought … end often by enslaving it'.[85]

Davies notes a potential path to resolving many of these puzzles, in making the 'apparently radical suggestion' that

> no single explanation for these cases will be found … on the basis that it is possible to decide whether to ignore the separate legal personality of the company in this

[77] C Bruner, 'The Enduring Ambivalence of Corporate Law' (2008) 59 *Alabama Law Review* 1385, 1432–33.

[78] Borg-Barthet (n 75) 58.

[79] cf the position of tort victims: H Hansmann and R Kraakman, 'Towards Unlimited Shareholder Liability for Corporate Torts' (1991) 100 *Yale Law Journal* 1879.

[80] P Blumberg, 'The Transformation of Modern Corporation Law: The Law of Corporate Groups' (2005) 37 *Connecticut Law Review* 605, 607–08.

[81] Davies and Freedland (n 17) 137.

[82] *Salomon v Salomon & Co Ltd* [1897] AC 22 (HL).

[83] P Davies, *Introduction to Company Law*, 2nd edn (Clarendon Law Series, Oxford, Oxford University Press, 2010) 32.

[84] F Easterbrook and D Fischel, 'Limited Liability and the Corporation' (1985) 52 *University of Chicago Law Review* 89, 89.

[85] *Berkey v Third Ave Ry.* 155 NE 58 (NY 1926), 61 as cited in A Crawley, 'Environmental Auditing and the *Good Samaritan* Doctrine: Implications for Parent Corporations' (1993) 28 *Georgia Law Review* 223, 223.

> class of case only on the basis of an understanding of the purpose of the rule which is alleged to require this step to be taken. This is true whether the rule in question is statutory, common law, or contained in a contract.[86]

This context-specific approach means that, for example, the resolution of a particular point will be 'a matter for employment lawyers and the vital interests of company law are not implicated, whichever way the decision turns out.'[87] Turning to specific examples of the group context just developed, the starting position is nonetheless the applicability of *Salomon v Salomon*.[88] There is no 'routine liability [of corporate group entities for each other], flowing simply from the fact of the existence of a parent and subsidiary relationship'.[89] This is not, however, because English law lacks the necessary conceptual apparatus: there are specific exceptions in both statute and at common law, marked out by a particular domain and additional requirements that are closely related to the purpose of the rules regulating that context.[90]

As regards statute, the Companies Act 2006, for example, imposes a range of obligations on shadow directors, defined as persons 'in accordance with whose directions or instructions the directors of a company are accustomed to act'.[91] This provision has been held to encompass corporate shareholders.[92] One context in which the provisions play an important role is wrongful trading,[93] the additional features to trigger parent liability being closely in line with the purpose of protecting creditors in the run-up to insolvency: '[T]he failure of the parent company to treat the management of the subsidiary as having an independent existence, plus negligent disregard by the parent of the interests of the subsidiary's creditors in the period before insolvency.'[94]

This limited, context-specific approach does not compromise the default position in company law: while a particular relationship in and of itself will not be enough to trigger liability, additional features in line with the purpose of a particular area justify the exception. Applying a single doctrine across all areas, on the other hand, would have asked the wrong questions, focusing on 'abstract, generalized ideas of entity separateness, and of "wrongful" conduct'.[95] Despite initial appearances, no significant doctrinal change is involved in achieving this result.[96]

The approach at common law is not dissimilar, with the ordinary threshold for

[86] Davies (n 83) 33.

[87] ibid.

[88] For a short-lived exception, see L Denning in *DHN Food Distributors v Tower Hamlets LBC* [1976] 1 WLR 852 (CA).

[89] Davies (n 83) 97.

[90] ibid 96–99, on which the following discussion builds.

[91] Companies Act s 251.

[92] *Re Hydrodan (Corby Ltd)* [1994] 2 BCLC 180, and *Re Paycheck Services 3 Ltd* [2009] 2 BCLC 309 (CA).

[93] Insolvency Act 1986 s 214.

[94] Davies (n 83) 97.

[95] Strasser (n 76) 657, 660–61.

[96] ibid 662.

ignoring the corporate veil set very high indeed.[97] That, however, is the *general* case; in the specific context of employer obligations different requirements may be in operation, as the most recent decision resulting from Cape Industries' asbestos manufacturing activities shows. In *Chandler v Cape*,[98] the claimant had contracted mesothelioma whilst working for a subsidiary of Cape plc; that contractual employer had ceased to exist by the time of the claim. The question therefore arose whether Mr Chandler could bring a direct claim against the parent company. Whilst a separate legal entity, the subsidiary had been managed as a 'branch of the defendant'[99] within the larger group of companies, the core business of which was the manufacture of asbestos-based products.[100] The court took the existence of a Group Medical Advisor and a long course of dealings between the entities as 'clear evidence that the Defendant was taking an active part in discussions relating to the health and safety of an employee of one of its subsidiaries'. There was no need to demonstrate full control over all activities of subsidiary, a focus on a particular employer function sufficed. 'It is enough … [to] establish that the Defendant either controlled or took overall responsibility for the measures adopted by Cape Products to protect its employees against harm from asbestos exposure.'[101] When it came to an application of the three-stage *Caparo* test[102] to determine whether the parent company owed a duty of care to the employee of its subsidiary, the court found that it had assumed such responsibilities.

In concluding his judgment, Wyn Williams J added a crucial note to 'dispel certain possible misunderstandings':

> [T]his case has not been presented on the basis that Cape Products was a sham—nothing more than a veil for the activities of the Defendant. Accordingly, this is not a case in which it would be appropriate to 'pierce the corporate veil'.[103]

The outcome on the facts of the case was not one of holding the parent entity liable for its subsidiary's obligations; strictly speaking it was found to have assumed a direct duty of care itself. Functionally speaking, this is nonetheless equivalent to the ideas developed in this subsection in general,[104] and the shadow director/wrongful trading scenario under section 214 of the Insolvency Act 1986 in particular.[105] The judge's final observation thus returns to the fact that the existence of separate legal entities, separated against creditor's claims by a corpo-

[97] *Adams v Cape Industries Plc* [1990] Ch 433 (CA).
[98] *Chandler v Cape Plc* [2012] EWCA Civ 525, [2012] 3 All ER 640; foreshadowed in US law by *Johnson v Abbe Engineering Co* 749 F.2d 1131 (5th Circuit, 1984) as noted by Strasser (n 76) 648.
[99] *Chandler* (n 98) [14].
[100] ibid [23], [24].
[101] ibid [49].
[102] ibid [72], [77]; *Caparo Industries plc v Dickman* [1992] 2 AC 605 (HL).
[103] ibid [66].
[104] Strasser (n 76) 648.
[105] Davies (n 83) 99. Written before *Chandler* (n 98), the relevant passage cites several cases, including that of a Cape subsidiary in South Africa, as examples: *Lubbe v Cape Plc* [2001] 1 WLR 1545 (HL).

rate veil, is not logically tied to the present unitary conceptualization of the employer. Domain-specific 'exceptions' to the corporate veil exist in a range of areas; their operation is closely aligned with the functional approach proposed.[106]

III. Autonomous Normativity, Autonomous Concepts?

The main aim of this contribution was to suggest that the development of a more flexible notion of the employer in response to the complexities of the employing enterprise identified by Paul Davies and Mark Freedland would not be incongruent with developments in the broader areas surrounding the legal notion of the employer. In returning to the three factors previously identified as key influences in shaping that notion as a substantively identical, singular entity across all domains of employment law, it thus hopes to have demonstrated the potential drawbacks of seeing labour law as a *conceptually* autonomous discipline. Indeed, as the law in each of the areas surveyed has developed beyond the original features that came to influence employment law, the case could be made out that an increased reference to (supposedly) 'external' developments would exert significant pressure for reform within employment law.

This assertion leaves us with an important underlying question as to how and why the unitary notion of the employer has continued to exert its influence over time. As Freedland and Davies have suggested, '[M]uch of the sustaining ideology for the unity of the employer and the bipolarity of the employment relation comes from within employment law.'[107] Put differently, the unitary notion may thus be linked to a particular normative underpinning of the discipline of labour law in general—if not explicitly, at least at a subconscious level. If the discipline's primary purpose is seen as the recalibration of a power inequality inherent in the relationship between 'the employer' and 'his' employees, between *the* master and *his* servants, a unitary notion of the employer is a logical corollary. When labour law's normative aim is understood as a rebalancing of power relations, the identification of a strong unitary entity as the bearer of equalizing legal duties becomes an important factor both in substantive and remedial terms.

Seen from this perspective, it is not difficult to imagine how increasing discussions by labour lawyers about a broader, even multi-level (and thus perhaps no longer autonomous), normativity of the discipline might thus support the underlying claim of the present chapter.[108] A fundamental (human) rights underpinning,[109] for example, might easily accommodate the potential range of entities

[106] This increasingly flexible approach to the purposive pursuit of particular regulatory aims is by no means limited to the examples discussed above. In EU competition law, for example, the ECJ has adopted a 'single economic entity doctrine' in dealing with infringements in corporate groups. See further R Whish and D Bailey, *Competition Law*, 12th edn (Oxford, Oxford University Press, 2012) 92ff.

[107] Davies and Freedland (n 1) 276.

[108] See eg the essays in H Collins, P Davies and R Rideout, *Legal Regulation of the Employment Relation* (London, Kluwer, 2000).

[109] See further Sandra Fredman's chapter in this volume.

to which different duties, correlative to the exercise of a particular right, would be ascribed as a consequence of the functional notion of the employer.

In concluding, it is important unequivocally to note that none of these conclusions should be read as distracting from the worker's perspective as the appropriate focus for the fundamental concerns of employment law, or indeed the broader significance of the distinctive *normativity* of employment law for a thorough and coherent understanding and operation of our discipline.[110] What the present chapter hopes to have achieved, on the other hand, is to question the extent to which a narrow *conceptual* focus—whether on a key concept, such as the worker, or in particular, on labour law as a conceptually autonomous discipline, to the exclusion of more recent developments in adjacent areas—may have come to hamper that larger enterprise. Put differently, the normative foundations of the subject should not be able to exert an unquestioned influence on the conceptual issue as to which apparatus could best achieve that aim.

Space limitations prohibit further development of this point; it should in any instance not be taken as a suggestion that there are no other good reasons for having a single, coherent concept of the employer—or indeed how such a coherent notion might nonetheless incorporate the more flexible approach outlined in this chapter. It is hoped that future work will be able to demonstrate how that shift towards an openly functional notion of the employer may be achieved.

[110] For recent discussion, see Freedland and Kountouris (n 22) 364 et seq ('The Personal Work Profile').

7

Uses and Misuses of 'Mutuality of Obligations' and the Autonomy of Labour Law

NICOLA COUNTOURIS

Leggendo non cerchiamo idee nuove, ma pensieri già da noi pensati, che acquistano sulla pagina un suggello di conferma.[1]

I. Introduction

This chapter was originally conceived as a paper for the conference held in Oxford in July 2013 on the topic 'Labour Law in Oxford: Past, Present, Future'. The conference programme suggested that the event was organized 'on the occasion of Professor Mark Freedland's retirement from his tutorial fellowship' to celebrate the discipline of labour law in general, and as shaped by Oxford labour lawyers in particular. The contribution of Oxford legal scholars to British labour law has been, and continues to be, distinguished and comprehensive, as that conference and this volume testify. Mark Freedland's crucial role in the development and flourishing of this *schola studiorum* is destined to be remembered as uniquely multidimensional and rich, as well as characteristically selfless and committed. While his research work has spanned across various legal fields, juridical institutions and legal systems, I think that it would not be inaccurate to suggest that his name is destined to be more closely associated with his ground-breaking work

* An earlier version of this chapter was presented in Oxford on 25 July 2013, at the Conference 'Labour Law in Oxford: Past, Present, Future'. I am particularly grateful to the organizers of the conference, and to Alan Bogg, Anne Davies and Mark Freedland in particular, for comments on earlier drafts of this chapter.

[1] C Pavese, *Il Mestiere di Vivere* (Turin, Einaudi, 1962) 134. Loosely translated as 'When reading we are not looking for new ideas, but [for] thoughts we have already thought of, that acquire a seal of confirmation on the [printed] page'.

on the contract of employment in English law. Throughout a long and fruitful (and ongoing) career, Mark Freedland has developed and coined—and generously shared with his contemporaries and with the next generations of labour lawyers—a goldmine of legal concepts, analytical devices, critical frameworks and normative arguments that have simultaneously and seamlessly shaped both *the* orthodox English law concept of contract of employment and *our* individual (and sometimes more heterodox and critical) understandings of the contract of employment. In particular, his original work on the concept of 'mutuality of obligations' in the labour law context has been acknowledged by his peers as perhaps one of the most important contributions to the modern understanding of the contract of employment.[2]

This chapter seeks to provide a critical reconstruction of how the original intuitions made by Mark Freedland in respect of the contribution of the 'mutuality' concept to the understanding of work relationships in general, and precarious work relations in particular, have been subject over the years to a long series of judicial transformations that have essentially distorted the original rationale that the author attached to the idea of 'mutuality of obligations', while at the same time distancing it from the mischief that his work was trying to address. That original mischief emerges clearly from the early pages of his seminal 1976 monograph *The Contract of Employment*, where the author, having briefly introduced the 'element of mutual obligations in respect of future services', went on to state, in unequivocal terms, that

> it is, in the view of this writer, a confusion of ideas to deny the existence of a contract of employment merely because the employment is for a short term and precarious. Neither of those factors is inconsistent with the existence of the contract of employment.[3]

The present chapter seeks to elaborate on the (few) uses and (many) misuses of the concept of mutuality of obligations that English labour law has developed over the years, while linking this specific analysis to the broader question of the 'autonomy of labour law'. Often, and variably, referred to in case law as 'an irreducible minimum … to create a contract of services',[4] 'an essential element of the contract of employment'[5] but also 'a necessary element in a "limb (b) contract"' (or 'worker' contract),[6] or 'the one important ingredient' for a contract

[2] There is virtually no labour law textbook that in analysing the concept of mutuality of obligation in the context of the contract of employment does not refer to Mark Freedland's seminal work in *The Contract of Employment* (Oxford, Clarendon Publishing, 1976).

[3] ibid 11. On a separate note, this may well be the first time a British legal author deploys the concept of precariousness in the labour law context, though it is arguable that, in his 1976 work, Freedland was predominantly referring to an idea of precariousness as equivalent to the casualization inherent to the succession of very short term contracts of service, rather than to the employment status precariousness that we tend to associate with post-*O'Kelly* labour markets.

[4] *Nethermere (St Neots) Limited v Taverna and Gardiner* [1984] ICR 612, 623 (Lord Kerr, dissenting); and more emphatically in *Carmichael and Another v National Power Plc* [1999] ICR 1226, 1230.

[5] *Stringfellow Restaurants Ltd v Nadine Quashie* [2012] EWCA Civ 1735, [85].

[6] *Byrne Bros (Formwork) Ltd v Baird and Others* [2002] ICR 667, 680.

of service to exist,[7] but also for any 'contract at all' or for 'a contract in the employment field' to exist,[8] mutuality has enjoyed an insuperable popularity in judicial reasoning, partly because of its unique characteristic of being credited, at the same time, as a legal '*test* … to found a contract [or] to found a contract of employment'[9] and as 'an essential *element*' of the structure of the contract of employment. Mutuality may well be the *lapis philosophorum* of English labour contract law, but the following pages will suggest that it is often used to turn gold into lead, rather than the other way round.

The present chapter is composed of four main sections. The following section briefly explores the concept of the autonomy of labour law, identifies its three main components and links them to the analysis of 'mutuality of obligations'. The third section begins by tracing the origins and subsequent development of 'mutuality of obligations' in English labour law, both from a doctrinal and from a jurisprudential perspective. This analysis explores the emergence of mutuality as a descriptive structural element of the contract of employment, but also its progressive transformation into a series of increasingly prescriptive and ubiquitous requirements or tests for identifying (and, by the same token, excluding) other facets of the contract of employment—and increasingly of contracts for personal work and services at large—such as contractuality, continuity, personality, bilaterality, and even (albeit in a more nuanced manner) subordination. In the following fourth section, the paper moves on to investigate the spread of the concept(s) of mutuality into other, mostly common law, jurisdictions with some brief references to European law. This part concludes by advancing the suggestion that while some particular manifestations of 'mutuality of obligations' appear to have transferred (or metastasized) to other legal systems, a number of the jurisdictions explored appear to have developed a certain resistance, if not outright immunity, to some or all of the more prescriptive and aggressive transmutations of the original English law versions of 'mutuality of obligations'. The fifth and final part queries whether the English law approach to 'mutuality' in the construction of personal work contracts is tenable and desirable from the point of view of conceptual clarity and heuristic viability, and in particular by reference to the discussion, developed by the chapters of the present collection, on the autonomy of labour law. In conclusion, this chapter tentatively suggests that by saying too much, mutuality is really saying too little to help our understanding of the structure of personal work contracts in general, and of the contract of employment in particular.

But before engaging in this analysis, it may be valuable briefly to discuss why 'mutuality' may be a valuable locus to explore the key questions underlying the present edited collection: is labour law autonomous, and, if so, in what sense?

[7] *O'Kelly and Others v Trusthouse Forte PLC* [1983] ICR 728, 743.

[8] *James v Greenwich London Borough Council* [2007] ICR 577, 582.

[9] *Singh v The Members of the Management Committee of the Bristol Sikh Temple and Others* (Appeal No UKEAT/0429/11/ZT) [25] (emphasis added).

II. The Autonomy of Labour Law

Autonomy is a complex term that deserves some clarification. Taken literally the term may suggest a total separation of an area of law from any other legal discipline. But as remarked by Lord Wedderburn, '[N]o branch of law can be "completely autonomous, within the body of the juridical order as a whole". Fortress labour law, like Fortress Wapping, cannot survive in total isolation.'[10] It is well accepted that labour law, both in Britain[11] and in the rest of Europe,[12] has relied heavily on contract and private law to shape fundamental building blocks of its edifice, and cornerstones such as the contract of employment. However, in most European systems, the original inner core of private law concepts has been progressively covered with several thick coats of self-standing philosophical rationales and legislative, collective and judicial intervention such as to emancipate this particular cornerstone, and arguably labour law as a whole, from its original private law vestiges, albeit without removing its influences altogether.[13] Self-standing as they may have been, it is also worth noting that these rationales were very much inspired by other legal and social disciplines, including the study of industrial relations and the sociology of law, that bolstered the 'worker protective' claims advanced by labour law. Paul Durand, speaking in respect of French labour law, captured the essence of this process when noting the progressive emergence of labour law worker protective principles and rules tasked with 'ne laisser au droit commun qu'une place subordonnée'.[14]

Labour law can thus be seen as entitled to make a rather credible and simultaneous claim to both active borrowing and autonomy, though it goes without saying that different legal traditions tend to strike different balances between the common law elements and the more properly understood labour law components of our discipline.[15] What is clear, however, is that labour law has certainly never embraced an idea of autonomy amounting to 'isolation'. As Collins put it: 'Although some fields of law such as contract and crime are marked by the quest of coherence according to a small set of principles, Labour Law, like other contextual fields such as Family Law, has never aspired to such conceptual unity.'[16] A contract of employment, in most legal systems, is both a '*contract*', and a 'contract *of employment*', with the latter formulation usually factoring in a

[10] Lord Wedderburn, 'Labour Law: From Here to Autonomy?' (1987) 16 *Industrial Law Journal* 1, 1–2.

[11] M Freedland, *The Personal Employment Contract* (Oxford, Oxford University Press, 2003) 4, and ch 2.

[12] M Freedland and N Kountouris, 'Towards a Comparative Theory of the Contractual Construction of Personal Work Relations in Europe' (2008) 37 *Industrial Law Journal* 49.

[13] ibid.

[14] P Durand, 'Le Particularisme du Droit du Travail' [1945] *Droit Social* 303.

[15] M Freedland and N Kountouris, *The Legal Construction of Personal Work Relations* (Oxford, Oxford University Publishing, 2011).

[16] H Collins, 'Labour Law as a Vocation' (1989) 105 *Law Quarterly Review* 463, 473.

series of normatively laden elements that serve to distance its formation, structure and functioning from a contract *tout court*.

With these caveats in mind, one could go on to suggest that the three main structural elements against which the autonomy of a discipline such as labour law ought to be evaluated are (a) the presence of a set of legal institutions[17] regulating a coherently identifiable social phenomenon or set of phenomena, (b) the presence of a set of original regulatory techniques and governance mechanisms, and (c) the existence of an original ideology underpinning the normative action and development of the discipline.[18]

In this context, 'mutuality of obligations', as it should become apparent in the following pages, is a useful concept to explore. As already noted by Anne Davies, properly understood 'mutuality of obligations is … an employment law requirement, not a contract law requirement'[19] and as such it could be seen as an original regulatory device deployed to structure the contract of employment, itself one of the key legal institutions of labour law. However the following pages will also reveal the extent to which both contractual law principles and contract law reasoning have shaped and continue to shape the development of 'mutuality', and force the English notion of contract of employment, and to a certain extent English labour law as a whole, to gravitate much more closely to its common contract law ideological nucleus than equivalent notions in other jurisdictions do, in a way that seriously detracts from a fully fledged claim to autonomy, to which both mutuality and the contract of employment would otherwise be entitled.

III. Mutuality of Obligations in English (Labour) Law

A. The Origins

The introductory section of this paper noted the relevance that modern judicial reasoning places on the concept and test of 'mutuality of obligations' in the construction of—mainly but not exclusively—contracts of employment. The present section attempts to reconstruct the origins of the concept, both in doctrinal and jurisprudential terms, but also to trace and map-out its evolutionary trajectory, mostly by reference to case law development.

[17] The term 'institutions' is used in the broad sense explored in Freedland and Kountouris (n 12) 51–53, where it was argued that the contract of employment was a central institution in labour law, functioning as both an analytical and a normative category.

[18] I have sought to engage with the concept of autonomy of European labour law in N Countouris, 'European Social Law as an Autonomous Legal Discipline' (2009) 28 *Yearbook of European Law* 95, on which this section partly draws.

[19] A Davies, 'The contract for intermittent employment' [2007] *Industrial Law Journal* 102, 104.

Many labour lawyers are likely to associate the emergence of 'mutuality of obligations' with the seminal work by Mark Freedland, *The Contract of Employment*[20] of 1976 and the 1980s cases of *O'Kelly*[21] and *Nethermere*.[22] Typically, most labour lawyers would also recognize that in the original work by Freedland mutuality had 'appeared with very different intentions'[23] to the ones later developed by English courts. It is sometimes suggested that Freedland's seminal work looked at mutuality, or more precisely at the parties to a contract of employment's 'exchange of mutual obligations for future performance',[24] for the specific reason of identifying an additional contractual element of the contract of employment that went beyond the mere 'exchange … of service against remuneration'.[25]

Freedland did, in fact, famously identify a 'two tiered structure'[26] for the contract of employment. But his main purpose was not that of introducing a second structural limb—certainly not a second hurdle—for a work relation to be classified as a contract of employment at its formation stage. His true intentions were apparent, in the view of the present author, from the pages of his 1976 book immediately preceding the famous 'two level structure' passage. In these pages Freedland noted some important conceptual lacunae in existing legal writings, still unduly anchoring the understanding of the contract of employment to general contract and commercial law principles, with 'neither judicial nor academic authorities [having] examined at all fully the structure of the mutual obligations of the contract of employment'. [27] From this observation he insisted on developing 'a theory dealing with [the structure of the contract of employment] in order to explain why there is a *cause of action for wrongful dismissal or wrongful departure of by the employee*',[28] and adding that '[t]his … is necessary to *the explanation of much of the law concerning breach of that contract*'.[29] So the rationale for developing the 'two tiered structure' theory of the contract of employment, with the second tier amounting to an 'exchange of mutual obligations for future performance', had much more to do with providing a sound conceptual basis for understanding the (changing) law on the breach and termination of the contract of employment, rather than the law on the formation of the contract of employment.

[20] Freedland (n 2). See eg the opening paragraphs in S Deakin and G Morris, *Labour Law* (Oxford, Hart Publishing, 2012) 164; and Davies (n 19) fn 3.

[21] *O'Kelly v Trusthouse Forte Plc* [1983] ICR 728.

[22] *Nethermere (St Neots) Ltd v Gardiner and Another* [1984] ICR 612.

[23] E McGaughey, 'Should Agency Workers Be treated Differently?' (LSE Legal Studies Working Paper No 7/2010) fn 76.

[24] Freedland (n 2) 20. Note that Freedland was also quite clear that the term mutual obligation was applicable to the second tier and not to the first one: 'At the first level there is an exchange of work and remuneration. At the second level there is an exchange of mutual obligations for future performance.'

[25] Deakin and Morris (n 20) 164.

[26] Freedland (n 2) 20.

[27] ibid 19.

[28] ibid.

[29] ibid 20. In this sense see also the concluding line in the first paragraph of p 21 of the monograph.

The reason why a labour lawyer in the 1970s would have been genuinely concerned with the way the (hitherto underexplored) structure of the contract of employment affected or shaped the understanding of the law on the breach and termination of this type of contract is that, around that time, English labour law was indeed going through an important evolutionary passage when it came to these aspects of the law, something that *The Contract of Employment* clearly reflected. For instance, the introduction of statutory notice periods in 1963,[30] of redundancy compensation in 1965,[31] of the first unfair dismissal protections with the Industrial Relations Act 1971, which were retained in 1974 and extended further the following year,[32] were clearly pushing English labour law away from both its more traditional voluntarist matrix but also from the 'employment (quasi) at will' paradigm that existed until then and that collective *laissez-faire* had at best masked and mitigated.[33] In other words, between 1963 and 1976 the standard employment relationship had entered a process that was progressively leading to a certain degree of (no doubt incomplete) stabilization and continuity. As later noted by Freedland and Davies,

> It may well be that the twenty years from 1963 to 1983 will in retrospect be regarded as the two decades which *saw the rise of the idea of job property in our labour law*—and also perhaps, its partial or complete fall.[34]

In the mid-1970s, this was a process that labour law was still failing fully to comprehend, and that Freedland's *The Contract of Employment* first sought to depict through novel legal concepts, including a concept of mutuality which could wrap together successive sequences of short-term assignments into a single and continuous contract of employment protected by the recently emerging law of unfair dismissal.

So to sum up this initial part of this section, the first steps of 'mutuality', at least in Freedland's work, were mostly those of a descriptive/analytical construct that was building on earlier contractual doctrines, such as the doctrine of consideration, which clearly informed the 'first tier' of 'exchange … of service against remuneration'[35] and which—by 1976—were already recognized by English courts, as the 1968 dictum by Mackenna J in *Ready Mixed* that '[t]here must be a wage or other remuneration. Otherwise there will be no consideration, and

[30] With the Contract of Employment Act 1963.
[31] Redundancy Payments Act 1965.
[32] Trade Union and Labour Relations Act 1974, sch 1
[33] There is a fascinating analysis of these underlying developments in the opening pages of ch 4 of P Davies and M Freedland, *Labour Law*, 2nd edn (London, Weidenfeld and Nicolson, 1984) see also 430–32. Their treatise of fixed-term contracts is also particularly significant, 446–48. To a certain extent, 19th- and early 20th-century trade unions had contributed to the spread of 'minute contracts' in certain industries as a means to circumvent the criminal and civil liabilities arising from the duty to give notice in the context of strikes: see SM Jacoby, 'The Duration of Indefinite Employment Contracts in the United States and England: An Historical Analysis' (1982) *Comparative Labor Law* 85, 98.
[34] See the opening line of ch 4 of Davies and Freedland (n 33) 428 (emphasis added).
[35] Freedland (n 2) 20.

without consideration no contract of any kind'[36] demonstrates. These existing pre-modern contractual elements were built upon by the introduction of the famous 'second tier' of mutuality for the sake of providing a more precise and lucid understanding of the slow but quite visible transformation of the employment contract into a more relational, continuous and open-ended one, and from there to understand the emerging new law of wrongful and, increasingly, unfair dismissal. If this reconstruction is correct, therefore, it would be right to say that in Freedland's work mutuality had nothing to do with the creation of a new hurdle for identifying contracts of employment (or with the creation of a new legal test), little to do with the formation of the contract of employment (even though for systematic reasons it was, perhaps inevitably, discussed in the chapter of his book dealing with 'Formation and Structure') and merely advanced the analytical suggestion that the emergence (through the development of wrongful and unfair dismissal law) of continuous employment relationships could be better understood by identifying a new supporting legal element in the construction of—increasingly relational—contracts of employment, ie that 'second tier' of mutuality of obligations to which we have eventually become accustomed. This element, as noted in the citation reproduced in the introduction,[37] was not to act as a prerequisite, or test, excluding short-term and precarious work from the protections of labour law, but rather it was to emerge as the *necessary implication* of increasingly more stable contractual employment relations. However, case law developments were soon going to turn this analysis on its head.

B. The Emergence of a Mutuality 'Test'

While the Court of Appeal judgments in *O'Kelly*[38] and *Nethermere*[39] are rightly perceived, for different reasons and in different ways, as the starting point of the judicial development of mutuality as a legal test, it is probably at the 1982 Employment Appeal Tribunal judgment in *Nethermere*[40] that one would have to look at in order to identify the missing link between the pre-modern notions of 'obligation … to accept offers of work',[41] which was already stigmatized by Atiyah as relevant to the existence of a contract of service (but one whose absence was, in cases involving daily labourers, 'of no particular significance'[42]) and the emergence of the 1980s concept of 'mutuality' as an element and test for the

[36] *Ready Mixed Concrete (South East) Ltd v Minister of Pensions and National Insurance* [1968] QB 497, 515.

[37] See above n 3.

[38] *O'Kelly v Trusthouse Forte plc* [1983] ICR 728.

[39] *Nethermere (St Neots) Ltd v Gardiner and another* [1984] ICR 612.

[40] *Nethermere (St Neots) Ltd v Gardiner and another* [1983] ICR 319.

[41] *Market Investigations Ltd v Minister of Social Security* [1969] 2 QB 173; *Airfix Footwear Ltd v Cope* [1978] ICR 1210, should probably be seen as such too.

[42] PS Atiyah, *Vicarious Liability in the Law of Torts* (London, Butterworths, 1967) 66, by reference to what Atiyah defined as 'the obligation to work' in the case of *O'Donnel v Clare County Council* (1912) 47 ILT 41 (Ct of Sess).

contract of employment. In the Employment Appeal Tribunal (EAT) judgment of *Nethermere* we can see, at the same time, a reference to this *retrospective* idea of mutual performance of obligations (ie that work performed over a period of time will be seen as performed under a contract of service) that can be found in earlier cases such as *Airfix Footwear*,[43] and its contestation in the form of a claim by the employer's counsel that 'the industrial tribunal misunderstood the ratio of the decision in *Airfix Footwear*' and that the

> analysis of the judgment shows that the case [of *Airfix*] did not decide that work performed consistently over a long period of time with an absence of mutual obligations could constitute a contract of service: a true analysis of the case shows that where the same quantity of work is accepted and performed over a long period, the proper inference is that there may be a mutual obligation to provide and perform it.[44]

The employer's side contestation ultimately suggested, as already noted by McGaughey,[45] that 'mutuality' ought to be understood as 'continuity' in the specific sense that 'mutual obligations are a crucial *pre-requisite* of a contract of service [and] that the reason for such a pre-condition is that a contract of service is a continuing relationship between employer and employee'[46] and that intermittent performance of work is therefore '*inconsistent* with the continuing obligations'.[47]

We know from the EAT judgment that, ultimately, the workers' interests were vindicated and this novel 'mutuality as a pre-requisite' argument dismissed, only by majority and thanks to 'the lay members'[48] relying on the 'business in own account' risk test. But the minority opinion—by Tudor Evans J—was willing to embrace the new legal argument that '[t]here was, briefly stated, no obligation upon the applicants to provide themselves to serve', and therefore no contract of service due to a lack of mutuality.[49]

When *Nethermere* reached the Court of Appeal in 1984, the majority of the Lord Justices (with Kerr LJ, as he then was, dissenting) eventually concluded that the homeworkers involved in the dispute could be legitimately categorized as 'employees', as the industrial tribunal had done to begin with. But when considering this appeal, the Court of Appeal had also before its eyes its earlier decision in *O'Kelly*,[50] taken in 1983 just after the EAT *Nethermere* judgment,

[43] The EAT in *Nethermere* quoting 'where work is done consistently over a substantial period a tribunal would be entitled to reach the conclusion that a contract of employment had been created between the parties': *Nethermere (St Neots) Ltd v Gardiner and Another* [1983] ICR 323.

[44] ibid 326.

[45] McGaughey (n 23) fn 76.

[46] *Nethermere (St Neots) Ltd v Gardiner and Another* [1983] ICR 326.

[47] ibid (emphasis added).

[48] ibid 327.

[49] ibid 328.

[50] Stephenson LJ is quite explicit when he opines that: '[W]e have to decide, in the light of this court's decision in *O'Kelly v. Trusthouse Forte PLC*, the difficult question whether, in agreement with the minority opinion of Tudor Evans J in the appeal tribunal but contrary to the opinion of all the other members of both tribunals, the preliminary issue [in favour of the applicants, Mrs Taverna and Mrs Gardiner, that they were both employees of the employer company]': *O'Kelly and Others v Trusthouse Forte PLC* [1984] ICR 612, 616–17.

and which drew upon that judgment in an extremely creative way, that effectively lent much more credit to the minority view of Tudor Evans J than to the majority decision itself. In *O'Kelly*, the Court of Appeal had no hesitation to refer to 'mutuality of obligation' as 'the *one* important ingredient'[51] for there being a contract of employment. This one important ingredient, in effect a test in everything but its name, was used to endorse the industrial tribunal finding that O'Kelly and the other 'regular casual' waiters involved in the case were operating under 'a purely commercial transaction for the supply and purchase of services for specific events, because there was no obligation for the company to provide further work and no obligation for the applicants to offer their further services'.[52] This reasoning was used both to defeat the existence of an 'umbrella contract' and to defeat the classification of each individual arrangement as a 'contract of service'.[53]

When considering *Nethermere*, the Court of Appeal built on its previous decision in *O'Kelly* to distance itself further from the pre-modern notion of mutual obligations exemplified in *Airfix* and to further embrace (and entrench) the newly emerged *O'Kelly*'s mutuality test. Stephenson LJ expressly noted that the *Airfix* interpretation given in the earlier tribunal judgement in *Nethermere* was a 'conclusion … open to criticism'[54] and condemned 'the *error* made by the appeal tribunal of deciding that no … mutual obligations were necessary and that the *Market Invetigations Ltd* … test provided a contract of service when there were no such obligations'.[55] So basically in *Nethermere* the Court of Appeal dismissed the appeal 'but for the [new] reasons … given, which are not those of the appeal tribunal but are those required by the majority judgments in *O'Kelly v Trusthouse Forte Plc*'.[56] It is also worth noting that in this decision the Court of Appeal first referred to McKenna J's view (that 'there must be a wage or other remuneration. Otherwise there will be no consideration, and without consideration no contract') as 'mutual obligations',[57] thus effectively using the same label of mutuality to address both 'consideration' and the new 'essential ingredient' of mutuality as 'continuity'. The absence of either limb would result in a failure to identify the relationship as one regulated by a contract of employment.

Fast forward these important developments by a number of years and, in the case of *Carmichael*, we can see the House of Lords explicitly endorsing the idea that mutuality is a 'rock' on which workers' claim to a 'contractual relationship of any kind' 'founders',[58] and an understanding that *Nethermere* introduced a requirement for an 'irreducible minimum of mutual obligation necessary to

[51] *O'Kelly and Others v Trusthouse Forte PLC* [1983] ICR 728, 754 (Ackner LJ) (emphasis added).
[52] ibid 744.
[53] ibid 762, 763 (Sir John Donaldson MR).
[54] *Nethermere (St Neots) Ltd v Gardiner and Another* [1984] ICR 612, 619.
[55] ibid 624.
[56] *Nethermere (St Neots) Ltd v Gardiner and Another* [1984] ICR 627.
[57] *Nethermere (St Neots) Ltd v Gardiner and Another* [1984] ICR 612, 623.
[58] *Carmichael and Another v National Power Plc* [1999] ICR 1226, 1229.

create a contract of service',[59] an expression that was only used in *Nethermere* in Lord Kerr's dissenting opinion, mentioned above, and that was now somewhat being 'upgraded'. What is also relevant is that in *Carmichael* mutuality—or rather the lack of it—was deployed to defeat the claim that an 'umbrella contract' could be established for the purposes of creating continuity between various successive contracts (on the status of which their Lordships maintained an open, if agnostic, mind).[60]

Within a matter of years English courts had remoulded and completely transformed a concept that, in its early doctrinal elaborations, was meant to provide an analytical insight into an increasingly continuous and stable notion of contract of employment. Now it was being used as a prescriptive element, and as a test, to assess the presence of a contract of employment, and this was being done at a time during which—for various reasons that are outside the scope of this chapter—arrangements for the provision of work and services in certain sectors of the labour markets were again becoming increasingly fragmented and precarious.

C. The Many Faces of 'Mutuality'

In the previous subsection we noted how a doctrinal device coined to provide a more accurate understanding of the implications of the increased stability in the provision of personal work was eventually developed, remoulded and applied in a completely different context to the detriment of what, by then, was a growing number of precarious and short term workers. This subsection seeks to offer an overview of the ways in which, in more recent years, mutuality has been used as a multi-tool to defeat various other claims pertaining to the establishment of contracts of employment or other workers' contracts. A good starting point is arguably the EAT decision in *James v Greenwich*, where Elias J, as he then was, provided a much more elaborate matrix of the impact that mutuality has on the fates of the contract of employment and on employment status. At paragraph 16 of his judgment, Elias J opined:

> 16. The authorities do not speak with one voice as to precisely what mutual obligations must be established. The relevant cases were analysed carefully by Langstaff J in *Cotswold Developments Construction Ltd v Williams* [2006] IRLR 181, paras 19–23. As he points out, sometimes the employer's duty is said to be to offer work, sometimes to provide pay. The critical feature, it seems to us, is that the nature of the duty must involve some obligation to work such as to locate the contract in the employment field. If there are no mutual obligations of any kind then there is simply no contract at all, as *Carmichael v National Power plc* [1999] ICR 1226 makes clear; if there are mutual obligations, and they relate in some way to the provision of, or payment for,

[59] ibid 1229–30.

[60] With Lord Irvine emphasizing: 'I repeat that no issue arises as to their status when actually working as guides': ibid 1231.

> work which must be personally provided by the worker, there will be a contract in the employment field; and if the nature and extent of the control is sufficient, it will be a contract of employment.[61]

In short, to paraphrase this paragraph of the judgment in *James v Greenwich*, mutuality can impact on an employment status claim in at least three separate, but interlinked, ways. Firstly, the absence of a 'mutual irreducible minimal obligation' can defeat any attempts to establish that the relationship is contractual, presumably on the basis of the conflation between 'mutuality' and 'consideration' discussed in the previous subsection. Secondly, 'the nature of those mutual obligations must be such as to give rise to a contract in the employment field', that is to say that if there is no mutuality, presumably in the form of mutual obligations for future performance, then the contract will not be seen as a contract for personal work. Thirdly, we are told that if the previous two limbs of mutuality exist, 'the issue of control determines whether that contract is a contract of employment or not', but even this small reassurance has suddenly been removed from us by the Court of Appeal in the recent case of *Stringfellow Restaurants Ltd v Quashie*, it which the following clarification was given:

> On reflection, it is clear that the last sentence … is too sweeping. Control is not the only issue. Even where the work-wage relationship is established and there is substantial control, there may be other features of the relationship which will entitle a tribunal to conclude that there is no contract of employment in place even during an individual engagement. *O'Kelly* and *Ready Mixed* provide examples.[62]

Other cases clearly suggest that 'it is necessary for a contract of employment to contain an obligation on the part of the employee to provide his services *personally*. Without such an irreducible minimum of obligation, it cannot be said that the contract is one of service',[63] thus juxtaposing, if not conflating, mutuality with 'personality'. And this while, according to the Court of Appeal in *Muschett*, the lack of mutuality (and at this stage it is difficult to understand which limb the authorities are referring to) is said not necessarily to exclude the establishment of 'a contract "personally to execute any work or labour" (ie … a contract for services)' with a user in a trilateral work arrangement,[64] while—at the same time—the fact 'that [the worker] was under no *obligation* to … work for [the user] and could terminate his engagement with [the user] at any time by giving notice to [the agency]'[65] means that no personal work contact can be established between the worker and the user for the purposes of gaining protection from anti-discrimination legislation. Just to make even clearer how much recent judgments are willing to read into the test and the elements of mutuality, one may add that mutuality is also understood as a necessary element for a 'limb (b)

[61] *James v Greenwich* [2007] ICR 577, 581.
[62] *Stringfellow Restaurants Ltd v Quashie* [2012] EWCA Civ 1735.
[63] *Express & Echo Publications Ltd. v Tanton* [1999] ICR 693, 699.
[64] *Muschett v HM Prison Service* [2010] EWCA Civ 25, with para 36 suggesting that 'such mutuality is not a condition of a contract for services'.
[65] ibid paras 35–36.

contract'[66] or 'worker' contract to exist, so that its absence will exclude workers from being covered by legislations such as the Minimum Wage Act 1998 or the Working Time Regulations.[67]

This section has explored the evolution, development and fragmentation of the concepts of 'mutuality of obligation'. The analysis has both verified and questioned the understanding of mutuality as an 'employment law requirement'. Its inception was clearly inspired by a pressing need to move beyond the analytical strictures provided by contract law reasoning in respect of 'untypical agreements'.[68] However, its evolution has been influenced by both contractual principles and contract law reasoning, and has no doubt failed in terms of delivering on its analytical potential (in that by saying too much about the contract of employment, it ends up saying too little) and has hindered the deployment of English employment protection legislation to the wider range of personal work relations present in modern labour markets.

IV. Mutuality of Obligations in a Comparative Perspective—Functional and Dysfunctional Equivalents

Can a single test, or even contractual element, perform so many functions? Has it become too laden and does it retain any purpose and conceptual coherence when it can be deployed in so many different ways (all typically resulting in added hurdles for atypical and precarious workers to prove employment status)? One could of course probe these questions in many different ways, but this section seeks to shed some light on them by exploring the approaches taken by other jurisdictions in respect of their uses of 'mutuality' or of other functionally equivalent concepts. We will begin by assessing the approach adopted by some common law jurisdictions and move on to elaborate on the approach taken by European law.

The Australian approach is quite clear and can be summarized as follows. Australia does recognize the concept of 'mutuality' in the construction of contracts of employment and academic authorities of the calibre of Stewart and

[66] *Byrne Bros (Formwork) Ltd v Baird and Others* [2002] ICR 667, 680.

[67] To this effect see the majority judgment in *A D Bly Construction Ltd v Mr A T Cochrane* (Appeal No UKEAT/0243/05/MAA), where at [40] it was held that '[T]he Claimant was not a worker on the footing that under the contract, the Respondent was not obliged to offer work and the Claimant was not obliged to do the work if offered. The finding of fact by the Tribunal at paragraph 7(4) of their Reasons that clause 23 of the contract reflected the true position precludes the Claimant from asserting that under the contract, he undertook to do or perform work or services. That, in our judgment, is fatal to his being classified as a "limb (b) worker".'

[68] Freedland (n 2) 19

Owens link it to the judgment in *Dietrich v Dare*.[69] However, in their more recent work they also note that 'the Australian understanding of this has never been as rigid as that in the United Kingdom'.[70] In advancing this claim they rely on the authority of *Forstaff v Chief Commissioner of State Revenue*, where

> Justice McDougall preferred to distinguish the British cases and express the Australian requirement of mutuality 'not as an obligation on the one side to provide and on the other to perform work, but as an obligation on the one side to perform work (or provide service) and on the other side to pay'. This was considered to be more consistent with the way in which the 'wage–work bargain' had been analysed in cases such as *Automatic Fire Sprinklers Pty Ltd v Watson* (1946) 72 CLR 435.[71]

This is certainly a far cry from the fragmented and multifaceted concept of mutuality discussed in the previous section.

South African labour law also offers an interesting benchmark for assessing the English law understanding of 'mutuality', not just because of the shared common law origin of the two systems, but also because of the influence that English doctrinal elaborations have had, over the years, on its development. In 2004, Benjamin noted that a 'seminal article written by Sir Otto-Kahn Freund, persuaded [South African courts] to reject the "control" test and adopt the approach that an employee is someone who is part of the employer's business … usually referred to as the "organization" or "integration" test'.[72] As a consequence of this, ever since *Smit v Workmen's Compensation Commissioners*, South African jurisprudence in this area of labour law had been effectively dominated by the so-called 'dominant impression' test[73] inviting adjudicators to consider all aspects of the contract, without limiting themselves to ascertaining the existence of a right of supervision or control, that was not seen as the conclusive element of the employee relationship. This test was strongly criticized by a number of academic authors, including Benjamin[74] and Brassey.[75] More recent court decisions engaged with this line of scholarship with the Labor Court of Appeal expressly endorsing Benjamin's critical analysis[76] and suggesting that:

[69] *Dietrich v Dare* (1980) 54 ALJR 388, as considered in A Stewart and R Owens, *The Nature, Prevalence and Regulation of Unpaid Work Experience, Internships and Trial Periods in Australia Experience or Exploitation? Report for the Fair Work Ombudsman* (University of Adelaide, 2013) 134, available at www.fairwork.gov.au/Publications/Research/UW-complete-report.pdf.

[70] R Owens and A Stewart, 'Internships, the Contract of Employment and the Scope of Labour Law' (Inaugural LLRN Conference, Barcelona, June 2013) 8, available at www.upf.edu/gredtiss/_pdf/2013-LLRNConf_OwensxStewart.pdf.

[71] *Forstaff v Chief Commissioner of State Revenue* (2004) 144 IR 1, [90], cited in Stewart and Owens (n 69) 135.

[72] P Benjamin, 'An Accident of History: Who Is (and Who Should Be) an Employee under South African Labor Law' (2004) *Industrial Law Journal* 787.

[73] *Smit v Workmen's Compensation Commissioner* 1979 (1) SA 51 (A); more recently considered in *SA Broadcasting Corporation v McKenzie* (1999) ILJ 585 (LAC); and *Somerset West Society for the Aged v Democratic Nursing Organisation of SA &others* (2001) ILJ 919 (LC).

[74] Benjamin (n 73).

[75] M Brassey, 'The Nature of Employment' [1990] *Industrial Law Journal* 919.

[76] *State Information Technology Agency (Pty) Ltd v Commission for Conciliation, Mediation & Arbitration & others* [2008] *Industrial Law Journal* 2234 (Labour Appeals Court) [10]–[11].

> [12] … when a court determines the question of an employment relationship, it must work with three primary criteria:
>
> 1. An employer's right to supervision and control;
>
> 2. Whether the employee forms an integral part of the organisation with the employer; and
>
> 3. The extent to which the employee was economically dependent upon the employer.[77]

But this is pretty much it. South African labour law is blissfully oblivious to our English law vagaries of 'mutuality of obligations'.

As for Indian labour law, in 2010 the Supreme Court endorsed the view, attributed to its former Justice Kuttyil Kurien Mathew, that

> [f]rom the contractual principle of mutuality of obligation, it was reasoned that if the employee can quit his job at will, then so too must the employer have the right to terminate the relationship for any or no reason. And there are a number of cases in which even contracts for permanent employment, ie for indefinite terms, have been held unenforceable on the ground that they lack mutuality of obligation. But these cases demonstrate that mutuality is a high-sounding phrase of little use as an analytical tool and it would seem clear *that mutuality of obligation is not an inexorable requirement and that lack of mutuality is simply, as many courts have come to recognize, an imperfect way of referring to the real obstacle to enforcing any kind of contractual limitation on the employer's right of discharge, ie lack of consideration.*[78]

Common law legal systems aside, it may be worth considering how other systems approach the element of continuity in employment relationships, and whether continuity in performance is seen as a strict *pre*requisite for a contract of employment to exist.

An interesting comparative angle is provided by the Italian notion of 'continuità ideale',[79] a concept that 'deploys its effects on a teleological, rather than temporal level, and is therefore different from the continuous or periodical execution of the performance, that is to say from the mere distribution over time of the fulfilment to the obligation'; continuity in the context of subordinate employment 'has to be understood not in its *material* sense but in the theoretical (*ideale*) one, as dependence or *functional availability*' of the worker 'in someone else's enterprise'.[80] These doctrinal insights are confirmed by the Italian Supreme Court explicitly accepting that the casual and intermittent nature of performance does not exclude that the work relation in question can be one of subordinate

[77] ibid [12].

[78] *Harjinder Singh v Punjab State Warehousing Corporation* [2010] SCR 591, para 21 (emphasis added).

[79] E Ghera, *Diritto del Lavoro* (Bari, Cacucci, 2000) 67. See N Countouris, *The Changing Law of the Employment Relationship* (Farnham, Ashgate 2007) 69.

[80] Ghera ibid (emphasis original).

employment.[81] This position is not altogether different from the one developed, in recent years, by Freedland, who has noted, for example, that

> although when I get into my taxi, neither I nor the taxi-driver necessarily expect that the taxi-meter rates will be held for longer than during the present journey to the station, when I take somebody into my employment under a contract of employment, that worker will have some sort of expectation that I will hold the agreed wage rates for some defined period or on some defined conditions.[82]

Finally it may be useful to assess our domestic notions of mutuality by reference to the benchmark of EU law. In this respect, one cannot fail to note that in the case of *Allonby*, the European Court of Justice came very close to explicitly suggesting that 'mutuality of obligations' plays no role in its assessment of who is a worker for the purposes of EU law. The Court held that:

> The formal classification of a self-employed person under national law does not exclude the possibility that a person must be classified as a worker within the meaning of Article 141(1) EC if his independence is merely notional, thereby disguising an employment relationship within the meaning of that article.
>
> In the case of teachers who are, vis-à-vis an intermediary undertaking, under an obligation to undertake an assignment at a college, it is necessary in particular to consider the extent of any limitation on their freedom to choose their timetable, and the place and content of their work. *The fact that no obligation is imposed on them to accept an assignment is of no consequence in that context*.[83]

In the earlier case of *Preston* the Court was equally dismissive of the relevance attributed in English court to the circumstance that 'after the completion of any contract, there is no obligation on either party to enter into further such contracts', resulting in the absence of an 'umbrella contract'[84] as long as the workers could be held to be in 'a stable employment relationship resulting from a succession of short-term contracts concluded at regular intervals in respect of the same employment'.[85]

Before indulging in the faux pas of misusing the comparative method in an unduly prescriptive way, it may be appropriate to draw some provisional conclusions in respect of the relevance and meaning of this set of comparative considerations. Although the examples discussed above clearly suggest that the legal construction of contracts of employment is not inextricably linked to any of the English notions of mutuality of obligations, this should not be seen as necessarily prescribing the demise of mutuality of obligations in English labour law.

[81] Cass Civ Sezione Lavoro, 10 luglio 1999, n 7304.

[82] M Freedland, 'Deductions, Red Herrings, and the Wage–Work Bargain' (1999) 28 *Industrial Law Journal* 255, 259.

[83] Case C-256/01 *Allonby v Accrington and Rossendale Community College* [2004] ECR I-873, paras 71–72 (emphasis added).

[84] Case C-78/98 *Preston v Wolverhampton Healthcare NHS Trust and Others* [2000] ECR I-3201, paras 30, 65.

[85] ibid para 72.

However, these comparative observations may lend themselves to assisting us in reaching three significant, and no less radical and problematic, sets of provisional conclusions on 'mutuality' and on its contribution to the autonomy of labour law that are discussed in the following, and final, section of this chapter.

V. Conclusions: Mutuality of Obligations and the Contested Autonomy of Labour Law

The second section of this chapter acknowledged that mutuality, properly understood, ought to be seen as an employment law requirement, rather than a contract law one. Its primary purpose is (or was intended to be) that of bringing to the fore in a meaningful way the relational aspects of the employment relationship that traditional contract law elements, such as contractual consideration, failed to acknowledge in any significant manner or shape. As noted in the opening paragraphs of section III, there is little doubt that this is how 'the second tier' of the 'two-tiered structure' coined by Freedland in *The Contract of Employment* was intended to operate. In his 2003 monograph *The Personal Employment Contract*, Freedland further clarified that, in his view

> the two level analysis should be regarded as applying to personal employment contracts generally and not just to contracts of employment strictly so called. … Semi-dependent workers' contracts are more likely to be of very short duration, but that is no reason to deny them a relational dimension.[86]

However, the analysis carried out in the second and third parts of section III identified a number of uses of the concept of mutuality that are hardly reconcilable with the autonomous function and rationale that was originally attached to the concept. On the contrary, mutuality has been used both (i) as a synonymous term of contractual consideration and (ii) as a prerequisite of contractual continuity (in a vast range of personal work relations) in a way that clearly defeats the purpose of the concept of mutuality as originally intended. This latter observation provides an interesting angle to enrich and question our appreciation of English labour law as an autonomous discipline (even with all the caveats and qualifications introduced in respect of the idea of 'autonomy' in section II above). Clearly the contract of employment can be seen as an original legal institution regulating a coherently identifiable social phenomenon or set of phenomena, and mutuality is obviously capable of being understood as an original regulatory techniques and governance mechanisms serving this original institution. However, the emphasis that English legal reasoning continues to place on the contractual arrangements underpinning personal work relations significantly

[86] Freedland (n 11) 91–92.

diminishes the claim to autonomy that mutuality, the contract of employment and UK labour law as a whole could potentially advance.

In this respect, the comparative enquiry of section IV provided a number of insights on the contractual strictures just outlined. Firstly, it is quite apparent that the importance of recognizing the elements of continuity and stability in employment relations is not inexorably connected with the English notion of 'mutual obligations for future performance'. A number of other legal notions of employee or worker, including the emerging EU 'worker' concept, reveal that the descriptive (and normative) value that English law attaches to continuity and stability is in fact wasted and pushed into an endless catch-22 when turned on its head and transformed into a (contractual) *prerequisite* for recognizing the existence of a contract of employment. Hence, 'mutuality as a precondition for contractuality' is a proposition that does not seem to attract much credit in most other jurisdictions.

Secondly, and perhaps more importantly, the idea of 'mutuality as a precondition for relationality' does not appear to withstand this kind of comparative scrutiny either. Several legal systems, including the EU legal system, are quite comfortable with the idea that a relationship in the employment field may well come into existence in the absence of a mutuality element, or in the presence of a 'non-mutuality clause', in individual contracts or in a succession of separate contracts. In fact, most foreign systems will go beyond this simple statement, and further accept the idea that in cases of discrepancy between the contract and the relationship, the reality of the latter ought to prevail over the formality of the former. The relationship between contractual formality and relational reality is an aspect of English labour law that English courts are just beginning to extricate. In line with other legal systems, they have sought to recognize the prevalence of the reality of the employment relationship over the legal fiction of the contractual arrangement when both parties have conspired to shape a contractual arrangement aimed at circumventing a legal requirement, as suggested by the traditional English sham doctrine under *Snook*.[87] But it is only in more recent times, with cases such as *Protectacoat*[88] and *Autoclenz*, that the English courts have moved on to recognize that when one of the parties, typically the employer, has abused its 'relative bargaining power' by unilaterally producing a written agreement that fails to reflect the 'true agreement', then 'the reality of the relationship' ought to prevail over the written documentation.[89] There is, however, a third set of cases where a mismatch between the written agreement and the reality of the relationship can manifest itself without being attributed, strictly speaking, to either a conspiracy between the two parties of the contract

[87] *Snook v London and West Riding Investments Ltd* [1967] 2 QB 786.

[88] *Firthglow Ltd (t/a Protectacoat) v Szilagyi* [2009] EWCA Civ 98.

[89] See *Autoclenz Ltd v Belcher and others* [2011] UKSC 41, paras 22, 35. On this line of cases see A Davies, 'Sensible Thinking about Sham Transactions *Protectacoat Firthglow Ltd v Szilagyi*' (2009) 38 *Industrial Law Journal* 318; and A Bogg, 'Sham Self-Employment in the Supreme Court' (2012) 41 *Industrial Law Journal* 328.

to dissimulate their real arrangements, or to a unilateral abuse of power on the part of the employer dictating 'what the written agreement will say and the contractor/employee must take it or leave it',[90] thus resulting in a 'legal fiction', to use the terminology used by Advocate General Geelhoed in his Opinion in *Allonby*.[91] These are the cases where, to borrow once more the Court's words in *Allonby*,[92] the contractual structure of the relationship is simply 'of no consequence' to the relationship itself in its specific context, though this admittedly requires a contextual analysis of the law that English courts have been traditionally reluctant to engage with.[93]

Bearing in mind these two points, a third provisional and highly normative conclusion may be tentatively put forward. The time might have come for English law to reassess the function of mutuality of obligations, as well as the fiction on which its current uses are premised. Arguably, the concept ought to embrace a more sober demeanour in which fewer, and arguably clearer, functions are assigned to it. And at the same time it ought to reshape itself to fit our modern, diverse, and increasingly fragmented and precarious labour markets. Mutuality understood as a contractually evidenced continuous and bilateral relationship between employer and employee and as a *prerequisite* for a contract of service, postulates a labour market in which employment relations develop along a paradigm of stability and subordination that is clearly increasingly challenged by the reality of contemporary human resource management arrangements. The time has arguably come for English labour law to recognize this and embrace a wider understanding of labour law as the law of personal work relations,[94] although admittedly such a shift may well require a new conceptualization of the third essential element of the concept of 'autonomy' embraced by this chapter, that is to say of the ideology underpinning the normative action and development of labour law itself.

[90] *Firthglow Ltd (t/a Protectacoat) v Szilagyi* [2009] EWCA Civ 98, para 52.

[91] ibid para 49.

[92] And here it may be worth noting that *Allonby* was not decided on the assumption that the employer was unilaterally imposing some kind of 'legal fiction', to borrow the terminology used by AG Geelhoed in para 49 of his Opinion (see also paras 37–38), but simply, as noted above, on the basis that 'the fact that no obligation is imposed on [the workers] to accept an assignment is of no consequence in that context'.

[93] An enlightening analysis of how specific contexts fail to be acknowledged by English courts can be found in E Albin, 'The Case of *Quashie*: Between the Legalisation of Sex Work and the Precariousness of Personal Service Work' (2013) 42 *Industrial Law Journal* 180, esp 183–86. The construction sector, as the plight of the black-listed 'self-employed' workers has amply demonstrated, provides another interesting example. See *Smith v Carillion (JM) Ltd & Anor* UKEAT/0081/13/MC.

[94] Freedland and Kountouris (n 15).

8

Migrants and Forced Labour: A Labour Law Response

CATHRYN COSTELLO*

I. Introduction

In this chapter, I reflect on the prevalence of discourse about slavery, servitude and forced labour in relation to migrant working. This discourse may be mistaken for pure political rhetoric, employing slavery analogies and the like to highlight injustice. However, as this chapter will illustrate, immigration law,[1] the immigration process and labour market structures may interact to create vulnerability to forced labour. Ten years ago, in the immediate wake of the Morecambe Bay tragedy,[2] Anderson and Rogaly identified key sources of vulnerability to forced labour amongst migrant workers.[3] Since then, further empirical evidence on forced labour in the UK has demonstrated that rather than simply powerful rhetoric, forced labour is the legally appropriate label for some migrants' (and indeed local workers') work relationships.[4]

* The author thanks Professor Mark Freedland for his support, insight and cooperation in developing the Migrants at Work project and this chapter, Professors Alan Bogg and ACL Davies and Dr Virginia Mantouvalou for most helpful comments, and Ms Emily Hancox for research and editorial assistance.

[1] By 'immigration law', I refer not only to formal laws on labour migration, but to the entire system of laws and admission control practices, which determine the terms and conditions of entry, residence, and work rights in the territory of any state.

[2] In February 2004, 21 Chinese migrant workers died picking cockles in the sea at Morecambe Bay. Their deaths raised awareness of the appalling working conditions in the industry where 'gangmasters' supplied migrant workers. See Oxfam GB, 'Turning the Tide: How to Best Protect Workers Employed by Gangmasters, Five Years after Morecambe Bay' (Oxfam Briefing Paper 2009); H Pai, 'The Lessons of Morecambe Bay Have not Been Learned', *The Guardian* 3 February 2014.

[3] B Anderson and B Rogaly, *Forced Labour and Migration to the UK* (Trades Union Congress, 2005).

[4] Equality and Human Rights Commission, *Inquiry into Recruitment and Employment in the Meat and Poultry Processing Sector* (Equality and Human Rights Commission, 2010); K Skrivankova, *Between Decent Work and Forced Labour: Examining the Continuum of Exploitation* (York, Joseph Rowntree Foundation, 2010); L Allamby and others, *Forced Labour in Northern Ireland: Exploiting*

The collection Mark Freedland and I edited on intersections between labour and migration law[5] was in part motivated by what we perceived as a gap in mainstream labour law scholarship.[6] The contributions of Oxford labour lawyers and migration scholars in that collection are a significant addition to this field. There were also some early acknowledgements of the importance of migration status for labour law. Notably, the 'radical and refugee'[7] Kahn-Freund wrote in 1967 of 'the branch of immigration and labour market legislation' where status was of increasing significance.[8] While the move from status to contract was the hallmark of the shift from ancient to modern law,[9] the rising significance of immigration status was a riposte to that account. Kahn-Freund was undoubtedly prescient in identifying the rise of immigration law as pertinent to labour law. However, one of the then features of immigration law was that it was attuned to allowing permanent settlement. Accordingly, he viewed immigration law as setting up disabilities principally in public rather than private law. Today's immigration law, in contrast, tends to create temporary, precarious statuses, which have a profound impact on work relations.[10] While this chapter is concerned with a form of labour relation characterized by extreme domination, to understand that end-point of forced labour, an attempt must be made to understand how immigration law pervades labour law.

Section II begins with some reflection on labour law's autonomy. As this chapter's subject matter ranges across immigration, criminal and human rights law, it seems useful to clarify the sense in which it is meaningful and useful to speak of labour law's autonomy, if any. I suggest that the autonomy claim is best understood as highlighting a distinctive set of normative concerns, which

Vulnerability (York, Joseph Rowntree Foundation, 2011); C Kagan and others, *Experiences of Forced Labour among Chinese Migrant Workers* (York, Joseph Rowntree Foundation, 2011); P Dwyer and others, *Forced Labour and UK Immigration Policy: Status Matters?* (York, Joseph Rowntree Foundation, 2011); M Lalani and H Metcalf, *Forced Labour in the UK: The Business Angle* (York, Joseph Rowntree Foundation, 2012); N Clark, *Detecting and Tackling Forced Labour in Europe* (York, Joseph Rowntree Foundation, 2013).

[5] See C Costello and M Freedland, *Migrants at Work: Immigration and Vulnerability in Labour Law* (Oxford, Oxford University Press, 2014).

[6] Notable early contributions were those of Mary Crock and Bernard Ryan: M Crock, 'Immigration and Labour Law: Targeting the Nation's Skills Needs' in A Frazer and others (eds), *Individual Contracts and Workplace Relations* (Working Paper No 50, ACCIRT, 1997); M Crock, 'Contract or Compact: Skilled Migration and the Dictates of Politics and Ideology' in M Crock and K Lyon (eds), *Nation Skilling: Migration, Labour and the Law* (Annandale, NSW, Desert Pea Press, 2002); B Ryan, *Labour Migration and Employment Rights* (Liverpool, Institute of Employment Rights, 2005).

[7] C Glasser 'Radicals and Refugees: The Foundation of the Modern Law Review and English Legal Scholarship' (1987) 50 *Modern Law Review* 688.

[8] O Kahn-Freund, 'A Note on Status and Contract in British Labour Law' (1967) 30 *Modern Law Review* 635.

[9] H Maine, *Ancient Law: Its Connection with the Early History of Society and its Relation to Modern Idea* (John Murray 1861).

[10] B Anderson, 'Migration, Immigration Controls and the Fashioning of Precarious Workers' (2010) 24 *Work, Employment and Society* 300; J Fudge, *The Precarious Migrant Status and Precarious Employment: The Paradox of International Rights for Migrant Workers* (Metropolis British Columbia Working Paper Series No 11-15, 2011) 5; S Marsden, 'The New Precariousness: Temporary Migrants and the Law of Canada' (2012) 27 *Canadian Journal of Law and Society* 209, 211.

in turn require particular institutional responses. Mark Freedland and I suggest that immigration law does challenge the autonomy of labour law, in that it divides both the purposes of labour law and its subjects.[11] Section III seeks to clarify 'forced labour'. I examine in turn the binary between 'free' and 'unfree' labour in political economy, and the notion of a continuum from free labour to the ultimate form of unfreedom, slavery. While both the binary and continuum approaches are illuminating, neither approach entirely befits the legal task of identifying the human rights violation that is forced labour. The distinct legal labels of 'slavery', 'servitude' and 'forced labour' are legal concepts embodying distinctive institutional forms of work relation. This part also explores how prohibitions on trafficking, in contrast, introduce a distinctive, potentially distortive focus on migration control and criminalization into this field. In light of the preceding discussion, Section IV examines how the migration process and immigration law create fertile conditions for forced labour. Some features of immigration law, such as precarious and irregular migration status are liable to increase dependency in work relations, which can induce domination. However, this part also considers how those with apparently secure migration status, namely EU citizens in the UK, are also vulnerable to forced labour.

In light of this analysis, Section V then critiques the current legal responses to forced labour. These responses should be of concern to labour lawyers, as they obscure general labour rights concerns, and the regulatory conditions that are fertile for forced labour. The UK exemplifies the tendency to obscure labour law concerns, with a Bill on 'modern slavery' going through Parliament at the time of writing, proposing life sentences for those convicted of human trafficking, slavery, forced labour and domestic servitude.[12] The criminal approach focuses on the outcome (the forced labour itself), rather than understanding the laws, practices and regulatory gaps that set up the vulnerability to forced labour. Accordingly, I contrast this criminal law approach with the labour law approach, taking into account the 2014 Protocol to the ILO Convention on Forced Labour.[13]

A third approach focuses on human rights law. As currently interpreted, the human rights approach is parasitic on the criminal law approach.[14] I argue that a more progressive (ie orthodox labour law) interpretation of human rights law on forced labour is appropriate and necessary. While some doubt whether international human rights norms are capable of challenging the role of immigra-

[11] M Freedland and C Costello, 'Migrants at Work and the Division of Labour Law' in Costello and Freedland (n 5).

[12] Home Office *Draft Modern Slavery Bill* (Cm 8770, 2013) 2: 'Modern slavery encompasses human trafficking, slavery, forced labour and domestic servitude.' Forced labour became a criminal offence under UK law: Coroners and Justice Act 2009, s 71 (England, Wales and Northern Ireland); Criminal Justice and Licensing Act 2010 s 47 (Scotland).

[13] ILO Protocol to the Forced Labour Convention 1930, ILO No 9A, 11 June 2014.

[14] Again, this is particularly vivid in the UK where the criminal prohibition refers directly to Art 4 ECHR. See V Mantouvalou, 'Modern Slavery: The UK Response' (2010) 39 *Industrial Law Journal* 425. See also V Stoyanova, 'The Obligation of Criminalizing Slavery, Servitude, Forced Labour and Human Trafficking under Article 4 of the European Convention on Human Rights and the Failures of the Domestic Criminal Law' (2014) *Cambridge Journal of International and Comparative Law* 1.

tion law in producing precarious employment,[15] I suggest that an important corrective role for human rights law should be embraced here. Moreover, the open texture of human rights law means that without the appropriate infusion of labour law values, the anti-trafficking frame may come to dominate human rights law.

A labour law approach should ideally entail three main elements, which are briefly sketched here. First, it should insulate labour rights from migration status. Secondly, it should regulate labour intermediaries. Thirdly, it should develop better collective and institutional protections for labour rights. Evidently this is not labour law as we find it in the UK today. However, the evidence of extreme labour exploitation and forced labour demands an urgent revisitation of the norms and institutions of labour law. This vision of a reformed labour law is in some senses an 'autonomous' one, in that it accepts the particularities of the values of the personal work relation and the need for particular institutions to make those commitments effective.

II. Labour Law and Immigration Law

A. Understanding the Autonomy Claim

There are at least three senses in which we may consider the 'autonomy' of labour law. Its autonomy could be thought to rest in being a body of law dealing with a discrete set of social relations or phenomena, namely employment relations. These were traditionally understood as characterized by subordination of the worker to the employer via a contract of employment, or more realistically today, characterized by a personal work relation.[16] In this sense, the autonomy claim rests on an empirical assumption of the distinctiveness of these forms of social relations. Just as 'family law' relates to a distinct set of human relations characterized by intimacy, unpaid labour and the domestic sphere, 'labour law' has a distinctive field of application. However, that labour law has a distinctive field of application is but the first step in understanding the autonomy claim. After all, in this weak sense, many domains of law are 'autonomous' in that they regulate an identifiable field of relations. Generally, the autonomy claim has two additional elements, in that it also refers to a distinctive set of legal institutions applicable to that set of relations and distinctive underlying normative principles.[17]

[15] J Fudge, 'Precarious Migrant Status and Precarious Employment: The Paradox of International Rights for Migrant Workers' (2012) 34 *Comparative Labor Law and Policy Journal* 95.

[16] Evidently, one of Mark Freedland's singular contributions has been to shed immense light on the distinctive nature of these relations. See M Freedland, *The Contract of Employment* (Oxford, Clarendon Press, 1976); M Freedland, *The Personal Employment Contract* (Oxford, Oxford University Press, 2005).

[17] This tripartite notion draws on N Countouris, 'European Social Law as an Autonomous Legal

Both the institutional and normative dimensions of the autonomy claim flow from an appreciation of the importance and particularity of the work relations subject to labour law's purview. This importance is rooted in the centrality of earnings for livelihood, the inequality of bargaining power between worker and employer,[18] and the importance of continuity of employment and dignity at work for well-being and self-worth.

These factors lead to a conception of labour law as having a worker-protective mission, and a focus on mechanisms, especially collective ones, to correct any inequality of bargaining power. In their crudest versions, the first sense of the autonomy claim has been undermined by the shifting boundaries between employment and other forms of work relations, while the second sense seems to be nostalgic for the heyday of collective bargaining and even 'collective *laissez-faire*' in the UK context. However, these legal and institutional changes make the reconsideration of the normative bases of labour law all the more important, and a revisitation of the material and institutional scope of labour law accordingly necessary. Few scholars have done as much as Mark Freedland in this regard.[19]

A comprehensive normative account of labour law would draw on a multiplicity of values. Notably, for Freedland and Kountouris, the rationales for labour law rest on the following normative commitments:

> (1) dignity and decent conditions for workers; (2) maximizing workers' access to the labour market and opportunities for skills development and capability building; and (3) controlling the costs and risks for employing entities and workers alike of entering into such arrangements by introducing and promoting elements of stability.[20]

While these values have a universal ring to them, their distinctiveness lies in being attuned to the particular context of personal work relations. As provided in their account, each of these values requires further specification, articulation and institutionalization in the work context.[21]

Discipline' [2009] *Yearbook of European Law* 95. Classic discussions of the autonomy of labour law include Lord Wedderburn 'Labour Law: From Here to Autonomy?' (1987) 16(1) *Industrial Law Journal* 1; P Davies and M Freedland, 'Employees, Workers, and the Autonomy of Labour Law' in H Collins, P Davies, and R Rideout (eds), *Legal Regulation of the Employment Relation* (London, Kluwer Law International, 2000).

[18] Even if we include within the scope of labour law work relations where formal subordination is not present, inequality of bargaining power seems inevitably a feature of work relations given the dependency of the worker on work for livelihood.

[19] See n 16.

[20] M Freedland and N Kountouris, *The Legal Construction of Personal Work Relations* (Oxford, Oxford University Press, 2011) 372.

[21] Notably, when they identify the importance of maximizing access to work opportunities, they seem to assume an identifiable population of workers who should enjoy such access. However, in world without open borders, we also assume that states dispose of a wide discretion to decide which migrant workers to admit, in other worlds, states decide amongst whom work opportunities should be distributed.

B. Freedom from Domination

Forced labour, where the worker's freedom is curtailed to an extreme extent, evidently offends the values of dignity, decency, capability building and stability. For the purposes of this chapter, which focuses on forced labour, the animating value is *freedom from domination*. Freedland and Kountouris refer to a version of dignity as a composite of autonomy and equality,[22] which would evidently embrace freedom from domination. My focus on non-domination is not to suggest that this value is fully realized once protections against forced labour are in place. Given that subordination is a common (if no longer defining) feature of the work relations within labour law's purview, subordination can become domination all too easily. Preventing subordination from becoming domination can be understood as central to labour law's worker-protective mission. Curtailing managerial prerogative takes on a particularly important rationale in light of the value of non-domination. For instance, avoiding domination requires various protections for both individual and collective worker voice.[23] Focusing on freedom from domination has affinities with a relational approach to autonomy in work, which can usefully move the discussion away from questions of consent vs. coercion, and onto an examination of whether the work relationship enhances or supports autonomy, or undermines it. Testing whether the relationship is consensual is pertinent, but the better approach looks at the whether the value of autonomy or non-domination is realized or undermined by the structures of the particular institutionalized relationship.[24]

Moreover, the value of non-domination is also helpful in identifying which forms of immigration control are ethical.[25] Immigration controls reflect a fundamental inequality between citizens and aliens. Liberal political theory tends to unravel when confronted with border controls, with notable liberal political theorists avoiding questions about the ethics of immigration policies, ignoring border controls, or bracketing them out.[26] Others aspire to open borders but accept migration control for prudential reasons;[27] or integrate a nationalist insider-preference.[28] All of these moves merely address the question of whether

[22] Freedland and Kountouris (n 20) 373.

[23] A Bogg and C Estlund, 'Freedom of Association and the Right to Contest: Getting Back to Basics' in A Bogg and T Novitz (eds), *Voices at Work* (Oxford, Oxford University Press, 2014) 141.

[24] See further J Nedelski, *Law's Relations: A Relational Theory of Self, Autonomy and Law* (Oxford, Oxford University Press, 2012).

[25] See I Honohan and M Hovdal-Moan (eds), 'Domination, Migration, Non-citizens' (2014) 17 *Critical Review of International Social and Political Philosophy* 1 (Special Edition).

[26] J Rawls, *A Theory of Justice* (Cambridge, MA, Harvard University Press 1971); J Rawls, *The Law of Peoples: with 'The Idea of Public Reason Revisited'* (Cambridge, MA, Harvard University Press 2001).

[27] J Carens, *The Ethics of Immigration* (Oxford, Oxford University Press, 2013).

[28] D Miller, 'Immigration: The Case for Limits' in A Cohen and C Wellman (eds), *Contemporary Debates in Applied Ethics* (Oxford, Blackwell Publishing, 2005); D Miller, 'Immigrants, Nations, and Citizenship' (2008) 16 *Journal of Political Philosophy* 371; R Pevnick, *Immigration and the Constraints of Justice: Between Open Borders and Absolute Sovereignty* (Cambridge, Cambridge University Press, 2011).

immigration controls are normatively defensible in the first instance. At this high level of generality, the discussion rarely engages with the forms of vulnerability and dependence some immigration laws may engender once migrants are admitted. A non-domination framework, in contrast, helps identify those aspects of immigration law that set up conditions whereby migrants are dominated in the host country,[29] which should be rejected even if we accept the premise of states' entitlement to determine admissions to the territory. Accordingly, a non-domination frame seems useful in the particular context of the way immigration law may create domination in work relations.

In focusing on non-domination, I assume a general commitment to this universal value. However, this value has a particular relational dimension, which demands different responses in different relational contexts. Valuing relational autonomy requires different norms and institutions in intimate relationships and in commodified work relationships, for instance. I also assume the particularity of personal work relations, in which subordination can all too easily become domination. In this context, the particular relation demands a particular set of institutional protections, in order to avoid domination. In this way, the universal value demands a particular (and in this sense distinctive or even perhaps autonomous) set of institutional responses and mechanisms. For instance, as will be discussed below in relation to the right to pay, even this most basic labour right requires a distinctive range of institutional supports in the context of personal work relations, in particular where intermediaries are involved as is often the case in relation to migrant working.[30]

C. Immigration Law and Labour Law

This contribution brings immigration law, *lato sensu*, into the labour law field. Focusing on immigration law assumes that it is predominantly the receiving state that regulates migration. That assumption is largely correct, reflecting the asymmetry built into the international system, with the right to leave one's own country being enshrined in international bills of rights, but no right to enter any particular state.[31] Admittedly, some sending countries do increasingly regulate the export of migrant workers, creating elaborate migrant export regimes and entering into webs of bilateral labour migration agreements.[32] Nonetheless, regulating migration remains predominantly in the hands of the receiving state.

[29] The focus of this piece is on an extreme form of labour domination, forced labour. The vulnerability of migrants to labour domination is connected with their alienage—migrants are not part of the polity. For a general examination of migrants' vulnerability to domination in the host polity, see M Benton *A Theory of Denizenship* (PhD thesis, University College London, 2010).

[30] See Section V.C.

[31] European Convention on Human Rights, Protocol No 4, Art 2; Universal Declaration of Human Rights, Art 132. See further S Benhabib, *The Rights of Others: Aliens, Residents, and Citizens* (Cambridge, Cambridge University Press, 2004).

[32] These agreements do often contain provisions that seek to determine the rights of migrant workers, in a manner that should attract the interest of labour lawyers.

The transformative exception is the EU, with a commitment to internal 'free movement' at its heart, and some aspects of entry and residence by so-called 'third-country nationals' now regulated at the EU level. All Member States have committed to realize EU citizenship and the internal market. In contrast, the UK participates selectively in EU asylum and immigration law as regards those from outside the EU. Broadly speaking, the UK has chosen to be bound by the 'first phase' of EU asylum law, but does not participate in the second phase, or in EU immigration law.[33] Some implications of this selective participation for labour rights are identified below.

While labour lawyers have traditionally tended not to integrate immigration law into their field of study, other disciplines have, in contrast, sought to examine how immigration, immigration law and labour markets interact. Immigration clearly affects the labour market, in that it affects labour supply. The 'supply' role of migration leads some to regard it as liable to instrumentalization by capital to undermine pay and conditions of local workers, particularly given labour market segmentation.[34] Bauder characterized immigration as a 'regulatory labour market tool'.[35] Immigration law, in this account, responds to, and in turn structures, demand for migrant labour, leading to the erosion of terms and conditions in the particular sectors or segments concerned. Immigration law creates a multiplicity of statuses, usually temporary, which determine not only the right to work, but determine the nature of the employment relations enjoyed. Accordingly, Anderson and Fudge have both refined the claim that immigration 'regulates' labour markets by demonstrating how the precariousness of migration status creates a precarious, 'ultra-flexible' workforce. [36] Immigration law nowadays combines with migratory processes to produce 'precarious workers' clustered in particular labour market segments.[37]

Two features of immigration law and the migration process are noteworthy at the outset. The first is the sectoral character of immigration law; the second is the prevalence of the use of labour intermediaries. We tend to find most migrant workers in low-wage sectors where enterprise relocation is difficult or impossible, such as care work, agriculture and horticulture, local transportation, catering

[33] C Costello and E Hancox, *Policy Primer: The UK, the Common European Asylum System and EU Immigration Law* (Oxford, Migration Observatory, 2014).

[34] See G Menz 'Employers and Migrant Legality: Liberalization of Service Provision, Transnational Posting, and the Bifurcation of the European Labour Market' in Costello and Freedland (n 5) citing the following: S Castles and G Kosack, *Immigrant Workers and Class Structure in Western Europe* (Oxford, Oxford University Press, 1973); M Castells, 'Immigrant Workers and Class Struggles in Advanced Capitalism: The Western European Experience' (1975) 5(10) *Politics and Society* 33; M Piore, *Birds of Passage: Migrant Labor and Industrial Societies* (Cambridge, Cambridge University Press, 1979).

[35] H Bauder, *Labor Movement: How Migration Regulates Labor Markets* (Oxford, Oxford University Press, 2006) 21. See also Castells (n 34); R Cohen, *The New Helots: Migrants in the International Division of Labour* (Gower, 1987).

[36] Anderson (n 10); Fudge (n 10).

[37] Anderson (n 10) 301.

and hospitality, and construction.[38] Immigration law often reflects this phenomenon, with diverse laws governing different forms of migration depending on the sectors concerned. Secondly, just as many employing enterprises are fragmented transnationally, so too are labour supply chains whereby workers come to the UK.

While the immigration law–labour law interactions are producing a new field of inquiry for labour law scholars, the interactions themselves are not new. Although today's controls on the movement of transnational labour are of relatively recent origin,[39] controls on forms of mobile labour have been central to labour laws in the past. Prior to the institutionalization of border controls as part of the consolidation of state and nation, forms of local mobility control, usually aimed at the poor and vagrants, predominated.[40] We are inclined all too often to imagine a past before migration, where homogenous nations formed bounded communities, with labour markets mapping neatly on to the same. Evidently a historical corrective is required. The regulation of labour mobility, in its various guises and manifestations, has always had a bearing on labour law.

Immigration law thus challenges labour law's autonomy. As Mark Freedland and I have argued, immigration law divides the objectives of labour law, diminishing the worker-protective aims, and privileging labour supply.[41] In this way, our account draws on political economy and legal analyses, both of which identify the strong tendency to regulate the supply of migrant workers in a way which privileges employers' 'need' for migrant workers over work-protective concerns.[42] We also identify how immigration law exacerbates existing divisions and further divides the subjects of labour law. In particular, migration status itself often determines work relations, so the 'migrant worker' is a distinctive subject in labour law. Moreover, migrants, often for legal and practical reasons, struggle to bring themselves within the existing protective categories in labour law ('employee' or 'worker' for instance), in a way that further divides labour law's personal scope. Accordingly, those who share the underlying values of labour law need to pay urgent and sustained attention to immigration law. As this chapter illustrates, migration status can create vulnerability in work relations, which under some conditions leads to forced labour.

[38] C Rienzo, *Briefing: Migrants in the UK Labour Market: An Overview* (Oxford, Migration Observatory, 2013).

[39] J Torpey *The Invention of the Passport: Surveillance, Citizenship and the State* (Cambridge, Cambridge University Press, 1990).

[40] B Anderson, *Us and Them? The Dangerous Politics of Immigration Control* (Oxford, Oxford University Press, 2013); B Anderson, 'Precarious Pasts, Precarious Futures' in Costello and Freedland (n 5).

[41] Freedland and Costello (n 11).

[42] Menz (n 34); Ruhs; ACL Davies, 'Migrant Workers in Agriculture: A Legal Perspective' in Costello and Freedland (n 5).

III. What Is 'Forced Labour'?

A. A Binary: 'Free' v 'Unfree Labour'?

Before we turn to examine how immigration law and the migration process create vulnerability to forced labour, that legal concept requires clarification. The notion of forced or compulsory labour evidently suggests contrasts with work undertaken consensually or voluntarily. This seems to suggest a simple binary, between coerced and voluntary work. Often, this is treated as mapping on to discussions about 'free' and 'unfree' labour. However, this section rejects any simple binary, and also the equation of 'forced' labour with 'unfree labour'.

The term 'unfree labour' certainly brings with it much useful scholarly reflection on labour relations. However, the term 'unfree labour' should not be conflated with 'forced labour'. 'Unfree labour' comes from accounts in political economy, which narrate the historical transition from 'unfree' to 'free' labour. According to this account, as workers gained the ability to sell their labour and institutions such as serfdom and slavery ended, work became 'free'. Commodified ('free') labour is thereby contrasted with 'unfree labour' in this account, but is by no means equated with true freedom, which remains elusive as long as control of the means of production remains out of the reach of workers.[43] The historical-determinist account of the move from unfree to commodified labour has been challenged, not least by a feminist account pointing out that not all forms of labour are commodified: work within the family and home often remains uncommodified, and indeed also undervalued generally. Much contemporary literature on unfree labour in development studies and critical geography focuses on the persistence of unfree labour relations in developing countries.[44] That this label is now commonly invoked to characterize migrant work relations in developed countries demonstrates how labour market deregulation, the migration process and immigration law are liable to affect labour relations, which are generally regarded as 'free'.

'Unfree labour' is not a legal concept, nor should it aspire to be. Its utility lies in its capacity to demonstrate the complex political economy of labour relations, often drawing on empirical research. Discussions of unfreedom, and the insights from empirical scholarship informed by this conceptual frame, can and should inform understandings of 'forced labour'. For instance, a recent scholarly survey has revealed that 'unfree labour in the contemporary era is constituted primarily, although not exclusively, by the constraints that are imposed on a person's ability to leave a particular arrangement—unfreedom at the point of exit'.[45] This chapter identifies constraints on exit as particularly important to

[43] K Strauss 'Coerced, Forced and Unfree Labour: Geographies of Exploitation in Contemporary Labour Market' (2012) 6(3) *Geography Compass* 137.

[44] S Barrientos, U Kothari, and N Phillips, 'Dynamics of Unfree Labour in the Contemporary Global Economy' (2013) 49(8) *Journal of Development Studies* 1037.

[45] ibid 1039.

understanding 'forced labour' in the legal sense, so there can be a helpful cross-fertilization here. However, the legal definitions need to be understood and tested on their own terms. Accordingly, although the assertion that '[u]nfree labour is … a broad category of which forced labour and slavery are subsets'[46] seems eminently plausible, it may well be that even this linkage is inappropriate, given the different natures of the claims regarding labour which is 'unfree' in a politico-economic sense, and that which is 'forced' in a legal sense. The prohibitions of 'forced labour' 'servitude' and 'slavery' belong in the legal realm.

B. A Continuum from Freedom to Domination?

Before we turn to examining the legal concept of 'forced labour', it is important to return to the value of non-domination. If autonomy and non-domination are important values in labour law, in particular if a relational autonomy approach is adopted, the notion of a continuum of different forms of labour relations, characterized by different *degrees* of freedom and unfreedom, might seem like the appropriate heuristic, rather than a simple binary.

The visual metaphor of the continuum has some explanatory force.[47] It illustrates gradations of domination, often without sharp distinctions between them in practice. Moreover, it reminds us that focusing on the worst forms of domination involving forced labour may often ignore other exploitative wrongs. A continuum also helps to understand the extent of domination experienced by the worker along one axis, which posits a situation where the worker is actually sold (ie she is a slave) at one end, to one where she is free to negotiate the terms under which she sells her work at the other. However, it is important to note that normal work relations are quite far from the free end of the continuum. There is a profound lack of autonomy in normal work relations, in particular at the outset, when most workers rarely negotiate terms and conditions.

The continuum, while useful, has its limitations, two of which I wish to highlight here. Firstly, a continuum does not identify causal connections. This chapter contends that without normal labour law protections, work relations can degenerate into forced labour. That is not an inevitable trajectory, but the empirical evidence suggests that the causes of forced labour are not merely villainous work-masters who constrain workers' liberty, but often a combination of regulatory conditions and gaps that undermine and constrain worker's rights, in particular their right to quit, creating conditions for forced labour. A continuum identifies a spectrum of domination, but does not trace the slide from one form to another, and how normal work relations can become forced labour without labour law protections.

[46] Strauss (n 43) 139.

[47] For a subtle and illuminating approach to a continuum, see Strauss (n 43). For a useful invocation is a more policy-orientated form, see Skrivankova (n 4).

Secondly, the continuum runs along a single axis, from freedom to slavery. However, the law does not only structure work relations along this axis. It can, and does, intervene in different ways to establish or indeed preclude distinctive institutional forms of work relations. Slavery was not simply near-complete domination of slave by slave-owner. Rather it was a legally established work relation or even institution, supported by various property, criminal and work-related laws, as too were serfdom and indentured servitude. Furthermore, the demise and ultimate abolition of these institutional forms did not simply involve removing the source of domination and allowing workers to be free in a negative sense. In addition to abolishing the particular institutions of property and contract which supported slavery, legal interventions were also required to ensure workers were protected from domination at work. Furthermore, the continuum is insensitive to relations between workers. For instance, workplace harassment can be characterized as a form of domination, which undermines worker autonomy.[48] The law's response is, and should be, a very particular one, in which identifying the harm of harassment and deciding how to address it take into account that the harasser may be a fellow-worker. The continuum ignores the important dimension of labour relations, which is the regulation of relations between workers.[49]

To recapitulate, claims pertaining to the autonomy of labour law have a strong normative dimension, as the work of Freedland and Kountouris exemplifies. For the purposes of this chapter, I focus on the value of non-domination, although any convincing account of labour law would need to draw on a multiplicity of values. However, this focus on non-domination often lends itself to a conceptualization of work relations along a continuum from freedom to slavery. While this continuum metaphor is illuminating, I contend that it fails to identify the extent to which different forms of work relations are legal institutions, not only distinguished by the their degree of freedom or voluntariness, but also institutionalized and underpinned by different regulatory forms, a distinctive law of slavery, serfdom and so on, as well as supporting structures in property, contract, criminal and other laws. This might seem more vivid when we look at largely defunct forms such as serfdom and slavery, but it is no less so with regard to less ancient forms such as indentured servitude and the master–servant relation. Modern labour law too was and is an institutional form, not simply a form of work relation characterized by freely entered into work relations under a contract of employment. Rather, workers' subordination was a trigger for various regulatory interventions, to counterbalance the relative lack of autonomy of the employee.

The continuum metaphor, focusing on freedom alone, ignores causal mechanisms, which lead to the slide to the domination end of the spectrum. One of

[48] This is not to suggest that that is the only other frame. See E Anderson, 'Recent Thinking About Sexual Harassment: A Review Essay' (2006) *Philosophy and Public Affairs* 284.

[49] See further G Mundlak, 'The Third Function of Labour Law: Distributing Labour Market Opportunities among Workers' in G Davidov and B Langille (eds), *The Idea of Labour Law* (Oxford, Oxford University Pressm 2011) 317.

the main contentions of this chapter is that forced labour in particular arises when the law creates and exacerbates vulnerability in work relations.

C. Slavery, Servitude and Forced Labour

Forced labour is a human rights violation, and indeed, a criminal offence in the UK. The prohibition of forced labour appears in Article 4 ECHR, alongside that of slavery and servitude. In interpreting these terms, the European Court of Human Rights (ECtHR) draws on other human rights and labour rights instruments. Each term will be considered in turn.

Article 4(1) ECHR states 'No one shall be held in slavery or servitude.' Both practices are prohibited absolutely. While 'forced labour' is also subject to absolute prohibition, some discrete practices are permitted which would otherwise be regarded as 'forced labour'.[50] Evidently, slavery is a form of near-complete domination, in that the slave-owner has some form of ownership of the slave. There has since 1926 been a consistent international legal definition of slavery as 'the status or condition of a person over whom any or all of the powers attaching to the right of ownership are exercised'.[51] The UN instruments on slavery also identify other 'practices similar to slavery', namely debt bondage, serfdom, servile marriage and child exploitation.[52] As slavery is formally abolished, there can be no de jure 'right of ownership' of a human being. De jure slavery then only persists if some remnant legal practice permits actual ownership, a rare occurrence today.[53]

There has been recent scholarly revisitation of the foundational definition of slavery, using property law theory to interpret the phrase 'powers attaching to the right of ownership' to include situations where people are treated 'like slaves' in that they are possessed (and so liable to being exploited, bought, sold and so on). This concept of de facto slavery turns on possession as the main hallmark of 'ownership'. This approach has garnered some judicial approval.[54] It facilitates findings of 'slavery' where people are 'possessed' by others, in a sense

[50] ECHR, Art 4(3).

[51] *Siliadin v France* (2006) 43 EHRR 16, para 122, citing League of Nations Slavery Convention 1926; Protocol Amending the Slavery Convention 1953; Supplementary Convention on the Abolition of Slavery, the Slave Trade, and Institutions and Practices Similar to Slavery (1956) 226 UNTS 3 (Supplementary Convention). The Supplementary Convention is replicated in substance as the definition of enslavement included in the 1998 Statue of the International Criminal Court. Note that under the Statute of the International Criminal Court, enslavement is a crime against humanity.

[52] Supplementary Convention 1956, Art 1, recognizes that the 'institutions and practices similar to slavery', ie debt bondage, serfdom, servile marriages or child exploitation, may be 'covered by the definition of slavery contained in article 1 of the Slavery Convention of 1926'.

[53] See *Hadijatou Mani Koraou v Republic of Niger*' Judgment No ECW/CCJ/JUD/06/08, ECOWAS Community Court of Justice, 27 October 2008. Allain characterizes the scenario as de jure slavery, and criticized the Court for treating it as 'enslavement'. See J Allain, 'Hadijatou Mani Koraou v Republic of Niger' (2009) 103 *American Journal of International Law* 311.

[54] See eg the High Court of Australia in *Tang* (2008) 237 CLR 1. See also J Allain and K Bales, 'Slavery and its Definition' (2012) 14(2) *Global Dialogue* 12.

found in some extreme scenarios where there is deprivation of liberty, freedom of movement and a comprehensive level of control such as to amount to 'possession'. The ECtHR adopted the UN definition in *Siliadin*,[55] emphasizing de jure ownership as an indication of slavery.[56] In *M and Others v Italy and Bulgaria* the ECtHR moved away from 'legal ownership' to referring to slavery as the 'exercise of genuine right of ownership and reduction of the status of the individual concerned to an "object"'.[57]

While slavery and forced labour are sometimes conflated, the better view, even if we endorse the move to include de facto slavery, would still mean that slavery is distinct from forced labour. As Cullen puts it, 'Control equating to possession [the threshold for slavery] goes beyond mere lack of voluntariness, as required to establish forced labour.'[58] Article 4(2) ECHR states that 'No one shall be required to perform forced or compulsory labour.' The ECtHR interprets 'forced or compulsory labour' in line with the definition provided in the ILO Convention against Forced Labour (No 29). Forced or compulsory labour accordingly means 'all work or service which is exacted from any person under the menace of any penalty and for which the said person has not offered himself voluntarily'.[59] The definition thus comprises two main elements: that the work or service is undertaken involuntarily, and that it is exacted under the menace of penalty. The requirement of involuntariness does not mean that entering into the work relation at the outset voluntarily means that labour is not 'forced'. The ILO accepts that, 'Many victims enter forced labour situations initially out of their own choice, albeit through fraud and deception, only to discover later that they are not free to withdraw their labour.'[60] The ability to exercise the right to quit thus becomes a litmus test for 'forced labour'.

Many of the Strasbourg cases on compulsory labour concern work performed under statutory obligations as part of professional training or service. The ECtHR has developed a fact-specific and context-sensitive jurisprudence, based on the 'normal' expectations of the sectors.[61] Regarding work in households, in *CN* the ECtHR sought to distinguish between work reasonably required in respect of mutual family assistance or cohabitation and prohibited 'forced labour'.[62] There may be good regulatory reasons for having a sharp legal notion of 'forced labour'

[55] *Siliadin* (n 51) para 122.

[56] *Siliadin* (n 51) para 122.

[57] See *M and Others v Italy and Bulgaria* (2013) 57 EHRR 29, para 149.

[58] H Cullen 'Contemporary International Legal Norms on Slavery'in J Allain (ed), *The Legal Understanding of Slavery: From the Historical to the Contemporary* (Oxford, Oxford University Press, 2012) 321.

[59] Convention Concerning Forced or Compulsory Labour 1930 (ILO No 29) 39 UNTS 55 cited in the following: *Van der Mussele v Belgium* (1984) 6 EHRR 163, para 32; *Siliadin* (n 51), para 30; *Stummer v Austria* (2012) 54 EHRR 11, para 118; *Graziani-Weiss v Austria* (2014) 58 EHRR 22, para 36.

[60] ILO, *The Cost of Coercion* (ILO, 2009) 6.

[61] *Van der Mussele* (n 59) para 32; *Steindel v Germany* App no 29878/07 (ECtHR, 14 September 2010); *Graziani-Weiss* (n 59).

[62] *CN and V v France* App no 67724/09 (ECtHR, 11 October 2012), para 74.

in order to distinguish normal work relations from those prohibited, treated as a violation of human rights and criminalized.[63] However, evoking the normally unpaid labour within families to obscure whether the work was undertaken voluntarily seems to leave domestic workers particularly vulnerable. We should recall that the French courts initially dealing with Siliadin's case had rejected the argument that Ms Siliadin had been held in slavery-like conditions on the basis that working long hours looking after children could not be regarded as labour exploitation, as mothers did this in the normal course of looking after their own children.[64]

On the facts of *CN*, the determination seems to have been questionable, in particular in finding that as the younger girl attended school and had time to do her homework, the extent of the labour she undertook was not sufficient to be regarded as a violation of Article 4 ECHR. This seems to conflate the quantity of work for the quality of the work relations. Moreover, rather than setting a test to examine whether, on the facts, the work was forced, the Court deemed it to be so, based on expectation of normal work in households. On this point, it would have been preferable to establish criteria or hallmarks of forced labour, but not foreclose the worker's own voice as to the nature of her predicament. The fact that she was also a minor suggests that the Court should have been wary of deeming her work to be voluntary. Perhaps the most disturbing aspect is treating her ability to complain about her predicament to a third party as an indication that she was not being subjected to forced labour. Again, it seems dubious to regard the ability to seek outside protection as indicative of the existence of voluntariness in the work relation itself.

Despite these concerns about the factual findings, the case law is helpful in taking a flexible approach to the 'menace of penalty'. In *Siliadin* the ECtHR considered that, although the applicant, a minor, was not threatened by a formal 'penalty', she understood herself to be at risk of being reported to the authorities for her irregular presence and arrested.[65] Similarly, in *CN*, while taking a rather bright-line approach to the notion of whether labour is voluntary, the Court opened up the notion of 'menace of penalty', accepting that the penalty need not be 'physical violence or restraint', but rather 'can also take subtler forms, of a psychological nature, such as threats to denounce victims to the police or immigration authorities when their employment status is illegal'.[66]

The ECtHR interprets 'servitude' as an aggravated form of forced labour, where the obligation to provide one's services is based on coercion.[67] Its hallmark was that 'in addition to the obligation to perform certain services for others there was an 'obligation for the "serf" to live on another person's property and

[63] Indeed, if there is to be a criminal offence of forced labour, then there are independent liberty-protective reasons for having a clearly delineated offence.

[64] Cited in Clark (n 4) 22.

[65] *Siliadin* (n 51) para 118.

[66] *CN* (n 62) para 77.

[67] *Seguin v France* App no 42400/98 (ECtHR, 16 April 2002); *Siliadin* (n 51), para 124.

the impossibility of altering his condition'.[68] There appears to be a conflation of servitude and serfdom here, not inappropriate on the facts given that the applicant was confined to the home, but conceptually misleading. While the institution of serfdom varied greatly across territories and over time, its basic feature was that serf's obligations to work for the landowner came by virtue of their inherited status of serf.[69] By virtue of its ascriptive status, the serf had no choice of employer and, usually, little prospect of exiting that status.[70]

In contrast, indentured servitude should not be seen as an ascriptive status in the way that serfdom was. The impossibility of altering serfdom may be contrasted with the notion of servitude, which was usually voluntarily entered into and time bound. Nonetheless, indentured servitude is a prohibited form of debt bondage, and debt bondage is a practice deemed 'similar to slavery' under UN instruments.[71] The reason seems to be that under indentured servitude, the employer purchases the worker's labour on long ill-defined terms, and the worker is indebted to the employer, in a way that means the work relation is characterized by domination. As Anderson has suggested, the tendency to reach for slavery analogies when discussing migrant workers today may be too hasty, when the most fitting analogy for today's tied labour migration would be indentured servitude.[72]

For servitude to be established, it is sufficient if the perceived inability to alter one's predicament is based on 'objective elements created or maintained by those responsible'.[73] In *Siliadin* the finding of 'servitude' was based on the fact that in addition to the forced labour, the applicant was a minor, lacked resources, and so was completely dependent on her employers. In *CN* the first applicant was deemed to be the victim of servitude (and forced labour), while the second was not.[74] The first applicant, the older of the two sisters, worked long hours and was socially isolated. In contrast, the younger sister attended school, and was given time to do her homework. On this basis, the unpaid chores she did were not

[68] *Siliadin* (n 51) para 123.

[69] This is reflected in the UN Supplementary Convention, which defines serfdom as 'the condition or status of a tenant who is by law, custom or agreement bound to live and labour on land belonging to another person and to render some determinate service to such other person, whether for reward or not, and is not free to change his status'.

[70] There were usually some mechanisms of manumission or buying freedom, or in some instances escaping and gaining freedom by operation of law. On the apparent ability of serfs in England to gain freedom by living in towns for a year and a day, see S Alsford, 'Urban Safe Havens for the Unfree in Medieval England: A Reconsideration' [2011] *Slavery and Abolition: A Journal of Slave and Post-Slave Studies* 363.

[71] The UN Supplementary Convention defines debt bondage as: '[T]he status or condition arising from a pledge by a debtor of his personal services or of those of a person under his control as security for a debt, if the value of those services as reasonably assessed is not applied towards the liquidation of the debt or the length and nature of those services are not respectively limited and defined.' The ILO approach also distinguishes between different forms of bonded labour, so that not all relations where a worker works to pay off debt will be regarded as forced labour. See J Lerche, 'A Global Alliance against Forced Labour? Unfree Labour, Neo-Liberal Globalization and the International Labour Organization' (2007) 7 *Journal of Agrarian Change* 425, 437.

[72] Anderson (n 40).

[73] *CN* (n 62) para 91.

[74] *CN* (n 62): on forced labour, see para 77; on servitude, paras 92–93.

regarded as undertaken involuntarily. The threshold of servitude was met in the first applicant's case as, in addition to forced labour, she felt that her condition was 'was permanent and could not change, especially as it lasted four years'.[75] As the younger girl attended school, she was able to alert the school nurse to her situation.

The ECHR definitions of forced labour draws from the ILO standards, and has been attuned to the subtle forms of coercion that may render work relations 'forced'. In that respect, labour lawyers should applaud. However, the ECtHR's next move, discussed further in Section V.A below, turns to criminal law to remedy forced labour. To understand how the criminal frame has come to dominate, we must understand the dominant tendencies in anti-trafficking law.

D. Trafficking and Smuggling: Criminalizing Border Crossings

The dominant definition of trafficking is that in the Palermo Trafficking Protocol to the UN Convention against Transnational Organized Crime (2000),[76] which is reproduced in the definition in the Council of Europe Convention on Action against Trafficking in Human Beings.[77]

The definition of trafficking focuses on the presence of coercion (force, deception, coercion, fraud, threats, abuse of power or position of vulnerability, and the giving of payments or benefits to a person in control of the victim) at the commencement of the labour relation or supply chain (recruitment, transportation, transfer, harbouring or receipt of a person) for the purposes of exploitation (broadly defined to include for forced labour, as well as prostitution, slavery or similar, or removal of organs). Trafficking has now been read into Article 4 ECHR. In *Rantsev v Cyrpus* the ECtHR held that Article 4 encompassed human trafficking.[78] Without identifying whether trafficking amounted to slavery, servitude or forced labour,[79] the ECtHR held that by its very nature and aim of exploitation, trafficking was 'based on the exercise of powers attaching to the right of ownership'.[80] The reasoning has been critiqued for conflating the different wrongs in Article 4 ECHR.[81] Moreover, Stoyanova argues persuasively that the human trafficking framework should be excised from Article 4 ECHR, as it incorpo-

[75] *CN* (n 62), para 92.

[76] Protocol to Prevent, Suppress and Punish Trafficking in Persons, Especially Women and Children (2004) 2237 UNTS 319 (the Trafficking Protocol); Convention Against Transnational Organised Crime 2000 (No 08-16) 2225 UNTS 209.

[77] Council of Europe Convention on Action against Trafficking in Human Beings 2005 (CETS No 197). See also Council Directive 2011/36/EU of 5 April 2011 on preventing and combating trafficking in human beings and protecting its victims [2011] OJ L101/1. Victims are to be granted access to 'existing schemes of compensation to victims of violent crimes of intent'. However, there are no provisions to enforce labour rights such as the right to backpay.

[78] *Rantsev v Cyprus and Russia* (2010) 51 EHRR 1, para 282.

[79] ibid para 282.

[80] ibid para 281.

[81] See J Allain, 'Rantsev v Cyprus and Russia: The European Court of Human Rights and Trafficking as Slavery' (2010) 10 *Human Rights Law Review* 546.

rates an anti-immigration and anti-prostitution ethos.[82] Nonetheless, the *Rantsev* case was promising in placing various positive duties on the state to prevent trafficking, as is discussed below.

Focusing on trafficking risks obscuring the fact that much forced labour is entered into apparently voluntarily, without any overt coercion at the outset. Admittedly, the UK criminalization of forced labour per se is portrayed as a response to that acknowledgement. However, prosecutorial guidance suggests that trafficking should be prosecuted rather than forced labour if the facts reveal both.[83] Moreover, when the Trafficking Protocol is read in light of its parent and sister instruments, a strong immigration-control ethos is evident.[84] The parent instrument is concerned only with transnational organized crime, while its sister Smuggling Protocol requires criminalization of providing assistance with illegal border crossings for gain.[85] Accordingly, one critique of the criminalization of trafficking and smuggling is that they amount to an extension and intensification of border controls.[86] The fact that victims of trafficking in the UK, along with refugees,[87] are prosecuted for immigration-related crimes, shores up this claim.[88]

The great energy and resources of anti-trafficking campaigns and policies have obscured the importance of migration for life plans and sometimes survival. Moreover, by focusing on prohibition of means of movement, they do little to protect migrants. By closing up migration opportunities and making migration more costly and dangerous, they can be seen as highly counterproductive, like many prohibition strategies. At the EU level, identified victims of trafficking are permitted to stay in order to testify against traffickers. Nonetheless, it is then assumed that the repatriation of trafficked migrants is appropriate. For repatriation we can often read deportation in practice, often to a home country the migrant actively sought to leave in the first place.[89]

By treating trafficking as the central case, we are invited to imagine that

[82] V Stoyanova, 'Dancing on the Borders of Article 4: Human Trafficking and the European Court of Human Rights in the *Rantsev* case' (2012) 30(2) *Netherlands Quarterly of Human Rights* 163.

[83] Crown Prosecution Service (CPS), *CPS Guidance: Slavery, Servitude and Forced or Compulsory Labour*: '[I]f there is evidence to support trafficking charges, it is important that the fact of trafficking is reflected in the charges [trafficking] should normally be charged in preference to [forced labour].'

[84] This contrasts with the Council of Europe Trafficking Convention, which the UK has also ratified. It applies to all trafficking, irrespective of whether it involves crossing international frontiers, or transnational organized crime.

[85] Protocol against the Smuggling of Migrants by Land, Sea and Air, Supplementing The United Nations Convention Against Transnational Organized Crime (2000) 2241 UNTS 507, Art 6.

[86] See J Hathaway, 'The Human Rights Quagmire of Human Trafficking' (2008) 49 *Virginia Journal of International Law* 6.

[87] See also *R v Mateta & Ors* [2013] EWCA Crim 1372, finding that such prosecutions of refugees violate Art 31 of the Convention Relating to the Status of Refugees 1951, whereby states undertake not to penalize refugees for irregular entry, under certain conditions.

[88] Council of Europe's Group of Experts against Trafficking in Human Beings (GRETA), *Report on UK* (GRETA 2012) 6.

[89] For instance, Sharma draws on the accounts of victims of trafficking who report the most coercive part of their migration process was the deportation following being 'rescued' as victims of trafficking. See N Sharma, 'Travel Agency: A Critique of Anti-Trafficking Campaigns' (2003) 21(3) *Refuge* 53.

migration is usually coerced, so that once the victim has assisted with the prosecution of her trafficker, she should be assisted to return home. Even if this vision held for trafficking, it certainly fails to capture the situation of many of those subject to forced labour, who have entered the UK voluntarily and legally. As will be demonstrated in the next section, the migration process and immigration laws create vulnerability to forced labour over time. The vulnerabilities create conditions in which exit options are foreclosed. In contrast, the anti-trafficking frame focuses on the start of the labour supply chain, and assumes that migration itself was coerced. In so doing, it obscures the predicament of many of those labouring under conditions of domination.

IV. How Do the Migration Process and Immigration Law Create the Conditions for Forced Labour?

Migrant workers are sometimes forcibly transported or tricked into migrating, kidnapped even, in which case they are properly characterized as victims of trafficking. That is not the main focus on this chapter. Rather, I am concerned to understand how migrant workers come to be in conditions of forced labour, even when they *appear* to enter into those work relationships voluntarily. Ten years ago, Anderson and Rogaly identified key sources of vulnerability to forced labour amongst migrant workers, namely 'dependency on recruiters for information and access to migration channels; immigration status and physical as well as psychological isolation'.[90] Further empirical evidence now illustrates the interactions between migration status and labour market structures as setting up the conditions for forced labour.[91] Given that immigration law creates so many diverse statuses, this part must of necessity make some generalizations. Its purpose is to illustrate the interactions between immigration law, the immigration process and labour market structures. It is not to suggest that all migrant workers are vulnerable to forced labour, but that by creating additional dependency on labour intermediaries and employers, and opportunities for domination, the conditions for forced labour are established.

A. The Migration Process

There are two common features of the migration process that should be borne in mind. Firstly, it is costly, requiring significant investment. Given the stark inequalities between income levels between sending and receiving states,

[90] Anderson and Rogaly (n 3).
[91] For a thorough account, see Dwyer and others (n 4).

migrants are often willing to take on significant debt, in various forms, in order to migrate.[92] There may be significant personal, familial or community investment in the migrants' journey, and migrants may have recourse to lenders, formal and informal, to fund their journeys.

Secondly, information asymmetries are also built into the migration process. The migrant may make a calculation based on success stories from previous migrants and returnees, or expected earnings based on her perceptions of a normal life and levels of opportunity in an affluent country. Cases of forced migration often involve exploiting these information asymmetries in order to create greater dependency and insecurity, for instance by misinforming migrants about pay, pay practices, their legal status or their labour rights in general.

Indebtedness and misinformation about likely life-conditions and earnings can together can lead to conditions of vulnerability to forced labour, in that exit options may be foreclosed. The manner in which migration status exacerbates this vulnerability to domination is explored below.

B. Intermediaries and the Long Chain

Immigration law makes the migration process much more costly. If a job offer or sponsor is required, then this means contact must be established in the host state before travel. For refugees and forced migrants, flight may be motivated by concern for survival, but as refugees are often unable to enter the UK legally,[93] they too must invest in particularly costly migration journeys using intermediaries.[94] An intermediary of some sort is often required in order to arrange the migration, whether that entails finding or acting as a visa sponsor, or assisting with circumvention of immigration controls. The law often characterizes the 'smuggler' who assists a migrant or refugee as a criminal,[95] while leaving unregulated many different forms of intermediaries in the labour supply chain. The role of intermediaries to facilitate migration and that of labour intermediaries coalesce here.[96] By hiring migrants through intermediaries, employing organizations almost invariably transfer the risks and costs associated with migration back onto the workers themselves.[97]

To understand the role of intermediaries, it is useful to recall the nature of the migration process outlined above, which is characterized by high costs and

[92] J O'Connell-Davidson, 'Troubling Freedom: Migration, Debt, and Modern Slavery' (2013) 1(2) *Migration Studies* 176.

[93] Refugee Convention, Art 31; *R v Uxbridge Magistrates Court and another ex parte Adimi* [1999] EWHC Admin 765, [1999] 4 All ER 520.

[94] J Morrison, *The Cost of Survival* (London, Refugee Council, 1998).

[95] Smuggling Protocol 2000.

[96] See generally S Ware Barrientos, '"Labour Chains": Analysing the Role of Labour Contractors in Global Production Networks' (2013) *Journal of Development Studies* 1058; J Fudge and K Strauss (eds), *Temporary Work, Agencies and Unfree Labour: Insecurity in the New World of Work* (New York, Routledge 2013).

[97] See Fudge and Strauss (n 96).

information asymmetries. Furthermore, recall that migrant workers are often concentrated at the bottom end of the labour market, where margins are low. Here, passing costs on to the worker can push the workers into exploitative work. If labour intermediaries are under-regulated, as is the case generally in the UK, small operators tend to proliferate, exacerbating these low margins.[98] This institutional structure tends to put the squeeze on wages, sometimes pushing them below minimum wage. In addition, this situation tends to induce agents to keep a roster of more workers than required, all paying fees to the agents, the fees being an important revenue source, with the wages being paid by the end-user being less negotiable.[99] If there are more workers than work, workers' earning will fail to meet the expectations based upon which they made their migration investment. Agents also tend to get into the business of providing accommodation and other services to migrant workers, extracting further 'rents' (literally and metaphorically) from these workers. Naturally this is a simplified account, but it recurs throughout the empirical literature. This is a 'business model' which can easily place workers at risk of forced labour.

As will be discussed further below, regulating labour intermediaries properly is central to a labour law response to forced labour.

C. Precarious Immigration Status

(i) The (Conditionally) Wanted: Ties and Temporariness

Some domination-inducing features of immigration law are highly visible, such as 'ties' that require migrant workers to remain in a particular job in order to retain or renew their immigration status. To give one example, the UK recently reintroduced a 'tie' in the system for domestic worker visas, under the scheme designed especially to allow wealthy transnational migrants bring their domestic workers into the UK with them.[100] The privileged wealthy migrant is wanted; his servants conditionally permitted. Given that the domestic setting itself makes workers particularly vulnerable to exploitation and abuse, the removal of the right to change employers has been framed by the NGO Kalayaan (which campaigns for and assists domestic workers) as a 'return to slavery for migrant workers'.[101]

[98] This account draws on J Allain and others, *Forced Labour's Business Models and Supply Chains* (York, Joseph Rowntree Foundation, 2013).

[99] ibid 51: very crudely, the more migrants a gangmaster has, the more income can be generated through these charges. It may not, therefore, be in a gangmaster's interest to find full-time work for, say, 10 people, when the gangmaster can recruit 30 people and find them part-time work. In the latter scenario, the gangmaster will make money from 30 rather than 10 sets of charges. For a similar analysis, see S Scott, G Craig and A Geddes, *Experiences of Forced Labour in the UK Food Industry* (York, Joseph Rowntree Foundation, 2012).

[100] Domestic Workers in a Private Household visa scheme. See J Fudge and K Strauss, 'Migrants, Unfree Labour, and the Legal Construction of Domestic Servitude: Migrant Domestic Workers in the UK' in Costello and Freedland (n 5).

[101] Kalayaan, *Government Proposes Return to Slavery for Migrant Domestic Workers in the UK* (Kalayaan Briefing 2011).

This form of tie is a vivid example of the more general phenomenon whereby migration status depends on employment. In all such cases, an additional layer of dependency on the employer is created.

The official rationale for ties to particular employers or sectors is often worker protective, in the protectionist sense of protecting the local workforce from competition by migrant workers. Labour migration is often constructed as permitted only to address temporary shortages in the domestic labour market.[102] To ensure that migrant workers only take up the posts in those sectors short of labour, various forms of 'tie' are institutionalized, which link residence rights to working for a particular employer, or in a particular sector or even place. Ties invariably create additional dependence between worker and employer, exacerbating the already unequal relationship. Immigration law in this respect changes the employment relationship, in a manner that should concern labour lawyers. Some ties seem to undermine the fundamental right to quit,[103] and so lead to tensions with the non-domination principle.

Ties are a feature of temporary labour migration programmes. As temporary programmes are becoming the norm, regular labour migrants usually have only a temporary right to stay to work.[104] Temporariness of migration status exacerbates the vulnerabilities we would recognize in any situation of fixed-term work. Moreover, that migration status creates additional dependency: if the worker is keen to renew that status, or acquire a more permanent migration status, that too will typically depend on further sponsorship by the employer. If migrants find they have to stay longer to pay off debt or recoup their investment in the migration process, their dependency is increased. A cycle of dependency can create longer stays: dependency means they may accept lower terms and conditions, meaning that a longer stay is needed. The migration process and immigration law together can foreclose exit and return. The very temporariness of migration status undermines attempts to leave.

In shaping a more dependent workforce, these forms of temporary labour migration tend to create greater demand for migrant workers, whose very migration status makes them more likely to accept terms and conditions that will undercut the local workforce.[105] The temporary right to stay of migrant workers makes them more likely to accept lower wages (if they have return to their home countries in mind) and accept conditions others would not.[106] In that way, the sector may come to be dominated by migrant workers. Temporary

[102] M Ruhs and B Anderson (eds), *Who Needs Migrant Workers? Labour Shortages, Immigration and Public Policy* (Oxford, Oxford University Press, 2010).

[103] *Kav LaOved v The Government of Israel* HCJ 4542/02. See futher E Albin, 'The Sectoral Regulatory Regime: When Work Migration Controls and the Sectorally Differentiated Labour Market Meet' in Costello and Freedland (n 5).

[104] S Castles, 'Guestworkers in Europe: A Resurrection?' (2006) 40 *International Migration Review* 741.

[105] Ruhs and Anderson (n 102) 1.

[106] V Ottonelli and T Torres, 'Inclusivist Egalitarian Liberalism and Temporary Migration: A Dilemma' (2012) 20 *Journal of Political Philosophy* 202.

status thus creates permanent demand, undermining the stated aims of ensuring that migrant labour is only used to address temporary shortages.[107] Positing this potential cycle of the degradation of labour standards does not mean it is inevitable, but it should give labour lawyers pause: the very measures built into immigration law ostensibly to protect local workers seem likely to undermine their position, possibly more than the alternatives.

(ii) The Unwanted—Asylum Seekers, Rejected Asylum Seekers and Refugees

Other categories of migrant lack even this limited work right. Asylum seekers have a particularly precarious, provisional residence status. They come to the UK to seek protection, but unless and until they are accepted as refugees, they are forced to endure harsh legal and material conditions. Over the past decades, a raft of measures has been imposed to make asylum seeking 'less attractive'. One manifestation of that approach is precluding asylum seekers from working.[108] When the UK combined this prohibition with deprivation of welfare benefits, the courts condemned the combined effects of these measures as liable to create extreme destitution of such severity that it would create 'inhuman and degrading' conditions in breach of Article 3 ECHR.[109] The right to work after one year is enshrined in the EU Directive on reception conditions for asylum seekers.[110] A recast version of that Directive would make the right to work available more quickly (after nine months), but the UK, partly for this reason, has decided not to opt in to that measure.

Asylum seekers seem particularly vulnerable to forced labour, as UK studies demonstrate.[111] Most asylum seekers in the UK have their asylum claims

[107] See further A Geddes and S Scott, 'UK Food Businesses' Reliance on Low-Wage Migrant Labour: A Case of Choice or Constraint?' in Ruhs and Anderson (n 102).

[108] Asylum seekers been precluded from working since 2002, and they are entitled to less than the standard rate to income support. Asylum support rates are set annually each year in accordance with what has been felt to be appropriate. In 2013, this amounted to 65% of the income support paid to those under 25 and 51% of that paid to those who are over 25. Further, asylum seekers are only eligible for no-choice accommodation. See Home Affairs Committee, *Asylum* (HC 2013–14, 71-I).

[109] *R (Limbuela) v Secretary of State for the Home Department* [2005] UKHL 66, [2006] AC 396. S Fredman, 'Human Rights Transformed: Positive Duties and Positive Rights' (Oxford Legal Studies Research Paper No 38/2006); Joseph Rowntree Charitable Trust Commissioners, *Moving On: From Destitution to Contribution* (York, Joseph Rowntree Charitable Trust, 2007); C O'Cinnéide, 'A Modest Proposal: Destitution, State Responsibility and the European Convention on Human Rights' (2008) 5 *European Human Rights Law Review* 583. The UK is not alone in providing asylum seekers with inadequate material support: in 2012, the Federal Constitutional Court of Germany, 18 July 2012 (1 BvL 10/10 and 1 BvL 2/11) held that payments to asylum seekers were insufficient to meet the requirements of human dignity and the social welfare state principle.

[110] Council Directive 2003/9 of 27 January 2003 laying down minimum standards for the reception of asylum seekers [2003] OJ L31/18 (Asylum Reception Conditions Directive).

[111] H Lewis and others, 'Precarious Lives: Experiences of Forced Labour among Refugees and Asylum Seekers in England" (University of Leeds, 2013). The authors describe as their 'most striking finding' that 'the experience of severely exploitative labour, including forced labour, is often unavoidable for refugees and asylum seekers in order to meet the basic needs of themselves and their families'.

rejected.[112] Rejected asylum seekers find themselves in an even more precarious position.[113] Their asylum support and housing entitlement are liable to withdrawal within 21 days of their rejection, so many are left destitute and homeless. Income support is available, but only under restricted conditions, such as if they agree to return voluntarily their country of origin.[114]

If at the end of the asylum process, a positive decision is issued, recognized refugees are usually afforded the same rights to work and social benefits as UK citizens, and leave to remain for five years.[115] One striking finding of the empirical literature is that recognized refugees may nonetheless fall victim to forced labour.[116] It seems that their previous precarious status means they have difficulty translating their secure status into a change in their material conditions. Many recognized refugees have experienced torture or trauma in the countries of origin, as well as inevitably perilous journeys to get to safety in the UK. The sometimes protracted asylum process may itself leave them yet further traumatized. Evidently for some, the security that refugee status is supposed to provide is illusory.

(iii) Illegality

The other factor to bear in mind is illegality. Some migrant workers lack legal permission to reside on the territory, or may have a right to reside but lack a right to work at all. Their migration status may permit them to work only part time, or in particular sectors, and if they exceed those conditions, their right to residence may be impaired. Usually, those without proper authorization of residence are under some legal constraints as to their work rights. Commonly, employers are legally prohibited from employing them.[117] Accordingly, irregular labour migrants often cluster in informal sectors. The extent to which these irregular workers are protected by labour law varies from state to state. In the UK, the common law doctrine of illegality, a doctrine itself riven with doctrinal instabilities, has been applied in a startling manner to deny labour law protections to vulnerable irregular migrant workers.[118] The most common response is

[112] S Blinder, *Migration to the UK: Asylum* (Oxford, Migration Observatory Briefing, 2013).

[113] A Bloch, 'Living in Fear: Rejected asylum seekers living as irregular migrants in England' (2013) *Journal of Ethnic and Migration Studies* 1.

[114] Immigration and Asylum Act 1999, s 4.

[115] Council Directive 2004/83 of 29 April 2004 on minimum standards for the qualification and status of third country nationals or stateless persons as refugees or as persons who otherwise need international protection and the content of the protection granted [2004] OJ L/304/12 (Qualification Directive).

[116] See P Dwyer and others (n 4).

[117] It is an offence to hiring an unauthorized worker under s 8 of the Asylum and Immigration Act 1996. See B Ryan, 'The Evolving Legal Regime on Unauthorized Work by Migrants in Britain' (2005) 27 *Comparative Labor Law and Policy Journal* 27.

[118] See further Freedland and Kountouris (n 19) 147–52 for a comparative discussion of 'illegality', citing as a paradigm case 'working as an immigrant without entitlement to work'. They contrast the mitigated approach under continental European legal systems to that in the UK under 'decisions such as *Vakante* … [which deny] basic anti-discrimination rights to asylum seekers falsely claiming that they had a right to work in the UK'. They cite *Vakante v Addey and Stanhope School* [2005] ICR 231

to call for a firewall between immigration status and labour rights, for worker-protective reasons.[119] (As is discussed further in Section V.C below, this move is part of my vision of a labour law response to forced labour.)

Unlike the common law doctrine of illegality, the EU Employer Sanctions Directive seeks to 'deal with' illegal working by focusing on employers, both penalizing and removing incentives to hire irregular migrants. Accordingly, it provides some minimal labour protections for 'illegal workers', in particular the right to enforce pay claims. If the rate of pay is unclear (as is often the case in irregular employment, where lack of transparency, unclear deductions and indeed deception are prevalent), pay is defined in a worker-protective manner. It is to be set at least as high as the relevant laws relating to minimum wage, by collective agreement or in accordance with established practice in a particular industry unless either the employer or the employee can prove differently.[120] While employers' sanctions are by no means unproblematic from a labour rights perspective,[121] the Directive seeks to reallocate the risks of breaching migration law in a more worker-protective manner than the UK approach, which allows the common law to infiltrate and undermine labour law.

Those with irregular, or potentially irregular, migration status are vulnerable to forced labour, if their exit options are precluded. It should be noted that migrants often find themselves moving from legal to illegal working, in particular when temporary migration status is for a short duration. As employers and intermediaries have considerable control over migration status, they can render workers irregular by pressuring them to do work in violation of their migration status. The knowledge that one is potentially, or soon-to-be, illegal is a pervasive feature of temporary immigration status.

D. Privileged Foreigners? EU Citizens

Another striking finding in the empirical literature is that forced labour persists even amongst migrant workers with a relatively secure right to live and work in

but note the developments up to the Supreme Court ruling in *Hounga v Allen* [2014] UKSC 47. For a critique of the Court of Appeal ruling in *Hounga*, see A Bogg and T Novitz, 'Race Discrimination and the Doctrine of Illegality' (2013) 129 *Law Quarterly Review* 12. On the Supreme Court ruling, see A Bogg and V Mantouvalou, 'Illegality, Human Rights and Employment: A Watershed Moment for the United Kingdom Supreme Court?' (*UK Constitutional Law Blog*, 13 March 2014) http://ukconstitutionallaworg/2014/03/13/alan-bogg-and-virginia-mantouvalou-illegality-human-rights-and-employment-a-watershed-moment-for-the-united-kingdom-supreme-court/ (accessed 20 March 2014).

[119] J Carens, 'The Rights of Irregular Migrants' (2008) 22(2) *Ethics and International Affairs* 163.

[120] Council Directive (EC) 2009/52 providing for minimum standards on sanctions and measures against employers of illegally staying third-country nationals [2009] OJ L168/24 (Employer Sanctions Directive), Art 6.

[121] M Wishnie, 'Prohibiting the Employment of Unauthorized Immigrants: The Experiment Fails' [2007] *University of Chicago Legal Forum* 193.

the UK, such as EU citizens.[122] In some instances, there may be a transitional explanation here too, but more research is certainly warranted to understand the dynamics of forced labour in these cases. That EU citizens with secure migration status seem to be so easily exploitable suggests that it is not only the formal ties that create conditions of domination, but the other structural features of the chain of supply. One insight of this literature is that the structures are now in place in the UK to make even migrants with a right to reside and work vulnerable to forced labour. A combination of low wages, proliferation of agents and agency working, and social exclusion seem to foster forced labour, in some cases, irrespective of secure migration status. One notable feature of the empirical literature is that EU citizens in the UK are liable to perceive themselves to be subject to normal immigration law, and understand compliance with mere bureaucratic requirements[123] as necessary in order to be 'legal'.[124] Agents and employers can exploit these misunderstandings, leading to conditions of dependency and insecurity, similar to those experienced by other immigrants.

(i) Compelled Self-employment

Sometimes immigration law places barriers on the right to work as an employee, but permits self-employment. At the EU level, freedom of establishment and the freedom to provide services were permitted in the Europe Agreements (the pre-accession association agreements between the EU and Central and Eastern European candidate countries), and are also a feature of the transitional arrangements for A2 migrants from Bulgaria and Romania.[125] The effect on domestic labour law has not been fully explored, but the following data point is illuminating. In the UK, the general rate of self-employment is about 14%. For workers from Bulgaria and Romania, for whom self-employment is legally more accessible than employment, over 50% were self-employed in 2013.[126] Of course, there are many possible explanations. At the very least, the transitional measures encouraged self-employment over employment. Workers took on roles that would normally have been subject to an employment relationship, but on a self-employed basis.

The spectre of sham self-employment comes to mind also. Under these conditions, it appears that employers may be constructing sham arrangements in order to avoid the immigration restrictions. These measures were adopted in the name

[122] On the susceptibility to forced labour of the so-called A8 nationals (EU citizens from countries which joined the EU in 2004, namely the Czech Republic, Estonia, Hungary, Latvia, Lithuania, Poland, Slovakia and Slovenia), see P Dwyer and others (n 4).

[123] Such as compliance with the Worker Registration Scheme that was applicable to A8 nationals which requires registration of employment with each new employer. After 12 months of continued registered employment without interruption, the A8 national was entitled to full EU free movement rights and exempt from registration.

[124] This contrasts with the foundational assumption in EU law that residence rights derive from the Treaty, so that domestic authorization is declaratory rather than constitutive of the rights in question. See Case 48/75 *Royer* [1976] ECR 497.

[125] Accession Treaty 2005.

[126] Migration Observatory, *Costs and 'Benefits': Benefits Tourism, What Does it Mean?* (Oxford, Migration Observatory Commentary, 2014).

of protecting local workers, yet a paradoxical effect may be anticipated. If sectors become dominated by self-employment, the marginalization of employment law increases. The injustice of the sham arrangement in this context is not merely that the worker is truly an employee, and so should enjoy the protections of employment law. The UK Supreme Court has accepted that proposition in *Autoclenz v Belcher*, a decision with great importance for migrant workers.[127] In addition, migrant workers who must be self-employed in order to have a regular migration status are in reality *more* dependent than a 'normal' worker in that they will normally be aware that if the true nature of the working relationship is revealed, they become deportable. If they sought to vindicate their rights based on a proper construction of their work relationship (ie 'employee') they could find themselves without a right of residence, and so be denuded of their labour rights on that basis. They are in an effective double-bind.

E. Migration Status and Forced Labour

The cases of forced labour involving migrant workers in the UK are diverse, but tend to share some common features. In this final section, I draw together the features outlined above to illustrate how the migration process and migration status create fertile conditions for forced labour. Of necessity, this account generalizes somewhat, and draws out some common features of the forced labour identified in the empirical literature. Its purpose is not to identify a typical scenario of forced labour, but rather to understand the various factors which contribute to vulnerability to forced labour. I draw here also on the ILO Indicators of Forced Labour.[128]

Often, the work relationship looks promisingly normal at the outset, with an agreed wage at least. However, deception or obfuscation mask the true terms of the work relation. A hallmark of forced labour is that although there may be an apparently voluntary acceptance of the work, the terms of that initial agreement are obscure, or there is deception involved. Where the terms are unclear or unknown, the transaction lacks voluntariness. The ILO includes deceptive recruitment in its explanation of forced labour, namely 'when a person is recruited using false promises about the work'.[129] The solution to deceptive recruitment is to regulate the labour supply chain, and ensure that terms and conditions are accurately, clearly and comprehensively described. A more basic labour right is hard to imagine, yet ensuring that it is respected for migrant

[127] A Bogg, 'Sham Self-Employment in the Supreme Court' (2012) 41 *Industrial Law Journal* 328. For an analysis as regards migrant workers in particular, see A Bogg and T Novitz, 'Links between Individual Employment Law and Collective Labour Law: Their Implications for Migrant Workers' in Costello and Freedland (n 5).

[128] ILO, *Hard to See, Harder to Count: Survey Guidelines to Estimate Forced Labour of Adults and Children* (Geneva, ILO, 2012) 14–16.

[129] ibid 14.

workers requires some institutional adaptations.[130] A right to a written statement of terms and conditions in combating this problem is only a limited solution, particularly as is often the case when the terms do not reflect the reality of the situation, and migrant workers are not in a strong position to ensure that they are treated according to the written terms. As is discussed further below, collective and institutional enforcement of labour rights takes on particular importance in this context.

These conditions will amount to forced labour if exit options are constrained and there is the 'menace of a penalty'. In the empirical literature, examples of threats of and actual violence abound. Retaining travel documents too recurs in the UK examples and is identified in the ILO Indicators. However, the legal definition does not require that exit be impossible, merely that exit be constrained by the 'menace of a penalty'. As the Strasbourg case law and the ILO Indicators demonstrate, the menace of a penalty requirement is an invitation to investigate the nature of the domination in the work relation. Psychological pressures, playing on fear of being deported, playing on migrants' misunderstanding of their migration status, reminding the migrant of her dependency on the employer for renewal of status, all seem apt to be characterized as a 'menace of a penalty'. The threats need not be overt—simply relying on immigration law to create additional dependency and using that dependency to create a climate of fear are appropriately characterized as the 'menace of a penalty'.

A further phenomenon observed is that the workers' obligations to the intermediary or the end-user often seem to increase as work continues, such as where debts accrue through placement and accommodation charges. If wages are not specified, and debts accrue, that may undermine the voluntariness of the transaction, and constrain exit. Vulnerability tends to beget further vulnerability as time goes on. Even without threats of violence or overt coercion, deception and obfuscation can create work relations that cannot be characterized as voluntary, and exit from which is constrained.

V. Forced Labour—The Legal Responses

As discussed above, forced labour is universally acknowledged as a human rights violation. Responding to forced labour has focused on criminalization, rather than identifying positive duties to protect and promote human rights more broadly. This part advocates clarifying positive duties beyond criminalization, and uses labour law to elucidate further the various guarantees that are necessary to avoid forced labour.

Of course, immigration law is a big part of the problem: as long as migration

[130] As discussed above, migrants workers seem particularly vulnerable to sham transactions (n 127).

status is precarious or absent, workers will be additionally vulnerable in their work relations. The most direct solution to that problem would be to reform immigration law, and increase opportunities for secure migration status. If that move is politically blocked, then insulating labour law from questions of migration status would be a good move, and not simply a second best one, for it would also serve the interests of local workers well. This forms the first desideratum of a labour law response to forced labour, discussed below.

A. Criminalization

The criminal law approach is exemplified in the current UK law.[131] Criminalization entails setting up particular and well-defined criminal offences, usually involving a degree of culpability and a high standard of proof in order to establish guilt. Criminal law enforcement typically involves police investigation and prosecutorial activities. In the normal course, selective enforcement due to scarce prosecutorial resources and often prolonged investigations focusing on instances where forced labour is combined with serious violence are to be anticipated.

The criminal law also tends to imagine the perpetrator as individually responsible for the forced labour. While criminal law's expressive and punitive character singles out wrong-doers in this way, this ignores how forced labour comes about, which as this chapter demonstrates, is not only because individual villainous employers and intermediaries kidnap and confine workers (although that does happen too), but rather because immigration law and the migration process, together with weak protections for basic labour rights, set up conditions for forced labour.

Inevitably, criminal laws are invoked ex post. The guilt or innocence of the accused is the central issue, rather than the prevention of the wrongs in question, or vindication of victims' rights. We could usefully recall that the gangmaster responsible for the Morecambe Bay drownings was convicted of manslaughter.[132] The criminal law 'worked' in that the wrong-doer was held accountable and publicly punished. But was that enough to prevent forced labour in the future? The negative response to that question may verge on the self-evident. The threat of detection, prosecution and punishment under the criminal law may have some general deterrent effect, but it is evidently not enough if the vulnerabilities to forced labour and its business model remain in place. Yet, the current UK moves on forced labour and 'modern slavery' suggest that a criminal law *is* being portrayed as sufficient.

[131] See n 12.

[132] CPS, 'CPS Sends Signal to Illegal Employers after Morecambe Bay Convictions' (CPS Press Release 117/2006).

B. Human Rights Protections

International human rights law offers no panaceas for migrants. While human rights apply to all within the state's jurisdiction, that body of law also acknowledges the state's right to control entry and residence. It even permits detention for immigration reasons, as a 'necessary adjunct' of the state's immigration control prerogatives.[133] To turn to human rights protection to protect migrants' rights will not assure their right to remain in their country of residence, although it does permit migrants to assert that time and ties to a host country should constrain the state's right to remove them.[134] Human rights law nonetheless offers two enticing features: forced labour is unequivocally a human rights violation, a violation of an absolute right at that. Moreover, human rights law offers ways to construct and identify positive duties on the state, and thereby develop approaches that engage with the practices that create the conditions for forced labour in the first place.

Where immigration law creates vulnerability to forced labour, there are two possible moves in human rights law. The first is to integrate immigration status into the definition of forced labour, treating threats of denunciation as 'menace of a penalty'. Denunciation for immigration law infractions is listed as an ILO indicator of forced labour.[135] The ECtHR has accepted this approach too.[136] However, it is one thing to accept on the facts of an individual case that threats of denunciation may amount to the menace of a penalty in an already involuntary work relationship. It is quite another to accept as a general proposition that placing migrants in that vulnerable position generally contributes to creating forced labour.

The second approach is to expand the positive duties of the state to avoid violations of human rights. Thus far, the Strasbourg jurisprudence has focused predominantly on the duty to criminalize forced labour, seeming to indicate that this exhausted the scope of the positive duty.[137] Fudge and Strauss note that 'while *Siliadin* has been celebrated as an object lesson of the capacity of human rights law to address, both symbolically and practically, labour abuse,[138] it also reveals the limitations and biases in this approach'.[139] However, in *Rantsev*, the Court did identify particular features of immigration law that set up vulnerability

[133] *Saadi v UK* (2008) 47 EHRR 17. See C Costello, 'Human Rights and the Elusive Universal Subject: Immigration Detention under International Human Rights and EU Law' (2012) *Indiana Journal of Global Legal Studies 257.*

[134] Art 8 ECHR works in this way but is not a trump card.

[135] ILO (n 127) 16.

[136] *Siliadin* (n 51); *CN* (n 62).

[137] While the Court does not exclude the possibility that positive duties may extend beyond criminalization and criminal investigation, thus far that has been the focus, as exemplified in *CN v UK* (2013) 56 EHRR 24.

[138] See Mantouvalou (n 13) 430.

[139] Fudge and Strauss (n 99).

to trafficking, and found Cyprus in violation of Article 4 ECHR inter alia on this basis.[140] Accordingly, it stated that:

> [I]n addition to criminal law measures to punish traffickers, Article 4 requires member States to put in place adequate measures regulating businesses often used as a cover for human trafficking. Furthermore, a State's immigration rules must address relevant concerns relating to encouragement, facilitation or tolerance of trafficking.[141]

Some further inspiration may be drawn from the Strasbourg case law on Article 3 ECHR, prohibiting torture, and inhuman and degrading treatment. The Court has accepted that certain categories of migrant, namely asylum seekers, are in a position of particular legally constructed vulnerability, and accordingly found the state responsible for their destitution.[142] The legal construction of the vulnerability in question is evident in the fact that the asylum seekers lacked effective work rights,[143] and other means of support. The UK House of Lords (as it then was) initiated this line of reasoning in *Limbuela*.[144] Strasbourg followed this line, reflecting how national courts can lead Strasbourg by jurisprudential innovation. The state was found in breach of Article 3 ECHR for creating conditions that rendered people liable to extreme destitution. The case concerned three asylum seekers, Mr Limbuela, Mr Tesema and Mr Adam. The latter two went on to be recognized as refugees.

The House of Lords held that the legal prohibition on working, together with the deprivation of welfare benefits, meant that some asylum seekers were liable to become destitute. Not all poverty is a violation of Article 3 ECHR, but in identifying how the law created the conditions where destitution was likely, the state became responsible for creating those conditions. The central question was whether

> the treatment to which the asylum-seeker [was] being subjected by the entire package of restrictions and deprivations that surround him is so severe that it can properly be described as inhuman or degrading treatment within the meaning of [Article 3 ECHR].[145]

The Court was keen to avoid situations where asylum seekers could only receive support once they were actually enduring inhuman and degrading conditions. Once a breach was an 'imminent prospect', there was a duty on the state to act.[146]

This case law suggests that the positive duty to avoid forced labour should focus on the conditions prior to labour becoming forced. If the state admits migrants to the territory under conditions that render them vulnerable, then it must act to mitigate that vulnerability. The approach demands an assessment of

[140] *Rantsev* (n 77).
[141] ibid para 284.
[142] *MSS v Belgium and Greece* (2011) 53 EHRR 28.
[143] Greece did permit asylum seekers to work, but the ECtHR was found that this right was practically ineffective.
[144] *R (Limbuela) v Secretary of State for the Home Department* [2005] UKHL 66, [2006] 1 AC 396.
[145] ibid [58] (Lord Hope).
[146] ibid [62] (Lord Hope).

the labour conditions before the threshold of forced labour has been crossed, refocusing attention on basic labour rights.

C. Labour Law

As this chapter demonstrates, the vulnerability of migrant workers to forced labour arises from many sources. Neither the criminal law approach, nor Article 4 ECHR as presently interpreted, address the causes of that vulnerability. Some sources of vulnerability seem more amenable to legal mitigation than others. If immigration law created more secure statuses for migrant workers, some of the additional dependency would be mitigated, for instance. Assuming wholesale reform of immigration law, or a move towards significantly liberalized international migration are blocked, this part suggests that a labour rights approach is most fruitful in avoiding forced labour. Positive human rights obligations aim to ensure that human rights violations do not happen in the first place, they identify how the regulatory environment should be developed to avoid forced labour, taking measures to ensure the threshold of forced labour is not crossed. This is where labour law comes in. Indeed, the newly agreed ILO Protocol embodies precisely this preventative ethos.

A new Protocol to ILO Convention 29 on Forced Labour was adopted in 2014,[147] and aims to make the prohibition on forced labour more effective. Noteworthy provisions for the purposes of this discussion include the general duty to 'prevent and eliminate' forced labour (Article 1(1)), and the duty to create a national policy and plan of action to that end 'in consultation with employers' and workers' organizations, which shall involve systematic action by the competent authorities and, as appropriate, in coordination with employers' and workers' organizations, as well as with other groups concerned' (Article 1(2). Specific efforts must be undertaken to ensure the coverage and enforcement of 'labour law as appropriate' to 'all workers and all sectors of the economy' (Article 2(c)(i)) and to strengthen labour inspection services (Article 2(c)(ii)). Specific protection, particularly for migrant workers, is required 'from possible abusive and fraudulent practices during the recruitment and placement process' (Article 2(d)).

The labour law approach to preventing forced labour fits with the ethos of the Protocol, but is more specific in that my argument is based on addressing the identified vulnerabilities in the UK context. The three basic main elements include, first, insulation of labour rights from migration status; secondly, better collective and institutional protections for labour rights; and thirdly, better regulation of intermediaries. Evidently this is not labour law as we find it in the UK today, but the evidence of extreme labour exploitation and forced labour demands an urgent revisitation of the norms and institutions of labour law.

[147] ILO Protocol To the Forced Labour Convention 1930, ILO No 9A, 11 June 2014.

Naturally, this is just a sketch and serious matters of regulatory design remain to be resolved.

The central feature of a labour law approach is that it is attuned to the need to ensure that work relations are institutionalized so that they do not degenerate into forced labour. The most basic labour rights, such as the right to pay, require a host of institutional supports in order to be practical and effective: Workers must know and understand their rates of pay; transparency is required; deductions must be regulated; individual and collective voice about pay must be ensured; arguably a mechanism to ensure a minimum decent wage is required. Of course, not all these are required to prevent forced labour, but the point is that in work relations characterized by power asymmetries, without institutional support, even basic labour rights like the right to pay may be ineffective. Given that intermediaries both muddy the duty-bearer, and undermine pay rates, their regulation is crucial.

(i) Insulating Labour Rights from Migration Status

This chapter illustrates that migration status is often precarious. This means that some migrants lack a right to work, and so are simply precluded from enforcing their labour rights, due to the doctrine of illegality. Even if they are de jure protected by labour law, their precarious status means they may be unlikely to complain about breaches. If their employer or intermediary effectively controls their migration status, that added dependency makes complaint unlikely, a fact employers and intermediaries can all too easily exploit. Moreover, it appears that even migrants with secure migration status in the UK do not complain about series breaches of labour rights. For instance, Barnard has identified a serious 'enforcement gap' concerning migrants from the Central and Eastern European countries that joined the EU in 2004.[148] The solution seems to be both a legal and institutional one. Legally, there are good reasons to insulate labour rights from migration status altogether. Institutionally, greater institutional enforcement of labour rights seems required, also separated from enforcement of immigration law. Naturally, these reforms would need careful calibration not to undermine migration control prerogatives, but the alternative too has an impact on migration control: as long as some migrant workers are unprotected by labour rights, the demand for their 'ultra-flexible' labour will increase. The aim of preventing the employment of irregular migrants is served by ensuring they are protected by labour law, and that too protects local workers' rights better.

The Protocol requires that efforts must be undertaken to ensure the coverage and enforcement of 'labour law as appropriate' to 'all workers and all sectors of the economy' (Article 2(c)(i)). It also requires that effective and appropriate remedies must be made available for all victims 'irrespective of their presence or legal status in the national territory' (Article 4(1)). However, rather than auto-

[148] C Barnard, 'Enforcement of Employment Rights by Migrant Workers in the UK: The Case of EU-8 Nationals' in Costello and Freedland (n 5).

matic immunity from prosecution for victims, or a prohibition on the criminalization of the victims of forced labour, Article 4(2) has a less robust protection. Instead it provides that:

> Each Member shall, in accordance with the basic principles of its legal system, take the necessary measures to ensure that competent authorities *are entitled not to prosecute or impose penalties* on victims of forced or compulsory labour for their involvement in unlawful activities which they have been compelled to commit as a direct consequence of being subjected to forced or compulsory labour.' (emphasis added)

On a literal reading, this requires states to confer a discretion not to prosecute victims who have been coerced. However, the requirement will be tempered by the requirement to act 'in accordance with the basic principles of its legal system'. Experience with the non-penalization clause under the 1951 Refugee Convention in the UK suggests that creating defences and relying on prosecutorial discretion to protect refugees from being prosecuted for immigration offences is inadequate.[149] To prevent penalization we should simply not criminalize the migrant.

(ii) Regulating Intermediaries: A Labour Law Approach

The Protocol requires specific protection, particularly for migrant workers, 'from possible abusive and fraudulent practices during the recruitment and placement process' (Article 2(d)). This is an acknowledgement of the wider problem of abusive practices by labour intermediaries, and the added vulnerability of agency workers.

Labour intermediaries come in diverse forms, and their regulation is a perennial concern for labour law. The ILO historically sought to reduce their role. As Fudge explains,

> [T]he economic crisis of the 1930s triggered action at an international level, and in 1933 the ILO adopted the *Fee-Charging Employment Agencies Convention,* 1936 (No 34), which prohibited fee-charging agencies and gave meaning to the maxim that 'labour is not a commodity'.[150]

The ILO 1997 Convention on Private Employment Agencies (No 181) reflects a shift in the perception of agencies generally at the ILO level, reflecting an acceptance of their pervasive role in labour markets.[151] The UK workforce has the highest proportion of temporary agency workers in the EU, by a large margin,

[149] See eg *R v Mateta and others* [2013] EWCA Crim 1372. See A Aliverti 'The Court of Appeal Quashes Convictions for Document Fraud against Asylum Seekers' (2013), available at: http://border-criminologies.law.ox.ac.uk/court-of-appeal-quashes-convictions.

[150] J Fudge, 'Global Care Chains: Employment Agencies, and the Conundrum of Jurisdiction: Decent Work for Domestic Workers in Canada" (2011) 23 *Canadian Journal of Women and the Law* 235.

[151] See further L Vosko, 'Legitimizing the Triangular Employment Relationship: Emerging International Labour Standards from a Comparative Perspective' (1997–98) 19 *Comparative Labour Law and Policy Journal* 43.

with a proliferation of small, local operators.[152] In the migration context, intermediaries are often transnational, or there may be chain of intermediaries from home to host country, or spread across further jurisdictions.[153] ILO research indicates that 'private agents' are the primary channel through which forced labour takes place.[154]

Being an agency worker of any form can increase vulnerability. It makes the work relationship triangular (if not even more complex), making the identification of the employer and accordingly the allocation of labour law duties difficult.[155] The EU Agency Workers Directive does not address this basic problem. Nor does the Directive properly regulate agents, who invariably take a cut. Its added-value is significant, but limited. To the extent that its conditions are met, it clarifies some of the allocation of labour law duties.[156]

Labour law usually precludes agents from charging workers for finding them jobs.[157] In the UK, levying such charges is a criminal offence.[158] However, that prohibition appears to be widely flouted. Moreover, it is found in legislation from which the regulatory conditions for agencies were excised in the mid-1990s.[159] Licensing can be effective, provided it captures the transnational nature of the labour chain and prevents costs being imposed on the worker, as Fudge has demonstrated concerning the supply of domestic workers in some Canadian provinces.[160]

The UK Gangmasters Licensing Authority (GLA), introduced by a private member's bill to avoid the abuse of workers subject to 'gang' labour after More-

[152] A Balch and S Scott, 'Labour Market Flexibility and Worker Security in an Age of Migration' in M Bommes and G Sciortino (eds), *Foggy Social Structures: Irregular Migration, European Labour Markets and the Welfare State* (Amsterdam, Amsterdam University Press, 2011); M Lalani and H Metcalf, *Forced Labour in the UK: The Business Angle* (York, Joseph Rowntree Foundation, 2012); Allain and others (n 97).

[153] While we may imagine migration as a straightforward unidirectional move from home to host state, many migrant workers form part of a class of mobile workers, moving from host state to host state. For instance, Fudge identifies how agencies in Canada recruit Philippina domestic workers from Hong Kong and Singapore when they wish to avoid worker-protective restrictions imposed by the Philippines, which only apply when workers are directly recruited from there. See Fudge (n 147).

[154] Report of the Director-General, *A Global Alliance Against Forced Labour: Global Report under the Follow-up to the ILO Declaration on Fundamental Principles and rights at Work 2005* (International Labour Conference 93rd Session 2005 Report I (B) 2005)

[155] N Kountouris, 'The Legal Determinants of Precariousness in Personal Work Relations: A European Perspective' (2012) 34 *Comparative Labour Law and Policy Journal* 21.

[156] Directive 2008/104/EC of 19 November 2008 on Temporary Agency Work [2008] OJ L327/9. The Directive guarantees the following working and employment conditions: equal treatment; access to information regarding vacancies; prohibition on agency fees; access to the amenities or collective facilities; and the inclusion of agency workers in the threshold for worker representation. See also N Countouris and R Horton, 'The Temporary Agency Work Directive: Another Broken Promise?' (2009) *Industrial Law Journal* 329. On agency work generally, see ACL Davies, 'The Implementation of the Directive on Temporary Agency Work in the UK: A Missed Opportunity' (2010) 1 *European Labour Law Journal* 303.

[157] Private Employment Agencies Convention 1997 (ILO Convention No 181), Art 7.

[158] Employment Agencies Act 1973, s 6.

[159] See further K Strauss, 'Unfree Labour and the Role of Temporary Agency Work in the United Kingdom' in Fudge and Strauss (eds) (n 95).

[160] Fudge (n 147).

cambe Bay, covers a limited range of sectors.[161] Within those limited sectors, though, it applies in a comprehensive manner, to any supply of workers in the UK (irrespective of where the gangmaster is based), taking a wide non-traditional understanding of 'worker'. As Davies explains, the provisions 'break out of the traditional labour law paradigm in which protection is reserved to individuals working under a contract of employment or a worker's contract, and—arguably—doing so on a lawful basis'.[162] Licensing depends on resources to monitor compliance with the conditions of the license, and appropriate sanctions for acting without a licence, and it appears that the GLA may be under-resourced. Moreover, there have been no moves to expand its remit, despite consistent calls to do so.[163]

(iii) Institutional Enforcement

Trade unions inevitably face difficulties in organizing migrant workers, especially temporary and irregular ones. This is particularly so in the UK, given low union membership and patchy coverage. This is not to discount the importance and potential of organizing migrant workers.[164] However, ordinarily, organizing migrant workers is more challenging than for local workers. Accordingly, institutional protections for labour rights are even more important. There again, the UK falls short: at present there is no single labour inspectorate,[165] and institutional protections of basic labour rights are weak, if not non-existent. The institutional architecture is ad hoc and fragmented.[166] In addition, there has been a steady move away from institutional protections for labour rights. The Wages Inspectorate was abolished in 1993,[167] and the Agricultural Wages Board was abolished in June 2013.[168] As discussed above in relation to intermediaries, licensing of employment agencies ended in 1994,[169] so there is no regulatory oversight

[161] It applies to the supply of workers to the agricultural, forestry, horticultural, shellfish gathering, food processing, and packaging industries by setting up and operating a licensing scheme for labour providers across the UK. Its mission is to safeguard the welfare and interests of workers while ensuring that labour providers operate within the law. See further M Wilkinson with G Craig and A Gaus, *Forced Labour in the UK and the Gangmasters Licensing Authority* (Hull University, 2010); K Strauss, 'Unfree Again: Social Reproduction, Flexible Labour Markets and the Resurgence of Gang Labour in the UK' (2013) 45(1) *Antipode* 180.

[162] Davies (n 41), citing *Allen v Hounga* [2012] EWCA Civ 609, [2012] IRLR 685 (at the time of writing, on appeal to the Supreme Court) discussed by Bogg and Novitz (n 116).

[163] For example, the Council of Europe group of experts against human trafficking advised that the 'GLA's scope of competence could be further extended to other sectors such as hospitality … and construction' See GRETA (n 87) para 100.

[164] See eg V Mantouvalou, 'Organising against Abuse and Exclusion: the Associational Rights of Undocumented Workers' in Costello and Freedland (n 5).

[165] For an overview of labour inspectorates in the UK (excluding Northern Ireland), see V Mantouvalou, *Study on Labour Inspection Sanctions and Remedies: The case of the United Kingdom* (ILO Working Document No 19, 2011).

[166] For an overview, see ibid.

[167] Trade Union Reform and Employment Rights Act 1993, s 35.

[168] Davies (n 41). Abolished by Enterprise and Regulatory Reform Act 2013, s 72 although the most recent Agricultural Wages Order remained in effect until 30 September 2013.

[169] Deregulation and Contracting Out Act 1994, s 35.

there any longer. The Employment Agencies Standards (EAS) Inspectorate has a limited remit, and takes a light-touch approach.[170] It has been suggested that the sharp difference between the EAS and the GLA cannot be justified.[171]

There is also the Health and Safety Executive to oversee health and safety standards.[172] Her Majesty's Revenue and Customs has a role in relation to the minimum wage.[173] The Equality and Human Rights Commission can examine some labour rights issues.[174] Noteworthy in this context is that the institution's report into recruitment into the meat and poultry sectors recommended additional institutional safeguards against forced labour, in particular noting the vulnerability of migrant agency workers. The recommendations included enhancing the remit of the GLA.[175]

The phenomenon of forced labour emerges when vulnerable migrant workers find themselves in work relationships the terms of which are unclear and exploitative, and where exit options are constrained. Those conditions emerge all too often as migrant workers often are loath to complain due to their migration status depending on employers and intermediaries, or due to indebtedness. Inability to understand or enforce basic labour rights such as the right to pay, to clarity about terms and conditions, and to limits on working time, create additional vulnerabilities and dependency, constraining exit options further. Without great collective or institutional enforcement of basic labour rights, these conditions seem unlikely to be rectified. Evidently, consideration should be given to the appropriate regulatory forms and mechanisms. But on any account, the current patchwork falls short. The 2014 Protocol obliges parties to strengthen labour inspection services (Article 2(c)(ii)). Together with the general duty to prevent forced labour (Article 1(1)), and develop national policies and action plans on forced labour (Article 2), these duties should trigger significant reform of institutional protections for labour rights.

VI. Conclusion

Forced labour is a human rights violation. The human rights law approach may seem promising, but two unhelpful moves dominate the current state of human rights law. While the Strasbourg case law helpfully places positive duties on

[170] Established by the Employment Agencies Act 1973. Later amended by the Conduct of Employment Agencies and Employment Business Regulations 2003 and the Employment Act 2008. See further M Wynn, 'Regulating Rogues? Employment Agency Enforcement and Sections 15–18 of the Employment Act 2008' (2009) 38(1) *Industrial Law Journal* 64.

[171] Wynn, ibid 72.

[172] Established by the Health and Safety at Work etc Act 1974.

[173] HMRC are appointed as enforcement officers under the National Minimum Wage Act 1998, s 13.

[174] Established by the Equality Act 2006.

[175] Equality and Human Rights Commission (n 10) Recommendation 25.

states to prevent forced labour, it has yet to develop a labour rights approach to combating forced labour. Moreover, the criminalization in the UK explicitly refers to the terms of Article 4 ECHR, giving the false impression that it exhausts the human rights duties to prevent forced labour. Both the criminal law approach and the human rights approach have also unhelpfully become intertwined with prohibitions on human trafficking. Trafficking focuses (as the term suggests) on the transportation of migrants across borders with the coercion at that stage. As this chapter demonstrates, this focus is unhelpfully narrow: if we are concerned about forced labour, we need to look at the entire labour supply chain, working conditions, and exit options of migrant and local workers. Moreover, the noise of trafficking discourse is liable to drown out a proper discussion on the causes of forced labour, which are more banal that the villainous portrayal of traffickers would suggest.

This account does not offer simple solutions. Migrants usually choose to migrate. They are, at least at the outset, strangers to the polity that sets the terms of their admission: migrants do not negotiate the terms and conditions of their entry and residence in the host state. As immigration law, at least in part, determines their work relations, they are liable to domination in a way that local workers are not. Given the failure to regulate transnational labour intermediaries (with the notable exception of 'gangmasters' in the UK), migrants may find themselves paying fees repeatedly in order to work. The extended supply chain renders them vulnerable to further exploitation. Step by step, the law creates vulnerability upon vulnerability. There are few Gordian knots: states could regulate labour intermediaries better, and set up systems to monitor and enforce labour rights for all workers on the territory, without comprising their migration control prerogatives. A general labour inspectorate would have much to recommend it over the current fragmented, patchy institutional disarray.

In the accounts of forced labour in the UK, the most basic labour rights are repeatedly flouted, including the right to pay, to clarity as to terms and conditions, and to limits on working time. Criminalizing forced labour seems like a spectacular sideshow compared to the real event, enforcing decent working conditions for all. Human rights law offers no panaceas, but in establishing positive duties on states to respect, protect and promote human rights, it allows us to investigate how vulnerability to forced labour is legally constructed and to require the state to address or at least mitigate that vulnerability. Labour law shows the way, with the new ILO Protocol identifying practical positive steps to be taken. What is the likelihood of such worker-protective developments?

The politics of the autonomy claim for labour law are also worth recalling. Collective *laissez-faire* in particular was rooted in a view of the state as hostile to the interests of labour, and liable to authoritarianism.[176] Similarly, Durand's 1945 account which so influenced Wedderburn[177] was premised on the autonomy

[176] R Dukes, 'Otto Kahn-Freund and Collective Laissez-Faire: An Edifice without a Keystone?' (2009) 72(2) *Modern Law Review* 220.

[177] Wedderburn (n 16) citing P Durand, *Le Particularism du Droit du Travail* (1945).

of collective actors and suspicion of state-imposed solutions. Today's political context makes revisiting the roots of the autonomy claim all the more urgent. Admittedly, some legal and institutional changes to labour law have been welcome adaptations in light of the wane of the standard employment relationship, which was premised on the male breadwinner model, and a sharp insider–outsider dichotomy in labour market participation. However, the move away from the standard employment relationship was also part of a neoliberal political turn. Its central tenet, never empirically well-founded, was that worker-protective legislation, in particular that on job security, was a drag on job creation.[178] If the laws and institutions of labour law have been dismantled with neoliberal ideological zeal, a normative response is all the more important.

Crucially, engaging with immigration law reveals a further authoritarian dimension to the neoliberal project. While the neoliberal project trades on liberal and libertarian values as regards markets, it also has a strong authoritarian dimension, relying on the state to police its edges.[179] The increasingly punitive and carceral aspects of migration control focused on 'outsiders' are politically coherent with the insecurity of economic life for 'insiders'. As states expose workers to greater economic risks, offering them 'security' from migrants becomes a spectacular distraction from the processes whereby all workers, both migrant and local, are made increasingly insecure and so vulnerable to exploitation and domination.

The labour law approach to forced labour advocated here is in this sense an 'autonomous' one, in that it accepts the particularities of the values of the personal work relation and the need for particular institutions to make those commitments effective. Asserting the autonomy of labour law is not a plea to insulate labour law from other domains, but rather to ensure that other areas of law do not sideline, distort and undermine labour law. That forced labour happens at all in the UK demonstrates the risks when some work relations are excluded from labour law's purview, or where its protections are ineffective. The normative core of labour law, seeking to avoid domination in work relations, demands that all workers in the territory enjoy labour rights.

[178] For an account of that process, see the discussion of 'stability' in Freedland and Kountouris (n 19) 379–81. The authors cite J Stiglitz, 'The Global Crisis, Social Protection and Jobs' [2009] *International Labour Review* 11: 'All of these so-called reforms have made our economic system less stable and less able to weather the storm.'

[179] See Menz (n 33).

Part III

Labour Law's Autonomy: Labour Law, Public Law and Human Rights

9

Labour Law as Public Law

ACL DAVIES*

I. Introduction

The impact of public law upon labour law was the subject of an important and interesting article by Paul Davies and Mark Freedland in 1997.[1] In that article, they identified three 'modes' of public law—pluralist, individualist and constitutional rights-based—and traced the varying degrees of influence of these modes on the labour law of the time. This chapter continues Davies and Freedland's exploration of the relationship between labour law and public law by applying the framework they set out to recent developments in the case law, and refining and developing the framework in various respects.

I will argue that judicial scrutiny of government action is generally more intensive in public law than it is in labour law because the judges perceive their role differently in the two disciplines. In public law, they see themselves as upholding the rule of law by keeping the government in check, whereas in labour law, they recognize that there is a balance to be struck between employers' and workers' interests and that there is a role for Parliament in deciding how this should be done. Thus, although there are important similarities between labour law and public law, the two disciplines are quite distinct. I will develop this argument by making three main claims.

First, as Davies and Freedland noted, the 'individualist' mode of public law, in which the aim is to protect individuals against encroachment by the state, remains highly relevant to labour law.[2] There are important and interesting analogies to be drawn between judicial review of government action on grounds of procedural fairness and substantive reasonableness, and the courts' assessment of employers' decisions on similar grounds in labour law. In general terms,

* I have benefited greatly from discussions with Alan Bogg and Mark Freedland about this paper. Responsibility for errors remains my own. This chapter considers developments up to 17 April 2014.

[1] P Davies and M Freedland, 'The Impact of Public Law on Labour Law, 1972–1997' (1997) 26 *Industrial Law Journal* 311.

[2] Ibid 318–27.

this part of the analysis shows—as Davies and Freedland found—that judicial scrutiny in public law tends to be more intensive than it is in labour law.

Second, Davies and Freedland anticipated that the 'constitutional rights-based' mode of public law would become more important over time.[3] This prediction has been borne out not, as they supposed, through EU law, but rather through the enactment of the Human Rights Act 1998 (HRA). I will argue that although this Act has had important effects in labour law, its impact is on public law is much more transformative. As with the 'individualist' mode, it seems that judicial scrutiny on human rights grounds is more intensive in public law than it is in labour law.

Third, I will add a new element to the Davies and Freedland framework by comparing the response of both public law and labour law to the contracting out of public services to the private sector. Here, public law has tended to step back: for example, the judges have been reluctant to treat private contractors as if they were performing public functions for the purposes of judicial review or the HRA. Labour law has fared somewhat better: the Court of Justice of the European Union (CJEU) has applied the Acquired Rights Directive (ARD) to various outsourcing situations so that employees have some protection during the process.[4] In this area, labour law offers more intensive scrutiny than public law. I suggest that this supports my overall argument because it demonstrates a judicial reluctance to extend public law scrutiny beyond purely public situations.

A few caveats are in order before I begin. First, my main focus will be on the case law in both disciplines, since this is where there is the greatest potential for comparison between them. This should not be taken to suggest, in general terms, that the common law of employment is a more important area of study than the statute law of employment. Second, although it is a worthwhile exercise in principle, I will not systematically separate 'public' and 'private' labour law—the labour law applicable to public sector workers and private sector workers, respectively—in my analysis.[5] Although both the government and the courts have tended to resist the emergence of separate employment principles for public sector workers, there are some examples of this in practice, but space precludes a detailed account of them in the present chapter.[6] And third, again for reasons of space, this chapter will seek merely to map out the territory for comparison between public law and labour law, with a view to engaging in deeper analysis—and, importantly, normative discussion of the material—in future work.

[3] Ibid 327–34.

[4] Directive 2001/23/EC.

[5] For an interesting recent exploration of this divide, see M Freedland and N Kountouris, 'Common Law and Voice', in A Bogg and T Novitz (eds), *Voices at Work* (forthcoming).

[6] For a recent decision in which this issue was debated, see *R(G) v X School Governors* [2011] UKSC 30, [2012] 1 AC 167.

II. Labour Law and Public Law in 'Individualist' Mode

The 'individualist' mode was one of three modes of public law identified by Davies and Freedland in their 1997 article.[7] They used this term to refer to public law's role in protecting individuals against the abuse of public power: in the terminology developed by Harlow and Rawlings, public law's 'red light' function.[8] It is worth noting that the 'individualist' mode is not entirely distinguishable from the 'constitutional rights-based' mode to be discussed in the next section, since nowadays much of the task of protecting individuals against encroachment by the state takes place through the HRA. However, as Davies and Freedland noted, the two modes of public law have different emphases and it is worth separating them for explanatory purposes.[9]

The idea of protecting the individual against the abuse of public power has obvious parallels in labour law, both in terms of protecting the individual against the employer and, more controversially, protecting the individual against his or her union. Based on a detailed examination of the case law, Davies and Freedland concluded that the 'individualist' mode had had considerable influence over labour law, although they noted that the courts were much more willing to embrace it in cases brought by individuals against trade unions than they were in cases brought by individuals against employers.[10]

In what follows, I will suggest that much the same conclusion could be drawn today: while public law continues to develop increasingly intensive scrutiny of government, labour law adopts a more 'hands-off' approach to employers in particular. I will examine two groups of cases: those involving procedural fairness and those in which reasonableness tests are applied.

A. Procedural Fairness

There is a long tradition at common law of requiring the government to observe basic principles of natural justice or procedural fairness in its decision-making. A natural justice case, *Ridge v Baldwin*, is often regarded as the starting-point for the modern revival of the judicial review jurisdiction.[11] The common law requires that the individual be given notice of the case against him or her and

[7] Davies and Freedland (n 1) 318–27. The third, 'pluralist', mode will not be discussed in this chapter because, as Davies and Freedland found in 1997, it remains the case today that there is limited evidence of it in either public law or labour law.

[8] C Harlow and R Rawlings, *Law and Administration*, 3rd edn (Cambridge, Cambridge University Press, 2009) ch 1.

[9] Davies and Freedland (n 1) 313.

[10] ibid 319. My focus will be on cases against employers since there have been few new cases against trade unions (outside the human rights context) since Davies and Freedland's article in 1997.

[11] *Ridge v Baldwin* [1964] AC 40.

an opportunity to be heard before an administrative decision affecting his or her important interests is taken (though this hearing need not always be oral), that the decision-maker be free from personal bias, and (in many cases, though not as a matter of general rule) that reasons be given for the decision.

The enactment of the HRA has brought Article 6 ECHR into play in this area, though this has given rise to difficulties for the courts. The requirements of Article 6 in terms of procedural fairness are not entirely clear but are probably somewhat more extensive than those at common law. For example, the decision-maker may need to be institutionally independent (or at least subject to 'full' review by an independent court)[12] and, depending on the seriousness of the case, the individual may be entitled to legal representation at the hearing.[13] However, the great uncertainty about Article 6 lies in its scope of application. An individual is entitled to an Article 6-compliant hearing when his or her 'civil rights or obligations' are being determined. Although the UK courts initially adopted a relaxed attitude to the applicability of Article 6,[14] they have become more reluctant to use it for fear that it might require extensive changes to traditional patterns of administrative decision-making.[15] The ECtHR's case-law on the point remains unclear.[16]

Interestingly, the common law's rules on procedural fairness have continued to develop even without direct reliance on Article 6.[17] Of course, this may be some sort of 'shadow' effect: perhaps the courts are anticipating (or mitigating) the impact of Article 6 by enhancing common law doctrines. But for present purposes what is important is the ongoing *development* of procedural scrutiny of administrative decision-making at common law. Two cases may be used to illustrate the point.

In *R (Smith) v Parole Board* the claimants were prisoners who had been released on licence but then recalled to prison for breaching their licence conditions.[18] In both cases, the Parole Board decided not to recommend their re-release. They sought judicial review of the Parole Board's decision on the grounds that they had not been afforded an oral hearing before that decision was taken. The House of Lords held that although an oral hearing was not required in every case, it should be offered where 'the prisoner seeks to challenge the truth or accuracy of the allegations that led to his recall, or seeks to provide an explanation for them which was not taken into account or was disputed when his recall was recommended by his supervising probation officer'.[19] The

[12] *Bryan v UK* (1996) 21 EHRR 342.
[13] *Ezeh v UK* (2004) 39 EHRR 1.
[14] *Begum v Tower Hamlets LBC* [2003] UKHL 5, [2003] 2 AC 430.
[15] *Ali v Birmingham City Council* [2010] UKSC 8, [2010] 2 AC 39.
[16] *Tsfayo v UK* (2009) 48 EHRR 18.
[17] For a useful overview, see P Craig, 'Perspectives on Process: Common Law, Statutory and Political' [2010] *Public Law* 275. The role of the common law is strongly emphasized in *Re Reilly* [2013] UKSC 61, [2013] 3 WLR 1020.
[18] *R (Smith) v Parole Board* [2005] UKHL 1, [2005] 1 WLR 350.
[19] ibid [68], per Lord Hope.

case was decided on common law grounds, largely because of the uncertainties surrounding the applicability of Article 6. The decision highlights the developing nature of procedural protection at common law. Although the Parole Board had, for many years, operated on the basis that there was no need to provide hearings in this type of case, the requirements of procedural fairness had, in effect, become more exacting over time.[20]

A second example is the recent decision of the Supreme Court in the *Bank Mellat* case.[21] The Treasury made an order under the Counter-Terrorism Act 2008 prohibiting anyone operating in the UK financial sector from having any dealings with the claimant Iranian bank, with a view to frustrating the funding of Iran's nuclear programme. The Supreme Court upheld the bank's substantive challenge to the order on the grounds that (despite considerable deference to the Treasury under the circumstances) it was disproportionate to single out one Iranian bank over others. For present purposes, the important feature of the case is the Supreme Court's ruling on procedural fairness. Here, it was held that it was unlawful to take this measure against the bank without first providing it with an opportunity to make representations, again as a matter of common law.[22] Although the measure took the form of an order laid before Parliament, the majority held that this did not preclude the implication of a duty to give the bank a hearing, because the measure was targeted at the bank, was serious in its effects and was based on factual assumptions that the bank might want to challenge.

These quite powerful public law decisions on procedural fairness can be contrasted with the position in labour law. In cases involving employers, there are three possible sources of procedural fairness norms: the express terms of the individual's contract of employment, implied terms in the contract of employment, or the 'reasonableness' test in the law of unfair dismissal.[23] Two main trends can be discerned in the case law here. First, in the common law of the contract of employment, there is no real equivalent of the gradual expansion of procedural protections in public law. Instead, the courts have largely sought to confine employees to their remedies in the statute law of unfair dismissal. Second, despite various attempts by government to encourage greater use of workplace procedures, the statute law of unfair dismissal involves a relatively 'light-touch' approach to procedural fairness. As a result, in terms of both the content of procedures and the methods for their enforcement, employment law lags behind public law.

Davies and Freedland suggested that the implied term of mutual trust and confidence might serve as a vehicle for developing public-law-like obligations

[20] ibid [63]–[68] (Lord Hope).

[21] *Bank Mellat v HM Treasury* [2013] UKSC 39, [2013] 3 WLR 179.

[22] ibid [28]–[49] (Lord Sumption).

[23] Public sector office-holders may be able to bring an application for judicial review and thus gain access to natural justice protections. For a recent example, see *R (Shoesmith) v Ofsted* [2011] EWCA Civ 642, [2011] ICR 1195, discussed by Freedland and Kountouris (n 5).

for employers, such as a duty to observe basic norms of procedural fairness.[24] In my view, it is important not to overstate the link between the implied term and public law. Although the content of the implied term has clear links to public law standards,[25] its underlying role is to maintain a successful long-term relationship between employer and employee. It thus reflects the relational nature of the contract of employment. As Freedland has argued in other contexts, public law is concerned with the review of discrete decisions and not with developments over time.[26]

The implied term has proved useful during the employment relationship. A good example of this is *Gogay*, in which the employer suspended the employee and told her that it was because she had been accused of child abuse.[27] The Court of Appeal held that the implied term had been breached because the employer should have considered options other than suspension and should have investigated the 'allegations' more fully before acting upon them. In *Eastwood* claims of this kind were held to survive the employee's subsequent dismissal.[28] However, where the case concerns the dismissal itself, the courts have shown themselves to be highly reluctant to make creative use of the implied term to develop procedural fairness norms, largely on policy grounds. Thus, in *Johnson* the House of Lords rejected the claimant's argument that he should be allowed to recover substantial damages in respect of his employer's alleged breach of the implied term of mutual trust and confidence in the manner of his dismissal.[29] A key element in the reasoning was the (much-contested) view that Parliament had provided a remedy in the statute law of unfair dismissal, with a limit on the damages that could be recovered, so the courts should not develop the common law to provide ways of 'getting round' that limit.[30] More surprisingly, in *Edwards* a majority in the Supreme Court applied the same reasoning to claims involving alleged breaches by employers of express terms entitling their employees to disciplinary procedures before dismissal.[31] It was held that such terms did not entitle the aggrieved employee to claim substantial damages (unless expressly agreed between the parties, which is unlikely) because it was thought that the parties included them in their contracts in order to satisfy the law of unfair dismissal, where the appropriate remedy for any breaches should be sought. Of course, simply enforcing the parties' agreed procedures would not necessarily fulfil the requirements of natural justice, nor would it constitute a vehicle for developing

[24] Davies and Freedland (n 1) 325.

[25] For an excellent overview, see AL Bogg, '*Bournemouth University Higher Education Corporation v Buckland*: Re-establishing Orthodoxy at the Expense of Coherence?' (2010) 39 *Industrial Law Journal* 408.

[26] MR Freedland, 'Government by Contract and Public Law' [1994] *Public Law* 86, 97.

[27] *Gogay v Hertfordshire CC* [2000] IRLR 703 (CA).

[28] *Eastwood v Magnox Electric Plc* [2004] UKHL 35, [2005] 1 AC 503. It is unclear how much of *Eastwood* (at least in relation to procedures leading up to dismissal) survives the decision in *Edwards v Chesterfield Royal Hospital NHS Foundation Trust* [2011] UKSC 58, [2012] 2 AC 22.

[29] *Johnson v Unisys Ltd* [2001] UKHL 13, [2003] 1 AC 518.

[30] ibid [37] (Lord Hoffmann).

[31] Above n 28.

general norms of procedural fairness in contracts of employment. Nevertheless, a refusal to uphold the *express* terms of a contract shows a remarkable reluctance on the part of the courts to intervene in this area.

As a result, employees have few options but to look to the law of unfair dismissal for procedural protections. As is well known, unfair dismissal law uses a 'band of reasonable responses' test to assess the employer's reaction to the situation in which it finds itself. It has long been accepted that the reasonableness enquiry has procedural as well as substantive dimensions,[32] and indeed one of the criticisms of this area of law is that tribunals and courts are more interested in whether the employer has observed fair procedures than they are in the substantive fairness of the dismissal.

The exact requirements of procedural fairness vary according to the employer's reason for the dismissal, so for simplicity I will focus on misconduct cases. In cases of this type, the requirements are laid down in a well-known quotation from the EAT's decision in *British Home Stores v Burchell*:

> What the tribunal have to decide every time is, broadly expressed, whether the employer who discharged the employee on the ground of the misconduct in question (usually, though not necessarily, dishonest conduct) entertained a reasonable suspicion amounting to a belief in the guilt of the employee of that misconduct at that time. That is really stating shortly and compendiously what is in fact more than one element. First of all, there must be established by the employer the fact of that belief; that the employer did believe it. Secondly, that the employer had in his mind reasonable grounds upon which to sustain that belief. And thirdly, we think, that the employer, at the stage at which he formed that belief on those grounds, at any rate at the final stage at which he formed that belief on those grounds, had carried out as much investigation into the matter as was reasonable in all the circumstances of the case.[33]

In subsequent cases, it has been accepted that employers should take greater care in investigating and hearing more serious allegations, for example, where they relate to the commission of a criminal offence and are likely to affect the individual's future employment prospects.[34] Practical guidance on disciplinary procedures is afforded by the ACAS Code of Practice, to which tribunals must have regard when deciding cases.[35] This indicates that the employer should give the employee written notice of allegations and invite him or her to a hearing at which he or she should be able to present a case (with a statutory right to be accompanied by a colleague or union official), with the further possibility of an appeal against the decision. In terms of remedies, it is possible for an employee to recover damages in respect of a dismissal that was procedurally but not substantively unfair, and the tribunal may increase damages by up to 25% if

[32] *Whitbread Plc v Hall* [2001] EWCA Civ 268, [2001] ICR 699.
[33] *British Home Stores Ltd v Burchell* [1980] ICR 303, 304.
[34] *Salford Royal NHS Foundation Trust v Roldan* [2010] EWCA Civ 522, [2010] ICR 1457.
[35] ACAS, *Code of Practice 1: Disciplinary and Grievance Procedures* (2009).

the employer unreasonably fails to comply with the ACAS Code.[36] However, this is subject to the general cap on unfair dismissal damages noted above.

In practical terms, there are strong similarities between natural justice and the procedural protections available in the law of unfair dismissal: the individual is entitled to notice of the case against him or her and has a right to be heard under both bodies of law. However, these similarities may mask deeper differences. First, the courts have long been clear that employees are not entitled to natural justice.[37] Second, the approach is different. In public law, although natural justice has no fixed content and must be adapted to the circumstances, it is for the court to determine whether the decision-maker gave the individual sufficient procedural protection. In employment law, procedural protections are derived from the 'band of reasonable responses' test and the ultimate question to be asked is whether or not any investigation by the employer was *reasonable* in all the circumstances of the case.[38] This encourages tribunals and courts to focus on the economic and practical constraints facing the employer. While courts are alert to these concerns in public law too, they seem to be less central to the enquiry. Put simply, there is a difference between asking whether the requirements of natural justice have been met (even if these are flexible), and whether an employer has behaved reasonably in a procedural sense.

B. Reasonableness

A second fertile area for comparison between labour law and public law in 'individualist' mode is the use of reasonableness tests in the two disciplines. Here, we see a similar phenomenon. While public law has developed a more intensive approach to the scrutiny of government decisions, labour law has tended to be more deferential to employers.

It goes without saying that the starting-point for reasonableness in public law is Lord Greene MR's judgment in the *Wednesbury* case: that a decision may only be struck down if it is 'so unreasonable that no reasonable' decision-maker could have made it.[39] Many commentators—and judges—now think that, with the advent of proportionality as a test in EU and HRA cases, the time has come to replace reasonableness with proportionality, though so far at least this change has not occurred.[40] What is important for present purposes is that public law cases rarely rely on the 'perversity' standard laid down in the *Wednesbury* case itself. Nowadays, the courts are much more likely to ask whether the decision

[36] Trade Union and Labour Relations (Consolidation) Act 1992 (TULRCA), s 207A.

[37] On this point see *McLory v Post Office* [1992] ICR 758. The position is different for office-holders in the public sector with access to judicial review: above n 23.

[38] *Whitbread Plc v Hall* [2001] ICR 699.

[39] *Associated Provincial Picture Houses Ltd v Wednesbury Corporation* [1948] 1 KB 223 (CA), 230.

[40] See eg *R (Association of British Civilian Internees (Far East Region)) v Secretary of State for Defence* [2003] EWCA Civ 473, [2003] QB 1397, and P Craig, 'Proportionality, Rationality and Review' [2010] *New Zealand Law Review* 265.

was 'rational' or 'reasonable',[41] and to recognize that the intensity of review under this test can vary according to the importance of what is at stake for the claimant.[42] The approach was summarized by Sir Thomas Bingham MR (as he then was) in *ex p Smith*:

> The court may not interfere with the exercise of an administrative discretion on substantive grounds save where the court is satisfied that the decision is unreasonable in the sense that it is beyond the range of responses open to a reasonable decision-maker. But in judging whether the decision-maker has exceeded this margin of appreciation the human rights context is important. The more substantial the interference with human rights, the more the court will require by way of justification before it is satisfied that the decision is reasonable in the sense outlined above.[43]

In judicial review, then, the judges recognize that more than one reasonable option may be open to the decision-maker, but emphasize that it is the decision-maker's responsibility to justify the decision, particularly where human rights are at stake. It is also important to note that the reasonableness test works alongside a raft of other requirements (proper purposes, relevant considerations, respect for legitimate expectations and so on), and therefore, in public law, it is never the only standard against which the decision must be evaluated.

In labour law, reasonableness tests are used in various areas but I will focus on two here: unfair dismissal and bonus cases. In unfair dismissal, tribunals are directed by statute to consider whether the employer 'acted reasonably or unreasonably' in treating the given reason as a reason for dismissing the employee under the circumstances.[44] As is well known, this test is subject to the interpretation placed upon it by the EAT in the *Iceland Frozen Foods* case:

> [T]he function of the industrial tribunal, as an industrial jury, is to determine whether in the particular circumstance of each case the decision to dismiss the employee fell within the band of reasonable responses which a reasonable employer might have adopted.[45]

This interpretation is clearly very similar to that in *ex p Smith*, quoted above. Indeed, in the *Turner* case Elias LJ made clear that the 'band of reasonable responses' is not a *Wednesbury* or 'perversity' test and should not be treated as such.[46] However, although both branches of law use similar formulations, a difference of emphasis remains. In the public law context, as we saw above, it is for the decision-maker to justify his or her decision. In labour law, there is no equivalent of this obligation: the burden of proof is formally neutral and the

[41] See eg *R v Chief Constable of Sussex, ex p International Trader's Ferry Ltd* [1999] 2 AC 418 (HL), 452 (Lord Cooke).

[42] *R v Ministry of Defence, ex p Smith* [1996] QB 517 (CA).

[43] ibid 554, quoting counsel's submission with approval.

[44] Employment Rights Act 1996, s 98(4).

[45] *Iceland Frozen Foods Ltd v Jones* [1983] ICR 17 (EAT), 25.

[46] *Turner v East Midlands Trains Ltd* [2012] EWCA Civ 1470, [2013] ICR 525 [18]. For a detailed analysis of standards of review in labour law, see D Cabrelli, 'The Hierarchy of Differing Behavioural Standards of Review in Labour Law' (2011) 40 *Industrial Law Journal* 146.

higher courts regularly remind tribunals that their role is to conduct a light-touch review of the employer's decision.[47]

Reasonableness is also used as a test in labour law in cases involving bonuses. In these cases, the employer generally has an express contractual power to award a bonus, but the employee challenges the way in which the power has been exercised. The courts have been willing to imply a requirement that the power be exercised reasonably. The most detailed discussion of reasonableness in this context can be found in *Clark v Nomura International*:

> I do not consider it is right that there be simply a contractual obligation on an employer to act reasonably in the exercise of his discretion, which would suggest that the court can simply substitute its own view for that of the employer. My conclusion is that the right test is one of irrationality or perversity (of which caprice or capriciousness would be a good example) ie that no reasonable employer would have exercised his discretion in this way.[48]

This formulation is, of course, immediately recognizable as a *Wednesbury* test, and it has become the standard test for use in bonus cases.[49] Thus, in this group of cases, the courts continue to use a test derived from public law even though it is no longer in general use in that field. It seems likely that this reflects a particular nervousness on the part of the courts about engaging in excessive scrutiny of decisions with obvious financial implications.

Thus, the picture in the reasonableness cases is somewhat more complicated than that in procedural fairness. In public law, the reasonableness test has become more intensive over time, with Lord Greene's original formulation nowadays being regarded as both too vague and too limited. In labour law, while the 'band of reasonable responses' test can be seen as similar to the modern public law approach to reasonableness in formulation, it is different in operation, and the 'old-fashioned' *Wednesbury* test is still invoked in certain types of case.

C. Conclusion

Overall, there are strong parallels between labour law in 'individualist' mode and public law, but the general tenor of decisions is more deferential to employers in labour law than it is to the government in public law.[50] I suggest that this reflects two main considerations. First, the courts regard their role in public law as one of keeping the government in check, and are increasingly sceptical about the capacity of Parliament to perform that task.[51] This results in greater judicial

[47] Employment Rights Act 1996, s 98(4)(b), and see *HSBC Bank Plc v Madden* [2000] ICR 1283 (CA).

[48] *Clark v Nomura International* [2000] IRLR 766 [40] (Burton J). See also *Keen v Commerzbank AG* [2006] EWCA Civ 1536; [2007] ICR 623.

[49] See eg *Mallone v BPB Industries Ltd* [2002] EWCA Civ 126, [2002] ICR 1045; *Horkulak v Cantor Fitzgerald International* [2004] EWCA Civ 1287, [2005] ICR 402.

[50] ACL Davies, 'Judicial Self-Restraint in Labour Law' (2009) 38 *Industrial Law Journal* 278.

[51] See eg *Bank Mellat* (n 21).

scrutiny of government decisions. In labour law, by contrast, as the case law on the implied term of mutual trust and confidence illustrates, the courts regard Parliament as having the primary responsibility for striking a balance between the interests of employers and workers, and are more reluctant to interfere. Second, and relatedly, the courts tend to regard employers' decisions as involving economic factors and thus as being beyond their expertise. This is particularly obvious in the bonus cases. The concern about the courts' lack of competence on economic issues also arises in public law, but less frequently.[52] The contrast between the two fields of law is even more striking when it is recalled that, in public law, tests such as reasonableness and procedural fairness form part of a barrage of requirements that a government decision must satisfy if it is to be upheld, whereas, in labour law, they are the central focus of many cases.

III. Labour Law and Public Law in 'Constitutional Rights-based' Mode

Davies and Freedland's article identified a third mode of public law: constitutional rights-based public law.[53] This mode is closely related to the 'individualist' mode, since it also involves protecting individuals against encroachment by the government, but the reasoning process differs because, in this mode, reliance is placed on fundamental rights. Davies and Freedland predicted that this mode might emerge in labour law via EU law, because of its emphasis on equality law and use of a proportionality test. What they could not have predicted was the enactment of the Human Rights Act 1998, and the extent to which this would transform the role of constitutional rights-based reasoning in English law.

I will argue in this section that this mode of reasoning features in both labour law and public law, but whereas it has been well received in public law, it has struggled to gain a foothold in labour law. The position is thus similar to that discussed above in respect of the individualist mode but, if anything, with a more marked difference between the two fields.

A. Public Law

In public law, the HRA has had a substantial impact. It has created a new ground of judicial review under section 6 which is invoked in many cases, some of which would have been argued differently pre-HRA, and some of which would not have been arguable at all pre-HRA. While some scholars have argued that the HRA has transformed the discipline as a whole (influencing 'non-HRA' doctrine

[52] See eg *R v Cambridge DHA, ex p B* [1995] 1 WLR 898 (CA).
[53] Above n 1, 327–34.

such as the *Wednesbury* test), others argue that these claims are exaggerated.[54] This debate need not detain us here. It is the reception of the HRA itself that is of interest for our purposes.

In a short chapter, it is impossible to give a complete picture of the role of the HRA in public law: some illustrative cases will have to suffice. In *Aguilar Quila* the applicants challenged the Secretary of State's refusal, under the immigration rules, to grant visas allowing them to enter the UK as spouses of British citizens because one of the parties to the marriage was under the age of 21.[55] The Supreme Court accepted that this decision infringed the applicants' Article 8 rights, declining to follow some older Strasbourg authority to the contrary,[56] and then turned its attention to justification under Article 8(2). The Secretary of State's aim, to deter forced marriages, was found to be legitimate, and prescribed by law, so attention turned to the question of necessity. Here, the Supreme Court found a rational connection between the policy and the aim, but held that the measure was disproportionate because it interfered with legitimate as well as forced marriages, and no attempt had been made to determine what proportion of marriages where one party was under 21 might have been forced.[57] This meant that the Secretary of State could not justify the interference with the applicants' legitimate marriages. What is significant about the case for present purposes is the Supreme Court's willingness to engage in rigorous scrutiny of the Secretary of State's decision in a politically sensitive area such as immigration, and to do so even though there was some uncertainty about the requirements of the ECtHR case law. The more 'traditional' approach to review was perhaps reflected in Lord Brown JSC's dissent, in which he said:

> The extent to which the rule will help combat forced marriage and the countervailing extent to which it will disrupt the lives of innocent couples adversely affected by it is largely a matter of judgment. Unless demonstrably wrong, this judgment should be rather for government than for the courts.[58]

Of course, by no means all HRA cases have had such dramatic results as *Aguilar Quila*. But even where the applicant does not succeed in establishing a violation of his or her Convention rights, the courts in public law cases have generally been quite willing to engage in detailed discussion of the Strasbourg jurisprudence and its potential relevance to the case, in accordance with section 2 HRA. A good example of this is the *Gillan* case, in which the applicants were stopped and searched under the Terrorism Act 2000.[59] This Act gave senior police officers a power under section 44 to authorize random stops and searches to look for

[54] Compare T Poole, 'The Reformation of English Administrative Law' (2009) 68 *Cambridge Law Journal* 142 with JNE Varuhas, 'The Reformation of English Administrative Law? "Rights", Rhetoric and Reality' (2013) 72 *Cambridge Law Journal* 369.

[55] *R (Aguilar Quila) v Secretary of State for the Home Department* [2011] UKSC 45, [2012] 1 AC 621.

[56] ibid [43] (Lord Wilson).

[57] ibid [58] (Lord Wilson).

[58] ibid [91] (Lord Brown).

[59] *R (Gillan) v Commissioner of Police of the Metropolis* [2006] UKHL 12, [2006] 2 AC 307.

articles connected with terrorism. The authorization, which had been confirmed by the Secretary of State under section 46, lasted for 28 days and covered the whole of the Metropolitan Police area. The House of Lords rejected the applicants' argument that their Article 8 rights had been infringed, holding that a superficial search did not interfere with personal autonomy, and even if Article 8 was infringed, the need to tackle the terrorism problem would be sufficient to justify the interference. Of particular concern in the case was the requirement that the interference (if any) with rights should be 'prescribed by law', given the wide discretion granted to police officers authorized to perform random searches. Lord Bingham held that the controls on that discretion were sufficient to ensure that it was not exercised arbitrarily, thereby meeting the 'prescribed by law' requirement:

> It is true that [the constable] need have no suspicion before stopping and searching a member of the public. This cannot, realistically, be interpreted as a warrant to stop and search people who are obviously not terrorist suspects, which would be futile and time-wasting. It is to ensure that a constable is not deterred from stopping and searching a person whom he does suspect as a potential terrorist by the fear that he could not show reasonable grounds for his suspicion.[60]

The ECtHR reached opposite conclusions in its ruling on the case.[61] It held that stop and search powers did interfere with personal autonomy and thus violated Article 8, and that the interference was not prescribed by law because it would be 'difficult if not impossible to prove' that a constable had acted improperly since there was no need for the constable to suspect the individual of anything before stopping him or her.[62] As some commentators have pointed out, the domestic courts have been rather more timid in the terrorism context (albeit with some notable exceptions, such as the well-known 'Belmarsh' case[63]) and have struggled to keep up with the ECtHR's tougher stance.[64] Nevertheless, even in a case such as *Gillan* the House of Lords recognized the relevance of the Convention and structured its reasoning accordingly, even if ultimately the ECtHR disagreed quite profoundly with its conclusions.

B. Labour Law

In labour law, the picture is rather different. Of course, as a statement of civil and political rights, the ECHR is inevitably somewhat limited in its relevance to labour law, but even where it does apply, some judges seem reluctant to engage with Convention rights in their decisions. There are three main areas in which

[60] ibid [35] (Lord Bingham).
[61] *Gillan v UK* (2010) 50 EHRR 45.
[62] ibid [86].
[63] *A v Secretary of State for the Home Department* [2004] UKHL 56, [2005] 2 AC 68.
[64] For a detailed account of the complex case-law in this area, see A Tomkins, 'National Security and the Role of the Court: A Changed Landscape?' (2010) 126 *Law Quarterly Review* 543.

the courts have been called upon to consider Convention rights: the dismissal of public sector workers and the potential application of Article 6;[65] unfair dismissal law more generally and the relevance of rights such as Articles 8 and 10 in certain cases;[66] and most importantly, the law on trade unions and industrial action and the influence of Article 11. For reasons of space, the discussion in this section will focus primarily on the Article 11 case law.

Article 11 has had a significant influence on UK labour law through decisions of the ECtHR, such as *Wilson v UK*[67] and *ASLEF v UK*,[68] which have led to (albeit sometimes inadequate) amendments of the relevant legislation.[69] However, for the purposes of comparison with public law, my interest is in the reception of the Convention by the domestic courts in labour law cases. In *Metrobus v Unite the Union* the Court of Appeal engaged in a lengthy discussion of Article 11 in the context of an appeal against the grant of an injunction to restrain industrial action, and concluded that Article 11 did not require a different construction of the various aspects of the balloting and notice provisions of which the union had fallen foul.[70] Of course, it would be simplistic to conclude that because the union lost the case, Article 11 was not properly considered. Two features of the decision are worthy of note. First, the judges were rather less confident in their handling of uncertainties in the Strasbourg case law. As is well known, the ECtHR's view of the right to strike has developed considerably in recent years. Initially, signatory states were given a wide margin of appreciation to determine what provisions should be in place to enable unions to 'strive' for protection of their members' interests.[71] Then, in *UNISON v UK*, the Court held that once a state had chosen a mechanism, such as industrial action, any restrictions on its exercise would be subject to the proportionality test.[72] And more recently, in the *Enerji* case, it was held that a ban on strikes in the Turkish civil service infringed Article 11.[73] However, Lloyd LJ was reluctant to place weight on *Enerji*, pointing out that it was not a Grand Chamber judgment and was relatively briefly reasoned (in contrast to *Demir*, an important recent decision on freedom of association and collective bargaining[74]):

[65] Above n 6.

[66] See eg *Turner* (n 46) and *Pay v Lancashire Probation Service* [2004] ICR 187 (EAT), *Pay v UK* (Admissibility) (2009) 48 EHRR SE2.

[67] *Wilson v UK* (2002) 35 EHRR 20.

[68] *ASLEF v UK* (2007) 45 EHRR 34.

[69] In response to *Wilson* (n 67) the government inserted or amended TULRCA 1992 s 145A, 145B, 146 and 152. For critique, see AL Bogg, 'Employment Relations Act 2004: Another False Dawn for Collectivism?' (2005) 34 *Industrial Law Journal* 72. In response to *ASLEF* (n 68), the government amended TULRCA 1992, s 174. For critique, see KD Ewing, 'Employment Act 2008: Implementing the *ASLEF* Decision—A Victory for the BNP?' (2009) 38 *Industrial Law Journal* 50.

[70] *Metrobus Ltd v Unite the Union* [2009] EWCA Civ 829, [2010] ICR 173.

[71] *Schmidt and Dahlström v Sweden* (1979–80) 1 EHRR 632.

[72] *UNISON v UK* (Admissibility) [2002] IRLR 497.

[73] *Enerji Yapi-Yol Sen v Turkey* (unreported), judgment 21 April 2009.

[74] *Demir v Turkey* (2009) 48 EHRR 54.

> It does not seem to me that it would be prudent to proceed on the basis that the less fully articulated judgment in the later case has developed the court's case law by the discrete further stage of recognising a right to take industrial action as an essential element in the rights afforded by article 11.[75]

While I agree that some care is required in interpreting and applying *Enerji*, not least because the facts of the case (a strike ban) were extreme, making it unclear what the case's implications might be for lesser forms of restriction,[76] Lloyd LJ's view seems unnecessarily cautious. It contrasts sharply with the Supreme Court's approach to uncertainties in the ECtHR's case law in *Aguilar Quila*, where the Court was prepared to disregard a decision that pointed quite clearly against the existence of the right being asserted by the applicants.[77] Although the classic formulation in *Ullah* requires the courts to follow 'clear and constant' Strasbourg jurisprudence, it seems clear from these examples that the courts place varying degrees of emphasis on this requirement.[78] Second, the Court of Appeal in *Metrobus* displayed strong deference to Parliament's role in determining how industrial action should be regulated. Lloyd LJ held that there was a margin of appreciation within which states could implement Article 11, and made it very clear that it was for Parliament to make the relevant choices, presenting the legislation as the product of a cross-party consensus:

> [T]he present state of the legislation is noteworthy in that it derives from provisions made first under a Conservative government, but it has been amended twice under a Labour government; in the respects relevant to this appeal the recent changes have been of important details but they have left the main structure of the legislation intact. It seems to me that this is an interesting example of the practical operation of a member state within the scope of the margin of appreciation.[79]

Although these are valid points,[80] what is missing from the discussion is any acknowledgement that the ECHR is a living instrument, so legislation that was once legitimate might need to be reconsidered in the light of new developments in the Court's case law.[81] But, most importantly for our purposes, it highlights the courts' different perception of their role in labour law as compared to public law. While there are plenty of deferential decisions in public law, as *Gillan* illustrates in the terrorism context, deference seems to be the default setting in *Metrobus*.

Metrobus is not quite the end of the story. In *RMT v Serco* Elias LJ stated (without reference to *Metrobus*) that the right to strike had been recognized as part of Article 11 by the ECtHR, albeit subject to restrictions under

[75] Above n 70, [35].

[76] A point borne out by the subsequent decision in *RMT v UK* (unreported), judgment 8 April 2014, discussed below.

[77] Above n 55.

[78] *R (Ullah) v Special Adjudicator* [2004] UKHL 26, [2004] 2 AC 323 [20] (Lord Bingham).

[79] Above n 70, [56].

[80] For subsequent discussion in the ECtHR, see *RMT* (n 75), [99].

[81] See eg *Demir* (n 74) [146].

Article 11(2).[82] Although the precedent set by *Metrobus* limited the Court of Appeal's scope to act on that recognition, Elias LJ did hold that those aspects of TULRCA restricting the right to strike should be construed neutrally rather than against unions,[83] as some older authority (emphasizing the law's provision of immunities rather than rights, and presenting them as 'privileges') had suggested.[84] While this decision is to be welcomed, and has encouraged some lower courts to scrutinize employers' applications for injunctions more rigorously, Simpson is right to caution that it is too early to regard the *Serco* decision as having transformed the judicial approach to this area of law.[85]

Since the decisions in these various cases, the ECtHR has revisited the right to strike in English law in the *RMT* judgment.[86] On one reading, this ruling vindicates Lloyd LJ's cautious approach. The Court held that the right to strike was protected by Article 11, but refused to decide whether or not it was an 'essential element' of the right,[87] and held that the margin of appreciation was variable depending on whether national restrictions struck 'at the core' of trade union activity.[88] It rejected a challenge to the notice provisions in English law as inadmissible (since the union had eventually been able to organize a strike) and held that Article 11 was not infringed by the ban on secondary action in English law because the union had been able to protect its members' interests in the particular case, and because the government was within the (wide) margin of appreciation on the matter. However, it is important to note the role played by the facts of the cases put before the Court in *RMT*. In both situations, the union had achieved some success for its members *despite* the restrictive legislation. Since the Court is not in the business of deciding hypotheticals, it is unlikely to find English law to be in breach of the Convention unless an applicant is able to show real detriment. The decision does not provide any grounds for stepping back from Elias LJ's judgment in *Serco*, though no doubt the courts will face arguments to that effect.

C. Conclusion

Surprisingly, then, we may draw much the same conclusion in relation to the constitutional rights-based mode as we did in relation to the 'individualist' mode. In public law, although there are many examples of deference shown to the government or Parliament, there are also plenty of examples of cases in which the courts engage in rigorous human rights scrutiny of decisions or legislation,

[82] *RMT v Serco Ltd* [2011] EWCA Civ 226, [2011] ICR 848.
[83] ibid [9].
[84] eg *Express Newspapers Ltd v McShane* [1979] ICR 210 (CA), 218 (Lord Denning MR).
[85] B Simpson, 'The Labour Injunction and Industrial Action Ballots' (2013) 42 *Industrial Law Journal* 54.
[86] Above n 76.
[87] ibid [84].
[88] ibid [87].

even in sensitive policy areas, and even where the Strasbourg jurisprudence is not entirely clear-cut. These decisions contrast with a more cautious approach in the labour law cases. And in broad terms, the explanation seems likely to be similar too: the courts regard labour law as a politically and economically sensitive subject that should be regulated primarily by Parliament.

IV. The Challenge of Outsourcing

The 'outsourcing' of traditionally public services to private sector providers has been a key development in public policy over the last 30 years. Although it was not addressed in the Davies and Freedland article, it has been a central theme of Freedland's public law scholarship.[89] In this part of the chapter, my aim is to examine how labour law and public law have dealt with the challenge of outsourcing. The discussion will reveal that while labour law has coped rather better with this phenomenon than has public law, the reason for the distinction is consistent with my earlier analysis of the judges' perception of their proper role in the two fields of law.

'Outsourcing' refers to three general types of activity: privatization, in which a public body is turned into a private firm once and for all (often with special regulatory arrangements); contracting out, in which the public body arranges for a private firm to provide a service after a competitive tendering process; and public–private partnerships, in which the public body enters into a long-term contract with a private firm to build and maintain a new asset such as a school or hospital.[90] All three activities present problems for labour law and public law. In labour law, workers may be expected to transfer to a new employer, giving rise to concerns about job security and the maintenance of their terms and conditions. In public law, there is uncertainty about the extent to which private firms engaged in the delivery of public services are, or should be, subject to public law norms.

A. Public Law

When a public body provides a public service directly, its decisions in relation to that public service are generally subject to judicial review and to review under the HRA. When a service is contracted out to a private provider, the public

[89] Freedland (n 26); 'Privatising *Carltona*: Part II of the Deregulation and Contracting Out Act 1994' [1995] *Public Law* 21; 'The Rule Against Delegation and the *Carltona* Doctrine in an Agency Context' [1996] *Public Law* 19; 'Public Law and Private Finance—Placing the Private Finance Initiative in a Public Frame' [1998] *Public Law* 288.

[90] See, generally, ACL Davies, *The Public Law of Government Contracts* (Oxford, Oxford University Press, 2008) ch 1.

authority remains subject to judicial review and HRA review in respect of at least some aspects of the service.[91] For example, if the public authority decided to stop providing the service altogether and to terminate the contract with the private provider, that decision might be reviewable at the suit of an affected service user. Problems arise, however, when the decision to which the service user objects (eg to evict him or her from social housing, or to close a residential home and relocate him or her to another home) is taken by the private contractor.

The leading authority on this situation under the HRA is the decision in *YL v Birmingham CC*.[92] The claimant in that case was threatened with eviction from privately run but publicly funded residential care because the care home alleged that her relatives engaged in disruptive behaviour when they visited her. She sought to bring a claim based on Article 8, relying on the possibility in section 6(3)(b) HRA of invoking Convention rights against a body 'certain of whose functions are functions of a public nature'. This provision is often described as having extended the HRA to 'hybrid' bodies, though this is rather unhelpful since—as the language of the section makes clear—the concern is not with the nature of the body (which might quite clearly be private) but with the nature of the functions it performs. The House of Lords split 3–2 on the result. The majority held that the mere fact that care was publicly funded was not sufficient to bring the contractor within the scope of the HRA.[93] Indeed, to do so would involve drawing unfortunate distinctions between publicly and privately funded residents within the same care home. Lord Neuberger in particular suggested that one of the aims behind the policy of contracting-out might be to escape from costly public sector obligations such as HRA compliance.[94] The claimant's only remedies lay against the public authority. Parliament has since reversed the decision in *YL* by statute in respect of care homes.[95]

The decision in *YL* indicates that 'mere' provision of services to the public under a contract with a public body is not sufficient to render a private contractor subject to the HRA. However, where the private provider is more closely involved, or 'enmeshed', in the public authority's performance of its public duties, the private provider may have HRA obligations of its own. For example, in *Weaver* a housing association was found to be subject to the HRA when terminating an individual's tenancy because of the role it played in activities with a 'public flavour', such as allocating social housing.[96]

In non-HRA cases, there is no equivalent of section 6(3)(b), but a similar approach has tended to prevail. Thus, in *Servite* the mere provision of residential accommodation under contract to a local authority was held not to render the contractor amenable to judicial review,[97] whereas in *Partnerships in Care* a

[91] ibid ch 8.
[92] *YL v Birmingham CC* [2007] UKHL 27, [2008] 1 AC 95.
[93] ibid [115] (Lord Mance).
[94] ibid [152] (Lord Neuberger).
[95] Health and Social Care Act 2008, s 145.
[96] *R (Weaver) v London & Quadrant Housing Trust* [2009] EWCA Civ 587, [2010] 1 WLR 363.
[97] *R v Servite Houses, ex p Goldsmith* (2001) 33 HLR 35.

private psychiatric hospital was held to be amenable to judicial review in respect of a decision to alter the type of care it provided, because its activities were heavily regulated by statute and because it was responsible for patients who were compulsorily detained.[98] This meant that it was 'enmeshed' in the exercise of public powers.

As commentators have noted, there are two main difficulties with these lines of case law.[99] First, the distinction between 'mere' provision of services and performance of public functions is elusive and generates unnecessary litigation. Second, the courts' refusal to impose HRA or public law obligations on contractors in service provision situations generates the anomalous result that a service provided directly by a public authority is subject to the full rigours of the HRA and judicial review, but as soon as it is contracted out, those obligations seem to disappear. Although an action may still lie against the public authority, this may not be effective in all situations. Under the HRA in particular, it seems at least plausible to suggest that section 6(3)(b) was designed to draw contracted-out public services into the Act's scope. Finally, although it is sometimes suggested that public law or HRA liability might be off-putting for contractors, this concern can be exaggerated. The risk of litigation could be factored into the contract price, and in practice it seems unlikely that the courts would take a particularly strict view of a 'mere' service provider's obligations under either public law or the HRA.

For all of these reasons, it is generally thought that public law has not risen particularly well to the challenge of contracting-out. Indeed, there is something to be said for the proposition that public law is becoming more rigorous (with the addition of the HRA, and developing common law norms in areas such as procedural fairness and legitimate expectations) whilst its scope of application (the public sector) is shrinking. The reason for this seems to be that traditionally, the courts have treated contract as the boundary between public and private law: if a contract is present, it is difficult to persuade them that there might also be public law issues. For example, where employees have sought judicial review of their public sector employer's decisions, they have generally failed unless they had no contractual relationship of any kind, or were an office-holder.[100] This can be seen to be related to the judges' perception of their role identified in the two previous sections of this chapter: they are keen to set standards for public bodies, but wary of doing so once the situation involves private firms and profit motives.[101]

[98] *R (A) v Partnerships in Care Ltd* [2002] EWHC 529 (Admin), [2002] 1 WLR 2610.

[99] See eg Davies (n 91), and P Craig, 'Contracting Out, the Human Rights Act and the Scope of Judicial Review' (2002) 118 *Law Quarterly Review* 551.

[100] Compare *R v Secretary of State for the Home Department, ex p Benwell* [1985] QB 554, with *R v East Berkshire HA, ex p Walsh* [1985] QB 152 (CA).

[101] Though some contractors are not-for-profit organizations.

B. Labour Law

Perhaps surprisingly, labour law has coped rather better with the phenomenon of contracting-out, but more by accident than by design. The Acquired Rights Directive (ARD) was intended to encourage workers to accept change at a time of considerable economic turmoil in the EU by offering protection to their jobs and working conditions when their employing entity was acquired by a new owner.[102] The Directive applies to 'public and private undertakings engaged in economic activities' and, in a substantial body of case law, the Court of Justice has held that the ARD protects workers in a variety of outsourcing situations (whether public or private).[103] This case law has inevitably been reflected in the domestic courts' decisions under the Transfer of Undertakings Regulations (TUPE), and to some extent in the drafting of those Regulations.[104] While this protection is far from perfect, it has made it harder for the government and its contracting partners to use outsourcing as a means of reducing labour costs.

In simple terms, the ARD seeks to achieve three main objectives: to ensure that workers are not dismissed by reason of the transfer,[105] to preserve the workers' contractual terms and conditions of employment as against the transferee,[106] and to require the transferee to observe applicable provisions of collective agreements in relation to the transferred workers[107] (and, if certain conditions are met, to recognize a trade union previously recognized by the transferor in respect of those workers[108]).[109] There are two crucial limitations on the effectiveness of these provisions.

First, dismissals are only precluded where they take place by reason of the transfer, implemented in TUPE as rendering a dismissal automatically unfair where the transfer is the 'sole or principal reason' for the dismissal.[110] They are not precluded when they take place for 'economic, technical or organisational reasons entailing changes in the workforce', often known as 'ETOR'. Under TUPE, dismissals for ETOR are potentially fair as either redundancies or for 'some other substantial reason'.[111] Similarly, contract variations are only precluded where they take place by reason of the transfer.[112] They are permitted if the terms of the contract allow the employer to vary it, or if they are for ETOR and they are

[102] Currently Directive 2001/23/EC, originally Directive 77/187/EEC. For history, see J Kenner, *EU Employment Law: From Rome to Amsterdam and Beyond* (Oxford, Hart Publishing 2003) ch 2.

[103] ARD, Art 1(1)(c). For an overview of the case-law, see ACL Davies, *EU Labour Law* (Cheltenham, Edward Elgar, 2012) 231.

[104] Transfer of Undertakings (Protection of Employment) Regulations 2006 (SI 2006/246), as amended.

[105] ARD, Art 4.

[106] ibid Art 3.

[107] ibid Art 3(3).

[108] ibid Art 6.

[109] The Directive also seeks to ensure that the transferor and transferee consult affected employees about the transfer: ibid Art 7.

[110] ibid Art 4(1); TUPE, r 7(1).

[111] TUPE, r 7(3).

[112] TUPE, r 4(4).

agreed by the employer and employee.[113] The significance of the ETOR exception is that it is broadly framed and creates a route for well-advised employers to disguise dismissals or contract variations that are, in fact, motivated primarily by the transfer.

Second, the provisions preserving the applicability of collective agreements to the transferee only have effect in the short term. TUPE has recently been amended to take advantage of the provision in the ARD that Member States may limit the applicability of collective agreements to a one-year period from the date of the transfer.[114] After the one-year period, TUPE now provides that the transferee may vary a term incorporated from a collective agreement (even if the reason for doing so is the transfer) provided that the overall balance of the contract is 'no less favourable' to the employee.[115] Moreover, new regulation 4A gives effect to the decision in *Alemo-Herron* by providing that the transferee is not bound by any changes to the collective agreement where these take place after the transfer and where the transferee is not a party to the collective bargaining process.[116] These changes are particularly significant in the outsourcing context because of the substantial difference in collective bargaining coverage as between the public and private sectors. One of the most harmful consequences of a transfer for many public sector employees is the move from a unionized to a non-unionized employer, so it is unfortunate that the law now offers little by way of 'portability' of collectively agreed terms and conditions.

Of course, the key question for present purposes is which forms of outsourcing are covered by the ARD? Although transfers of public activities between public bodies are expressly excluded from the Directive,[117] transfers of non-public activities between public bodies are caught,[118] as are transactions between public bodies and private firms or voluntary bodies. Moreover, the Court of Justice has interpreted the concept of a 'transfer' broadly to cover three key outsourcing transactions (whether the transferor is a private firm or a public body): where the transferor contracts out to private firm A;[119] where the contract is re-tendered and private firm A loses the contract to private firm B (even though there is no direct relationship between A and B);[120] and where the transferor brings the service back in-house.[121] The privatization of a public service may also be covered

[113] TUPE, r 4(5).
[114] ARD, Art 3(3).
[115] TUPE, r 4(5B).
[116] Case C-426/11 *Alemo-Herron v Parkwood Leisure Ltd* [2013] ECR 0 (itself a public to private case). See J Prassl, 'Freedom of Contract as a General Principle of EU Law? Transfers of Undertakings and the Protection of Employer Rights in EU Labour Law' (2013) 42 *Industrial Law Journal* 434.
[117] ARD, Art 1(1)(c).
[118] Case C-108/10 *Scattolon v Ministero dell'Istruzione* [2011] ECR I-7491.
[119] Case C-392/92 *Schmidt v Spar- und Leihkasse der früheren Ämter Bordesholm* [1994] ECR I-1311.
[120] Case C-13/95 *Süzen v Zehnacker Gebäudereinigung GmbH Krankenhausservice* [1997] ECR I-1259.
[121] Case C-127/96 *Francisco Hernández Vidal SA v Gómez Pérez* [1998] ECR I-8179.

by the ARD.[122] However, the Court's broad interpretation of a 'transfer' has been somewhat undermined by its approach to the related question of what constitutes an 'entity', now codified in the ARD itself.[123] There must be a transfer of 'an economic entity which retains its identity, meaning an organised grouping of resources which has the objective of pursuing an economic activity'.[124] Here, the Court divides 'entities' into those that are asset intensive and those that are labour intensive. If the 'entity' is deemed to be labour intensive, a transfer will only have taken place if the workforce has transferred.[125] However, this is highly problematic because it may be hard to classify a particular business as asset or labour intensive, and because it offers another easy loophole to avoid the ARD: if the transferee of a labour-intensive business does not want to comply with the ARD, it could simply refuse to take on the transferor's workers, thereby defeating the very purpose of the ARD.[126]

Given the complexities of the CJEU's case law, the Labour government sought to clarify the position by introducing the concept of a 'service provision change' into TUPE, rule 3(1)(b):

> … that is a situation in which—
> (i) activities cease to be carried out by a person ('a client') on his own behalf and are carried out instead by another person on the client's behalf ('a contractor');
> (ii) activities cease to be carried out by a contractor on a client's behalf (whether or not those activities had previously been carried out by the client on his own behalf) and are carried out instead by another person ('a subsequent contractor') on the client's behalf; or
> (iii) activities cease to be carried out by a contractor or a subsequent contractor on a client's behalf (whether or not those activities had previously been carried out by the client on his own behalf) and are carried out instead by the client on his own behalf,
> and in which the conditions set out in paragraph (3) are satisfied.

These activities must be 'fundamentally the same',[127] and, under rule 3(3):

> (a) immediately before the service provision change—
> (i) there is an organised grouping of employees situated in Great Britain which has as its principal purpose the carrying out of the activities concerned on behalf of the client;
> (ii) the client intends that the activities will, following the service provision change, be carried out by the transferee other than in connection with a single specific event or task of short-term duration; and
> (b) the activities concerned do not consist wholly or mainly of the supply of goods for the client's use.

[122] Case C-4/01 *Martin v South Bank University* [2003] ECR I-12859.
[123] *Süzen* (n 120).
[124] ARD, Art 1(1)(b).
[125] *Süzen* (n 120).
[126] Davies (n 103) 232–34; P Davies, 'Taken to the Cleaners? Contracting Out of Services Yet Again' (1997) 26 *Industrial Law Journal* 193, 196.
[127] TUPE, r 3(2A).

This set of provisions is generally regarded by the courts as somewhat broader than the requirements of EU law.[128] Perhaps the most obvious example of this is that the focus of rule 3(3) is on the 'entity'—the 'organised grouping' and its purpose—without importing the troublesome distinction between asset- or labour-intensive activities.[129] A recent proposal by the Coalition government to repeal the concept of a service provision change (as unnecessary 'gold-plating' of the ARD) was roundly criticized by commentators and was subsequently withdrawn.[130]

Despite these (and other) problems and limitations, the protection afforded by the ARD and TUPE is worth having. Although the present government's Code of Practice on workforce matters in outsourcing is less worker protective than that of the previous Labour government, public bodies remain committed to ensuring that their contractors observe various good employment practices.[131] Contractors are usually repeat players, bidding regularly for government contracts, so maintaining a good reputation is important to them. Thus, both sides have strong incentives to avoid litigation and bad publicity. This may make them somewhat less inclined to try to exploit TUPE's many loopholes.

C. Conclusion

Proponents of outsourcing in the public sector argue that one of its main benefits is cost control. This is particularly attractive in times of austerity. However, there are different ways in which outsourcing might contribute to cost cutting. For example, private firms competing to win government business might come up with innovative (and cheaper) ways of delivering the service, drawing on their particular expertise. But some forms of cost cutting linked to outsourcing—like those examined in this section—are much more controversial. Is it acceptable to cut costs by withdrawing human rights protection from service users, or by reducing the terms and conditions of employment of the workers delivering the service? As we have seen, labour law (by the happy accident of the ARD, and some bold moves by the CJEU) has placed some obstacles in the way of the latter form of cost cutting. Public law, by contrast, has struggled to address the former, in part at least because once a situation involves a private contractor as well as a public authority, the courts are much less willing to intervene.

[128] *Hunter v McCarrick* [2012] EWCA Civ 1399, [2013] ICR 235.

[129] C Wynn-Evans, 'In Defence of Service Provision Changes?' (2013) 42 *Industrial Law Journal* 152.

[130] Department for Business Innovation & Skills, *Transfer of Undertakings (Protection of Employment) Regulations 2006: Consultation on Proposed Changes to the Regulations*, (January 2013, URN 13/533); *Transfer of Undertakings (Protection of Employment) Regulations 2006: Government Response to Consultation* (September 2013, URN 13/1023). For critique, see Wynn-Evans (n 129).

[131] Compare Cabinet Office, *Code of Practice: Workforce Matters in Public Sector Service Contracts* (2005) with Cabinet Office, *Principles Of Good Employment Practice* (December 2010).

V. Conclusions

In a short chapter, it is not possible to conduct a comprehensive analysis of every point at which the disciplines of public law and labour law might intersect. But I hope that I have done enough to demonstrate that this remains as fruitful a line of enquiry today as it proved to be for Davies and Freedland in 1997. In structural terms, the two disciplines share important similarities: a concern with the protection of the individual against a (more powerful) entity, be that the government or the employer, which manifests itself in the adoption of similar legal doctrines, such as reasonableness tests; and a concern with the protection of Convention rights. Both disciplines also face a significant challenge brought about by the shrinking of the public sector due to the outsourcing of various activities to the private sector, with associated threats to the rights of service users and to the jobs and pay of workers providing the service.

In examining these structural similarities, I have identified a broad difference between the courts' approach in public law and their approach in labour law, which could usefully be tested more fully in future research. In public law, the courts perceive themselves as one of the main mechanisms for holding the government to account. Although they recognize that their task is one of reviewing, rather than taking, government decisions, and that they have less expertise and legitimacy to intervene in some areas than in others, their general approach to scrutiny is quite rigorous. In labour law, by contrast, the courts regard the subject as having important economic and political dimensions and this leads them to exercise a degree of self-restraint when taking decisions. Thus, for example, their human rights scrutiny is less rigorous and there is a greater tendency to rely on traditional 'light-touch' reasonableness tests. They regard the government and Parliament as having the primary role in striking a balance between the interests of workers and unions on the one hand, and employers on the other. Public law's ineffectual response to outsourcing tends to confirm this view, because the judges' perception of their proper role alters once the case involves a private firm under contract to the government.

What are the implications of this for the autonomy of labour law? On one level, it might be argued that I have demonstrated labour law's lack of autonomy: the courts' differing approaches in labour law and public law can be explained (as I have done elsewhere) using familiar ideas of judicial 'deference' or self-restraint from the public law literature.[132] On a deeper level, though, the discussion has shown that while labour law is something of a 'magpie' subject, borrowing strategies and concepts from other disciplines such as public law, the courts tend to alter and adjust those strategies and concepts to bring them into line with a particular judicial ethos in the field of labour law. This ethos has at its heart a strong emphasis on the employer's economic freedom. As a result, the

[132] Davies (n 50).

courts' approach to labour law cases would probably be more familiar to private lawyers than it is to public lawyers, though of course there is also plenty of scope for debate and discussion about the impact of private law subjects, like contract, on labour law.[133] The judicial emphasis on the employer's economic freedom conflicts in an obvious and direct way with the emphasis on *limiting* the employer's economic freedom adopted by the vast majority of academics (and many other actors) in the field of labour law. In turn, this helps to explain why long-standing calls for labour law to be procedurally autonomous—to have a fully separate system of labour tribunals or courts—remain relevant today.[134] As Wedderburn put it over 25 years ago:

> It may well be that a new and constructive relationship between law and industrial relations in Britain depends in tomorrow's labour market and social conditions even more upon reform of labour tribunals than upon substantive law reform.[135]

[133] See, further, ACL Davies, 'Employment Law', in E Simpson and M Stewart (eds), *Sham Transactions* (Oxford, Oxford University Press, 2013), and the chapter by Hugh Collins in this volume.

[134] See eg WEJ McCarthy, 'The Case for Labour Courts' (1990) 21 IRJ 98, Lord Wedderburn, 'Labour Law: From Here to Autonomy?' (1987) 16 *Industrial Law Journal* 1. As I have argued elsewhere, this issue is increasingly relevant to labour law at the EU level: ACL Davies, 'The Court of Justice as a Labour Court' (2011-12) 14 *Cambridge Yearbook of European Legal Studies* 145.

[135] Wedderburn (n 134) 28.

10

Equality Law: Labour Law or an Autonomous Field?

SANDRA FREDMAN

I. Introduction

The absence of a written constitution and bill of rights in the UK has meant that, unlike in most countries, anti-discrimination law developed as an integral part of labour law. Although education and goods and services were within the scope of anti-discrimination legislation from the start, the conceptual development happened largely within labour law. The powerful influence of EU law did nothing to change this: given the limited competence of the EU, employment, vocational training and occupational social security remained the main focus until the beginning of the 21st century. Before 2000, too, the ECHR was a shadowy presence. The equality guarantee in Article 14 ECHR was widely regarded as of little use, given that it is a parasitic right, limited to discrimination in the enjoyment of other convention rights, and the ECtHR was frequently reluctant to rely on Article 14 if breach of a substantive right had already been shown.

The advent of the Human Rights Act 1998 (HRA), which simply incorporated Convention rights, including Article 14, did little to convince many in the field that the right to equality is a human right. Indeed, when the three equality commissions were merged in 2006, it was only as a late afterthought that the newly refashioned commission was given jurisdiction over human rights. Many anti-discrimination lawyers and equality specialists still do not consider themselves human rights experts. The major equality instruments in international law[1] remain relatively unknown. While Article 14 ECHR is increasingly adjudicated in domestic courts, the interaction with anti-discrimination law is still unwieldy.

This paper aims to explore what the late arrival of legal human rights protec-

[1] Convention on the Elimination of Discrimination against Women; Convention on the Elimination of Racial Discrimination; Convention on the Rights of the Child; Convention on the Rights of People with Disabilities.

tion in the UK has meant for equality law. How has the right to equality in the UK been shaped by its roots in labour law, and, conversely, in what ways has the newly acquired human rights regime influenced labour law? On the assumption that the human rights jurisdiction came of age a decade after the HRA came into force in 2000, this paper focuses on a close analysis of some of the major equality cases in the highest courts in the UK and in the ECtHR since 2010. Such an analysis reveals two main arenas of contestation. The first concerns the rights-holder, and the corresponding duty-bearer. Labour law's preoccupation with the employment relationship is challenged by the basic premise of human rights, namely that human rights inhere in everyone, simply by virtue of their humanity. On the other hand, the human rights regime generally assumes that it is only the state that is bound, leaving the obligations of the private employer in limbo. Yet it is into the interstices of all these settled relationships that the most vulnerable fall, and it is here that the right to equality should have the most traction.

The second major cause of friction concerns the role of justification. Whereas under Article 14, the proportionality analysis is integrated into the definition of discrimination, the anti-discrimination statutes have built up a rigid divide between discrimination that can be justified and discrimination that cannot. This divide is under increasing pressure, particularly with the introduction of additional protected characteristics such as religion, age and disability.

Closer examination reveals that both these issues have a similar background concern: to create appropriate limits to the responsibilities of duty bearers to rights holders. It is argued here that this issue should not receive the same answer in equality law as it does in labour law. Duties should not be limited to relationships of subordination, but should fall on anyone with the power to discriminate. Similarly, limits on the duty not to discriminate should not be based on an employer's economic interests. Appropriate limits to the right not to be discriminated against should derive from human rights considerations, particularly the need to protect the rights of others.

Before elaborating on this argument, it is important to note that the ECHR does not on the face of it sit easily with labour law. The guarantee of equality in Article 14 ECHR does not in itself have traction in employment cases because it does not have an independent existence. Instead, for Article 14 to apply, the facts of a case must fall within the ambit of another substantive provision of the Convention or its protocols.[2] An employment situation must therefore fall within the ambit of one of the substantive rights, such as Article 4 (freedom from slavery and compulsory labour); Article 8 (right to private life); Article 9 (freedom of religion and belief); Article 10 (right to freedom of speech); or Article 11 (right to freedom of association). Yet if the substantive right has been breached in its own right, then the Court is often tempted to avoid having to make a decision under Article 14.

[2] See eg *Eweida v UK* [2013] 57 EHRR 8, para 85.

In practice, some of the most contested cases have concerned the right to freedom of religion and belief. Indeed, the introduction of 'religion and belief' as a ground of discrimination has been a major source of contestation, throwing human rights and labour law together in ways which had possibly not been contemplated in advance. This is seen in both *Jivraj*,[3] which was decided under domestic and EU labour law, and in the conjoined *Eweida*[4] group of cases, which were decided under the ECHR. The more recent non-employment cases of *Wilkinson*[5] and *Bull*,[6] decided by the domestic courts under the HRA, are of particular interest as a contrast to the employment cases. The interaction between the right to freedom of religion and the right not to be discriminated against on grounds of religion remains to be worked through; not to mention the even more problematic set of relationships between freedom of religion, and the right not to be discriminated against on other grounds, such as sex and sexual orientation. It is these cases that form the substance of the discussion below.

II. From Worker to Rights-Bearer

Labour law's traditional preoccupation with the employment relationship at first glance differs strikingly from the human rights approach. Whereas labour law regulates the relationship between employers and workers, human rights law addresses the relationship between the state and individuals. From the point of view of the rights-bearer, these approaches appear to diverge radically. To qualify for labour rights, an individual must fit within the definition of a worker. Although the boundaries of the personal scope of labour law have been contested,[7] the employment relationship has traditionally been defined as a relationship of subordination, at its core at least. The assumption that entitlements must arise out of the employment relationship changes radically in the human rights arena. Human rights inhere in their subjects because of their inherent humanity and regardless of their status.[8]

A very different perspective is gained if we focus on the duty-bearer rather than the rights-holder. In both contexts, the concern is to justify imposing such duties. Why is the duty paradigmatically placed on the state in relation to human

[3] *Jivraj v Hashwani* [2011] UKSC 40, [2011] 1 WLR 1872.

[4] *Eweida v UK* (n 2).

[5] *Black v Wilkinson* [2013] EWCA Civ 820, [2013] 1 WLR 2490.

[6] *Bull v Hall* [2013] UKSC 73, [2013] 1 WLR 3741.

[7] For the foremost critique of these assumptions, see M Freedland and N Kountouris, *The Legal Construction of Personal Work Relations* (Oxford, Oxford University Press, 2011); see further S Fredman and J Fudge, 'The Legal Construction of Personal Work Relations and Gender' (2013) 7 *Jerusalem Review of Legal Studies* (2013) 112–22.

[8] Under Art 1 ECHR, states must 'secure to everyone within their jurisdiction the rights and freedoms' in the Convention. See eg *Siliadin v France* (2006) 43 EHRR 16, where the Court found a breach of the rights under Art 4 prohibiting slavery and forced labour of a young woman who was an illegal migrant in France. Some human rights obligations, such as the right to vote, are usually confined to citizens. See eg the EU Charter of Fundamental Rights, which distinguishes citizens' rights and human rights.

rights, and on the employer in relation to labour rights? The answer in each context is surprisingly similar. It seems that it has to do with both power and burdens. The state must be restrained by human rights obligations because of its power to interfere in the freedom of individuals. The employer must be subject to duties towards workers because it exercises power over them and is therefore in a position to provide for them: hence the focus on subordination. The correlative of this principle, however, is that the ordinary individual should not be burdened with duties to fulfil human rights because this would unduly interfere with her individual freedom.

The rights to equality and non-discrimination challenge all these assumptions. Discrimination constitutes an exercise of power which can take place in myriad sets of relationships, which include but do not exhaust the familiar nexuses of state–individual or employer–worker. If the reluctance to impose human rights duties on individuals arises from the imperative of protecting individual freedom, the real question should be: in what circumstances should individuals be free to discriminate against others? Since both labour law and human rights law insist that power brings with it responsibility, the response could be that the right not to be subjected to discrimination places correlative duties on anyone who is in a position to discriminate. It is true that the word 'individual' disguises a wide spectrum of actors, from powerful corporations to private individuals. It may be that some individuals are simply not in a position to affect others through discriminatory actions; whereas others, such as public corporations, have vast power to do so. However, this is captured by the focus on placing the duty on anyone who is in a position to discriminate against another. For example, should an elderly person, who is herself vulnerable and compromised, be permitted to discriminate against her carer on racial grounds? From the carer's perspective, the effect of the discrimination might be every bit as powerful as if this had been inflicted by a large corporation.

Of course, instead of asking when it is justifiable for an individual to discriminate against others, it is possible to ask the question from the converse perspective: ie when it is justifiable for the law to interfere with a person's freedom to discriminate against others? But anti-discrimination laws have already signalled that society's acceptance of discrimination by private actors can be curtailed. The question, then, is not so much whether such private action should be limited, but why the boundaries of such regulation should be determined by the particularities of the personal scope of labour law.

Both labour law and human rights law in the UK reflect the ways in which the right to equality disrupts the settled relationships, whether that of employer–employee or state–individual. Since anti-discrimination law in the UK grew out of labour law, the starting point has always been that the right not to be discriminated against arises from the employment relationship. However, even then, the scope of anti-discrimination law was cast more widely than that of labour law, to include education, and goods, facilities and services to the public. In addition, within labour law, the anti-discrimination statutes from the start included protection for those employed under a contract for services to do the work personally. The Equality Act 2010 (EA 2010), which repeats previous definitions, states that 'employment' means 'employment under a contract of employment, a contract of apprenticeship *or a contract personally to do work*'.[9] Moreover, the statutes make particular provision for certain categories that fall outside of the conventional employment relationship, including police officers, partners,[10] barristers,[11] advocates, etc. Notably, barristers are not permitted to discriminate against pupils or prospective tenants; but in addition, those instructing a barrister cannot discriminate against a barrister by subjecting him or her to any detriment.[12] Furthermore, a principal cannot discriminate against a contract worker, the paradigmatic case being that an end-user (or 'principal') cannot discriminate against an agency worker, provided the latter is employed by an agency which has supplied her under a contract with the end-user.[13]

This ambivalence is similarly reflected in EU law. Given its roots in the creation of a common market, it is not surprising that the equality instruments from the start focused on the worker and the employment relationship. This is to some extent reflected in the case law of the European Court of Justice. Thus in *Allonby*[14] the Court directly transposed its definition of worker from its free movement of workers' jurisprudence to the characterization of 'worker' for the purposes of the right to equal pay for work of equal value in Article 157 of the Treaty on the Functioning of the European Union (TFEU) (then Article 141). Quoting a freedom of movement of workers case, *Lawrie Blum*,[15] it held that 'a person who, for a certain period of time, performs services for and under the direction of another person in return for which he receives remuneration' 'must be considered as a worker'.[16]

However, as equality law matured within EU law, a more inclusive approach found voice. The Race Directive was the first discrimination directive to reach beyond employment, to include housing, social security, etc. Even within the labour market, the Race Directive[17] appears to have a different scope than that of Article 157 TFEU, which was at issue in the *Allonby* case. Whereas Article 157 TFEU relates to the relationship between the employer and the worker, the Race Directive uses the wider concept of 'employment or occupation'.[18] Picking up on these cues in the *Firma Feryn*[19] case, Advocate General Maduro stated that the Directive

[9] EA 2010, s 83(2) (emphasis added).
[10] ibid s 44.
[11] ibid s 47.
[12] ibid s 47(4).
[13] ibid s 41(5).
[14] C-256/01 *Allonby v Accrington & Rossendale College* [2004] ECR I-873.
[15] C-66/85 *Lawrie-Blum v Land Baden-Württemberg* [1986] ECR 2121.
[16] *Allonby v Accrington & Rossendale College* (n 14) para 67.
[17] Council Directive 2000/43/EC of 29 June 2000 implementing the principle of equal treatment between persons irrespective of racial or ethnic origin [2000] OJ L180.
[18] Freedland and Kountouris (n 7) 61.
[19] Case C-54/07 *Centrum voor gelijkheid van kansen en voor racismebestrijding v Firma Feryn NV* [2008] ECR I-5187.

> must be understood in the framework of a wider policy 'to foster conditions for a socially inclusive labour market' (recital 8 in the preamble to the Directive) and 'to ensure the development of democratic and tolerant societies which allow the participation of all persons irrespective of racial or ethnic origin' (recital 12).[20]

The Employment Directive[21] similarly uses the concept of 'employment or occupation'[22] and its preamble, like that of the Race Directive, refers to 'the need to foster a labour market favourable to social integration (recital 8)' and points out that discrimination can undermine EU treaty objectives in relation to raising the standard of living, economic and social cohesion and free movement of workers.[23]

The extent to which discrimination law should reflect the assumptions of labour law on the one hand or human rights law on the other continues to be subject to fierce contestation. The two most prominent cases decided since 2010 came down firmly on the side of the labour law approach. Both concern work relationships that fall outside of the normal spectrum of employment protection. *Jivraj*[24] was concerned with whether a commercial arbitrator could claim to have been discriminated against on religious grounds in circumstances in which a commercial contract specified that the arbitrator should be a member of the Ismaili community. *X v Mid Sussex CAB*[25] addressed the issue of whether a voluntary worker could claim that she had been discriminated against on grounds of disability. In both cases, the Supreme Court found that the relationship did not fall within the scope of discrimination law. Neither accepted the contention that the case fell within the definition of 'occupation' for the purposes of either domestic or EU law.

Both cases are notable for their unquestioned adherence to the view that that the right not to be discriminated against should operate within the same parameters as employment protection rights, ie that it should arise out of the employment relationship rather than being an independent human right. In *Jivraj* the Supreme Court, drawing heavily on the *Allonby* case, accepted the respondent's contention that EU law draws a clear distinction between those who are employed and those who are independent providers of services who are not in a relationship of subordination with the person who receives the services. This is despite the fact, noted above, that the Race Directive arguably has a wider scope than the right to equal pay for equal work in Article 157 TFEU, which was at issue in *Allonby*.[26] Moreover, the scope of domestic law was construed much more narrowly than had previously been generally accepted. In particular, Lord Clarke held that, contrary to the common understanding, the words 'employ-

[20] ibid Opinion of AG Maduro, para 14.
[21] Council Directive 2000/78/EC of 27 November 2000 establishing a general framework for equal treatment in employment and occupation [2000] OJ L303/16.
[22] ibid Art 1.
[23] ibid recital 11.
[24] *Jivraj* (n 3).
[25] *X v Mid Sussex Citizens Advice Bureau* [2012] UKSC 59, [2013] 1 All ER 1038.
[26] Freedland and Kountouris (n 7).

ment under a contract personally to do work' in UK anti-discrimination legislation did not apply to all contracts personally to do work. Instead, he insisted that the scope was narrowed by the words 'employment under', which in turn required a relationship of subordination. Thus, he stated:

> If the approach in *Allonby* is applied to a contract between the parties to an arbitration and the arbitrator (or arbitrators), it is in my opinion plain that the arbitrators' role is not one of employment under a contract personally to do work. Although an arbitrator may be providing services for the purposes of VAT and he of course receives fees for his work, and although he renders personal services which he cannot delegate, he does not perform those services or earn his fees for and under the direction of the parties as contemplated in para 67 of *Allonby* . He is rather in the category of an independent provider of services who is not in a relationship of subordination with the parties who receive his services, as described in para 68.[27]

Lord Clarke preferred not to speculate on what the position might be in other factual contexts. But he took the view that it would be 'surprising' if 'a customer who engages a person on a one-off contract as, say, a plumber, would be subject to the whole gamut of discrimination legislation'.[28] Individual choice by customers was not addressed by the Directive. Thus the applicability of the Directive and the domestic regulations to such groups as solicitors, plumbers, accountants or doctors depended entirely on whether they could be said to be subordinate workers as defined by *Allonby*. One way or another, it was not sufficient simply to ask whether there is a contract to do the work personally.[29] A similar narrow construction was given to the reference to the 'conditions for access to employment, to self-employment or to occupation, including selection criteria and recruitment conditions' in Article 3(1)(a) of Directive 2000/78. This was concerned only with preventing discrimination 'from qualifying or setting up as a solicitor, plumber, greengrocer or arbitrator. It was not concerned with discrimination by a customer who prefers to contract with one of their competitors once they have set up in business.'[30]

The *CAB* case reflects a similar assumption that the right not to be discriminated against should operate only within the settled parameters of labour law. The applicant worked as a voluntary advisor for the Mid Sussex Citizens Advice Bureau (CAB). Having completed the CAB's extensive training requirements, she signed a volunteer agreement headed: 'This agreement is binding in honour only and is not a contract of employment or legally binding.' She worked as a voluntary advisor from November 2006, carrying out a wide range of advice duties, generally attending between one and three days a week. In May 2007, she claimed, she was asked to cease acting as a volunteer in circumstances amounting to discrimination against her on the grounds of disability. However, although her claim was heard by an employment tribunal, the EAT, the Court of Appeal

[27] *X v Mid Sussex Citizens Advice Bureau* (n 25) [40].
[28] *Jivraj* (n 3) [46].
[29] ibid.
[30] ibid [49].

and the Supreme Court, none of them addressed the substance of her claim. The employment tribunal concluded that no legally binding contract came into existence, and this was not contested in the Supreme Court. Instead, all of these courts held that, as a volunteer, she was outside of the scope of protection against discrimination on grounds of disability.

The absence of a contract at first glance appeared to be fatal to her claim. Under the regulations then in force, and now under the EA 2010, 'employment' means 'employment under a contract of service or of apprenticeship or a contract personally to do any work, and related expressions are to be construed accordingly'.[31] Nor did she fall into any of the specific categories of office bearers in the 2010 Act. However, as in *Jivraj*, she argued that EU law had a wider scope than employment and referred too to 'occupation'. EU Directive 2000/78 states expressly that it applies, inter alia, to '(a) conditions for access to employment, to self-employment or to occupation, including selection criteria and recruitment conditions, whatever the branch of activity and at all levels of the professional hierarchy, including promotion'.[32] The Supreme Court dismissed this argument. Although the concept of occupation had never previously been examined in EU law, the Supreme Court held, following *Jivraj*, that the Directive only applied to selection criteria rather than to practice of the occupation itself.

Both these cases raise fundamental questions of principle. What background principle would justify the result, which is to permit discrimination against a voluntary worker on the one hand, and a commercial arbitrator on the other, on the basis that one has no contract and the other is not subordinate? Lord Dyson in the *CAB* case took the view that there was a clear divide between moral and legal obligations:

> Any responsible organisation aims to combat discrimination on the grounds of disability—or indeed any other characteristic protected by the EA 2010—and will do so for the benefit of persons serving or wishing to serve as volunteers in the organisation no less than anyone else. But the present appeal is not about this moral imperative. It is about whether, under European Union and domestic law, discrimination against volunteers, or some categories of volunteer, on the grounds of disability is currently unlawful and if so how the relevant volunteers are to be defined.[33]

However, the background moral principle need not be wholly excluded by an apparently technical interpretation of positive law, especially given the background requirement to construe legislation in the light of human rights commitments. A human rights approach, having started with the recognition of the human right not to be discriminated against on grounds of disability, race, gender or other protected ground, would insist that the law be interpreted in this light. The line between the legal and moral imperative is often a matter of interpretation, and judicial choice of interpretive materials. In this case, there

[31] *X v Mid Sussex Citizens Advice Bureau* (n 25) [10].
[32] Council Directive 2000/78/EC (n 21) Art 3(1)(a).
[33] *X v Mid Sussex Citizens Advice Bureau* (n 25) [1].

are plenty of legitimate interpretive possibilities within the texts of both EU and domestic law which could be drawn on. One is the inclusion of 'occupation' in EU law. The other is the choice of precedent.

More importantly, for our purposes, the normative approach can drive the descriptive. In other words, many of the open-textured terms can but need not be interpreted to fulfil the background principle that discrimination law should be limited to those who are in a subordinate relationship. This is clearly evidenced in *Jivraj*, where despite many signals to the contrary, the Supreme Court persistently chose the narrower interpretation. As Freedland and Kountouris powerfully show, by interpreting 'employment under a contract of service or … personally to do work' to require subordinate employment even in relation to the reference to 'personally to do work', the Court effectively required a contract of service in all circumstances, rendering the latter words otiose. In addition, they show that to construe 'occupation' to apply solely to the criteria for selection leads to the strange result that, having set up in one's occupation free of discrimination, one can then be subjected to discrimination. It is also reduces the scope of the Race and Employment Directives to that of the equal pay provisions in Article 157 TFEU.[34] This problem is not mitigated by taking the view that, while there is a requirement of subordination and dependence both in relation to workers and employees, there is a difference of degree, with the intensity of subordination progressively weakening as one moves from employee to worker.[35] The argument here is that the very principle of subordination, even if arguably suitable in labour law, is inappropriate as a criterion for personal scope in discrimination law.

Nevertheless, in the *CAB* case, the limited view of 'occupation' taken in *Jivraj* was endorsed. The Supreme Court rejected the applicant's more purposeful approach, which focused on the general statement in the preamble of the Directive, proclaiming its purpose as being to 'lay down a general framework for combating discrimination on the grounds of religion or belief, disability, age or sexual orientation as regards employment and occupation, with a view to putting into effect in the member states the principle of equal treatment'.

The Court's restrictive interpretation of the law is therefore not purely technical. What background principle could be isolated to make sense of the result? In Tushnet's admittedly controversial words, is there 'a substantial interest in allowing private decision-makers a sphere within which they [can] exercise unattractive preferences?'[36] One approach extrapolates from the employment context. Christopher McCrudden takes the view that domestic and EU anti-discrimination law are fundamentally asymmetric: the law protects employees and not employers; consumers rather than providers of services. Employees

[34] M Freedland and N Kountouris, 'Employment Equality and Personal Work Relations—A Critique of *Jivraj v Hashwani*' (2012) 41 *Industrial Law Journal* 56.

[35] *Byrne Brothers (Formwork) Ltd v Baird* [2002] IRLR 96 (Employment Appeal Tribunal).

[36] M Tushnet, '*Shelley v Kraemer* and Theories of Equality' (1988) 33 *New York Law School Law Review* 383, 388.

can discriminate against employers; and consumers may discriminate against providers of services. 'The asymmetry appears to be based on a view that employees and consumers (but not employers or service providers) are "vulnerable", and therefore they are appropriately protected by the legislation.'[37] It is not clear whether this is meant to be purely descriptive or also normative. From a descriptive perspective, it is not wholly accurate. As we have seen, there are some situations, such as that of a barrister, in which the provider of services is protected. Even putting aside these as somewhat isolated examples, this does not explain why voluntary workers are not protected. This highlights the problems of transplanting the concept of vulnerability from employment to the context of discrimination. Whereas the voluntary worker is arguably not vulnerable in the sense of standing to lose her source of income, she is certainly vulnerable to discrimination. This is underscored by the situation of the arbitrator. If commercial contracts routinely required arbitrators to be white, we would be surprised if the law did not regard this as unlawfully discriminatory. Would we have been satisfied to permit an arbitration clause to exclude all blacks from being hired as a commercial arbitrator in relation to the contract in question? Framing the question in this way highlights the similarities between *Jivraj* and the *CAB* case and *Shelley v Kraemer*,[38] which concerned a restrictive covenant barring blacks from owning or occupying property in an area of St Louis, Missouri, discussed further below. Importantly, however, this does not mean that this protection is absolute. It simply means that the claim should not be foreclosed at the threshold question of who should be the right-holder. Instead, potential limits should be determined at the proportionality stage. For example, it is quite conceivable that different kinds of justifications for race and religion might be acceptable. This is discussed further below.

III. From Employer to Duty-Bearer

Just as the right to equality disrupts settled ideas about the employer–worker relationship within human rights law, so the right to equality destabilizes the presumption that the primary sphere of human rights law is the relationship between the state and the individual. The need to restrict the exercise of private power in a discriminatory manner has been addressed in various ways within human rights law in different jurisdictions. One is to make horizontal application explicit. Thus section 9 of the South African Constitution prohibits discrimination both by the state and by other persons. A second is to regard the enforcement of private contracts as itself a form of state action. This was the approach of

[37] C McCrudden, 'Two Views of Subordination: The Personal Scope of Employment Discrimination Law in *Jivraj v Hashwani*' (2012) 41 *Industrial Law Journal* 30, 32–33.

[38] *Shelley v Kraemer* 334 US 1 (1948).

the US Supreme Court in the famous case of *Shelley v Kraemer*,[39] which, as we saw above, concerned a restrictive covenant barring blacks from owning or occupying property in an area of St Louis, Missouri. The question before the US Supreme Court was not directly whether the state could prevent individuals from discriminating on grounds of race or colour. Instead, the Court held that judicial enforcement of such discrimination was a form of state action and therefore prohibited by the equal protection clause of the Fourteenth Amendment. This idea is reflected too in the HRA 1998, which includes courts in the definition of the state for the purposes of liability. A court which endorses private contractual power to discriminate contrary to Article 14 of the ECHR would in principle engage the HRA. A third and closely related approach is through the duty to protect. Under this principle, the state has a duty not just to refrain from breaching human rights, but also to protect individuals against breach of their rights by other individuals.[40] One way of fulfilling this duty is through statutory prohibitions on discrimination by private actors. For example, the South African Constitution requires the state to enact anti-discrimination legislation. This has the important implication that, to the extent that anti-discrimination statutes are seen as a fulfilment of the duty to protect, they can be scrutinized for their human rights compliance.

The ECtHR has recently developed the last approach, giving it the opportunity to determine whether labour laws place appropriate obligations on private parties. This can be seen in *Eweida*,[41] where two of the applicants, Eweida and MacFarlane, were employed by private employers. Notably, in both these cases, the Court chose to deal with the issue directly under Article 9 (freedom of religion and belief) rather than Article 14 (non-discrimination) together with Article 9. The Court held:

> Where, as for the first and fourth applicants, the acts complained of were carried out by private companies and were not therefore directly attributable to the respondent State, the Court must consider the issues in terms of the positive obligation on the state authorities to secure the rights under art 9 to those within their jurisdiction.[42]

This was elaborated by Judges Bratza and Thór Björgvinsson when they summed up the background principles in their joint, partly dissenting, opinion:

> Where, as in the case of the first and fourth applicants, the acts complained of were not directly attributable to the respondent State, the central question is not whether the interference was necessary in a democratic society or whether the state complied with its negative obligations flowing directly from art 9, but whether the state was in breach of its positive obligations to secure art 9 rights through its legal system.[43]

The ECtHR regarded this as an instance of the state's positive duty to protect

[39] ibid.
[40] See eg *Z v United Kingdom* (2002) 34 EHRR 3.
[41] *Eweida v UK* (n 2).
[42] ibid para 84.
[43] ibid para OI-2(3).

individuals against breach of their rights by other individuals. This meant that, instead of cutting off cases at the threshold, the Court was able to deal with these issues as part of a substantive proportionality determination.

The employment discrimination cases can also be contrasted with discrimination cases outside the employment context, where the threshold question of both right-holder and duty-bearer have not loomed large, allowing the Court to reach the substantive issues. Of particular note is the case of *Bull v Hall*,[44] decided by the Supreme Court in 2013. In this case, Mr and Mrs Bull, proprietors of a small hotel, refused to let a double room to a same-sex couple on the grounds that, according to their sincerely held religious belief, sexual relations outside of marriage were sinful. The Bulls believed that marriage could only take place between a man and a woman, and that the fact that Mr Hall and Mr Preddy were civil partners was irrelevant. As Lady Hale pointed out, this was a claim by private individuals against other private individuals; and although there were also human rights in play, Mr Hall and Mr Preddy could not assert their rights directly against Mr and Mrs Bull, but only against the state.[45] However, they could assert their rights directly against the proprietors under anti-discrimination legislation, in this case, the Equality Act (Sexual Orientation) Regulations 2007, which applied explicitly to providers of services such as hoteliers.[46] Thus there were no threshold barriers and the substance of the claim could immediately be dealt with. Nor was the HRA entirely out of the picture. If the outcome were to conflict with Mr and Mrs Bull's right to freedom of religion in Article 9 ECHR, then the Court would be obliged to read the regulations in a way which was compatible with their rights.[47] In the event, the Supreme Court held that the hoteliers had indeed discriminated unlawfully against Mr Hall and Mr Preddy and that this did not infringe Article 9. Rather than dismissing the case for technical reasons linked to the relationship between the right-holder and the duty-bearer, as has been done in the employment cases, the Court was able to deal appropriately with the substantive issues.[48]

IV. Adjusting the Burdens: The Role of Justification

The sophisticated development of conceptions of discrimination under statutory anti-discrimination laws contrasts markedly with the broad brush formulae of constitutional equality guarantees. But in both cases, again, there is a strong if not frequently articulated concern with limiting the burdens on the duty bearer.

[44] *Bull v Hall* (n 6).
[45] ibid [5].
[46] Equality Act (Sexual Orientation) Regulations 2007, reg 4(1)–(2).
[47] HRA 1998, s 3(1).
[48] See also *Black and Morgan v Wilkinson* (n 5).

At constitutional level, this manifests itself in the form of judicial deference to the state; or, at ECHR level, of the margin of appreciation. From the labour law perspective, it is reflected in conceptions of employer prerogative. At both levels, it is mediated through the principle of justification. This can either be internal to the concept of equality; or operate as a defence. Thus the primary guiding principle behind Article 14 is that not all distinctions are discriminatory, but only those for which there is no objective and proportionate justification. This compares with the statutory structure, which regards justification as a potential defence to a prima facie finding of some types of discrimination.

Here, too, the right to equality disrupts the settled assumptions within labour law. With most employment protection, the balance is between the employer's economic interests and the worker's interests in job stability, self-respect, and decent terms and conditions. However, in the case of the right to equality, a wider range of interests is at stake, including the public interest, and the rights and interests of others. Nevertheless, the origins of discrimination law in labour law have meant that the justification defence for discrimination under statutory discrimination law has been calibrated primarily to reflect the conflict between the employer's economic interests and those of the employee. This is reflected in the structure of the legislation. As we have seen, under a human rights analysis, all kinds of discrimination can be justified under the proportionality analysis in Article 14 ECHR and other substantive rights. However, under the statutory regime, whereas indirect discrimination can be justified, both EU and UK law have been resistant to the possibility of allowing direct discrimination to be justified.[49] This resistance reflects the appropriate concern that such a defence would permit employers to justify blatant discrimination on grounds that it furthered their economic interests, for example, because of the prejudices of customers or consumers, or, because it is simply more costly, as in the case of equal pay or pregnancy discrimination.[50]

However, with the expansion into other grounds of discrimination and beyond employment per se, this rigid refusal to contemplate a defence for direct discrimination has proved problematic. Not only has it made it impossible to pursue affirmative action policies. It has also meant that there is no medium for achieving a nuanced balance between different rights and interests. Arguably, the knowledge that, once established, direct discrimination cannot be justified tempts courts to foreclose the issue at the threshold stage of determining whether the individuals involved are rights-holders and duty-bearers. The *CAB* case certainly gives rise to the suspicion that one motivating factor was the concern that, if volunteers were included in the scope of anti-discrimination legislation, this would give them an absolute right not to be discriminated against.

In practice, there are a growing number of ways in which direct discrimination can indeed be justified. It has always been possible to justify direct race

[49] See eg *R (E) v JFS Governing Body* [2009] UKSC 15, [2010] 2 AC 728.

[50] See eg T Gill and K Monaghan, 'Justification in Direct Sex Discrimination Law: Taboo Upheld' [2003] 32 *Industrial Law Journal* 115.

and sex discrimination where sex or race is a genuine occupational qualification. This has now been extended to most of the protected characteristics, subject to a proportionality requirement.[51] Equal pay legislation has always permitted employers to justify differences of pay for equal work by reference to a material factor that is not itself the difference in sex. The Disability Discrimination Act permitted direct discrimination on grounds of disability to be justified,[52] and although the EA 2010 removes this possibility for direct discrimination strictly defined, it is retained for the newly coined concept of discrimination arising from disability, found in section 15 of the EA 2010. The disability legislation also allows a balancing through the application of the principle of reasonable adjustment. After 2000, with the introduction of the three new protected characteristics of age, religion or belief, and sexual orientation, the possible justifications have multiplied. Age discrimination can be justified for a variety of statutory reasons, and discrimination on grounds of gender and sexual orientation can be justified for specific religious reasons.

This makes it particularly important to be in a position to shape a justification defence that is context sensitive without permitting costs arguments to trump equality or reintroducing the very stereotypes that direct discrimination aims to eliminate. The key issue is therefore the standard of scrutiny and how it is applied. This requires careful consideration of which aims are legitimate. One approach could be to specify a fixed list of potentially legitimating reasons;[53] another is to insist that the ends reflect a 'pressing state interest'.[54] Equally important is the standard of scrutiny to determine whether the means 'fit' the ends. Must the discrimination be necessary to achieve the legitimate aim, or is a lesser standard of fit acceptable? This in turn necessitates a determination of what kind of evidence needs to be produced to support a justification claim.

The different approaches under anti-discrimination and human rights law, respectively, are well illustrated by contrasting *Jivraj*, which was decided under the anti-discrimination legislation, and *Eweida*, a human rights case. The justification defence for religion or belief, framed as an exception for a 'genuine occupational qualification' operates in two circumstances: in order to permit discrimination against an individual on the basis of religion; and in order to permit religiously motivated discrimination against individuals on the grounds of their sex or sexual orientation. The EU Directive permits Member States to permit a difference of treatment based on a person's religion or belief in the case of occupational activities within churches or other organizations with an ethos based on religion or belief, provided that a person's religion or belief constitute a 'genuine, legitimate and justified occupational requirement having regard to the organisation's ethos'.[55] The domestic application of the Directive, now found in

[51] EA 2010, sch 9, pt 1.
[52] Disability Discrimination Act 1995, s 5(1).
[53] See eg ECHR, Arts 9(2), 10(2) and 11(2).
[54] *Johnson v California* 543 US 499 (2005).
[55] Council Directive 2000/78/EC (n 21) Art 4(2).

the EA 2010, states that a person with an ethos based on religion or belief may set a requirement of a particular religion or belief provided that, in the context of the work, it is, inter alia, a proportionate means of achieving a legitimate aim. In *Jivraj* the standard of review for this defence was a central point of difference between the Court of Appeal and the Supreme Court. The Court of Appeal determined that the necessity standard was the appropriate one. Applying this standard to the role of arbitrator, it held, since an arbitrator needed to know the law of the land, that being a member of the Ismaili community was not necessary. It therefore upheld the claim of discrimination. In the Supreme Court, Lord Clarke, despite having decided that an arbiter was not within the scope of the anti-discrimination legislation, went on to consider whether the genuine occupational qualification exception applied. Crucially, he held that the standard of necessity was too strict:

> I am not persuaded that the test is one of necessity. The question is whether, in all the circumstances the provision that all the arbitrators should be respected members of the Ismaili community was legitimate and justified. In my opinion it was. The approach of the Court of Appeal seems to me to be too legalistic and technical. The parties could properly regard arbitration before three Ismailis as likely to involve a procedure in which the parties could have confidence and as likely to lead to conclusions of fact in which they could have particular confidence.[56]

The result was that the interests of those who employed the arbitrator were given precedence, even though the very fact of having more confidence in one group than another was arguably based on prejudicial stereotypes. The costs to those excluded on grounds of their religion were not factored in.

This can be contrasted with the *Eweida* case, which was decided as a human rights case in the ECtHR. In relation to Chaplin and Ladele, because the employer was the state, the court applied the justification test in Article 9(2), which required proof that the limitation was 'necessary in a democratic society' in pursuit of one of the aims set out in Article 9(2).[57] So far as Ms Eweida was concerned, although the Court regarded the actual weighing process as falling within the margin of appreciation, and therefore requiring a measure of deference to domestic decision-making bodies, it held that the balance in this case had been struck in the wrong place. This is important because in this case, the conflict was the familiar one between the employer's business interests, in the form of its corporate image, and the applicant's basic human right. Although the domestic courts had taken the view that the corporate interests could justify the restriction in this case, the ECtHR took the opposite view. It is worth setting out the Court's balancing process in some detail:

> On one side of the scales was Ms Eweida's desire to manifest her religious belief. As previously noted, this is a fundamental right: because a healthy democratic society needs to tolerate and sustain pluralism and diversity; but also because of the value

[56] *Jivraj* (n 3) [70].
[57] *Eweida* (n 2) para 98.

> to an individual who has made religion a central tenet of his or her life to be able to communicate that belief to others. On the other side of the scales was the employer's wish to project a certain corporate image. The Court considers that, while this aim was undoubtedly legitimate, the domestic courts accorded it too much weight. Ms Eweida's cross was discreet and cannot have detracted from her professional appearance. There was no evidence that the wearing of other, previously authorised, items of religious clothing, such as turbans and hijabs, by other employees, had any negative impact on British Airways' brand or image. Moreover, the fact that the company was able to amend the uniform code to allow for the visible wearing of religious symbolic jewellery demonstrates that the earlier prohibition was not of crucial importance.[58]

Given that there was no real encroachment on the interests of third parties, the Court held that the state was in breach of its positive obligation under Article 9 ECHR.

This contrasts with the other three complainants in the conjoined cases heard with *Eweida*, where there was the possibility of a real encroachment on the rights and interests of others. In the case of Ms Chaplin, the employer's reason for restricting the wearing of a cross was to reduce the risk of injury when handling patients. Here, while her freedom to manifest her religion should weigh heavily in the balance, the protection of health and safety in a hospital ward was inherently of a greater magnitude than the corporate image factor which had been put forward by British Airways. Moreover, there was a wider margin of appreciation, given that hospital managers were better placed to make decisions about clinical safety than an international court, which had heard no direct evidence.[59]

The Court's reasoning in relation to Ms Ladelle and Mr McFarlane is particularly important. Here the Court put the spotlight on whether the complainants should be permitted to use their work situation to discriminate against gay people. This required an assessment first of the legitimacy of the objective and then of whether the means were proportionate. So far as the legitimacy of the objective was concerned, the Court had no doubt that the local authority's policy of promoting non-discrimination against same-sex couples was a legitimate one. It then went on to determine whether the means used to pursue this aim were proportionate. It acknowledged the strength of the applicant's religious conviction and the fact that the consequences for her were serious, including the possibility of losing her job. On the other hand, it recognized that

> the local authority's policy aimed to secure the rights of others which are also protected under the Convention. The Court generally allows the national authorities a wide margin of appreciation when it comes to striking a balance between competing Convention rights. In all the circumstances, the Court does not consider that the national authorities, that is the local authority employer which brought the disciplinary proceedings and also the domestic courts which rejected the applicant's discrimination claim, exceeded the margin of appreciation available to them. It cannot, therefore,

[58] ibid para 92.
[59] ibid para 99.

be said that there has been a violation of art 14 taken in conjunction with art 9 in respect of the third applicant.[60]

V. Conclusion: Convergence or Sui Generis?

This chapter has briefly explored whether the right to equality is a part of labour law or should better be regarded as an aspect of human rights law or constitutes an autonomous field in its own right. It has been argued that the right to equality unsettles the assumptions in both labour law, where the focus is on an employer–worker relationship, and human rights law, which emphasizes the relationship between the state and individual. But whereas human rights law has gradually been overcoming these limitations, labour law in the UK has been moving in the opposite direction.

While the right not to be discriminated against in a work situation remains embedded in labour law, the scope of anti-discrimination law has always extended beyond work to include education and goods, facilities and services. With the arrival of domesticated human rights law, the right to equality can be asserted in an even wider range of cases, often in parallel to labour law, and with different scopes and standards of review. This has made the focus on the employment relationship particularly discordant with the underlying aims of the equality, which do not cohere well with the principle that protection should be aligned with subordinate status. Discrimination constitutes an exercise of power which can take place in a many sets of relationships, well beyond that of employment. While this was given limited recognition by the use of legislative terms such as 'contract for personal services' and 'occupation,' the Supreme Court in *Jivraj* and the *CAB* cases decisively shut down these avenues of expansion. It has been argued here that the background question should be: in what circumstances should individuals be free to discriminate against others? Since both labour law and human rights law insist that power brings with it responsibility, the right not to be subjected to discrimination should place correlative duties on anyone who is in a position to discriminate, whether directly or indirectly, and regardless of whether they are in an employment relationship or not. At the same time, a properly nuanced proportionality measure, calibrated at a strict standard of review, should be used to balance the freedom of the duty-bearer against the rights of the right-holder. In particular, limits on the duty not to discriminate should not be based on an employer's economic interests. Appropriate limits to the right not to be discriminated against should derive from human rights considerations, particularly the need to protect the rights and interests of others.

[60] ibid para 106.

11

Labour Law as Human Rights Law: A Critique of the Use of 'Dignity' by Freedland and Kountouris

CHRISTOPHER MCCRUDDEN

I. Introduction

In their recent book, *The Legal Construction of Personal Work Relations*,[1] Mark Freedland and Nicola Kountouris present an ambitious study of the personal scope of (what they would not want to call) 'employment' law. The book does this within a broader argument that calls for the reconceptualization of labour law as a whole, and it is this broader argument on which I shall focus in this chapter. Their aim, in urging us to see labour law through the lens of 'dignity' is to bring labour law and human rights law into closer alignment than has sometimes been the case in the past. Increasingly, dignity is seen as providing *a*, sometimes *the*, foundation of human rights law, particularly in Europe.[2] I shall suggest that whilst the aim of constructing a new set of foundations for labour law is a worthy and increasingly urgent task, the concepts on which Freedland and Kountouris seek to build their project pose significant difficulties. In particular, their espousal of 'dignity' presents problems that must be addressed if their reconceptualization is not to prove a blind alley.

* I am indebted to Alan Bogg and Anne Davies for comments on an earlier draft of this chapter.

[1] M Freedland and N Kountouris, *The Legal Construction of Personal Work Relations* (Oxford, Oxford University Press, 2011).

[2] See eg JP Costa, 'Human Dignity in the Jurisprudence of the European Court of Human Rights' in C McCrudden (ed), *Understanding Human Dignity* (Oxford, Oxford University Press, 2013) 393.

II. The Freedland–Kountouris Thesis

The Freedland–Kountouris view of the function of labour law, which I take to be a normative rather than a descriptive thesis,[3] is presented throughout the book in a particular form. (The particular quotation that follows is presented early in the book, but is repeated frequently throughout in similar terms.) The 'function of labour law as a whole,' they say, is one of

> maximizing the dignity accorded to workers in personal work relations and optimizing their capabilities in and through those relations while recognizing the importance of stability in the relations between workers and those for whom they work.[4]

We see here three of the central concepts on which Freedland and Kountouris seek to build: 'dignity', 'capabilities' and 'stability'. In their critical chapter 9 they set out their important idea of 'personality at work', and it is here that they present the most sustained analysis of these three concepts and how they relate to the function of labour law more generally. Labour regulation 'should aspire to establishing strong protections' in terms of 'dignity', 'stability', and capabilities'. These three concepts, they suggest, 'could be used as a basis to reshape and inform the regulation which labour law deploys'.[5] Indeed, they 'may well serve as a normative and moral *raison d'être* for labour law in the twenty-first century'.[6]

In what follows, I shall focus primarily on examining the concept of 'dignity' in their analysis, leaving it to others to consider whether the concepts of 'capabilities' and 'stability' establish a firmer foundation for future labour law regulation. I focus on the issue of 'dignity' not only because it is apparently central to the Freedland–Kountouris schema,[7] but also because there appears to have been a relatively sudden increase in the extent to which 'dignity' has become a part of EU employment law,[8] as well as current labour law scholarship, not only in Britain, but also in the wider European and American contexts.[9] On a

[3] This is made clear where they 'advocate the importance of refocusing the normative rationale for labour regulation'. Freedland and Kountouris (n 1) 372.

[4] ibid 49.

[5] ibid 372.

[6] ibid 376.

[7] 'Dignity' is mentioned at least 23 times in the text of the book, in comparison with Mark Freedland's 2003 book, *The Personal Employment Contract* (Oxford, Oxford University Press, 2003), in which it is mentioned only three times.

[8] 'Dignity' is to be found in the employment-related provisions of the EU Charter of Fundamental Rights (Art 31(1) provides: 'Every worker has the right to working conditions which respect his or her health, safety, and dignity'), union legislation (eg Art 1 of Recommendation 92/441/EEC, COM(91) 161 final requires Member States to 'recognise the basic right of a person to sufficient resources and social assistance to live in a manner consistent with human dignity'), and CJEU jurisprudence, see eg Case C-413/99 *Baumbast* [2002] ECR I-7091, para 50.

[9] See eg DC Yamada, 'Human Dignity and American Employment Law' (2009) 43 *University of Richmond Law Review* 523, Suffolk University Law School Research Paper No 08-36, www.ssrn.com/abstract=1299176; G Davidov, 'A Purposive Interpretation of the National Minimum Wage Act' (2009) 72 *Modern Law Review* 581; and J Gross and L Compa, *Human Rights in Labor and Employment Relations: International and Domestic Perspectives* (Ithaca, NY, ILR Press, 2009).

more personal level, I have been working on trying to understand the concept of dignity in human rights discourse more generally;[10] its emergence (or, perhaps, it would be better to say, *re*-emergence[11]) in the field of labour regulation raises important questions about how far labour law is becoming a part of human rights law, giving an added edge to the long-debated issue of the autonomy of labour law.

III. Dignity: Why Now in Labour Law?

The use of the language of dignity in the labour context is not, of course, a new phenomenon, so why does the discussion about human dignity appear to have become so much more intense over the last few years? As an issue in the history of ideas, the reason for the relatively recent pervasiveness of dignity discourse is interesting and problematic. Several explanations have been advanced, relying partly on the relative failures of alternative ethical approaches to gain sufficient traction to support an increasingly challenged set of legal requirements, partly on the accretion of new responsibilities on employers and others that require a rethinking of the theoretical underpinnings of labour law if they are to be accommodated, and partly on the growth of human rights and the increasingly pervasive influence of human rights law on the interpretation of domestic and EU labour law. It is the third of these that I shall focus on for the moment.

Dignity's role is to supply a value, or a set of values, that other approaches do not, or do not fully capture, such as autonomy, or solidarity, for example. One explanation for the increasing importance and salience of debates about dignity in labour law relates to the role of dignity in the discourse of human rights in general. With the increased political salience of human rights, and the increased use in litigation of human rights language, has come increasing attention on the theoretical underpinnings of human rights. This has tended to demonstrate how contested the foundations of human rights are. The familiar story is that when the Universal Declaration of Human Rights was being drafted in 1948 the participants were able to agree on what they were against, but not on *why* they were against these violations. Human dignity, so the story goes, was inserted as a placeholder when those drafting the Declaration failed to agree on any single foundation.[12] (That is not to say that dignity was a placeholder when inserted into national constitutions drafted at much the same time; there is now historical

[10] C McCrudden, 'In Pursuit of Human Dignity: An Introduction to Current Debates' in McCrudden (ed) (n 2) 1.

[11] The use of the idea of the 'dignity of labour' has roots stretching back to the 19th century.

[12] I have discussed this in C McCrudden, 'Human Dignity and Judicial Interpretation of Human Rights' (2008) 19 *European Journal of International Law* 655.

evidence that dignity in the German Basic Law may well have had a particular substantive meaning.[13])

Since the 1970s at least, the human rights enterprise has become both more powerful and more controversial, legally, politically and ethically, and this absence of a clear agreement on the foundations has threatened to undermine the project. Many human rights instruments now invoke dignity. Perhaps the most recent in the European context is the EU Charter of Fundamental Rights.[14] The meaning of dignity in these contexts is currently the subject of considerable debate and litigation.[15] As practical use of concrete rights proceeds, nagging questions about foundations come to the surface and beg for further discussion. From this has come the urge to revisit the concept of human dignity, in order to examine whether it is more than a placeholder and whether it can provide the necessary foundational principle for human rights.

To the extent that labour law is influenced by developments in human rights law, the role of dignity as a foundational principle is likely to flow from human rights to labour. A crude count of the number of contributions in the *Industrial Law Journal* mentioning 'dignity' and 'human rights' between 1973 and 2013 appears to support this view.

IV. Dignity in Legal Texts

In their analysis, Freedland and Kountouris present 'dignity' initially as firmly linked to existing legal texts: ILO texts (eg the ILO Declaration of Philadelphia, and the ILO 'Decent Work' Agenda), international and European human rights texts (eg the Universal Declaration of Human Rights, and the EU Charter of Fundamental Rights), and national constitutions (eg the German, Italian and South African constitutions). Indeed, the frequency of the use of dignity in such contexts is said to be a reason why the concept of dignity 'does not need much introduction to social scientists in general and lawyers and labour lawyers in particular'.[16] This is an important point because it means that 'dignity' already has an important history of use and interpretation that cannot but influence how it will be understood in the future—a point I return to subsequently.

Freedland and Kountouris do not present the use of dignity in these contexts as the prologue to a detailed exegesis of how dignity has been interpreted in the labour law context by those charged with enforcing ILO, EU, human rights or national constitutional law. Indeed, there is no reference to how 'dignity'

[13] See eg C Goos, '*Würde des Menschen*: Restoring Human Dignity in Post-Nazi Germany' in McCrudden (ed) (n 2) 79.

[14] EU Charter of Fundamental Rights, Art 1.

[15] See eg Case C-34/10 *Brüstle v Greenpeace eV* [2011] ECR I-09821.

[16] Freedland and Kountouris (n 1) 372.

has been interpreted in these or other legal contexts at all, beyond a somewhat contentious statement that its interpretation has been based on '*slightly* different meanings', a point that some would contest.[17] The application of 'dignity' by these bodies is not of central concern to the authors because it is clear that their project is more in the nature of building the foundations of labour regulation on a particular *philosophical* understanding of 'dignity'.

V. Philosophical Understandings of 'Dignity'

We need, therefore, to consider what the philosophical understanding of Freedland and Kountouris consists of. For Freedland and Kountouris, the 'notion' of dignity is seen as 'something of a composite concept,'[18] 'ultimately amounting to a conceptual amalgam of the concept of personal autonomy and equality',[19] and being essentially 'the synthesis of these two concepts'. [20]

Leaving aside the tricky question of whether 'composite', 'amalgam' and 'synthesis' mean precisely the same thing, we can nevertheless discern that, for Freedland and Kountouris, the meaning of 'dignity' is entirely encompassed by these two other concepts, 'autonomy' and 'equality'. There is, in other words, no additional meaning that 'dignity' brings into our discourse that is not encompassed by some combination of 'autonomy' and 'equality'; 'dignity' is simply a way of describing a particular combined configuration of these two concepts. This is confirmed by their explicit rejection of the alternative view (which they consider is how 'dignity' is 'typically seen'), that dignity, autonomy and equality are 'notionally distinct'.[21] How convincing is 'dignity' conceived as an amalgamation of 'autonomy' and 'equality'? I shall first consider how far 'dignity' conceived as either 'autonomy' or as 'equality' is convincing, before turning to the issue of whether in combination they are convincing.

VI. Griffin's Human Rights

It is important to note that, in support of their own understanding of 'dignity', Freedland and Kountouris draw particularly on the work of the noted Oxford philosopher James Griffin, whose major work on this topic was published in 2008 with the title, *On Human Rights*.[22] Griffin's view of what grounds human

[17] McCrudden (n 12).
[18] Freedland and Kountouris (n 1) 373.
[19] ibid.
[20] ibid 374.
[21] ibid 373.
[22] J Griffin, *On Human Rights* (Oxford, Oxford University Press, 2008).

rights is based on the concept of the dignity of the human person. It is a controversial understanding, one that concentrates on emphasizing the importance of a particular conception of human persons, whom Griffin understands 'as normative agents'. 'The dignity [of persons],' he writes, 'is then seen as deriving from the value we attach to our normative agency.'[23] Human rights are those claims that defend 'personhood' understood in this way, as the 'protection of a component of normative agency'.[24] The effect of this is to create a significantly more restricted approach to what constitutes 'human rights' than do approaches that ground human rights on ideas of justice or fairness, and he is particularly sceptical of arguments that seek to ground human rights in general or specific human rights on the idea of distributive justice.

Although he denies it,[25] Griffin's understanding of human rights is, like that of Freedland and Kountouris, one based on what might be characterized as 'top-down' rather than one that stresses the significance of social practices in constituting the meaning of values, a 'bottom-up' approach. When, as he finds to be the case, Griffin identifies a significant mismatch between the best philosophical theory of human rights and legal or political practice, theory trumps practice, meaning that if existing legal practice of what constitutes 'human rights' goes beyond what the theory would justify as such, then we should be prepared to say that the legal practice is misleading and wrong. This leads to a particularly important analysis in which, with brutal candour, he sets out examples of what legal and political practice would regard as human rights but would be unacceptable or dubious under his approach. He regards 'some of the claims to welfare rights' as 'hardly credible'.[26] The right of every worker 'to promotion or upward mobility in his employment' is also 'incredible'.[27] On Griffin's account, 'there is no right to work'.[28] There is no right to 'the highest attainable standard of physical and mental health'.[29] In the 'debatable cases' category, he includes 'equal pay for equal work', 'just conditions of work' and 'promotion on merit',[30] concluding that 'in the end the argument goes against their being human rights'.[31] Griffin's account is also hostile to the idea of collective right-holders, and hence of collective rights. With this brief account of Griffin, we can return to consider the two elements that Freedland and Kountouris consider to make up their conception of 'dignity': 'autonomy' and 'equality'.

[23] ibid 200.
[24] ibid 210.
[25] ibid 29.
[26] ibid 206.
[27] ibid 206–07.
[28] ibid 207.
[29] ibid 208.
[30] ibid 209.
[31] ibid.

VII. Dignity as 'Autonomy'

Dignity as freedom or autonomy is a popular conception of dignity, particularly in the United States. One prominent philosophical version of this has been advanced by Griffin, who argues that human dignity consists in one particular interest, an interest in freedom. Freedland and Kountouris appear to adopt a similar understanding of autonomy, one that 'encompasses both the ability to take decisions about the life to pursue (including of course, one's working life), and the possibility of doing so in the absence of any undue constraints'.[32] For these authors, this vision of autonomy 'has a number of essential components that readily translate into legal rights and entitlements', such as the protection of 'fundamental human rights'.

John Tasioulas outlines several difficulties with Griffin's approach, but there are essentially three.[33] First, it seems to present an impoverished understanding of the grounds of human rights to see them as purely protecting freedom. From Griffin's perspective, therefore, the reason why torture constitutes a violation of human rights is that it undermines the capacity of the person tortured to make decisions and stick to them. Tasioulas considers that the fact that torture is incredibly painful is not, in Griffin's argument, relevant to it being a violation of human rights, and that this is fundamentally mistaken. To view labour regulation as based on 'autonomy', in this sense, seems equally mistaken. For example, it would seem to present a peculiar view of why we protect someone in employment from being discriminated against to view such protection as important because it undermines the capacity of a person to make decisions; don't we instead usually say that such protection is important because discrimination is 'unfair' or 'unjust'?[34]

Second, Tasioulas argues, a focus exclusively on freedom means that human rights standards do not protect human beings incapable of agency. At the extreme, some of the most vulnerable, such as those in a permanent vegetative state, lack any capacity for agency and would thus not attract the protection of Griffin's human rights, but are nevertheless protected by existing human rights law and practice. An emphasis on dignity as freedom and autonomy alone also appears to pose significant difficulties as a foundation for a significantly robust understanding of labour rights for the same reason. Taking the employment discrimination example a little further, we protect some disabled workers, for example those suffering from reduced mental capacity, in spite (indeed, *because*) of their reduced agency.

A third concern with making 'autonomy' central to 'dignity' is the extent

[32] Freedland and Kountouris (n 1) 374.

[33] J Tasioulas, 'Human Dignity as a Foundation for Human Rights' in McCrudden (ed) (n 2) 291.

[34] I am here concerned with Griffin's approach, rather than with how Freedland and Kountouris use Griffin. So, for example, they envisage autonomy working *in tandem* with equality, and so it would be open to them (even if not Griffin) to characterize the right to non-discrimination in this way.

to which it reduces the importance of relationality to a fully developed understanding of 'dignity', and undermines the importance of 'relationality' in the labour law context if labour regulation is seen as based on this understanding of 'dignity'. Labour regulation is surely better thought of protecting *relational* aspects of human flourishing in order to maximize the recognition and protection of our dignity, rather than as protecting the exercise of autonomy. This is not to say that a relational approach is incapable of coexisting with all understandings of autonomy. A focus on autonomy does not have to adopt a conception of the individual as ruggedly individualistic. Indeed, one can argue that autonomy often results from the existence of certain kinds of supportive relationships, but if this understanding of 'autonomy' is what is thought to be important, then this needs to be made clearer than it is at the moment. There is, for example, no explicit reliance on the understanding of autonomy developed by Joseph Raz, which may supply a more suitable framework in this regard.[35]

In short, we have seen that in several respects Griffin's approach denies the label of 'human rights' to some well-established labour rights, and Freedland and Kountouris do not explain how they can rely on Griffin's autonomy-based approach whilst arguing at one and the same time for 'a right to free, decent, suitable, and rewarding work', and a 'general entitlement to work that can help a person in her personal and professional progression',[36] both rights that Griffin appears explicitly to reject, based on his approach to autonomy. This is not to say that arguments cannot be made that what Griffin's understanding of dignity leaves out might be picked up by the use of other concepts, such as equality, or by basing human rights on ideas of capabilities; it is only to say that the problems in using Griffin are not identified, let alone addressed.

VIII. Dignity as 'Equality'

What of dignity as 'equality'? One of the best-known recent attempts to link 'dignity with 'equality' is that put forward by Jeremy Waldron, who argues in his recent book that modern understandings of dignity take the intuition that dignity is about status and combine it with modern commitments to equality.[37] We can easily imagine situations, he argues, where high-ranking people in society have a vote, low-ranking people do not, and then we decide to give the vote to everybody. We decide to treat everybody as having the high rank. Or, to take another example, high-ranking people are punished humanely and allowed to give evidence freely in court, but low-ranking people are punished

[35] See J Raz, *The Morality of Freedom* (Oxford, Oxford University Press, 1988) ch 15.
[36] Freedland and Kountouris (n 1) 374.
[37] J Waldron, *Dignity, Rank & Rights, with commentaries by Wai Chee Dimnock, Don Herzog, Michael Rosen*, ed M Dan-Cohen (Oxford, Oxford University Press, 2012).

savagely and give evidence only under torture, and then we decide to confer the high rank on everybody.

Michael Rosen is sceptical of Waldron's equal-status-based conception of dignity.[38] Adopting an egalitarian, status-based conception of dignity requires a decision as to which of the characteristics of high status are going to be attributed to people when everybody has this high status. Clearly, if those with high status have previously required their dignity to be recognized by having people kow-tow to them, then we are unlikely to want to generalize that requirement to everyone. In addition, the idea that we can generalize high-status privileges may misunderstand the nature of the privilege in question; at least some privileges require there to be inequality. So which aspects of a high status are the ones that are essential to that high status, and therefore part of one's dignity?

The authors do not mention Waldron's views, or the criticisms that might be made of them, in their discussion of the relationship between 'dignity' and 'equality'. Indeed, they eschew the need to adopt or promote any particular conception of equality ('we do not feel overly prescriptive in respect of a particular equality model'[39]), finding potentially suitable approaches in Amartya Sen's capabilities approach, a revised Rawlsian account, and Gerry Cohen's understanding of equality of opportunity as ensuring protection from unchosen disadvantages. Had they felt the need to be more prescriptive, they would almost certainly have run into trouble. To take but one example: how well would Cohen's 'protection from unchosen disadvantages' cope with claims to conscientious objection by workers, based on philosophical or religious beliefs, a right to which the authors appear to be committed.[40]

As I have said, the authors avoid dealing with problems such as these by defining their interest in 'dignity' as useful but limited in its focus: 'our work', they say, is concerned 'with the justification, or rather the lack of it, for disparate regulatory protection for different typologies of providers of personal services.'[41] They are interested, they say, in 'why some typologies of providers of personal work are left outside employment protection legislation', and 'dignity' 'provides a powerful antidote to the main justifications as to why some workers should not be endowed with the protection of employment or labour law'. So, after being told that 'autonomy' and 'equality' are what together make up their concept of dignity, we are now told that we should not be too concerned to pin down the meaning of either concept because the primary function of 'dignity' is to challenge exclusions from protections rather than itself form the basis for any general system.[42]

However, were we not earlier told that 'dignity' 'may well' provide the basis of a general revision of labour law *as a whole*? The absence of rigorous analysis

[38] M Rosen, 'Dignity: The Case Against' in McCrudden (ed) (n 2) 143.
[39] Freedland and Kountouris (n 1) 374.
[40] ibid.
[41] ibid 375.
[42] We shall consider subsequently whether this more limited role for dignity is successful.

and critical reflection on the meaning of and reasons for the assertion of human dignity could then leave a vacuum to be filled, which has its advantages and disadvantages. On the one hand, an open-textured idea of dignity has been seen by some as providing space for dialogue in a pluralistic society among those who fundamentally disagree.[43] Dignity, in this understanding, marks out a space for dialogue about the proper shape and weight of labour law rather than supplying a particular template. On the other hand, Jürgen Habermas identified the dangers of such open-ended concepts, in a rather impenetrable phrase, as the likely 'colonization of the lifeworld' by strategic rationality,[44] potentially distorting the recognition of human dignity and the protection of the rights founded on it. In other words, the interests of the law, or of politics, would fill the vacuum shaping the meaning of dignity in practice, and not always with benign consequences. Whether the advantages are outweighed by the disadvantages depends, above all, on the exercise of power, an issue that needs to be systematically considered if a conception of dignity as apparently as open ended as the one proposed by Freedland and Kountouris is adopted.

IX. Personhood as Moral Worth

Leaving that problem to one side for the moment, and accepting the more limited role that 'dignity' is to play in the Freedland–Kountouris scheme, what is the basis for their understanding of dignity in this more limited context? My suspicion is that the Freedland–Kountouris formulation is based on a mostly unarticulated understanding of personhood, one in which dignity is a kind of basic moral status, the intrinsic worth of being a human being. The answer appears to be, as they say, that 'the concept of dignity … goes hand-in-hand with the idea of personality in work'.[45] The authors' reference in this context to Griffin's work on personhood as the basis for a defensible understanding of human rights supports this view.

If I am correct in this, however, then the concept of 'dignity' that we see emerging is one in which both 'equality' and 'autonomy' have to be understood against the background of a strong concept of 'personhood'. Indeed, I think we can go further, although this is not made explicit and therefore requires a degree of reconstruction of their views, and say that their conception of dignity is one in which both 'equality' and 'autonomy' have to be *filtered through* the idea of 'personhood', because it is an individual's personhood that provides the basis for being able to claim equality and autonomy. But if that is the case, then why do we need, except for rhetorical purposes, any reference to 'equality' or 'autonomy'

[43] For a discussion, see C McCrudden, 'Introduction' in McCrudden (ed) (n 2) 12–15.

[44] J Habermas, *The Theory of Communicative Action*, vol 2: *Life-World and System: A Critique of Functionalist Reason*, trans T McCarthy (Boston, Beacon Press, 1987) 325.

[45] Freedland and Kountouris (n 1) 375.

in the definition of dignity at all? Isn't it the case that, for Freedland and Kountouris, it is 'personhood' that is actually doing all the normative heavy lifting in their concept of 'dignity'?

Assuming that I am correct that it is the concept of 'personhood' that is critical to their understanding of dignity, then their argument appears to amount to the following: we should treat others in the context of work relations in the way that is conducive to respecting them as 'human persons'. In arriving at this conclusion, we can finally arrive at a position where labour regulation takes on the same understanding of its foundations as human rights theory does. Labour law effectively becomes human rights law, with the same theoretical foundations, and loses any specific understandings of its role and functions that departs from this new understanding. But there are several problems with this approach.

The first problem is that the concept of 'human personhood' is deeply contested, and the absence of consensus on such a critical concept, were it to become central to labour regulation, may well conflict with the value of stability that Freedland and Kountouris also espouse. In particular, different understandings of the 'human person' are likely to engender very considerable differences in political ideology, and hence affect profoundly the very starting point for considering how far the state should intervene through legal regulation.

Dignity discourse invites openness to the posing of the question of what it is to be human in our public and communal discourse. Such a dialogue is all the more important because some consider that there is something irreducible about the human person that cannot be fully captured (Sedmak and others use the word 'mystery'[46]). This means that there is always going to be a need for discussion, the likelihood of disagreement, and a certain under-determination. The very nature of what we are talking about—the human person—means that we should never presume to be able to specify dignity beyond contestation. But that leaves open the possibility that it will be 'captured', as I have suggested earlier.

All this also has important implications for the extent to which, even if we agree that dignity is a foundation for rights, dignity provides any guide for action, and this is the second problem. The more general and open-ended one's conception of dignity, the more steps removed we are from being able to specify the contours of rights: rights with what content, whose responsibility it is to accord those rights, what kind of remedy for rights violations is appropriate, and how does the state fit in? Even if we all agreed on the foundations and meaning of human dignity, there would still be a rich difference of understandings about how exactly that principle should be instantiated in specific contexts, with respect to specific persons, and in specific cultures.[47]

[46] C Sedmak, 'Human Dignity, Interiority, and Poverty' in McCrudden (ed) (n 2) 559.

[47] This is not to say that agreements on what actions to take are not possible even where there are deep disagreements on foundations.

X. Personalism and 'Personality in Work'

A different problem is that it is unclear how far Freedland and Kountouris, intentionally or unintentionally, are edging towards grounding their conception of labour law on what has been called 'personalism'. This may explain their passing (if highly qualified) reference to Pope Benedict's 2009 encyclical *Caritas in Veritate*. Recent expositions of dignity from a 'personalist' perspective seem to me more in line with the substantive vision that Freedland and Kountouris seek to espouse than with Griffin's approach. Thomas Williams has identified the core of personalism as a school of thought or intellectual movement that 'focuses on the reality of the person … and on his unique dignity, insisting on the radical distinction between persons and all other beings (nonpersons)'.[48] But there is more to it than that. Williams sets out the distinctive characteristics of personalism as not only including 'an insistence on the radical difference between persons and nonpersons' and 'an affirmation of the dignity of persons', but also 'a concern for the person's subjectivity, attention to the person as object of human action to be treated as an end and never as a mere means, and particular regard for the social (relational) nature of the person'.

Using a phrase borrowed from Margaret Farley, one could call the requirements of respect for dignity that the authors appear to espouse 'obligating features of personhood'.[49] These are dimensions of personal dignity that indicate not only *that* we should show respect toward one another but *what* it will mean to show such respect. Farley identifies two such features: autonomy (the capacity to be self-determining and not have one's life simply shaped by other persons or external powers), but also, crucially, relationality (the fact that persons cannot survive, thrive or even exist as persons without some fundamental relatedness to other persons). David Hollenbach, in addition, suggests we add 'basic needs', such as the need for food or healthcare, as a third obligating feature of personhood that will help specify the meaning of human dignity and what respect for dignity requires.[50] Is Freedland and Kountouris's idea of 'personality in work' in fact this vision of 'personalism' at work?

Even if that is so, however, a lot more work needs to be done to articulate why any particular form of labour regulation is required to meet an understanding of the requirements of human personhood. Why is it an 'obligating feature of personhood' for a greater range of service providers to be protected by *labour* law?[51]

[48] TD Williams, *Who Is My Neighbour? Personalism and the Foundations of Human Rights* (Washington, DC, The Catholic University of American Press, 2005) 108.

[49] MA Farley, 'A Feminist Version of Respect for Persons' (1993) 9 *Journal of Feminist Studies in Religion* 183–98.

[50] D Hollenbach, 'Human Dignity: Experience and History, Practical Reason and Faith' in McCrudden (ed) (n 2) 123.

[51] This is an issue I discuss in C McCrudden, 'Two Views of Subordination: The Personal Scope of Employment Discrimination Law in *Jivraj v Hashwani*' (2012) 41 *Industrial Law Journal* 30.

More generally, we need to be alert to the possibility that 'personalism' has itself served as the basis for highly authoritarian conceptions of the role of the state, one in which individuals were prohibited from choosing a path that was regarded by the state as one of diminished personhood. Let me give only one example, an extreme one, it is true, to illustrate the point. Referring to Edward Mounier, the French philosopher/politician of the 1930s and 1940s, Kevin Schmiesing recounts how,

> Because the nature of personhood demanded sociality, Mounier believed that coercion might be employed to achieve that end. His idea of freedom as not merely the ability to choose, but the act of choosing rightly, lent itself to being distorted into a political principle that permitted governmental intervention to force citizens 'to act freely'. The importance of interpersonal cooperation and the destructive nature of individualism, moreover, justified the use of state power for the purpose of enforcing social values in the economic sphere.[52]

No doubt, at this point, Freedland and Kountouris would want to draw on their commitment to autonomy and capabilities to prevent such a development, but that argument merely emphasizes the work that needs to be done to explain how the different bits of the theory hang together.

XI. Labour Law as European Human Rights Law

My final point is to come back to the issue of methodology in the Freedland-Kountouris analysis of dignity, in particular their preference for philosophical analysis rather than conceptual analysis of how the legal and political practice that deals with labour law handles cases in the context of claims about dignity. Their assumption, I think, is that the language of dignity can be restricted to the field of scholarly normative analysis, rather than serve as a substantial resource for litigation or judicial interpretation, and that the latter can indeed be isolated from the former. That is, I think, unrealistic. The impulse to bring 'dignity' into litigation in the European context is likely to increase. Without specifically adopting 'dignity' language, there has been recent scholarship that views the ECtHR as the new defender of labour rights, and sees that Court as an increasingly important source of labour law protection, as opposed to the CJEU.[53] Were labour law to be more clearly founded on the foundations of human dignity, it is arguable that litigants would feel that human rights courts would be even more prepared to embrace labour rights as human rights.

[52] K Schmiesing, 'A History of Personalism' (1 December 2000) www.ssrn.com/abstract=1851661, 17.

[53] See eg K Ewing, 'Preface' in B Bercussion, *European Labour Law*, 2nd edn (Cambridge, Cambridge University Press, 2009) xii.

This is a potential problem because the 'popular' view of dignity appears to differ from that which Freedland-Kountouris would prefer. Although the ECtHR does adopt the view that the concept of 'human dignity' underpins all the rights protected by the Convention, the Court is notably cautious in bringing forward 'dignity' arguments in support of their conclusions in employment rights cases, except in cases of the most extreme type, such as under Article 3 ECHR,[54] prohibiting torture and inhuman and degrading treatment, and Article 4 ECHR, prohibiting slavery, servitude and forced labour.[55] With that exception the small number of applications explains why the Court, at least until recently, has not needed to have recourse to human dignity. In contrast, the approach the Court takes in cases under Article 11, protecting the right to 'freedom of peaceful assembly and to freedom of association with others, including the right to form and to join trade unions for the protection of his interests', is not to adopt an analysis based on 'dignity'. The effect is that, if labour rights have to be based on 'dignity' to succeed in being recognized as rights, but if 'dignity' only applies in extreme circumstances, labour rights may struggle for recognition by human rights courts. In practice, dignity in the ECtHR may be closer to ideas of 'humiliation' and extreme restrictions on autonomy than to anything more useful for labour law purposes.[56]

XII. Conclusion

How, if at all, does my argument directly relate to the overall theme of this book, namely the autonomy of labour law? My intuition is that Freedland and Kountouris consider that they can have their cake and eat it: retaining a significant degree of autonomy for labour regulation, whilst piggy-backing on the conceptual richness (and, for the moment at least, greater popularity) of human rights, by linking labour law to human rights, via human dignity. In other words, they seek to argue that the relationship between dignity and labour regulation may provide a foundation for more specific ethical principles relevant to workplace

[54] For a detailed discussion of the relevant jurisprudence, see Costa (n 2) 396–97.

[55] The first judgment, in the case of *Siliadin v France* (2006) 43 EHRR 16, concerned a case of 'domestic slavery', or so-called 'modern slavery'. The Court held that the treatment inflicted on the applicant, a 15-year-old girl coming to Paris from Africa, amounted not just to forced labour but to servitude. The Court went further by stating that the exploitation of a person in such circumstances was contrary to human dignity. This important judgment was confirmed by the Court's judgment in the case of *Rantsev v Cyprus and the Russian Federation* (2010) 51 EHRR 56, in which a young woman was forced into human trafficking and transferred from Russia to Cyprus in order to become a prostitute. She eventually died in uncertain circumstances. The Court decided that trafficking of human beings is covered by Art 4 of the Convention. Art 4 was found to have been violated in this case, and the judgment states that the phenomenon 'threatens the human dignity and the fundamental freedoms of its victims' (para 282).

[56] An interpretation of dignity that may, or may not, apply to the interpretation of dignity in the EU Charter of Fundamental Rights, Art 1.

relations, articulated in a form that much more closely parallels human rights claims.

However, unintentionally I assume, the position that Freedland and Kountouris adopt in their book may fundamentally challenge the 'autonomy' of labour law by positing its foundational unity with human rights law, and a thin one at that. In drawing on a set of common theoretical foundations, seeking a closer relationship between labour law and human rights law, Freedland and Kountouris are potentially risking the crown jewels: sacrificing labour law's collectivist and solidarity-based roots for a much thinner set of individualist foundations, and at the same time risking a significant loss of labour law's autonomy by encouraging the importation of human rights principles into areas of labour law that seem unsuited to human rights as they are currently understood.

A significant reason for these problems arises from the under-theorized understanding of human dignity that Freedland and Kountouris embrace. For dignity to be fit for purpose in labour law theory and practice, it needs to be understood as a more complex conception than the one that Freedland and Kountouris appear to envisage, and a thicker one than human rights law appears to adopt. If dignity is to be used in labour law, a conception of dignity needs to be developed that supports the richer view of the human person that labour law in Europe currently encompasses. Only by making clear that the understanding of dignity that provides a foundation for labour law differs significantly from some understandings (including judicial understandings) of dignity in the human rights context can the twin dangers of loss of autonomy and thin foundations be avoided.

Assuming that neither loss of autonomy nor thin foundations is what Freedland and Kountouris desire, an important challenge for their future work would be to provide that richer conception of dignity, one that sets it apart from the more attenuated understanding of dignity that human rights are sometimes seen as based on. That would be a significant undertaking, one with the potential of immense promise, one where labour law theory would provide a provocation to human rights theory to develop a richer conception of the human person in the human rights context itself. But this strategy is not without its costs: creating greater distance between human rights and labour law will not serve to provide the legitimacy to labour law that a closer identification between the two seeks to achieve.

12

The EU Internal Market and Domestic Labour Law: Looking Beyond Autonomy

PHIL SYRPIS and TONIA NOVITZ

I. Introduction

In this chapter, we aim to shed some light on the impact that the European Union has had on labour law in the UK. It is important to note at the outset that the focus of this chapter is not 'EU labour law'. It is well known that competence of the EU in the labour law sphere has evolved with each revision of the Treaties. Over the years, a significant amount of legislation, together with a number of statements of social rights, and a series of guidelines and other softer forms of law, have emerged from the EU, be that via labyrinthine EU legislative procedures, via the growing number of OMC-type processes, or (occasionally) via the agreements reached at European level by the social partners. 'EU labour law' has had a substantial and positive impact on national labour laws, especially in the discrimination law field, but also in relation to health and safety (including the regulation of working time) and worker participation law (including transfers of undertakings). The relationship between what may be termed the labour law governance structures at EU and Member State levels is worthy of, and has received, close scholarly attention.[1] However, it is not the focus of this chapter.

Instead, this chapter focuses on the impact that 'EU internal market law' is apt to have on national systems of labour law. The 'logic' of EU internal market law can and does have the capacity to have profound effects on labour law structures within the Member States. We argue that it is not only important that labour lawyers are aware of these developments—in the wake of the *Viking* and *Laval*

[1] See eg C Barnard, *EU Employment Law*, 4th edn (Oxford, Oxford University Press, 2012); and J Kenner, *EU Employment Law: From Rome to Amsterdam and Beyond* (Oxford, Hart Publishing, 2003).

decisions of the Court of Justice,[2] they could not very well remain unaware—but also that labour lawyers bring insights from their discipline to bear on the political debate on internal market management within the EU.

As early as 1996, Mark Freedland observed that 'the shift of focus from national to European labour law serves to widen the conceptual as well as geographical frontiers of the subject', noting that it remains important to heed 'a warning against a loss of attention to the traditional concerns of labour law',[3] including 'crucial areas of social and economic contestation'.[4] Bearing these words in mind, this contribution has three substantive sections. In the first, we sketch out the objectives of the EU internal market. In the second, we explore the dynamic relationship between the Court of Justice and the legislative institutions at EU level, and examine the way in which the balance between the 'economic' and the 'social' is translated into more concrete policy prescriptions as a result of the interventions of the judiciary and the legislature.[5] In the final section, we reflect on the lessons for labour law and labour lawyers. In much the same way as labour law in the UK does not operate free from pressures exerted by the 'ordinary' common law, it cannot escape 'ordinary' EU internal market law. This reality should give labour lawyers cause to stop and think, but should not lead to despair. Just as it is not unrealistic to suppose that insights from labour law may shape the development of the common law,[6] it is also not unrealistic to expect labour lawyers to feed into the debate about the policy priorities within the internal market, and about the institutional structures to be utilized in the realization of those priorities. However, labour lawyers need to understand the systems in which those debates occur, and to make their arguments in a way that, while it may of course be highly critical of, is nevertheless sensitive to, the logic of those systems.

[2] See Case C-438/05 *International Transport Workers' Federation (ITF) and Finnish Seamen's Union (FSU) v Viking Line* [2008] ECR I-10779 (hereinafter '*Viking*'); and Case C-341/05 *Laval un Partneri v Svenska Byggnadsarbetareförbundet* [2008] ECR I-11767 (hereinafter '*Laval*'). For comment, see A Davies, 'One Step Forward, Two Steps Back? The *Viking* and *Laval* Cases in the ECJ' (2008) 37 *Industrial Law Journal* 126; and P Syrpis and T Novitz, 'Economic and social rights in conflict: Political and judicial approaches to their reconciliation' (2008) 33 *European Law Review* 411.

[3] M Freedland, 'Employment Policy' in P Davies, A Lyon-Caen, S Sciarra and S Simitis (eds), *Liber Amicorum for Lord Wedderburn—European Community Labour Law: Principles and Perspectives* (Oxford, Oxford University Press, 1996) 276.

[4] ibid 279.

[5] The 'integrationist', 'economic' and 'social' rationales for EU intervention in domestic labour law are explored in P Syrpis, *EU Intervention in Domestic Labour Law* (Oxford, Oxford University Press, 2007) esp ch 2. In very simple terms, the economic rationale is concerned with the size of the pie, while the social rationale is concerned with the distribution of the slices.

[6] See eg M Freedland and N Kountouris, *The Legal Construction of Personal Work Relations* (Oxford, Oxford University Press, 2011).

II. The Objectives of EU Internal Market Law

One of the core tasks that the EU Treaties identify for the EU is the establishment of an internal market. In the process of the construction of the internal market,[7] certain national policy choices will be mandated and/or encouraged, while others will be prohibited and/or discouraged. These consequences will be the result of the impact that such policy choices have, or are perceived to have, on the establishment and functioning of the internal market.

The Treaty of Lisbon, which came into force in 2009, made some substantial changes to the common provisions of the Treaties. The changes are such as to invite some reflection on whether the objectives of internal market law, which emerge as a result of the way in which the text of the Treaties is interpreted by the Court, may be said to have shifted towards 'the social'.[8]

The new Article 2 TEU states that:

> The Union is founded on the values of respect for human dignity, freedom, democracy, equality, the rule of law and respect for human rights, including the rights of persons belonging to minorities. These values are common to the Member States in a society in which pluralism, non-discrimination, tolerance, justice, solidarity and equality between women and men prevail.

The new Article 6 TEU affirms the Union's commitment to human rights. It states for the first time that the rights, freedoms and principles set out in the Charter of Fundamental Rights of the European Union 'shall have the same legal value as the Treaties'. It also makes provision for the EU to accede to the European Convention for the Protection of Human Rights and Fundamental Freedoms 1950 (ECHR); and states, in much the same way as in previous Treaties, that fundamental rights 'shall constitute general principles of the Union's law'.

Further, the underexplored Articles 7–17 TFEU introduce a proliferation of integration principles, requiring the integration of a wide range of EU policy objectives. Thus, Article 7 TFEU states that the Union shall 'ensure consistency between its policies and activities, taking all of its objectives into account', and Article 9 TFEU on social policy integration reads as follows:

> In defining and implementing its policies and activities, the Union shall take into account requirements linked to the promotion of a high level of employment, the guarantee of adequate social protection, the fight against social exclusion, and a high level of education, training and protection of human health.

The new Article 3(3) TEU describes the internal market in the following way:

[7] See M Egan, *Constructing a European Market* (Oxford, Oxford University Press, 2001).

[8] See N Bruun, K Lörcher and I Schömann (eds), *The Lisbon Treaty and Social Europe* (Oxford, Hart Publishing, 2012); C Semmelmann, 'The European Union's Economic Constitution under the Lisbon Treaty: Soul-searching among Lawyers Shifts the Focus to Procedure' (2010) 35 *European Law Review* 516; and P Syrpis, 'The Lisbon Treaty: Much Ado … But About What?' (2008) 37 *Industrial Law Journal* 219.

> The Union shall establish an internal market. It shall work for the sustainable development of Europe based on balanced economic growth and price stability, a highly competitive social market economy, aiming at full employment and social progress, and a high level of protection and improvement of the quality of the environment. It shall promote scientific and technological advance. It shall combat social exclusion and discrimination, and shall promote social justice and protection, equality between women and men, solidarity between generations and protection of the rights of the child. It shall promote economic, social and territorial cohesion, and solidarity among Member States. It shall respect its rich cultural and linguistic diversity, and shall ensure that Europe's cultural heritage is safeguarded and enhanced.

Seemingly as a response to French public opinion, the reference to the internal market is no longer, as it was under the ill-fated Constitutional Treaty, accompanied by the words 'where competition is free and undistorted'. There is, however, a Protocol on the internal market and competition, which states that 'the internal market as set out in Art 3 of the Treaty on European Union includes a system ensuring that competition is not distorted'. Legally, it is of course correct to state that, as Article 51 TEU gives equal weight to the Treaty and Protocols, this change should not be of any significance. However, when the change is taken together with the other changes that Treaty of Lisbon made to the statements of the values and aims and objectives of the Union, it is possible to detect a distinct change in emphasis towards the social.[9] According to the House of Lords Committee charged with tracing the impact of the new Treaty framework, this may be 'likely to have some effect on the way in which other provisions of the Treaty are interpreted, not only by the Court of Justice but also by the other institutions when undertaking their tasks'.[10]

According to the settled case law of the Court, which of course long predates the Treaty of Lisbon, the establishment and functioning of the internal market involves the elimination of barriers to free movement and distortions of competition. Under the framework set out in the Treaty and developed by the Court, once an activity is characterized as a barrier or a distortion, it is held to be unlawful, unless it is justifiable and proportionate.

For many years, the Court managed to avoid conflicts between internal market norms and national labour laws, maintaining a certain autonomy for labour law. In *Seco* and *Rush Portuguesa*, in the context of the transnational provision of services, it felt able to hold that:

> Community law does not preclude Member States from extending their legislation, or collective labour agreements entered into by both sides of industry, to any person

[9] See in particular the references to 'human dignity' in Art 2 TEU; and to 'a highly competitive *social* market economy' (our emphasis) in Art 3(3) TEU. See further F Dorssemont, 'Values and Objectives' in Bruun, Lörcher and Schömann (n 8); and F Costamagna, 'The Internal Market and the Welfare State after the Lisbon Treaty', OSE Research Paper 4/2011.

[10] House of Lords European Committee Report, *The Treaty of Lisbon: An Impact Assessment* (2008) ch 2.7–2.16.

> who is employed, even temporarily, within their territory, no matter in which country the employer is established.[11]

In *Albany International*, in similar vein, it held that collective negotiations between management and labour must 'by virtue of their nature and purpose' be regarded as falling outside the scope of the competition law provisions of the Treaty.[12]

However, the *Viking* and *Laval* cases destroyed any cosy assumptions to the effect that labour law may in some way be insulated from the internal market case law of the Court. In *Viking* and *Laval* the Court's stance did not appear to be overtly hostile to 'the social', or indeed to the position of trade unions. The Court made reference to the aims and objectives of the then Community in acknowledging that

> since the Community has thus not only an economic but also a social purpose, the rights under the provisions of the Treaty on the free movement of goods, persons, services and capital must be balanced against the objectives pursued by social policy.[13]

It also felt able to hold that 'the right to take collection action' must 'be recognised as a fundamental right which forms an integral part of the general principles of law the observance of which the Court ensures'.[14] Nevertheless, in *Viking* the Court concluded that the collective action of trade unions was liable to restrict the exercise of enterprises' free movement rights, and that while the protection of workers is, in general, able to serve as a justification for restrictions on free movement rights, the legality of industrial action turns on the ability of unions to convince courts that the action 'does not impose disproportionate limitations on the employer's cross border activities'.[15] In *Laval*, where posted workers were involved, the Court conceded that 'in principle' action aimed at prevention of social dumping could be permissible,[16] but considered that action connected to negotiations on rates of pay for such workers could not be justified on public interest grounds since this would make it 'impossible or excessively difficult' for service providers to determine their obligations.[17] This collision between internal market law and national labour laws has attracted a significant body of research across Europe.

[11] See Joined Cases 62 and 63/81 *Seco v EVI* [1982] ECR 223, para 14; and Case C-113/89 *Rush Portuguesa* [1990] ECR I-1417, para 18. Paul Davies has stated that the Court in *Rush* committed 'a basic error of the craft of judicial decision-making' by answering a question which was not necessary for its decision; P Davies, 'The Posted Workers Directive and the EC Treaty' (2002) 31 *Industrial Law Journal* 298, 300.

[12] Case C-67/96 *Albany International* [1999] ECR I-5751, para 60. See further S McCrystal and P Syrpis, 'Competition Law and Worker Voice: Competition Law Impediments to Collective Bargaining in Australia and the European Union' in A Bogg and T Novitz (eds), *Voices at Work: Continuity and Change in the Common Law World* (Oxford, Oxford University Press, 2014).

[13] *Viking* (n 2) para 79; *Laval* (n 2) para 105.

[14] *Viking* (n 2) para 44; *Laval* (n 2) para 91.

[15] A Davies, 'One Step Forward, Two Steps Back? The *Viking* and *Laval* Cases in the ECJ' (2008) 37 *Industrial Law Journal* 126, 145.

[16] *Laval* (n 2) para 107.

[17] ibid paras 110–11.

Under the legal framework established by the Court, the need to provide justifications for national labour laws and for the actions of trade unions only arises once it becomes apparent that these laws and actions are creating obstacles to the establishment of the internal market, within the meaning of the relevant Treaty provisions. *Viking* and *Laval* (and the subsequent cases) took a very broad view on this crucial question. First, the Court held very clearly that the actions of trade unions fall within the scope of the free movement provisions, despite significant doubts over the extent to which the free movement provisions should be able to catch the conduct of non-state actors.[18] Second, and more important, the Court chose to define the 'barrier to free movement' very broadly, holding that a barrier exists whenever an out-of-state service-provider faces a situation which has the effect of making the exercise of rights to freedom of establishment 'less attractive'.[19] The fact that undertakings may be 'forced' into 'negotiations with the trade unions of unspecified duration', and would not be able to ascertain in advance the minimum wage rates to be paid to workers, was said to confirm for the Court that a restriction on the freedom to provide services within the meaning of the Treaties had occurred,[20] thereby triggering the need to provide a justification. At the justification stage, the Court was prepared to countenance arguments to the effect that restrictions could in principle be justified on the ground of the protection of workers, but applied the proportionality test strictly, insisting that the state (and the trade unions) be able to demonstrate first, that any restrictive action was suitable for ensuring the attainment of the legitimate objective pursued, and secondly, that it did not go beyond what was necessary to achieve that objective.

The key point to take away from this brief discussion is that the establishment of the internal market within Europe is a complex exercise involving a number of political choices. The framework is set by the Treaties. A set of politically salient choices made by the Court—regarding whether trade unions should fall within the ambit of the free movement provisions of the Treaties, the definition of a barrier to free movement, and the justification and proportionality of national laws and actions—have, as *Viking* and *Laval* amply illustrate, played an important part in shaping the market. The next section of this chapter moves beyond an analysis of the Court's approach to the free movement provisions of the Treaties, and examines in detail the impact of legislative interventions on the evolution of the internal market.

[18] See *Viking* (n 2) paras 33–37. It is worth noting that an argument to the effect that the purpose of the dispute was to enable Laval to circumvent Swedish law, and that the dispute was therefore artificial, was also rejected by the Court. For more on 'abuse of law' in the internal market context, see R de la Feria and S Vogenauer (eds), *Prohibition of Abuse of Law: A New General Principle of EU Law* (Oxford, Hart Publishing, 2011).

[19] See eg *Viking* (n 2) para 72; *Laval* (n 2) para 99.

[20] *Laval* (n 2) para 100.

III. The Role of the Court and the Legislative Institutions

In this section, we explore the dynamic relationship between the EU's legislative institutions and the Court of Justice.[21] The relationship is, in public law terms, controversial, and it is important for both lawyers and political scientists to understand it, in order better to understand the mechanisms through which EU internal market law is created. The legislative institutions are, in principle, able to act in order to advise the Court in arriving at what they consider to be an appropriate balance between 'the social' and 'the economic', and between integration and diversity. But, as we shall see, the nature of the relationship between the judiciary and the legislature means that legislative interventions often have rather unpredictable effects.

Clearly, both the judiciary and the legislature have a role to play in shaping the internal market. Among the Court's tasks is to 'ensure that in the interpretation and application of the Treaties the law is observed'.[22] It is entirely uncontroversial to state that alongside interpretation of the Treaties, interpretation of acts of the EU institutions and review of the legality or validity of legislative acts of the EU institutions[23] fall within the jurisdiction of the Court. However, the legislative institutions also have a role. Within the limits set out in the Treaties (and policed by the Court), the legislative institutions are specifically authorized to act in a range of ways so as to attain the objectives set out in the Treaties. There are a number of desirable features that legislation may be able to offer, when compared with the alternative—incremental judicial elaboration of the EU's constitutional texts. Legislation can offer structure, detail and certainty in a way that is at least unusual in the case of judicial elaboration. It is also likely, though this claim deserves close scrutiny at the European level, that legislation will have more of a claim to democratic legitimacy.[24]

The intersection between EU internal market law and labour law provides a fascinating illustration of the dynamic relationship between the judiciary and the legislature. The governments of the Member States have played, and will continue to play, the key role in relation to Treaty amendments.[25] The latest in a long line of Treaty amendments occurred at Lisbon in 2009, and several of the key changes to the Treaty structure were referred to above. It is certainly

[21] This section of the chapter draws in part on P Syrpis (ed), *The Judiciary, the Legislature and the EU Internal Market* (Cambridge, Cambridge University Press, 2012).

[22] Art 19(1) TEU.

[23] Cases may come before the Court either from national courts via the Art 267 TFEU preliminary rulings procedure, or directly via Art 263 TFEU. A third category of cases comes to the Court via Art 258 TFEU. Such cases are brought by the Commission against Member States, where Member States have failed to fulfil an obligation under the Treaties.

[24] It is also possible to argue that European-level action—by either the legislature or the judiciary—has a stronger claim to democratic legitimacy if it respects democratic choices made at the level of the Member State.

[25] See Art 48 TEU.

possible, as the House of Lords Select Committee suggested, that these changes will have an effect on the case law of the Court in some areas, in particular in relation to the all-important balances between integration and autonomy, and between the economic and the social. Further speculation will be deferred until such time as the case law develops.

Instead, our focus is on the impact that the passage of secondary legislation has on the case law of the Court. The cases we refer to here—*Rüffert*, *Alemo-Herron* and *Commission v Germany*—are likely to be familiar to readers. Our focus is specifically on the effect that the existence of secondary legislation has on the argumentation before, and of, the Court; in particular in relation to the all-important balance between the economic and the social in the internal market. At first blush, this might appear to be a rather strange line of enquiry. There is, after all, a hierarchy of norms in the EU, and it seems clear that the Court's interpretation of the primary law of the EU should not be influenced by the passage of secondary legislation. It is also clear that the Court has the power to annul legislation that is contrary to the Treaties.[26] Further, in its interpretation of EU legislation, it seems almost trite to say that the Court should use the Treaties as its touchstone, and that it is able, within the (admittedly contested) limits of judicial propriety, to strain the meaning of legislation so that it most closely corresponds with its conception of the dictates of the Treaties.

However, the opposing argument cannot easily be dismissed. The argument is that the influence of the political institutions on the meaning of key concepts introduced in the Treaties cannot sensibly be limited to their role in Treaty revision, frequent though such revision has been. Thus, the internal market concept should not be defined solely by the Court, but is a political matter on which national governments, the Commission, the European Parliament and a range of other stakeholders—including labour lawyers—have relevant and valuable input.[27] In its case law, the Court should not be guided merely by the words of the Treaties and its own instincts, but should also strive to reflect the will—perhaps the 'democratic will'—expressed by the political institutions. It should take care to 'avoid intrusion on the perceived proper domain of political judgment'.[28] It should read secondary legislation in a literal way (in particular, perhaps, where the legislature has 'sanctioned' particular restrictions on free movement), and should even, perhaps, be prepared to adjust its own interpretation of the dictates of the Treaties in the light of the stance adopted by the legislature. Thus, in the words of Paul Craig, '[W]here the Community legislature has given considered thought to the more particular meaning to be accorded

[26] 'The Community legislature has no dispensing power in respect of the Treaty': P Davies, 'The Posted Workers Directive and the EC Treaty' (2002) 31 *Industrial Law Journal* 298, 301.

[27] See eg K Armstrong and S Bulmer, *The Governance of the Single European Market* (Manchester, Manchester University Press, 1998).

[28] S Weatherill, 'Supply of and Demand for Internal Market Regulation: Strategies, Preferences and Interpretation' in N Nic Shuibhne (ed), *Regulating the Internal Market* (Cheltenham, Edward Elgar, 2006) 38.

to a right laid down in a Treaty article and expressed this through Community legislation, the Community courts should treat this with respect'.[29]

As it turns out, the Court's case law is rather difficult to make sense of in constitutional terms. It is certainly willing to interpret EU legislation creatively, so that the scope and meaning of the legislation come to correspond with the Court's, often controversial, conception of the demands of primary law. On occasion, it strays into more constitutionally contentious territory. Thus, we see instances of the Court privileging legislation over the Treaties, by allowing legislation to affect its reading of the Treaties; but conversely, we also see instances of the Court privileging the Treaties over legislation, by questioning the very applicability of legislation in certain contexts. Examples are provided below. Frustratingly, however, we are denied an overt rationalization for the Court's inconsistent approach.

The first case we consider is *Rüffert*,[30] one of a number of cases in which the Court has wrestled with the Posted Workers Directive (PWD). Article 3(1) of that Directive lays down 'a nucleus of mandatory rules for minimum protection' to be observed in the host country by employers who post workers there. Article 3(7) provides that paragraphs 1–6 'are not to prevent application of terms and conditions of employment which are more favourable to workers'. Controversially, in *Laval*, Article 3(7) was interpreted in such a way that the result was that, under the PWD, 'the level of protection which must be guaranteed to workers posted to the territory of the host Member State is limited, in principle, to that provided for in Article 3(1)'.[31] A lot has already been written about that;[32] to be fair to the Court, it did at least opt for an interpretation that accords with the internal market legal basis under which the Directive was enacted. Our aim here is to draw attention to an earlier paragraph in *Laval*, in a section of the judgment titled 'The possibilities available to the Member States for determining the terms and conditions of employment applicable to posted workers, including minimum rates of pay', and to tease out the nature of the relationship between the PWD (as interpreted by the Court) and the free movement provisions of the Treaties. In *Laval* the Court took pains to point out that

> since the purpose of Directive 96/71 is not to harmonise systems for establishing terms and conditions of employment in the Member States, the latter are free to choose a system at the national level which is not expressly mentioned among those provided for in that Directive, provided that it does not hinder the provision of services between the Member States.[33]

[29] P Craig, *EU Administrative Law* (Oxford, Oxford University Press, 2006) 520.

[30] Case C-346/06 *Rüffert v Land Niedersachsen* [2008] ECR I-1989.

[31] *Laval* (n 2) para 81. The one exception is where workers already enjoy more favourable terms and conditions of employment pursuant to the law or collective agreements applicable in the 'home' Member State.

[32] See eg C Kilpatrick, 'Laval's Regulatory Conundrum: Collective Standard-setting and the Court's New Approach to Posted Workers' (2009) 34 *European Law Review* 844.

[33] *Laval* (n 2) para 68.

Later in the judgment, 'the collective action at issue' in the case was assessed 'from the point of view of Article 49 EC [now Article 56 TFEU]'. The clear implication is that a national system going beyond the terms of the PWD might nevertheless be compatible with the Treaties, and therefore be lawful, provided that it does not infringe, or lead to infringements of, Article 56 TFEU.

This conceptualization of the relationship between the PWD and Article 56 TFEU did not endure. In *Rüffert* the issue was whether Article 56 TFEU precluded an authority of a Member State from requiring a contracting authority to designate as contractors only those that agree in writing to pay employees at least the wage provided for in the collective agreement in force at the place where those services are performed. The Court began by stating that 'in order to give a useful answer to the national court, it is necessary to take into consideration the provisions of Directive 96/71'.[34] It then proceeded to analyse the PWD, and was able, following the approach it had adopted in *Laval*, to conclude, at paragraph 35, that the national rules at issue were not compatible with (its interpretation of) the Directive. The following paragraph is intriguing. The Court stated that

> that interpretation of Directive 96/71 is confirmed by reading it in the light of Article 49 EC, since that Directive seeks in particular to bring about the freedom to provide services, which is one of the fundamental freedoms guaranteed by the Treaty.[35]

The burden of the paragraphs which follow seems to be to show that the measure in question 'is capable of constituting a restriction' and that 'it cannot be considered to be justified', but it is significant that this is stated to amount to an interpretation of the Directive in the light of Article 56 TFEU, rather than an independent analysis of the Treaty provisions. The strong suggestion is that the limits of national autonomy are set by the Court's controversial interpretation of the PWD (read in the light of the Treaties), and that the freedom of states to choose a system which goes beyond the PWD, which the Court took care to preserve in paragraph 68 of *Laval*, is illusory.

Constitutionally, *Rüffert* is interesting for two reasons. First, the interpretation of the PWD in *Rüffert*, as in *Laval*, serves the interests of service-providers at the expense of national systems of labour law. Secondly, this controversial interpretation of the PWD, in *Rüffert*, unlike in *Laval*, influenced the Court's reading of the scope for national action under Article 56 TFEU.

The second case to consider is *Alemo-Herron*.[36] It is possible to see the case simply as another instance of a controversial interpretation of a Directive; this time Directive 2001/23, the Directive that codifies Directive 77/187 on the approximation of the laws of the Member States relating to the safeguarding of employees' rights in the event of transfers of undertakings (hereinafter the 'TUPE Directive'). Like the PWD, the TUPE Directive had been assumed to be a

[34] *Rüffert* (n 30) para 18.
[35] ibid para 36. This approach—considering the Directive 'interpreted in the light of the Article 49 EC'—is repeated in para 43, and in the Court's conclusion.
[36] Case C-426/11 *Alemo-Herron v Parkwood Leisure* (18 July 2013).

minimum-standard-setting directive on which Member States were free to build; Article 8 of the Directive, rather like Article 3(7) of the PWD, states explicitly that the Directive does not 'affect the right of Member States to apply or introduce laws, regulations or administrative provisions which are more favourable to employees'.[37] The question at issue in *Alemo-Herron* was whether the UK was precluded, by the Directive, from allowing standard common law principles to apply which enabled dynamic clauses referring to collective agreements negotiated and agreed after the date of the transfer to be enforceable against the transferee.[38] The Court chose to interpret the Directive, notwithstanding the existence of Article 8, as indeed precluding a Member State from providing that dynamic clauses are enforceable against the transferee 'where that transferee does not have the possibility of participating in the negotiation process of such collective agreements concluded after the date of the transfer'.[39] The Court chose to characterize the Directive as one that

> does not aim solely to safeguard the interests of the employees in the event of transfer of an undertaking, but seeks to ensure a fair balance between the interests of those employees, on the one hand, and those of the transferee, on the other.[40]

Taken with the interpretation of the PWD in *Laval* and *Rüffert*, this seems to be illustrative of a trend: Directives, adopted in order to redress an imbalance between the economic and the social in the internal market context, are being interpreted by the Court in a way that is more sensitive to the interests of service-providers and transferee employers than to the interests of workers.

There is, however, another dimension to the case. This concerns the relationship between the Directive at issue and primary law—this time not the text of the Treaties, but Article 16 of the Charter of Fundamental Rights. The UK's attempt to go beyond the minimum required by the Directive was held not only to be impossible under the Directive, but also to fall foul of Article 16 of the Charter, on the freedom to conduct a business. It is entirely unobjectionable for the Court to seek to ensure that its interpretation of Directives is in conformity not only with the Treaties, but also with fundamental rights, as protected via, for example, the Charter.[41] In *Alemo-Herron* the Court interpreted the TUPE Directive in the light of the Treaties and the Charter, with the impact of Article 16 of the Charter being to prevent Member States from imposing obligations on the

[37] On the social objectives of the TUPE Directive, see M Shanks, 'Introductory Article: The Social Policy of the European Communities' (1977) 14 *Common Market Law Review* 375; and B Hepple, 'The Crisis in EEC Labour Law' (1987) 16 *Industrial Law Journal* 77.

[38] *Alemo-Herron* (n 36) para 20.

[39] ibid para 37. Notably, the transferee would not have that 'possibility' because of the transferee's choice not to participate in collective bargaining, the latter being protected as a species of an employer's negative freedom of association.

[40] ibid para 25. In this respect, it builds on Case C-499/04 *Werhof* [2006] ECR I-2397.

[41] The paragraphs dealing with the Charter are introduced in this way: 'It is settled case-law that the provisions of Directive 2001/23 must be interpreted in a manner consistent with the fundamental rights as set out by the Charter of Fundamental Rights of the European Union'; see *Alemo-Herron* (n 36) para 30.

transferee beyond those specified in the TUPE Directive where the transferee can 'neither assert its interests effectively in a contractual process nor negotiate the aspects determining changes in working conditions for its employees with a view to its future economic activity'.[42] Thus, the Court used the fundamental rights protected in the Charter to strengthen its argument that Member States could not, at least in the given circumstances, go beyond the TUPE Directive in terms of the level of protection for employees in the event of a transfer of undertakings. One wonders whether the result may have been different had the Court chosen to focus on other Charter rights, such as Article 28, on the right of collective bargaining and action.

In constitutional terms it is unproblematic for the Court to use its interpretation of the Charter to buttress its reading of the Directive in the way that it did (though the UK 'opt-out' from the Charter does, potentially, muddy the waters). The substantive result, however, is rather similar to that in *Rüffert*—in each case the Court's interpretation of EU law, be that the relevant Directive, the relevant Treaty Article, or indeed the Charter, operates so as to restrict the freedom of Member States to go beyond minimum standards established under the Directives in question; or, to put this another way, to restrict national autonomy to set high labour standards.

The final example is *Commission v Germany*.[43] In the case, the Commission brought an action against Germany, on the grounds that Germany had failed to fulfil its obligations under the relevant public procurement Directives (92/50/EEC and 2004/18/EC). The specific problem was that local authorities had awarded service contracts of above a certain threshold size, in respect of occupational old-age pensions, directly to bodies referred to in a collective agreement, and without the call for tenders at EU level demanded by the relevant Directives. At paragraphs 68–105, the Court held that the contract awards at issue fell within the relevant public procurement Directives. It concluded, on the basis of a detailed analysis of the text of the Directives, that the various requirements and thresholds in the Directives were met, and therefore held that Germany had infringed its EU law obligations by not providing for a system which complies with the criteria set out in the EU secondary legislation.

More interesting for our purposes is the preceding section of the judgment (paragraphs 36–67), in which the Court discusses the 'applicability' of the relevant Directives. It is worth pausing to reflect on what the Court might mean here, and to note that the Court did not discuss the applicability of the PWD and the TUPE Directive in either *Rüffert* or *Alemo-Herron*. Given that the legality of the Directives was not at issue, the only possibility is if a higher norm of EU law—for example, the Treaties, or a fundamental right of equivalent status—in some way prevented the application of the Directives in the particular circum-

[42] *Alemo-Herron* (n 36) para 34. J Prassl, 'Freedom of Contract as a General Principle of EU Law? Transfers of Undertakings and the Protection of Employer Rights in EU Labour Law (Case C-426/11 *Alemo Herron v Parkwood Leisure*)' (2013) 42 *Industrial Law Journal* 434.

[43] Case C-271/08 *Commission v Germany* [2010] ECR I-7091.

stances at issue. Rather like in the famous citizenship case of *Baumbast*,[44] what the Court has in mind is an intensive enquiry as to whether the implementation of the Directives in the particular circumstances of the case is in accordance with the principle of proportionality. This sort of approach falls short—but only just short—of a review of the Directives themselves. The clear inference is that were the Court to conclude that compliance with the public procurement Directives in the particular circumstances at issue was irreconcilable with a higher norm of EU law, the Directives would not apply. The result of such an intrusive application of the proportionality test on the part of the Court is 'an appreciable decrease' in the 'effective regulatory competence' of the EU legislature.[45] Intriguingly, the higher norm at issue in *Commission v Germany* was not an economic norm found in the Treaty, but rather the fundamental right to bargain collectively.

Labour lawyers should be encouraged to see that the Court is prepared to investigate the applicability of EU legislation on the grounds that it may infringe the fundamental right to bargain collectively. However, once again, they will have been bitterly disappointed by the substantive result of the *Commission v Germany* case. The Court, as in *Viking* and *Laval*, referred to a 'reconciliation' between 'the requirements related to the attainment of the social objective pursued here by the parties to the collective bargaining' and 'the requirements stemming from Directives 92/50 and 2004/18'.[46] This was said to require verification as to whether

> a fair balance was struck in the account taken of the respective interests involved, namely enhancement of the level of the retirement pensions of the workers concerned, on the one hand, and attainment of the freedom of establishment and the freedom to provide services, and opening-up to competition at European Union level, on the other.[47]

However, the 'balancing process' was not undertaken properly. For the Court, the reconciliation was said to involve an assessment of whether the objectives of the German scheme could be accommodated within the framework of the EU law Directives in question. Given that framework, the result was inevitable. The Court noted that the German scheme, while pursuing a legitimate social objective, 'effectively disapplies the rules stemming from Directive 92/50 and 2004/18 completely, and for an indefinite period … a fact which the Federal Republic of Germany has not denied'.[48] The lack of engagement with the rationale for the Directives, and the corresponding lack of an attempt to comply with their terms, was enough to condemn the German rules. The Court's argument was simply that the Directives were able to apply, as a result of the fact that it would be possible to accommodate the various social objectives of the German scheme within the Directives.

[44] See Case C-413/99 *Baumbast* [2002] ECR I-7091.

[45] M Dougan, 'The Constitutional Dimension to the Case Law on Union Citizenship' (2006) 31 *European Law Review* 613, 640.

[46] *Commission v Germany* (n 43) para 51.

[47] ibid para 52.

[48] ibid para 53.

However, as Advocate General Trstenjak argued in *Commission v Germany* itself, it would be possible, and in the interests of fair balance, necessary, to undertake the reconciliation in a fundamentally different way. This involves starting from a different point, and assessing not whether the social objectives of the national scheme may be accommodated within the framework of the Directives, but rather whether the objectives of the EU Directives may be accommodated in a way which more fully respects the fundamental rights protected by EU primary law. In the light of the fact that the Court's enquiry (at paragraphs 36–67) relates to the applicability of the Directives in the context of a higher norm of EU law (the fundamental right to bargain collectively), the analysis should not have focused on whether the requirements of the German scheme were justified and proportionate, but instead on the very different question of whether the requirements in the Directives were justified and proportionate.

The Advocate General's approach was rich in promise. She seemed to have correctly identified the rather one-sided attempt by the Court to balance fundamental freedoms and fundamental rights—or economic freedoms and social rights—in *Viking* and *Laval*. She, it seemed, was advocating an approach that examined not only whether, and to what extent, social rights may have to yield to economic freedoms (the Court imposes a considerable burden on the party seeking to show that restrictions on economic freedoms are justified and proportionate), but also whether, and to what extent, economic freedoms may have to yield to social rights. Such an approach, in which there is no relationship of hierarchy between the fundamental freedoms guaranteed by the Treaties and the fundamental rights in the Charter, clearly accords with the new text of the Treaties, in particular Article 6 TEU.[49]

However, her Opinion did not take the symmetrical approach she advocated to its logical conclusion.[50] Thus—despite the focus on the applicability of the relevant Directives in both the Advocate General's Opinion and the Court's judgment—we were denied the opportunity to see an in-depth examination either of whether the application of the Directives in the circumstances at issue was appropriate and necessary for the achievement of the EU's free movement goals, or of whether any restrictions on fundamental social rights were proportionate.[51]

This section has shed light on the complexity involved in seeking to balance the economic and social goals of the EU, in those areas in which the fundamental freedoms in the Treaties and fundamental rights protected in the Charter are supplemented by secondary legislation. Both primary and secondary law fall to be interpreted by the Court—and it is not only the interpretation of the relevant texts themselves, but also of the relationships between them (whether one should be interpreted in the light of the other, and whether the limits of secondary legis-

[49] *Commission v Germany* (n 43) Opinion of AG Trstenjak, paras 179–99.

[50] ibid paras 203–04.

[51] See further P Syrpis, 'Reconciling Economic Freedoms and Social Rights—The Potential of *Commission v Germany* (Case C-271/08, judgment of 15 July 2010)' (2011) 40 *Industrial Law Journal* 222.

lation should coincide with the limits of the Treaties and the limits of Charter rights) that create political controversy. The degree to which secondary legislation, and the application of secondary legislation by the Member States, should be subject to close scrutiny by the Court, and what that scrutiny should entail, are also matters for debate.

Three cases were examined in this section: *Rüffert*, *Alemo-Herron* and *Commission v Germany*. In each of those cases, despite many promising signs, the results were profoundly disappointing for labour lawyers and trade unionists.[52] The final section considers how they may choose to respond.

IV. Conclusion: The Autonomy of Labour Law?

Labour lawyers have tended to greet the intrusion of the internal market into the domain of labour law with dismay; and, given the outcome of the cases in which national labour law systems have collided with internal market principles, such a reaction is rational and predictable. For many labour lawyers, the best way to secure a balance between the economic and the social is via the maintenance of an autonomous sphere for labour law. There is thus, among the labour law community, a nostalgia for the breadth of the Court's formulation in *Rush*,[53] and a desire to extend the exemption from the application of competition law carved out in *Albany* more broadly to the whole of the internal market arena.[54]

Our argument is that such an isolationist approach, while in many respects appealing, is misguided. The EU internal market permeates all areas of national life, so that there is, to borrow former judge Koen Lenaerts' famous phrase, 'no nucleus of sovereignty' which the Member States can invoke against the EU.[55] There is, in fact, no reason of principle located within the logic of the EU legal order why national labour law rules should be exempt from the rules governing the EU internal market, while other important spheres of national policy (including those in relation to which the legislative institutions of the EU lack the competence to act) are routinely scrutinized at EU level. The arguments to reinstate *Rush* and extend *Albany* ultimately lack conviction.

[52] The ETUC, for example, greeted the judgment in *Commission v Germany* with the headline, 'Economic Freedoms vs Fundamental Rights: The Dark Series Continues', see www.etuc.org/a/7521.

[53] See eg the comment in KD Ewing and J Hendy (eds), *The New Spectre Haunting Europe—The ECJ, Trade Union Rights and the British Government* (Institute of Employment Rights, 2009) and A Bücker and W Warneck (eds) *Viking-Laval-Rüffert: Consequences and Policy Perspectives* (Brussels, European Trade Union Institute, *2010*). *cf R* Blanpain and A Swiatkowski (eds) (2009) 69 *Bulletin of Comparative Labour Relations*.

[54] See the arguments raised in *Viking* (n 2) paras 48–50. For a strong defence of the autonomy rationale, see Freedland's chapter in this volume.

[55] K Lenaerts, 'Constitutionalism and the Many Faces of Federalism' (1990) 38 *American Journal of Comparative Law* 205, 220.

It would, of course, be foolish not to acknowledge the risks inherent in abandoning arguments from autonomy which have been a lodestar in the development of labour law as a discipline. This chapter is full of examples of the Court's half-hearted attempts to balance the economic and the social; the rhetoric of balance and symmetry may well be present, but the decided cases point very clearly towards a systematic preference for the economic over the social. This preference manifests itself in relation to the way in which the Treaties and the Charter are interpreted; in the way in which secondary legislation is interpreted; in the way in which linkages are made between the scope of primary and secondary law; and in the way in which the balance between the economic and the social is first conceptualized, and then applied (eg in the Court's justification and proportionality case law).

Nevertheless, labour lawyers can respond, and indeed have responded, in a range of ways, addressing not only the Court, but also the legislative institutions of the EU, Member State governments and trade unions. Arguments have focused on the EU legal order itself, and on the relationships between that legal order and other international legal orders, such as those developed by the Council of Europe and the ILO, which make a stronger commitment to the social. First, given the existing Treaty framework, which, via Article 6 TEU, includes a strong commitment to fundamental rights, the case law of the Court can be effectively critiqued. Labour lawyers are able to point—as we hope we have done here—to flaws in the reasoning of the Court, to inconsistencies in the Court's approach, and to the extent of the effects that the Court's choices are apt to have on the social fabric of the Member States.[56] The failure of the Court to comply with basic standards regarding freedom of association established by the ILO can also be highlighted so as to exert pressure.[57] Secondly, using these external frames of reference, labour lawyers are able to provide advice to the EU legislature, with the aim of making social legislation more effective, protecting it from legal challenge, and ensuring that its substance cannot be interpreted away by the Court.[58] Particular attention can be devoted to the adoption of legislation

[56] See also C Barnard, 'The UK and Posted Workers: The Effect of *Commission v Luxembourg* on the Territorial Application of British Labour Law' (2009) 38 *Industrial Law Journal* 122; Davies (n 2); S Evju, 'Revisiting the Posted Workers Directive: Conflict of Laws and Laws in Contrast' (2009–10) 12 *Cambridge Yearbook of European Law* 151; and Kilpatrick (n 32). Another example is the symposium in C Barnard (ed) (2008) 10 *Cambridge Yearbook of European Law*. For continuing further study of the flawed reasoning in the Court's jurisprudence and its impacts, see E Ales and T Novitz (eds), *Collective Action and Fundamental Freedoms in Europe: Striking the Balance* (Intersentia, Brussels, 2010); A Bücker and W Warneck (eds), *Reconciling Fundamental Social Rights and Economic Freedoms after Viking, Laval and Rüffert* (Baden-Baden, Nomos, 2011); J Cremers, *In Search of Cheap Labour in Europe: Working and Living conditions of Posted Workers* (Brussels, CLR/EFBWW/International Books, 2011); and S Evju (ed), *Cross-Border Services, Posting of Workers, and Multilevel Governance* (Oslo, University of Oslo Press, 2013).

[57] See the drafting by J Hendy QC and others of the *Application by the British Air Line Pilots Association to the ILO* (2009); and K Apps, 'Damages Claims Against Trade Unions after Viking and Laval' (2009) 34 *European Law Review* 141.

[58] See M Houwerzijl, SSM Peters and Y Jorens, *Study on the Protection of Workers' rights in Subcontracting Processes in the European Union* (Brussels, European Commission, 2012). Note also

under the social provisions of the Treaties—*Rüffert* and *Alemo-Herron* serve only to confirm that legislation adopted under internal market, rather than social, legal bases will not be interpreted so as to further the interests of workers. And thirdly, labour lawyers can give advice to trade unions and Member States seeking to protect social rights and interests, on how best to avoid and negotiate collisions with EU internal market norms.[59] It seems too early to measure accurately the success of these efforts; it is sufficient to note that they are underway.

Despite the text of the Treaties, little more than lip-service appears to have been paid to the idea that there is no hierarchy between the fundamental freedoms enshrined in the Treaties, and the fundamental rights to be found in the Charter and in the general principles of EU law that the Court is committed to protect. Labour lawyers are right to point to the dire consequences of the disregard for the social; and to demand a reorientation of the Court's case law. In order to do so effectively, they must properly understand the dynamics of internal market making, and show sensitivity to the concerns of service-providers. In the current crisis, national systems of labour law are coming under ever-increasing pressure, not only as a result of EU internal market law, but also as a result of the policies demanded by the EU in the attempt save the eurozone.

Many have responded by calling for a revision of the text of the Treaties, and for a constitutional privileging of the social over the economic.[60] We fear that such calls are doomed to fail in the current political climate. Even a proposal as innocuous as the Commission's Monti II Regulation, which did little more than reiterate the constitutional equivalence between the freedom of establishment and the freedom to provide services and the fundamental right to take collective action, faced strong opposition (from both left and right), and failed to be adopted by the European Parliament and the Council of Ministers.[61]

Houwerzijl's contribution to the FORMULA project study led by Evju, the working papers for which are available at www.jus.uio.no/ifp/english/research/projects/freemov/.

[59] An example of exceptionally helpful technical comment as to the scope of union liability under EU law is Apps (n 57). For a broader view of this rebalancing and advisory task in a wider range of respects, see the continuing work of M Freedland in N Countouris and M Freedland (eds), *Resocializing Europe: In a Time of Crisis* (Cambridge, Cambridge University Press, 2013).

[60] Since 2008, the ETUC has been calling for a social progress clause, in the form of a Protocol attached to the Treaties and with the same legal value as the Treaties 'to redress the balance between economic freedoms and fundamental social rights'. This clause aims to make it clear that the single market is not an end in itself, but is established to achieve social progress for the peoples of the Union; and goes on to state that in the event of conflict, social rights are to take precedence over economic freedoms. See www.etuc.org/IMG/pdf/social_progress_protocolEN.pdf.

[61] The key provision, Art 2, reads as follows: 'The exercise of the freedom of establishment and the freedom to provide services enshrined in the Treaty shall respect the fundamental right to take collective action, including the right or freedom to strike, and conversely, the exercise of the fundamental right to take collective action, including the right or freedom to strike, shall respect these economic freedoms.' See, for critical comment, KD Ewing, *The Draft Monti II Regulation: An Inadequate Response to Viking and Laval* (Liverpool, Institute of Employment Rights, 2012) available at: www.ier.org.uk/sites/ier.org.uk/files/The%20Draft%20Monti%2011%20Regulation%20by%20Keith%20Ewing%20March%202012.pdf. See for rejection by 19 national parliaments under the so-called 'yellow card' procedure: www.europolitics.info/social/commission-withdraws-monti-ii-proposal-art342821-25.html.

Instead, we argue that the current Treaty framework, and the current conceptualization of the relationship between the economic and the social, is probably as good as it is going to get. The relationship between the economic and the social is destined not to be comfortable, and there will frequently be significant tensions. These will be exacerbated in times of crisis. Labour lawyers need to be vigilant about the various aspects of the balancing process, and to strive to ensure that, within the EU internal market, social rights are afforded the protection they deserve.

Part IV

Labour Law's Autonomy: Labour Law, Commercial Law and Economic Theory

13

Labour Law as the Law of the Business Enterprise

ALICE CARSE and WANJIRU NJOYA

I. Introduction

In a recent analysis of the challenges facing global markets and the contribution made by the corporation as 'the central instrument in economics' to growth, prosperity and human flourishing, Colin Mayer highlights the capacity of large corporations to destroy communities and destabilize economies with never-ending cycles of booms and busts, each successive economic crisis worse than the one preceding it and the worst probably still to come.[1] Mayer depicts the frantic and ultimately futile attempts by regulators to contain the damage through corporate governance reforms as 'trying to control the whale by tickling its tail'.[2] Indeed regulatory interventions seem to succeed only in triggering and exacerbating a fresh crisis: '[I]n the cyclical way markets work, the origins of the 2008 financial crisis may be found in the solutions to the previous market crisis.'[3] Rather than concentrating on the superficial fixes that preoccupy regulators, such as encouraging shareholder activism and aligning the interests of directors with those of shareholders by linking executive pay to shareholder returns, measures that are likely only to aggravate the whale, Mayer turns the spotlight onto the overarching normative questions concerning the 'obligations, responsibilities and commitment' between the corporation, its stakeholders and the wider society.

[1] C Mayer, *Firm Commitment: Why the Corporation Is Failing Us and How to Restore Trust in It* (Oxford, Oxford University Press, 2013).

[2] ibid 4.

[3] T Clarke, 'Corporate Governance Causes of the Global Financial Crisis' in W Sun, J Stewart and D Pollard (eds), *Corporate Governance and the Global Financial Crisis: International Perspectives* (Cambridge, Cambridge University Press, 2012) 28, 29 arguing that the regulatory responses to the dotcom and Enron crises triggered the 2008 global financial crisis. Mayer suggests that the recourse to taxpayer reserves to rescue 'too big to fail' banks in the 2008 crisis ($856 billion was offered by the UK government; $7.74 trillion in the US: Clarke, 44) is now on course to precipitate an even more epic crisis unless the underlying ethos of regulating corporations is reconsidered (Mayer (n 1) 34–39).

It is in that spirit, appreciating the need to reconceptualize the corporation as a resource that can contribute to the overall welfare of society, that this chapter evaluates the legal interpretations of the relationship between workers and the business enterprise. The discussion therefore rejects the orthodox theory of the firm with its exclusive focus on shareholders as the embodiment of the corporate interest, and relies instead on alternative theories that emphasize the productive function of co-operation amongst all stakeholders. Our concern is with one particular form of business enterprise: the incorporated entity with separate legal personality or the limited liability corporation.[4]

Following Deakin, we view the corporation as a legal institution designed to resolve collective action problems between stakeholders and to serve as a repository of collectively held rights; for this purpose we adopt Deakin's definition of the corporation as 'a shared resource whose sustainability depends on the participation of multiple constituencies in its governance (not just shareholders, but employees, core suppliers and customers)'.[5] This definition accounts for the empirical fact that all stakeholders have investments in the corporation that give rise to claims akin to property rights in relation to corporate assets. The corporation is viewed as a 'commons' in the sense that within it is pooled all the various contributions of its stakeholders to create a commonly held resource in which they all have 'multiple, overlapping and often conflicting property rights or property-type claims'.[6] The framework of overlapping property rights is central to our thesis, as we argue in this chapter that the proprietary structure of corporate law serves as a useful complement to the contract of employment in understanding the nature of workers' entitlements in the business enterprise and allowing those claims to be vindicated in courts of law.

This theoretical starting point enables us to address the concerns highlighted by Mayer: the widespread condemnation and mistrust of large corporations and their tendency to extract value for absentee shareholders while destroying the foundations from which that value was created. Indeed, Deakin's reason for reconstructing the corporation as commons is designed to address this problem by offering insights into how 'such 'over-exploitation of shared resources—the "tragedy of the commons"—can be overcome through forms of collective resource use and management'.[7] From this perspective, law has a dual function in regulating the corporation. First, law specifies the claims that stakeholders may make on the firm, and second, more importantly, law maintains the commons by 'preserving and sustaining the firm's asset pool as a source of

[4] Corporate law is selected for discussion to enable a detailed analysis of the specific rules establishing the nature of directors' fiduciary duties. North American discourse uses the term 'corporation' where the term 'company' is used in the UK and other common law jurisdictions: we use the two terms synonymously.

[5] S Deakin, 'The Corporation as Commons: Rethinking Property Rights, Governance and Sustainability in the Business Enterprise' (2012) 37 *Queen's Law Journal* 339.

[6] ibid 381.

[7] ibid 368.

productive value'.[8] Understanding the corporation as commons does not privilege any single stakeholder group over the rest.[9] As Mayer points out, long-term commitment to all stakeholders requires moving beyond both shareholder primacy and stakeholder theories as traditionally conceptualized, to the extent that the protagonists wage battle on behalf of a particular constituency to the exclusion of others. Rather than a quest for dominance by particular interest groups, the focus should be on the commitment of all corporate participants to each other and to the wider society.[10]

As a first step towards that goal the chapter explores the common ground between labour law and corporate law, focusing on the nature of workers' entitlements in the corporation. We challenge 'the convention that the wires of company law and labour law must not be crossed'[11] by drawing insights from corporate law to institutionalize labour's traditional goal of employment protection. To test the application of this approach to legal disputes we compare two doctrinal examples—the scope of unfair dismissal protection during economic dismissals and the interpretation of directors' duties in corporate law. In both cases, the law displays an excessive deference to managerial prerogative expressed through emanations of what is sometimes loosely referred to as the business judgment rule, ie the principle that judges do not second-guess business decisions. In corporate law, the directors of a company 'must exercise their discretion bona fide in what they consider—not what a court may consider—is in the best interests of the company'.[12] In labour law, this principle is reflected in the 'band of reasonable responses' in testing the fairness of dismissal.[13] Courts do not substitute their own views of what they would have considered to be fair or the priority they would have accorded to saving jobs during organizational restructuring. Focusing on recent case law in the UK and Canada, we show the scope for purposive interpretation of legislation in order to expand the ideals of fairness and legitimate expectations to resolve these problems in a way that recognizes the true value of workers' claims and interests in the business enterprise.

II. Overview of the Argument

The discussion explores two main themes: first, the specialized interpretations

[8] ibid.

[9] 'Viewing one user group as having priority over the others in the use it can make of common resources and in its power to hold the managers of the resource to account is not compatible with the maintenance of the resource over time' (ibid 377, 378).

[10] Mayer (n 1) 6.

[11] A convention depicted by Lord Wedderburn as a constraint on research in both fields of the common law: Wedderburn of Charlton, *The Future of Company Law: Fat Cats, Corporate Governance and Workers* (Liverpool, Institute of Employment Rights, 2004) 41.

[12] *Re Smith & Fawcett* [1942] Ch 304, 306.

[13] ACL Davies, 'Judicial Self Restraint in Labour Law' (2009) *Industrial Law Journal* 278.

of workers' rights in labour law; and second, the recognition in corporate law of non-contractual or extra-contractual entitlements which may arise from informal interactions between corporate participants. In exploring these themes we treat labour law and corporate law as autonomous but interdependent domains of law, viewing each field as 'strong enough to mix on equal terms with other bodies of law'.[14] Although neither field is able straightforwardly to adopt the doctrinal apparatus of the other, both fields may nevertheless be influenced positively by progressive interpretations of the worker's relationship with the enterprise.

The discussion proceeds as follows. Section III describes the heightened judicial deference to managerial prerogative in the context of economic dismissals. Economic dismissals are subject to a legislative test of fairness, creating an entitlement to job security that was envisaged as being 'proprietary in nature'.[15] Yet today, Lord Denning's observation in relation to the Industrial Relations Act 1971 that 'the Act gives an employee a right in his job which is akin to a right in property'[16] seems to have no impact when workers are routinely fired purely as a cost-cutting measure. The extent of this problem is illustrated in Section IV by reference to redundancy law. Section V turns to corporate law, evaluating the normative implications of understanding the firm as an economic institution that co-ordinates the transactions and relationships between workers, shareholders, managers and other participants in industrial activity. The focus is on the law regulating directors' duties. Section VI compares the judicial interpretation of worker-protective concepts in labour law and company law, considering the scope for judicial creativity in safeguarding workers' legitimate expectations of job security. We contrast case law developments in Canada and the UK, focusing on the implied term of mutual trust and confidence in labour law and the concept of unfair prejudice claims in corporate law.[17] We conclude by acknowledging the challenges posed by economic determinism and uncritical faith in self-correcting markets, and argue that if law is to find effective responses to the challenges outlined by Mayer, then we must call all doctrinal hands to the deck. Corporate law and labour law reinforce and complement each other in ways that may prove powerful in validating workers' entitlements during economic restructuring.

[14] P Davies and M Freedland, 'Employees, Workers, and the Autonomy of Labour Law' in H Collins, PL Davies and R Rideout (eds), *Legal Regulation of the Employment Relation* (London, Kluwer Law International, 2000) 267.

[15] 'Job property is the interest, viewed as proprietary in nature, which a worker has in the continuation of his employment as the result of legal measures or social systems which protect the expectation and security of continued employment': Paul Davies and Mark Freedland, *Labour Law: Text and Materials*, 2nd edn (London, Weidenfeld and Nicolson, 1984) 428 detailing the rise and subsequent fall of this idea. This followed on the heels of the Redundancy Payments Act 1965 which was specifically targeted at redundancy, unlike the 'unfair dismissal' concept which extended generally to all forms of termination of employment.

[16] *Brindle v HW Smith (Cabinets) Ltd* [1973] 1 All ER 230, 231.

[17] For a recent discussion of case law developments in mutual trust and confidence, see A Bogg, '*Bournemouth University Higher Education Corporation v Buckland*: Re-establishing Orthodoxy at the Expense of Coherence?' (2010) *Industrial Law Journal* 408; for a discussion of unfair prejudice, see P Davies, *Company Law* (Oxford, Oxford University Press, 2010).

III. Managerial Prerogative and Economic Dismissals

The common law has traditionally facilitated business enterprise by upholding the managerial prerogative to hire and fire.[18] This prerogative is most robustly defended when dismissals are occasioned by the sale of a business or insolvency or a reduction in the number of staff in response to unfavourable market conditions.[19] Economic dismissals in the UK are now subject to a legislative safeguard of fairness.[20] The statutory provisions that relate to economic dismissals fall into three categories. First, there are provisions prescribing the circumstances in which employees are entitled to financial protection such as the right to a redundancy payment. Another example, which is not limited to employees who have been the victim of an economic dismissal, is the preferential treatment given to any claim to remuneration by an employee whose employer has become insolvent and the right to claim payments from the National Insurance Fund. Second, there are provisions that mitigate economic dismissals in certain circumstances where a business is sold as a going concern. This category is the domain of the Transfer of Undertakings (Protection of Employment) Regulations 2006 implementing the European Acquired Rights Directive. The third category, statutory unfair dismissal, recognizes various reasons why economic dismissals can be fair: redundancy is a potentially fair reason for dismissal. It is also well established that a 'necessary re-organisation' of the business can amount to 'some other substantial reason', ie a potentially fair reason for dismissal. Economic, technical or organizational reasons for dismissal are also prima facie fair under EU law.[21]

From its earliest inception the unfair dismissal legislation incorporated elements of what might be viewed as an ulterior purpose, that of efficiently managing the termination of employment particularly where unionized workers were deemed likely to take industrial action. As Howe observes, 'industrial justice was not just a post hoc rationale on the part of theorists but actively adopted by both political parties, and the members of the tribunal system, as providing the basis for Britain's unfair dismissal [legislation]'.[22] Yet over time,

[18] Primarily through its interpretation of freedom of contract and the employer's property rights: S Anderman, 'Termination of Employment: Whose Property Rights?' in C Barnard, S Deakin and G Morris (eds), *The Future of Labour Law: Liber Amicorum Sir Bob Hepple* (Oxford, Hart Publishing, 2004) 101.

[19] '[A]n employer is entitled to reorganise his business so as to improve its efficiency and in so doing to propose to his staff a change in the terms and conditions of their employments: and to dispense with their services if they disagree': *Johnson v Nottinghamshire Combined Police Authority* [1974] ICR 170.

[20] The Redundancy Payments Act 1965 and the Industrial Relations Act 1971.

[21] Such as the Acquired Rights Directive, Council Directive 77/187/EEC on approximation of the laws of the Member States related to the events of transfers of undertakings, businesses or parts of businesses [1977] OJ L061 026.

[22] J Howe, 'Poles Apart? The Contestation between the Ideas of No Fault Dismissal and Unfair Dismissal for Protecting Job Security' (2013) 42 *Industrial Law Journal* 122, 132.

the efficiency aims have been increasingly emphasized and legitimized, so that the test of fairness in dismissal can no longer be said to be concerned with job security in the traditional sense.[23] Although the legislative framework of fairness in dismissal now extends to a wide range of situations under various EU Directives, economic dismissals in the UK are now subject only to a relatively weak form of procedural fairness. Taking redundancy as an example, an employer is required to engage in meaningful consultation with employees who are at risk of redundancy, as well as collective consultation where the statutory threshold is met,[24] but there is no obligation on the employer to act so as to implement any of the views expressed by the employees or trade unions. In practice, in many cases the consultation procedure provides employees with little more than fair warning of impending redundancies and the opportunity to seek alternative employment. Further, as discussed below, the test of fairness in selection for redundancy does not provide employees with a strong level of protection. Moreover, although EU law has expanded the scope of these unfair dismissal rights it may be observed that the protective framework of collective redundancies is weaker in the UK than in other European jurisdictions because the definition of what amounts to an employment relationship, and who is an employee falling within the protective scope of the Collective Redundancies Directive, are matters to be determined according to national law.[25]

The legitimization of efficiency as a primary concern for labour law is part of a broader trend that has seen the early focus on employment protection incrementally replaced with a commitment to the liberal market ideals of flexibility, competitiveness and profitability.[26] These market ideals seem at first sight to be inconsistent with the protectionist traditions of labour law and more strongly aligned with the shareholder primacy norms underlying corporate law.[27] By viewing labour law as a regulatory framework designed to promote efficiency by reducing transaction costs, the goals of labour law are strongly identified with those of the law of the business enterprise. The unifying theme is that of prioritizing managerial adaptability in order to facilitate organizational restructuring. The effect is to abandon the interests of workers. Promoting an 'equity

[23] H Collins, 'The Meaning of Job Security' (1991) 20 *Industrial Law Journal* 227.

[24] Trade Union and Labour Relations (Consolidation) Act 1992, pt IV c II.

[25] Council Directive 98/59/EC of 20 July 1998 on the approximation of the laws of the Member States relating to collective redundancies [1998] OJ L225, 16. On the difficulties arising in harmonising labour law, see Otto Kahn-Freund, 'On Uses and Misuses of Comparative Law' (1974) 37 *Modern Law Review* 1.

[26] 'The purpose is instrumental: to improve the competitiveness of businesses. The rights are not accorded to workers out of respect for basic values or to ensure compliance with ideal standards of fairness and justice. Instead, the legal rights are justified primarily because it is believed that they will contribute to the enhancement of efficient business methods, innovation, improvements in design, more successful marketing, and so forth': Hugh Collins, 'Is There a Third Way in Labour Law' in J Conaghan, RM Fischel and K Klare (eds), *Labour Law in an Era of Globalisation* (Oxford, Oxford University Press, 2002) 455.

[27] 'The starting point for many labour lawyers is that traditional judicial values—individualism, freedom of contract, and property rights—tend to align with the interests of employers rather than with those of employees and trade unions': Davies (n 13) 279.

culture' which encourages constant organizational and institutional restructuring exacerbates the fragmentation of work relationships.[28] As activist institutional and foreign investors increase pressures on management to maximize returns to shareholders, combined with greater exposure of firms to global product market competition, there is greater preoccupation with the costs of labour and the perceived need to minimize those costs.[29] Nothing could surely be more pernicious in its effects on trust, loyalty and commitment between all stakeholders than for managers to refer to their own employees as 'the headcount' whose levels must be constantly kept in check in order to keep costs as low as possible.[30] From that perspective the termination of employment relationships for economic reasons is regarded as no different from the termination of any other type of commercial arrangement, subject to no special or social expectations other than those agreed in the contract. Labour law's autonomy as a juridical system that emerged to differentiate and thereby safeguard workers' interests seems to be undermined.[31]

In seeking common ground between labour law and corporate law we must emphasize that we are by no means defending this unholy alliance with the ideology of efficiency as shareholder-value maximization. We do not view a dogmatic commitment to profiteering as being in any way representative of the overall narrative offered by the law of the business enterprise in relation to stakeholder interests. Instead we contest the prevailing degree of judicial deference by arguing that it rests upon a failure to appreciate the full value of labour to the business enterprise, illustrating this failure by reference to redundancy and directors' duties.

IV. Fairness in Dismissal: The Case of Redundancy

The law relating to redundancy represents the context in which notions of job

[28] R Sennett, *The Culture of the New Capitalism* (New Haven, Yale University Press, 2010).

[29] W Brown and P Edwards, 'Researching the Changing Workplace' in W Brown, A Bryson, J Forth and K Whitfield (eds), *The Evolution of the Modern Workplace* (Cambridge, Cambridge University Press, 2009) 1–21.

[30] Hence writing to redundant workers in these terms: 'As you are aware, in order to remain competitive within a challenging trading environment, it is necessary for the Company to ensure its costs and headcount are kept to the lowest practical level. Consequently, it is currently proving necessary for the Company to consider critically possible headcount and cost reductions on an ongoing basis and therefore to restructure the entire sales team. … I regret that one of the possible consequences of this perpetual review process is that your current position has been identified as one which the business may be unable to justify in the current climate. It is with regret therefore that we have to confirm that we are considering making your current position redundant.' This letter precipitated the (unsuccessful) unfair dismissal claim in *Samsung Electronics (UK) Ltd v Mote-D'Cruz* [2012] UKEAT 0039_11_0103.

[31] Lord Wedderburn, 'Labour Law: From Here to Autonomy?' (1987) 16 *Industrial Law Journal* 1.

security as a proprietary interest are most compelling.[32] It is also a context in which consultation and negotiation with employees is particularly widespread.[33] The 2011 Workplace Employment Relations Study (WERS) First Findings Report found that in up to 40% of workplaces the consultation and negotiation process during redundancy made a difference to the eventual outcome by prompting managers to alter their original proposals.[34] The willingness to make such alterations is significant given the apprehension that managers might approach negotiation with a predominant focus on their preferred options.[35] While the extent of consultation is to be welcomed, nevertheless the consultation is limited in its effect by focusing on procedural issues surrounding the implementation of redundancies, and not the more fundamental issue of whether the redundancies are inevitable in the first place. In that sense redundancy consultation does not challenge managerial prerogative and numerical flexibility regarding workforce size. Employees are still unlikely to be consulted on matters that affect the financial or strategic future of the employing entity, such as venturing into new products or services, or corporate restructuring, such as transfers of undertakings or mergers.[36]

The statutory definition of redundancy applies to situations where the whole business or a particular workplace has closed or is closing or where there is or is expected to be a diminution or cessation in the need for a particular

[32] The Redundancy Payments Act of 1965 was hailed as 'treating employment as a property right, by awarding compensation when positions disappeared for economic reasons': M Bennett, 'Montana's Employment Protection: A Comparative Critique of Montana's Wrongful Discharge from Employment Act in Light of the United Kingdom's Unfair Dismissal Law' (1996) 57 *Montana Law Review* 115, 117–18.

[33] B Van Wanrooy, H Bewley, A Bryson, J Forth, S Freeth, L Stokes and S Wood, *The 2011 Workplace Employment Relations Study: first Findings*, Workplace Employment Relations Study (WERS), BIS/13/535 (Department for Business, Innovation & Skills, 2013). Regarding the sample, WERS surveyed 'all British workplaces with 5 or more employees. This population accounts for 35% of all workplaces and 90% of all employees in Britain' (4, 5).

[34] 'In most cases (87%), managers had consulted with employees or their representatives before making anyone redundant' with such consultation going up to 95% of managers where redundancies affected two or more employees (ibid 20). Influence of consultation on the outcome included alternatives to redundancy, reduction in number of redundancies, strategies for redeployment or criteria for selection.

[35] WERS reports that from the managers' perspective '43% of managers in 2011 said that their usual approach was to use the [joint consultative committee] to seek solutions to problems, 38% said that it was to seek feedback on a range of options and 19% said that it was to seek feedback on their preferred option. The percentage of managers who said their usual approach was to focus on their preferred solution stood at 13% in 2011. … Among employee representatives who sat on joint consultative committees, the percentage who considered that managers typically focused consultation around a preferred option rose from 8% in 2004 to 30% in 2011' (ibid 21).

[36] WERS shows that 'changes in work techniques and the introduction of new technology were—along with the introduction of new products or services—the items on which managers were least likely to consult or negotiate with staff or their representatives' (20). Under the Information and Consultation Regs 2004 employees must be consulted on: (a) the recent and probable development of the undertaking's activities and economic situation; (b) the situation, structure and probable development of employment within the undertaking and on any anticipatory measures envisaged, in particular, where there is a threat to employment within the undertaking; and (c) decisions likely to lead to substantial changes in work organisation or in contractual relations (Reg 20(1)).

kind of work. The employee whose workplace has closed or is closing or who is employed by a business which has closed or is closing is unlikely to have much success arguing that there was not a genuine redundancy situation. The majority of case law on section 139 of the Employment Rights Act 1996 relates to the diminution or cessation in the need for a particular type of work, in which context there are two difficulties facing employees who challenge their dismissal. First, it is difficult for the employee, who may not have been involved in the management of the business, to argue that the employer has incorrectly determined that there was a need for a diminution or cessation of the need for a particular kind of work. Second, the statutory definition does not include a situation where there is no change in the amount of a particular kind of work but due to a reorganization fewer employees are required to do the work.

The procedural protection given to employees in redundancy dismissals is based upon good industrial practice as experienced by the lay members of the Employment Appeal Tribunal (EAT) as set out in the judgment of the EAT in *Williams v Compare Maxam Ltd*.[37] It is trite law that good practice involves giving employees and trade unions as much warning as possible of the impending redundancies, meaningful consultation with employees and trade unions on the redundancies and selection criteria, the use of objective selection criteria and attempts to find suitable alternative employment as an alternative to dismissal. While this approach could potentially safeguard job security in the sense of dignity at work and offering the opportunity and support to find alternative employment, courts and employment tribunals have increasingly construed these elements of good practice narrowly, deferring to managerial discretion in making business decisions. Although it is finding new forms of expression, this deference is not itself a recent development. Traditionally managerial discretion has been upheld in relation to two aspects of a redundancy procedure: the pool from which candidates are selected for redundancy, and how they are scored. When an employer has genuinely applied its mind to the constitution of the pool it would be difficult for an employee to challenge it.[38] Further, in *British Aerospace v Green* the Court of Appeal held that whilst an employment tribunal will have to consider whether a system of scoring and marking was fair, if that system is to function effectively it must not be 'scrutinised officiously'.[39] These decisions show the EAT and Court of Appeal restraining employment tribunals from interfering with ring-fenced areas of managerial discretion.

In recent years, such deference to managerial discretion has extended its reach to other aspects of the redundancy procedure. In *Morgan v Welsh Rugby Union*[40] the claimant was made redundant as a result of an internal reorganization. The employer interviewed two candidates for a new post following the reorganization: the claimant and another who did not meet the job descrip-

[37] *Williams v Compare Maxam Ltd* [1982] ICR 156 (EAT).
[38] *Taymech Limited v Ryan* [1994] UKEAT/663/94.
[39] *British Aerospace v Green* [1995] IRLR 433 (CA).
[40] *Morgan v Welsh Rugby Union* [2011] ILR 376 (EAT).

tion and minimum qualifications for the new role. The employer also departed from the set format for the interview. There was no objectivity in the rehiring process which was attendant upon the reorganization, nor was the claimant given any useful or reliable information about the form that process would take. The employment tribunal found that the claimant's dismissal for redundancy was fair despite the irregularities in the reorganizational process. In upholding that finding the EAT distinguished the situation from that in *Williams*, stating that the procedural fairness required by *Williams* did not address the situation where there were *new* internal roles to be filled. Further, the EAT recognized that the employer will need to be forward looking and consider what will be required in the new role. Thus, it will not necessarily be bound by the job description or purely objective selection criteria. It is significant that the EAT held that a tribunal should keep carefully in mind that deciding which candidate will perform best in the new role is likely to involve a 'substantial element of judgment'. Taken at its lowest point, this judgment is pragmatic because it recognizes that a suitable candidate for a job should not be unsuccessful because he or she does not have a level of qualification which was originally stated in the job description. At its highest point, *Morgan* permits an employer to change the job description to suit the candidate which it prefers following a business reorganization in the knowledge that its decision cannot be successfully challenged before the employment tribunal. The notion of fairness during redundancy therefore fades away after the first early stages of the reorganizational process.

Morgan has been applied in subsequent cases, thus according even further deference to managerial discretion. In *Samsung Electronics (UK) Ltd v Mote-D'Cruz* the EAT, following *Morgan*, held that the employer is not obliged to use objective criteria and certainly not when interviewing candidates for suitable alternative employment.[41] By splitting the reorganization into two stages, the first involving dismissals for redundancy and the second involving rehiring into alternative roles, it is thus possible effectively to avoid the requirements of procedural fairness altogether. *Morgan* and *Samsung* were applied by the EAT in *Mitchells of Lancaster v Tattersall* in which it held that the respondent employer had not acted unfairly in selecting the claimant for redundancy on the basis that 'losing him would cause least damage to the Respondent's business' because the claimant's back-office role 'was not a role that generated revenue'.[42] This was deemed by the candidate to be 'indefensibly subjective' and hence unfair. The EAT held that it was not unfair for the respondent's board of directors to consider the skills of all of the employees in the pool for redundancy and decide who had the relevant skills to bring in revenue. There is in any event a further hurdle to be faced by those employees who successfully establish that they have been unfairly dismissed: a *Polkey* deduction may be applied to the compensatory award to reflect the fact that the employee would have been dismissed even if the employer

[41] *Samsung Electronics (UK) Ltd v Mote-D'Cruz* [2012] UKEAT 0039_11_0103.
[42] *Mitchells of Lancaster v Tattersall* [2012] UKEAT 0605_11_2905.

had carried out a fair procedure.[43] Collins observes that this permits an employer to disregard a fair procedure without having to be concerned about financial consequences when a particular employee is bound to have been dismissed.[44] In those circumstances the employee who has received a statutory redundancy payment (therefore cancelling out their entitlement to a basic award) will have to be content with a finding of unfair dismissal.

The law therefore seems to be lethargic about protecting the job security of individuals in particular jobs. In that context managerial discretion is ring fenced and is increasingly becoming an area into which an employment tribunal will not intrude. The removal of lay wing members from unfair dismissal cases in the employment tribunal, resulting in the loss of their practical expertise, creates the potential for even greater deference to managerial discretion. Lack of specialized expertise in the subject matter is one of the key factors prompting judges to defer to the decision-maker's discretion[45] and the role of practical knowledge and experience of workplace conventions was a key part of the rationale for including lay members in the tribunal.[46]

The function of 'fairness' in economic dismissals seems to carry greater weight when the goal is not to protect particular jobs, but to safeguard other elements necessary in giving effect to the efficient functioning of labour markets. This is borne out in the EAT's decision in *USDAW v Ethel Austin Ltd and others* which involved mass redundancies.[47] Former employees of Woolworths who had been employed in stores where there were fewer than 20 employees, too few to trigger the obligation to collectively consult, claimed that they were entitled to a protective award similarly to their colleagues employed in larger stores. The EAT adopted a purposive construction of the legislation to 'delete' that part of the statutory language which required employees to work 'at one establishment', holding that the employees at the smaller branches were entitled to the protective award.[48] This approach was intended to give effect to the core objective of the EU Directive on collective redundancies, namely to safeguard workers' right to employment security. Employment security in this context denotes financial security as well as the idea of adaptability or employability in facilitating transition to new jobs.[49] The EAT decision in this case reflects the operation of what

[43] *Polkey v AE Dayton Services Ltd* [1987] UKHL 8.

[44] H Collins, K Ewing and A McColgan, *Labour Law* (Cambridge, Cambridge University Press, 2012) ch 15.

[45] '[T]he view that employers' decisions should be respected because employers know best how to run their own businesses' is more likely to prevail in the absence of lay representatives from both employer and employee/union sides: Davies (n 13) 290.

[46] As Howe (n 22) 131 points out: 'The rationale for choosing one lay representative from an employer perspective and another from a union background was aimed to achieve just decision making not based on legal principles but upon custom and practice in British industrial relations.'

[47] *USDAW v Ethel Austin Ltd and others* UKEAT/0547/12/KN, 30 May 2013.

[48] s 188 of the Trade Union and Labour Relations (Consolidation) Act 1992.

[49] This reflects the motivation behind the UK's first Redundancy Payments Act 1965: '[T]he main aim of the Redundancy Payments Act was not, as it might seem, to recognize a kind of property right in jobs, but to ensure that employees displaced from declining industries were given incentives to abandon resistance to technological change, and to enhance job security by granting displaced

Collins calls the social costs policy consideration in redundancy protection:[50] a recognition that if employees are permitted to bring a claim against their former employer, this will reduce the social costs of economic dismissals.[51] The courts therefore seem willing to give effect to core values of employment protection when dealing with large-scale collective redundancies. The overriding influence of European law certainly plays a part in this, but it also reflects an awareness that allowing large corporate employers to externalize the costs of job losses through unregulated job dislocation would, beyond a certain point, become inimical to efficiency and hence unjustifiable if efficiency is to be taken as the gold standard. We consider this sensitivity to the efficiency requirements of the wider labour market to be a useful point of comparison in evaluating the insights that may be gained from tracing similar developments in corporate law, where market efficiency often explicitly influences judicial reasoning.

V. Corporate Law and Directors' Duties

Since the nineteenth century the courts in considering directors' fiduciary duties to act in the best interests of the company have acknowledged the interdependence between corporate success and the welfare of workers, in the sense that profits are most effectively maximized by encouraging workers to exert themselves on behalf of the enterprise. As pronounced in 1883 by Bowen LJ:

> A railway company, or the directors of the company, might send down all the porters at a railway station to have tea in the country at the expense of the company. Why should they not? It is for the directors to judge, provided it is a matter which is reasonably incidental to the carrying on of the business of the company, and a company which always treated its employees with Draconian severity, and never allowed them a single inch more than the strict letter of the bond, would soon find itself deserted—at all events, unless labour was very much more easy to obtain in the market than it often is. The law does not say that there are to be no cakes and ale, but there are to be no cakes and ale except such as are required for the benefit of the company.[52]

workers a form of compensation which would assist them in the job search': S Deakin and G Morris, *Labour Law*, 4th edn (Oxford, Hart Publishing, 2005) 391.

[50] Collins (n 44).

[51] The Court of Appeal has referred the question to the Court of Justice of the European Union, 22 January 2014.

[52] On making payments to employees that are not strictly required by their employment contracts, the courts have expressed approval subject to the approval of shareholders: 'Not only have [the directors] done nothing wrong, but I confess I think the company have done what nine companies out of ten would do, and do without the least objection being made. They have paid, perhaps liberally, perhaps not at all too liberally, persons who have served them faithfully. But that, of course, does not get rid of the difficulty. As soon as a question is raised by a dissentient shareholder, … sympathy must be cut adrift, and we have simply to consider what the law is': *Hutton v West Cork Railway Co* (1883) 23 ChD 654.

There can be little doubt that even the most avaricious shareholders would find it within themselves to accept this interpretation of labour's interests in the company: cakes and ale to keep the workers happy. The modern 'enlightened shareholder value' (ESV) approach now codified in section 172 of the Companies Act 2006 holds that stakeholder interests are intrinsic to corporate success, but does not go further to recognize the importance of building high levels of trust in the shareholder–stakeholder relationship, nor does it acknowledge the role directors can play in co-ordinating that relationship to create the genuine partnerships on which co-operative team production depends.

In their team production theory of corporate law Margaret Blair and Lynn Stout address the ideas behind ESV, emphasizing the value of co-operation in the new economy where the knowledge and creativity of workers are essential to corporate success and all members of the team are interdependent.[53] Corporate productivity requires the 'combined investment and coordinated effort' of all participants.[54] Blair and Stout argue that directors are not agents for any particular constituency, but more akin to trustees charged with safeguarding the beneficial interests of all members of the corporate team. The Blair–Stout thesis explains why individual contracts are unable fully to account for labour investments: the whole is greater than the sum of its parts, so it is impossible for any contract to fully capture the parties' overlapping and sometimes conflicting claims and entitlements. Blair and Stout depict the corporation as a 'mediating hierarchy' in which all these claims and entitlements are vested and resolved. The board of directors, independent of all the stakeholder-investors, lies at the apex of that hierarchy and has the function of allocating the distribution of returns equitably amongst the members. In this role directors are in the position of trustees for all stakeholders.[55]

This approach complements Deakin's theory of the corporation as commons by suggesting that all claims, not just shareholder claims, are encompassed within the corporation's internal governance structures. The role of directors is to enable the preservation of corporate assets for the benefit of all its stakeholders and society as a whole, to safeguard the investments of all participants in corporate enterprise. The challenge for law is then to find effective means of holding them accountable by reference to their fiduciary obligation to promote the best interests of all corporate participants.[56] Blair and Stout do not envisage employee claims

[53] M Blair and L Stout, 'A Team Production Theory of Corporate Law' (1999) 85 *Virginia Law Review* 247.

[54] ibid 249.

[55] Blair and Stout demonstrate that although the corporation as a mediating hierarchy is poorly designed to deal with agency costs between directors and shareholders, it is able efficiently to respond to the challenges of team production: 'While this legal structure may increase agency costs, it may also provide an efficient (albeit second-best) solution to the contracting problems that arise in team production' (ibid 255).

[56] '[T]he legal requirement that public corporations be managed under the supervision of a board of directors has evolved not to reduce agency costs—indeed, such a requirement may exacerbate them—but to encourage the firm-specific investment essential to certain forms of team production. In other words, boards exist not to protect shareholders per se, but to protect the enterprise-specific

becoming more important than shareholder claims; they advocate complete independence of the director decision-makers who are 'free to mediate among competing interests'.[57] Deakin pins this down further by defining a corporate stakeholder as 'one who makes an input of value to the firm and as a result has an investment which is at risk if the firm fails, along with a claim to exercise voice in the firm's governance'.[58] Judicial oversight of directors' decisions would then not rely on specification of a class or category of claimants entitled to challenge directors' decisions, but would instead focus on the existence of inputs in the firm which are unduly exposed to risk.

An example of how this can be translated into vindicating corporate law claims may be drawn from the Canada Business Corporations Act, which grants the court discretion to allow any 'proper person' to bring a derivative action challenging directors' decisions.[59] The Canadian Supreme Court has recently echoed the Blair–Stout interpretation of the fiduciary duty of directors, by treating all stakeholders as beneficiaries of that duty:

> The duty of the directors to act in the best interests of the corporation comprehends a duty to treat individual stakeholders affected by corporate actions equitably and fairly. There are no absolute rules. In each case, the question is whether, in all the circumstances, the directors acted in the best interests of the corporation, having regard to all relevant considerations, including, but not confined to, the need to treat affected stakeholders in a fair manner, commensurate with the corporation's duties as a responsible corporate citizen.[60]

The Court went on to observe that:

> There is no principle that one set of interests—for example the interests of shareholders—should prevail over another set of interests. Everything depends on the

investments of all the members of the corporate "team," including shareholders, managers, rank and file employees, and possibly other groups, such as creditors' (ibid 253).

[57] ibid 327.

[58] *Deakin* (n 5) 368

[59] This is in stark contrast to the UK Companies Act 2006 which only allows a 'member' (a shareholder) to bring a derivative claim under s 260 or to seek an unfair prejudice remedy under s 994. S 238 of the Canada Business Corporations Act, the definitional section in relation to corporate remedies, defines a 'complainant' as a shareholder, creditor, director, officer or 'any other person who, in the discretion of a court, is a proper person to make an application under this Part'; s 239(1) of the Canada Business Corporations Act provides that 'a complainant may apply to a court for leave to bring an action in the name and on behalf of a corporation or any of its subsidiaries, or intervene in an action to which any such body corporate is a party, for the purpose of prosecuting, defending or discontinuing the action on behalf of the body corporate'; under s 239(2) in giving leave the court must be satisfied that the complainant is acting in good faith and that the action is in the interests of the corporation: in practice such complainants are required to show a direct financial interest in the corporation and are likely to be shareholders, creditors or directors, including employees who are also shareholders/officers of the corporation: *Naneff v Con-Crete Holdings Ltd* (1995), 23 OR (3d) 48 (CA); for discussion see M Marin, 'Disembedding Corporate Governance: The Crisis of Shareholder Primacy in the UK and Canada' (2013) 39 *Queen's Law Journal* 223; the 'discretion' vested in the courts means that, for reasons discussed by Lord Wedderburn, judges are unlikely to see employees as 'proper' applicants (Wedderburn (n 31) 13–16).

[60] *BCE Inc (Arrangement relatif d) (Re)* [2008] 3 SCR 560 para 82. For the treatment of stakeholders as beneficiaries, see *Peoples Department Stores Inc (Trustee of) v Wise* [2004] 3 SCR 461.

> particular situation faced by the directors and whether, having regard to that situation, they exercised business judgment in a responsible way.[61]

This case involved a conflict between the interests of debenture holders and shareholders in the context of a proposed leveraged buyout of BCE Inc. The buyout was to be funded largely by debt guaranteed by a wholly owned subsidiary of BCE, and while the shareholders favoured the arrangement the debenture holders deemed it to be unfair as it would devalue their bonds. Based on these facts it would have been open to the Court to confine itself to considering the fairness of the proposed arrangement, but since the debenture holders also sought a remedy for oppression or unfair prejudice to their interests, the Court considered more generally the nature of directors' duties to the corporation's stakeholders.[62] Indeed, to the extent that the Supreme Court does not confine its language to creditor interests but speaks more broadly of stakeholders and even adverts to a requirement to be a 'good corporate citizen', the decision has come under scathing attack.[63] The Court ruled that:

> Directors or other corporate actors may make corporate decisions or seek to resolve conflicts in a way that abusively or unfairly maximizes a particular group's interest at the expense of other stakeholders. The corporation and shareholders are entitled to maximize profit and share value, to be sure, but not by treating individual stakeholders unfairly.[64]

The origin of this approach, emphasizing fairness amongst corporate participants, is not difficult to trace to its roots in English company law. These roots lie in the robust protection of minority shareholders, who will be protected by the courts even when the 'wrong' they are complaining about is perfectly lawful and explicitly contemplated by the terms of their formal contracts.[65] The Canadian Supreme Court in *BCE* addresses the nature of stakeholders' reasonable expectations by reference to the following extract from Lord Wilberforce's speech in *Ebrahimi v Westbourne Galleries*:

> A limited company is more than a mere legal entity, with a personality in law of its own: … there is room in company law for recognition of the fact that behind it, or amongst it, there are individuals, with rights, expectations and obligations inter se which are not necessarily submerged in the company structure.[66]

[61] ibid para 84.

[62] The Canada Business Corporation Act allows any 'complainant' to seek a remedy for oppression (s 241) While the definition of 'complainant' includes a discretion to allow any 'proper person' to apply, the interests alleged to have been unfairly prejudiced are confined to 'the interests of any security holder, creditor, director or officer'.

[63] For a critique of the *BCE* decision, see JG Macintosh, 'BCE and the Peoples' Corporate Law: Learning to Live on Quicksand' (2009) 48 *Canadian Business Law Journal* 255. This revives the debate on the role of directors following the separation of ownership and control: E Merrick Dodd Jr, 'For Whom Are Corporate Managers Trustees?' (1932) 45 *Harvard Law Review* 1145; AA Berle Jr, 'For Whom Corporate Managers Are Trustees: A Note' (1932) 45 *Harvard Law Review* 1365.

[64] *BCE Inc* (n 60) para 64.

[65] P Davies and S Worthington, *Gower & Davies Principles of Modern Company Law*, 9th edn (London, Sweet & Maxwell, 2012) 723–24.

[66] *Ebrahimi v Westbourne Galleries* [1973] AC 360, 379 (Lord Wilberforce).

Lord Wilberforce is referring specifically to the interests of *shareholders* on a petition to wind up a small quasi-partnership (only three shareholders) on 'just and equitable' grounds. The Canadian Supreme Court extends that interpretation, applying the principles set out by Lord Wilberforce to an evaluation of the reasonable expectations of 'affected stakeholders' in a large corporation (a telecommunications corporation worth Can$52 billion). Attempts to apply legal principles developed in the context of very small business associations to the affairs of a large publicly held corporation have received a frosty reception from the UK courts, which expect shareholders to simply sell up if they are not happy but will be enormously sympathetic to minority shareholders in small private companies with no external market for their shares and therefore no ready exit.[67]

The greater willingness in Canada to apply these principles outside the fact situation contemplated by *Ebrahimi* is partly explained by the fact that the Canada Business Corporations Act allows creditors to seek unfair prejudice remedies (unlike the law in the UK[68]), and partly by the commitment of Canadian judges to let the statute speak for itself without reading common-law-derived restrictions into it.[69] Added to this is a discernibly creative element in *BCE* as there is nothing in the dicta to suggest that such reasonable expectations can only arise in relation to creditors. The court clearly states that: 'What is just and equitable is judged by the reasonable expectations of the stakeholders in the context and in regard to the relationships at play.'[70] It is true that the scope for directors in the UK to respond to interests other than those of shareholders is more constrained than it is in the US or Canada.[71] It is not simply that in the UK company legislation does not allow non-shareholders to bring claims against directors; it is more that the courts read restrictions into legislation to make it accord with the common law, perhaps appropriately so because the Companies Act 2006 is a codifying statute.[72] Yet we must look outside the legislative provisions to understand the full import of the constraints facing the courts, as it is plain to see that a Canadian-style stakeholder revolution would have to do

[67] Even though the Companies Act does not itself preclude such actions or explicitly state that unfair prejudice is only available to minority shareholders in small firms. This rule emanates from case law: *Re Legal Costs Negotiators* [1999] 2 BCLC 720.

[68] Although in a very small one-person firm the 'creditor' and 'shareholder' may be one and the same person and may be successful in claiming, qua shareholder, a remedy for a loss suffered in his capacity as creditor: *Gamlestaden Fastigheter AB v Baltic Partners Ltd & Ors* (Jersey) [2007] UKPC 26.

[69] 'The common law courts, under both contractarian and letters patent corporate statutes, failed to find any principled approaches to the problem of minority shareholder protection. Canadian legislatures have created some': B Welling, L Smith and LI Rotman, *Canadian Corporate Law*, 4th edn (Toronto, LexisNexis, Markham, 2010) 453.

[70] *BCE Inc*, n 60, para 59.

[71] See JC Coffee and BS Black, 'Hail Brittania? Institutional Investor Behavior Under Limited Regulation' (1994) 92 *Michigan Law Review* 1997.

[72] s 170(3): the general duties are based on certain common law rules and equitable principles as they apply in relation to directors and have effect in place of those rules and principles as regards the duties owed to a company by a director; s 170(4): the general duties shall be interpreted and applied in the same way as common law rules or equitable principles, and regard shall be had to the corresponding common law rules and equitable principles in interpreting and applying the general duties.

battle with the strongly shareholder-centric rules of takeover regulation[73] and the financial ethos of the City of London.[74]

Two further observations may be made on this point. First, although section 172 soothes shareholder-primacy fever with the balm of ESV it does not advance the common law much further than its historical position.[75] Second, it must be acknowledged that as long as the law vests in shareholders the right to hire and fire directors by a simple majority vote, making directors' own position somewhat precarious (at least in theory), directors are likely quite naturally to prioritize shareholder interests. For these reasons it is perhaps instructive that in the US, the context in which Blair and Stout advance their mediating hierarchy view of the role of directors in free exercise of an independent discretion, directors have greater ability to take defensive action through 'just say no' defences to hostile takeovers such as the infamous poison pills which are automatically triggered to unleash death and destruction to the corporation if an attempt is made to wrest control from the incumbent managers.[76] In Canada the closely held structure of large corporations with dominant shareholders, predominantly family-controlled, means directors are less exposed than they are in the UK to the threat of hostile takeovers.[77] The UK remains, as Lord Wedderburn described it, a shareholders' city state,[78] although as Deakin points out this is attributable

[73] For a discussion of the shareholder-oriented takeover regulations, see A Johnston and W Njoya, 'Employee Voice in Corporate Control Transactions' in T Novitz and A Bogg (eds), *Voices at Work: Continuity and Change in the Common Law World* (Oxford, Oxford University Press, 2014). We do not explore here the possibility of simply amending the Companies Act to allow stakeholders to bring derivative actions, not because such a development seems unlikely but because even in the Canadian context, where in theory any stakeholder may seek leave to sue on behalf of the corporation, this does not in practice occur. The reasons may at least partly be understood by reference to Lord Wedderburn's description ((n 31) 1) of the structures of the common law.

[74] S Deakin, R Hobbs, S Konzelman and F Wilkinson, 'Anglo-American Corporate Governance and the Employment Relationship: A Case to Answer?' ESRC Centre for Business Research, University of Cambridge Working Paper No 308, June 2005.

[75] Indeed enforcement by stakeholders is expressly ruled out in the Companies Act 2006: directors' duties are owed to the company (s 170) and only members may seek permission to enforce those duties (s 261). It has always been open, at common law, for directors to take employee interests into account and even to give some kind of priority to those interests as long as they could demonstrate that it would ultimately be in the best interests of shareholders: in *Parke v Daily News* [1962] Ch 927 such an attempt failed utterly because the company was insolvent and so the ex gratia payment to employees could not conceivably yield any benefit for the corporation or its shareholders. The same is generally true in US law, where the Delaware position is reflected in the dicta in *Unocal Corp v Mesa Petroleum Co*, 493 A2d 946 (Del 1985): the board of directors 'may have regard for various constituencies in discharging its responsibilities' but 'concern for non-stockholder interests is inappropriate when … the object no longer is to protect or maintain the corporate enterprise but to sell it to the highest bidder' (182). Enlightened shareholder value makes the difference that now directors have a duty to take into account stakeholder interests.

[76] M Kahan and EB Rock, 'How I Learned to Stop Worrying and Love the Pill: Adaptive Responses to Takeover Law' (2002) 69 *University of Chicago Law Review* 871.

[77] R Morck and B Yeung, 'Some Obstacles to Good Corporate Governance in Canada and How to Overcome Them' (2006) Research Study Report Commissioned by the Task Force to Modernize Securities Legislation in Canada, available at www.tfmsl.ca/docs/V4(5)%20Morck.pdf .

[78] Lord Wedderburn, 'The Social Responsibility of Companies' (1985) 15 *Melbourne University Law Review* 4; see also by the same author *The Future of Company Law* (n 11).

not to company law but to the financialization of corporate governance.[79] It is not suggested here that these differences are insignificant or that we can ignore the political economy of global capitalism altogether.[80] Nevertheless by looking at comparable jurisdictions we are able to better understand the potential for employee interests to be safeguarded within the broader conceptual framework of the law regulating business enterprise.[81] In all common law jurisdictions the operation of some form of business-judgment rule or deference to the directors' decision-making authority means that where all the considerations are finely balanced the court will not attempt to second-guess the result arrived at by directors, but by noticing that the different degrees of deference are based on statutes which do not have significant differences in their wording, some scope may be delineated for the courts to adopt a more purposive interpretation of the law.

VI. Purposive Interpretation

The court in *BCE Inc* came out strongly in favour of stakeholder interests, but recognized that ultimately the decision has to be one for the directors and the court will not interfere with the directors' decision to prefer one stakeholder interest over another.[82] Like the reasonableness test in unfair dismissal law, which encompasses a 'range of reasonable responses', the courts will not find the directors to be in breach of duty just because the judge would have chosen a different alternative.[83] Mayer observes that if courts are hesitant to wade into the murky waters of business judgment when the applicable benchmarks are straightforward and well-established (shareholder value or fairness in dismissal), then the introduction of a 'broad, contextual concept' of directors duties is likely to exacerbate the difficulties: '[E]xtend the obligation to customers, employees, and communities, grant directors discretion over how to balance these conflicting

[79] 'The idea that the surplus should be returned to the shareholders on a regular basis owes little or nothing to the legal framework of company law. It owes much more to late twentieth century finance theory, which argued that companies should distribute "free cash flow" to shareholders in order to promote capital efficiency, and to the practice of listed companies in some countries (most notably the USA and UK from the early 1980s onwards) of rewarding shareholders through increased dividend payments, and in particular through share buy-backs': Deakin (n 5) 357.

[80] On this see H Arthurs and C Mummé, 'From Governance to Political Economy: Insights from a Study of Relations Between Corporations and Workers' in C Williams and P Zumbansen (eds), *The Embedded Firm: Corporate Governance, Labor, and Finance Capitalism* (Cambridge, Cambridge University Press, 2011)

[81] M Blair and M Roe, *Employees and Corporate Governance* (Washington DC, Brookings Institution Press, 1999).

[82] '[W]here it is impossible to please all stakeholders, it will be irrelevant that the directors rejected alternative transactions that were no more beneficial than the chosen one': *BCE Inc* (n 60) para 82.

[83] *Iceland Frozen Foods v Jones* [1983] ICR 17. Under the 'band of reasonable responses' test the courts 'emphasise the fact that more than one decision by an employer might be reasonable. The tribunal should not necessarily find the dismissal to be unfair just because it would have decided the case differently': Davies (n 13) 291.

claims, and there will be next to nothing that is legally enforceable.'[84] Mayer thinks that given this reality 'the law cannot of itself solve the problem', at least not by the simple expedient of allowing stakeholders to bring derivative claims against directors on behalf of the corporation. Indeed the main criticism in Canadian reaction to *BCE* is that such a duty to resolve conflicting interests is impossible for a court to review.[85] Critics insist that a single clear standard (eg shareholder value maximization) is required to make ex post evaluation by judicial review feasible.[86]

This is not because critics consider judges to be unable to solve complex legal problems. It is more that there are limits to how much can be achieved by judicial discretion on questions touching upon the balance of power between labour and capital, as the weight of the common law tradition makes it virtually impossible for legislation to achieve a result that seems to be fundamentally at odds with deeply rooted common law ideals such as freedom of contract and the sanctity of private (shareholder) property.[87] Simple tests make for straightforward judicial review—in relation to fairness in dismissal, the law is straightforward if it is accepted that economic reasons constitute fair and justifiable grounds. It would be easier still if the court only had to quantify the appropriate amount of compensation without troubling to inquire into the reasons for dismissal.[88] Yet this would come at the expense of justice, as recognized in the context of public law where courts have developed standards of review such as proportionality that allow an incisive review of complex decisions where rights are at stake.[89] A balancing test such as that put forward by the Canadian Supreme Court admittedly requires review based on 'a broad, contextual concept'[90] where 'there are no absolute rules and no principle that one set of interests should prevail over another'[91] but this does not prevent the Supreme Court from seizing the mantle. This provides an example to emulate in challenging the complacency with which the law accepts efficiency or flexibility as justifications for yielding the ground to managerial prerogative.[92]

[84] Mayer (n 1) 42.

[85] There are of course many other difficulties, which are addressed by Lord Wedderburn in 'Employees, Partnership and Company Law' [2002] 31(2) *Industrial Law Journal* 99; here we focus on the issue regarding the accountability of directors. For a critique of *BCE Inc*, see E Iacobucci 'Indeterminacy and the Canadian Supreme Court's Approach to Corporate Fiduciary Duties' (2009) 48 *Canadian Business Law Journal* 232.

[86] The fear is that if directors are not accountable to shareholders, assessed by reference to whether they have maximized shareholder returns, then they will be accountable to nobody and it will be impossible to evaluate their performance: see eg Iacobucci, ibid.

[87] S Anderman, 'The Interpretation of Protective Employment Statutes and Contracts of Employment' (2000) 29 *Industrial Law Journal* 223; and Anderman (n) 18, remarking that judges interpreting unfair dismissal legislation 'seem unable to adjust to the reality of labour legislation as an intended moderator of employer property rights' (127).

[88] This is the justification for the 'no-fault' dismissal proposals discussed by Howe (n 22).

[89] Davies (n 13).

[90] *BCE Inc* (n 60) para 38.

[91] ibid para 84.

[92] 'If we take the view, as a working hypothesis, that the law actively shapes the operation of business firms within the economy rather than simply responding to their existence, it becomes necessary to specify more precisely how that is done': Deakin (n 5) 355.

VII. Legitimate Expectations

A potential foundation for a more interventionist approach in defending workers' entitlements when jobs are at risk is presented by the implied term of mutual trust and confidence (MTC): '[T]he employer shall not, without reasonable and proper cause, conduct itself in a manner calculated or likely to destroy or seriously damage the relationship of confidence and trust between employer and employee.'[93] The idea of MTC has the advantage of being more powerful than ESV in capturing the importance of co-operation and partnership in the employer–employee relationship.[94] Yet as Judy Fudge shows in analysing the influence of MTC in Canada and the UK, the first hurdle to be faced in applying MTC to job security is the common law conviction that termination of employment lies beyond the boundaries of the courts' review jurisdiction. Labour law is disastrously inhibited by the strictures of the contract of employment when it comes to the termination of employment.[95] Although MTC has transformed the rights and obligations during the subsistence of the contract of employment, all bets are off once the firing decision is made. MTC remains vulnerable to being modified or even excluded by agreement between the parties[96] and more importantly it stops short of encroaching upon the zone of dismissal either in relation to the manner of dismissal or the decision to effect the dismissal.[97] Again we see greater willingness on the part of the Canadian judiciary to strike at the heart of termination by extending notions of good faith to the manner of dismissal. Fudge shows that the obligation of good faith plays an important analytical role in 'imposing limitations on employers' right to terminate' in Canadian law.[98] This, however, does not affect the principle that damages for wrongful dismissal are awarded only in respect of breach of the duty to give

[93] *Woods v WM Car Services (Peterborough) Ltd* [1981] ICR 666, 670. For discussion, see D Brodie, 'Mutual Trust and the Values of the Employment Contract' (2001) 30 *Industrial Law Journal* 84.

[94] 'Instead of the image of master and faithful servant that informed the earlier legal construction of the contract of employment, the law tries to present the employment relationship as one between equals, where both parties need to co-operate, to assist each other in good faith, to use the powers and responsibilities conferred by the contract for proper purposes, and to treat each other with dignity and respect': Collins et al (n 44) 142.

[95] J Fudge, 'The Spectre of Addis in Contracts of Employment in Canada and the UK' (2007) 36 *Industrial Law Journal* 51.

[96] The vulnerability of employee claims which rest on contract has long been recognized. See A Fox, *Beyond Contract: Work, Power and Trust Relations* (London, Faber, 1974); Davies and Freedland (n 15) 318–47. Nor indeed has contract always constituted the legal basis of workers' claims: S Deakin, *The Law of the Labour Market: Industrialization, Employment, and Legal Evolution* (Oxford, Oxford University Press, 2005).

[97] *Johnson v Unisys* [2001] UKHL 13, by creating the so-called '*Johnson* exclusion zone', has established that: 'The exclusion of the claim for wrongful dismissal comprised three elements: the zone applied to claims based on the implied term of mutual trust and confidence that were in substance claims about the manner of dismissal; and it applied to claims regarding psychiatric loss, either in tort or contract, caused by the manner of dismissal; and perhaps, more generally, it applied to any claims that would circumvent the statutory cap on compensation for unfair dismissal': H Collins, 'Compensation for Dismissal: In Search of Principle' (2012) 41 *Industrial Law Journal* 208, 210.

[98] Fudge (n 95) 55.

reasonable notice. All that good faith does is to affect the length of notice that would be deemed reasonable in the circumstances.[99] In Canada, as in the UK, the 'spectre of Addis' still haunts the common law.[100]

By turning to corporate law it may be possible in an analytical sense to bypass *Addis* in order to explore potential ways to extend the values underlying MTC to more informal extra-contractual obligations that may give rise to legitimate expectations. In corporate law, claims based on legitimate expectations are enforced without the requirement that the expectation should arise within the framework of a contractual relationship.[101] Although this principle has legislative roots in the unfair prejudice doctrine, the role of judicial law-making in the courts' equitable jurisdiction emerges clearly when we compare the divergent directions taken by the case law in the UK and Canada. In the UK the unfair prejudice petition exists to safeguard shareholder interests.[102] Case law suggests that this remedy will ordinarily be restricted to minority shareholders, as majority shareholders would be expected to be in control or to have ways of resolving their own problems by asserting control.[103] Apart from restricting the remedy to minority shareholders the courts further restrict it to the context of very small undertakings with only a few members where much reliance is placed on informal unwritten understandings between the parties and it would be inequitable to rely on the formal agreement between them as 'the precise provisions of the articles may seem almost irrelevant to the petitioner's sense of grievance'.[104] Here the courts recognize a legitimate expectation that 'arises out of a fundamental understanding between the shareholders which formed the basis of their association but was not put into contractual form'.[105] The courts look to 'the bargain which the members of the company had struck, a bargain which, in its totality, might be located in informal, non-legally enforceable understandings between the members as well as in the company's formal constitution'.[106] Paul Davies suggests that these restrictions on the availability of the remedy, not required by the wording of the statute, reflect the 'traditionally non-interventionist attitude of judges in relation to the internal affairs of companies' and especially their reticence in deciding issues of 'fairness' in the conduct of corporate affairs, although he suggests that more recently 'we have witnessed a partial

[99] ibid 66: '[I]n Canada the length of notice will be increased if an employer behaves badly when terminating an employee' based on the principle enunciated in *Wallace v United Grain Growers* [1997] 3 SCR 701.

[100] For the UK position, see Collins (n 97).

[101] For a more detailed analysis of the meaning and implications of legitimate expectations in the context of employee claims to job security, see I Skandalis, *Balancing Employer and Employee Interests: Legitimate Expectations and Proportionality under the Acquired Rights Directive* (DPhil thesis, Oxford University, 2013).

[102] A shareholder may petition for relief on grounds that 'the company's affairs are being or have been conducted in a manner which is unfairly prejudicial to the interest of its members': s 994 Companies Act 2006.

[103] *Re Legal Costs Negotiators* [1999] 2 BCLC 720.

[104] Davies and Worthington (n 65) 726.

[105] *Re Saul D Harrison & Sons Plc* [1995] 1 BCLC 14, 19.

[106] Davies and Worthington (n 65) 727.

revolution in judicial attitudes' in terms of the range of conduct which they are prepared to treat as unfairly prejudicial.[107] In Canada the courts do not read any such restrictions into the availability of the unfair prejudice remedy in relation to the size of the corporation or the identity of the complainant; the complainant need not be a shareholder, much less a minority shareholder.[108] Even when an agreement expressly provides for the termination of the employment of a director or officer of the corporation, the expectation of MTC arising outside the formal agreement may give rise to a reasonable expectation of 'a partnership in spirit if not in law' which would make termination amount to oppression or unfair prejudice.[109] The remedy is broadly construed 'to enforce not just what is legal but what is fair … what is just and equitable is judged by the reasonable expectations of the stakeholders in the context and in regard to the relationships at play'.[110]

The question then arises as to the potential for similar interpretations in the context of the employment relationship. As Fudge points out:

> [T]here is nothing inevitable about contract law that limits the employing entity's liability under the contract of employment for the losses suffered by the employee from wrongful termination of the employment relationship; it is a choice made by judges about whose expectations the law should vindicate.[111]

The informal understandings and expectations in the employment relationship are analogous to those between shareholders. In corporate law, when disputes arise in the contractual relationship between majority and minority shareholders the courts suffer no inhibitions in going outside the contractual agreement, express or implied. This is so even when the shareholders also have an employment relationship in that they are working for the corporation and the unfair prejudice arises from what is in effect a wrongful dismissal.[112] Although the articles of association are generally construed like any other contract[113] the courts will forge beyond contract to achieve fairness by giving effect to the parties' extra-contractual expectations. It may well be that judicial boldness in defending minority shareholder rights is implicitly driven by the proprietary nature of shareholder interests; property rights are more robustly defended than contractual rights in the sense that they cannot be fully vindicated by a remedy in

[107] ibid 721, 722.

[108] A complainant may apply for relief on grounds that the affairs of the corporation are being conducted in a manner 'that is oppressive or unfairly prejudicial to or that unfairly disregards the interests of any security holder, creditor, director or officer' (s 241).

[109] *Deluce v Air Canada* (1999) 98 DLR (4th) 509.

[110] *BCE Inc* (n 60) 565.

[111] Fudge (n 95) 53.

[112] *Deluce v Air Canada* (1999) 98 DLR (4th) 509.

[113] Companies Act 2006 s 33(1): the provisions of a company's constitution bind the company and its members to the same extent as if there were covenants on the part of the company and of each member to observe those provisions.

damages.[114] This presents no great challenge for our argument.[115] Although it is not customary for courts to think about non-shareholder rights as property rights, in fact the Redundancy Payments Act 1965 and the Industrial Relations Act 1971 were introduced to defend workers' proprietary interest in their jobs by challenging the validity of the dismissal itself as an expropriation rather than simply leaving the dismissed employee to a contractual remedy in damages.[116]

For these reasons we suggest that the discourse of corporate law may be beneficial in defining the legal claims of workers, by suggesting a modified analytical framework within which economic dismissals which defeat the legitimate expectations of employees may be impugned on the basis of legal principles that lie outside the law of contract. In defining such legitimate expectations we view workers as being in an analogous position to minority shareholders who are vulnerable to exploitation and expropriation.[117] Similarly to minority shareholders, the expectations of both worker and employer are in constant flux, are often informal and are never fully reflected in explicit or implicit contracts. If it is the case that a stakeholder may acquire a reasonable expectation that the directors will safeguard their economic interests by not placing those interests needlessly at risk, this suggests an approach by which employee claims may be understood as reasonable expectations based upon reliance on explicit or implicit promises made on behalf of the firm.[118] Such a reasonable expectation would not amount simply to what the employee would like in an ideal world, such as a secure job for life; it refers instead to what the employee has been led to expect taking all the relevant circumstances into account. Guidance as to the relevant factors may be drawn from the criteria set out in *BCE* as being pertinent in ascertaining the reasonable expectations of stakeholders: the size, nature and structure of the corporation; the relationship between the parties; past practice; whether the stakeholder has taken any preventative steps to mitigate the harm suffered; representations and agreements between the parties and fairness as between all stakeholders.[119] It is a matter of assessing the evidence in each case

[114] Indeed the Australian High Court has stated that the reason why minority shareholders will be protected from being frozen out by the majority is because forcing out the minority would amount to expropriation: *Gambotto v WCP Ltd* (1995) 182 CLR 432.

[115] W Njoya, *Property in Work: The Employment Relationship in the Anglo-American Firm* (Aldershot, Ashgate, 2007).

[116] Howe (n 22).

[117] JW Singer, 'The Reliance Interest in Property' (1988) 40 *Stanford Law Review* 611; see also M Blair, *Ownership and Control: Rethinking Corporate Governance for the Twenty-First Century* (Washington DC, Brookings Institute, 1995).

[118] This approach is reflected in the Canadian Supreme Court decision in *BCE Inc (Arrangement relatif d) (Re)* [2008] 3 SCR 560 where the Court recognizes that 'boards can exercise their business judgment about what interests are relevant to the "best interests of the corporation" as they see it (including stakeholders with potentially relevant "reasonable expectations" about board decisions), and consider those interests in fulfilling their fiduciary duty': E Iacobucci, 'Indeterminacy and the Canadian Supreme Court's Approach to Corporate Fiduciary Duties' (2009) 48 *Canadian Business Law Journal* 232, 244.

[119] *BCE Inc* (n 60) para 96–100, assessing the reasonable expectations of creditors in language which is highly pertinent to the issues which it is suggested here would be relevant in assessing employees' claims.

based on the relationship and conduct between the parties as well as commercial and market realities. If this seems likely to entail too much uncertainty, it should be remembered that it would amount to no more than the courts are already accustomed to deliberating in the context of MTC, strengthened by the principle that the deliberation need not shy away from the zone of dismissal.

VIII. Conclusion: Efficiency and the Law of the Business Enterprise

This chapter has examined the interplay between the regulatory goals of labour law and the law of the business enterprise, an interaction that is most dynamic when decision-making during business reorganization affects labour interests. This was presented as an opportunity to explore alternative ways of defining workers' entitlements and expressing the normative demands of employment protection. The chapter undertook such an exploration by focusing on unfair dismissal rights during economic dismissals and the entitlement of employees to have their interests taken into account by directors in exercise of their fiduciary duties. The discussion began by arguing that deference to managerial prerogative reflects a broader non-interventionist judicial stance and the assumption that only the lightest regulation of business reorganization, if any, is appropriate in order to ensure flexible adaptation to rapidly changing global economic conditions. This is assumed to be the only rational response to prevailing financial constraints, so that minimizing labour costs whenever possible is seen as the only possible response when faced with overwhelming pressure to maximize shareholder returns. As suggested by Mayer, this is a form of economic determinism that assumes helplessness in the face of 'the market', and it must be determinedly resisted if effective policy responses to successive corporate crises are to be forged.[120]

An effective way for the law to respond to Mayer's challenge is by constructing the legal framework on a theory of the corporation as commons, which recognizes both the value as well as the limitations of neoclassical economic principles. Economic principles greatly advance our understanding of corporate law, but must not be uncritically institutionalized in the legal framework. The insistence that that markets cannot be improved upon as a mechanism for allocating resources, and that regulatory intervention must always be viewed as a misguided attempt to interfere with superior market forces cannot be relied upon

[120] As compellingly depicted by Mayer (n 1) 1: 'By eulogizing the merits of markets, the laws of economics apparently condemn us to control by forces that are both anonymous and beyond our reach, and restrict our attempts to pursue a better life. The world is, according to economics, what the markets make of it and none of us, not even for the most part governments, has the power to dispute their will.' Mayer argues that far from being hostage to market forces, we are able to influence and respond through tailored legal intervention.

as a basis for policy prescriptions.[121] As Deakin shows, sustainable productive and competitive corporations are incompatible with the automatic prioritization of shareholder value because the ideology of shareholder primacy bears no empirical relationship to the realities of team production and collective asset pooling that are observed in modern corporations. The implication for labour law is that while it is legitimate for law to promote flexibility and efficiency in market institutions, it does not follow that employment protection during economic dismissals is impossible to achieve or not worth pursuing.

In sum, institutional or organizational restructuring that proceeds at the expense of employment security is unsustainable in the long term. This at least partly explains the existence of income security protection such as redundancy payments and guarantee payments in insolvency. Fairness in dismissal during organizational restructuring is in turn intended to reinforce these measures. To build upon and strengthen that legal framework it is crucial to give effect to the legitimate expectations of employees. This will help to fill in the gaps in the existing legal framework created by unacceptably weak formulations of job security. In drawing upon corporate law to underpin the legitimate expectations of workers the autonomy of labour law as a discipline devoted to worker-protective goals such as job security must also be borne in mind. Labour law's autonomy requires that it should resist being transformed into an objective set of rules designed merely to 'balance' the interests of the worker with the goals of the employing enterprise. Yet autonomy as an independent juridical system also implies the ability and confidence to interact with those aspects of the law of the business enterprise which lend force to labour's own essential goals, in the ways demonstrated in this chapter.[122] Through this interaction, corporate law in turn acquires greater depth in its interpretation of enlightened shareholder value as a benchmark in promoting the long-term success of the corporation in the interests of all its stakeholders, preserving the corporation as a resource that will continue to drive growth and prosperity for society as a whole.

[121] J Kay, *The Truth About Markets: Why Some Nations Are Rich but Most Remain Poor* (London, Penguin Books, 2003).

[122] This methodology is derived from the observation of Davies and Freedland ((n 14) 25): 'We are used to prizing the autonomy of labour law from civil law principles. If, however, the personal scope of labour law is to extend into commercial relationships. … then labour law principles will often have to be blended with private and commercial law principles if an appropriate scheme of regulation is to be achieved. Having established its right to autonomy, labour law should regard itself as strong enough to mix on equal terms with other bodies of law.'

14

Conceptualizing the Employer as Fiduciary: Mission Impossible?

JILL MURRAY*

I. Introduction

This chapter aims to explicate the current interface between the common law of employment and the equitable concept of fiduciary obligation. By mapping fiduciary law onto a number of concepts, relationships and circumstances highlighted by modern employment law discourse and jurisprudence, the concept of the employer owing a fiduciary obligation to the employee is examined.

This enquiry may be seen as heretical in two ways. Insofar as the employment relationship has any fiduciary element at all, it has been traditionally identified as taking the form of an *employee's* fiduciary obligation to their *employer*. And any attempt to extend the operation of fiduciary principles beyond historically recognized categories smacks of the much-criticized 'craze' for confecting grounds for equitable remedies on the basis of loosely conceived injustices. Such an approach has met with the liveliest judicial and academic disapproval in Anglo-Australian equity.[1] As Viscount Simmonds put it, substantive law cannot be said to mean something it does not simply because we want it to.[2]

This chapter attempts to avoid doing this by utilizing accepted equitable principles and approaches to demonstrate that there may well be a sphere within which the employer should be required to forego self-interest in favour of

* Thanks to Professor Michael Bryan, Mary Gardiner and the editors for their comments on an earlier draft, and to Rose Gardiner Kennedy for her research assistance into Australian asbestos manufacture. I am solely responsible for the final content and all the remaining errors.

[1] AF Mason, 'The Place of Equity and Equitable Remedies in the Contemporary Common Law World' [1994] 110 *Law Quarterly Review* 238, 248; S Worthington, 'Fiduciaries: When Is Self-Denial Obligatory?' (1999) 58(3) *Cambridge Law Journall* 500; R Flannigan, 'The Boundaries of Fiduciary Accountability' (2004) *New Zealand Law Review* 215; P Birks, 'The Content of the Fiduciary Obligation' (2000) 34(1) *Israel Law Review* 3; *Breen v Williams* (hereinafter '*Breen v Williams*') [1996] HCA 57, (1996) 186 CLR 71; *Bristol & West Building Society v Mothew* (hereinafter '*Mothew*') [1996] EWCA Civ 533, [1998] Ch 1

[2] *Chapman v Chapman* [1954] UKHL 1, AC 429, 444

the employee. But it is recognized that this analysis raises questions of fact and degree which necessarily call for normative and other value judgements. Where appropriate and available, guidance is taken from the existing case law, particularly the way the competing economic interests of the employer and the employee are balanced.[3]

In making this argument, it is necessary to give concrete examples of ways in which the employer may be regarded as breaching a fiduciary obligation to the employee, a task which that condemnation as unprincipled, a mere listing of moral outrages.[4] However, some support can be gained from equity's insistence that a purist approach based on lofty principle is not appropriate in this field of law:[5] fiduciary law is grounded in its engagement with the factual circumstances of particular cases.

At the same time, it is not appropriate to proceed as if fiduciary law involves little more than the pragmatic application of remedies in individual cases in the absence of underpinning principle. On the contrary, the field is marked by detailed application of the enigmatic and occasionally contradictory fiduciary rules and a strong insistence on the need for the principled development of the law. The starting point of this article is therefore the principles and policies as equity, brought into alignment with contemporary labour law jurisprudence and discourse in order to explicate the possible fiduciary obligations of the employer.

II. The Concept of Fiduciary Obligation

The origins of the concept of the fiduciary lie in the institution of the trust, and the unique potential for opportunistic behaviour afforded to the legal owner of the trust property.[6] Prior to the evolution of equity's supervision of the trustee, neither the donor of the property nor the intended beneficiary was able to supervise the trustee's management of trust property—the donor was no longer the legal owner of the property, and the beneficiary might not even be aware of their beneficial interest in it. The common law offered no effective remedy for misuse of the property, nor any overarching mechanism to discourage treacherous behaviour by the trustee.

Equity developed rules to perform both these functions: it obliged trustees strictly to set aside self-interest to the extent required by the terms of the trust. Broadly, a trustee is not, in the absence of fully informed consent, to place themselves in a position where there was an actual or potential conflict between their personal interests or their duty to others in relation to their responsibilities

[3] M Freedland, *The Personal Employment Contract* (Oxford, Oxford University Press, 2003) 177.
[4] Worthington (n 1).
[5] *Harris v Digital Pulse* (2003) NSWCA 10, 56 NSWLR 298.
[6] See generally PD Finn, *Fiduciary Obligations* (The Law Book Company Ltd 1977) 1; S Worthington, *Equity*, 2nd edn (Oxford, Oxford University Press, 2006) 63–64.

under the terms of the trust. And the trustee is not to make any unauthorized profit from their position without the fully informed consent of the beneficiary.[7]

The trustee is the fiduciary par excellence: the foundational concept underpinning the trustee's obligations has been variously expressed as a 'duty of single-minded loyalty',[8] a requirement of 'disinterestedness',[9] 'self-denial'[10] and 'altruism.'[11] It is hard to disagree with Birks' observation that equity's fiduciary concept cannot be readily paraphrased.[12] Despite continuing attempts to clarify and unify the field, such as Finn's more recent focus on one party having a 'legitimate expectation' that the other will act in their interests,[13] Conaglen's view that our understanding of the concept is 'very confused' is apt.[14]

Over time, the fiduciary concept was extended to trustee-like relationships where equity found that the strict fiduciary obligations should also be enforced. The legal rules and principles underpinning this extension are difficult to state with precision—indeed, senior jurists have argued that the fiduciary concept cannot and should not be subject to precise definition.[15] To the extent that there is guidance as to the circumstances in which fiduciary obligations are imposed or arise, it can 'only be stated in the most general terms'[16] and the courts should not be constrained by 'verbal formulae'.[17]

Despite this reluctance to formulate a bright-line definition of fiduciary, there are several broad statements that continue to influence judicial decision-making in the field. Mason J's dissenting decision in the *Hospital Products* case remains the lodestone in Australian law,[18] and is frequently cited as authoritative in international jurisprudence:[19]

> The critical feature of these relationships is that the fiduciary undertakes or agrees to act for or on behalf of or in the interests of another person in the exercise of a power or discretion which will affect the interests of that other person in a legal or practical sense. The relationship between the parties is therefore one which gives the fiduciary a special opportunity to exercise the power or discretion to the detriment of that other person who is accordingly vulnerable to abuse by the fiduciary of his position. The expressions 'for', 'on behalf of' and 'in the interests of' signify that the

[7] *Boardman v Phipps* [1967] 2 AC 46.

[8] P Millett, 'Equity's Place in the Law of Commerce' [1998] 114 *Law Quarterly Review* 214, 217/18.

[9] Birks (n 1) 17.

[10] Worthington (n 1).

[11] Birks (n 1) 12.

[12] Birks (n 1).

[13] See eg *Gibson Motorsport Merchandise Pty Ltd v Forbes* [2006] FCAFC 44, [12], (2006) 149 FCR 569 (Finn J).

[14] M Conaglen, *Fiduciary Loyalty: Protecting the Due Performance of Non-Fiduciary Duties* (Oxford, Hart Publishing, 2010) v.

[15] *Breen v Williams* (1996) HCA 57, [22]

[16] *Hospital Products v United States Surgical Corporation* (hereafter *Hospital Products*)[1984] HCA 64, [37], (1984) 156 CLR 41.

[17] *Coomber v Coomber* (CA) [1911] 1 Ch 723, 728

[18] See eg *Concut v Worrell* [2000] HCA 64, [17], (2000) 176 ALR 693 and *Pilmer v Duke Group, Ltd* (hereinafter '*Pilmer v Duke*') [2001] HCA 31, [70]; 207 CLR 165.

[19] See eg *Ranson v Customer Services plc* [2012] EWCA Civ 841, [25].

> fiduciary acts in a 'representative' character in the exercise of his responsibility, to adopt an expression used by the Court of Appeal.[20]

Millett J's definition, with its subtle differences to the Australian text quoted above, has been similarly influential:

> A fiduciary is someone who has undertaken to act for or on behalf of another in a particular matter in circumstances which give rise to a relationship of trust and confidence. The distinguishing obligation of a fiduciary is the obligation of loyalty. The principal is entitled to the single-minded loyalty of his fiduciary.[21]

We will see that these broad definitions are augmented by a number of rules, qualifications and explications. One is relevant to this general introduction: it is now more correct to refer to the ascription of fiduciary obligations, rather than to speak of 'the fiduciary' or an all-encompassing fiduciary relationship. This is because, generally speaking, people are not fiduciaries for all purposes.[22] The question today is whether or not a person's role may contain a *sphere of responsibility* within which that person must not permit a conflict to arise between their interests and those of their principal.

As Lord Millett points out, there are different kinds of fiduciary obligations—those arising from relationships of trust and confidence, those arising on the receipt of confidential information, and those arising from relations of dependence.[23] All three are potentially relevant to the employment relationship, but the focus of this paper will be in fiduciary obligations that arise in circumstances of trust and confidence.

III. The Fiduciary Obligations of the Employee

Equity has obviated some of the need to apply external definitions to the case-by-case determination of claims by establishing a catalogue of relationships that are presumed to give rise to fiduciary obligations.[24] The recognized categories capture archetypal or structural features of particular relationships on the basis of widely accepted legal narratives about, inter alia, the nature of power and vulnerability within those relationships. The modern view is that inclusion on this list simply represents an initial taxonomic step, as the character and scope

[20] *Hospital Products* (n 16) [68], endorsed *Pilmer v Duke* (n 18) [70].

[21] *Mothew* (n 1) 18.

[22] *Breen v Williams* (n 1) 82; *NZ Netherlands Societies 'Oranje' Inc v Kuys* [1973] UKPC 7, (1973) 1 WLR 1126, 2 All ER 1222, 1229–30; see generally M Conaglen, *Fiduciary Loyalty Protecting the Due Performance of Non-Fiduciary Duties* (Oxford, Hart Publishing, 2010).

[23] Millett (n 8).

[24] *Hospital Products* (n 16) [28]; *News Ltd v Australian Rugby Football League* [1996] FCA 870; (1996) 64 FCR 410.

of fiduciary obligations can only be determined having close regard to the facts of each case.[25] The list of recognized categories is not closed,[26] and the content of the list has been subject to some evolutionary change.[27]

At some point in the twentieth century, the relationship between employee and employer consolidated its position on the list of accepted fiduciary relationships.[28] (Lord Millett points out that a 1921 Victorian Supreme Court decision on a servant's obligations to his master pre-dated the inclusion of employee–employer in the catalogue of recognized fiduciary relationships.[29]) It is the employee who is thus identified as presumptively owing fiduciary obligations to the employer, as the trustee does to the beneficiary, the director to the company, the lawyer to client, agent to principal, and so on. [30]

This categorization of the employment relationship as 'normally fiduciary' led to the relatively routine ascription of fiduciary obligations to the employee: it is 'clear beyond question that an employee is in a fiduciary relationship with his employer'.[31] A relevant conflict between duty and interest attracting equity's remedies was a commonplace once certain facts were ascertained:

> Were it not for one feature [the employer had claimed exemplary damages for the employees' fiduciary breach], this case would be unremarkable amongst the many of its type which come into the Equity court: employees resolve to go into business for themselves in competition with their employer; they decide to give their new venture a head start by remaining in employment and diverting to themselves their employer's business opportunities until they are economically secure enough to declare their hands, throw up their employment and compete openly. No one doubts that the employees have breached their contractual and fiduciary duties of loyalty to their employer and that they are liable for damages, an account of profits or equitable compensation.[32]

The jurisprudence frequently specifies that it is senior employees who are more likely to owe fiduciary obligations to their employers.[33] Brodie has criticized this notion as legally flawed and 'hugely problematic' as a tool for distinguishing between employees for the purposes of fiduciary analysis. The concept is none-

[25] *Mothew* (n 1); *Breen v Williams* (n 1) 82.

[26] *Tufton v Sperni* [1952] 2 TLR 439, referred to *Hospital Products* (n 16) [67].

[27] J Edelman, 'When Do Fiduciary Obligations Arise?' (2010) 126 *Law Quarterly Review* 302, 304, 316.

[28] *Reading v Attorney General* [1951] UKHL 1, 4, (1951) AC 507; *Concut v Worrell* [2000] HCA 64; 75 ALJR 312, [17]; JRF Lehane, 'Fiduciaries in a Commercial Context' in PD Finn (ed), *Essays in Equity* (The Law Book Company, 1985) 96.

[29] Millett (n 8). Jurisprudence on the servant's fiduciary obligations as agent dates from the 18th century: GHL Fridman, *Fridman's Law of Agency*, 5th edn (London, Butterworths, 1983) 6.

[30] *Hospital Products* (n 16) [28], [68]

[31] *Stoelwinder v Southern Health* [2001] FCA 115, [39].

[32] *Digital Pulse Pty Ltd v Christopher Harris and Others* (2002) [2002] NSWSC 33, [1]166 FLR 421.

[33] *Collidge v Freeport* [2007] EWHC 1216 (QB); *Main v Able Tours Pty Ltd* [2010] WASCA 59, [104]. M Freedland, 'High Trust, Pensions and the Contract of Employment' (1984) 13(1) *Industrial Law Journal* 24; R Flannigan, 'The Fiduciary Obligation' (1989) *Oxford Journal of Legal Studies* 9(3) 285; M Freedland and N Kountouris, *The Legal Construction of Personal Work Relations* (Oxford, Oxford University Press, 2011) 190.

theless tenacious and continues to be supported on the grounds that more senior employees have greater access to the inner workings of the business and a commensurately greater capacity to harm the employer or take inappropriate advantage of their position.[34] Whether this remains the case in the age of Wikileaks and Edward Snowden is debatable.

However, the employment relationship has now shifted to the very periphery of the list of recognized categories of fiduciary and possibly even beyond it altogether.[35] A new orthodoxy has emerged, or is emerging, based on the view that the employment relationship 'does not necessarily' give rise to fiduciary obligations based on the authoritative decision of Elias J in *Nottingham University v Fishel*:[36]

> The hallmark of a fiduciary obligation in an employment context is therefore a particular contractual obligation which requires the law to impose a duty positively to act in the best interests of the employer.[37]

Elias J notes that 'the essence of the employment relationship is not typically fiduciary at all'[38] because the contract of employment is not designed to ensure that the employee acts in the exclusive interests of the employer in a general sense, and the employer is able to negotiate contract terms which provide it with the capacity adequately to supervise and control the employee's discretionary acts.[39] Thus Dr Fishel could not be held to account as fiduciary in relation to work he was not contracted to do for the University. The employee's implied contractual duty of fidelity, derived from the contract of employment's genesis in the master–servant relationship,[40] must not be equated with the higher equitable standard of fiduciary obligation.

Does this mean that each claimed breach of employee fiduciary obligation is to be determined de novo, as if the employment relationship is no longer a category recognized by equity? The answer appears to be that it does not: the former clear-cut inclusion of the employee on the list of recognized fiduciaries still points towards a well-recognized pathway for the ascription of fiduciary responsibilities to the employer in certain common circumstances, provided post-*Fishel* that these can be tied to an aspect of the work for which the employee has been contracted. Contemporary decisions disclose that while the employment relationship may not be 'designed' to ensure that the employee subjugates

[34] *VUT v Wilson and Others* [2004] VSC 33, [145],(2004)60 IPR 392.

[35] But see eg *Hodgson v Amcor Ltd* [2012] VSC 94, [1346].

[36] *Nottingham University v Fishel* (2000) EWHC 221 (QB), [2001] RPC 2 (hereinafter '*Fishel*'), *Samsung Semiconductor Europe v Docherty* [2011] CSOH, 2011 SLT 806: *Lonmar Global Risks Ltd v West* (hereafter *Lonmar Global Risks*) [2010] EWHC 2878 (QB); *University of Western Australia v Gray* (2008) FCA 448.

[37] *Lonmar Global Risks* (n 36) [152].

[38] *Fishel* (n 36) [90].

[39] ibid.

[40] O Kahn-Freund, 'Blackstone's Neglected Child: The Contract of Employment' (1977) 93 *Law Quarterly Review* 508; S Deakin and F Wilkinson, *The Law of the Labour Market: Industrialisation, Employment and Legal Evolution* (Oxford, Oxford University Press, 2005) 17 et seq.

self-interest in favour of the employer as Elias J argues, employees continue to be held to account as fiduciaries where the employee engaged in actions which the courts are prepared to recognizes as breaches of the fiduciary obligation.[41] This is evident in the recent Scottish decision in *Samsung Semiconductor v Docherty* (*Samsung*),[42] which follows Elias J's approach to the letter, yet reaches a conclusion which maintains strong continuities with the historical flow of decisions holding defaulting employees to account for illegitimately competing with their employer.

IV. The Rationales for the Employee's Fiduciary Obligations

In what ways, then, and to what extent do the principles and rules of equity shape these decisions?

First, as noted above, while the *Fishel* decision and those adopting its logic have firmly disapproved of any automatic ascription of a general fiduciary obligation owed by the employee to the employer, equity does continue to recognize the employee–employer relationship as a known type. One ramification of this is that a full argument about all of the elements of the fiduciary definition is not always necessary in holding employees to account as fiduciaries: in particular, little is said about the employee's actual or inferred undertaking to act in the interests of the employer.

Like most elements of the fiduciary definition, the voluntary undertaking aspect is the subject of controversy. Some are adamant that no fiduciary obligation can be imposed in the absence of a voluntary undertaking, while others conceive the obligation as imposed by law in circumstances where it is necessary to meet equitable principles to do so.[43] A reading of the Australian and English cases shows that the employee's undertaking to act in the employer's interests is routinely imputed in the absence of explicit undertaking.[44] In *Samsung* the court speaks of fiduciary obligations 'arising out of the relationship between the parties' even where there had been no explicit reference to fiduciary obligations in the contract negotiations.[45]

It seems that the employee's implied contractual duty of fidelity may act as a kind of scaffolding upon which the employee's fiduciary duty can be erected. For many years, the employee's fiduciary duty was closely associated with, and

[41] Perhaps particularly so in Australia, where 'the fiduciary character of the employee is well-recognised', *Charltons CIC Pty Ltd v Fitzgerald* [2013] NSWSC 350, [40].

[42] *Buitendag v Ravensthorpe Nickel Operations Pty Ltd* [2012] WASC 425.

[43] See A Duggan, 'Contracts, Fiduciaries and the Primacy of the Deal', in E Bant and M Harding (eds), *Exploring Private Law* (Cambridge, Cambridge University Press, 2010) 275.

[44] eg *Harris v Digital Pulse* [2003] NSWCA 10, [43].

[45] *Samsung Semiconductor v Docherty* [2011] CSOH 32, [30].

even conflated, with the employee's contractual duty of fidelity.[46] As recently as 2002 the NSW Supreme Court held that:

> An employee has a duty to act in the interests of the employer with good faith and fidelity. The duty is implied in every contract of employment. … In addition, *the duty* is imposed upon every employee by the law of fiduciaries, the relationship of employer and employee being recognized as a paradigmatic fiduciary relationship.[47]

This eliding of contractual and equitable obligation is juridically incorrect, as decisively explained by Elias J in *Fishel*,[48] but the two concepts remain intertwined.

The *Fishel* decision itself offers an example of the kind of shorthand reckoning available because of this close interconnection between common law and equity. The facts of the case need not be repeated in full here. It will be recalled that Dr Fishel did not have to set aside self-interest in relation to his own outside work, but he was required to account as fiduciary for his role in deploying other University assets in those ventures. Dr Fishel instructed University employees under his supervision to work in his overseas ventures and received payment for this service from these international clinics. Elias J said this aspect of the case had to be 'viewed in a different light', because Dr Fishel was under a contractual obligation (the details of which were not discussed) to manage these staff in the interests of the University, whereas he was under no contractual duty to work solely for the University in relation to his own labour.[49]

This rationale takes us to the point at which Dr Fishel can be found to have breached his contract of employment's implied term of fidelity, and probably other express terms as well. But what exactly is the rationale for the further step that these actions were a breach of fiduciary obligation to the University? Elias J makes clear that there can be no employee fiduciary obligation without a contractual hook on which to hang a breach; here, apparently, the implied contractual obligation of fidelity is utilized. However, the existence of the implied term cannot of itself be a rationale for the imposition of fiduciary obligations, otherwise every employee would be subject to fiduciary obligations for this reason. It is not entirely clear from this decision where the line between contractual implied term and fiduciary obligation is drawn and what it is about the circumstances that justify equity's intervention in this way.

Of course, reasoning aside, the finding of breach of fiduciary obligation served the practical purposes of giving the University an otherwise unavailable avenue to seek a remedy: no common law damages were available for the breach of the contract's implied term of fidelity because the University suffered no loss, but equity could order an account of profits for the breach of fiduciary obligation.

The second point drawn from the jurisprudence is that equity, in construing

[46] *Robb v Green* [1895] 2 QB 315, 319; *Prebble v Reeves* [1910] VLR 97.
[47] *Digital Pulse Pty Ltd v Harris and Others* [2002] NSWSC 33 (my emphasis).
[48] *Fishel* (n 36) [96].
[49] ibid [115].

the employer's vulnerability to the employee, does not limit its focus to the employer in the narrow sense of the contractual entity which has engaged the employee. Instead, Equity tends to envision a broader sphere with more extensive metaphorical, geographic and temporal boundaries than the contract itself: an employee's fiduciary obligations are conceived of as applying to the employer's business interests (present and future) more generally.[50] A useful example of this kind of elaboration is found in *Digital Pulse*:

> The obligations imposed by the duty are not coterminous with the employee's normal working hours: they govern all the activities of the employee, whenever undertaken, which are *within the sphere of the employer's business operations and which could materially affect the employer's business interests.* Whether a particular activity could materially affect the employer's business interests is a question of fact and degree.[51]

The concepts used here—the 'employer's business operations' and the 'employer's business interests'—are not synonymous with the legal identity of the employing entity and almost certainly extend beyond the scope of any individual job within the employer's business. It is possible that even senior employees may be unaware of the full scope of their employer's 'business operations … and interests' to which equity may require their highest fidelity. The sphere of fiduciary responsibility, where it exists, is thus a fluid realm, not bounded by time, into which a vast range of employee actions detrimental to the employer may be found to have strayed. Great flexibility is therefore available for the courts to monitor and police employee behaviour in order to protect the vulnerable employer's interests as equity has chosen to define them.

In contrast to these expansionary elements in the principles of fiduciary law, the courts exhibit a great deal of caution in holding employees to account to the fiduciary standard. One reason for this is the long-standing view that not every act of the fiduciary is subject to the fiduciary obligation;[52] and not every breach of fiduciary obligation calls for the intervention of equity.[53] A more significant constraint is imposed by competing policy objectives: the employment fiduciary cases, and those dealing with the contractual implied duty of fidelity, walk a fine line between the Scylla of condoning employee treachery against the employer and the Charybdis of stifling freedom of contract, autonomy and entrepreneurship in economic affairs, to adopt the language of Lord Greene MR.[54] Indeed, even where the employee has been held to breach a fiduciary obligation, the employee's liability may be reduced having regard to the employee's entrepre-

[50] Finn (n 6) 266 et seq includes a duty not to 'inflict actual harm on an employer's business' in his list of eight fiduciary obligations of good faith.

[51] *Digital Pulse Pty Ltd v Christopher Harris and Others* [2002] NSWSC 33, [20]– [21] (my emphasis). In *Hivac*, the court spoke of the need to protect 'the employer's business' (178); in *Lamb v Evans* [1892] 1 Ch 218 the fiduciary duty was not to use materials gained in employment against the 'interests of the employer' (266).

[52] *Breen v Williams* (n 1) 82.

[53] *In Re Coomber* [1911] 1 Ch 723, 728–29; LS Sealy, 'Fiduciary Relationships' [1962] *Cambridge Law Journal* 69.

[54] *Hivac Ltd v Park Royal Scientific Instruments Ltd and Others* [1946] 1 Ch 169, 178.

neurial or professional skill and effort where this is relevant to a profit arising from the breach.[55] Equity's insistence that it should not impose fiduciary obligations in relationships between commercial parties[56] and those at arm's length is another sign of the influence of a normative outlook based on liberal market values. [57]

Equity thus demarcates legitimate from illegitimate competitive assaults on the employer.[58] The reason for this is not that the employer's interests are construed narrowly, or that the employee is somehow a second-class fiduciary who can get away with breaches of trust; rather, the logic which constructs the employer as vulnerable supports a view of the employee as a legitimate market actor in his/her own right requiring equity to weigh carefully the competing economic interests.

The emphasis on the terms of the contract, crystallized in the *Fishel* decision, accords with this normative vision of the market inhabited by freely contracting parties. Employees may be required to subjugate their interests to their employer's, but only in relation to the job they have contracted to do. Both parties are regarded as free to contract accordingly.

V. The Employer as Fiduciary

A. Overview

On the face of it, it is difficult to view the employer as owing a fiduciary obligation to the employee. Depending on one's theoretical outlook, employment in a capitalist economy necessarily involves exploitation, or at the least gives rise to distinct pluralist interests mediated through the common law and statute. The employment relationship is often seen as a creature of contract and, according to classical contract theory and much common law jurisprudence, this invites the conclusion that the parties have consciously determined an agreed division of risk, power and discretion between them, augmented by the judge-made implied terms specific to the employment relationship. On this view, there is no need or room for equity to supervise abuses of discretionary power within the relationship: employees may be presumed to be structurally aware of their contractual vulnerability in a way the beneficiary to a trust could never be.

A similar conclusion seems inevitable if we adopt Finn's expectation analysis. While many would accept that an employer has a legitimate expectation that

[55] *Warman International v Dwyer* [1995] HCA 18, [33]; (1995) 182 CLR 544; *Boardman v Phipps* [1996] UKHL 2, [1967] 2 AC 46, 19.

[56] Criticized as a 'red herring' given the range of commercial relationships within which fiduciary obligations are routinely found. JRF Lehane, in Finn (n 6) 104.

[57] *Henry v Walker* (1958) 100 CLR 342, [15]; *Hospital Products* (n 16) 235, Millett (n 8) 217–18.

[58] See eg *Ranson v Customer Systems PLC* [2012] EWCA Civ 841, [19].

its employees will not undermine the integrity of the employing enterprise or make hidden profits out of their jobs, it is counterintuitive to expect that an employer was under an equivalent obligation to their employees' interests first in any general sense. When an employer suggests a change in a worker's pay-rate, for example, the common view would be that employees should expect that the employer's decision was shaped by self-interest. And an enterprise with more than one employee raises the question of how the utmost loyalty could in practice be owed by the employer to each and every member of the staff.

Further, the contract of employment does not place an obligation of loyalty on the employer: there is no contractual equivalent for the employer of the employee's contractual duty of fidelity. The implied contractual term which requires both parties to a contract of employment not to act in a way that is likely to destroy or seriously damage the relationship of trust and confidence between the employer and employee (abbreviated here to the implied term of mutual trust and confidence)[59] does not perform this function.[60] (In Australian law, the High Court is yet to affirm the term's existence.[61]) There is an a misleading coincidence of language here—the contractual term's reference to a relationship of trust and confidence, and the language of equity about relationships of trust and confidence that give rise to fiduciary obligations.[62] In fact, the two concepts are distinct.

Although the implied term of mutual trust and confidence is associated with a duty to act in good faith, and one facet of the fiduciary obligation is a requirement to act in good faith, good faith is not the essence of the fiduciary concept, as we have seen. It cannot be equated with an obligation of loyalty,[63] and thus fiduciary duties may be breached in the absence of bad faith.[64] The essence of the implied term of mutual trust and confidence is that it is directed towards 'the proper functioning of the contract': it requires a balancing of interests where discretionary power is available under the terms of the contract. While this balancing must be done in good faith, the contractual duty of good faith is narrower than that of the 'unique' fiduciary obligation.[65]

The same conclusion is reached through different reasoning by Lewison LJ, who adopts a more reductive argument against the idea that the implied contractual term gives rise to fiduciary obligations. Because the term of mutual trust and confidence is a default term in all employment contracts, and because all

[59] *Malik and Mahmud v Bank of Credit and Commerce International* (SA) (*Malik*) [1997] UKHL 23; [1998] AC 20.

[60] *Fishel* (n 36) [96].

[61] A majority of the Full Federal Court held the term to exist in *Commonwealth Bank of Australia v Barker* [2013] FCAFC 83 and leave has been granted to appeal this decision to the High Court.

[62] *Neary v Dean of Westminster* [1999] IRLR 288.

[63] *Fishel* (n 36) [92].

[64] *Chan v Zacharia* [1984] HCA 36, (1984) 154 CLR 178; *Boardman v Phipps* [1996] UKHL 2, [1967] 2 AC 46.

[65] *Fishel* (n 36) [90]; R Nolan and M Conaglen, 'Good Faith: What Does it Mean for Fiduciaries?' in Bant and Harding (eds) (n 43) 319.

employees are not fiduciaries, it cannot be correct that the implied term supports the ascription of fiduciary obligations.[66]

Brodie goes a step further and argues that the existence of the implied term of mutual trust and confidence *precludes* the existence of any fiduciary obligation on the employer.[67] Certainly it has been held by one leading jurist that the capacity to have regard to one's own interests is an 'over-whelming obstacle' to a finding that fiduciary obligations also exist.[68] However, it is surely correct that the right to act self-interestedly in the performance of the contract is 'not inconsistent with more limited fiduciary duties' if it can be shown that there is a coexisting obligation to favour the interests of the other party within this more limited field.[69] As we have seen, the employee's contractual duty of loyalty is not absolute and so the employee has some room for self-interest (eg by planning a new business while still employed),[70] yet at a certain point fiduciary obligations are held to exist despite this capacity for lawful competition with the employer.

A reasoned case can be made for the employer as fiduciary, based on the ways in which the employment relationship is treated by orthodox equitable principles. As we have seen, the relationship is a recognizable type from which generalizations can be derived, which suggests that equity is in a position to recognize structural features of the relationship relevant to the fiduciary concept. As shown above, although the status of employee as presumptive fiduciary is no longer the starting premise of equity's analysis, elements of the older, generalized approach remain important, particularly in relation to the issue of the undertaking to act in the other party's interests. Further, equity accepts that a fiduciary is not a fiduciary for all purposes: as argued above, the employee's fiduciary obligation largely survives in its traditional form within a relationship that is predominantly governed by the common law and statute and within which the employee has no over-arching responsibilities to put the interests of the 'vulnerable' employer first. This means that all the factors considered above as pointing to the employer as not owing a fiduciary obligation to the employee may be valid, yet there still may exist some sphere within which it can be argued the employer must prefer the interests of the employee. Although this argument suggests that the employer may owe fiduciary duties to more than one employee, equity allows the fiduciary concept to extend to circumstances of this kind.[71]

Finally, one of the key arguments against the concept of the employee's fiduciary obligation is based on a view of contract law which may no longer predominate in relation to the contract of employment: in particular, it is difficult to exclude fiduciary obligations on the grounds that had the employee wanted

[66] *Ranson v Customer Services plc* [2012] EWCA Civ 841, [40].

[67] D Brodie, 'The Employment Relationship and Fiduciary Obligations' (2012) 16 *Edinburgh Law Review*, 198, 209.

[68] *Hospital Products* (n 16). This aspect of Mason J's decision has not been explicitly endorsed by the High Court.

[69] *News Ltd v Australian Rugby Union Football League* [1996] FCA 870, [134].

[70] *Robb v Green* [1895] 2 QB 1, 15.

[71] *Kelly v Cooper Associates* (1992) UKPC 30, [1993] AC 205.

to protect themselves from employer discretionary power he/she would have shaped the contract accordingly, when elsewhere the law is inclined to have regard to imbalances of power when construing contractual terms governing the employment relationship.[72]

B. The Outer Limits of Employer Autonomy

It will be recalled that in certain circumstances, equity imposes fiduciary obligations to protect the realm of the employer's business and its interest broadly defined in jurisprudence that is strongly influenced by liberal principles of the free market. On this worldview, economic actors are autonomous, self-interested and mobile, and it will be recalled that both the common law and equity balance out the competing market interests of workers and employers even within the sphere of fiduciary responsibility. In drawing the line between legitimate and illegitimate competition equity recognizes the employee as an autonomous, self-interested and mobile economic actor in his/her own right. It is this aspect of existing equitable principle that provides the foundation for an argument for the employer's fiduciary obligation to the employee.

The essence of the contract of employment is that it is a contract for personal service through which the employer gains access to the embodied labour of the employee. Whatever the contractual terms, however narrowly focused upon a particular set of tasks it may be, the employer always gains practical access to all of the worker's skills, knowledge, technical abilities, personal attributes, and other human and social capital well captured in the notion of capabilities.[73] The employer's access to this bundle of assets comprising the employee's economic being is for the limited purpose of the performance of that particular contract, yet the contract provides great discretionary power to affect the 'legal and practical' interests of the worker far beyond that contract's terms. Employees are unable to monitor all the potential employer incursions into the integrity of their economic being, and the circumstances ensure that the employer is subject to the same kind of temptation faced by the trustee to misapply or make unauthorized use of its special access. These structural circumstances, taken as a whole, support the imposition of limited fiduciary duties on the employer and explain why the various common law remedies applied are either insufficient or inappropriate.

What can be said to stand for the employer's undertaking to act in the interests of the employee in relation to this sphere? Normally there will be no conscious or actual undertaking, because of the counterintuitive factors discussed above,

[72] AL Bogg, 'Sham Self-Employment in the Supreme Court' (2012) 41(3) *Industrial Law Journal* 328; *Autoclenz Ltd v Belcher and Others* (hereinafter '*Autoclenz*') [2011] UKSC 41, [2011] 4 All ER 745.

[73] A Sen, *Development as Freedom* (Oxford, Oxford University Press, 2001); Deakin and Wilkinson (n 40); K Stone, *From Widgets to Digits: Employment Regulation for the Changing Workplace* (Cambridge, Cambridge University Press, 2004).

but this is not required by equity as we saw in the discussion of the employee's undertaking above. An undertaking would only be imputed to the employer based on a structural understanding of the relationship, grounded in the facts of the particular case, where the requirement of loyalty was seen as normatively essential in all the circumstances. How this normative vision might be constructed is considered in the following section.

Before turning to an analysis of labour law discourse which bears on the normative task proposed here, two other possible avenues for the ascription of fiduciary obligations to the employer will be briefly outlined. The first is the conception of the employment relationship as a form of co-operative partnership.

One of Brodie's arguments against the employment relationship as fiduciary (chiefly in relation to the employee) is that the implied contractual term of mutual trust and confidence may exclude fiduciary duties because relationships of reciprocity are less likely to be found to be fiduciary in character.[74] However, partnership[75] and joint venture[76] sometimes give rise to fiduciary obligations, despite their 'horizontal' character.[77] In the latter case, where there is 'an association of persons for the purposes of … [an undertaking] for mutual profit, with each participant usually (but not necessarily) contributing money, property or skill'[78] each party owes a fiduciary obligation to the other in respect of the mutual enterprise.[79]

Is it possible that employment could be conceived of as taking a relevantly co-operative form? Certainly the language of partnership was in the late twentieth century increasingly applied to employment relationships as noted in Napier's seminal article in the 1970s, in which he described shifting common law perceptions of the employment relationship away from a 'conflict and subordination' model towards one more focused on 'common interest and partnership'.[80] Contractually, the employee has long been held to be required to co-operate with the smooth running of the enterprise, and the implied term of mutual trust and confidence may place obligations of co-operation on the employer in terms of the performance of the contract. These developments were echoed in public policy during the 1990s, with the then government's flagship 'Partnership at Work', and employee share ownership[81] and mutualization of state enterprises are currently undergoing something of a revival in the UK. It is too early to say what the new status of 'employee shareholder' might mean in this context.[82]

[74] Brodie (n 67) 209.

[75] *Helmore v Smith* (1886) 35 Ch D 436 CA, 444.

[76] *United Dominions Corporation Ltd v Brian Pty Ltd* [1985] HCA 49; (1985) 157 CLR 1.

[77] *News Ltd and Others v Australian Rugby Football League Ltd and Others* [1996] FCA 870

[78] *United Dominions* (n 76), 10–11.

[79] But this does not extend to a duty to inform colleagues of the benefits of joining a workers' co-operative: *Morris v Hanley* [2003] NSWSC 523.

[80] B Napier, 'Judicial Attitudes towards the Employment Relationship: Some Recent Developments' (1977) 6 *Industrial Law Journal* 1, 17

[81] Deakin and Wilkinson (n 40) 326 et seq.

[82] J Prassl, 'Employee Shareholder "Status": Dismantling the Contract of Employment' (2013) *Industrial Law Journal* 42(4) 307.

However, none of these developments amounts to the imposition of a requirement for subjugation of self-interest by the employer: on the contrary, the common law implied term of co-operation has tended to operate in the service of the interests of the employer.[83] Napier himself notes that the developments he observed should not be overstated. And the concepts of 'third way' politics[84], including partnership at work, are now regarded with a more jaundiced eye.[85] While there are many adherents to the various schools of human resource management that advocate an essentially unitarist view of the workplace, employees and their employer have at least in some respects differing interests. It is unlikely even in circumstances where employees invest capital in an employing entity that there is a total excision of these differing interests. The reality is that the political policies advocating a partnership approach to employment relations rarely rise above the level of rhetoric, and the key levers of control and subservience remain critical to employment relations under the veneer of unitarism.[86]

A second possibility is that the ad hoc, fact-based approach may disclose fiduciary obligations. Whether such a relationship exists will turn upon a case-by-case analysis of the interpersonal dynamics between the employer and employee, or the two persons engaged in the exchange of labour whatever their legal status. That the courts are open to construing employment in such terms is evident in the following decision of Nourse LJ, which dealt with an employee who mortgaged her house to help her financially struggling employer. The court noted that the relationship between an employer and a junior employee

> is clearly one which is capable of developing into a relationship of trust and confidence with the attendant risk of abuse, particularly in the case of a very small business where the parties are accustomed to work closely together.[87]

Some factual scenarios in settled labour law cases disclose key trust-like features. In an Australian case of tragic dimensions, 16-year-old James Annetts sought work at an outback cattle station. His mother told the station manager that she would only agree if the employer guaranteed the safety of her son. The employer agreed, but in breach of these undertakings posted the boy to work alone in charge of a remote cattle station. James died of thirst and exhaustion after getting lost in the desert. Hayne J noted that James had been 'entrusted' to the company in response to its 'solemn assurance' of his safety, and that because of the employer's breach of this assurance James had died an 'horrific death'.[88]

In particular cases such as this we see something approaching an express

[83] *Secretary of State for Employment v ASLEF* (No 2) [1972] ICR 19, CA; *Adami v Maison de Luxe Ltd* [1924] HCA 45; (1924) 35 CLR 143.

[84] H Collins, 'Regulating the Employment Relationship for Competitiveness' (2001) 30(1) *Industrial Law Journal* 17.

[85] See eg Deakin and Wilkinson (n 40) 327 et seq.

[86] ibid 102 et seq.

[87] *Credit Lyonnais Bank Nederland NV v Burch* [1996] EWCA Civ 1292, (1997) P&CR 384, 391.

[88] *Tame v NSW; Annetts v Australian Stations Pty Ltd* [2002] HCA 35, [37], [239], [361].

undertaking to withhold self-interest in relation to James' employment, the requisite capacity to alter the interests of James legally and practically, James' vulnerability to this discretion, and his utter inability to supervise his employer's management of him. The employer's decision to profit from the misuse of unskilled junior staff represented a relevant conflict of interest between its commercial objectives and its duty to James. An ad hoc argument for the employer's fiduciary obligation in such circumstances could succeed.

The primary focus of this chapter, however, is at the general level. That is, just as equity balances out competing competitive ambitions in relation to the realm of the present and future business interests of the employer, it may be persuaded to protect the narrow but critical sphere of the employee's fragile, dynamic economic capacity upon which the employee's present and future labour market participation depends.

C. Interfaces with Labour Law

This section aims to align some of the core insights of labour law scholarship and jurisprudence with the fiduciary concepts outlined above. Part of the definition of fiduciary obligation includes the notion of one party's power to 'affect the interests of [the other] in a legal or practical sense',[89] which carries with it the idea of the vulnerability of the other party to this power. Labour law discourse provides a number of different ways of understanding the vulnerability of the employee, three of which are considered below. It is recognized at the outset that this discussion is speculative, because whether or not equity would adopt or be influenced by any or all of these perspectives has not been tested. And it also must be admitted that even within the labour law academy there exists a range of philosophical, ideological and personal perspectives which are not easily reconciled into a coherent whole which equity could apply in any simple way.

Yet it remains clear that adjudication of fiduciary matters has regularly relied upon at least some reference to external frameworks of understanding. Facts do not come before the court labelled with the terms of legal principle, and the notions of power and vulnerability need to be constructed from the factual material before the court. A good example of this complex interpretive task is the UK Court of Appeal's consideration of whether or not company directors who were required to join a trade union were in breach of their fiduciary obligation to the company. In that case, the majority followed its sense of prevailing industry practice to decide that union membership and company directorship could coexist without a breach of fiduciary obligation. [90]

The fundamental insight of what might be called traditional labour law scholarship is that the employment relationship generally involves a power imbalance,

[89] *Hospital Products* (n 16) 238.

[90] *Boulting Brothers v Association of Cinematograph, Television and Allied Technicians* [1963] 2 QB 606.

with the employer in the ascendancy.[91] The contract of employment, as a result of its feudal roots, is regarded as cementing the subservience of the employee to the discretionary power of the employer. At different times, and in different ways, various labour law discourses have explicated the multifaceted ways in which the employer's superior power may manifest itself, some of which are suggestive of examples of a relevant conflict of interest requiring the employer to act within that particular sphere in the sole interests of the employee should a fiduciary duty be found. Three examples are briefly considered here. The first construes the employee as vulnerable to physical harm, the second to invasion of fundamental human rights and the third to an unconscionable exploitation of the employee in ways which damage the worker's capacity to integrate work and family life.

Physical harm at work is regulated by contract and elaborate statutory provisions which place the employer under an obligation to exercise reasonable care. However, cases where the employer knowingly or recklessly impairs the worker's health and hence their capacity to engage in work into the future are not appropriately seen as simply a failure to act in accordance with the common law and statutory standard of reasonable care. Such actions exhibit classical features of a breach of trust not because of the employer's intention, which is irrelevant to equity, but because the temptation to utilize human labour provided for a limited purpose in a way that is catastrophically destructive of the worker's entrepreneurial capabilities is inherent in the employment relationship, and there is no way in which the employee can protect themselves by supervising the employer's decisions to permit or cause harm.

An example is found in the actions of James Hardie, the Australian company that produced and sold asbestos products for much of the twentieth century. Litigation over claims for compensation in tort have revealed that the company made 'a conscious decision of management' not to warn its employees and customers of the dangers they knew were inherent in the use of asbestos in order to shore up profits and ensure the product was not removed from the market.[92] The company was able to control information about its deadly product, including withholding critical safety messages that would have saved workers' lives. Such circumstances meet the test for the imputation of fiduciary obligations proposed by Birks, who argued that:

> [C]ircumstances triggering the duty to act [are] … such as to indicate a real and sensible temptation to sacrifice that duty to self-interest and an equally real and sensible reason why that danger cannot be monitored by ordinary vigilance.[93]

A second lens through which to view the possible impact of the employer on

[91] Otto Kahn-Freund, *Labour and the Law* (Stevens and Co, 1972); K Wedderburn, *The Worker and the Law* (Harmondsworth, Penguin Books, 1965).

[92] Evidence of the harm caused by asbestos was known to the company by at least the 1950s. See eg *Rolls Royce Industrial Power (Pacific) v James Hardie and Co Pty Ltd* [1999] NSW Dust Diseases Tribunal; 18 NSWCCR 653, [125].

[93] Birks (n 1) 38.

the legal and practical interests of the employee is that provided by human rights law and discourse. This approach suggests that the notion of the worker's economic being proposed here should be understood to include not just the physical capacity to continue to engage in economic activity but also the very autonomy and dignity of the worker. Egregious cases of slavery and near-enslavement of vulnerable domestic workers have come to the attention of the courts in Canada[94] and France.[95] Instances of severe exploitation include deprivation of liberty, threats of deportation if the worker does not co-operate, no personal time or space, as well as actual violence and harassment. In such cases, the employer has rationally advanced its interests by creating a source of cheap, compliant and always-available labour, but arguably equity should impose an outer limit on the employer's autonomy and safeguard the integrity of the worker's economic capacity with which it is entrusted.

The idea that a worker in these circumstances could protect themselves either through the initial contract or via later legal proceedings to retrieve their common law and statutory entitlements is untenable. The young claimant in *Hounga v Allen*, for example, had lived with her employers as a domestic worker for 18 months but did not know the address of the house for the purposes of service of legal documents.[96] Orthodox fiduciary principles suggest that the employer should be held to account to prevent others from exploitative access to the worker's labour, with the boundary drawn at the point at which the employer presses its power advantage to damage or destroy the fundamental human rights of the worker.

A third elaboration of the potential impact of the employer calls attention to the evolving boundaries of the concept of 'economic interest'. Traditional labour law's construction of the worker as a man unencumbered by domestic care responsibilities has been deconstructed and a sophisticated commentary on the need to view the work/life boundary in an integrated sense has evolved. The permeability of work to domestic care responsibilities has become a major theme in the public legal regulation of work.[97] Should the ideas underpinning the novel construction of working time as 'time out of life' ever become naturalized in legal discourse generally, then the way in which employer actions such as 'hours theft' are viewed might shift this issue into the fiduciary context. In the feminist vision of the worker as an economic being, integration of paid work and domestic care would be essential to maintain the worker's full economic capabilities.[98] On this view, a relevant misuse of power would be the unconscionable imposition of grossly excessive working time in ways that damage the worker's capacity to maintain all their social obligations to work and family.

[94] *Mustaji v Tjin* 1996 CanLii 1907 (BA CA).

[95] V Mantouvalou, 'Servitude and Forced Labour in the 21st Century: The Human Rights of Domestic Workers' (2006) 35(4) *Industrial Law Journal* 395.

[96] *Hounga v Allen* [2012] EWCA Civ 609, [2].

[97] J Conaghan and K Rittich (eds), *Labour Law, Work and Family: Critical and Comparative Perspectives* (Oxford, Oxford University Press, 2005).

[98] S Fredman, *Women and the Law* (Oxford, Oxford University Press, 1997).

These three ways of construing power and vulnerability provide one basis of operationalizing the concept of the employer's fiduciary obligation to the employee. Another is to examine particular instances of employer power to affect the interests of the employee, focusing on the legal forms of engagement themselves. The employer has power over the content of mode of the contract, power during the operation of the contract, power to manipulate corporate form and an extra-contractual power to control in the absence of contract. The ramification of each for the employer's putative fiduciary obligation is considered below.

(i) The Employer's Power over Content and Mode of Contract

It will be recalled that the recent narrowing of the employee's fiduciary obligation centred on the long-standing stricture that the fiduciary relationship must mould itself to the terms of the contract. In traditional equitable analysis, it is assumed that the employer is in a position to secure the terms necessary to control the potentially errant employee's abuse of power. As Simms puts it, fiduciary obligations deal with problems of control, and in the employment relationship the 'control mechanism' is the contract of employment itself.[99]

However, when it comes to the employee's role in the making of the contract of employment, labour law jurisprudence and scholarship may take a different view. Employment contracts are seen as 'contracts of adhesion' which employees are offered on a 'take it or leave it' basis.[100] The important Supreme Court decision in *Autoclenz v Belcher*[101] provides the highest authority for the view that even in the face of a signed, written contract the court should 'focus on the reality of the situation.'[102] Lord Clarke stated that 'while employment is a matter of contract, the factual matrix in which the contract is cast is not ordinarily the same as that of an arm's length commercial contract'.[103]

The Supreme Court accepted that 'frequently organisations are in a position to dictate the written terms which the other party has to accept'.[104] As Bogg argues, decisions such as this suggest that the common law of employment is evolving into a sub-branch of the general law. This developing common law view suggests that equity should not defer to the contract of employment as the instrument of control of discretionary power: *Autoclenz* exposes the contract as an expression of unilateral employer power in the case of these vulnerable workers, suggesting that in fact there is a juridical space within which fiduciary law can, and should, operate.

The employer's power extends to both the content of the contract and the very

[99] V Simms, 'Is Employment a Fiduciary Relationship?' (2001) 30(1) *Industrial Law Journal* 101, 106.

[100] I MacNeil, 'The Many Futures of Contract' (1973–74) 47 *Southern California Law Review* 691 (1974), 770.

[101] *Autoclenz* (n 72)

[102] ibid [22].

[103] ibid [33].

[104] ibid [34].

mode of contracting itself. Many statutory protections for workers are restricted to those who are technically employees, creating an incentive for employers to 'game' the contractual status of their workforce in order to avoid compliance costs.[105] Freedland has mapped the terrain of the contract for personal work in forensic detail,[106] and generally the various literatures on precarious employment articulate forms of vulnerability caused by contemporary employment practices.[107] This discourse highlights numerous ways in which work can be legally structured to shift responsibility for risk from the employer to the employee, whilst maintaining effective employer control. This article cannot do justice to the richness and complexity of these observations.[108]

Modern employment practices have created a borderland between the contract of employment and self-employment.[109] Vulnerable workers may be required to incorporate as an owner–operator business even if they continue to labour for a single enterprise and be deemed wholly responsible for their own insurance, taxation and so on. The common law is occasionally asked and able to tear away the façade of independence and reveal the true subordinate character of the relationship,[110] but such cases are generally speaking rare because of the hurdles facing ordinary workers in bringing civil actions and the paucity of meaningful remedies for common law breaches. This means that the conversion of employees to the status of independent contractors, if performed in a technically correct manner, will generally result in the successful removal of the worker from the protective sphere of the contract of employment. The social and economic meaning of such outsourcing might differ in different settings, creating one set of dynamics for, say, a highly qualified information technology consultant, and another set for a truck driver[111] or cleaner.[112] The disastrous personal and societal consequences that may flow from an employer's decision to outsource vulnerable workers in this way are discussed by Glasbeek in his searing analysis of *Brambles v Anders Transport*.[113]

A second issue highlighted in labour law discourse is an entity's decision to engage labour through an intermediary such as a labour hire agency, thus creating a tripartite set of 'parties' whose legal statuses may vary according to the facts of the arrangement.[114] McCann identifies this triangular work relation-

[105] S Deakin, 'The Changing Concept of the Employer in Labour Law' (2001) 30(1) *Industrial Law Journal* 72.

[106] Freedland (n 3).

[107] eg J Fudge and R Owens (eds), *Precarious Work, Women and the New Economy* (Oxford, Hart Publishing, 2006).

[108] eg D McCann *Regulating Flexible Work* (Oxford, Oxford University Press, 2008).

[109] *Sweeney v Boylan Nominees* [2006] HCA 19, (2006) 226 CLR 161 (Kirby J).

[110] *Hollis v Vabu* [2001] HCA 44; 207 CLR 41.

[111] *Andar Transport Pty Ltd v Brambles Ltd* [2004] HCA 28; (2004) 217 CLR 424.

[112] *Damevski v Guidice* [2004] FCFCA 252.

[113] H Glasbeek, 'The Legal Pulverisation of Social Issues: *Andar Transport v Brambles Ltd*' (2005) 13 *Tort Law Journal* 217.

[114] Freedland (n 3) 39.

ship as 'the most profound' challenge to labour law norms.[115] There may be a relationship of employer and employee between the labour hire company and the worker, but this is not necessarily the case. In Australia, a common form of contracting, if properly instituted, ensures that such workers are legally regarded as self-employed, the employee of neither the agency nor the host firm.[116] As Freedland and other have argued, where an agency worker is placed into a host business they may become subject to the day-to-day authority of that business, in the absence of any legal connection with that authority.[117] Deakin describes the fracturing of the traditional concept of the employer:

> The legal meaning of the employer is not synonymous with the sociological or economic idea of the 'enterprise' … nor with the workplace, ie the physical site where work is carried out.[118]

In a recent Australian case typical of many, a labour hire worker was racially abused by his supervisor in the host firm, and his employment with the labour hire agency was terminated after he posted a notice at the workplace calling for all workers to be treated with dignity. The employee's claim under the 'adverse action' provisions of the national statute was refused because he was not an employee of the host.[119]

The third way in which the employer may exercise its power over the mode of contracting is to obtain labour through a series of casual engagements whereby the worker's contract begins and ends each time they work with no ongoing legal obligation to provide or accept work.[120] The common law regards this kind of work as intermittent, although labour law research discloses a different reality. In Australia, for example, the concept of the 'long-term casual' is so pervasive that statute now recognizes the difference between workers who have worked intermittently but with regular hours for a certain period and 'true casuals' for certain limited purposes.[121]

The fiduciary principles may be enlivened in such cases as these where, through the use of grossly exploitative contracting practices, the employer seeks to conceal a *subsisting relationship* through which labour is exchanged for wages. The vulnerable worker 'requested' to resign and tender for their former job as a company, for example, could argue that the employer's contracting-out action breached a pre-existing fiduciary obligation based on their existing relationship of trust and confidence. It may be that the racially abused agency worker could argue that a fiduciary obligation had arisen between him and the host firm,

[115] McCann (n 108) 168.
[116] *Re ODCO v Building Workers Industrial Union of Australia* (1989) FCA 336.
[117] Freedland (n 3) 35.
[118] Deakin (n 105).
[119] *Vij v Cordina Chicken* [2012] FMCA 483.
[120] ACL Davies, 'Casual Workers and Continuity of Employment' (2006) 35 *Industrial Law Journal*, 196; McCann (n 108) 180.
[121] See eg *Fair Work Act* (Cth) 2009, s 384; R Owens, 'Working Precariously, the Safety Net after the Work Choices Act' (2006) 19 *Australian Journal of Labour Law* 161.

notwithstanding his common law legal relationship with the labour hire firm. And the casual employee whose long-term commitment to the firm is relied upon by the employer may argue that the legal construction of their employment as intermittent is a fiduciary breach.

The implied undertaking to forego self-interest required by equity could be derived from the fact that the employer or managing entity in the case of the host firm continues to accept the labour of the workers—over years in some cases—and obtains the benefit of control provided by the reality of subservience. For particularly vulnerable workers, the problem of supervising whether or not the employer is engaging in abusive contracting practices is acute. Most ordinary workers, and even those in more senior grades, have little idea of the nuances of employment contracting or of the critical significance of the indicia of the contract of employment for their statutory and common law protection.

The possibility that labour contracting practices could give rise to fiduciary obligations exists because equity's fiduciary concept exists independently of the common law of contract. Where a relationship is contractually based, there is a strong view that the fiduciary obligation should be consistent with the scope and terms of the contract, but a contractual relationship is not a prerequisite for the imputation of fiduciary obligations. Fiduciary obligations have been held to arise 'between parties who have not reached and who may never reach agreement on contractual terms'.[122] Equity's vigorous interrogation of the facts of each case is a methodology well placed to look beneath the common law strategems, where it is appropriate to do so, to protect against opportunistic breaches of the principal's interests within the narrow sphere identified.

Of course, the space in which such disinterested loyalty could operate would be narrow, because by and large the law expects and condones employer behaviour that is self-serving and even severely exploitative in this arena.

(ii) Employer Power During the Performance of the Contract

In addition to seeing the contract of employment as the product of a relationship of power imbalance, labour law also differs from classical contract theory by highlighting the contract of employment as indeterminate. Relational contract theory from the 1970s identified the employment contract as one in which the specific terms of the contractual deal cannot actually be identified in advance.[123] The flexibility to determine duties and responsibilities over time is essential when contracting for all but the most Tayloristic of management systems or the most basic of human labour. The implied contractual duty to obey provides the employer with control of the employee throughout the life of the contract,

[122] *United Dominions* (n 76). The post-contractual operation of fiduciary obligations is less clear. Obligations of confidence subsist, and there is some authority that senior employees who resign in order to further their illegitimate competition with the employer may still be regarded as fiduciaries. *Canadian Aero Service Ltd v O'Malley* [1974] SCR 592, 40 DLR (3d) 371; but see *Dolphin v Simonet* [2001] EWHC 415 Ch [95].

[123] MacNeil (n 100), 745 et seq.

and as Collins and others so clearly spell out, the employer fills the gaps through the ongoing exercise of managerial prerogative through authority structures that govern and give content to the relationship as circumstances require.[124]

The employee is vulnerable to the employer's capricious or unreasonable use of this managerial power.[125] Many of the leading UK cases on breach of the implied contractual term of mutual trust and confidence by the employer deal with such actions.[126] Is there any aspect of the exercise of managerial prerogative which might be characterized as subject to a fiduciary obligation?

One possibility arises in circumstances where the employer has created, or has allowed to exist, a system of actual workplace control that is disassociated from the real source of employer power as established in the contract. In Freedland's terms, the legal structure and the social reality of the organization are at odds.[127] Such a scenario enables the employer to exploit the labour of its employees as efficiently as if the managerial structure were real, then deny legal responsibility for decisions taken. A strict contractual analysis of this situation does not assist the employee, who would be seen by the court as having voluntarily submitted to the instructions in the absence of a legally binding requirement to do so.

The employment law cases are replete with examples of this collision between strict legal reasoning and the reality of power relations in the workplace.[128] This mismatch of real workplace power and the common law's regulation of it may give rise to a relevant conflict of interest where a fiduciary duty exists. It is argued here that a higher obligation should apply to the employer not to create a conflict between its own interests and its duty to the employee in relation to the exercise of workplace power. That is, the employee has a legitimate expectation or is entitled to trust that the employer has authorized the creation of the managerial systems to which the employee is routinely subject in the workplace.

The employee's problems of supervising the employer's use of its discretionary powers in this regard are formidable. What amounts to an illusory governance structure would be undetectable unless and until the matter were finally determined in court, by which time employees may have already submitted to the workplace directions. There is little chance of a vulnerable employee interrogating their apparent 'boss' as to that person's actual legal capacity to command the employee. And there is a real risk of an employer deciding to avoid their legal obligations in this way, or to fail to regulate properly the management processes within the entity.

In one case, an employee whose duties including responding to emergency

[124] See H Collins, 'Market Power, Bureaucratic Power and the Contract of Employment' (1986) Industrial Law Journal 1; H Collins, *Employment Law*, 2nd edn (Oxford, Oxford University Press, 2010) 10.

[125] Collins, *Employment Law* (n 124) 11.

[126] D Brodie, 'Fair Dealing in the World of Work' (2014) 43(1) *Industrial Law Journal* 29; J Riley, 'Siblings but not Twins: Making Sense of "Mutual Trust and Confidence"' (2012) 36(2) *Melbourne University Law Review* 521.

[127] Freedland (n 3) 45.

[128] see eg *Francis v South Sydney Rugby League Football Club* [2002] FCA 1306.

callouts to fix security problems at a university worked on-call at the direction of his manager but, unbeknownst to him, without the correct administrative approval required by the university's policies and the university's collective agreement.[129] Evidence showed that the employee's expertise and work ethic were utilized by the employer on countless occasions, even by telephone when the worker was on holidays in America. However, because the technically correct procedure for the granting of permission to offer staff on-call duties was not followed, he was ineligible to overtime payments for the work performed out of hours. A similar outcome was reached in a dispute over a term implied in fact in a contract of employment: in *Griggs v Noris* an aircraft engineer believed he had a verbal agreement with his employer that he would be awarded time off in lieu of overtime payments. He worked some 4,798 hours of unpaid overtime and was too busy to take time off in lieu of payment.[130] When his contract was terminated, he sought to be paid out for the overtime worked, arguing that a term implied in fact in his contract should be held to require to the employer to honour the purported agreement. The majority of the court held that no such term could be implied because it was not necessary to the business efficacy of the contract, an element of the test for implication by fact in Australia.[131]

In both cases, the employer permitted the exercise of actual power for its own benefit and then refused to accept that it had legally authorized the directives. It is arguable that these cases expose a space within which the employer should prefer the interests of the employee over their own: the benefits accrued could be seen as unconscionable, and breach of fiduciary duty provides an appropriate lens through which to capture the particular problems of supervision and breach of trust through unauthorized use of the employee's economic capacity. From the pragmatic perspective, no contractual remedy was available to the workers, given that the findings about the 'true' legal character of the power relations at the workplace led to the unsatisfactory conclusion that both employees had voluntarily gifted their labour to their respective employers ex-contractually.

(iii) The Employer's Power to Manipulate Corporate Form

The employer may affect the interests of the employee through its capacity to alter corporate form. Obviously this kind of metamorphosis is integral to the free operation of the market, and it would be contrary to the public interest and legal principle to suggest that capital could not mutate into different economic structures to respond to the changing environmental factors and owner preference. The task here is to see whether or not it is possible to identify ways in which a relevant conflict of interest of sufficient gravity may arise where it is arguable that equity's intervention is appropriate.

[129] *Royal Melbourne Institute of Technology v National Tertiary Education Industry Union* [2011] FCA 34; (2011) 203 IR 294.

[130] *Griggs v Norris Group* (2006) SASC 23, (2006) 94 SASR 126.

[131] *BP Refinery (Westerport) Ltd v Shire of Hastings* [1977] UKPC 13, (1977) 180 CLR 266.

One way in which the employer can exercise its discretion is the way it deals with its assets. Whether or not the employer treats accrued employee entitlements as part of the general operating funds of the company can have an impact on employees in the event of insolvency.[132] These circumstances provide a close analogy to the institutional dynamics of the trust. Employees are volunteers in the sense that they have no option but to trust that their employer will hold these retrospectively earned entitlements for their benefit, a vulnerability recognized in relation to the pension fund in *Mettoy Pension Trustees Ltd v Evans*.[133] The severe problems of supervision are akin to those of the beneficiary to a trust. Writing from an Australian perspective, Burgess and Lewer argue that the mere fact that the company retains the funds covering the accrued entitlements 'places a strong fiduciary responsibility' on the employer not to divert the funds for its own purposes, but it is unlikely that this is correct. This is an area in which employees and their trade unions could attempt to create an express trust over the funds removed from workers' pay for these future benefits by specifying that the funds were to be separately held in a special account and devoted solely of the workers' future benefit.[134]

Corporate form-shifting has at times been an anti-union tactic: whether such actions could be construed as a breach of employer fiduciary obligation would depend upon the emphasis placed on fundamental labour rights in the court's application of fiduciary concepts to the facts. One example is the bitter industrial dispute between the Maritime Union of Australia and the company running the docks, which involved complex corporate stratagems leading to the existing workforce being employed by a financially precarious 'shell' employment-only entity. Although the workers were not actually transferred to another legal entity, the security of their employment was undermined without their knowledge or agreement. The ultimate aim appeared to be to provoke industrial action and then terminate the contract with the shell employing entity, to enable the company to bring in a new non-unionized workforce.[135]

A second example is provided by the James Hardie group of companies which, despite knowing that two subsidiaries would be subject to multimillion-dollar claims for death and illness arising from asbestos exposure, separated off those entities and reconstituted the core of the corporation in the Netherlands. A Medical Research Fund and Compensation Foundation was left to deal with the claims, but it had been underfunded by hundreds of millions of dollars. The company directors were held to have breached their corporate law duties by informing the Australian Stock Exchange that the Foundation had sufficient

[132] J Burgess and J Lewer, 'Protecting Employee Entitlements: Corporate Governance and Industrial Democracy in Australia' (2006) 32(4) *Australian Bulletin of Labour* 365.

[133] *Mettoy Pension Trustees Ltd v Evans* [1991] 2 All ER 513 held on particular facts that employer had fiduciary obligation to use occupational pension fund surplus for benefit of workers not the company

[134] *Re Kayford Ltd* [1975] 1 WLR 279.

[135] For a full discussion, see G Orr, 'Conspiracy on the Waterfront' (1998) 11 *Australian Journal of Labour Law* 2.

funds to cover all claims.[136] However, the corporate restructuring was entirely effective in that the two vulnerable subsidiaries had indemnified the parent company against any future claims and it was held to have no legal obligation to top up the fund.[137] Eventually public and political pressure led to a voluntary settlement of more money for the Foundation.

This is possibly a more fruitful set of circumstances from which to argue that there is a relevant conflict of interest representing a breach of the employer's fiduciary obligation than the breach of freedom of association principles in the dock workers' case. Corporate actions to avoid payment of compensation for legitimate claims in contract and tort, in circumstances where the company knowingly caused those breaches, arguably occupies a sphere in which the employer should prefer the interests of the employees to those of itself. The remedy sought would be quantifiable and monetary in nature, and the interests clearly economic.

(iv) Power in the Absence of Contract

Recent attention in both Australia and the UK has been paid to exploitative unpaid work engagements.[138] One example in both countries is the use of unpaid interns who actually perform work of significant value for the employer under the guise of industry training or work experience. Unpaid work in its various guises generally exists beyond the regulation of contract law: lack of consideration and intention to create legal relations mean that no contract has been formed between the parties. English law is more likely to recognize non-traditional payments as adequate consideration in relation to volunteer labour,[139] but generally such labour exists beyond the regulation of the common law. Economic exploitation in such circumstances where the relevant fiduciary indicia are present may give rise to a breach of fiduciary obligation. The case of law graduates asked to work without pay researching complex matters for a firm while competing for a single job might be an example of such a case.

The case of *Allen v Hounga* provides a stark example of the capacity to exploit labour in the absence of an enforceable contract, in that case because the contract was void on the grounds of illegality.[140] Fiduciary obligations may be imputed to the employer if any of the rationales for doing so discussed in this chapter are adopted, as equity's remedial intervention is not dependent upon the exist-

[136] *Australian Securities and Investments Commission v Hellicar* [2012] HCA 17.

[137] These events were subject to a Judicial Enquiry which made critical findings of the company and its directors: D Jackson QC, *Report of the Special Commission of Inquiry into the Medical Research Fund and Compensation Foundation* (Parliament of New South Wales 2004)

[138] A Stewart and R Owens, 'Experience or Exploitation? The Nature, Prevalence and Regulation of Unpaid Work, Work Experience, Internships and Trial Periods in Australia', Fair Work Ombudsman, Sydney, 2013. www.fairwork.gov.au/about-us/publications/pages/research-reports (accessed 31 March 2014); P Walker, 'Unpaid Interns: 100 Firms Being Investigated by HMRC', *The Guardian* 12 April 2013.

[139] J Murray, 'The Legal Regulation of Volunteer Work', in C Arup and others (eds), *Labour Law and Labour Market Regulation* (The Federation Press, 2006) 696.

[140] *Allen v Hounga* [2012] EWCA Civ 609; A Bogg and T A Novitz, 'Race Discrimination and the Doctrine of Illegality' (2013) 129 *Law Quarterly Review* 12.

ence of a valid contract. However, the equitable 'clean hands' maxim may be used against the claimant.

VI. Cross-cutting Policies and Principles

There is near unanimity in Anglo-Australian law that any kind of expansion of the application of fiduciary concepts, particularly in the Canadian sense, is not to be countenanced.[141] In the past, Canadian courts have found fiduciary obligations to exist in a range of non-traditional categories where a relationship of 'power dependency' is evident on the facts.[142] Cases include exploitative abuse of power in relationships between doctor and patient,[143] student and school board, parent and child,[144] and immigrant domestic worker and householder.[145]

More recently, even Canadian law has evolved to narrow the scope for the ascription of fiduciary obligations by moving away from a loose test based largely around relationships of around ascendancy and vulnerability.[146] In *Galambos v Perez* an employee donated a significant sum of money to the employer's business, initially without the employer's knowledge. At first instance, the employee was construed as vulnerable to the employer's influence and the employer was held to have breached a fiduciary obligation. But the Supreme Court held that some form of voluntary undertaking to act in the interests of the other, or circumstances giving rise to an implicit undertaking had to be disclosed on the evidence before a fiduciary obligation, could be held to exist. On the facts of this case, the employee knew more about financial matters than the employer and could not be characterized to be appropriately vulnerable.[147]

The Anglo-Australian position against expansion has several distinct if interrelated concerns. One goes to the relationship between fiduciary obligation and the duties arising under contract law and tort: it is argued that fiduciary law, if not checked, will 'swallow whole contract and tort law' by creating 'new forms of civil wrong'.[148] Judges in Australia, for example, have pointedly refuse to follow Canadian principles by stating that where a relationship is properly regulated by tort and contract, there is 'no room' for the operation of equity.[149] A second concern with what is regarded as the unprincipled expansion of the fiduciary concept is that it might drag equity away from its primary concern

[141] For example, *Breen v Williams* (n 1) 83.
[142] *Hogkinson v Simms* (1995) 117 DLR (4th) 161, 178.
[143] *McInerney v MacDonald* [1992] 2 SCR 138.
[144] *M(K) v M(H)* [1992] 3 SCR 6.
[145] *Mustaji v Tjin* 1996 CanLII 1907 (BC CA).
[146] M McInnes, 'A New Direction for the Canadian Law of the Fiduciary Relationship?' (2010) 126 *Law Quarterly Review* 185.
[147] *Galambos v Perez* (2009) SCC 48; [2009] 3 SCR 247, [79].
[148] Worthington (n 1), 500.
[149] *Breen v Williams* (n 1) 93.

with economic interests.[150] And thirdly, there is concern that expansion might lead to the ascription of some kind of free-standing positive duty to act in good faith in certain relationships, thus overturning the principle that the fiduciary obligations are proscriptive only.[151] How compelling are these arguments against the notion of the employer's fiduciary obligation to the employee?

The idea that where contract and tort operate there is no room for equity is not applied with vigour in the cases of the employee's fiduciary obligation to the employer: employees are routinely held to account as fiduciaries in circumstances where there is a concurrent breach of the common law. Dr Fishel's deployment of university staff in his overseas ventures, for example, is both a breach of his contractual duties and his fiduciary obligation to use the assets of the university for its benefit alone. Conaglen argues that this is a feature of fiduciary law more generally, and points to decision in *Commonwealth Bank of Australia v Smith* where the bank manager had acted both negligently and in breach of his fiduciary obligation, and equitable remedies were ordered.[152]

This view accords with another set of strongly expressed views from within equity jurisprudence and academic discourse that equity and the common law are juridically distinct: '[T]he foundation and ambit of the fiduciary obligation are conceptually distinct from the foundation and ambit of contract and tort.'[153] The fiduciary relationship has a 'different character from the contract itself'.[154]

What of the requirement that equity limits the scope of fiduciary obligations to economic interests? In Australian law, it is clear that 'economic' is taken to mean 'monetary' in a rather narrow sense. Thus, the court which held doctors were not under a general fiduciary obligation to their patients stated that doctors *could* be held to account as fiduciaries if, for example, they prescribed drugs to a patient in return for a kickback from the pharmaceutical company, or held undisclosed shares in a health facility to which they referred their patient. Interpersonal relationships giving rise to abuse, as in *Paramasivam v Flynn*, cannot be dealt with in fiduciary law, because inter alia the interest is not economic.[155]

It is arguable that the sphere of protection by fiduciary principles proposed here is a quintessentially economic one, and the broad range of actions which relevantly impact upon that realm should be recognized as such.

In relation to the prohibition of prescriptive rules. In general terms, and recognizing that every case would need to determine a specific fiduciary obligation or obligations based on the specific facts, the fiduciary obligation formulated here involves a negative obligation not to act to damage or destroy the employee's economic capabilities with which it is necessarily entrusted when it engages labour.

[150] *Paramasivam v Flynn* (1998) FCA 1711; (1998) 160 ALR 203.

[151] Notwithstanding *Item Software v Fassihi*, which held that a director had an obligation to expose his own wrong-doing; see Nolan and Conaglen (n 65) 324; *Pilmer v Duke* (n 18) 198.

[152] *Commonwealth Bank of Australia v Smith* (1991) 102 ALR 453; Conaglen (n 22).

[153] Extract from *Norberg v Wynrib* [1992] SCR 226, 272; *Pilmer v Duke* (n 18); Congalen (n 22) 59.

[154] Conaglen (n 22) quoting Privy Council in *Re Goldcorp Exchange* [1994] UKPC 3, n 15 59.

[155] *Paramasivam v Flynn* (n 150).

On balance, it seems likely, given all the complex issues and cross-cutting principles, that although an intellectual case can be made which aligns equitable concepts and certain aspects of employer power as understood in labour law, equity would be reluctant to extend fiduciary remedies for the employee in circumstances where common law remedies are available and suitable. This leaves the practical focus on circumstances where (absent a wholesale adoption of the logic that the essence of the employee's economic being should be protected by equity as the employer's business interests are) fiduciary duties may arise in the interstices between contracts, where contract law provides no effective remedy or where there is no valid contract at all. And it would be no stretch of current principle at all to apply a fiduciary lens to the protection of accrued employee entitlements and possibly even to the manipulation of corporate form where this is done to avoid statutory or common law liability.

VII. Conclusion

It has been argued here that the engagement of labour, whether through a contract of employment or otherwise, necessarily involves a relationship of trust and confidence requiring the employing entity to place the interests of the worker above their own within a particular, narrow sphere. This sphere has been defined as the bundle of assets inherent in the employee to which the employer necessarily gains complete access, irrespective of any limited purpose for which the labour is provided. Just as equity continues to deter inappropriate misuse of access to the employer's business interests by the employee, it is argued here that existing principles of law require that a fiduciary duty be imputed to the employer in respect of the employee's capacity to engage in future economic activity as an 'entrepreneur marketing their own human capital in the market place'.[156]

Just what would constitute the boundaries of this narrow sphere depends on normative and ideological judgments, but equity is used to making these in its rich jurisprudence on the fiduciary obligations of the employee and cognate cases. Labour law scholarship has conclusively demonstrated the changed social conditions which would support the evolution of the law as proposed here.

The fragmentation of many of the legal norms of employment has had a paradoxical dual impact on the interface between equity and the common law of employment. On one hand, the senior employee is now less likely to be called to account for disloyalty, particularly in English law,[157] and the contract is upheld as the appropriate 'control mechanism' to manage power in the relationship. This accords with the long-run trend away from the employee's status as the

[156] Stone (n 73) 112.
[157] Brodie (n 67).

loyal servant in a job for life. But at the same time, more vulnerable workers are less likely to be seen, by the common law at least, through the lens of the contract they signed, and it is arguable that the new modes of vulnerability (or newly revived methods of exploitation) create a space in which the employer could be held to account to the fiduciary standard. Equity's flexible methods in assessing all the facts and dynamics of the relationship in question, not limited to the actual contractual engagement, is particularly relevant here.

There are thus contrapuntal patterns of retreat and potential evolution in the interaction between common law, the common law of employment and fiduciary law, and hence the autonomies of the individual fields. A further dimension can be added, as although the fiduciary concept is part of private law, equity's regime is directed at a public end, as Worthington and Flanagan emphasize.[158] The purpose of the fiduciary concept is to deter opportunistic breach of an undertaking of trust in circumstances where ordinary vigilance cannot fully protect the vulnerable party.[159] This public purpose places the question of the employer's putative fiduciary obligation to the employee squarely in the normative territory mapped by Fredman in her argument that employers' duties should not be conceived of as limited to their contractual obligations, because of the broader social and economic power they wield. Employers should be held to account, she argues, because of the 'civic responsibility which attaches to those with power'.[160] This chapter has argued that it is possible there is a role for equity in establishing the outer boundaries of employer autonomy through the productive evolution of the fiduciary concept, a legal tool which could serve this broader social function.

[158] Worthington (n 1); Flannigan (n 33).

[159] Flannigan (n 33) 322.

[160] S Fredman, 'Women at Work: The Broken Promise of Flexicurity' (2004) 33(4) *Industrial Law Journal*, 299, 301.

15

Efficiency Arguments for the Collective Representation of Workers: A Sketch

PAUL DAVIES

I. Why Worry About the Question?

The classic works in the UK relating to the collective representation of workers (in the UK tradition, predominantly via collective bargaining with employers) have rarely paid much attention to the efficiency impacts of the mechanisms for giving employees collective voice. In *The System of Industrial Relations in Great Britain*, edited by Hugh Clegg and Alan Flanders in 1954,[1] the editors analyse both collective bargaining and joint consultation. The chapter by Flanders on collective bargaining presents that method of providing employee voice as something which, from the middle of the nineteenth century onwards, was imposed upon employers, either by trade unions acting alone or by trade unions and pro-worker governments acting together. The main benefit to employers from collective bargaining is seen to be industrial peace. Recognizing and doing deals with the union removes the threat of industrial action and so removes one of the threats to undisturbed productive activity—just as a minimum level of political stability at country level can be seen as a precondition for successful production. However, there are only hints at possible benefits to the employer of recognizing and doing deals with the union, as compared with the situation where there is no collective representation of workers via trade unions and, thus, no demand for collective bargaining.[2]

The chapter by Hugh Clegg and Norman Chester on consultation commit-

[1] H Clegg and A Flander, *The System of Industrial Relations in Great Britain* (Oxford, Basil Blackwell, 1954) ch 5 (collective bargaining) and ch 6 (joint consultation).

[2] There are undeveloped suggestions that employers benefit from taking piece work rates out of competition among employers (via multi-employer collective bargaining) and that unions can assist employers by becoming, in the modern phrase, managers of discontent: Clegg and Flander (ibid) 268–72.

tees is more open to the potential benefits to employers of collective representation, but the story there presented is, at best, of promise unfulfilled. Collective consultation was crushed because of the inability of those involved to find a way of making it compatible with collective bargaining. The Joint Production Committees, which government and unions fostered during the Second World War, did not make an effective transition into the post-war world of resurgent collective bargaining but rather sank under the weight of the 'suspicions and ignorance' of managers, trade unionists and workers.[3] In the later version of *The System*, written by Clegg alone in 1972, Clegg explained the decline of consultation committees and their absorption into workplace bargaining as the triumph of the pluralist frame of reference.[4] Employers and unions, both committed to maximizing their own welfare through collective bargaining, were unable sustain co-operation in consultative committees. The establishment- and enterprise-level space for collective employee voice had been effectively occupied by collective bargaining and consultation mechanisms were squeezed out.

Turning to the more important question of the societal benefits of collective employee voice, the traditional arguments have not turned on efficiency either. Those arguments (again predominantly in relation to voice through collective bargaining) have been either distributional or democratic. So, collective bargaining is often presented as achieving a larger share of the firm's revenues for the workers (through the union wage premium),[5] implicitly at the cost of a reduction in the proportion going to the firm's owners (though the analysis is sometimes rather vague as to whether it is the firm's owners or the consumers of its products who carry the bulk of the costs of collective bargaining). More attractively, collective bargaining is not presented simply as a collective version of individual bargaining (in which the employees do better because they have managed to exclude competing offers of service), but as an extension of the democratic imperative from the political sphere into the industrial. One of the crucial benefits of collective bargaining, on this approach, is that it gives the workers the opportunity to participate in the setting of the rules which govern the workplace, irrespective of the size of the financial benefit that collective bargaining confers on them.[6] On this view, collective representation is as impor-

[3] ibid 344.

[4] H Clegg, *The System of Industrial Relations in Great Britain*, 2nd edn (Basil Blackwell, Oxford, 1972) 185 et seq.

[5] For (relatively) recent estimates of this, see D Blanchflower and A Bryson, 'Union Relative Wage Effects in the United States and the United Kingdom' in A Eaton (ed), *Proceedings of the 56th Annual Meeting of the Industrial Relations Research Association* (Champaign, IL, Industrial Relations Research Association, 2004) 133. For a particular example, consider this comment in an obituary of Bob Crow, General Secretary of the RMT union, in relation to London underground workers: 'To his members, however, he was a working-class hero who succeeded in driving up pay … and expanded his union's membership against the tide of declining trade unionism', *Financial Times* 11 March 2014.

[6] The classic expression of this analysis is A Flanders, 'Collective Bargaining: A Theoretical Analysis' in A Flanders, *Management and Unions* (London, Faber, 1970) 213, a paper first published in 1968. This criticizes the Webbs (S and B Webb, *Industrial Democracy* (London, Longmans Green, 1902) 173) for seeing collective bargaining simply as a mechanism whereby the co-ordination costs of employees in individual bargaining are overcome.

tant as a protection against abuse of power as it is as a generator of higher rewards.[7] Of course, these two rationales are not incompatible with one another.

The purpose of this piece is not to question either of the rationales given in the previous paragraph, but to explore the question of whether a case can be made for collective employee voice on efficiency grounds. The first step is to stipulate what is meant by 'efficiency' in this argument. Efficiency is defined for the purposes of this chapter as arranging governance rights in the company so as to minimize its costs of production.[8] The proposition is that a company's contribution to society is maximized if, for whatever level of production the market or regulation determines is desirable, the resources consumed by the company to produce that output are minimized. Other possible definitions of 'efficiency' are available, but this is the one stipulated here. The company is a legal construct aimed at facilitating the acquisition and co-ordination of inputs (financial, material and human) that a business needs to produce outputs. It is suggested, therefore, that the proposed definition of efficiency is an appropriate test to apply to governance arrangements within companies. The applicable rules and institutions may facilitate or hinder acquisition and co-ordination, and thus raise or lower the company's costs of production. As it has been put, good corporate law 'reduces the ongoing costs of organising through the corporate form by facilitating coordination among participants in corporate enterprise and constraining value-reducing forms of opportunism among the constituencies of the corporate enterprise'.[9]

It is further suggested that government and managers (and possibly shareholders) may today be as interested in the efficiency implications of the institutions of collective employee voice as in their distributional outcomes, and this means that workers and unions have an interest in efficiency (as defined) as well. Why has this situation come about? In large part it is because the secular decline in union membership and collective bargaining coverage has reduced the capacity of the union movement to secure the extension of collective bargaining via self-help and has reduced the political incentives for government to take vigorous steps to promote collective bargaining.[10] Thus, both of the main drivers of the expansion of collective bargaining identified by Flanders in the 1950s today operate more weakly than in the heyday of that institution and this situ-

[7] See for a powerful articulation of this rationale H Collins, 'Market Power, Bureaucratic Power, and the Contract of Employment' (1986) 15 *Industrial Law Journal* 1.

[8] Readers will have noticed the shift from 'firm' to 'company'. For the rest of the chapter I will assume the employer is a company. The same issues arise in relation to non-corporate employers but, so as not to complicate the argument and because most of the relevant employers are corporations, will confine myself to companies.

[9] R Kraakman and others, *The Anatomy of Corporate Law*, 2nd edn (Oxford, Oxford University Press, 2009) 2. This approach is, of course, in the tradition established by R Coase, 'The Nature of the Firm' (1937) 4 *Economica* 386.

[10] The union recognition procedure in Trade Union and Labour Relations (Consolidation) Act 1992 sch 1A, inserted by the Employment Relations Act 1999, demonstrates both that governmental support has not completely disappeared but also the limited nature of that support. See A Bogg, *The Democratic Aspects of Trade Union Recognition* (Oxford, Hart Publishing, 2009).

ation seems likely to continue in the future.[11] In addition, and partly a cause of the development just mentioned, global competition has sharpened companies' interests in efficiency as the areas of national economies sheltered from competition (especially from outside the jurisdiction) have been substantially reduced. An efficiency rationale, if one could be established, might operate so as both to reduce employer caution in relation to the mechanisms of collective worker voice and encourage government to be more proactive in introducing support for the voice mechanisms. Employers might be thought to have a natural interest in reducing the costs of production, whilst government has an interest in increasing the competitiveness of productive enterprises, because it benefits in terms of tax revenues and the political dividend from job creation.

However, the credibility of the efficiency argument can by no means be taken for granted. It needs to be explored in some detail. What is the theory behind the claims that worker voice reduces companies' costs of production? Is there any empirical evidence to back up the theoretical claims? This chapter will explore the empirical evidence mainly through an analysis of the German system of worker voice, which contains three main elements: board-level employee representation, works councils and collective bargaining. It will be argued that there is reasonably strong empirical evidence to support the efficiency claims for the German system. An attempt will be made to isolate the conditions under which those efficiency results obtain in Germany. This gives rise to the final, and perhaps crucial, question. In a system where those conditions do not obtain, what would be costs of establishing those conditions so as to capture the efficiency gains which are currently foregone? Are the costs of change likely to be greater than the efficiency gains, and, even if they are not, are the necessary changes likely to be opposed successfully by the incumbents in the current system?

How does this chapter relate to the notion of the 'autonomy' of labour law? In so far as autonomy means that labour law struggled against and at least partially succeeded in escaping from the legal concepts of the common (or civil) law, such as freedom of contract and restraint of trade, this chapter has nothing to contribute, because it is not about legal concepts but rather institutional design. In so far as autonomy means that the rationales underlying labour law were unique to that body of law, then this chapter is at odds with such a notion of autonomy. However, in terms of underlying policies, the claim of labour law to autonomous status was closely linked to the idea that the predominant purpose of labour law was to promote collective bargaining.[12] This is clearly no longer

[11] The force of this argument was recognized some years ago by R Hyman, 'Is there a Case for Statutory Works Councils in Britain?' in A McColgan (ed), *The Future of Labour Law* (London, Pinter, 1996)—with a response by John Kelly. The latest WERS survey shows a continuing decline in union density and collective bargaining coverage, but at a much slower rate than in earlier surveys, Workplace Employment Relations Study, *The 2011 Workplace Employment Relations Study: First Findings* (URN 13/1010, 2013).

[12] O Kahn-Freund, 'Labour Law' in O Kahn-Freund, *Selected Writings* (London, Stevens & Sons, 1978), a paper first published in 1959.

a sustainable notion of the function of labour law.[13] By contrast, older views of the drivers of labour law polices (such as industrial democracy) or newer ones (such as protection of human rights) did not present claims that were unique to labour law. They represented rather the extension into the world of work of ideas of general social value. The same claim can be made for the notion of efficiency, around which this chapter revolves.

What might be argued in relation to efficiency is a rather different point. This is that efficiency is a goal which it is difficult for labour law to adopt because it is inconsistent with the core policies of the subject. This is not an argument that the core policies of labour law are idiosyncratic to that subject, but rather that labour law must reject efficiency as a goal if it is to pursue those (non-idiosyncratic) core policies. This is a large question, which cannot be explored here. Suffice it to say that the argument seems to underplay very substantially the extent to which efficiency is already established as a goal of labour law.[14] In any event, the goals of this chapter are more modest: it is to explore the efficiency claims for voice-at-work mechanisms, given the particular definition of efficiency stipulated for.

The chapter proceeds as follows. Section II deals with worker voice in corporate law and so focuses on the form of governance known to corporate law scholars as control rights. The claims of law and economics scholarship that employees are in most cases efficiently excluded from control rights are shown not to be as conclusive as is generally taken to be the case. Section III analyses the open-ended nature of the contract of employment and analyses the potential value to both employees and employers of allocating governance rights to employees. Section IV takes the notion of governance rights beyond the control rights known to corporate law and discusses the potential role of sub-board participation mechanisms, such as works councils and collective bargaining. Section V describes the German system of codetermination as a case-study of a governance system containing board representation, works councils and collective bargaining. Section VI considers the empirical evidence about the efficiency of the German system. Section VII considers the extent to which the German system is capable of generalization. Section VIII concludes.

II. Worker Voice and the Law and Economics of Corporation Law

Over the past three decades or so, the economic analysis of law has transformed

[13] P Davies and M Freedland, *Labour Legislation and Public Policy* (Oxford, Oxford University Press, 1993).

[14] See G Davidov, 'The Goals of Regulating Work: Between Universalism and Selectivity' (2014) 64 *University of Toronto Law Journal* 1, who identifies a trend in the goals of labour law away from selective towards universal goals, the two main examples of the latter in his discussion being 'efficiency' and 'human freedom and capabilities'.

the study of corporate law—and indeed many other fields of legal research. By and large labour or employment law has remained resistant to this trend.[15] Work has either continued within the existing paradigms or, where advances have been made, they have focused on distributional questions. Fairness rather than efficiency has been the acid test.

Whatever the explanations for this lack of this engagement with economic concepts, some opportunities to open up old questions in novel ways were in danger of being lost to labour lawyers. Take, for example, the idea of the company as a 'nexus of contracts', one of the foundational ideas of the law and economics school in relation to companies.[16] This idea seeks to explain the function of separate corporate personality in the following way. As a separate legal person, the company facilitates contracting among all the providers of inputs to the corporation (and indeed the purchasers of outputs). By contracting with the company, which acts, so to speak, as a central counterparty, the suppliers and purchasers are enabled, functionally and cheaply, to contract with each other.[17]

For labour lawyers the important implication is that, by itself, the nexus of contracts theory tells one nothing about where control rights should be allocated in the company. (For the purposes of this essay I take control rights to be the rights to appoint or remove directors or to give them instructions as to how to conduct the management of the business.) Indeed, it undermines one of the historically potent rationales for the allocation of control rights to shareholders, ie that they are the owners of the company. There is no obvious basis in this contracting theory upon which control rights are allocated (either wholly or in part) to shareholders. Shareholders are just one among several groups of people whose inputs are necessary for production (at least in most cases).[18] Shareholders are contractors with, not owners of, the corporation. Control rights, therefore, cannot be claimed by the shareholders on the grounds that they are owners of the company: the nexus of contracts theory does not need to assign ownership of the company to anyone—though it does need to do something about control rights.[19]

[15] See M Wachter, 'Neoclassical Labor Economics: Its Implications for Labor and Employment Law' in C Estlund and M Wachter (eds), *Research Handbook on the Economics of Labor and Employment Law* (Cheltenham, Edward Elgar, 2013) ch 2. For notable exceptions in the UK, see ACL Davies, *Perspectives on Labour Law*, 1st edn (Cambridge, Cambridge University Press, 2004); much of the *oeuvre* of Simon Deakin and some of the work of Hugh Collins, eg H Collins, 'Regulating the Employment Relationship for Competitiveness' (2001) 31 *Industrial Law Journal* 17 and H Collins, 'Justifications and Techniques of Legal Regulation of the Employment Relation' in H Collins, P Davies and R Rideout (eds), *Legal Regulation of the Employment Relation* (The Hague, Kluwer, 2000).

[16] M Jensen and W Meckling, 'Theory of the Firm: Management Behavior, Agency Costs and Ownership Structure' (1976) 3 *Journal of Law and Economics* 305.

[17] Separate legal personality, together with limited liability, also functions so as to separate business assets from shareholders' personal assets and to focus business creditors on the corporate assets and personal creditors on the shareholders' assets—but that is not an argument relevant to the present discussion. See H Hansmann and R Kraakman, 'The Essential Role of Organizational Law' (2000) 110 *Yale Law Journal* 387.

[18] Under certain, rather rare, conditions a business could be financed wholly by debt and internal cash flows, and so not need shareholders and risk capital.

[19] English doctrine, in any event, abandoned the idea that the shareholders own the company (as opposed to their shares) more than half a century ago in *Short v Treasury Commissioners* [1948]

In order to decide on the allocation of control rights (and thus to decide whether shareholders should have them exclusively, be required to share them with other contracting groups or be entirely excluded from control rights), some additional level of theorizing is required. It is true that the mainstream of law and economics theory as applied to corporations does have a rationale for allocating control rights exclusively to shareholders. This is that shareholders, by contrast with any other contracting group, are in the worst position to protect their interests by contract and have the best incentives to exercise control rights efficiently. Therefore, if the objective is to minimize the sum of the company's costs of contracting and costs of governance, the shareholders get exclusive control rights in most situations.[20] Shareholders are residual claimants because they earn remuneration on their investment only after other groups (who have fixed contractual claims on the company) have been paid off. Ordinary shareholders, at any rate, do not normally have a contractual (or any other) right to a return on their investment (short of a winding up of the company), but receive one only to the extent that the company earns profits and the directors decide to make a distribution to them.[21] The rule that shareholders are remunerated out of profits means that the claims of other groups have to be met before a profit is struck and a potential for distribution created. It is clear enough that the shareholders come last in the liquidation of the company and this is also broadly true when the company is a going concern, because of the 'no distribution except out of profits' rule.[22] Because of their lack of a fixed claim and residual status, shareholders have the strongest incentives to drive down the company's costs of production. Every pound of net cost saved is a pound of profit earned, which will inure to the benefit of the shareholders via either a distribution or the share price. Nor can shareholders contract for rights of return, without changing the function they perform in corporate finance, ie the provision of risk capital.[23]

This is an argument which says that control rights are allocated to shareholders because they will make best use of them (by pressing for managerial action which minimizes the company's costs of production). The point can also

AC 534 (HL). The real objection to the nationalization statute in that case was that the state obtained control of the company without paying a control premium.

[20] See H Hansmann, *The Ownership of Enterprise* (Cambridge, MA, Harvard University Press, 1996) pt I, who also provides a rationale for the cases where shareholders are excluded from or share control rights.

[21] The prospect of a distribution may cause the company's share price to increase and investors can thus obtain a return by selling part of their holdings before a distribution is made. However, if it were clear that a company would never make a distribution (eg where it is ineluctably prohibited from doing so), there is no reason to supposed that profits earned by the company would have an impact on the share price.

[22] Given the 'no distribution except out of profits' rule, investors who want a reliable contractual entitlement to a regular return need to provide debt to the company; by the same token, where debt is substituted for equity, the contractual commitment of the company to the debt-holder impairs the loss-absorbing capacity which attaches to the reduced equity.

[23] Of course, shareholders can contract for dividend rights and preference shareholders often do so, but typically preference shares are also non-voting shares, ie their holders have no control rights but rely on their contractual entitlements instead.

be put negatively. Without control rights the company's cost of ordinary share capital would increase. Investment via the acquisition of ordinary shares consists of handing over a chunk of money in exchange for shares which normally carry no right to a return (short of liquidation) but an expectation of a return, if the company makes profits and the directors decide to pay out part of that profit. Without control rights the power of shareholders to protect their expectations would be much reduced. Consequently, without the ability to choose those who are, or those who monitor, the management and make distribution decisions (the members of the board), shareholders would pay less for the company's shares because the risk of no or an inadequate return would increase. Investors would thus protect themselves against loss of control rights by paying less for their shares, but society would suffer because companies would have a reduced capacity to raise risk capital.

By contrast, standard law and economics theory views employees as able to contract for protection against opportunistic behaviour by others in the nexus of contracts with the company, and for the same reason they have weaker incentives than shareholders to exercise control rights efficiently. This is partly because less turns for them on the efficient exercise of their control right (since they have contractual entitlements which the company is obliged to meet except in extremis) and partly because their incentives, as prior rather than residual claimants, are to enhance their contractual entitlements, irrespective of the impact of that enhancement on efficiency.

Overall, the argument is that society will benefit from allocating control rights exclusively to shareholders, because the persons with control rights are then those with the biggest incentives to reduce the company's costs of production. The dominance of this theory amongst law and economic scholars may seem to present a gloomy picture for the labour lawyer. But, like many an economic theory, examining when the theory does not apply proves to be as illuminating as examining when it does. In particular, once one relaxes the assumption that all claimants other than shareholders have fixed contractual claims on the corporation under fully specified contracts, then some important questions can be asked. How do the arguments for allocating control rights exclusively to shareholders fare when other groups have incomplete contractual protection? Are employees' interests confined to the short-term maximization of their rents or do they have a long-term interest in the competitive efficiency of the enterprise?

III. The Open-ended Nature of the Contract of Employment and Governance Rights

Let us start the process of reverse-engineering the standard law and economics argument by examining whether the contract of employment is a fully specified contract, so that employees do not need control rights to protect themselves against opportunism. The law and economics school, at least in its early manifestations, tended to treat the contract of employment as a fully specified contract. On the reward side, this appears a plausible argument. Entitlements as to wages, bonuses, hours and holidays are normally spelled out, although, in the case of bonuses, the provisions normally provide for a way of calculating the bonus rather than a commitment to a fixed amount of payment. Even on the reward side, however, the contract rarely seeks to specify more than current entitlements. Commitments to wage increases are uncommon, even more so commitments to promotion. These lie, as far as the employee is concerned, in the realm of expectation, not contract. This may not matter in a short-term employment contact that is expected to be ended before such questions arise, or if the costs of job change are minimal, because the employee can enforce his or her expectations through exit. In contracts that are expected to be of long duration, however, perhaps because of human capital investment by the employee (discussed below), the result is that important elements of the reward side of the contract are not fully specified.

On the task side the contract often does not achieve even the level of specification found on the reward side, whilst the provisions for termination of the contract normally vest a high level of discretion in the employer about the continuity of the employment. It is in the employer's interest that the contract of employment should contain these elements of discretion. The employer wishes to control what the employee is required to do in the light of how matters develop in the future. It will be unwilling to tie itself down with a limited and specific job description. Consequently job descriptions tend to be either short and vague or very long and detailed, specifying more tasks than any one person could possibly discharge in a working week, so that the employer retains a discretion as to which items to choose for actual performance from time to time. If the job description is framed as a concise analysis of what the job entails at the point of hiring, the tasks actually performed tend to diverge quite quickly from those listed. Quite apart from the undesirability (from the employer's point of view) of defining the employee's tasks very precisely, it is difficult for the employer to specify the quality of the employee's performance of those tasks, except in very general terms. Often the quality issue is simply not addressed, except in procedural terms, eg a periodic appraisal mechanism. In short, the contract of employment is a potentially long-term relational contract, whose core features on the task side can be spelled out at the time of hiring only to a limited extent.[24] This contractual gap was partly filled by implied terms developed at common law, but these terms were necessarily standards rather than rules[25] and so diffi-

[24] S Deakin and G Morris, *Labour Law*, 6th edn (Oxford, Hart Publishing, 2012) ch 4.3.

[25] The central ones bearing on the current discussion were the employee's implied duties to: obey lawful orders, take reasonable care in the performance of the contract, to act loyally towards the interests of the employer and to serve the employer faithfully. See M Freedland and N Kountouris, *The Legal Construction of Personal Work Relations* (Oxford, Oxford University Press, 2011) ch 4.1.B.

cult to apply on a self-enforcing basis and unattractive to apply via litigation in the courts, except upon termination of the contract. The implied terms might be formulated in a pro-employer way but low-cost and effective enforcement of those terms was not usually available to the employer, at least in modern times (ie with the growth of statutory controls over termination by the employer).

Reserving contractual discretion as to how the employee is to discharge the task side of the contract makes abundant good sense from the employer's point of view, and may have some advantages for the employee who is not risk averse. Nevertheless, converting a contractual commitment to work into the effective deployment of labour power is a challenge for the employer. Traditionally, this was done by creating a layer of inferior managers,[26] whose task was to monitor and direct the activities of the large number of bottom-level employees, and by assigning those managers a social status clearly superior to the 'hands' they directed.[27] This proved an unsustainable general solution to the employers' problem, partly because it became expensive to maintain additional layers of management and partly, as jobs became more skilled and conferred high levels of discretion on employees, low-level managers were often unable to observe how well the worker was performing the assigned tasks until after they had been completed—and perhaps not even then.[28] Alternatively, employers might design financial incentives to induce the level of effort desired, but it was often difficult to identify a measurable payment metric that was both appropriate and not open to manipulation by the employee.[29] Again, this problem became more prominent with the increased technical sophistication of jobs. In modern times, 'human resource management' techniques are a response to this issue, with mixed results.

If, therefore, the reward side of the contract is not fully specified, the claim of employees to governance rights cannot be set aside as superfluous. Equally, if the task side is even more open-ended and the monitoring costs of the employer are high, the employer has an interest in the internalization by the workforce of effective working practices. These positions give rise to the possibility that the following type of 'deal' could be arrived at between employer and employee. Employees would commit to discharge the task side of the work contract in a way which promoted the employer's needs for productive output, in exchange for the employer's commitment to take into account the interests of the employees in the exercise of its managerial discretions, notably when taking decisions which impact on wage increases, promotion and continuity of employment. Employees would internalize the need to work co-operatively (rather than be monitored or subject to financial inducements related to their work performance) whilst

[26] These were the charge-hands and foremen so prominent in 19th-century factories.

[27] The implied duty to obey lawful orders was clearly central in this context.

[28] As Fox remarked, '[P]erformance of the discretionary content requires, not trained obedience to specific external controls, but the exercise of wisdom, judgement, expertise': A Fox, *Beyond Contract: Work, Power and Trust Relations* (London, Faber & Faber, 1974) 19.

[29] 'Payment by results' reward systems, at one time popular in industrial production, for example, tended to allow work groups to capture all the efficiency gains from technical innovation, thus reducing the incentives for companies to make such investments: Clegg (n 4) 178–80.

employers would commit to giving employee interests an independent weight when exercising their discretions. This could be referred to as 'the mutual co-operation deal'.

This type of deal might be particularly valuable in industries or occupations where the employer needs to induce employees to make investment in firm-specific skills ('firm-specific human capital investment' (FSHCI)). A firm-specific skill has either no, or much less, value when deployed on behalf of another employer, because the most extensive exercise of the skill depends upon its use in conjunction with the particular physical assets or routines that the current employer has established. Loss of a job thus means loss of the opportunity to deploy the skill, either at all or as effectively as in the previous employment, and thus future employment at a lower wage. An employee is more likely to expend time or resources in FSHCI if there is some concomitant commitment on the part of the employer to increase wages to reflect the skills acquired and to maintain the employment.[30]

Two clarifications of the 'mutual cooperation deal' should be made. At one level, such a deal would build on developments well established in relation to the contract of employment and the implied term of trust and confidence. However, it would go substantially beyond that. First, the implied term of trust and confidence is essentially a way of controlling opportunistic behaviour within the confines of the contract of employment. The mutual co-operation deal, whilst controlling opportunistic behaviour, would also promote forward-looking solutions to work-related problems, where opportunism was absent. Second, the deal would cover matters normally well outside the confines of the contract of employment, such as the setting of corporate strategy. Third, the deal is likely to need the elaboration of a governance structure which no contractually implied term could generate.

The second clarification is that the mutual co-operation deal is not an expression of the unitary frame of reference. It does not require that employees share the employer's goals and interests in the enterprise. Both workers and employers (ie management assumed to be accountable to shareholder interests) may continue to have interests which diverge from one another in various ways. The question which is posed is whether both employer and employee can each more effectively advance their own interests by defining areas of co-operation which exist alongside areas of conflict. That worker and employer interests in the enterprise are partly congruent and partly conflicting is surely now well established.[31] The question for this chapter is whether it is possible to design institutions which expand the areas of co-operation (in order to reduce the company's costs of production) without denying the likely conflicts between

[30] M Blair and L Stout, 'A Team Production Theory of Corporate Law' (1999) 85 *Virginia Law Review* 24.

[31] J Bélinger and P Edwards, 'The Conditions Promoting Compromise in the Workplace' (2007) 45 *British Journal of Industrial Relations* 713, identifying technology, exposure to the market and institutions as the operative factors in relation to conflict and co-operation *within* collective bargaining.

employers and workers over the distribution of the increased revenues resulting from successful co-operation.

It might be asked whether the deal I propose could be set out in a contract, thus obviating the need for governance structures. It is unlikely that this arrangement would be (or even could be) cast into contractual form. Specifying what the exchange of mutual regard undertakings would mean in all future situations which might arise would be beyond the capacity of the parties to imagine and expensive to translate into contractual language, even if possible to imagine.[32] Indeed, it is likely that the terms of the arrangement would not be set out explicitly at all, but would be discernible only from repeated interactions amongst the parties involved, giving rise to what economists call 'implicit contracts'.[33] Precisely because ex ante specification of the deal is so difficult, it is likely to express itself in the creation of governance arrangements that handle problems and issues as and when they arise.

Governance arrangements also have a central role to play in verifying whether the parties are adhering to the underlying deal. For example, from an enforcement point of view, an obvious difficulty with the mutual co-operation deal that is not enforceable as a contract is that the exchanges under it are not synchronous. The parties cannot enforce the arrangement through self-help, ie by refusing to perform if the other party is not ready to perform, because simultaneous exchanges are not expected to occur. In particular, whilst the employee commitment is more or less continuous—co-operation is required in principle in all working periods—the employer's commitments are episodic, ie they are triggered mainly when managerial decisions bearing on wages or continuity of employment fall to be taken. Some sort of control arrangement is thus needed to protect the party who performs first, and this builds an argument for a governance arrangement. Governance rights are particularly important for the employees for verification purposes. The employer may not be able to observe accurately the effort of individual employees but it is probably well placed to gauge the productivity of the workforce as a whole through its management information systems.

For employees the matter is more complex. The employer's commitment is not likely to consist of an undertaking never to dismiss employees for economic reasons or always to promote employees or raise their wages whenever asked to do so. Rather, it is a promise to exercise its discretions in a way that takes appro-

[32] The standard impediments to specifying completely long-term contracts—bounded rationality and transaction costs—apply strongly in this situation. See O Williamson, 'Transaction-Cost Economics: The Governance of Contractual Relations' (1979) 22 *Journal of Law and Economics* 233.

[33] See eg A Shleifer and R Summers, 'Breach of Trust in Hostile Takeovers' in A Auerbach (ed), *Corporate Takeovers: Causes and Consequences* (Chicago and London, University of Chicago Press, 1988). The term 'implicit contract', like its bed-fellow 'agency costs', is apt to cause misunderstanding between lawyers and economists because the term means different things in each discipline. Lawyers tend to think of implicit contracts as contracts the terms of which have to be deduced by the court from the behaviour of the parties, whereas for an economist an implicit contract is an agreement the terms of which are not observable by third parties (with any accuracy), including by a court. So, for a lawyer, an implicit contract is not a contract at all.

priate account of the interests of employees in continued employment or wage increases in return for co-operative working or FSHCI. Whenever the employer wishes to take decisions in these areas which do not fully comply with the employees' wishes, it will normally have plausible reasons for so deciding—often relating to the economic state of the company. However, given the asymmetry of information between employees and managers, it may well be very difficult for the employees to judge whether the employer is acting opportunistically or has arrived at a defensible decision after fully considering the employees' interests. Governance rights may provide the employees with reliable information to make that judgement. In addition, governance rights not only protect employees ex post (after they have performed) against employer opportunism but they will also have the ex ante effect of helping to set the conditions under which the employees are willing to make their initial commitments. For example, an employee is more likely to engage in FSHCI, in the expectation of higher wages in the future, if she knows there is in place some governance mechanism that can scrutinize the employer's subsequent wage decisions.

However, verification is only one, perhaps a secondary, function of governance institutions. The governance institution may constitute part of the process through which the mutual co-operation commitments are expressed. Thus, in their classic theoretical analysis of works councils, Freeman and Lazear show that the information rights of works councils can not only operate as a verification tool for employees (incidentally also reducing the level of strategic industrial action), but also encourage the communication of information from employees to management, which gives rise to better-informed management decisions. Equally, consultation rights for employees may lead to the emergence in the consultation process of new solutions to problems facing the firm or the improvement of existing solutions, whilst also assuring employees that their interests are being taken into account in managerial decision-making.[34]

The above paragraphs have been aimed at disposing of the argument that employees have complete contracts with the company and so can protect themselves through the contracting mechanism and do not need recourse to governance rights. However, even at a theoretical level, this is not enough to make out the case for allocating governance rights to employees. Employees might be very poor monitors of management, so that introducing them onto the board might reduce the overall quality of the supervision of management. Or employees might be equally good monitors but allocating control rights to them and to shareholders jointly might produce a very high level of conflict between the two groups on the board, again reducing the quality of the board's supervision of management. The most efficient allocation is one that minimizes the combined costs of contracting and of governance:[35] if the governance costs of allocating employees control rights are very high, then it might be less costly

[34] RB Freeman and E P Lazear, 'An Economic Analysis of Works Councils' in J Rogers and W Streek (eds), *Works Councils* (Chicago and London, University of Chicago Press, 1995).

[35] Hansmann (n 20) pt I.

for the company to exclude employees from control rights even at the cost of less efficient working practices. We will return to this point in Section VI, since it is essentially an empirical point.

IV. Governance Mechanisms in Corporate and Labour Law

One potential conclusion from the argument in the previous section is that allocating employees governance rights might reduce the company's costs of contracting for labour inputs, because it could be part of an overall deal in which employees work more effectively to deliver the output the employer is seeking, in exchange for a greater input by employees into managerial decision-making. The next question is: what sort of governance rights are we thinking of? The corporate law debate revolves around what we have termed control rights, ie the right to appoint and remove and instruct the board of the company.[36] Governance rights, however, need not be so narrowly conceived when the employment relationship is considered. Labour lawyers tend to have a broader concept of governance rights. Employee representation at board level is included, to be sure, but so also are collective bargaining and works councils. All three can be thought of as institutions of joint regulation, but potentially operating at different levels of decision-making within the company or covering different subject-matters. As we shall see in our case-study of Germany, it is the interrelationships among these various institutions that give the overall governance arrangements their particular character.

The institutional value of the board, from the point of view of employee governance, is that it captures the high-level strategic decision making within the company.[37] As the UK Corporate Governance Code puts it:

> The board's role is to provide entrepreneurial leadership of the company within a framework of prudent and effective controls which enables risk to be assessed and managed. The board should set the company's strategic aims, ensure that the necessary financial and human resources are in place for the company to meet its objectives and review management performance. The board should set the company's values and standards and ensure that its obligations to its shareholders and others are understood and met.[38]

[36] The corporate lawyers' concept of governance strategies might also embrace situations where the employees have rights to take decisions directly (rather than through representatives) and systems in which (some of) the board members are made sensitive to the employee interests through mechanisms other than their being appointed by the employees. See Kraakman and others (n 9) 39. For simplicity, however, we will concentrate on the core appointment, removal and instruction rights.

[37] Most corporate decisions are taken solely by the board. In the case of a small number of 'fundamental' decisions shareholder approval is required as well, but even then the right to initiate the decision is, de jure or de facto, with the board.

[38] Financial Reporting Council, *UK Corporate Governance Code* (London, 2012) A.1 (Supporting Principle).

To be sure, not all boards work in this way. Some may be captured by the company's management or by a controlling shareholder. Nevertheless, the board has formal power to approve the company's strategy and there is no other institution within the corporate structure with the potential to enable employees to have an input into corporate strategic decisions. Those decisions will certainly include some decisions of significance to employees under a mutual co-operation arrangement. In particular, high-level decisions about the location of investment might well impact in due course on the competitiveness of particular establishments operated by the company and thus on the availability of continued employment or promotion opportunities in those establishments.[39] However, many decisions salient to employees will never reach board level. The board meets episodically, perhaps for one day each month, and has time only for matters of overall importance for the company (or the group of companies it controls). The size of wage increases in a particular establishment or enterprise, for example, is likely to be left with lower-level management in the normal run of things, as are many other matters relating to terms and conditions of employment or which impact upon terms and conditions of employment. These are matters more likely to be captured by the governance mechanisms which labour lawyers have studied, namely collective bargaining and works councils.

It thus seems plausible to assert that a fully developed system of employee governance, forming part of a deal in which the employees commit to co-operative forms of working, might involve participation at both board and sub-board levels and the involvement at sub-board level might focus on works councils or collective bargaining or both. Employee governance rights which operate only at sub-board or only at board level are unlikely to provide sufficient support for a fully effective co-operation arrangement, but each is arguably a necessary ingredient in a complete structure.

The next part of this chapter will analyse employee governance rights in Germany. There are three main reasons for choosing Germany as the country to examine more closely. First, it has an employee governance system that displays all three elements (board, works council and collective bargaining) which seem relevant—though it is not unique in that respect. Second, Germany has the strongest system of governance rights for employees of all the EU countries. It is unique in having near-parity representation at board level in companies with more than 2,000 employees, and its works councils have a particularly impressive set of information, consultation and co-decision rights. Finally, and most important for this chapter, there is now a growing body of empirical evidence about the efficiency effects of the German system. This will be examined in the Section VI.

[39] Lord Wedderburn and P Davies, 'The Land of Industrial Democracy' (1977) 6 *Industrial Law Journal* 197.

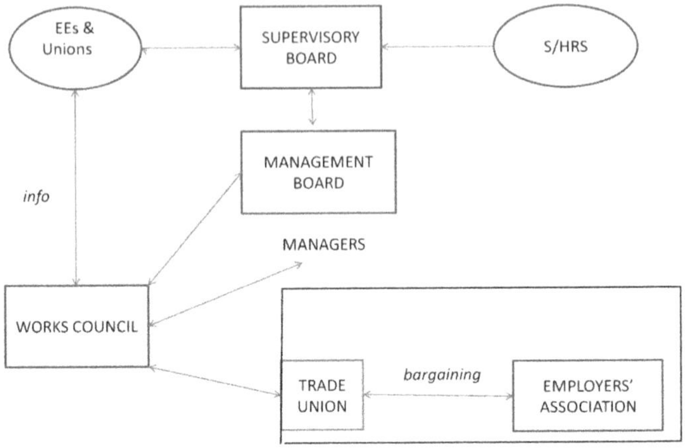

Figure 1. German codetermination.

V. The German System of Employee Participation

The three elements of German codetermination are shown clearly in Figure 1, as are the complexities of their interrelationships. The first element is the appointment of employee representatives to the supervisory board.[40] In companies with more than 2,000 employees (outside the iron, steel and coal industries)[41] the employee representatives constitute one-half of the supervisory board and the shareholder representatives the other half, but the shareholder representatives can insist on their choice of the chair of the board, who has the casting vote in cases of deadlock.[42] All employee representatives are elected by the workforce of the company (either directly or indirectly via delegates), and so a crucial

[40] In Germany a two-tier board is mandatory. Employee representation is on the upper—or supervisory—board. The supervisory board appoints the members of the management board. The division of function between supervisory and management boards in a two-tier system is not bound to take a particular form. The German company law of 1937 (which influenced the post-war legislation) took a noticeably constrained view of the functions of the supervisory board. In 2002, however, the rules were amended so that what the supervisory board of a listed German company is now expected to do vis-à-vis the management board is not markedly different from how a UK one-tier board functions vis-à-vis the management of a UK listed company—except that the UK management is not formally organized in a separate board but are members of the one-tier board along with the non-executive directors. Even this difference is attenuated by the fact that members of the management board often attend meetings of the German supervisory board, even if they are not members of it. See M Roth, 'Corporate Boards in Germany' in P Davies and others (eds), *Corporate Boards in Law and Practice* (Oxford, Oxford University Press, 2013) 276–78, 282–83.

[41] To reduce length I leave on one side those three industries' (even stronger) provisions as well as those weaker ones applying to companies with fewer than 2000 employees.

[42] Codetermination Act 1976 § 27. Hence the term 'quasi-parity' codetermination, in contrast to the full parity operating in the iron, coal and steel industries.

issue becomes the allocation of nomination rights. The union has nomination rights over a minority of the employee representatives (the larger the board, the smaller the de facto proportion of union nominees)[43] but the union must give the workforce a choice of nominees for election (ie there must be more union nominees than union places). Nomination rights for the remainder of the board lie with the employees (one-fifth of the workforce or 100 employees), though in practice the works council will have substantial influence over the selection of those nominated. The union-nominated representatives need not be employees of the company (and normally are not) but the other employee representatives are required to be employees.[44]

The formal role of the supervisory board is not altered where quasi-parity codetermination applies (but see below) and the formal legal duties of the employee representatives are no different from those of the shareholder representatives.[45] The supervisory board appoints the members of the managing board. To constrain the shareholder representatives' powers of appointment (when coupled with the chair's casting vote), appointments to the managing board require (on a first vote) two-thirds support (ie some element of support from the employee representatives) from the supervisory board. This is an important mechanism for making the senior executives of the company sensitive to the interests of the employees and the trade union in the company. If the two-thirds level of support is not achieved, a later vote can be held after a further month, at which only simple majority support is required. However, the nomination power for this later election is confined to a supervisory board subcommittee consisting of equal numbers of employee and shareholder representatives. The institutional pressures are thus towards appointments to the managing board on which both shareholder and employee representatives agree.[46]

The second element is the works council. This operates within the company but at sub-board level.[47] The members of the works council are elected by the employees with more than six months' service, must be employees of the company and any employee may nominate a candidate. However, the union

[43] Two union nominees out of 6 or 8 employee representatives in the case of 12 or 16 member boards and 3 out of 10 in the case of 20 member boards (Codetermination Act § 7). The size of the board is determined by the number of employees in the company and the formula can lead to large and unwieldy boards. The average board size across Europe as a whole is no more than the smallest board permitted under quasi-parity codetermination. See P Davies, K Hopt, R Nowak and G van Solinge 'General Report' in Davies et al (eds) (n 40) 15.

[44] Codetermination Act 1976, §§ 15–16.

[45] However, those board member duties are owed to the 'company', which is not traditionally conceived of as being identical with the shareholders but as embracing a range of other groups as well, so that the board formally has power to balance all group interests in the way it considers appropriate: see Roth (n 40) 262–63.

[46] Codetermination Act § 31. The fact that the employee representatives must include one member of the 'executive staff' (§ 15(2))—in effect the leading white-collar workers—may help the shareholders build support for proposed member of the management board.

[47] Works Constitution Act. In fact, there is a hierarchy of works councils, operating establishment, enterprise and group level, but this account will ignore that complication.

represented within the plant also has nomination rights.[48] Most works councillors, at least in large companies, are union members,[49] and, since most employee board representatives are also works council members, union influence carries through to that level as well. It is mandatory for a works council to be set up in establishments with five or more employees, upon request by three or more employees or a trade union represented within the establishment.[50] The powers of the works council are legally defined and wide ranging but exclude the core subjects of collective bargaining (basic wages, hours and holidays). Those powers range, in ascending order, from rights to information about the financial affairs of the company; rights to consultation over personnel planning (including works processes and job allocation); and consent rights to 'social matters' such as payment methods, performance-related pay, allocation of working hours (unless these are covered by collective agreement); and veto rights over dismissals. Since these powers are legally granted, they are legally sanctioned and in fact the works council is forbidden to use industrial action to enforce its rights (or to any other end).[51] Where the works council has a consent or veto right, a failure to agree can be resolved or a veto removed by a third party, such as an arbitration board or the labour court.

Collective bargaining in Germany deals with the usual core subjects of bargaining in any country, but its crucial characteristic for present purposes is that it is conducted outside the enterprise on a multi-employer basis and thus with an employers' association. Typically, the bargaining covers a particular industry in a particular region of the country.

From the above short account of the elements of German codetermination it appears that it creates a complex set of interrelationships among the employee representatives in the three governance institutions and between different levels of management and those representatives (Figure 2). The potential for these

• Ee reps on SB	⇔	Shr reps/top management
• Supervisory board	⇔	Works council
• Works council	⇔	Plant management
• Works council	⇔	Trade union & collective bargaining
• Trade unions	⇔	SB/top management and employers association

Figure 2. Interrelationships.

[48] ibid §§ 8 and 14.

[49] Overall, about three-quarters of works council members were union members in 1990: W Müller-Jentsch, 'Germany: From Collective Voice to Co-Management' in Rogers and Streek (n 34) table 3.2.

[50] Above n 47, §§ 1 and 17. In fact works councils are ubiquitous in larger companies but only about 35% of the total number of eligible companies have one: Müller-Jentsch (n 49) 56.

[51] ibid § 74.

relationships to support long-term co-operative deals can be identified along the following lines. The size of the employee representation on the supervisory board and that board's appointment rights over the management board give the employees the power to influence corporate strategy so that it does not cut across implicit contracts between workers and employer (the details of which are probably settled at lower levels within the company). Information obtained at supervisory board level is fed to the works council and this reduces the information asymmetry between works council and plant or company management. That lower level management is less likely to behave opportunistically in dealing with the works council (whether in relation to the council's information, consultation or decision rights) for two reasons. Plant or company management statements may verifiable by the council through the information it has received via the supervisory board, so that lower management has an incentive not to exaggerate. The top management of the company will wish to maintain at least a minimum level of support from the employee representatives at board level in order to secure the continuation of their own jobs and those representatives may be influenced by the views of the works council about how it has been treated by lower-level management. The legal rights of the works council thus provide a platform from which the co-operative deal can be fashioned.

Nevertheless, there is nothing in the above which guarantees that the works council and lower-level management will work co-operatively rather than antagonistically. For example, the works council might perceive the best interests of the employees to be served by its adopting an obstructive attitude towards the exercise of its legal rights, in exchange for concessions in areas not covered by their statutory powers. However, there is one feature of the German arrangements which reduces this risk. This is that the high-powered distributional conflicts are allocated to collective bargaining, which takes place outside the plant on a multi-employer basis. Whilst the works council has decision or consultation rights over a number of wages and hours issues, these matters are framed within the context provided by collective bargaining (assuming the employer is a member of the employers' association). So, whilst council/management relations display a mixture of co-operative and conflictual elements, the risk is reduced that conflict will become the dominant characteristic of that relationship and stymie co-operative initiatives.

On the other hand, the design of the arrangement is clearly not that union and works council be put in hermetically sealed boxes.[52] In addition to the union's formal rights to initiate the establishment of a works council, to enter the plant and to attend works council meetings if one-quarter of the members of the council so request,[53] we have seen that there is substantial overlap between union and works council membership. Nevertheless, there is a risk inherent

[52] For a contrast between Germany and France in this respect, see R Gumbrall-McCormick and R Hyman, 'Embedded Collectivism? Workplace Representation in France and Germany' (2006) 37 *Industrial Relations Journal* 473.

[53] Above n 47, §§ 2(2), 17(3) and 31.

in these arrangements that the union will seek to make the works council its puppet or, alternatively, set up a rival in-plant institution for the representation of the workers' interests. In either case, the high-powered distributional conflicts, instead of being resolved through multi-employer bargaining, might enter the plant and undermine the co-operative elements in the works council's relationship with management. Yet, the works council and the union have strong incentives not to allow either of these developments to occur, because each will maximize its influence if they work together in separate, but linked, spheres. The works council may need expertise which only the union can provide (or provide at reasonable cost), whilst the union needs representation within the plant to build membership. At times the works council and the union have been in danger of becoming rivals for employee support within the enterprise, but by and large unions have adopted the strategy or working through, rather than against, the works council.[54] Equally, the union has an interest in the works council not venturing into the field of high-powered distributional conflict but leaving that to collective bargaining, for otherwise the role on the union might be significantly undermined.

Neither is it guaranteed that the presence of employee representatives on the board will not generate a high degree of conflict. Whilst the shareholder representatives can always break deadlock in their favour and this may encourage the employee representatives to seek agreement, it is easily conceivable that those representatives might think that their prestige with their electorate would be enhanced by pushing matters to a deadlock rather than in seeking consensus. So, it is conceivable that quasi-parity codetermination will lead to high levels of conflict between shareholder and employee representatives at board level and that the quality of board decisions on corporate strategy will suffer.

VI. Empirical Studies of the German System

It is thus possible to construct a plausible argument in favour of an efficiency view of the German codetermination system. It is equally clear that the design of the system does not guarantee an outcome which reduces the company's costs of production. Employee representatives, both at board and lower levels, might use their powers so as to raise, rather than reduce, the company's costs of contracting for labour. Higher wages might be compounded by lower levels of effort rather than offset by higher levels of productivity.[55] Board-level employees might slow

[54] Müller-Jentsch (n 49) 64. Works Constitution Act § 2 in fact imposes an obligation on the works council to work co-operatively with the union for the good of the employees and the enterprise. There is no corresponding obligation on the union.

[55] Brian Cheffins has a game-theoretic model in which it is shown that, whilst the joint surplus of employers and employees is maximized by sticking to the co-operative deal, the welfare of either party is maximized by defecting from the deal, provided that the other party does not defect:

down the process of formulating and implementing revised corporate strategies as the business environment changes. Even if labour codetermination reduces the company's costs of contacting for labour, it may increase its costs of contracting for capital, and the net balance of those cost movements may be negative. It is therefore of the utmost significance to look at the empirical evidence that might cast light on these questions.

Let us look first at the board-level evidence. There is a long tradition in Germany of qualitative studies of the operation of boards under quasi-parity codetermination. These studies are not that useful from our point of view, partly because observational work on boards (whether in Germany or elsewhere) is hard to do, given the difficulties of obtaining sufficient access, and the studies therefore tend to be based on interviews and questionnaires rather than real-time observation. Nevertheless, these studies do rebut one hypothesis about the functioning of boards under codetermination. One might think that codetermined boards would discharge the same functions as before they were codetermined but display high levels of conflict between employee and shareholder representatives. In fact, overt conflict, involving the use of the chair's casting vote is rare and consensus reached after perhaps hard bargaining between the two groups is the norm. On the other hand, the functions of the board do change, in that more time under codetermination is spent on strategic issues which impinge rather directly on the interests of the employees and less time on strategic issues which lack this quality.

In Katharina Pistor's perceptive analysis of these studies, codetermination is a 'socio-political model with governance externalities'.[56] By this she means that the studies show that quasi-parity codetermination has functioned as an effective way of handling the relations between capital and labour, but has operated less effectively as a mechanism for reducing the agency costs[57] of shareholders as against the management of the company. The codetermined board is a less effective way of making managers responsive to the interests of the shareholders, because, in general, the shareholder influence on the supervisory board is diluted and, in particular, because managers can build coalitions with the employee representatives against the shareholder representatives in some situations.[58]

B Cheffins, *Company Law: Theory Structure and Operation* (Oxford, Oxford University Press, 1997) 578–80. Consequently, the constant risk of defection needs to be addressed through governance arrangements which provide that defection will be quickly identified and appropriately punished.

[56] This is the title of her chapter in M Blair and M Roe (eds), *Employees and Corporate Governance* (Washington, DC, Brookings Institution, 1999).

[57] In this context agency costs arise because shareholders, especially dispersed shareholders, run the risk that the management of the company will not loyally pursue the shareholders' interests but rather management's own interests or the interests of some other stakeholder group. To combat this, shareholders may incur costs in the monitoring of management action. The agency costs of shareholders are thus the sum of the post-monitoring 'disloyalty' costs (assuming the monitoring is not wholly successful) plus the costs of the monitoring. The same analysis can be applied to the employees, especially where there is an implicit contract in place which exposes employees to managerial opportunism.

[58] It is sometimes suggested that, for this reason, concentrated shareholding is associated with

However, the codetermined board has operated so as to reduce the agency costs of the employees as against the shareholders and managers of the firm. This analysis nicely frames the issue, but does not tell us whether overall the sum of the employees' and the shareholders' agency costs is reduced.

More recent statistical studies have focused, not on board behaviour, but on seeking to demonstrate associations between the elements of the codetermination system and positive or negative indicators of firm performance. This work has become possible as the range and quality of data sets has improved, but it is not without its own problems, notably the problem of endogeneity.[59] Even taking these studies at face value, a survey of them by Frick and Lehman published in 2006 concluded that no positive or negative association between codetermined boards and the overall value of the firm had been shown.[60] Although disappointing for the advocates of codetermined boards, this conclusion can be read as providing no grounds for arguing that Germany would benefit from changing its current board-level arrangements.

More recently, Maug and colleagues[61] have shown an association between quasi-parity boards, on the one hand, and wage levels and job security among white-collar and skilled blue-collar workers, on the other. As compared with similar companies without quasi-parity codetermination, quasi-parity companies were associated with lower wages levels (to the extent of 3%) but higher levels of employment (some 15%) in periods after the company in question had suffered an economic shock. They interpret these findings as evidence of an 'implicit contract' between these groups of workers and the management of the firms under which lower wages were traded for higher job security. More important for our purposes, they explain the absence of such an association in firms without parity codetermination as evidence that parity codetermination gives the employees a method of verifying and enforcing ex post management's adherence to the 'contract'. This is therefore a study which supports the view that board-level representation at parity facilitates the conclusion of long-term deals between management and workers because it controls ex post opportunism on the part of the management. What these authors have demonstrated is not, of course, a classic example of a deal based on co-operative working or FSHCI. That analysis usually assumes that employee co-operation or investment will

strong forms of employee representation on the board. Controlling shareholders have less need for a board to protect their interests because they have the capacity and incentive to deal with management directly. See M Gelter, 'The Dark Side of Shareholder Influence: Managerial Autonomy and Stakeholder Orientation in Comparative Corporate Governance' (2009) 50 *Harvard Journal of International Law* 129.

[59] R Adams and others, 'The Role of Boards of Directors in Corporate Governance' (2010) 48 *Journal of Economic Literature* 58.

[60] B Frick and E Lehman, 'Corporate Governance in Germany: Ownership, Codetermination and Firm Performance in a Stakeholder Economy' in H Gospel and A Pendleton (eds), *Corporate Governance and Labour Management* (Oxford, Oxford University Press, 2006).

[61] E Maug and others, 'Labor Representation in Governance as an Insurance Mechanism' (2013) European Corporate Governance Institute (ECGI) Finance Working Paper No 411/2014, http://papers.ssrn.com/sol3/papers.cfm?abstract_id=2399399 (accessed 24 March 2014).

show itself in higher wages, whereas the opposite is true in this study. Whilst it is conceivable that workers under the classical model will wish to take out the value of their co-operation in the form of increased job security, rather than higher wages, it is difficult to explain why workers should enter into a deal which reduces their wages from the level that would otherwise obtain.[62] To establish this, it would be necessary to show that the benefit to the employer of co-operative working did not cover the cost to the company of the job security commitment and that the balance of the cost was covered by the reduction in wages. However, the data for the study in question did not permit this hypothesis to be tested.

Turning to works councils, the results of the statistical analyses are richer, but still not conclusive on the overall balance of costs and benefits to the firm. There is substantial support for the propositions that works councils are associated with higher wages, higher productivity, the same level of investment and lower profitability than in firms without works councils.[63] At first sight such findings are strongly in favour of the efficiency of works councils. Lower profitability is not necessarily a finding against the efficiency impact of works councils. It might be a purely distributional point, ie works councils have an impact on the distribution of the company's revenues as between shareholders and workers (in favour of workers) *at the same time* as they lower the company's costs of contracting for labour. In other words, works councils might both raise the joint surplus and divide the resulting surplus between workers and shareholders in a pro-worker way. From the point of view of the efficiency test adopted in this piece, however, the distributional effect of works councils is irrelevant and only the productivity effect is important.

However, it is possible that the adverse distributional impact on the shareholders has efficiency implications for the company. If lower profitability means less by way of distributions to the shareholders (as the lack of impact of works councils on the level of investment suggests), then the amount of equity capital the company will be able to remunerate at an appropriate level will be less than at higher levels of profitability. Shareholders will have an expected rate of return on their equity investment, depending on the riskiness of the company's activities, and so lower profits may mean a constrained ability to remunerate equity capital. This may not matter if the company can substitute debt[64] for equity or has a highly cash generative business so that it can finance investment from internal sources. However, where recourse to these substitutes is constrained,

[62] The authors explain the lack of the insurance arrangement in relation to blue-collar workers on grounds of their de facto under-representation at board level.

[63] Frick and Lehman (n 60); J Addison and others, 'Works Councils in Germany: Their Effects on Establishment Performance' (2001) 53 *Oxford Economic Papers* 659.

[64] Though increased leverage may raise the company's risk profile and thus its cost of equity capital, so that the amount of equity capital the company can remunerate is further reduced. Finance theory predicts precisely this consequence, though at moderate levels of debt (ie low bankruptcy risk) the tax shield for interest payments on debt may mean that more debt reduces the company's overall cost of capital.

the company may find that its ability to finance future positive-value projects is also constrained by lower profitability. This distributional finding may be linked to the traditionally smaller part played in corporate finance by equity and the correspondingly large part played by debt and retained earnings in the funding of German companies as compared with UK companies.[65] Unfortunately, the works councils studies did not have access to the data necessary to assess whether the distributional impact on shareholders of works councils generated costs for companies in terms of higher financing costs and, if so, whether those costs outweighed the productivity gains.

The third important element in the German system is the location of collective bargaining outside the company at multi-employer level. Not all companies that have works councils[66] are covered by collective bargaining arrangements. Taking advantage of this fact, Hübler and Jirjahn[67] compared wage levels and productivity arrangements in companies with works councils which were and were not covered by collective bargaining. They found that in covered companies the level of wages was lower and productivity was higher than in uncovered companies. They interpret this result as showing that, where high-conflict distributional issues are not dealt with through collective bargaining and where they necessarily have to be dealt with through works agreements concluded with the works councils, the works council focuses on those high-conflict issues, to the detriment of its ability to reach co-operative deals with the employer on the task side of the contract. This study thus offers strong support for the Freeman and Lazear conclusion from their theoretical model that firm-level collective bargaining is likely to hinder the conclusion of co-operative deals.[68]

VII. Can the German System Be Generalized?

The empirical evidence about the German system suggests, overall, that it is a system in which the employees' governance rights over the corporation facilitate long-term implicit contracts between employees and managers[69] and that the impact of the system on the production costs of German companies is not negative and may well be positive. Should other countries seek to emulate the German arrangements? Even if the empirical studies had come up with a more

[65] C Mayer and I Alexander, 'Banks and Securities Markets: Corporate Financing in Germany and the UK' (1990) 4 *Journal of the Japanese and International Economies* 450.

[66] And not all companies eligible to have works councils in fact have them (n 50).

[67] O Hübler and U Jirjahn, 'Works Councils and Collective Bargaining in Germany: The Impact of Productivity on Wages' (2003) 50 *Scottish Journal of Political Economy* 471.

[68] Freeman and Lazear (n 34) 32.

[69] This evidence may be thought to be stronger in relation to works councils than in relation to quasi-parity codetermination, but, given the interrelationships identified in Section V, it would be unwise to conclude that works councils would have the same effects if quasi-parity representation at board level were reduced.

ringing endorsement of the German system, the question of transposition raises many difficult questions. Just because a particular set of arrangements may well be functional in Germany, it does not follow that it will be functional in another country with different background institutions. On the other hand, just to state the banality that an institution from country A may operate very differently in country B hardly provides great insight into the factors which might affect the transferability of the institution in question. The institution may not be functional in country B, but maybe it will. How can one assess which is the more likely outcome?[70]

It is sometimes suggested that there is a market answer to this question, which removes the need for developed institutional analysis. It has been pointed out that it is rare (though not unknown) for employees to be allocated control rights in the corporation in the absence of mandatory law requiring this. If, it is said, control sharing were functional, we would see it more frequently. More to the point, shareholders would wish to assign employees a share of control rights in order to reduce the company's costs of production. However, a moment's thought shows that this argument is unconvincing. We have already noted that, although employee governance sharing may lower the company's costs of production, it also has a distributional effect which is adverse to shareholders. In other words, shareholders may be better off with a larger slice of a smaller pie than with a smaller share of a larger pie. If they judge that to be the case, they will oppose moves on the part of the managers to introduce control sharing.[71] Consequently, mandatory law may be necessary to achieve the introduction of control sharing over shareholder opposition for the benefit of society as a whole.

In addition, it is far from clear that the steps necessary to introduce effective control sharing lie wholly within the powers of the company. To be sure, the company can alter its internal governance and propose the establishment of works councils to the employees, but it may be beyond its powers to shape the level of collective bargaining or the attitude of trade unions towards the introduction of works councils. The Freeman and Lazear model suggests that, left to themselves, management will want a works council with too little power and trade unions a works council with too much. Management beholden to shareholders will want to reduce the power of the council to a level below the optimum (because of its distributional impact), whilst the union will want to maximize its institutional power, even though an over-powerful works council may fail to promote co-operative deals.[72] Finally the 'varieties of capitalism' literature[73] suggests that there are complementarities not only between corporate

[70] See on comparative law as a tool of law reform the masterly piece by Otto Kahn-Freund, 'On Uses and Misuses of Comparative Law' (1974) 37 *Modern Law Review* 1.

[71] Shareholders are likely to be in a strong position to oppose such voluntary moves since they would inevitably require amendment to the articles of association which, in most countries, requires a shareholder resolution, normally on a supermajority basis.

[72] Freeman and Lazear (n 34) 29.

[73] P Hall and D Soskice 'An Introduction to Varieties of Capitalism' in P Hall and D Soskice (eds), *Varieties of Capitalism* (Oxford, Oxford University Press, 2001).

governance arrangements in a company and its labour governance institutions, but also with other co-ordination mechanism in society at large in the case of 'co-ordinated market' economies, such as Germany. Those larger societal institutions include employers' associations and the system of education and training a society has put in place. But these societal institutions will be outside the reach of individual companies. For all these reasons, an appropriately calibrated market solution is unlikely to emerge.

Although a legislature has the formal power to overcome sectional shareholder opposition and excessive union demands by introducing, and calibrating, mandatory control sharing, it too (and the government controlling the legislature) will need to have a convincing answer to the ex ante question, ie will the benefits of the reform exceed its costs? Government may worry about the distributional impact on shareholders, if shareholders are a politically powerful group,[74] but, even where government's sole concern is with efficiency, it will need to conclude that the efficiency gains of the new arrangements will be substantial before it expends political capital and scarce legislative time introducing them. The expected opposition may be high and expected benefits of the new system may be uncertain. Take, for example, a jurisdiction with existing institutions not unlike those in the UK. In such a jurisdiction, the intra-plant representation space has been occupied by adversarial collective bargaining; there is no history of workplace-based works councils elected by the employees as a whole; and no significant history of worker representation on the board, even on a voluntary basis; and a history of generally adversarial union/employer relations. In such a case, the degree of institutional upheaval involved in moving to the German system may appear to be high and benefits of such a shift distinctly uncertain. How is collective bargaining not only to be moved to a multi-employer level but the unions induced to vacate a space in which they are already established in exchange for the new role of acting in conjunction with an employee-based works council?[75] How are shareholders to be convinced that parity representation on the board for employees will not entail a significant dilution of their control rights over the company without any corresponding efficiency gains? And so on.

Understanding the development of the German system will provide little help in answering these questions. What is now referred to as the German 'system' was not designed as a coherent whole. Its three constituent parts—board-level representation, works councils and multi-employer collective bargaining—have come together over the years into their current configuration and, arguably, operate so as to reduce the costs of production of German companies. However, no one started with a grand design of the current configuration.[76] Only after

[74] Institutional shareholders; families.

[75] In the UK even the policy of supplementing in-plant collective bargaining with works councils with information and consultation rights has proved daunting to implement and the results so far are far from encouraging for the proponents of such a move: M Hall and J Purcell, *Consultation at Work* (Oxford, Oxford University Press, 2012).

[76] This is not to say that, when major reforms in the system were put in place at different times, the authors did not have grand visions of what they would achieve—simply that those grand visions

a long and turbulent history did the current system emerge from its disparate elements. Defeat in two world wars, a period of totalitarian rule, and significant social discontent in the late 1960s have all contributed to the 'system' as we now see it. And there is no reason to think that today's configuration is necessarily the end-point of its development. Wolfgang Streek has been particularly gloomy in his assessment of recent changes in the German system, especially the decline of multi-employer collective bargaining.[77] Whilst the current German system could conceivably be regarded as a good point to aim it, its history provides no clues as to how to get there from the starting points at which other countries are likely to be located.

On the other hand, it is easy to underestimate the possibilities of change in societies with a more stable history over the past century. Even though victorious in both world wars, the UK suffered the strains of war and post-war reconstruction and those strains induced significant change. However, that change tended to work with the grain of existing institutions and to ratify their centrality. After both world wars the position of collective bargaining as the primary method of providing employee voice was reinforced.[78] When in the 1980s the governments of Mrs Thatcher sought to destroy the post-Second World War settlement, that occurred only after political support for it had been undermined by its association with high levels of industrial conflict, high inflation and low productivity. Even this significant policy shift took the form of undermining the dominance of collective bargaining in favour of individual 'bargaining' rather than the creation of alternative collective representation mechanisms.[79] Thus, it was apparently more feasible for a major shift in perception about the value of collective bargaining to lead to the legislative undermining of that institution rather than to the creation of a new, potentially more efficient, set of replacement institutions.

The above simply reinforces one of the simpler lessons to be drawn from 'path dependency theory'.[80] The chances of a reform taking place turn not on the expected benefits of the reform but on the balance between the expected

were not what the current system appears to achieve. See eg Ruth Dukes' analysis of the ideas of Sinzheimer in relation to the reforms of the 1920s: R Dukes, 'Hugo Sinzheimer and the Constitutional Function of Labour Law' in G Davidov and B Langille (eds), *The Idea of Labour Law* (Oxford, Oxford University Press, 2011).

[77] See W Streek, *Re-forming Capitalism* (Oxford, Oxford University Press, 2009) ch 6 ('Corporate Governance: The Decline of Germany Inc') and ch 10 ('Time's Up: Positive Externalities Turning Negative'). See also W Streek, 'The Study of Organized Interests: Before "The Century" and After' in C Crouch and W Streeck (eds), *The Diversity of Democracy* (Cheltenham, Edward Elgar, 2006) ch 1, stressing the contingent nature of German employers' commitment to corporatist institutions and the shift in role of the works councils in recent decades from 'market constraining' institutions to institutions which provide employers with a co-operative labour force. In addition, the power of the union may have lessened as against the works council. But he acknowledges the potential for German codetermination to provide an effective, high-value, competitive strategy in a globalized world.

[78] Davies and Freedland (n 13) ch 1.

[79] ibid ch 9.

[80] L Bebchuk and M Roe 'A Theory of Path Dependency in Corporate Ownership and Governance' (1999) 52 *Stanford Law Review* 126.

benefits and expected costs. Even if the expected benefits of a proposed reform are the same in two countries A and B, the country with the lower expected costs of reform (A) is more likely to implement than the country with the higher expected costs (B). B may be expected to continue without the reform until the expected benefits exceed the expected costs, for example, as the existing system becomes increasingly dysfunctional for B. In the meantime, the competitive advantages of A over B will be strengthened. Even this puts the cost–benefit analysis in too simple a form and if countries do choose sometimes to take significant immediate losses for longer term gains (partly because the size of those losses may not be clear ex ante),[81] nevertheless it must be unlikely that a country will embark on wholesale introduction of new institutions whose successful operation depends on the adoption of behaviours and attitudes on the part of trade unions, workers and manager which are at odds with those generated in the system which is being replaced. The history of the wartime joint production committees, recounted at the beginning of this chapter, and the more recent failure of employee-based institutions mandated by EU law to take root in UK workplaces,[82] are pieces of evidence which show the difficulties of comprehensive institutional change in industrial relations.

VIII. Conclusion

This chapter has suggested that that labour lawyers should not hold back from engagement with law and economics scholarship. Although that scholarship, at least as applied to the corporation, has shown little interest in engaging with distributional questions, which might be thought to be at the heart of labour law, the efficiency argument is not one that labour lawyers are bound to 'lose'. As efficiency considerations obtain more and more prominence in policy debate, labour lawyers need to be able to engage with these arguments. Quite apart from policy-making, there is something intellectually limiting about a refusal to analyse the implications for one's discipline of a major intellectual development, no matter how unpalatable it may seem at first sight. 'Autonomy' should not mean failure to engage. Even distributional arguments might be more persuasive if coupled with arguments from positive economics, designed to demonstrate the likely outcomes proposed reforms, which do not always coincide with the

[81] See C Crouch, *Capitalist Diversity and Change* (Oxford, Oxford University Press, 2005) putting a powerful case for the role of 'institutional entrepreneurs' in producing radical change in societies.

[82] M Hall and J Purcell, *Consultation at Work* (Oxford, Oxford University Press, 2012). This is not to say that more modest 'nudges' of UK labour or corporate law in a particular direction might not lead to increases in economic efficiency. See S Deakin, *The Legal Framework Governing Business Firms and its Implications for Manufacturing Scale and Performance: The UK Experience in International Perspective* (2013) University of Cambridge Faculty of Law Research Paper No 15/2014, http://papers.ssrn.com/sol3/papers.cfm?abstract_id=2394724 (accessed 24 March 2014).

predictions of the reformers or those opposed to the reforms.[83] That, however, is a debate for another day. What this chapter has sought to do is, first, to show that the law and economics analysis of the corporation does not exclude an efficiency argument in favour of governance rights for employees and, second, to take a first step towards identifying the conditions under which such efficiencies might be realized. As to the second point, it has been shown that it is unlikely the market will cause employee governance to emerge where it would be efficient, but also that the efficiency of employee governance is highly sensitive to both the overall configuration of the mechanisms for employee voice in the company and, probably, to societal co-ordination mechanisms existing outside the company. This makes it more than usually uncertain whether the transposition of a governance system from one jurisdiction to another will generate the efficiencies associated with that system in the jurisdiction in which it is embedded.[84]

[83] For a recent example of such work, see S Deakin and others, *Do Labour Laws Increase Equality at the Expense of Higher Unemployment? The Experience of Six OECD Countries, 1970–2010* (2013) Centre for Business Research, University of Cambridge Working Paper No 442, http://papers.ssrn.com/sol3/papers.cfm?abstract_id=2345821 (accessed 25 March 2014).

[84] From an efficiency perspective it is therefore a matter of relief that the European Union failed in its attempts to impose an unsophisticated and uniform system of board-level employee representation on companies through the draft Fifth Company Law Directive (now abandoned) or the European Company, where employee board-level representation is a conditional and default rather than a mandatory rule, but equally that the 'board neutrality' rule in the Takeover Directive was made optional.

16

Labour Law on the Plateau: Towards Regulatory Policy for Endogenous Norms

DEIRDRE McCANN*

I. Introduction

This chapter investigates the post-crisis evolution of a pivotal transnational labour law narrative: that of the World Bank. The recent evolution of the Bank's account of labour law initially offered models of minimal regulation. After the crisis, however, it has generated more elaborate depictions of legitimate, or desired, labour regulation. Yet this crucial transnational institution remains unsettled on the substantive content of these expanded frameworks and on the nature and functioning of the norms that they embody. This chapter tracks the evolution of the imagery of labour law generated by the World Bank over the last decade, from the Doing Business project to the 2013 *World Development Report*. The broader purpose is to take this evolution as an opportunity to consider the notions of legal regulation of markets that have been elevated by the crisis and the pertinence of contemporary labour regulation scholarship to international legal policy narratives.

In doing so, the chapter addresses the autonomy of labour law in both discourse and institutional function. At the discursive level, it attends to the reception of legal regulation in economic policy and research narratives, and in particular to their rendition of the form, dynamics and objectives of legal regulation. On the institutional dimension, the paper argues that the regulatory policy of the World Bank and the ILO can usefully be conceived of as dynamic processes of institutional convergence and divergence. More broadly, the chapter explores an important refashioning of the Bank's vision of labour

* I am grateful to comments on this paper by participants at the Oxford Labour Law conference, in particular by Hugh Collins, Paul Davies and Simon Deakin, and by Judy Fudge, Joe Hermer and David Kucera.

law—grounded in the image of a 'regulatory plateau'—that embraces the benefits of regulation and embeds a more sophisticated conception of the operation of regulatory regimes.

In this regard, the chapter contributes to a line of legal scholarship that has tracked and assessed the trajectory of transnational labour law narratives. Rittich, centrally, has examined the influence of regulatory narratives generated by international financial institutions (IFIs) on the nature and function of legal regulation[1] and, more recently, the diversification of international-level sources of labour law guidance.[2] The chapter is also a contribution to the evolving academic reflections, including by the author, on the narratives of labour regulation that are generated by economic theoretical research and policy discourses,[3] and is aligned with recent work that offers a neo-institutional account of legal regulation in which legal rules are rendered as endogenous to the market.[4] The chapter points to key limitations that should be addressed for a more robust and effective vision of labour regulation at the international level.

II. Quantified Flexibility: The Decline and Fall of the Employing Workers Index

During much of the last decade, the Doing Business project was the World Bank's flagship engagement with labour regulation.[5] The project is now familiar.[6] It evaluates a range of 'business regulations' from around 190 countries using a set of indicators that quantify and compare sub-fields of legal regulation

[1] K Rittich, 'Rights, Risk, and Reward: Governance Norms in the International Order and the Problem of Precarious Work' in J Fudge and R Owens (eds), *Precarious Work, Women, and the New Economy: The Challenge to Legal Norms* (Oxford, Hart Publishing, 2006).

[2] K Rittich, 'Precarious Work and the Fragmentation of International Labour Law' [2014] *London Review of International Law* (forthcoming).

[3] S Deakin and P Sarkar, 'Assessing the Long-Run Economic Impact of Labour Law Systems: A Theoretical Reappraisal and Analysis of New Time Series Data' (2008) 39 *Industrial Relations Journal* 453; S Deakin, 'The Evidence-Based Case for Labour Regulation' in S Lee and D McCann (eds), *Regulating for Decent Work: New Directions in Labour Market Regulation* (Basingstoke, Palgrave Macmillan/International Labour Organization, 2011); S Lee and D McCann, 'New Directions in Labour Regulation Research' and 'The Impact of Labour Regulations: Measuring the Effectiveness of Legal Norms in a Developing Country' in Lee and McCann (eds), *Regulating for Decent Work*; S Lee and D McCann 'Regulatory Indeterminacy and Protection in Contemporary Labour Markets: Innovation in Research and Policy' in D McCann et al, *Creative Labour Regulation: Indeterminacy and Protection in an Uncertain World* (Basingstoke, Palgrave Macmillan/International Labour Organization, 2014).

[4] Deakin (n 3).

[5] www.doingbusiness.org.

[6] KE Davis and MB Kruse, 'Taking the Measure of Law: The Case of the *Doing Business* Project' (2007) 32(4) *Law and Social Inquiry* 1095; J Berg and S Cazes, 'Policymaking Gone Awry: The Labor Market Regulations of the *Doing Business* Indicators' (2008) 29(4) *Comparative Labor Law and Policy Journal* 349; Lee and McCann, 'New Directions' (n 3); P Bakvis, 'The World Bank's *Doing Business* Report: A Last Fling for the Washington Consensus?' (2009) 15(3–4) *Transfer: European Review of Labour and Research* 419.

(starting a business; dealing with construction permits; getting electricity; registering property; paying taxes; trading across borders; getting credit; protecting investors; enforcing contracts; resolving insolvency; and employing workers).[7] The project provides an overall aggregate ranking in an Ease of Doing Business Index, disseminates its results through a series of annual reports[8], and identifies, celebrates and rewards countries whose regulatory frameworks are most favourable to the 'business environment'.[9] The project's engagement with labour regulation is through the Employing Workers Index (EWI), which measures and compares laws on 'hiring' (fixed-term contracts; minimum wages); working hours (night work, weekly rest, weekly hours, paid annual leave); and redundancy. Each sub-indice ranges from 0 to 100 and is a simple average of a set of binominal indicators that assess elements of domestic labour law regimes.[10] Based ostensibly on the work of Botero and colleagues,[11] the EWI can be situated in the trend towards research projects that quantify and compare labour regulations.[12]

The Doing Business project has been the subject of intense and sustained criticism, which has ultimately triggered an ongoing process of reform. The most damaging criticisms have been directed at the project's engagement with labour regulation.[13] For present purposes, two key themes can be identified among the assessments of the EWI's conception and design. These interrogate two interlinked set of assumptions that are encoded in the Index's methodology and associated rhetoric on (i) the substantive scope of legitimate labour regulation, and (ii) the nature, functioning and effects of regulatory frameworks.

To elaborate on the first theme, it is commonly observed that the account of the legitimate subject-matter of labour regulation offered by the Doing Business project is highly constrained.[14] Less frequently observed is that this sparse portrait is grounded in a conviction that labour rights can be neatly divided into the fundamental and the residual. The core/non-core narrative enshrined by the

[7] World Bank, 'Doing Business: A Joint Publication and Project by the World Bank and IFC' www.doingbusiness.org/~/media/GIAWB/Doing%20Business/Documents/Miscellaneous/What-is-Doing-Business.pdf (accessed 15 June 2014).

[8] Most recently, World Bank, *Doing Business 2014: Understanding Regulations for Small and Medium-Size Enterprises* (Washington DC, World Bank, 2013).

[9] See country rankings at www.doingbusiness.org/rankings (accessed 15 June 2014). Prior annual reports have identified 'Top Reformers,' which were designated members of a 'Doing Business Reformers' Club.' See World Bank *Doing Business 2007: How to Reform*, 2, Table 1.1; *Celebrating Reform 2009: Doing Business Case Studies* (2009) 1. The project currently identifies 'most improved economies': www.doingbusiness.org/Reforms (accessed 15 June 2014).

[10] See further Davis and Kruse (n 6); Berg and Cazes (n 6).

[11] JC Botero et al, 'The Regulation of Labour' (2004) 119(4) *Quarterly Journal of Economics* 1339.

[12] See also S Deakin, P Lele and M Siems, 'The Evolution of Labour Law: Calibrating and Comparing Regulatory Regimes' (2007) 146 *International Labour Review* 133; Deakin and Sarkar (n 3); R Mitchell et al, 'The Evolution of Labour Law in Australia: Measuring the Change' (2001) 23 *Australian Journal of Labour Law* 1; P Gahan et al, 'Economic Globalization and Convergence in Labor Market Regulation: An Empirical Assessment' (2012) *American Journal of Comparative Law* 60(3) 703.

[13] See works cited in n 6.

[14] Ibid.

ILO in its 1998 Declaration on Fundamental Rights and Principles at Work has been pivotal to the conceptual framing, methodology and rhetorical stridency of the Doing Business project.[15] Unleashed by the ILO into the sphere of international labour regulation policy, the Declaration's assertion that the rights to freedom of association and collective bargaining and to protection from forced labour and child labour are fundamental has had consequences that have been predictable, yet perhaps unexpectedly enduring. Among the most substantial is that a rendition of fundamentality is at the heart of both methodology and policy discourse in Doing Business. The core/non-core distinction is embedded in the selection of the regulatory subjects measured by the EWI sub-indices, which target only non-core elements of transnational and domestic labour law schema (employment protection, minimum wages, working time). At the rhetorical level, it is a point of honour in the Doing Business literature that none of the 'core' entitlements are subject to quantification, measurement or ranking.[16] Non-core regimes, in contrast, have explicitly been conceived of as harbourers of damaging economic impacts.[17]

The 1998 Declaration was condemned, most prominently by Alston, as the ill-judged bifurcation of what was conceived of as an integrated international labour code.[18] Other contributions have stressed that the regulatory objectives subordinated by the Declaration, and more broadly during the core rights era, are centrally those towards the improvement of working conditions.[19] For present purposes, the pivotal consequence of the Declaration is that the World Bank grasped the core/non-core duality—in the kind of deployment feared by Alston and others—to profoundly diminish non-core rights.

The transmission of the core/non-core schema illuminates the analysis of the institutional autonomy of labour law at the international level. The recent history of international labour law has been characterized by Rittich as a process of fragmentation in which competing or converging norms and regulatory guidance are transmitted by a multiplying array of actors.[20] Within this analytical frame-

[15] See also D McCann, 'New Frontiers of Regulation: Domestic Work, Working Conditions, and the Holistic Assessment of Nonstandard Work Norms' (2012) 34(1) *Comparative Labour Law and Policy Journal* 167.

[16] Most recently, World Bank, *Doing Business 2014* (n 8) 122, n 2.

[17] S Lee and D McCann, 'Measuring Labour Market Institutions: Conceptual and Methodological Questions on "Working-Hour Rigidity"' in J Berg and D Kucera (eds), *In Defence of Labour Market Institutions: Cultivating Justice in the Developing World* (Basingstoke, Palgrave/ILO, 2008). See eg World Bank, *The World Development Report: A Better Investment Climate for Everyone* (Washington DC, World Bank, 2004). The *Doing Business* literature now asserts that the indices 'are fully consistent with' ILO conventions, World Bank, *Doing Business 2014* (n 8) 118.

[18] P Alston and J Heenan, 'The Shrinking of the International Labor Code: An Unintended Consequence of the 1998 ILO Declaration on Fundamental Principles and Rights at Work?' (2004) 36 *New York University Journal of International Law and Politics* 221; P Alston, 'Facing Up to the Complexities of the ILO's Core Labour Standards Agenda' (2005) *European Journal of International Law* 467. See also J Fudge, 'The New Discourse of Labour Rights: From Social to Fundamental Rights?' (2007) 29(1) *Comparative Labor Law and Policy Journal* 29.

[19] McCann (n 15).

[20] Rittich (n 1).

work, the relationship between the ILO and World Bank in the decade from the Declaration to the global financial crisis can be read as signalling not merely a convergence of narratives but an institutional convergence, which pivots on the role of these two institutions in fashioning and disseminating regulatory policy. On closer analysis, further, this institutional convergence can be understood to embody layers of interaction that have, in aggregate, curbed the institutional autonomy of the ILO.

First, the Doing Business project relays an account of the economic impact of labour regulation, including on regulatory subjects shared with the ILO's standards. Predicting labour's regulation's economic effects is a role on which the World Bank has long staked a claim. Yet Doing Business has not merely reiterated the familiar—abstract—narrative of labour regulation's inhibiting effects. The project has also, second, propelled a convergence in legal policy strategy towards detailed guidance on the design of legal frameworks. As has been argued elsewhere, the EWI has translated open-textured flexibility narratives into detailed prescriptions for legal design, sending a 'message to law' to legal policy actors.[21] This advisory role had previously been assumed to be primarily the domain of the ILO, at least at the level of generic global guidance (guided by the regulatory frameworks that are suggested by the standards). Third, on the most fundamental level, a claim was staked in the Doing Business project that narratives of the relevance and status of the ILO's standards could be co-piloted by the World Bank. The borrowing of the core/non-core dichotomy by Doing Business can therefore be identified, with hindsight, as the death-knell of the ILO's unchallenged pre-eminence in the international labour law arena. The outcome is that the Organization no longer assuredly governs its own discourses on legal regulation, including as they relate to ILO norms.

The Doing Business project therefore shifted the Bank onto institutional and legal policy terrain conventionally occupied by the ILO. In this analysis, Doing Business elevated the ILO, by integrating its standards and concepts (decent work, fundamental rights and principles) into the economic debates on labour regulation. The Declaration has also helped substantially to shield the most precarious of the fundamental rights from the sights of the IFIs, namely the right collectively to bargain. Yet it simultaneously diminished the Organization's normative authority by destabilizing already neglected discourses on the role of the ILO's non-core standards in contemporary economic life (including regulatory objectives that are co-pursued through collective bargaining). In the transmission of the core/non-core narrative, the ILO set the frame but was unable or unwilling to dictate the path of the engagement.

Such paths of convergence with the Bank, and other transnational legal policy and adjudicative institutions, appear to be exercising an internal paralysis among ILO policy and legal actors. The first report of the new Director-General of the ILO to the June 2013 International Labour Conference revealed an internal

[21] McCann (n 15).

unease over the normative dimension of the ILO's work.[22] The report admits to a fraught internal debate—'described by some as a crisis'[23]—centred on standard-setting. The focus of the DG's Report is partly on the future of the Organization's oversight mechanisms and standard-setting, but also embraces the dissemination of existing norms. It is particularly notable that the Report in part attributes the normative crisis to institutional and discursive convergence:

> [P]aradoxically, one of the reasons cited for the emergence of controversy at this point in the ILO's history is precisely that the outputs of the supervisory system are increasingly influential as a reference point in numerous settings outside the ILO itself.[24]

The second key theme that unites prominent criticisms of Doing Business is the limitations of the EWI in capturing the nature, functioning and therefore impact of labour market regulations. Certain of the Index's deficiencies in this regard are technical: they are grounded in a misreading of legal systems as a whole or the interaction of the internal components of labour law systems.[25] The Index does not recognize functional equivalents of statutory regulation, for instance, thereby downgrading regimes that regulate predominantly via bargaining.[26] It also misreads how certain components of regulatory sub-fields interact and whether the classification of legal data will accurately capture the measurement goals of the sub-indices.[27]

Given the Bank's subsequent conversion to the merits of labour regulation, traced in the following section, the most salient critiques of Doing Business are the overarching analyses that probe the theoretical underpinnings of the project.[28] This literature has argued that Doing Business rests on a model of development that, by neglecting most of the benefits of regulation, embeds the tenets of orthodox economic theory.[29] The critique embraces the assessment of labour standards in the EWI, which is configured to restate, in quantified form, orthodox economic theory's stark dichotomy between regulation and deregulation.[30] As Davies and Freedland have observed in their investigation of labour law's autonomy, the deregulatory account of labour law holds there to be 'a

[22] International Labour Organization, *Towards the ILO Centenary: Realities, Renewal and Tripartite Commitment*, Report of the Director-General, International Labour Conference, 102nd Session, 2013 (ILO, 2013).

[23] Ibid 19.

[24] Ibid 20.

[25] Berg and Cazes (n 6); Deakin and Sarkar (n 3); Lee and McCann (n 17).

[26] Ibid.

[27] Lee and McCann (n 17). With respect to weekly hours, for example, it is apparent that the Rigidity of Hours indice is intended to capture regulatory frameworks in which extensive working hours are permitted during periods of no more than two months a year: World Bank, *Doing Business 2014* (n 9). Yet the data and indice capture without distinction regulatory frameworks that contain time-limited extensions and those (eg the US) that place no limit (other than overtime premia) on weekly hours. For details on the Rigidity of Hours sub-indice, see 'Employing Workers Methodology', www.doingbusiness.org/methodology/employing-workers (accessed 15 June 2014).

[28] Berg and Cazes (n 6); Independent Evaluation Group, *Doing Business: An Independent Evaluation* (Washington DC, World Bank, 2008); Lee and McCann (n 17).

[29] Ibid.

[30] Ibid.

simple, direct, relationship between the removal of the protections of labour law and the creation of jobs'.[31] Resting on a default model of the perfectly competitive market, labour regulations are assumed inexorably to raise unemployment and informal employment and to impede growth.[32] Although complicated by its tolerance of the right collectively to bargain, Doing Business absorbs and reflects the orthodox account, by advising constrained expectations of the intensity of non-core regulation (in the sense of demands on the employer, whether administrative, financial, organizational, etc).

The details of how the EWI sub-indices prize minimal regulation have been extensively mapped in the literature.[33] In the 'difficulty of hiring' sub-indice, for example, restrictions on the purposes or maximum cumulative duration of fixed-term contracts are downgraded while redundancy regulations rank highest when their costs (advance notice requirements, severance payments and penalties for terminating redundant workers) are minimal.[34] In consequence, the EWI generates an account of the intensity of labour law much diminished from the frameworks and regulatory techniques that are embedded in the related international norms and in most domestic-level regimes.[35] This deregulatory orientation has endured despite periodic adjustments to the methodology. To single out an illustration derived from the 2014 dataset, for example, it is apparent that the highest score under the 'Rigidity of Hours' sub-indice can be accorded to legal systems that permit weekly hours uninhibited by constraints other than a rest day.[36]

Scholarly work has also identified orthodox economic theory to harbour a—more elusive—theory of how regulatory frameworks operate. Deakin has prised a discrete account of law from orthodox theory.[37] In this account, he points out, legal regulation emerges as an 'an external force imposed upon an otherwise "unregulated" market'.[38] Since laws operate as an external imposition on market relations, legal rules therefore appear as exogenous to the labour market. This narrative, further, carries an associated assumption about the operation of laws: that they are 'complete', in the sense of certain in scope of application and self-executing.[39] A formalist narrative implicitly depicts labour law frameworks as static and constrained: the influence of legal standards is assumed to be deter-

[31] PL Davies and M Freedland, 'Employees, Workers, and the Autonomy of Labour Law' in H Collins, PL Davies and R Rideout (eds), *Legal Regulation of the Employment Relation* (Kluwer, 2000) 270.

[32] Deakin (n 3).

[33] See in particular Berg and Cazes (n 8); Lee and McCann (n 17).

[34] See 'Employing Workers Methodology' (n 27).

[35] On working time, see Lee and McCann (n 17) 41-42, Table 3.1.

[36] 'Data Points and Details, 2014,' available from www.doingbusiness.org/data/exploretopics/employing-workers (accessed 15 June 2014). See further n 27.

[37] Deakin (n 3).

[38] Ibid 35.

[39] Ibid. See also Lee and McCann's analysis of this model as configuring legal frameworks as comprehensive (protecting all workers within their formal ambit) and complete (workers are entitled to the full array of legal protections, to the maximum permissible extent), 'The Impact of Labour Regulations' (n 3).

mined by their textual and institutional parameters.[40] In this account, therefore, labour law is understood as autonomous from economic and social systems, to the detriment of an accurate conception of its functioning.

This account of labour law's autonomy is particularly stark in the quantified version of the flexibility narrative that is embedded in certain indicator projects. This reading of labour law frameworks underpins the incapacity of the Doing Business indices to capture the de facto influence of regulatory frameworks. This limitation is common, and unobjectionable, in quantification projects.[41] It is less persuasive, however, when fuelling guidance on policy reform. In the policy arena, the formalist narrative is particularly pertinent to the account in the Doing Business literature of the relevance of law to the informal economy. Centrally to the conception of legal regulation in low-income economies, the World Bank has crafted an image of legal regulation as entirely distinct from the informal economy.[42] This 'pessimistic' account of labour law's promise[43] hinges on a clear-cut dichotomy between the 'formal' and 'informal' economies. It thereby ignores evolving formalization within formal settings.[44] Most pertinently to the concerns of this paper, labour standards emerge as unknown or entirely irrelevant to informal workers.[45] Yet labour law systems are better understood to harbour dynamic capacities beyond their textual demands, which encompass an influence in informal settings (see further the discussion of 'institutional dynamism' in Section III below).

The post-crisis history of the EWI has been a story of decline. Forcefully criticized in the research literature[46] and subsequently by the Bank's own Independent Evaluation Group (IEG),[47] the Doing Business project was further discredited by an Independent Panel of Experts that reported in the summer of 2013.[48] The EWI has been pivotal to this decline. Since the IEG report, it has been downplayed in Doing Business.[49] The Index is no longer integrated into countries' overall rankings,[50] Bank units are prohibited from taking it into account

[40] Lee and McCann, ibid.

[41] Deakin and Sarkar (n 3).

[42] Lee and McCann (n 17). See World Bank (n 17).

[43] Lee and McCann, 'The Impact of Labour Regulations' (n 3).

[44] See eg Kamala Sankaran, 'Flexibility and Informalisation of Employment Relationships' in J Fudge, S McCrystal and K Sankaran, *Challenging the Legal Boundaries of Work Regulation* (Oxford, Hart Publishing, 2012).

[45] eg World Bank *Doing Business 2006: Creating Jobs* (Washington DC, World Bank, 2005).

[46] See n 6.

[47] Independent Evaluation Group, *Doing Business: An Independent Evaluation* (Washington DC, World Bank, 2008).

[48] Independent Review Panel, *Independent Panel Review of the Doing Business Report* (Washington DC, World Bank, 2013).

[49] World Bank, 'Revisions to the Doing Business Employing Workers Indicator' (Memorandum, 27 April 2009) www.doingbusiness.org/methodology/~/media/FPDKM/Doing%20Business/Documents/Methodology/EWI/EWI-revisions.pdf (accessed 15 June 2014); World Bank, 'Guidance Note for World Bank Group Staff on the Use of the Doing Business Employing Workers Indicator for Policy Advice' (3 October 2009), www.doingbusiness.org/methodology/~/media/fpdkm/doing%20 business/documents/methodology/ewi/ewi-guidance-note.pdf (accessed 15 June 2014).

[50] See World Bank, *Doing Business 2014* (n 8) 2.

as an element of loan conditionality,[51] and it has been exiled to an Annex of the annual reports.[52] The Independent Panel concluded that the Doing Business project should endure (albeit renamed), but that it should be redesigned to respond to the criticisms of its reliability and validity, including by jettisoning the aggregate ranking.[53] Further, the Panel recommended that a careful reconsideration of the EWI methodology should be undertaken, outside of the Doing Business project, and should incorporate protective goals. [54]

More recently, the regulatory drama of the World Bank has offered both a more expansive picture of the substantive scope of legitimate labour regulation and a more sophisticated understanding of the nature and functioning of legal frameworks and of their potential economic effects. The 2013 *World Development Report* (*WDR2013*) both confirmed the diminished internal influence of the *Doing Business* project and unveiled a new narrative on the scope, purpose and functioning of labour market regulation. This volte-face is the subject of the following section.

III. From Underregulation Bias to the Regulatory Plateau: The *World Development Report 2013*

WDR2013, entitled *Jobs*, acknowledges that growth does not inevitably translate into employment.[55] (Private) employment creation is the heartbeat of the Report's development model: 'Jobs are the cornerstone of development, and development policies are needed for jobs.'[56] More prominently than the Bank's earlier literature, the *Report* acknowledges a set of social objectives for employment: for the individual (earnings, benefits, self-esteem, happiness) and societal-level gains that include investment in the education and health of children, providing alternatives to violence, raising living standards and—notably—ensuring both productivity and social cohesion.[57] The Report builds on this insight to contribute to the existing typologies of 'good jobs'. It debuts a novel variant on the avail-

[51] World Bank, 'Guidance Note' (n 49). In 2013, the Independent Review Panel noted that '[f]ortunately, the indicator's use in loan conditionality seems to have ended after its suspension' (n 48) 35.

[52] See World Bank, *Doing Business 2014* (n 9), Annex, 119–22. Data is still gathered and made available on the *Doing Business* website (n 36). The Bank continues explicitly to evaluate and classify domestic norms (classified as 'excessively flexible,' 'balanced' and 'excessively rigid'); see World Bank, *Doing Business 2014*, Annex.

[53] The Independent Review Panel (n 48) 4 suggested instead that the cardinal values for each of the indicators be emphasized. The Panel also called for the project's title to be changed, a peer-review process introduced, the methodology reformed, and the project relocated within the World Bank. See 'Recommendations' 4–6, 20–22.

[54] ibid 36.

[55] World Bank, *World Development Report 2013: Jobs* (Washington DC, World Bank 2012).

[56] ibid 3.

[57] ibid 2.

able models,[58] which it labels 'good jobs for development'.[59] These are jobs with 'the highest payoff to society':[60]

> [S]ome jobs also have spill overs on the living standards of others, on aggregate productivity, or on social cohesion. When spill overs are positive, the job has a greater value to society than it has to the person who holds it.[61]

WDR2013 recommends a three-layered policy blueprint for cultivating good jobs for development:

- *Fundamentals* are identified as a prerequisite for job creation in the private sector.[62] The central policy fundamentals are identified as macroeconomic stability, an enabling business environment, human capital and the rule of law.
- *Labour policies* convert growth into jobs. These are defined as 'policies and institutions' that include labour market regulation, collective bargaining, active labour market programmes and social insurance.[63]
- *Policy priorities.* Policy actors are called on to establish the priorities that will support good jobs for development. In this stratum of the policy pyramid, restraints on the private sector in its job creation role are attributed to market imperfections and institutional failures.[64] Policy priorities allow policy actors to remove these restraints and to identify the types of jobs that generate optimal development outcomes.

WDR2013 has been welcomed in the policy sphere for focusing on the persistent unemployment that has characterized the post-crisis period.[65] The 'good jobs for development' paradigm also holds some promise.[66] Typologies of 'good jobs' in the academic literature have been elaborated primarily in the context of the advanced industrialized economies and are ripe to be extended to low-income countries. Most saliently for this chapter, the *Report* also offers a substantial recalibration of the Bank's engagement with labour law. Departing from the Doing Business model of minimal regulation, it showcases a novel appreciation of the labour regulation/employment nexus and of the functioning and capacities of regulatory frameworks. The purpose of this section is to evaluate the *Report*'s conception of labour regulation and to explore its parallels with certain advances in the research literature.

[58] See in particular Arne L Kalleberg, *Good Jobs, Bad Jobs: The Rise of Polarized and Precarious Employment Systems in the United States, 1970s to 2000s* (New York, Russell Sage Foundation, 2011).

[59] World Bank, *World Development Report 2013* (n 55) Part 2.

[60] ibid 159.

[61] ibid.

[62] ibid 257.

[63] ibid.

[64] ibid.

[65] P Bakvis, 'World Bank Jobs Report: Detailed Analysis,' 2 October 2012, www.tuc.org.uk/international-issues/globalisation/international-development/global-economic-justice-campaigns/world (accessed 15 June 2014).

[66] Although see Bakvis' reservations about the concept of 'good jobs for development' as a replacement for 'decent work' (ibid).

The recent labour regulation literature has reassessed neoclassical theory's rendering of the relation between legal and economic systems and the economic impacts of labour laws. In part the advances in this literature are methodological. Deakin has highlighted that refinements in the cross-national measurement of labour regulations and in time series and panel data econometrics are sustaining more sophisticated assessments of the economic impact of labour legislation.[67] These research findings suggest that the effects of legal regulations on growth, employment and informal employment are not those predicted by orthodox economic theory.[68] Macleod's recent survey of empirical evidence on the impact of employment protection legislation (EPL), for example, has concluded that theoretical predictions about negative employment impacts lack empirical grounding.[69] Similarly, minimum wage laws have been found to have no negative impact on employment and even to enhance productivity.[70]

To argue that the potential benefits of labour regulations—both economic and social—should be more explicitly considered in analyses of the impacts of labour law, Lee and McCann have offered a model for conceptualizing optimal labour regulation.[71] Failure to take into account the benefits of regulation generates what the authors characterize as an 'underregulation bias'. This insight is reproduced in graphic form in Figure 1, which recognizes that the net benefits of labour regulations can be jeopardized both by regulations that are too onerous, or ill-designed, and those that are too minimal. In Figure 1, the minimalist approach—underregulation—for Country A is represented as *Da*' and the optimal degree of regulation as *Da**.

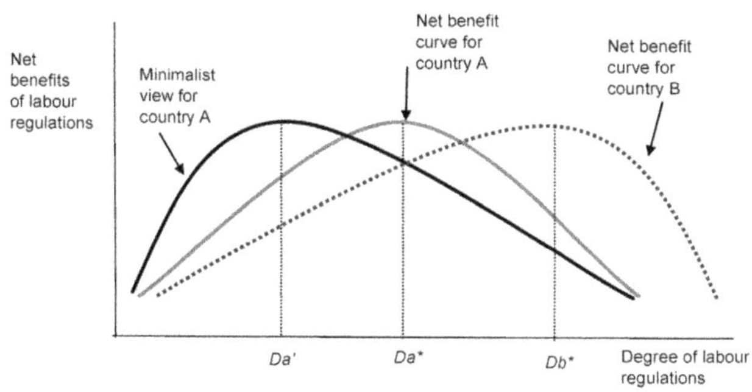

Figure 1. Net benefits of labour regulations: an illustration.

Source: Lee and McCann 'New Directions' (n 3), Figure 1.1, adapted from E Olin Wright, 'Beneficial Constraints: Beneficial for Whom?' (2004) 2 *Socio-Economic Review* 407.

[67] Deakin (n 3).

[68] ibid.

[69] W Bentley Macleod, 'Great Expectations: Law, Employment Contracts, and Labour Market Performance,' (2011) 4(b) *Handbook of Labor Economics* 1591.

[70] See International Labour Organization, *Global Wage Report 2010/2011: Wage Policies in Times of Crisis* (Geneva, ILO, 2010).

[71] Lee and McCann 'Regulatory Indeterminacy' (n 3).

WDR2013 to a degree parallels the scholarly literature's reassessment of the economic impacts of labour regulation. The *Report* acknowledges the substantial research findings that indicate that labour regulations do not inhibit job creation.[72] Mirroring the conclusions of the research literature, it observes that the '[e]stimated effects [of labour regulations] prove to be relatively modest in most cases—certainly more modest than the intensity of the debate would suggest'.[73] The *Report* concludes that 'Overall, labor policies and institutions are neither the major obstacle nor the magic bullet for creating good jobs for development in most countries.'[74]

To reach this conclusion, *WDR2013* ventures beyond the boundaries of neoclassical labour economics, to entertain alternative explanations for poor employment outcomes. To this end, it acknowledges that the crucial constraints on job creation often lie beyond the labour market:

> When faced with jobs challenges, policy makers tend to look first at labor policies as either the solution or the problem. … But the main constraints to the [*sic*] job creation often lie outside the labor market, and a clear approach is needed to support appropriate policy responses.[75]

Rationales are offered for poor employment outcomes in countries at a range of income levels.[76] Thus in agrarian economies, the *Report* suggests, low productivity in smallholder farming is most likely to be attributable to deficiencies in agricultural research and extension.[77] In higher-income countries in which a lack of competition in the advanced technology sector is suggested to contribute to youth unemployment, '[c]ronyism and political favouritism' are credited as the most likely culprits.[78]

The *Report* also responds to calls for the Bank to take account of the benefits of regulation. In doing so, the *WDR2013* offers a similar analysis to Lee and McCann's account of underregulation bias and optimum labour regulation, in this case expressed in an imagery of apt labour regulation as a plateau. The *Report* acknowledges the risk that labour regulations may not only be too rigid but also too lax, and that both rigid and weak regulatory frameworks can have detrimental effects on productivity.[79] Between these extremes, the Bank suggests, lies a plateau of regulation of appropriate intensity and form. Labour policies

[72] The Report cites T Boeri, B Helppie and M Macis, 'Labour Regulations in Developing Countries: A Review of the Evidence and Directions for Future Research', World Bank Social Protection Discussion Paper No 0833 (Washington DC, World Bank, 2008); R Freeman, 'Labor Regulations, Unions and Social Protection in Developing Countries: Market Distortions or Efficient Institutions?' in D Rodrik and M Rosenzweig (eds), *Handbook of Development Economics*, vol 5 (Amsterdam, Elsevier, 2009) 4657; G Betcherman, 'Labor Market Institutions: A Review of the Literature', Background Paper for the World Development Report 2013 (Washington DC, World Bank, 2012).

[73] World Bank, *World Development Report 2013* (n 55) 259.

[74] ibid.

[75] ibid 257.

[76] See the Bank's typology of 'job challenges', ibid 18–19, 20 (Figure 14).

[77] ibid 25.

[78] ibid 25–26.

[79] ibid 258.

that are not to undermine job creation, while maximizing development payoffs from jobs, must remain on this plateau:

> Excessive or insufficient interventions can certainly have detrimental effects on productivity. But in between these extremes lies a 'plateau' where effects enhancing and undermining efficiency can be found side by side and most of the impact is redistributive.[80]

This plateau is encircled by 'cliffs' that denote errors of contrasting genres:

> Labour policy should avoid two cliffs: the distortionary interventions that clog the creation of jobs in cities and in global value chains, and the lack of mechanisms for voice and protection from the most vulnerable workers, regardless of whether they are wage earners.[81]

As Section II has suggested, inflexible labour laws have long haunted the regulatory visions of the World Bank. Rigidity's appearance in *WDR2013* as one of the cliffs of the regulatory plateau is therefore unexceptional. The *Report* cautions that: 'Policies should seek to avoid the distortive interventions that stifle labor reallocation and undermine the creation of jobs in functional cities and global value chains.'[82]

The novelty of this post-crisis phase of the Bank's engagement with labour law—central to this chapter—is its discovery of the risks of weak labour regulation: 'This cliff may be less visible than excessive labour market rigidity, but it is no less real.'[83] Signalling an awareness of the potential for underregulation bias, the report explicitly rejects minimal regulation: 'If rules that are too weak, or not enforced, the problems of poor information, unequal bargaining power, or inadequate risk management remain unaddressed.'[84] This risk of underregulation, further, encompasses the social goals of regulation. This second 'cliff' is stated to presage low living standards and disrupted social cohesion.[85]

The significance of *WDR2013*, and of the image of the regulatory plateau, should not be understated. The *Report* harbours a markedly more sophisticated conception of labour regulation—including of its protective objectives—than the models generated by the Doing Business project. As such, it signals a substantial post-crisis shift in the World Bank's tolerance of legal intervention in labour markets. It remains to be seen if this stance will be sustained in the Bank's legal policy discourses. The 2014 *World Development Report—Risk and Opportunity* is less exuberant: at points it recalls pre-crisis language on the hazards of regulation and the limited scope of feasible intervention ('While in many areas regulations can be excessive and disruptive of market forces, stronger regulations are needed

[80] ibid.
[81] ibid 22.
[82] ibid 257.
[83] ibid 27.
[84] ibid 263.
[85] ibid 22.

for workplace safety, consumer protection and environmental preservation').[86] In contrast, the Independent Panel of Experts that reviewed Doing Business suggested *WDR2013* as a guide for the redesign of the project, highlighting the *Report*'s assertion that regulation can be pitched at a range of levels and varieties on the plateau.[87]

Yet the inclusion of labour regulation on the menu of policy-makers—beyond a bland commitment to dismantling legal protections—inevitably generates a set of complex dilemmas about the form, intensity and functioning of legal regulation. The World Bank's warmer embrace of labour law and of cognate regulatory frameworks is a crucial uncertainty in mapping the trajectory of international labour law narratives. Retaining the framework of analysis used in Section II, two dimensions can be distinguished, namely the substantive scope and the functioning of regulation.

On the substantive dimension of the regulatory plateau, it is evident that it hosts the 1998 Declaration's fundamental rights. *WDR2013* devotes ample space to lauding the spread of collective bargaining onto virgin territory. China's decade of legislative reform on trade unions, labour contracts and dispute resolution is warmly endorsed.[88] These legislative reforms are credited with a rapid growth in unionized workers and in the coverage of wage and collective agreements. The *Report* also recognizes the research findings that the Chinese reforms have encouraged the direct election of union representatives and a growth in local and sectoral collective agreements. [89]

More significant is that *WDR2013* extends the Bank's vision of labour law's domain beyond the core to what, at points, seems an open-ended catalogue of rights. This expansion stems from an—inchoate if intriguing—theory of the status of labour rights and of the normative foundation of jobs. Social rights emerge in the *Report* not merely as the preferred adjuncts of a job, but rather as prerequisites: 'All countries have subscribed to a set of universal rights. … Thus, some work activities are widely viewed as unacceptable and should not be treated as jobs.'[90]

This normative restriction on the nature of a job governs the breadth of the plateau. The concept of 'good jobs for development' is tied to a strikingly

[86] World Bank, *World Development Report: Risk and Opportunity—Managing Risk for Development* (Washington DC, World Bank, 2014) 27. The 2014 Report also cites 'labor market regulations that purport to defend workers' interests but wind up protecting only a few and contributing to the roots of a large informal sector' (40).

[87] Independent Review Panel (n 48) 36. *WDR2013* has also had a visible external influence: see eg International Monetary Fund, 'Jobs and Growth: Analytical and Operational Considerations for the Fund' (14 March 2013) www.imf.org/external/np/pp/eng/2013/031413.pdf (accessed 15 June 2015).

[88] World Bank, *World Development Report 2013* (n 55) 266, Box 8.3.

[89] Chang Hee Lee and Mingwei Liu, 'Collective Bargaining in Transition: Measuring the Effects of Collective Voice in China' in S Hayter (ed), *The Role of Collective Bargaining in the Global Economy: Negotiating for Social Justice* (Cheltenham, Edward Elgar, 2011) and *Measuring the Effects of the Collective Voice Mechanism and the Labour Contract Law: A Survey of Labour Relations and Human Resource Management Practices in China* (Geneva, ILO, 2011).

[90] World Bank, *World Development Report 2013* (n 55) 155.

expansive raft of international norms, which are characterized as embodying 'basic human rights'.[91] These norms are extensive in both subject-matter and source: a reference to rights from international and regional frameworks[92] is elaborated to embrace a range of international human rights instruments[93] and regional regimes that include the European Convention on Human Rights,[94] the European Social Charter[95] and the Inter-American Convention on Human Rights.[96] *WDR2013* also sidesteps the reservations about the status of working conditions rights that emerged in the pre-crisis era.[97] The inclusion of Article 23 of the Universal Declaration of Human Rights among the normative preconditions of a job extends the objectives of legitimate regulation to just and favourable working conditions, protection against unemployment, and remuneration that ensures 'an existence worthy of human dignity' for the worker and his family.[98] Throughout, further, the *Report* assumes the viability of EPL and minimum wage frameworks that are more protective than the minimal interventions foreseen in the Doing Business literature.[99] With respect to the ILO, as would be expected, the *Report* references the 1998 Declaration and therefore the fundamental standards.[100] Yet international labour standards (ILS) beyond the fundamental conventions are also recognized, including, explicitly, instruments on working time, social security, health and safety, and labour inspection.[101]

The World Bank's image of the good job therefore encroaches on the ILO's normative domain. Yet, to return to the question of institutional autonomy addressed in the pre-crisis era in Section II, it is revealing that the regulatory expansion in *WDR2013* is realized primarily through recourse to human rights

[91] ibid 65.

[92] ibid 156.

[93] Convention on the Elimination of all Forms of Discrimination Against Women, 18 December 1979, 1249 UNTS 13, (1980) 19 ILM 33, entered into force 3 September 1981; Convention on the Rights of the Child, 20 November 1989, 1577 UNTS 3, (1989) 28 ILM 1448, entered into force 2 September 1990; the International Convention on the Protection of the Rights of All Migrant Workers and Members of their Families, 18 December 1990, 2220 UNTS 93, (1991) 30 ILM 1517, entered into force 1 July 2003; International Convention on the Protection and Promotion of the Rights and Dignity of Persons with Disabilities, GA res 61/106, Annex I, UN GAOR, 61st Sess, Supp No 49, 65, UN Doc A/61/49 (13 December 2006), 46 ILM 443.

[94] Convention for the Protection of Human Rights and Fundamental Freedoms, 4 November 1950, Europ TC No 5; 213 UNTS 221.

[95] European Social Charter, 18 October 1961, 529 UNTS 89; Europ TS No 35.

[96] American Convention on Human Rights, 22 November 1969, (1970) 9 ILM 673, entered into force 18 July 1978. The expansive treatment of labour rights in *WDR2013* is uneven. In the Glossary, for example, 'rights' are defined to include only the core labour standards and health and safety at work (330).

[97] McCann (n 15).

[98] Universal Declaration of Human Rights, 10 December 1989, UNGA Res 217 A (III) (1948).

[99] eg World Bank *World Development Report 2013* (n 55) 260–63.

[100] Freedom of Association and Protection of the Right to Organise Convention, 1948 (No 87); Right to Organise and Collective Bargaining Convention, 1949 (No 98); Forced Labour Convention, 1930 (No 29); Abolition of Forced Labour Convention, 1957 (No 105); Minimum Age Convention, 1973 (No 138); Worst Forms of Child Labour Convention, 1999 (No 182); Equal Remuneration Convention, 1951 (No 100); Discrimination (Employment and Occupation) Convention, 1958 (No 111).

[101] World Bank, *World Development Report 2013* (n 55) 156.

instruments.[102] Most conspicuously, the *Report* does not engage with a comparable expansion in the ILO's legal policy narrative. The ILO's 2008 Declaration on Social Justice for a Fair Globalization was adopted just prior to the global financial crisis and has shaped the ILO's response. This Declaration, of equal status to its 1998 antecedent, asserts the breadth of the ILO's policy realm. It highlights the four 'strategic objectives' in which the work of the ILO has been configured since the end of the last century: fundamental principles and rights, employment, social protection and social dialogue.[103] These objectives are then characterized—in a formula akin to the concept of indivisibility[104]—as 'inseparable, interrelated and mutually supportive'.[105] The ILO has therefore elevated non-core objectives of labour law frameworks within its guiding regulatory policy discourse. The Declaration also recentred the improvement of working conditions by explicit reference to one of the Organization's foundational texts, the Declaration of Philadelphia, specifically to a call for 'policies in regard to wages and earnings, hours and other conditions of work calculated to ensure a just share of the fruits of progress to all and a minimum living wage to all employed and in need of such protection'.[106]

Yet *WDR2013*, despite initiating a comparable broadening of the substantive scope of legitimate labour regulation, does not make any reference to the 2008 Declaration. Thus the expanded regulatory terrain of the World Bank is not mapped to the ILO's elaboration of the relative status of core and non-core rights. This omission suggests that the institutional convergence between these global policy actors has stalled since the crisis. The regulatory narratives of the institutions continue to proceed in similar trajectories, yet with limited shared reference points. As a result, the ILO's normative discourses are more autonomous, yet less influential. This institutional divergence threatens the influence of ILS on the World Bank's rendition of labour regulation on the plateau. It also hints at a diminished status for the ILO, at least in the Bank's policy discourses.[107] It also threatens to obscure ILO normative frameworks and policy discourses that could suggest regulatory strategies, standards and outcomes for regulation on the plateau. Certainly the ILO's minimum wages[108] and employment protection[109] standards do not trouble the *WDR2013* analysis of the parameters of the kindred domestic legal frameworks (see further Section IV.A below).[110]

[102] See in particular ibid 156.
[103] ILO, *Decent Work* (Geneva, ILO, 1999).
[104] On indivisibility and the 1998 *Declaration*, see Alston (n 18); Alston and Heenan (n 18).
[105] *Declaration on Social Justice for a Fair Globalization 2008*, Part I.B.
[106] ibid Part I.A(ii).
[107] It remains to be seen whether this trend will be reversed. The Independent Review Panel (n 48) 36 recommended that the Bank 's future quantification work should be pursued jointly with the International Labour Organisation.
[108] Minimum Wage-Fixing Machinery Convention, 1928 (No 26), Minimum Wage Fixing Convention, 1970 (No 131) and, as relevant, the Minimum Wage Fixing Machinery (Agriculture) Convention, 1951 (No 99), Plantations Convention, 1958 (No 110), Arts 24 and 25, and Social Policy (Basic Aims and Standards) Convention, 1962 (No 117) Art 10.
[109] Termination of Employment Convention, 1982 (No 158).
[110] World Bank, *World Development Report 2013* (n 55) 260–63.

On the nature and functioning of legal regulation, second, Section IV identified as a key criticism of the Doing Business methodology that it does not account for the de facto influence of legal rules on the practices of working life and, therefore, for the effectiveness of legal norms. One of the central contributions of the recent literature is to pinpoint legal effectiveness as a key dilemma of contemporary labour market regulation.[111] Comparable doubts about the effective functioning of legal frameworks haunt the World Bank's new appreciation of labour regulation. As a starting point, the familiar chasm is discerned between 'law on the books' and 'law in practice':[112]

> Even in countries that have ratified the core labour standards and have laws on the books, children work in harmful conditions, discrimination happens in access to jobs and in pay, forced labor persists, and freedom of association is limited. Commitments in treaties, conventions, and laws may not change the institutions, practices, and behaviours that affect workers' rights on their own.[113]

Such deficiencies are explained as a function of a set of limitations of regulatory design. The Report lists the features of legal frameworks that preclude protected status.[114] Legislative exceptions are illustrated by the widespread exclusion of domestic workers, family workers, workers in small enterprises and in export zones, and unpaid family workers in agriculture and enterprises.[115] The complexities of regulating tripartite relations are acknowledged in an observation that the growth in agency-supplied labour 'complicates legal accountability'.[116] The *Report* also notes the constraints on workers in the informal economy accessing adjudication mechanisms.[117] Each of these factors impedes effective regulation and has been well documented in the precarious work and informality literatures.[118] Yet this analysis neither captures the broader challenges of conceptualizing the

[111] See eg M Piore and A Schrank, 'Toward Managed Flexibility: The Revival of Labour Inspection in the Latin World' (2008) 147(1) *International Labour Review* 1; Lee and McCann 'Measuring Labour Market Institutions' (n 17); D Weil and C Mallo, 'Regulating Labour Standards Via Supply Chains: Combining Public/Private Interventions to Improve Workplace Compliance' 2007 45(4) *British Journal of Industrial Relations* 791; T Teklè (ed), *Labour Law and Worker Protection in Developing Countries* (Oxford, Hart Publishing, 2010); J Howe, T Hardy and S Cooney, 'Mandate, Discretion and Professionalisation at an Employment Standards Enforcement Agency: An Antipodean Experience' (2013) 35 *Law & Policy* 81.

[112] World Bank, *World Development Report 2013* (n 55) 156–57.

[113] ibid 156.

[114] ibid.

[115] The Report cites ILO, *Coverage of Domestic Workers by Key Working Conditions Laws* (ILO, 2011); Fredman 'Anti-Discrimination Laws and Work in the Developing World: A Thematic Overview', Background Paper for the *WDR2013* (Washington DC, World Bank, 2012).

[116] World Bank, *World Development Report 2013* (n 55) 156.

[117] ibid.

[118] See eg L Vosko (ed), *Precarious Employment: Understanding Labour Market Insecurity in Canada* (McGill-Queen's University Press, 2000); J Fudge and L Vosko, 'By Whose Standards? Re-regulating the Canadian Labour Market' (2001) 22 *Economic and Industrial Democracy* 271; Fudge and Owens (eds) (n 1); D McCann, *Regulating Flexible Work* (Oxford, Oxford University Press, 2008); Teklè (n 111); Fudge, McCrystal and Sankaran (n 44).

complex operation of contemporary labour law frameworks nor suggests the future of regulatory design. These issues are addressed in the following section.

IV. Towards Regulatory Policy for Endogenous Norms

Given the promise that *WDR2013* holds for international labour regulation policy, it is worth taking seriously the Bank's image of the regulatory plateau as the locus of apt labour regulation. The remainder of this section investigates the imagery of the plateau. Its aim is to reflect on the needs of a regulatory policy that is poised at the international level: having global resonance, acknowledging the diversity of country conditions, and responding to the demands of fragmented labour markets and of low-income settings. To offer a contribution to this multifaceted debate, this section considers whether the insights of the recent labour regulation literature can enrich the project of regulation on the plateau. It centres on three conceptions of the operation of legal frameworks that have emerged from recent insights on regulation: regulatory indeterminacy, institutional dynamism and the holistic assessment of precarious work regulation.

A. Regulatory Indeterminacy and the Edges of the Plateau

As related in Section II, the regulation research has exposed a conception of legal norms that is embedded in conventional economic narratives: external impositions on an otherwise well-functioning market that are self-executing and protect all workers within their formal scope.[119] A contrasting imagery, grounded in the neo-institutional tradition, offers an alternative depiction of legal frameworks in which legal rules are recognized as endogenous and context dependent.[120] As Deakin has elaborated:

> In this approach, legal rules are understood as devices for coordinating the expectations of actors under conditions of uncertainty. Laws are not simply imposed in a top-down fashion but, just as often, crystallize conventions which first emerge at the level of exchange relations before being formalized in contractual agreements and, at a further level, legal texts. … To understand labour law in this way is to see it not as an external force imposed upon an otherwise 'unregulated' market, but as endogenous to market processes and political structures.[121]

Conceiving of legal rules as endogenous norms in this way has implications for understanding their influence on the practice of working relations. In Deakin's

[119] Deakin (n 3); Lee and McCann, 'The Impact of Labour Regulations' (n 3).
[120] Deakin (n 3).
[121] ibid 35.

words, 'the operation of legal rules depends upon contextual factors which vary across time and space'.[122] The recognition that labour regulations are endogenous and their effects context-dependent therefore precludes any universally applicable threshold for 'good' labour regulations.[123] There is no reason, that is to say, to assume that the benefits curve in Figure 1 (above) will be identical across countries. In fact it would be expected that the curve would vary, as illustrated by the curve for Country B in Figure 1. This insight is reflected in the recent literature on the recognition of the indeterminacy of legal norms. The notion of regulatory indeterminacy emerged in the work of Deakin and Sarkar to convey that the economic effects of labour law reform projects are a priori indeterminate[124] and has since been developed by Lee and McCann into a notion of 'protective indeterminacy', to capture indeterminacy in the protective strength of labour regulations.[125] Regulatory indeterminacy implies that that translation of legal standards into working practices depends upon factors beyond law.

WDR2013 recognizes the potential for fluctuation in the effects of legal norms, both cross-national and temporal: '[The e]dges of plateau vary across countries and even within countries over time, as conditions change.'[126] In this regard, the *Report* partially integrates the insights of the research literature. Regulatory indeterminacy inevitably renders the optimal form and intensity of laws on the regulatory plateau difficult to predict. The project of mapping the edges of the plateau therefore becomes crucial to the Bank's renewed assessment of labour regulation. In *WDR2013*, this quest is centred substantially on EPL and minimum wage regulations: 'The main challenge is to set EPL and minimum wages so that they address the imperfections in the labor market without falling off the plateau.'[127] The range of countries that host appropriate legal frameworks appears to be fairly extensive: 'Many countries appear to set EPL and minimum wages in a range where impacts on employment or productivity are modest.'[128] The crucial challenge, however, is not to identify the potential scope of the plateau but instead to solve the intricate puzzle of fixing its edges at country level.

In this regard, the indications of the Bank's assessment of the edges of the plateau in *WDR2013* are not fully convincing. The rim of the plateau is conveyed primarily as an assertion about the effects of two labour law projects: EPL at state-level in India and minimum wage legislation in Colombia. To illustrate rigid legislation, the report contends that (i) Indian states with 'more restrictive' EPL have significantly lower employment and output and that (ii) increases in the Colombian minimum wage in the late 1990s resulted in substantial employment loss.[129] Yet the evidence cited in support of the *Report*'s contentions is

[122] ibid 35–36.
[123] Lee and McCann 'Regulatory Indeterminacy' (n 3) 16–17.
[124] Deakin and Sarkar (n 3).
[125] Lee and McCann 'Regulatory Indeterminacy' (n 3).
[126] World Bank, *World Development Report 2013* (n 55) 263.
[127] ibid.
[128] ibid 262.
[129] ibid 262–63.

strikingly slim. Evidence on the effects of state laws in India is drawn primarily from the work of Ahsan and Pagés;[130] the other studies cited are not directly relevant.[131] The assessment of the effects of the Colombian minimum wage is based on Kucera and Roncolato,[132] who explicitly stress that the Colombian case is not representative and conclude that it is best understood as an illustration that 'badly designed and implemented labour regulations can have negative repercussions'.[133] Most significantly, the Bank's assessment does not account for the range of alternative explanations for economic impacts, even those reflected in more sophisticated analyses elsewhere in the Report (see Section III above).[134] It can be suggested that careful measurement is needed to identify apt regulatory systems for a particular country context that will generate the optimal degree of regulation on the benefits curve. More broadly, the abstract and static depiction of legal measures characteristic of conventional economic theory should be replaced by models that capture the intricacies of regulatory design and implementation.[135] Detailed knowledge of the context (institutional frameworks, enforcement mechanisms, social norms, etc) is therefore necessary for the effects of labour law reforms to be predicted.[136]

B. Institutional Dynamism

A second dimension of regulation on the plateau is hinted at by an aside in *WDR2013* on the operation of legal regulation in the informal economy. The *Report* mentions in passing the evidence of 'lighthouse effects' of minimum wage reforms, through which increases in the minimum wage function as a reference wage for the informal economy.[137] This observation is a partial recognition of

[130] A Ahsan and C Pagés, 'Are All Labor Regulations Equal? Evidence from Indian Manufacturing' (2009) 37 *Journal of Comparative Economics* 62.

[131] On India, the Report cites a cross-national comparison of Asian countries that does not compare Indian state-level legislation: W Carlin and M Schaffer, 'A Comparison of Business Environment Constraints between Formal Sector Firms and Rural and Informal Sector Firms' (Washington DC, World Bank, 2011), cited in World Bank, *More and Better Jobs in the South* (Washington DC, World Bank, 2011).

[132] D Kucera and L Roncolato, 'Informal Employment: Two Contested Policy Issues' (2008) 147(4) *International Labour Review* 321.

[133] ibid 338. Columbia's minimum wage, already among the highest in the region, was increased during the late-1990s recession. Kucera and Roncolato compare Lemos' findings on Brazil, which found higher minimum wage to reduce earnings inequality without reducing employment for either workers generally or for vulnerable workers: S Lemos, 'Minimum Wage Effects across the Private and Public Sectors in Brazil' (2007) 43(4) *Journal of Development Studies* 700.

[134] Kucera and Roncolato (n 132), for example, note that the effects of minimum wage increases on formal employment depend on a range of factors that include the difference between minimum and prevailing wages (citing C Saget, *Wage Fixing in the Informal Economy: Evidence from Brazil, India, Indonesia and South Africa*, Conditions of Work and Employment Series No 16 (ILO, 2006) and F Eyraud and C Saget, 'The Revival of Minimum Wage Setting Institutions,' in Berg and Kucera (n 17)).

[135] Lee and McCann, 'Measuring Labour Market Institutions' (n 17).

[136] Deakin (n 3).

[137] World Bank, *World Development Report 2013* (n 55), 260–61, citing PR Souza and PE Baltar,

a phenomenon that has a more significant potential for regulatory policy on endogenous norms. It was noted in Section II above that the formalist policy narrative on the economic impact of labour regulation reads labour law frameworks as static and constrained. This literature assumes that the influence of legal frameworks is determined by their textual and institutional parameters. Recent contributions suggest, however, that labour law systems are better understood to harbour dynamic capacities beyond their formal demands.

Lee and McCann have proposed the notion of institutional dynamism to account for the capacity of legal frameworks to operate beyond their formal parameters.[138] Intended for analytical, measurement and policy purposes, institutional dynamism can be classified as external or internal in form. External dynamism denotes the influence of labour law norms beyond their formal reach. It therefore embraces the range of processes alluded to in *WDR2013*—and as yet imperfectly understood—through which labour norms take effect in informal settings (adherence to norms of social behaviour, awareness of statutory standards,[139] etc) In its internal form, institutional dynamism denotes the capacity of regulatory regimes to host multiple interactions between a range of institutions. A key illustration is the operation of 'ripple effects', through which increases in the minimum wage affect wages above the minimum level.[140]

The notion of institutional dynamism offers a useful imagery of legal norms, which can inform regulation on the plateau. It has been argued to be both a significant component of regulatory indeterminacy and a gateway to improved protective outcomes.[141] Yet *WDR2013* does not fully grasp the dynamic potential of regulatory frameworks. The 'pessimistic' account of domestic frameworks outlined in Section II, which disregards informal economies as sites of regulatory intervention, has been tempered. Envisaging a protective future for the informal economy, the *Report* asserts that vulnerable workers should have mechanisms for voice and protection 'regardless of whether they are wage earners'.[142] In elaborating the needs of workers in informal relations, however, the *Report* centres primarily on social protection frameworks[143] (although noting the evolving role

'Salario Minimo e Taxa de Salarios no Brasil' (1980) 10 *Pesquisa e Planejamento Economico* 1045; T Boeri, P Garibaldi and M Ribeiro, 'The Lighthouse Effect and Beyond' (2011) 57 *Review of Income and Wealth* S54; and M Neri, G Gonzaga and J Márcio Camargo, 'Salário Mínimo, Efeito Farol e Pobreza' (2001) 21(2) *Revista de Economia Política* 79.

[138] Lee and McCann 'Regulatory Indeterminacy' (n 3).

[139] On legal awareness, see further Lee and McCann 'The Impact of Labour Regulations' (n 3).

[140] R Freeman, 'The Minimum Wage as a Redistributive Tool' (1996) 106 (May) *Economic Journal* 639; ILO *Global Wage Report 2010/2011: Wage Policies in Times of* Crisis (ILO, 2010); D Grimshaw, J Rubery and G Bosch, 'The Pay Equity Effects of Minimum Wages: A Comparative Industrial Relations Approach' in McCann et al, *Creative Labour Regulation* (n 3); S Lee and K Sobeck, 'Low-Wage Work: A Global Perspective' (2012) 151(3) *International Labour Review* 141; S Lee and M Gerecke, 'Regulatory Indeterminacy and Institutional Design in Minimum Wages: Decentralization, Coordination, and Politics in Asian Minimum Wages' (3rd *Regulating for Decent Work* Conference, Geneva, 2013).

[141] Lee and McCann 'Regulatory Indeterminacy' (n 3).

[142] World Bank, *World Development Report 2013* (n 55) 22.

[143] See in particular ibid 272–76.

of associations of self-employed workers in protecting legal rights, through negotiating with governments, for example, or pursuing litigation strategies in areas such as the construction of malls, harassment or confiscation of inventories).[144]

Other interventions that act on informal working relations, however, are not fully integrated into the analysis. The regulatory plateau model would benefit from considering mechanisms that are tailored to improving the quality of jobs in informal work. Minimum wage legislation is an obvious candidate as a site of experimentation with institutional dynamism in both forms. Recent research on Europe has found ripple effects of minimum wage legislation to enhance pay equity, through their impact on low-wage employment, gender pay inequality and wage compression in the lower half of the wage structure. Grimshaw, Rubery and Bosch have found an association between ripple effects and strong—dual or inclusive[145]—industrial relations systems, and observe that unions with defined pay equity strategies can heighten these effects.[146] Ripple effects are also worth investigating in low-income countries. They can be substantial where minimum wages are used by workers as basis for wage negotiation.[147] This phenomenon has recently been observed in Asian countries, including the Philippines, China and Vietnam,[148] and strengthens the negotiation role of associations of informal workers that is already foreseen by the Bank. This evidence points to a significant, if neglected, policy role for the minimum wage, in which it is available to integrate into formalization and poverty alleviation strategies in low-income countries.[149]

C. The Holistic Analysis of Precarious Work Regulation

Finally, the World Bank's new policy discourse on labour regulation is conspicuously tentative in its treatment of non-standard forms of work.[150] *WDR2013* calls for legal protections for 'the most vulnerable'.[151] The analysis neglects, however, the tendency of non-standard configurations both to disrupt the certainties of conventional regulatory frameworks and also, in recent decades, to propel labour law towards novel regulatory forms. This neglect is more broadly resonant of contemporary labour regulation policy.[152] Yet the recent research has cited the accelerating fragmentation of labour markets as one of the key drivers of

[144] ibid 266–67.
[145] D Gallie, *Employment Regimes and the Quality of Work* (Oxford, Oxford University Press, 2007).
[146] Grimshaw, Rubery and Bosch (n 140).
[147] Lee and Gerecke (n 140); ILO, *Global Wage Report 2010/2011* (n 140).
[148] Lee and Gerecke (n 140).
[149] See also T Dinkelman and V Ranchod, 'Evidence on the Impact of Minimum Wage Laws in an Informal Sector: Domestic Workers in South Africa,' (2012) 99(1) *Journal of Development Economics* 27.
[150] Bakvis (n 65).
[151] World Bank, *World Development Report 2013* (n 55) 257.
[152] McCann (n 15).

regulatory indeterminacy and has elaborated these fragmentation processes to include both heightened recourse to non-standard working arrangements and the intersecting pressures that generate informality.[153] This fragmentation generates a divergent application of legal entitlements and obligations, thus triggering substantial variation in the effectiveness of regulatory frameworks.

Yet labour market fragmentation is challenging to conceptualize in research, and in particular to capture through the use of empirical methods,[154] thus inhibiting an accurate understanding of the nature and influence of labour regulation on the plateau. As a contribution towards unravelling the complexities of this project at the conceptual level, a holistic analysis of non-standard work regulation has been proposed to suggest that the nature and effects of labour law should be understood to be in part defined by the legal treatment of non-standard workers.[155] In consequence, it is contended, analyses of labour law sub-fields should no longer focus exclusively on generally applicable norms; instead, they should be expanded to integrate the governance of non-standard work. The holistic strategy, further, can readily be expanded to embrace analyses of the regulation of informal working relations. This conceptual strategy expands the analysis of regulation to embrace protective lacunae and also the bespoke norms that have been devised to protect workers in non-standard and informal relations. It thereby offers a more accurate and comprehensive understanding of the evolution of labour law.

The primary contribution of *WDR2013* on non-standard work was noted in Section III: the Bank acknowledges the tendency of multipartite working relations to repel labour law's protective reach.[156] Yet no solution is tendered for this problem, and regulatory options already under experimentation are ignored (specific allocation of legal obligations, joint liability, restrictions on the supply of agency work, etc).[157] The legal policy response to informality, further, is confined to efforts to expand social protection and representation and negotiation by associations of the self-employed. A holistic analysis of the regulation of non-standard work and the informal economy would further refine the paradigm of the regulatory plateau to advance effective regulation. This is an arena, for example, in which the Bank's recent neglect of ILO non-core standards, outlined in Section III, obscures regulatory techniques. Regulatory strategies that are widely deployed in European domestic legal orders can be derived from the ILO's non-standard work instruments.[158] Conventional forms of regulation

[153] Lee and McCann, 'Regulatory Indeterminacy' (n 3).

[154] A key features of Botero et al's methodology is that is based on the assumption that legal standards are applied to a 'standard' worker and employer, Botero et al (n 11); see also Berg and Cazes (n 6).

[155] McCann (n 15).

[156] World Bank, *World Development Report 2013* (n 55) 156.

[157] Limiting abuse by employment intermediaries is suggested in the Report's 'Overview' but not subsequently investigated, ibid 27.

[158] eg Home Work Convention, 1996 (No 177); Part-Time Work Convention, 1994 (No 175), Domestic Workers Convention, 2011 (No 189).

also remain relevant. The potential of the minimum wage as a site of experimentation with external dynamism was outlined in Section IV.B. The regulatory plateau model would also benefit from absorbing formalization strategies of the kind advocated by Fenwick et al[159] and, more recently, in McCann and Murray's investigation of domestic work as an entry-point for the legal regulation of informal working relations.[160]

V. Conclusions

The regulatory trajectory of the crisis era can be portrayed, schematically, as an early embrace of forceful market regulation upended by a reversion to the deregulatory orthodoxy. It is notable, then, that the progression of the World Bank's account of labour regulation over this period has been towards a tentative embrace of protective goals. Building on Rittich's analysis of the fragmentation of international labour law, this chapter has assumed that the World Bank, having adopted a guiding role in disseminating labour governance norms,[161] will be crucial to labour law's future. It is therefore essential that scholarly accounts of labour regulation accurately capture the imagery of labour law generated by this institution.

The chapter has suggested that a critical relationship within the international legal policy scene—between the World Bank and ILO—is best understood as a dynamic process of institutional convergence and divergence. This interaction, further, can be read to generate a conversation about the objectives, format and tenor of labour market regulation. Within this frame, the chapter has reappraised the Doing Business project as substantially pivoting on the core/non-core narrative donated by the ILO. The declining fortunes of Doing Business, sealed by *WDR2013*, heralded a pronounced shift in World Bank discourses towards an imagery of a regulatory plateau.

The plateau narrative is open to more expansive substantive policy goals than its antecedents and hosts a more sophisticated understanding of the nature, functioning and economic effects of legal regulation. Yet the precise content of the favoured regulatory frameworks has yet to emerge. A halt in the Bank's institutional dance with the ILO has exiled ILS, distancing a useful source of regulatory models. Further, in recognizing the potential for fluctuating effects, the Bank offers a glimpse of Deakin's analysis of legal regulation, of endogenous norms with context-dependent impacts. Yet it does not fully confront the challenges of regulatory design for endogenous norms. *WDR2013* ushered the Bank into the

[159] C Fenwick et al, *Labour and Labour-Related Laws in Micro and Small Enterprises: Innovative Regulatory Approaches*, ILO SEED Working Paper No 81 (Geneva, ILO, 2007).

[160] D McCann and J Murray, 'Prompting Formalisation through Labour Market Regulation: A 'Framed Flexibility' Model for Domestic Work' (2014) 43(3) *Industrial Law Journal* 319.

[161] For an account of its rise, see in particular Rittich (n 1).

uncertain world of contextualized labour regulation. This chapter has raised a set of crucial challenges for conceptualizing such legal frameworks, of indeterminate outcomes, dynamic norms and the destabilizing presence of precarious work. It has suggested that the response should be a sustained, and more curious, engagement with the complexities and capacities of labour regulation.

INDEX

NB – Legislation, cases, publications and organisations cited refer to the UK unless otherwise indicated.

www.ingramcontent.com/pod-product-compliance
Ingram Content Group UK Ltd.
Pitfield, Milton Keynes, MK11 3LW, UK
UKHW020131290926
15471UKWH00003B/409

9 781509 914142